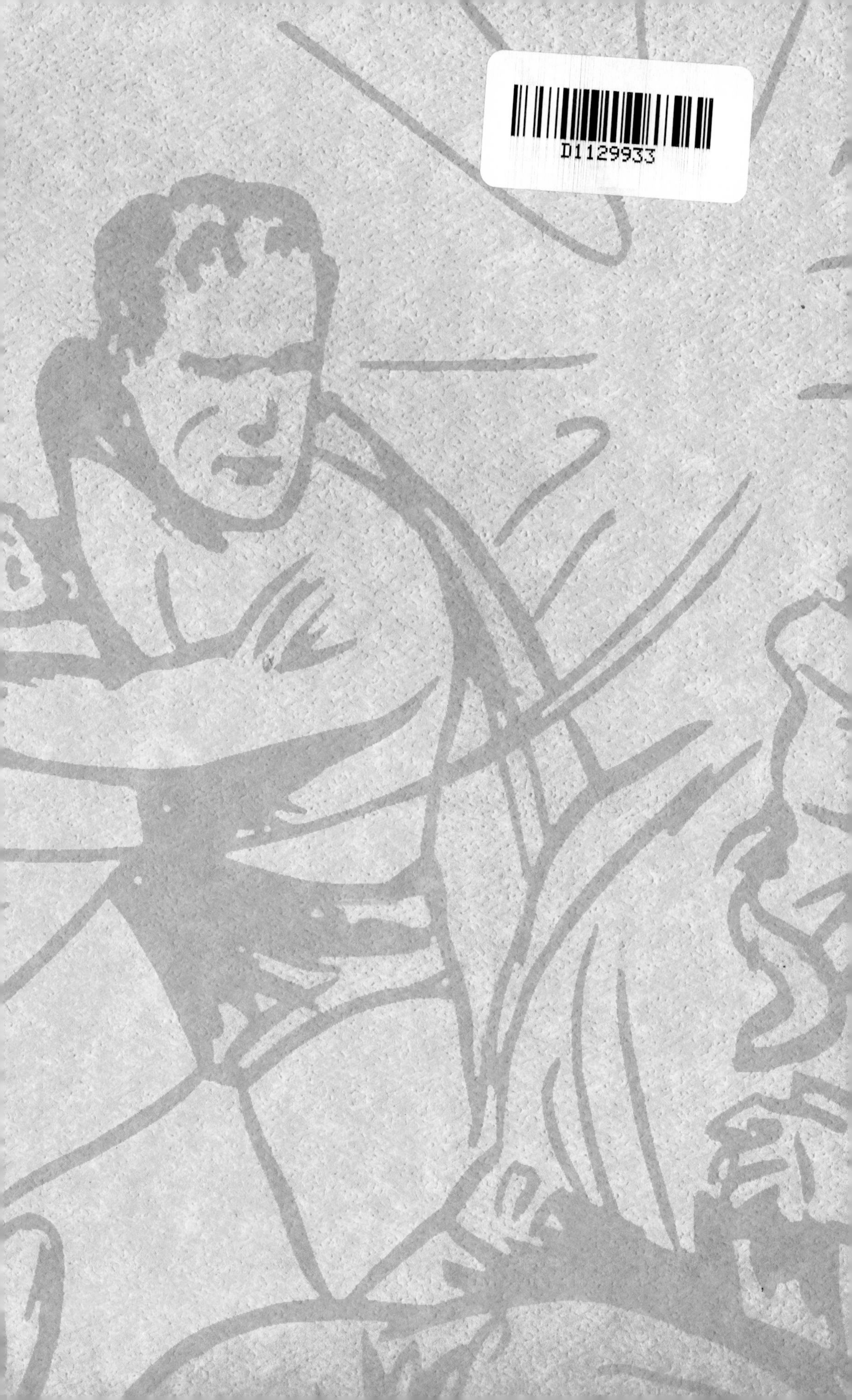

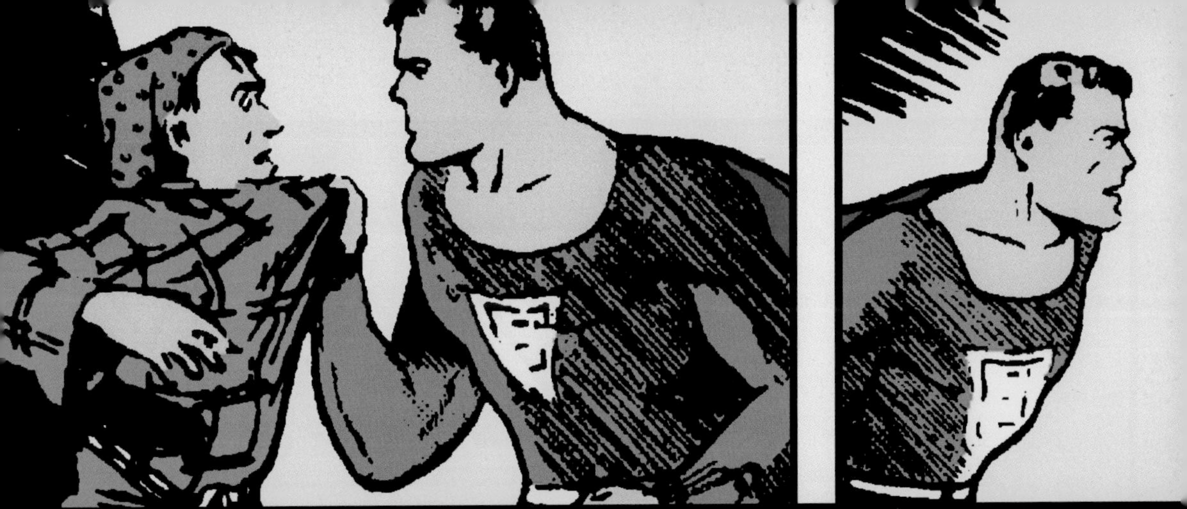

The two creators were forced to hire new artists keep up with all the production: Paul Cassidy, Wayne Boring, Leo Nowak and John Sikela.

Drafted into World War II in 1943, Siegel continued to write comics from the front, but new writers like Don Cameron, Alvin Schwartz and Bill Finger were hired to lend a hand.

All the while, Superman faced enemies like the Ultra-Humanite, Lex Luthor, Mr. Mxyztplk and the Prankster. Against those threats, the hero gained new abilities. Leaping from building to building? Now, he flies. His strength and invincibility increased, and super-senses appeared.

As the character grew, DC Comics' editors started to expand his universe. They added more science-fiction elements to the series, making Superman an alien. In 1949, he finally discovered that he is from Krypton and that remains of his home world are deadly to him.

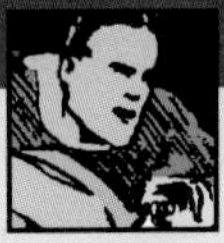

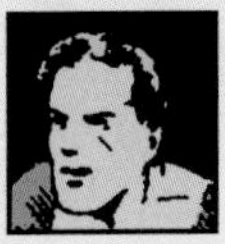

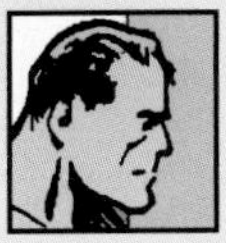

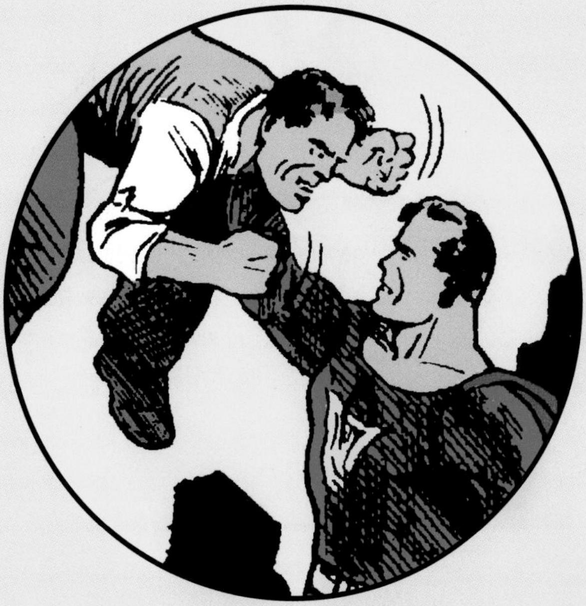

TOUGH IS PUTTING MILDLY THE TREATMENT YOU'RE GOING TO GET!

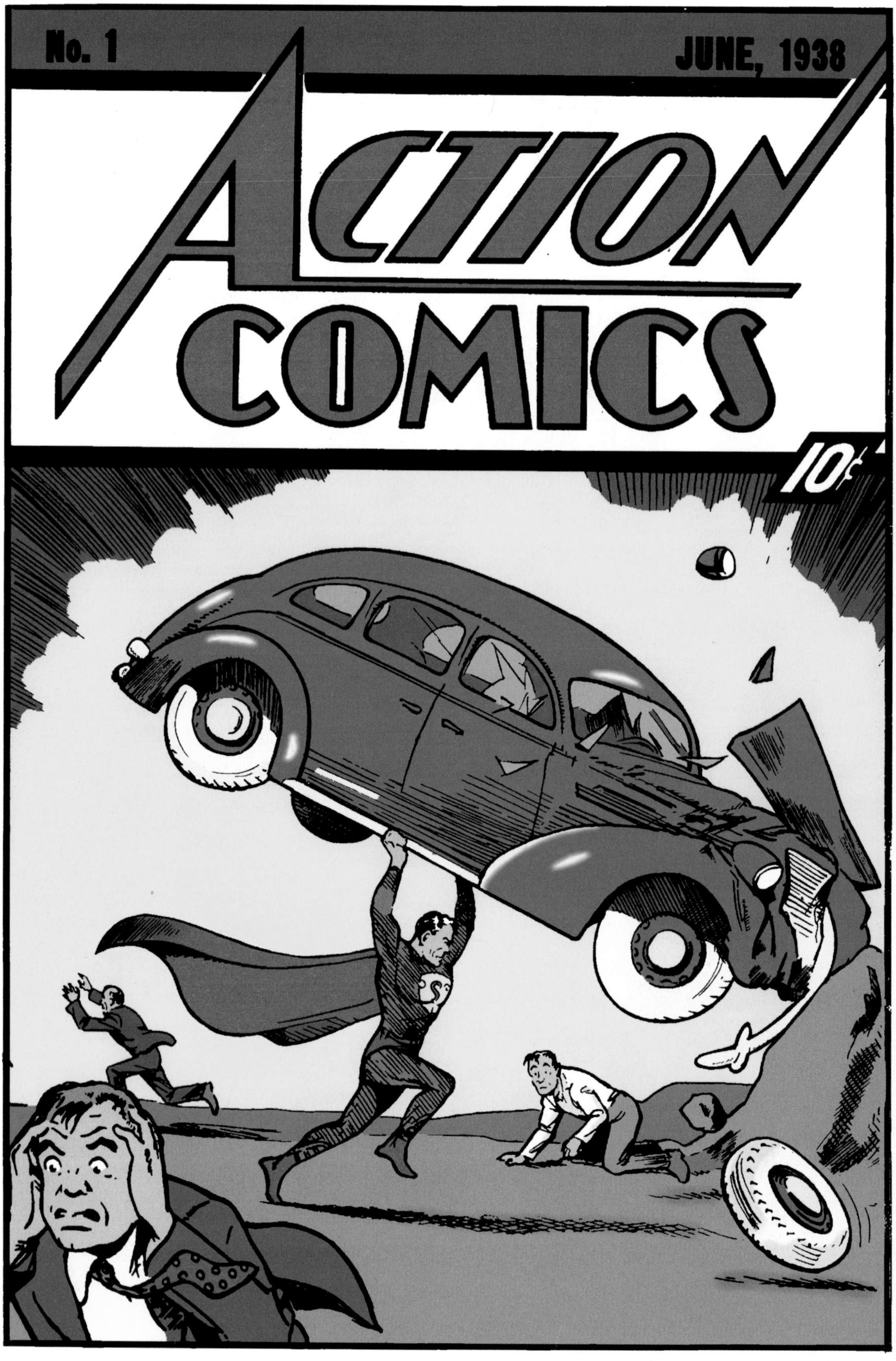
No. 1
JUNE, 1938
ACTION COMICS
10¢

SUPERMAN

A CELEBRATION OF 75 YEARS

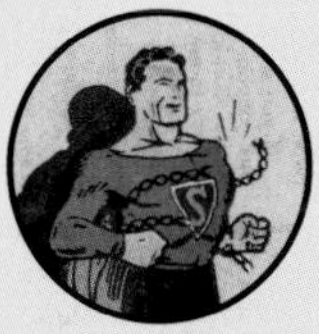

SUPERMAN CREATED BY JERRY SIEGEL AND JOE SHUSTER

BY SPECIAL ARRANGEMENT WITH THE JERRY SIEGEL FAMILY

HEARING POLICE-SIRENS, SUPERMAN
HURRIEDLY DONS STREET-CLOTHES OVER
HIS UNIFORM.

BY WELDING SHUT THE BULLET-HOLES
WITH MY FINGERS, I CHOKED OFF THE
FIRE! NOW TO INHALE A LUNGFUL OF
WATER-VAPOR FROM THIS CLOUD!

DC COMICS

VIN SULLIVAN
WHITNEY ELLSWORTH
JACK SCHIFF
MORT WEISINGER
JULIUS SCHWARTZ
MIKE CARLIN
EDDIE BERGANZA
CHARLES KOCHMAN
MATT IDELSON
WIL MOSS
JENNIFER FRANK
TOM PALMER, JR.
Editors — Original Series

ROBIN WILDMAN
Editor

ROBBIN BROSTERMAN
Design Director — Books

RANDALL DAHLK
Publication Design

BOB HARRAS
*Senior VP — Editor-in-Chief,
DC Comics*

DIANE NELSON
President

DAN DIDIO and JIM LEE
Co-Publishers

GEOFF JOHNS
Chief Creative Officer

JOHN ROOD
*Executive VP — Sales,
Marketing & Business
Development*

AMY GENKINS
*Senior VP — Business
& Legal Affairs*

NAIRI GARDINER
Senior VP — Finance

JEFF BOISON
VP — Publishing Planning

MARK CHIARELLO
VP — Art Direction & Design

JOHN CUNNINGHAM
VP — Marketing

TERRI CUNNINGHAM
VP — Editorial Administration

ALISON GILL
*Senior VP — Manufacturing
& Operations*

HANK KANALZ
*Senior VP — Vertigo
& Integrated Publishing*

JAY KOGAN
*VP — Business & Legal
Affairs, Publishing*

JACK MAHAN
*VP — Business Affairs,
Talent*

NICK NAPOLITANO
*VP — Manufacturing
Administration*

SUE POHJA
VP — Book Sales

COURTNEY SIMMONS
Senior VP — Publicity

BOB WAYNE
Senior VP — Sales

SUPERMAN: A CELEBRATION OF 75 YEARS
Published by DC Comics. Copyright © 2013 DC Comics. All Rights Reserved.
Originally published in single magazine form in ACTION COMICS #1-2, 242, 544, 775, 900, 0; LOOK MAGAZINE #27; SUPERMAN #17, 53, 76, 129, 141, 149, 247, 400; SUPERMAN (VOL. II)
#11, 75; SUPERMAN ANNUAL #11; MYTHOLOGY: THE DC COMICS ART OF ALEX ROSS Copyright © 1938, 1940, 1942, 1952, 1958, 1959, 1960, 1961, 1972, 1983, 1984, 1985, 1987, 1993,
2001, 2003, 2011, 2012 DC Comics. All Rights Reserved. All characters, their distinctive likenesses and related elements featured in this publication are trademarks of DC Comics. The stories,
characters and incidents featured in this publication are entirely fictional. DC Comics does not read or accept unsolicited ideas, stories or artwork.
DC Comics, 1700 Broadway, New York, NY 10019. A Warner Bros. Entertainment Company. Printed by RR Donnelley, Salem, VA, USA. 10/25/13. First Printing.
ISBN: 978-1-4012-4704-1

Library of Congress Cataloging-in-Publication Data
Superman : a Celebration of 75 Years.
pages cm
"Superman created by Jerry Siegel and Joe Shuster."
ISBN 978-1-4012-4704-1
1. Superman (Fictitious character) — Comic books, strips, etc. 2. Graphic novels.
PN6728.S9S79 2013
741.5'973 — dc23

SUSTAINABLE
FORESTRY
INITIATIVE

Certified Sourcing
www.sfiprogram.org
SFI-01042
APPLIES TO TEXT STOCK ONLY

TABLE OF CONTENTS

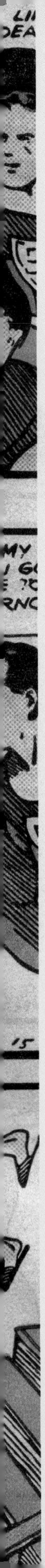

PART I • 1938-1950
CHAMPION OF THE OPPRESSED

In January 1933, two teenagers from Cleveland, Jerry Siegel and Joe Shuster, self-published an illustrated novel titled "Reign of the Superman." In this story, a mad scientist transforms a vagrant into a telepathic being who attempts to conquer the world.

Determined to break into the comic book industry, Siegel took this idea and remodeled his concept. His new "Superman" would not be an evil character, but a real hero. His powers would be physical, not mental. Brick by brick, by trading thoughts and ideas, Siegel and Shuster modeled the Superman we know today.

From 1933 to 1938, prototype after prototype, the first super hero took shape. Meanwhile, Siegel and Shuster worked on other creations such as detective Slam Bradley, musketeer Henri Duval and the supernatural Dr. Occult. All these characters were published by a young company named National Allied Publications, which would ultimately become DC Comics.

In 1938, National launched a new monthly comic book: ACTION COMICS. For the first issue, the editors chose to give the previously rejected Superman strip a chance. Right from the start, many of the essential elements are in place. We are introduced to shy reporter Clark Kent, his co-worker Lois Lane, whom he secretly loves, and his spectacular abilities — though not yet as powerful as they would eventually become.

The story is firmly set in the reality of its time: Superman fights for justice and against the consequences of the Great Depression, while in the background, there are rumblings of war. Siegel and Shuster would later address the war head-on in a spread drawn for *Look* magazine in 1940, which shows Superman toting Adolf Hitler and Joseph Stalin off to a United Nations tribunal.

Quickly, ACTION COMICS proved to be a hit and Superman became the new star of the book. The success was so phenomenal that imitations appeared mere weeks after ACTION COMICS #1. Issue after issue, Superman's popularity grew stronger — so strong that a year later the publisher decided to launch a second series dedicated to the hero. Simply titled SUPERMAN, the new monthly started with reprints of early Superman strips before going to original material.

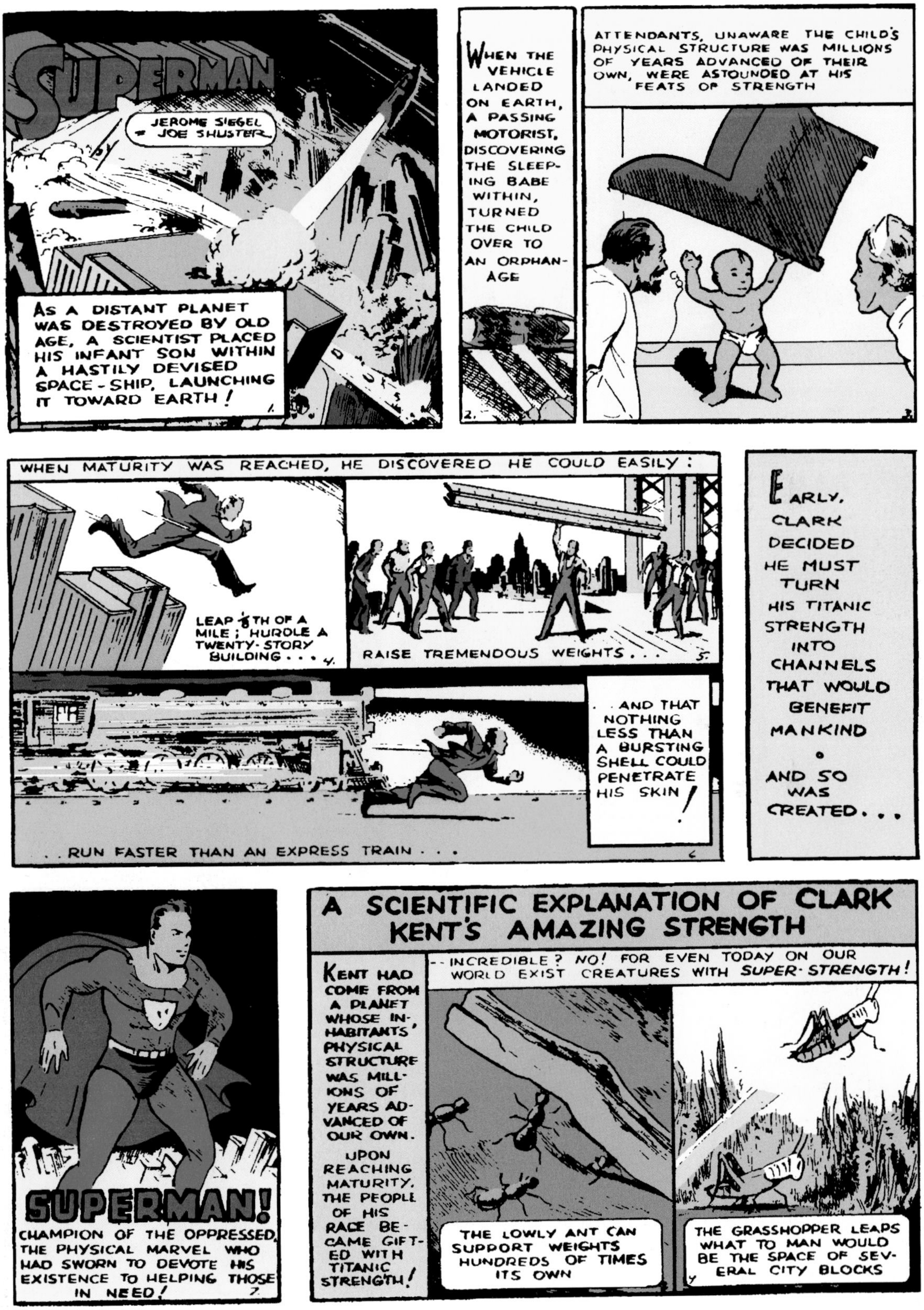
SUPERMAN
BY JEROME SIEGEL + JOE SHUSTER
AS A DISTANT PLANET WAS DESTROYED BY OLD AGE, A SCIENTIST PLACED HIS INFANT SON WITHIN A HASTILY DEVISED SPACE-SHIP, LAUNCHING IT TOWARD EARTH! 1.
WHEN THE VEHICLE LANDED ON EARTH, A PASSING MOTORIST, DISCOVERING THE SLEEPING BABE WITHIN, TURNED THE CHILD OVER TO AN ORPHANAGE 2.
ATTENDANTS, UNAWARE THE CHILD'S PHYSICAL STRUCTURE WAS MILLIONS OF YEARS ADVANCED OF THEIR OWN, WERE ASTOUNDED AT HIS FEATS OF STRENGTH 3.
WHEN MATURITY WAS REACHED, HE DISCOVERED HE COULD EASILY:
LEAP 1/8TH OF A MILE; HURDLE A TWENTY-STORY BUILDING . . . 4.
RAISE TREMENDOUS WEIGHTS . . . 5.
. . RUN FASTER THAN AN EXPRESS TRAIN . . .
. . AND THAT NOTHING LESS THAN A BURSTING SHELL COULD PENETRATE HIS SKIN! 6
EARLY, CLARK DECIDED HE MUST TURN HIS TITANIC STRENGTH INTO CHANNELS THAT WOULD BENEFIT MANKIND
AND SO WAS CREATED . . .
SUPERMAN!
CHAMPION OF THE OPPRESSED, THE PHYSICAL MARVEL WHO HAD SWORN TO DEVOTE HIS EXISTENCE TO HELPING THOSE IN NEED! 7.
A SCIENTIFIC EXPLANATION OF CLARK KENT'S AMAZING STRENGTH
KENT HAD COME FROM A PLANET WHOSE INHABITANTS' PHYSICAL STRUCTURE WAS MILLIONS OF YEARS ADVANCED OF OUR OWN.
UPON REACHING MATURITY, THE PEOPLE OF HIS RACE BECAME GIFTED WITH TITANIC STRENGTH!
-- INCREDIBLE? NO! FOR EVEN TODAY ON OUR WORLD EXIST CREATURES WITH SUPER-STRENGTH!
THE LOWLY ANT CAN SUPPORT WEIGHTS HUNDREDS OF TIMES ITS OWN
THE GRASSHOPPER LEAPS WHAT TO MAN WOULD BE THE SPACE OF SEVERAL CITY BLOCKS

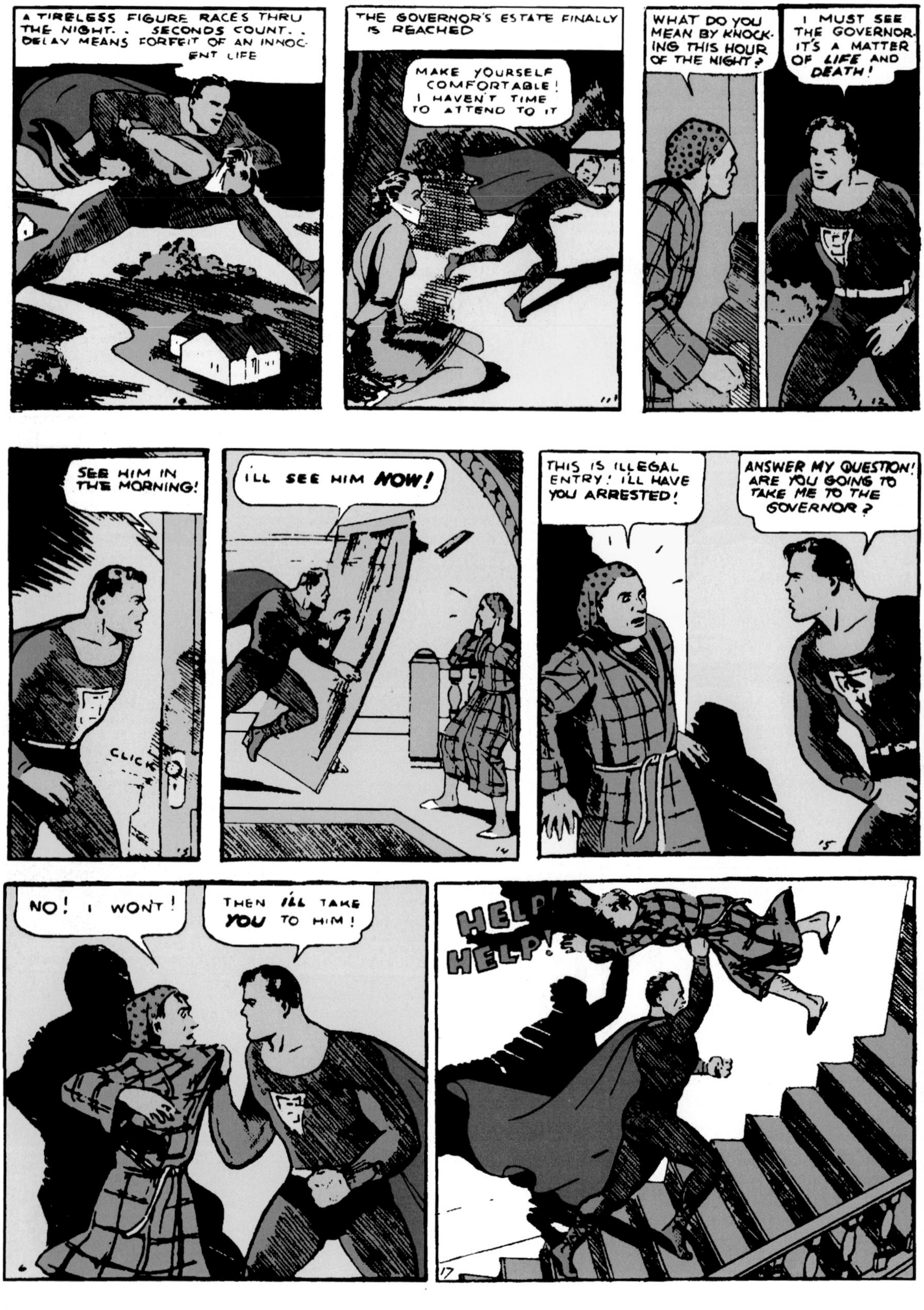
A TIRELESS FIGURE RACES THRU THE NIGHT. . SECONDS COUNT. . DELAY MEANS FORFEIT OF AN INNOCENT LIFE
THE GOVERNOR'S ESTATE FINALLY IS REACHED
MAKE YOURSELF COMFORTABLE! I HAVEN'T TIME TO ATTEND TO IT
WHAT DO YOU MEAN BY KNOCKING THIS HOUR OF THE NIGHT?
I MUST SEE THE GOVERNOR. IT'S A MATTER OF *LIFE* AND *DEATH*!
SEE HIM IN THE MORNING!
CLICK
I'LL SEE HIM *NOW*!
THIS IS ILLEGAL ENTRY! I'LL HAVE YOU ARRESTED!
ANSWER MY QUESTION! ARE YOU GOING TO TAKE ME TO THE GOVERNOR?
NO! I WON'T!
THEN *I'LL* TAKE *YOU* TO HIM!
HEL
HELP!

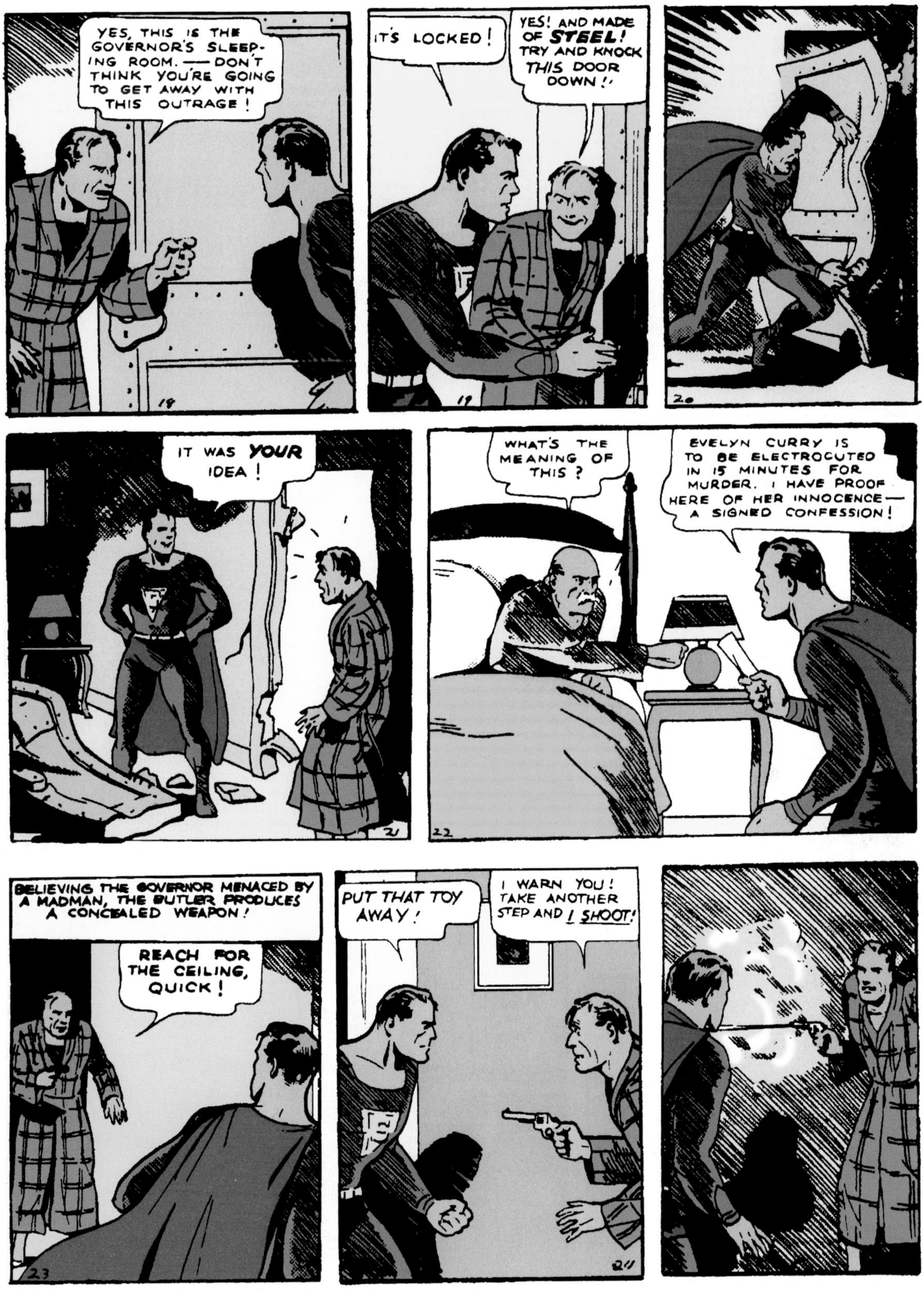
YES, THIS IS THE GOVERNOR'S SLEEPING ROOM. — DON'T THINK YOU'RE GOING TO GET AWAY WITH THIS OUTRAGE!
IT'S LOCKED!
YES! AND MADE OF STEEL! TRY AND KNOCK THIS DOOR DOWN!
IT WAS YOUR IDEA!
WHAT'S THE MEANING OF THIS?
EVELYN CURRY IS TO BE ELECTROCUTED IN 15 MINUTES FOR MURDER. I HAVE PROOF HERE OF HER INNOCENCE — A SIGNED CONFESSION!
BELIEVING THE GOVERNOR MENACED BY A MADMAN, THE BUTLER PRODUCES A CONCEALED WEAPON!
REACH FOR THE CEILING, QUICK!
PUT THAT TOY AWAY!
I WARN YOU! TAKE ANOTHER STEP AND I SHOOT!

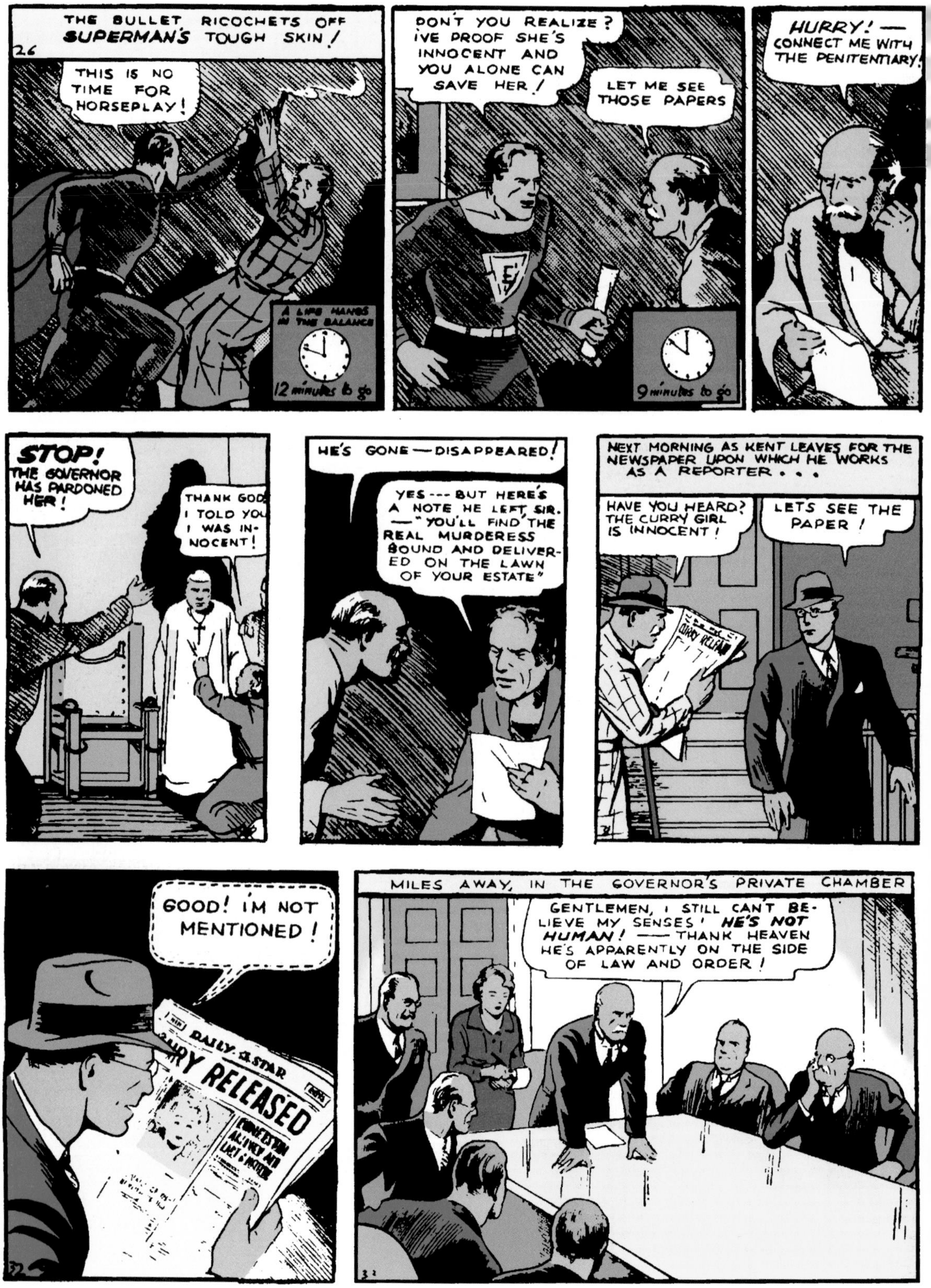
THE BULLET RICOCHETS OFF SUPERMAN'S TOUGH SKIN!
THIS IS NO TIME FOR HORSEPLAY!
A LIFE HANGS IN THE BALANCE
12 minutes to go
DON'T YOU REALIZE? I'VE PROOF SHE'S INNOCENT AND YOU ALONE CAN SAVE HER!
LET ME SEE THOSE PAPERS
9 minutes to go
HURRY! — CONNECT ME WITH THE PENITENTIARY!
STOP! THE GOVERNOR HAS PARDONED HER!
THANK GOD! I TOLD YOU I WAS INNOCENT!
HE'S GONE — DISAPPEARED!
YES --- BUT HERE'S A NOTE HE LEFT, SIR. —"YOU'LL FIND THE REAL MURDERESS BOUND AND DELIVERED ON THE LAWN OF YOUR ESTATE"
NEXT MORNING AS KENT LEAVES FOR THE NEWSPAPER UPON WHICH HE WORKS AS A REPORTER . . .
HAVE YOU HEARD? THE CURRY GIRL IS INNOCENT!
LET'S SEE THE PAPER!
GOOD! I'M NOT MENTIONED!
DAILY STAR
RY RELEASED
MILES AWAY, IN THE GOVERNOR'S PRIVATE CHAMBER
GENTLEMEN, I STILL CAN'T BELIEVE MY SENSES! HE'S NOT HUMAN! — THANK HEAVEN HE'S APPARENTLY ON THE SIDE OF LAW AND ORDER!

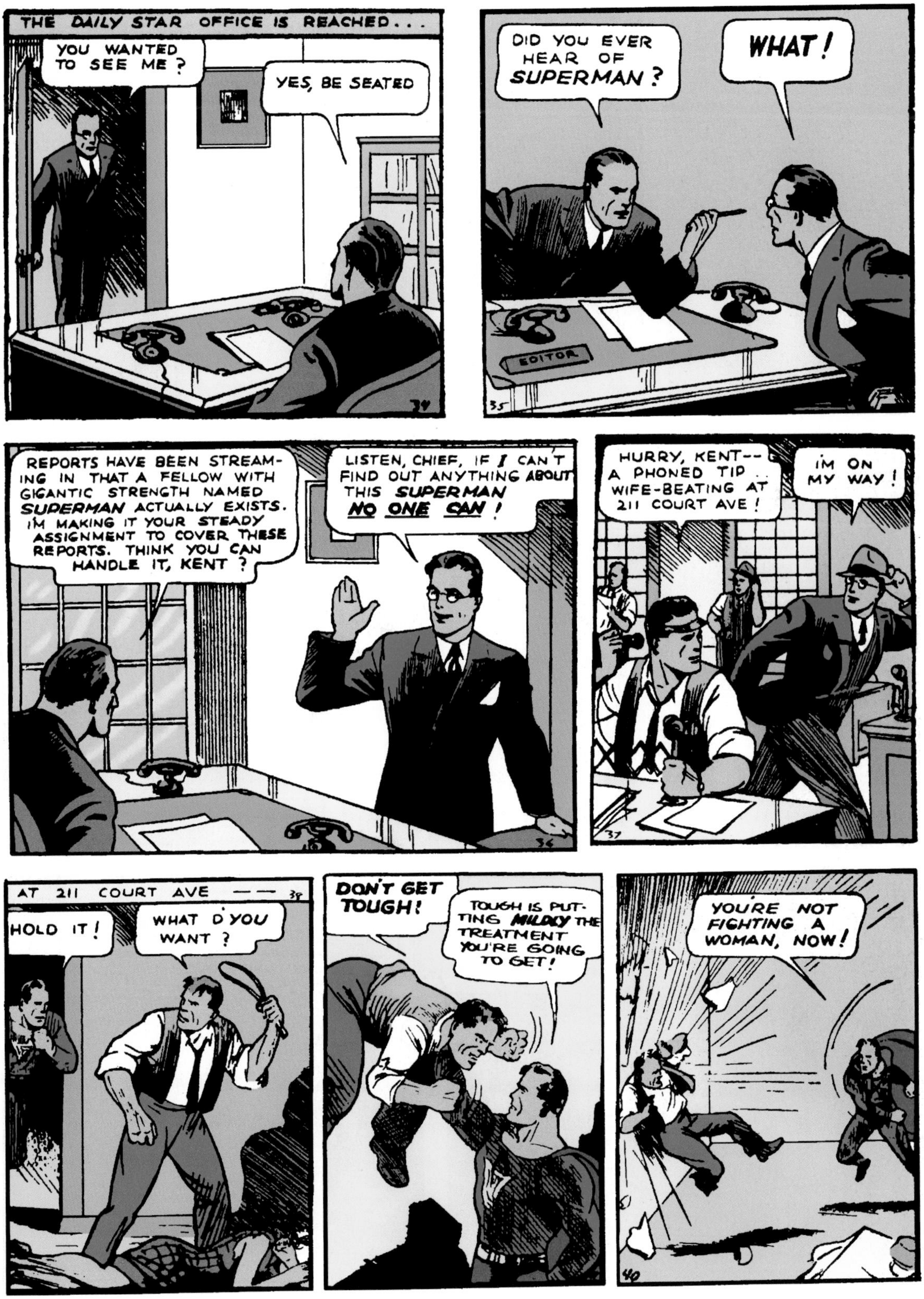
THE DAILY STAR OFFICE IS REACHED...
YOU WANTED TO SEE ME?
YES, BE SEATED
DID YOU EVER HEAR OF SUPERMAN?
WHAT!
EDITOR
REPORTS HAVE BEEN STREAMING IN THAT A FELLOW WITH GIGANTIC STRENGTH NAMED SUPERMAN ACTUALLY EXISTS. I'M MAKING IT YOUR STEADY ASSIGNMENT TO COVER THESE REPORTS. THINK YOU CAN HANDLE IT, KENT?
LISTEN, CHIEF, IF I CAN'T FIND OUT ANYTHING ABOUT THIS SUPERMAN NO ONE CAN!
HURRY, KENT-- A PHONED TIP.. WIFE-BEATING AT 211 COURT AVE!
I'M ON MY WAY!
AT 211 COURT AVE --
HOLD IT!
WHAT D'YOU WANT?
DON'T GET TOUGH!
TOUGH IS PUTTING MILDLY THE TREATMENT YOU'RE GOING TO GET!
YOU'RE NOT FIGHTING A WOMAN, NOW!

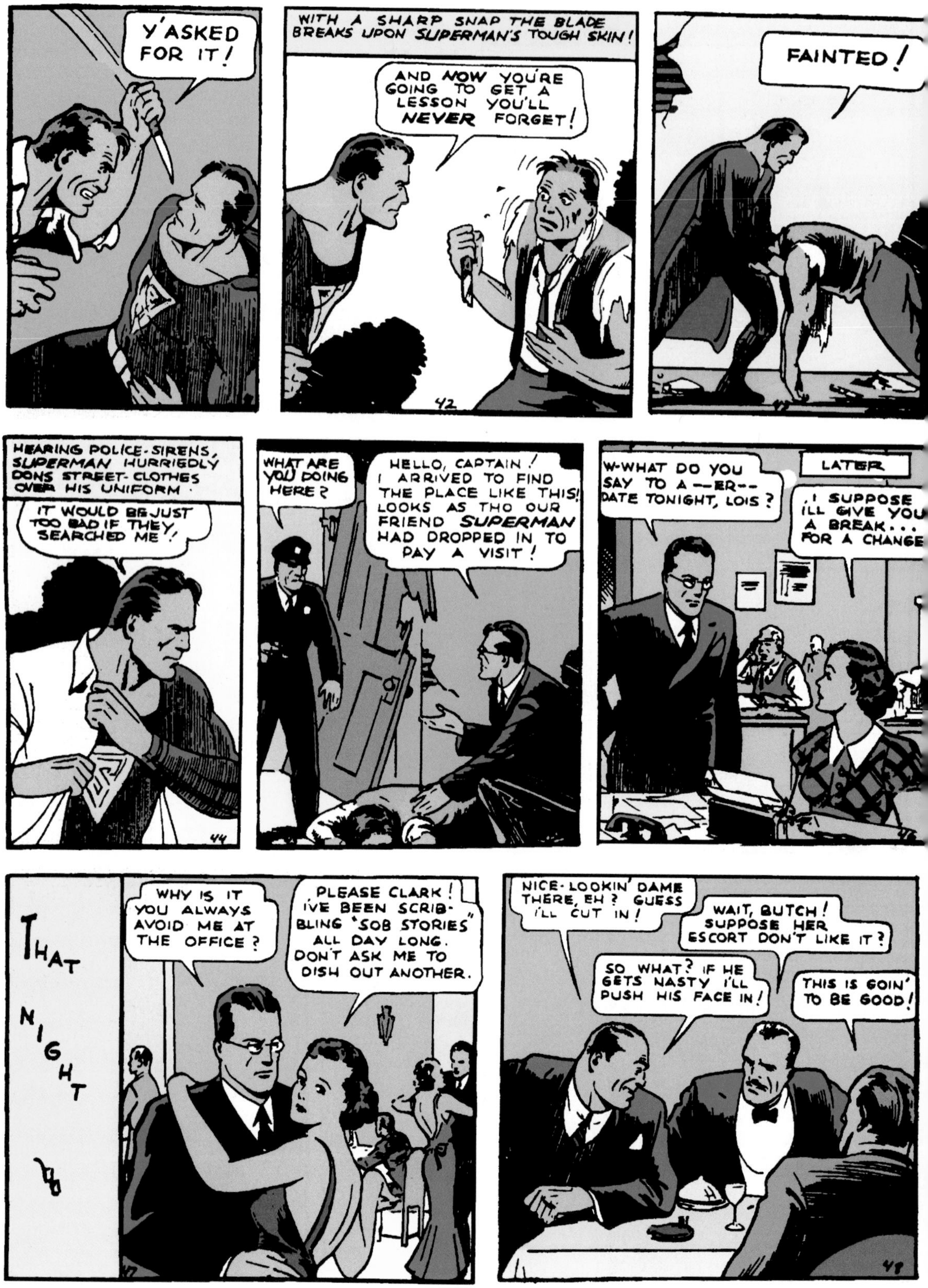
Y'ASKED FOR IT!
WITH A SHARP SNAP THE BLADE BREAKS UPON SUPERMAN'S TOUGH SKIN!
AND NOW YOU'RE GOING TO GET A LESSON YOU'LL NEVER FORGET!
42
FAINTED!
HEARING POLICE-SIRENS, SUPERMAN HURRIEDLY DONS STREET-CLOTHES OVER HIS UNIFORM.
IT WOULD BE JUST TOO BAD IF THEY SEARCHED ME!
44
WHAT ARE YOU DOING HERE?
HELLO, CAPTAIN! I ARRIVED TO FIND THE PLACE LIKE THIS! LOOKS AS THO OUR FRIEND SUPERMAN HAD DROPPED IN TO PAY A VISIT!
W-WHAT DO YOU SAY TO A --ER-- DATE TONIGHT, LOIS?
LATER
I SUPPOSE I'LL GIVE YOU A BREAK... FOR A CHANGE
THAT NIGHT
WHY IS IT YOU ALWAYS AVOID ME AT THE OFFICE?
PLEASE CLARK! I'VE BEEN SCRIBBLING "SOB STORIES" ALL DAY LONG. DON'T ASK ME TO DISH OUT ANOTHER.
47
NICE-LOOKIN' DAME THERE, EH? GUESS I'LL CUT IN!
WAIT, BUTCH! SUPPOSE HER ESCORT DON'T LIKE IT?
SO WHAT? IF HE GETS NASTY I'LL PUSH HIS FACE IN!
THIS IS GOIN' TO BE GOOD!
48

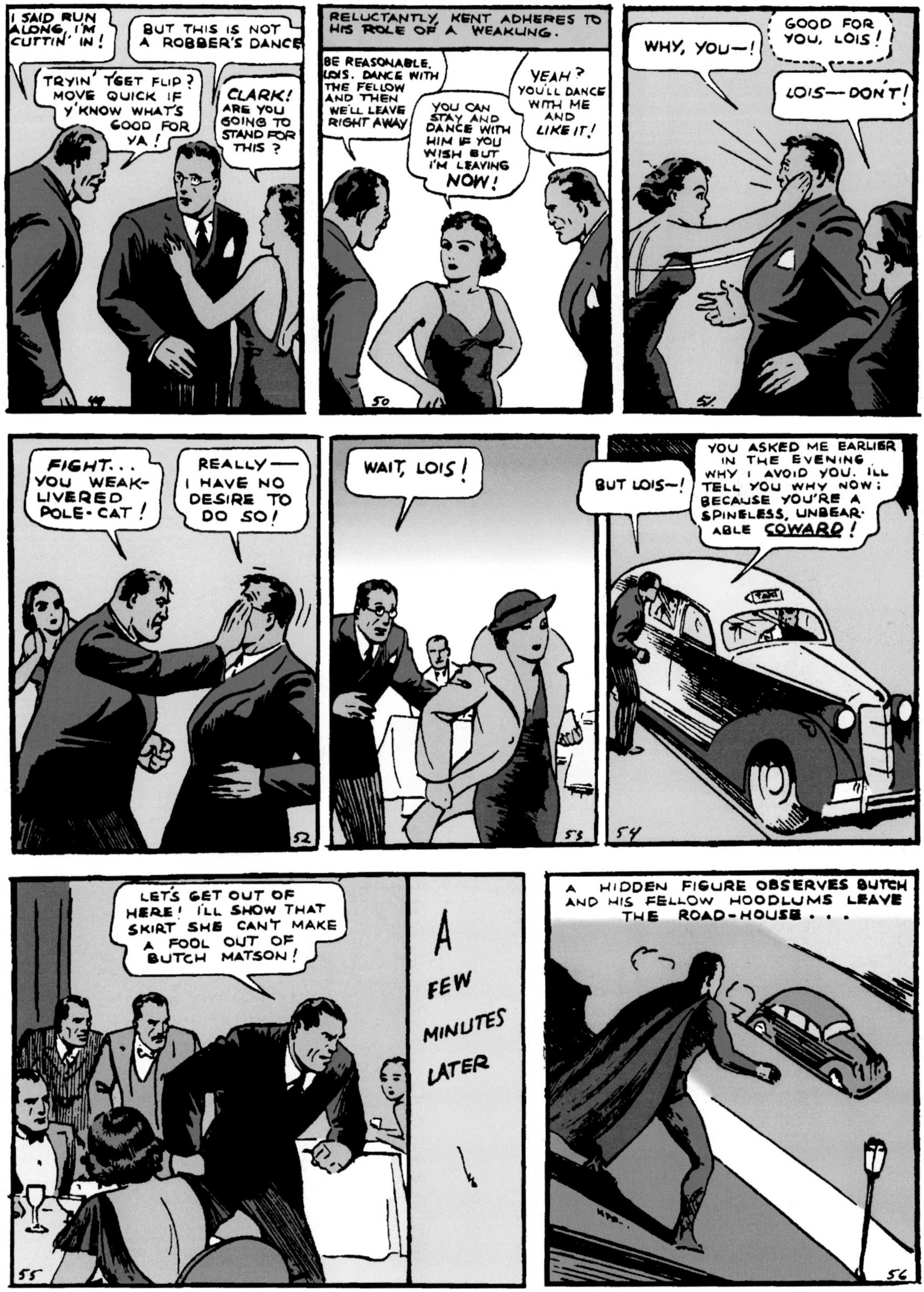

I SAID RUN ALONG, I'M CUTTIN' IN!
BUT THIS IS NOT A ROBBER'S DANCE
TRYIN' T'GET FLIP? MOVE QUICK IF Y'KNOW WHAT'S GOOD FOR YA!
CLARK! ARE YOU GOING TO STAND FOR THIS?
49
RELUCTANTLY, KENT ADHERES TO HIS ROLE OF A WEAKLING.
BE REASONABLE, LOIS. DANCE WITH THE FELLOW AND THEN WE'LL LEAVE RIGHT AWAY
YOU CAN STAY AND DANCE WITH HIM IF YOU WISH BUT I'M LEAVING NOW!
YEAH? YOU'LL DANCE WITH ME AND LIKE IT!
50
WHY, YOU—!
GOOD FOR YOU, LOIS!
LOIS—DON'T!
51
FIGHT... YOU WEAK-LIVERED POLE-CAT!
REALLY— I HAVE NO DESIRE TO DO SO!
52
WAIT, LOIS!
53
BUT LOIS—!
YOU ASKED ME EARLIER IN THE EVENING WHY I AVOID YOU. I'LL TELL YOU WHY NOW: BECAUSE YOU'RE A SPINELESS, UNBEARABLE COWARD!
TAXI
54
LET'S GET OUT OF HERE! I'LL SHOW THAT SKIRT SHE CAN'T MAKE A FOOL OUT OF BUTCH MATSON!
55
A FEW MINUTES LATER
A HIDDEN FIGURE OBSERVES BUTCH AND HIS FELLOW HOODLUMS LEAVE THE ROAD-HOUSE...
56

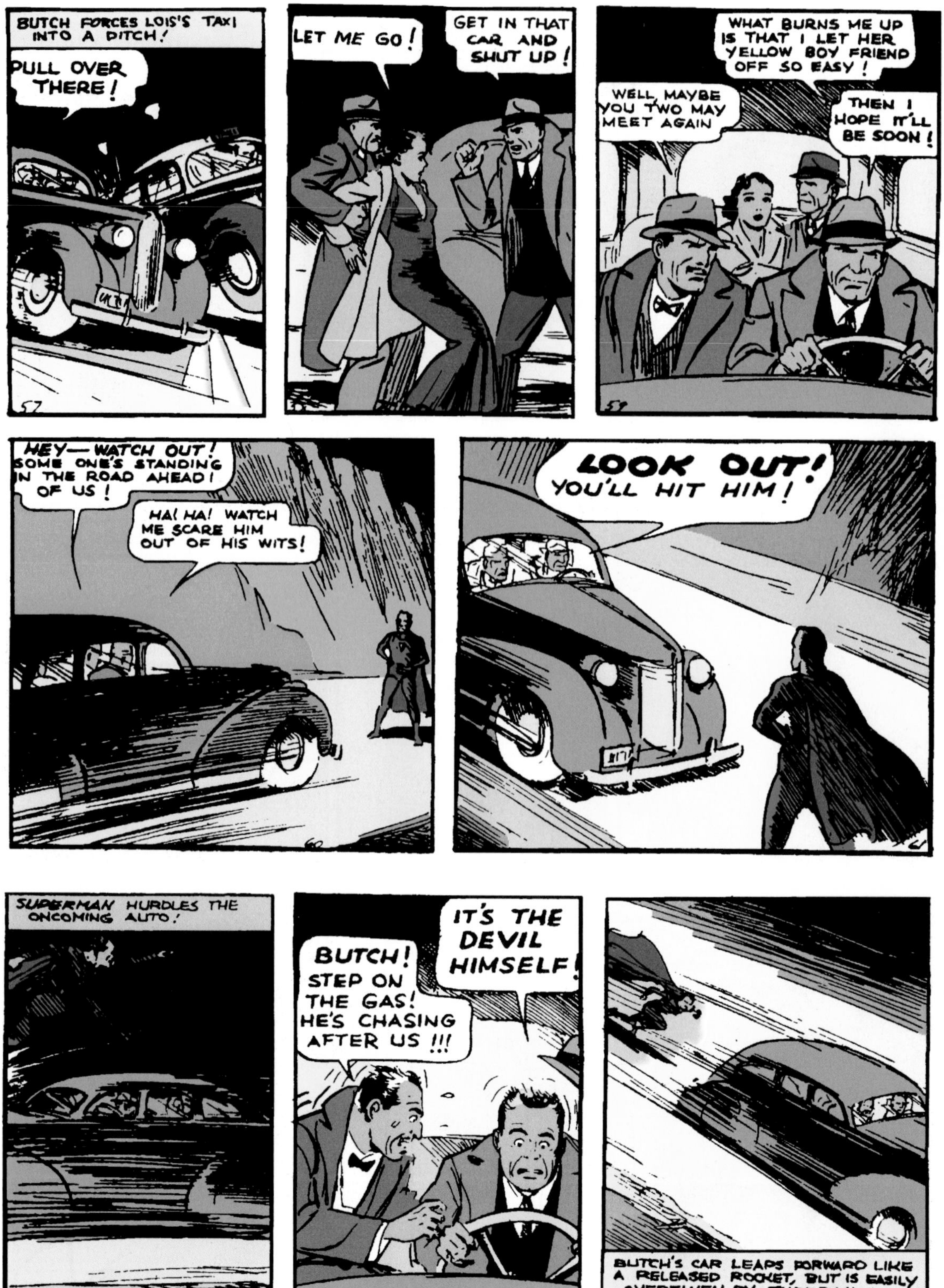
BUTCH FORCES LOIS'S TAXI INTO A DITCH!
PULL OVER THERE!
LET ME GO!
GET IN THAT CAR AND SHUT UP!
WHAT BURNS ME UP IS THAT I LET HER YELLOW BOY FRIEND OFF SO EASY!
WELL, MAYBE YOU TWO MAY MEET AGAIN
THEN I HOPE IT'LL BE SOON!
HEY—WATCH OUT! SOME ONE'S STANDING IN THE ROAD AHEAD OF US!
HA! HA! WATCH ME SCARE HIM OUT OF HIS WITS!
LOOK OUT! YOU'LL HIT HIM!
SUPERMAN HURDLES THE ONCOMING AUTO!
BUTCH! STEP ON THE GAS! HE'S CHASING AFTER US !!!
IT'S THE DEVIL HIMSELF!
BUTCH'S CAR LEAPS FORWARD LIKE A RELEASED ROCKET, BUT IS EASILY OVERTAKEN BY SUPERMAN

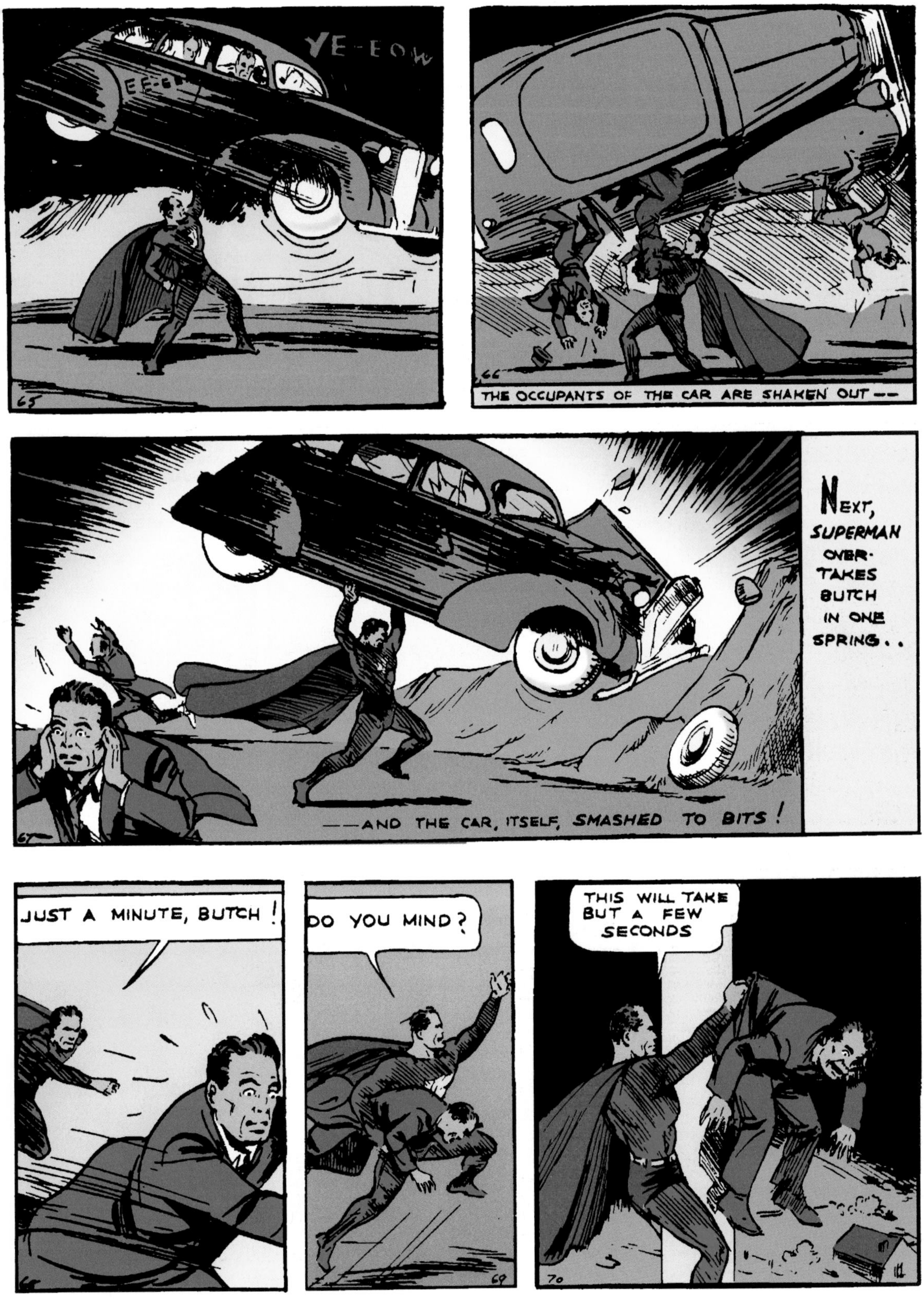
YE-EOW
EE-E
THE OCCUPANTS OF THE CAR ARE SHAKEN OUT --
NEXT, SUPERMAN OVER-TAKES BUTCH IN ONE SPRING . .
---AND THE CAR, ITSELF, SMASHED TO BITS!
JUST A MINUTE, BUTCH!
DO YOU MIND?
THIS WILL TAKE BUT A FEW SECONDS

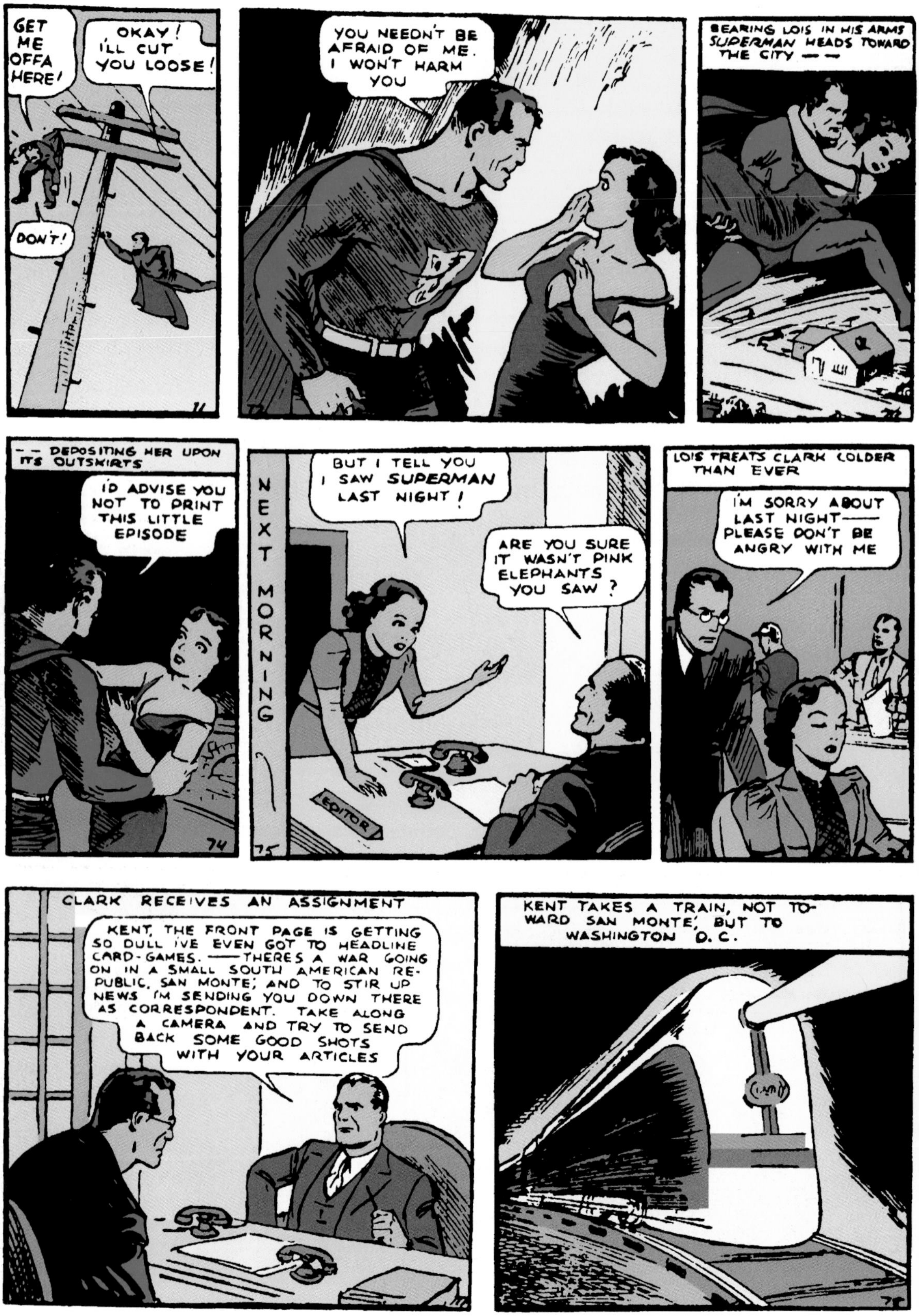
GET ME OFFA HERE!
OKAY! I'LL CUT YOU LOOSE!
DON'T!
YOU NEEDN'T BE AFRAID OF ME. I WON'T HARM YOU
BEARING LOIS IN HIS ARMS SUPERMAN HEADS TOWARD THE CITY — —
— — DEPOSITING HER UPON ITS OUTSKIRTS
I'D ADVISE YOU NOT TO PRINT THIS LITTLE EPISODE
NEXT MORNING
BUT I TELL YOU I SAW SUPERMAN LAST NIGHT!
ARE YOU SURE IT WASN'T PINK ELEPHANTS YOU SAW?
EDITOR
LOIS TREATS CLARK COLDER THAN EVER
I'M SORRY ABOUT LAST NIGHT—— PLEASE DON'T BE ANGRY WITH ME
CLARK RECEIVES AN ASSIGNMENT
KENT, THE FRONT PAGE IS GETTING SO DULL I'VE EVEN GOT TO HEADLINE CARD-GAMES. ——THERES A WAR GOING ON IN A SMALL SOUTH AMERICAN REPUBLIC, SAN MONTE; AND TO STIR UP NEWS I'M SENDING YOU DOWN THERE AS CORRESPONDENT. TAKE ALONG A CAMERA AND TRY TO SEND BACK SOME GOOD SHOTS WITH YOUR ARTICLES
KENT TAKES A TRAIN, NOT TOWARD SAN MONTE, BUT TO WASHINGTON D. C.

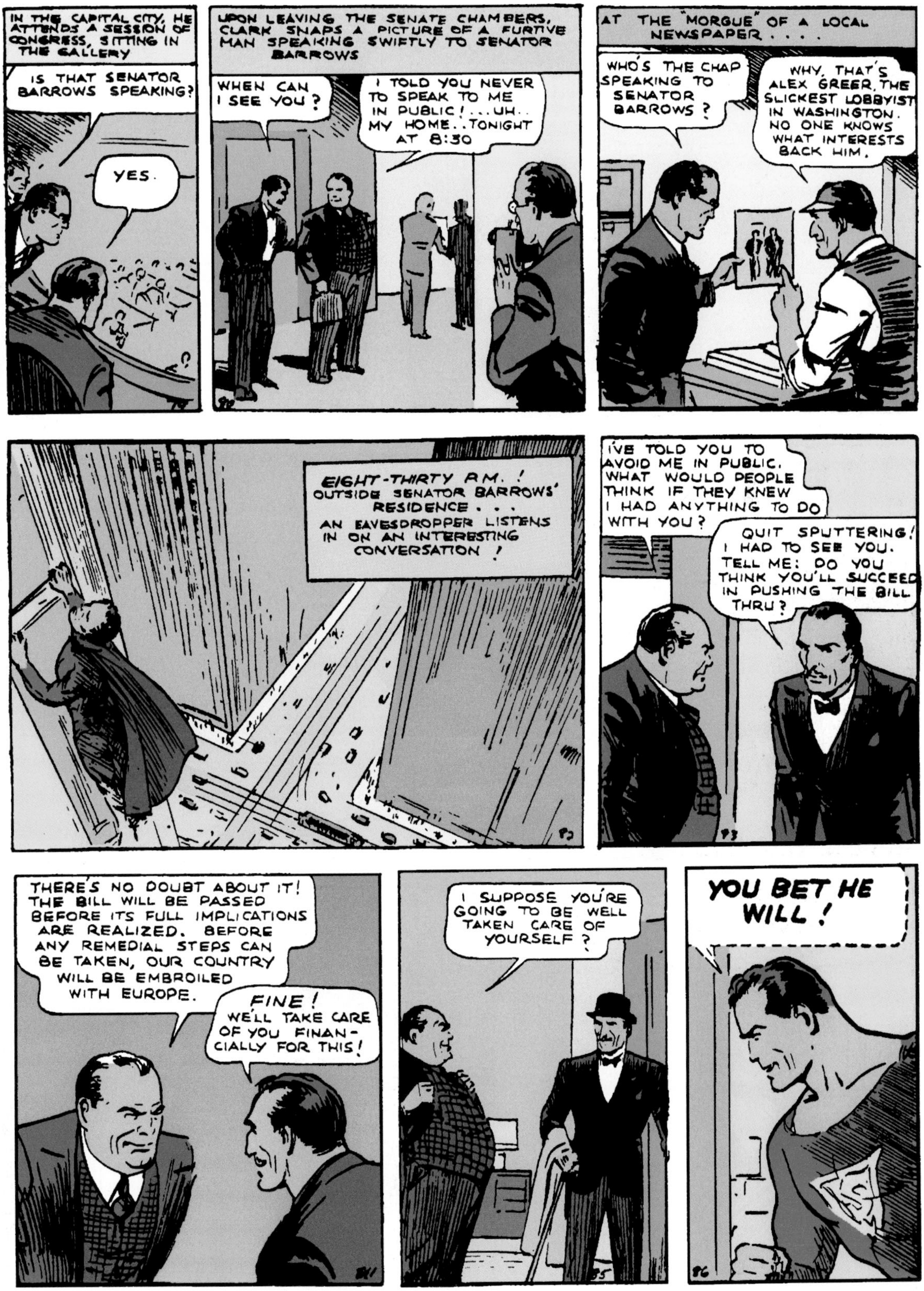
IN THE CAPITAL CITY, HE ATTENDS A SESSION OF CONGRESS, SITTING IN THE GALLERY
IS THAT SENATOR BARROWS SPEAKING?
YES.
UPON LEAVING THE SENATE CHAMBERS, CLARK SNAPS A PICTURE OF A FURTIVE MAN SPEAKING SWIFTLY TO SENATOR BARROWS
WHEN CAN I SEE YOU?
I TOLD YOU NEVER TO SPEAK TO ME IN PUBLIC!...UH.. MY HOME..TONIGHT AT 8:30
AT THE "MORGUE" OF A LOCAL NEWSPAPER . . . .
WHO'S THE CHAP SPEAKING TO SENATOR BARROWS?
WHY, THAT'S ALEX GREER, THE SLICKEST LOBBYIST IN WASHINGTON. NO ONE KNOWS WHAT INTERESTS BACK HIM.
EIGHT-THIRTY P.M.! OUTSIDE SENATOR BARROWS' RESIDENCE . . . AN EAVESDROPPER LISTENS IN ON AN INTERESTING CONVERSATION!
I'VE TOLD YOU TO AVOID ME IN PUBLIC. WHAT WOULD PEOPLE THINK IF THEY KNEW I HAD ANYTHING TO DO WITH YOU?
QUIT SPUTTERING! I HAD TO SEE YOU. TELL ME: DO YOU THINK YOU'LL SUCCEED IN PUSHING THE BILL THRU?
THERE'S NO DOUBT ABOUT IT! THE BILL WILL BE PASSED BEFORE ITS FULL IMPLICATIONS ARE REALIZED. BEFORE ANY REMEDIAL STEPS CAN BE TAKEN, OUR COUNTRY WILL BE EMBROILED WITH EUROPE.
FINE! WE'LL TAKE CARE OF YOU FINANCIALLY FOR THIS!
I SUPPOSE YOU'RE GOING TO BE WELL TAKEN CARE OF YOURSELF?
YOU BET HE WILL!

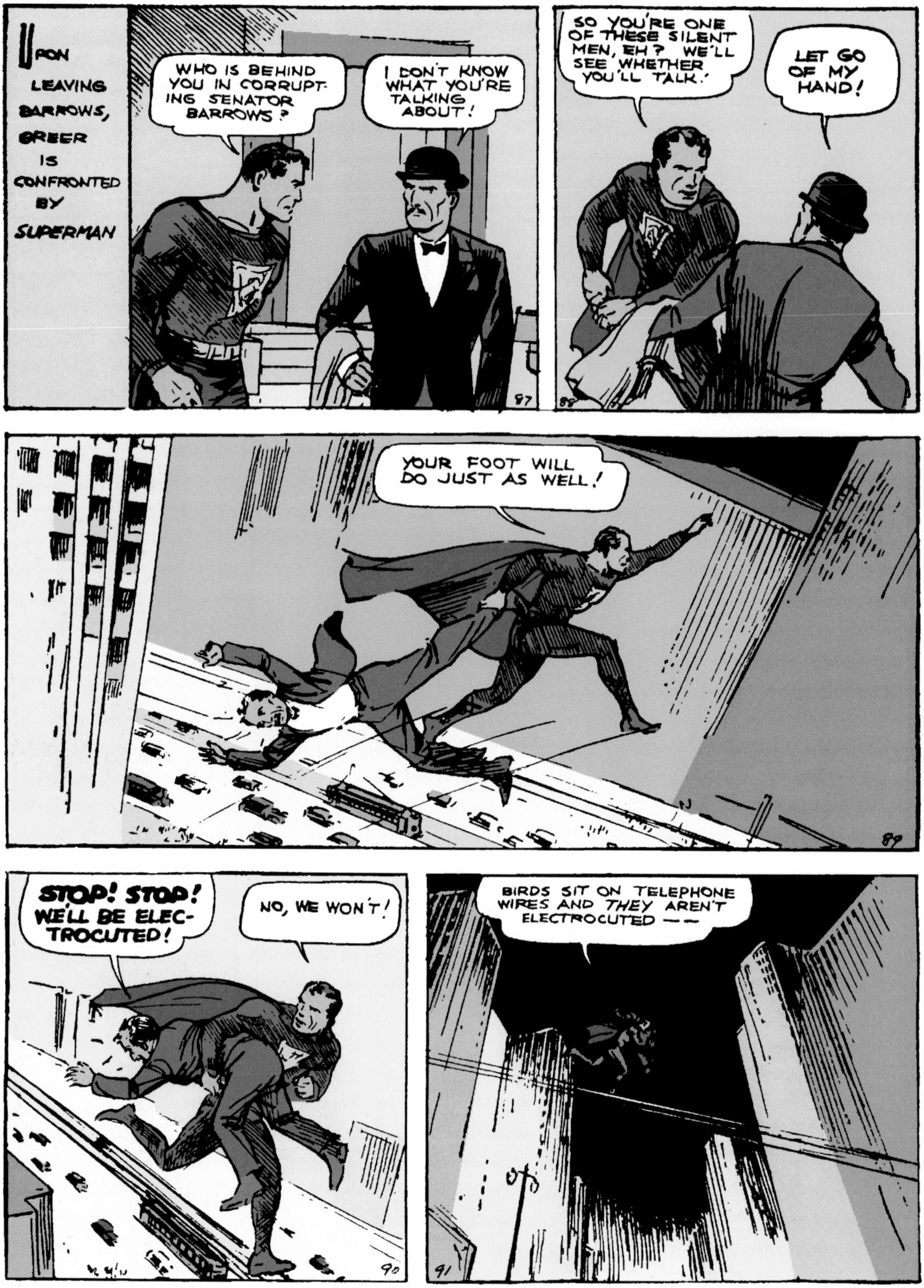
UPON LEAVING BARROWS, GREER IS CONFRONTED BY SUPERMAN
WHO IS BEHIND YOU IN CORRUPTING SENATOR BARROWS?
I DON'T KNOW WHAT YOU'RE TALKING ABOUT!
87
SO YOU'RE ONE OF THESE SILENT MEN, EH? WE'LL SEE WHETHER YOU'LL TALK.
LET GO OF MY HAND!
88
YOUR FOOT WILL DO JUST AS WELL!
89
STOP! STOP! WE'LL BE ELECTROCUTED!
NO, WE WON'T!
90
BIRDS SIT ON TELEPHONE WIRES AND THEY AREN'T ELECTROCUTED ——
91

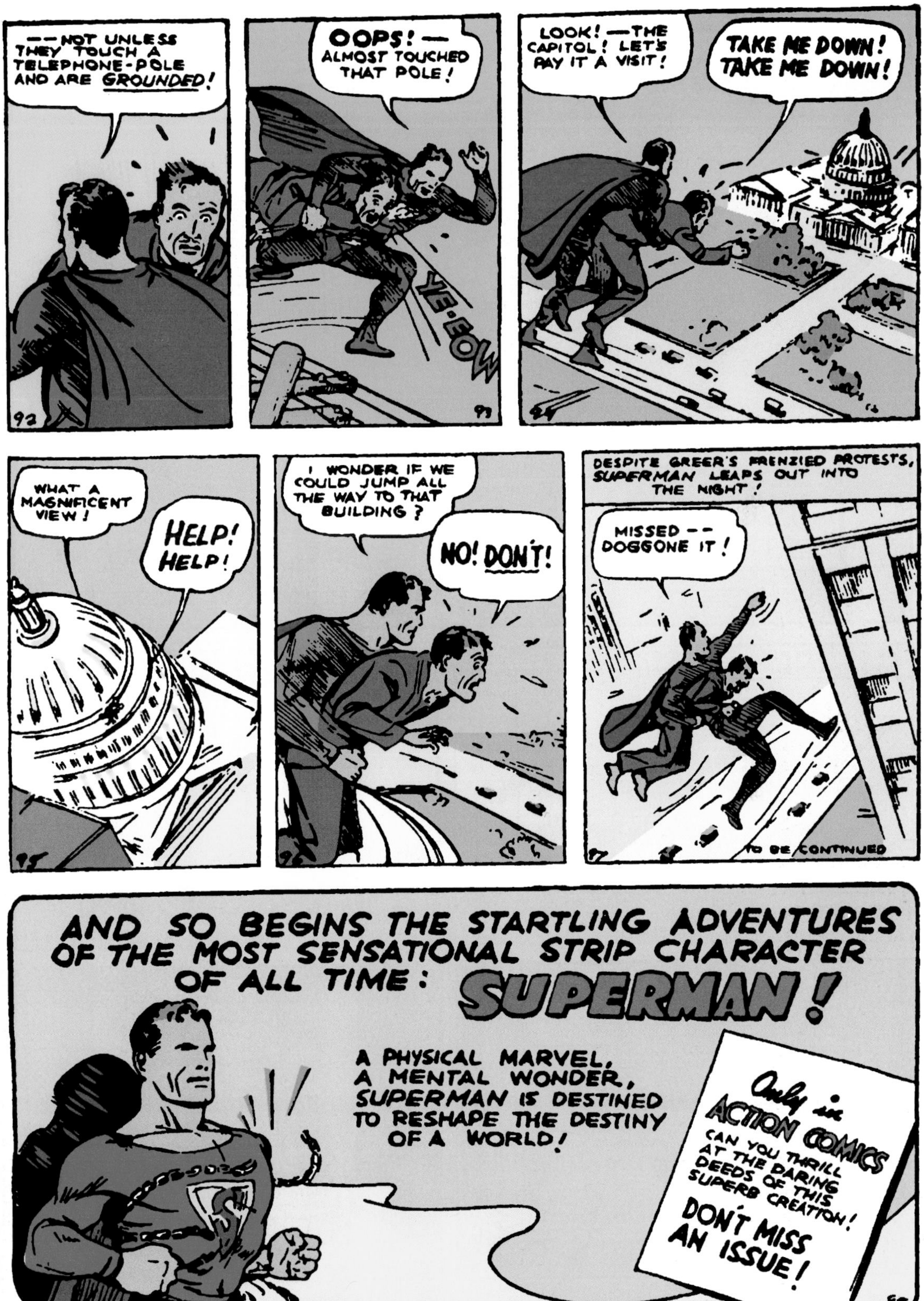

--NOT UNLESS THEY TOUCH A TELEPHONE-POLE AND ARE GROUNDED!
92
OOPS!— ALMOST TOUCHED THAT POLE!
YE-EOW
93
LOOK! —THE CAPITOL! LET'S PAY IT A VISIT!
TAKE ME DOWN! TAKE ME DOWN!
94
WHAT A MAGNIFICENT VIEW!
HELP! HELP!
95
I WONDER IF WE COULD JUMP ALL THE WAY TO THAT BUILDING?
NO! DON'T!
96
DESPITE GREER'S FRENZIED PROTESTS, SUPERMAN LEAPS OUT INTO THE NIGHT!
MISSED -- DOGGONE IT!
97
TO BE CONTINUED
AND SO BEGINS THE STARTLING ADVENTURES OF THE MOST SENSATIONAL STRIP CHARACTER OF ALL TIME: SUPERMAN!
A PHYSICAL MARVEL, A MENTAL WONDER, SUPERMAN IS DESTINED TO RESHAPE THE DESTINY OF A WORLD!
Only in ACTION COMICS CAN YOU THRILL AT THE DARING DEEDS OF THIS SUPERB CREATION!
DON'T MISS AN ISSUE!
98

SUPERMAN

by JEROME SIEGEL and JOE SHUSTER

As they topple like a plummet to the street below, eighty stories distant, Greer shrieks insanely the entire length of the building!

As they strike the sidewalk, it bursts into fragments!

2.

SAY! WASN'T THAT FUN? -- LET'S DO IT AGAIN!

NO! I'LL TALK! -- THE MAN BEHIND THE THREATENING WAR IS EMIL NORVELL, THE MUNITIONS MAGNATE. YOU'LL FIND HIM AT HIS LEXINGTON PARK ESTATE!

3.

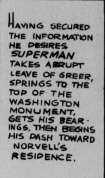

Having secured the information he desires Superman takes abrupt leave of Greer, springs to the top of the Washington Monument, gets his bearings, then begins his dash toward Norvell's residence.

4.

MEANWHILE

I CAN'T EXPLAIN OVER THE PHONE, NORVELL, BUT YOU'RE ABOUT TO RECEIVE A VISIT FROM THE MOST DANGEROUS MAN ALIVE!

DON'T WORRY, GREER! -- I'LL TAKE CERTAIN PRECAUTIONS TO INSURE HE DOESN'T REMAIN ALIVE LONG!

6.

22

FIVE MINUTES ELAPSE -- THEN . . . . . . SUPERMAN STEPS THRU THE WINDOW OF EMIL NORVELL'S STUDY AND CALMLY CONFRONTS HIM . . .

WHETHER YOU LIKE IT OR NOT, NORVELL, YOU'RE COMING WITH ME!

SORRY, BUT I HAVE OTHER PLANS!

AS HE SPEAKS, THE MUNITIONS MANUFACTURER SURREPTITIOUSLY REACHES BEHIND HIM TO PRESS A BUTTON ON HIS DESK.

WHAT ARE YOU HOLDING BEHIND YOU? -- GIVE IT TO ME!

ALL RIGHT BOYS! -- HE ASKED FOR IT! LET HIM HAVE IT!!

INSTANTLY SEVERAL PANELS ABOUT THE ROOM SLIDE ASIDE AND OUT STEP A NUMBER OF ARMED GUARDS!

NEXT MOMENT SUPERMAN IS THE CENTER OF A DEAFENING MACHINE-GUN BARRAGE!

UNHARMED BY THE RAIN OF MACHINE-GUN BULLETS, SUPERMAN STREAKS TOWARD HIS WOULD-BE MURDERERS!

GOOD HEAVENS! HE WON'T DIE!

GLAD I CAN'T SAY THE SAME FOR YOU!

A MOMENT LATER A DOZEN BODIES FLY HEADLONG OUT THE WINDOW INTO THE NIGHT, THE MACHINE-GUNS WRAPPED FIRMLY ABOUT THEIR NECKS!

YOU SEE HOW EFFORTLESSLY I CRUSH THIS BAR OF IRON IN MY HAND? -- THAT BAR COULD JUST AS EASILY BE YOUR NECK! . . . NOW, FOR THE LAST TIME: ARE YOU COMING WITH ME?

YES! YES! IMMEDIATELY!

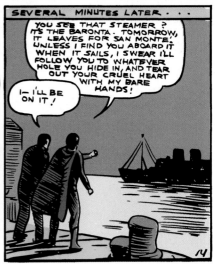

SEVERAL MINUTES LATER . . .

YOU SEE THAT STEAMER? IT'S THE BARONTA. TOMORROW, IT LEAVES FOR SAN MONTE! UNLESS I FIND YOU ABOARD IT WHEN IT SAILS, I SWEAR I'LL FOLLOW YOU TO WHATEVER HOLE YOU HIDE IN, AND TEAR OUT YOUR CRUEL HEART WITH MY BARE HANDS!

I-- I'LL BE ON IT!

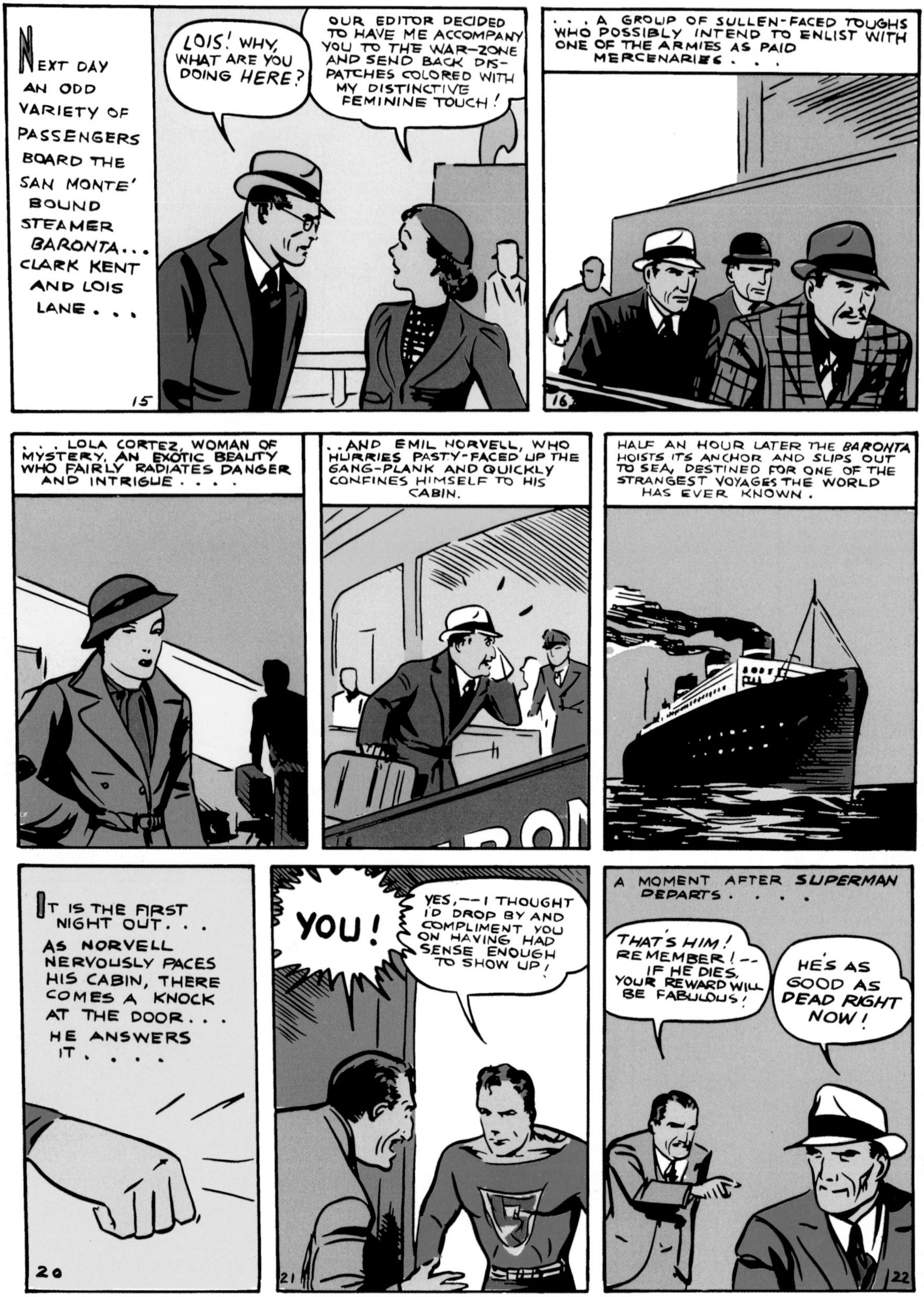
NEXT DAY AN ODD VARIETY OF PASSENGERS BOARD THE SAN MONTE' BOUND STEAMER BARONTA... CLARK KENT AND LOIS LANE . . .
LOIS! WHY, WHAT ARE YOU DOING HERE?
OUR EDITOR DECIDED TO HAVE ME ACCOMPANY YOU TO THE WAR-ZONE AND SEND BACK DISPATCHES COLORED WITH MY DISTINCTIVE FEMININE TOUCH!
15
. . . A GROUP OF SULLEN-FACED TOUGHS WHO POSSIBLY INTEND TO ENLIST WITH ONE OF THE ARMIES AS PAID MERCENARIES . . .
16
. . . LOLA CORTEZ, WOMAN OF MYSTERY, AN EXOTIC BEAUTY WHO FAIRLY RADIATES DANGER AND INTRIGUE . . . .
. . AND EMIL NORVELL, WHO HURRIES PASTY-FACED UP THE GANG-PLANK AND QUICKLY CONFINES HIMSELF TO HIS CABIN.
HALF AN HOUR LATER THE BARONTA HOISTS ITS ANCHOR AND SLIPS OUT TO SEA, DESTINED FOR ONE OF THE STRANGEST VOYAGES THE WORLD HAS EVER KNOWN.
IT IS THE FIRST NIGHT OUT. . . AS NORVELL NERVOUSLY PACES HIS CABIN, THERE COMES A KNOCK AT THE DOOR. . . HE ANSWERS IT . . . .
20
YOU!
YES,--I THOUGHT I'D DROP BY AND COMPLIMENT YOU ON HAVING HAD SENSE ENOUGH TO SHOW UP!
21
A MOMENT AFTER SUPERMAN DEPARTS . . . .
THAT'S HIM! REMEMBER!-- IF HE DIES, YOUR REWARD WILL BE FABULOUS!
HE'S AS GOOD AS DEAD RIGHT NOW!
22

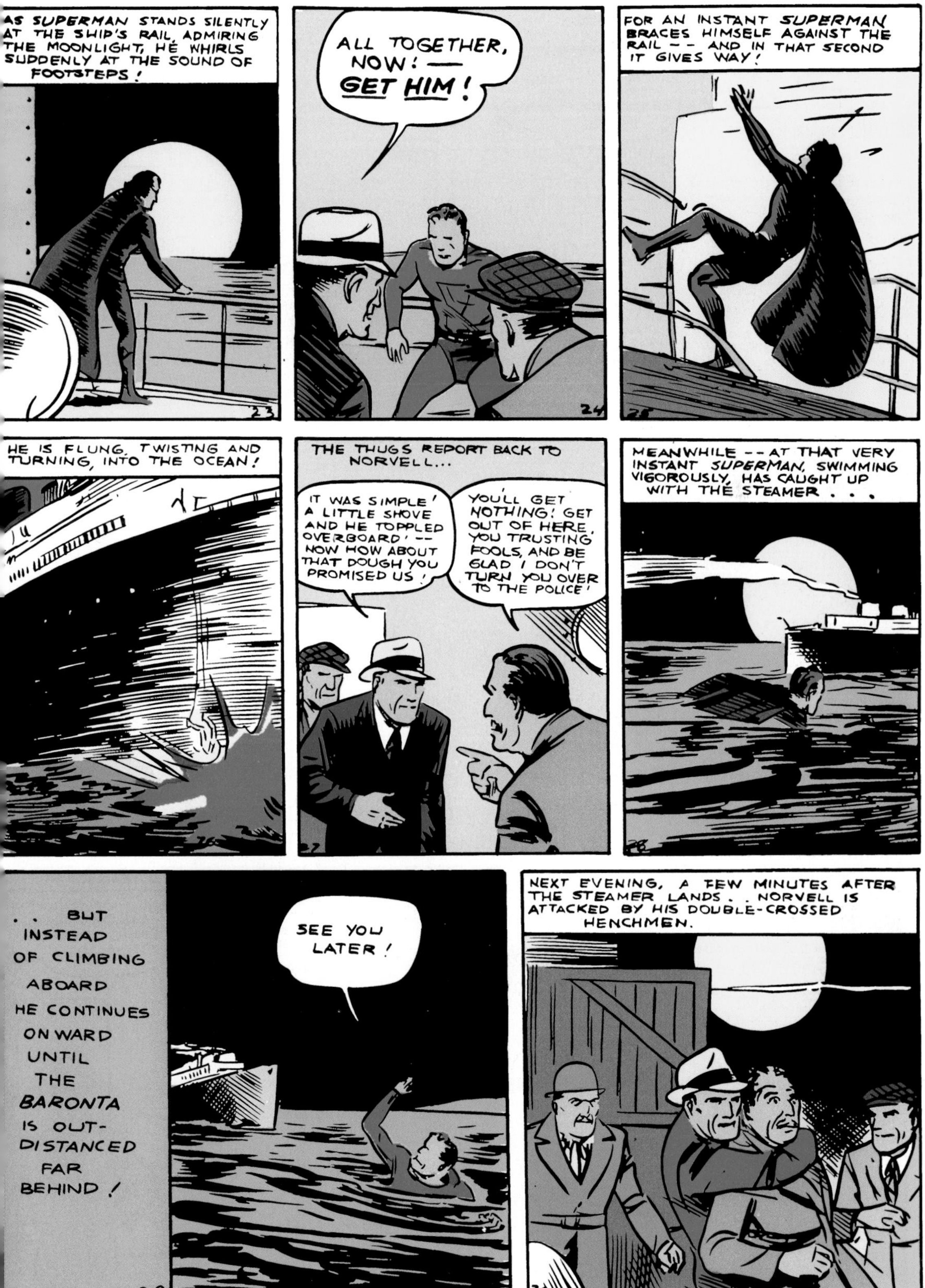
AS SUPERMAN STANDS SILENTLY AT THE SHIP'S RAIL, ADMIRING THE MOONLIGHT, HE WHIRLS SUDDENLY AT THE SOUND OF FOOTSTEPS!
ALL TOGETHER, NOW! — GET HIM!
FOR AN INSTANT SUPERMAN BRACES HIMSELF AGAINST THE RAIL -- AND IN THAT SECOND IT GIVES WAY!
HE IS FLUNG, TWISTING AND TURNING, INTO THE OCEAN!
THE THUGS REPORT BACK TO NORVELL...
IT WAS SIMPLE! A LITTLE SHOVE AND HE TOPPLED OVERBOARD! -- NOW HOW ABOUT THAT DOUGH YOU PROMISED US!
YOU'LL GET NOTHING! GET OUT OF HERE, YOU TRUSTING FOOLS, AND BE GLAD I DON'T TURN YOU OVER TO THE POLICE!
MEANWHILE -- AT THAT VERY INSTANT SUPERMAN, SWIMMING VIGOROUSLY, HAS CAUGHT UP WITH THE STEAMER . . .
. . BUT INSTEAD OF CLIMBING ABOARD HE CONTINUES ON WARD UNTIL THE BARONTA IS OUT-DISTANCED FAR BEHIND!
SEE YOU LATER!
NEXT EVENING, A FEW MINUTES AFTER THE STEAMER LANDS . . NORVELL IS ATTACKED BY HIS DOUBLE-CROSSED HENCHMEN.

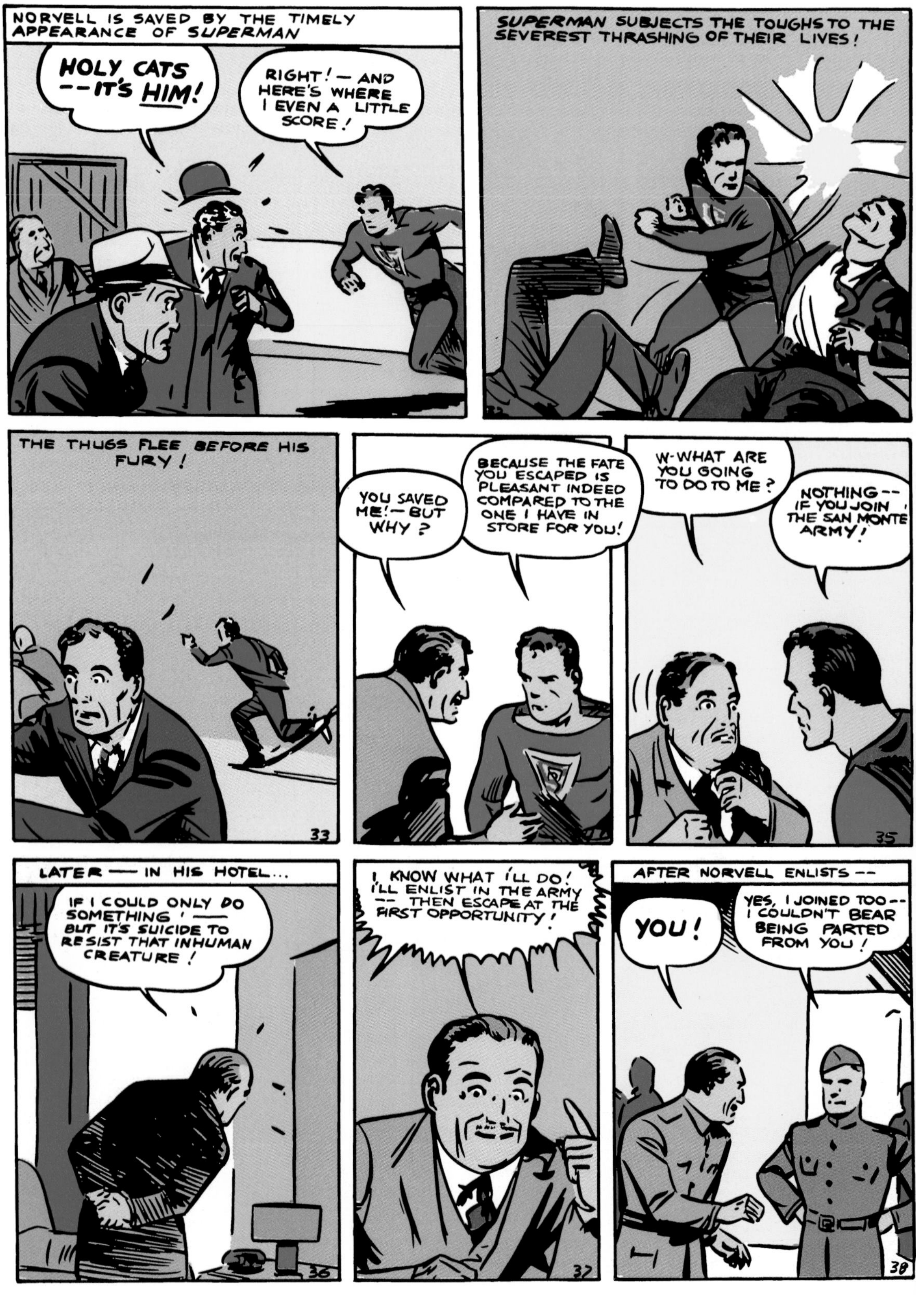
NORVELL IS SAVED BY THE TIMELY APPEARANCE OF SUPERMAN
HOLY CATS --IT'S HIM!
RIGHT! — AND HERE'S WHERE I EVEN A LITTLE SCORE!
SUPERMAN SUBJECTS THE TOUGHS TO THE SEVEREST THRASHING OF THEIR LIVES!
THE THUGS FLEE BEFORE HIS FURY!
33
YOU SAVED ME!—BUT WHY?
BECAUSE THE FATE YOU ESCAPED IS PLEASANT INDEED COMPARED TO THE ONE I HAVE IN STORE FOR YOU!
W-WHAT ARE YOU GOING TO DO TO ME?
NOTHING-- IF YOU JOIN THE SAN MONTE ARMY!
35
LATER — IN HIS HOTEL...
IF I COULD ONLY DO SOMETHING! — BUT IT'S SUICIDE TO RESIST THAT INHUMAN CREATURE!
36
I KNOW WHAT I'LL DO! I'LL ENLIST IN THE ARMY -- THEN ESCAPE AT THE FIRST OPPORTUNITY!
37
AFTER NORVELL ENLISTS --
YOU!
YES, I JOINED TOO-- I COULDN'T BEAR BEING PARTED FROM YOU!
38

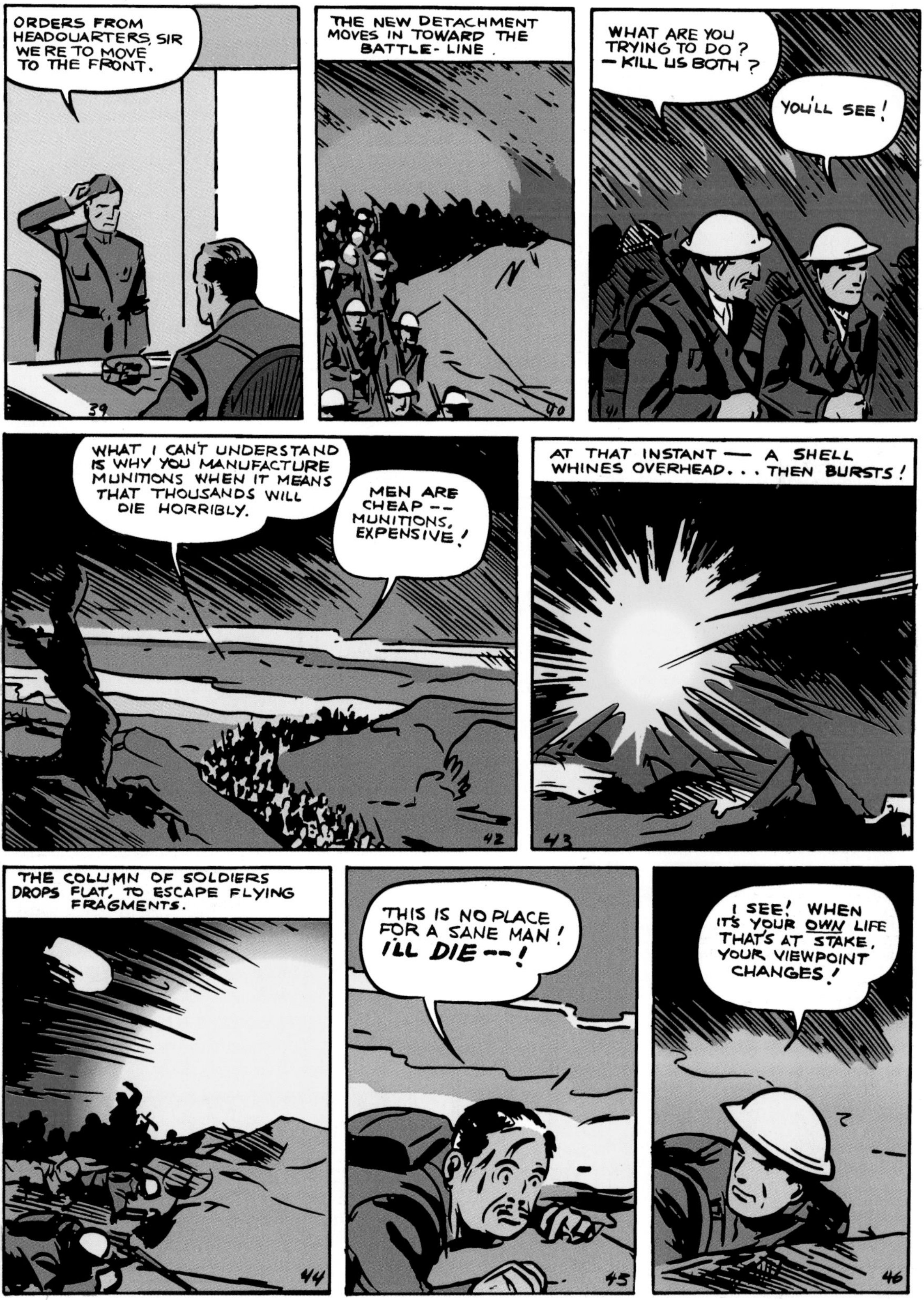
ORDERS FROM HEADQUARTERS, SIR WE'RE TO MOVE TO THE FRONT.
39
THE NEW DETACHMENT MOVES IN TOWARD THE BATTLE-LINE.
40
WHAT ARE YOU TRYING TO DO? —KILL US BOTH?
YOU'LL SEE!
41
WHAT I CAN'T UNDERSTAND IS WHY YOU MANUFACTURE MUNITIONS WHEN IT MEANS THAT THOUSANDS WILL DIE HORRIBLY.
MEN ARE CHEAP -- MUNITIONS, EXPENSIVE!
42
AT THAT INSTANT — A SHELL WHINES OVERHEAD... THEN BURSTS!
43
THE COLUMN OF SOLDIERS DROPS FLAT, TO ESCAPE FLYING FRAGMENTS.
44
THIS IS NO PLACE FOR A SANE MAN! I'LL DIE --!
45
I SEE! WHEN IT'S YOUR OWN LIFE THAT'S AT STAKE, YOUR VIEWPOINT CHANGES!
46

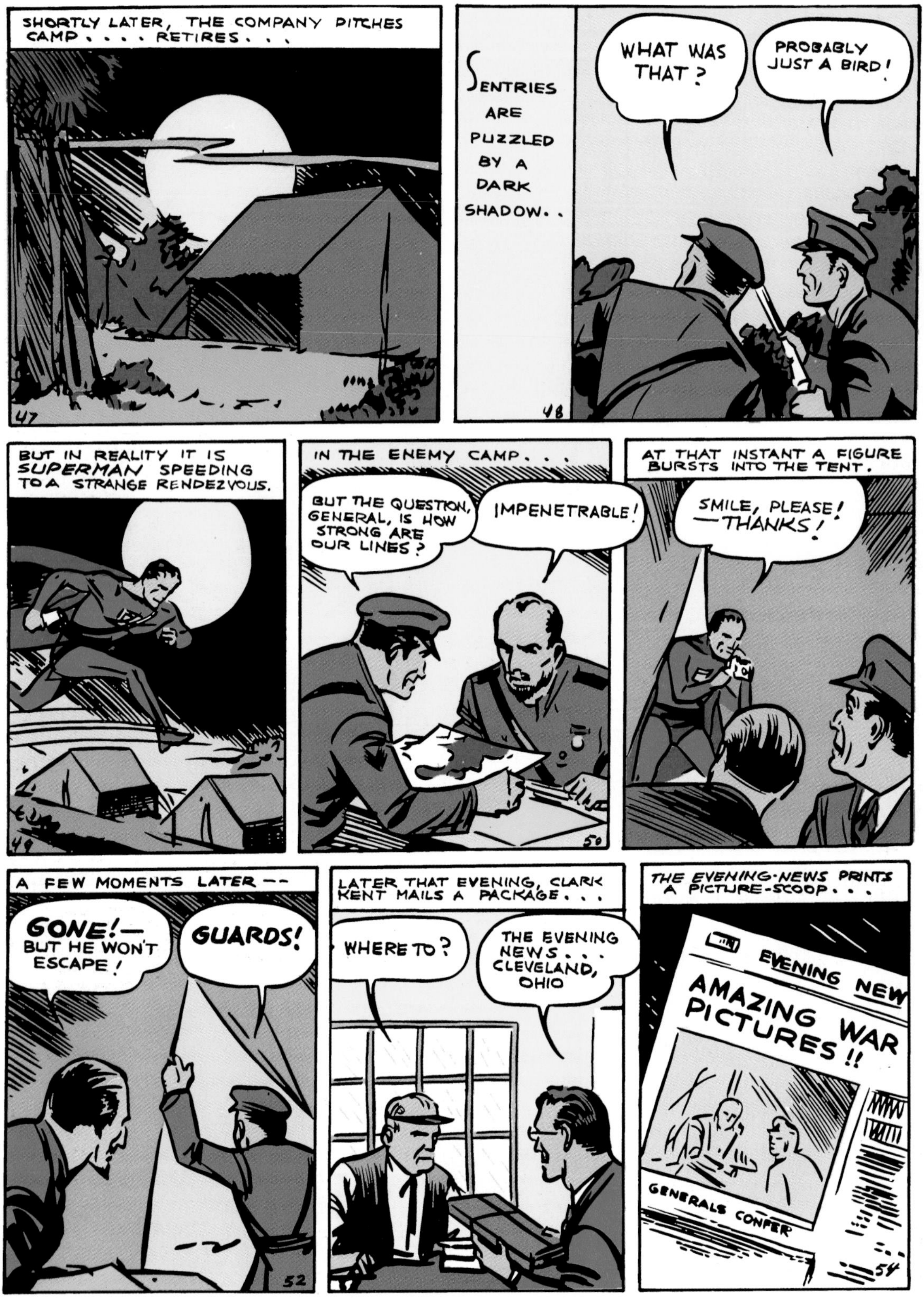
SHORTLY LATER, THE COMPANY PITCHES CAMP.... RETIRES...
SENTRIES ARE PUZZLED BY A DARK SHADOW..
WHAT WAS THAT?
PROBABLY JUST A BIRD!
BUT IN REALITY IT IS SUPERMAN SPEEDING TO A STRANGE RENDEZVOUS.
IN THE ENEMY CAMP...
BUT THE QUESTION, GENERAL, IS HOW STRONG ARE OUR LINES?
IMPENETRABLE!
AT THAT INSTANT A FIGURE BURSTS INTO THE TENT.
SMILE, PLEASE! —THANKS!
A FEW MOMENTS LATER --
GONE!— BUT HE WON'T ESCAPE!
GUARDS!
LATER THAT EVENING, CLARK KENT MAILS A PACKAGE...
WHERE TO?
THE EVENING NEWS... CLEVELAND, OHIO
THE EVENING-NEWS PRINTS A PICTURE-SCOOP...
EVENING NEW
AMAZING WAR PICTURES!!
GENERALS CONFER

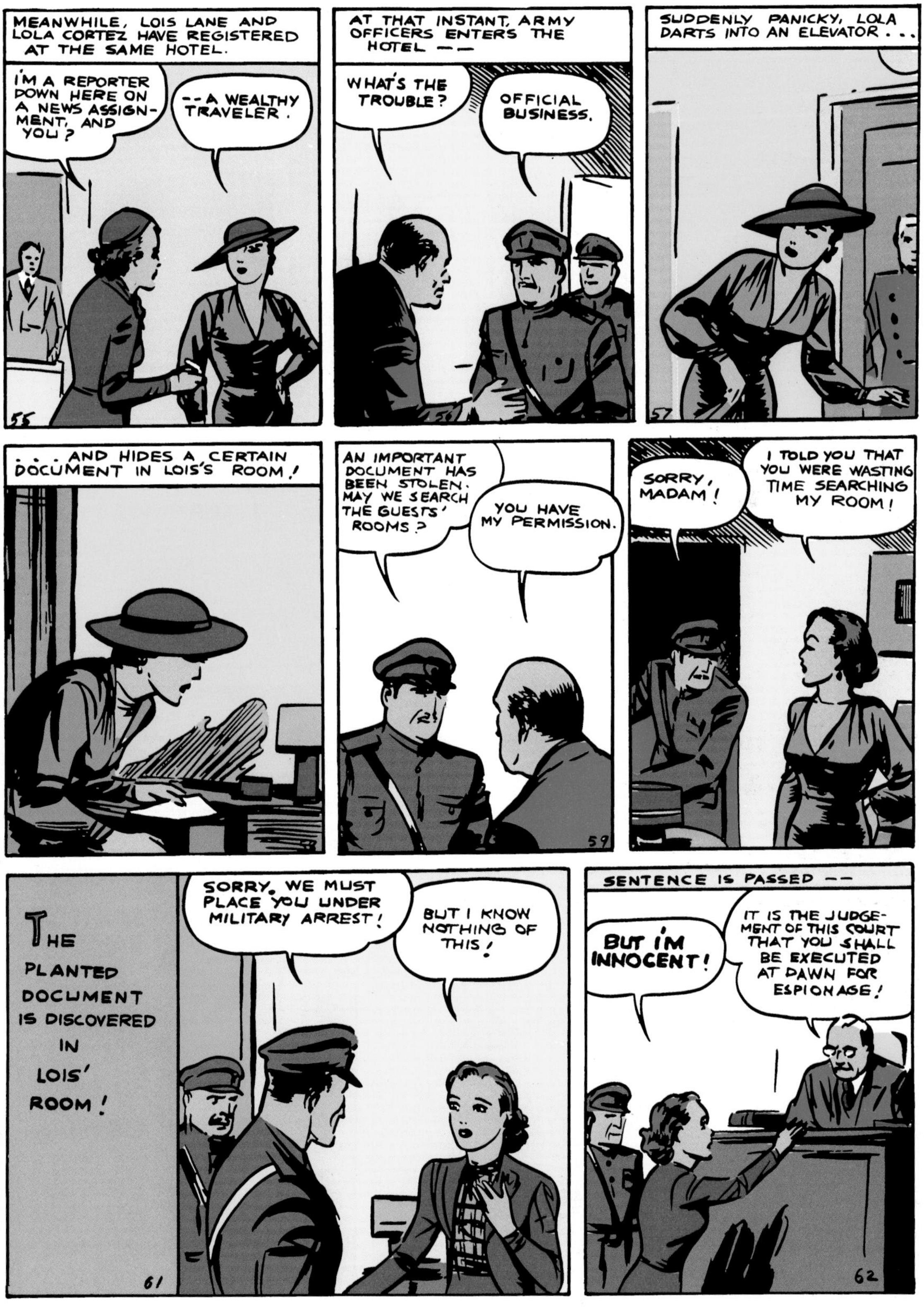
MEANWHILE, LOIS LANE AND LOLA CORTEZ HAVE REGISTERED AT THE SAME HOTEL.
I'M A REPORTER DOWN HERE ON A NEWS ASSIGNMENT, AND YOU?
--A WEALTHY TRAVELER.
AT THAT INSTANT, ARMY OFFICERS ENTERS THE HOTEL --
WHAT'S THE TROUBLE?
OFFICIAL BUSINESS.
SUDDENLY PANICKY, LOLA DARTS INTO AN ELEVATOR . . .
. . . AND HIDES A CERTAIN DOCUMENT IN LOIS'S ROOM!
AN IMPORTANT DOCUMENT HAS BEEN STOLEN. MAY WE SEARCH THE GUESTS' ROOMS?
YOU HAVE MY PERMISSION.
SORRY, MADAM!
I TOLD YOU THAT YOU WERE WASTING TIME SEARCHING MY ROOM!
THE PLANTED DOCUMENT IS DISCOVERED IN LOIS' ROOM!
SORRY. WE MUST PLACE YOU UNDER MILITARY ARREST!
BUT I KNOW NOTHING OF THIS!
SENTENCE IS PASSED --
BUT I'M INNOCENT!
IT IS THE JUDGEMENT OF THIS COURT THAT YOU SHALL BE EXECUTED AT DAWN FOR ESPIONAGE!

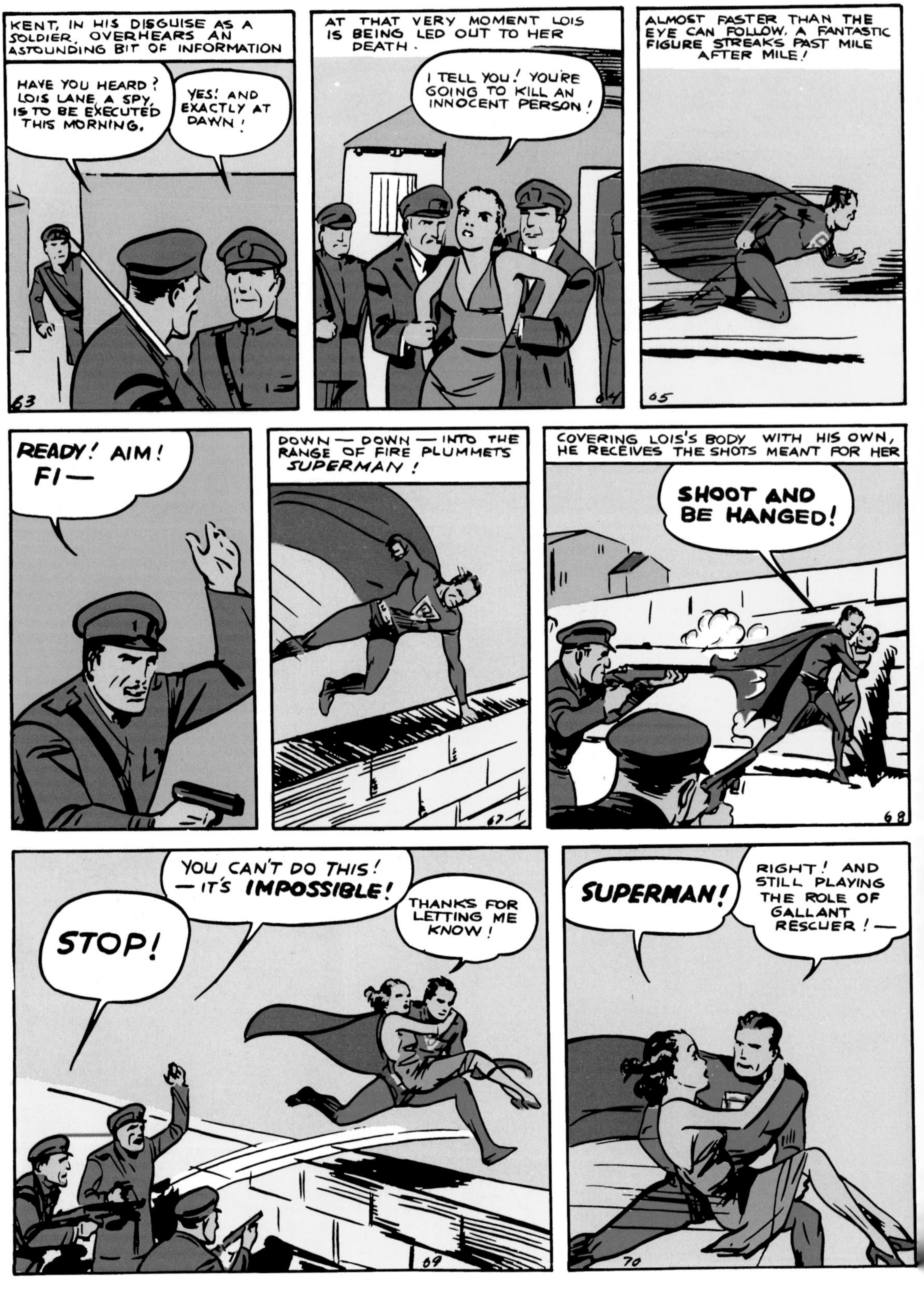
KENT, IN HIS DISGUISE AS A SOLDIER, OVERHEARS AN ASTOUNDING BIT OF INFORMATION
HAVE YOU HEARD? LOIS LANE, A SPY, IS TO BE EXECUTED THIS MORNING.
YES! AND EXACTLY AT DAWN!
AT THAT VERY MOMENT LOIS IS BEING LED OUT TO HER DEATH.
I TELL YOU! YOU'RE GOING TO KILL AN INNOCENT PERSON!
ALMOST FASTER THAN THE EYE CAN FOLLOW, A FANTASTIC FIGURE STREAKS PAST MILE AFTER MILE!
READY! AIM! FI—
DOWN — DOWN — INTO THE RANGE OF FIRE PLUMMETS SUPERMAN!
COVERING LOIS'S BODY WITH HIS OWN, HE RECEIVES THE SHOTS MEANT FOR HER
SHOOT AND BE HANGED!
STOP!
YOU CAN'T DO THIS! — IT'S IMPOSSIBLE!
THANKS FOR LETTING ME KNOW!
SUPERMAN!
RIGHT! AND STILL PLAYING THE ROLE OF GALLANT RESCUER! —

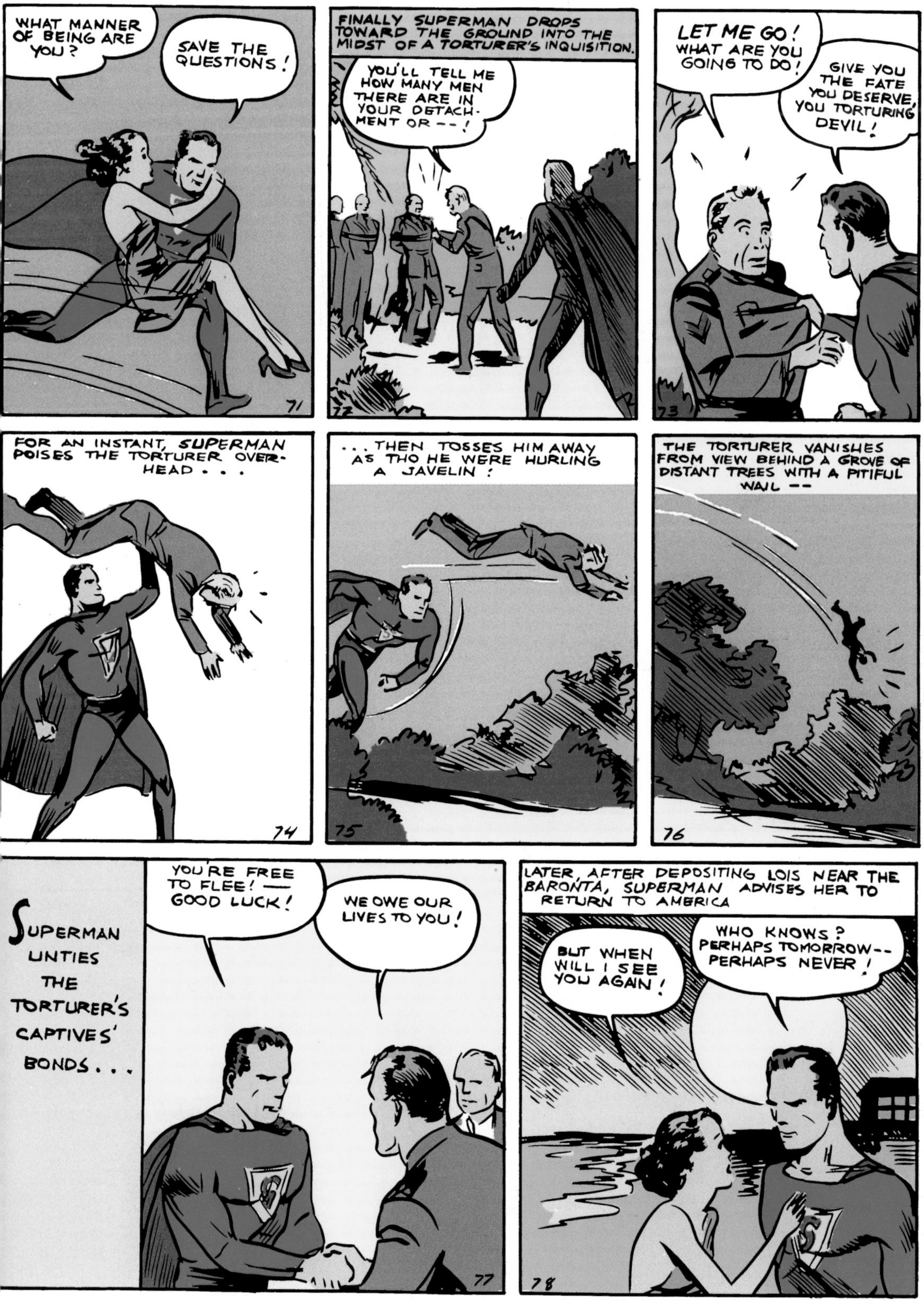
WHAT MANNER OF BEING ARE YOU?
SAVE THE QUESTIONS!
71
FINALLY SUPERMAN DROPS TOWARD THE GROUND INTO THE MIDST OF A TORTURER'S INQUISITION.
YOU'LL TELL ME HOW MANY MEN THERE ARE IN YOUR DETACHMENT OR --!
72
LET ME GO! WHAT ARE YOU GOING TO DO!
GIVE YOU THE FATE YOU DESERVE, YOU TORTURING DEVIL!
73
FOR AN INSTANT, SUPERMAN POISES THE TORTURER OVERHEAD . . .
74
. . . THEN TOSSES HIM AWAY AS THO HE WERE HURLING A JAVELIN!
75
THE TORTURER VANISHES FROM VIEW BEHIND A GROVE OF DISTANT TREES WITH A PITIFUL WAIL --
76
SUPERMAN UNTIES THE TORTURER'S CAPTIVES' BONDS . . .
YOU'RE FREE TO FLEE! — GOOD LUCK!
WE OWE OUR LIVES TO YOU!
77
LATER, AFTER DEPOSITING LOIS NEAR THE BARONTA, SUPERMAN ADVISES HER TO RETURN TO AMERICA
BUT WHEN WILL I SEE YOU AGAIN!
WHO KNOWS? PERHAPS TOMORROW-- PERHAPS NEVER!
78

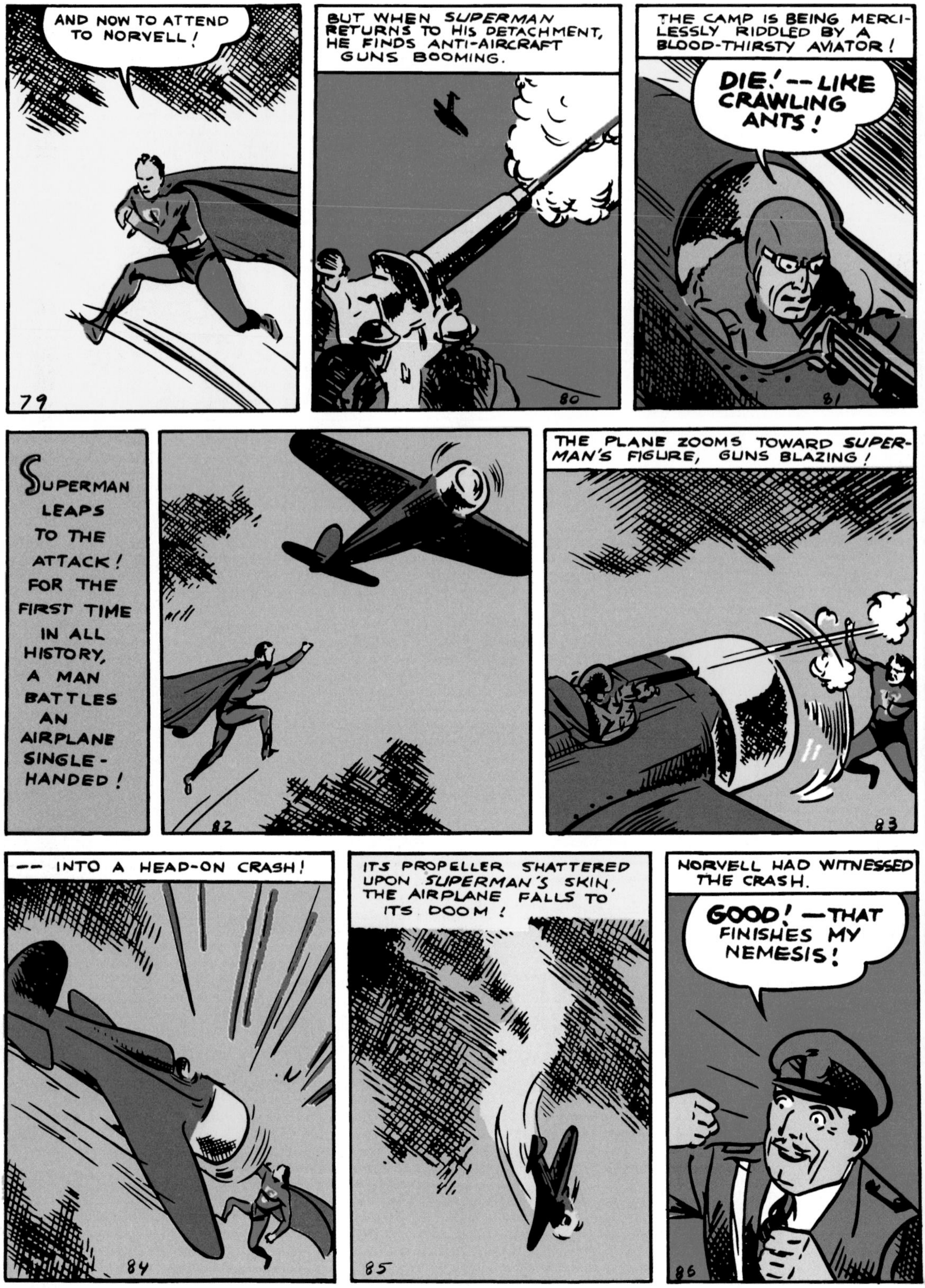
AND NOW TO ATTEND TO NORVELL!
BUT WHEN SUPERMAN RETURNS TO HIS DETACHMENT, HE FINDS ANTI-AIRCRAFT GUNS BOOMING.
THE CAMP IS BEING MERCILESSLY RIDDLED BY A BLOOD-THIRSTY AVIATOR!
DIE! --LIKE CRAWLING ANTS!
SUPERMAN LEAPS TO THE ATTACK! FOR THE FIRST TIME IN ALL HISTORY, A MAN BATTLES AN AIRPLANE SINGLE-HANDED!
THE PLANE ZOOMS TOWARD SUPERMAN'S FIGURE, GUNS BLAZING!
-- INTO A HEAD-ON CRASH!
ITS PROPELLER SHATTERED UPON SUPERMAN'S SKIN, THE AIRPLANE FALLS TO ITS DOOM!
NORVELL HAD WITNESSED THE CRASH.
GOOD! —THAT FINISHES MY NEMESIS!

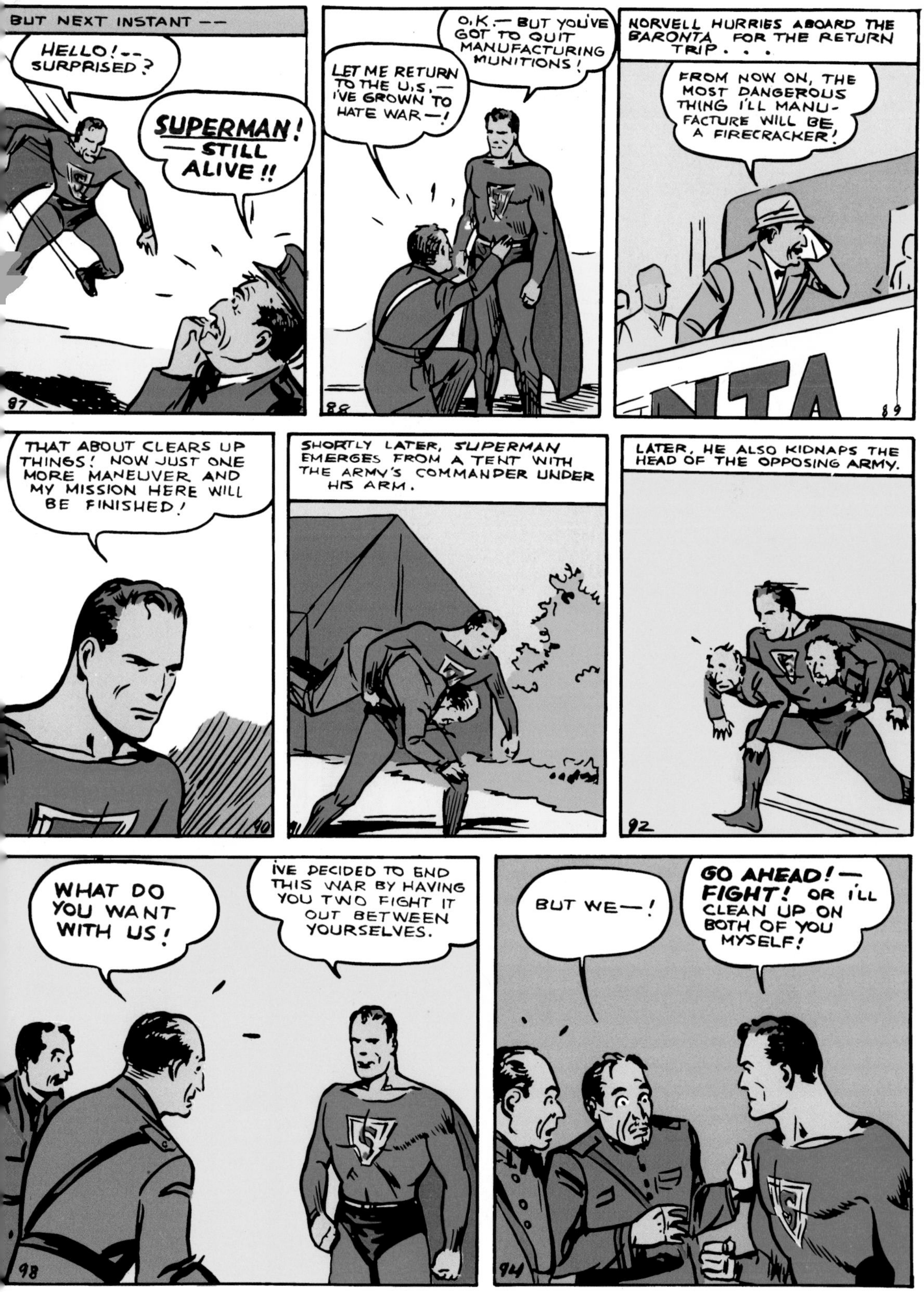
BUT NEXT INSTANT --
HELLO! -- SURPRISED?
SUPERMAN! — STILL ALIVE!!
LET ME RETURN TO THE U.S. — I'VE GROWN TO HATE WAR —!
O.K. — BUT YOU'VE GOT TO QUIT MANUFACTURING MUNITIONS!
NORVELL HURRIES ABOARD THE BARONTA FOR THE RETURN TRIP . . .
FROM NOW ON, THE MOST DANGEROUS THING I'LL MANUFACTURE WILL BE A FIRECRACKER!
NTA
THAT ABOUT CLEARS UP THINGS! NOW JUST ONE MORE MANEUVER AND MY MISSION HERE WILL BE FINISHED!
SHORTLY LATER, SUPERMAN EMERGES FROM A TENT WITH THE ARMY'S COMMANDER UNDER HIS ARM.
LATER, HE ALSO KIDNAPS THE HEAD OF THE OPPOSING ARMY.
WHAT DO YOU WANT WITH US!
I'VE DECIDED TO END THIS WAR BY HAVING YOU TWO FIGHT IT OUT BETWEEN YOURSELVES.
BUT WE —!
GO AHEAD! — FIGHT! OR I'LL CLEAN UP ON BOTH OF YOU MYSELF!

BUT WHY SHOULD WE FIGHT ?
WE'RE NOT ANGRY AT EACH OTHER!
95
THEN WHY ARE YOUR ARMIES BATTLING ?
96
I DON'T KNOW! CAN YOU TELL ME ?
NO. CAN YOU ?
97
GENTLEMEN, IT'S OBVIOUS YOU'VE BEEN FIGHTING ONLY TO PROMOTE THE SALE OF MUNITIONS! — WHY NOT SHAKE HANDS AND MAKE UP ?
98
AND SO, DUE TO THE CONCILIATORY EFFORTS OF SUPERMAN, THE WAR IS HALTED.
99
WHEN KENT REPORTS BACK TO HIS EDITOR . .
SINCE YOU'VE BEEN GONE, THERE'S BEEN NO SUPERMAN NEWS. MAYBE HE'S RETIRED FOR GOOD!
SOMEHOW, CHIEF, I'VE A HUNCH HE'LL MAKE HIS APPEARANCE AGAIN-- SOON!
THE END
100

SUPERMAN

JERRY SIEGEL AND JOE SHUSTER

THE NAZIS CLAIM THE WESTWALL IS INVULNERABLE— WELL, HERE'S WHERE I FIND OUT!

TOWARD THE SIEGFRIED LINE RACES **SUPERMAN**, SAVIOR OF THE HELPLESS AND OPPRESSED, AS SHELLS BURST ON ALL SIDES OF HIM!

WITHIN THE UNDERGROUND FORTIFICATIONS...

IT'S INCREDIBLE! WE'VE SCORED DIRECT HITS AND STILL HE KEEPS COMING ON!

KEEP FIRING! ACH! THAT INHUMAN CREATURE HAS **GOT TO BE STOPPED!**

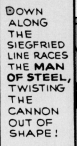

DOWN ALONG THE SIEGFRIED LINE RACES THE **MAN OF STEEL,** TWISTING THE CANNON OUT OF SHAPE!

JUST LET 'EM TRY FIRING **NOW!**

...THEN TEARING THE TOP OFF THE CONCRETE WESTWALL, SHOUTS AN INVITATION BACK TOWARD THE MAGINOT LINE TO THE FRENCH FORCES...

COME AND GET 'EM!

A TERRIFIC LEAP CARRIES **SUPERMAN** FAR INTO GERMANY... BUT AS HE HURTLES THRU THE AIR, A FIGHTING PLANE SWOOPS TOWARD HIM GUNS BLAZING...

LOOKING FOR TROUBLE, EH?

WELL, HERE IT IS!

HIMMEL! VOS IS DISS?

SHORTLY AFTER, THE **MAN OF TOMORROW** STREAKS DOWN THROUGH THE CEILING OF HITLER'S RETREAT...

ZOOM-M

WHEN THE DICTATOR'S GUARDS OFFER OPPOSITION, THEY FIND THE LONE INTRUDER TOO MUCH FOR THEM!

KILL THE SWINE! DON'T LET HIM TOUCH ME!

I'LL GET AROUND TO YOU IN A FEW SECONDS!

I'D LIKE TO LAND A STRICTLY NON-ARYAN SOCK ON YOUR JAW, BUT THERE'S NO TIME FOR THAT! YOU'RE COMING WITH ME WHILE I VISIT A CERTAIN PAL OF YOURS.

PUT ME DOWN! YOU'RE HURTING ME!

EASTWARD RACES SUPERMAN WITH HIS UNWILLING BURDEN, AT A CLIP THAT WOULD OUTDISTANCE THE FASTEST PLANE . . . . !

DON'T FIRE! HE'S HOLDING THE FUEHRER HOSTAGE!

MOSCOW, RUSSIA— AS STALIN REVIEWS HIS TROOPS FROM ATOP A BALCONY, THE MAN OF STEEL'S FIGURE PLUMMETS FROM THE SKY PLUCKING HIM FROM HIS PERCH...

JOE, MEET ADOLF!

WHAT—??

AS SUPERMAN RACES INTO THE MASSED MARCHERS, THE TROOPS SCATTER IN CONFUSION!

THAT'S RIGHT! CLEAR THE WAY!

WHERE ARE YOU TAKING US?

NEXT STOP— GENEVA, SWITZERLAND!

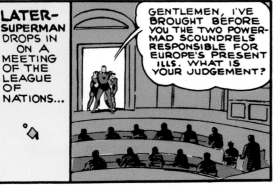

LATER— SUPERMAN DROPS IN ON A MEETING OF THE LEAGUE OF NATIONS...

GENTLEMEN, I'VE BROUGHT BEFORE YOU THE TWO POWER-MAD SCOUNDRELS RESPONSIBLE FOR EUROPE'S PRESENT ILLS. WHAT IS YOUR JUDGEMENT?

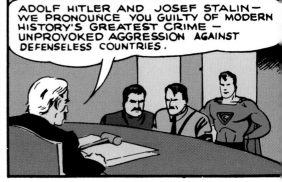

ADOLF HITLER AND JOSEF STALIN— WE PRONOUNCE YOU GUILTY OF MODERN HISTORY'S GREATEST CRIME— UNPROVOKED AGGRESSION AGAINST DEFENSELESS COUNTRIES.

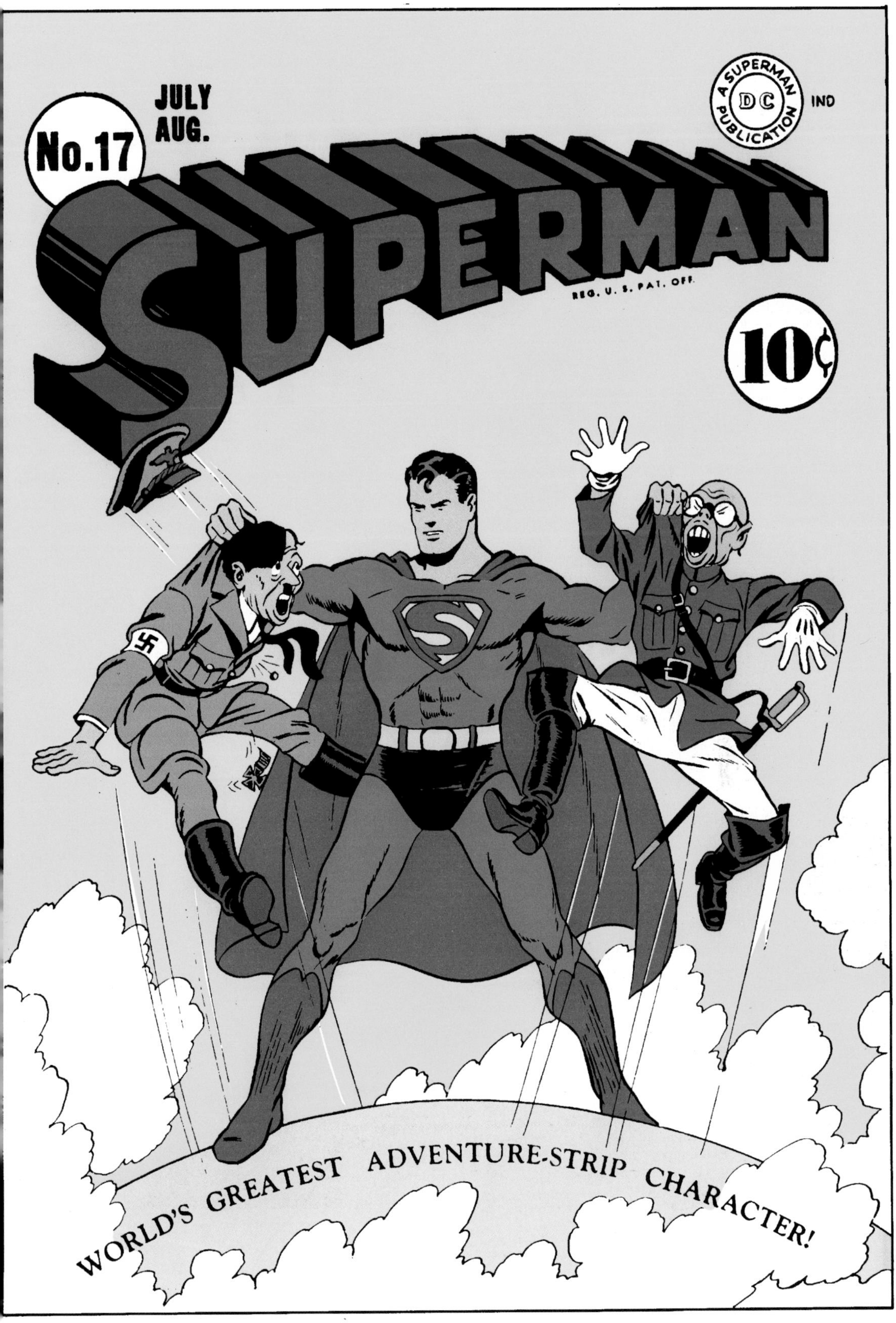

No.17
JULY
AUG.
A SUPERMAN
DC
PUBLICATION
IND
SUPERMAN
REG. U. S. PAT. OFF.
10¢
WORLD'S GREATEST ADVENTURE-STRIP CHARACTER!

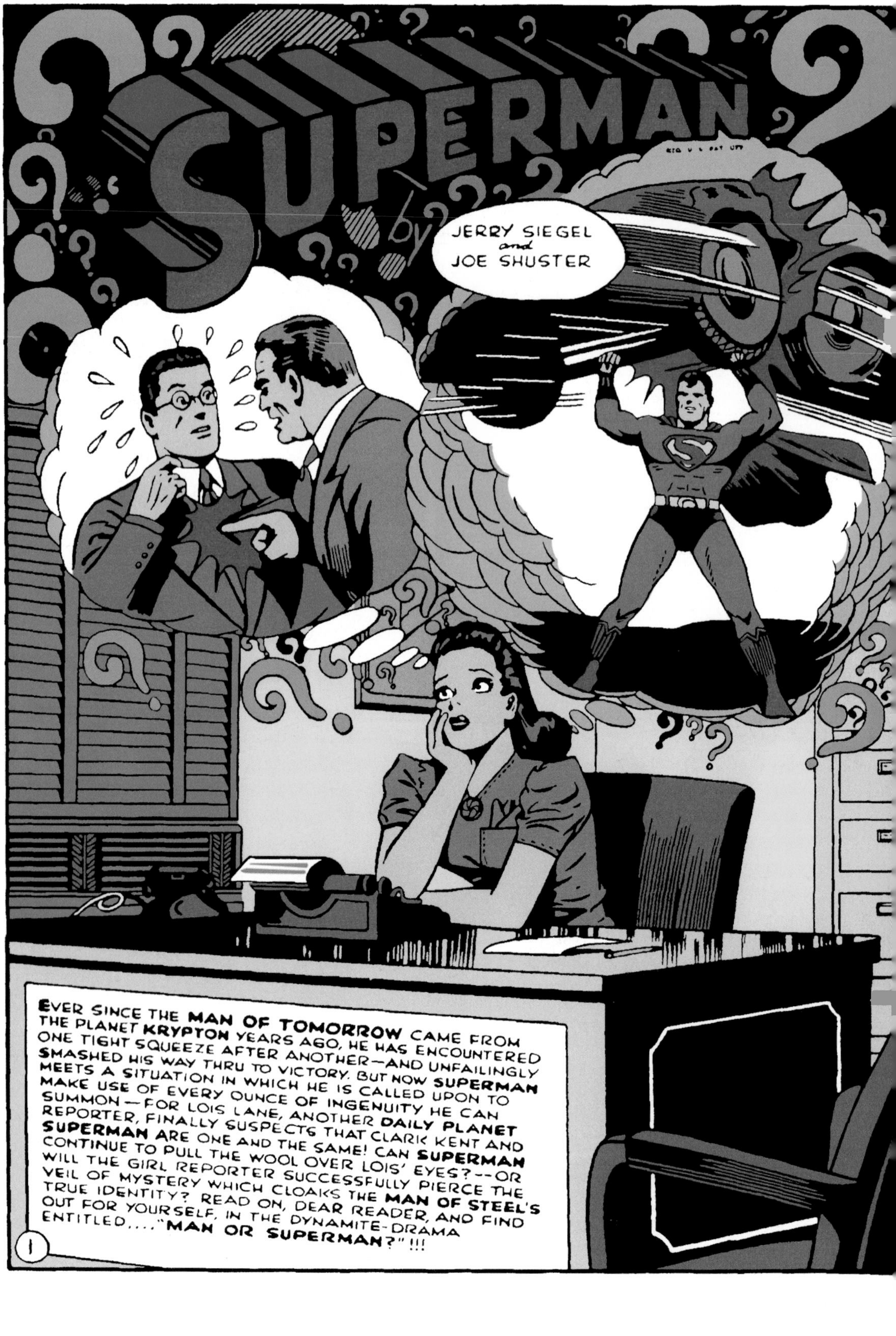
SUPERMAN
by
JERRY SIEGEL and JOE SHUSTER
EVER SINCE THE MAN OF TOMORROW CAME FROM THE PLANET KRYPTON YEARS AGO, HE HAS ENCOUNTERED ONE TIGHT SQUEEZE AFTER ANOTHER—AND UNFAILINGLY SMASHED HIS WAY THRU TO VICTORY. BUT NOW SUPERMAN MEETS A SITUATION IN WHICH HE IS CALLED UPON TO MAKE USE OF EVERY OUNCE OF INGENUITY HE CAN SUMMON—FOR LOIS LANE, ANOTHER DAILY PLANET REPORTER, FINALLY SUSPECTS THAT CLARK KENT AND SUPERMAN ARE ONE AND THE SAME! CAN SUPERMAN CONTINUE TO PULL THE WOOL OVER LOIS' EYES?--OR WILL THE GIRL REPORTER SUCCESSFULLY PIERCE THE VEIL OF MYSTERY WHICH CLOAKS THE MAN OF STEEL'S TRUE IDENTITY? READ ON, DEAR READER, AND FIND OUT FOR YOURSELF, IN THE DYNAMITE-DRAMA ENTITLED...."MAN OR SUPERMAN?"!!!
1

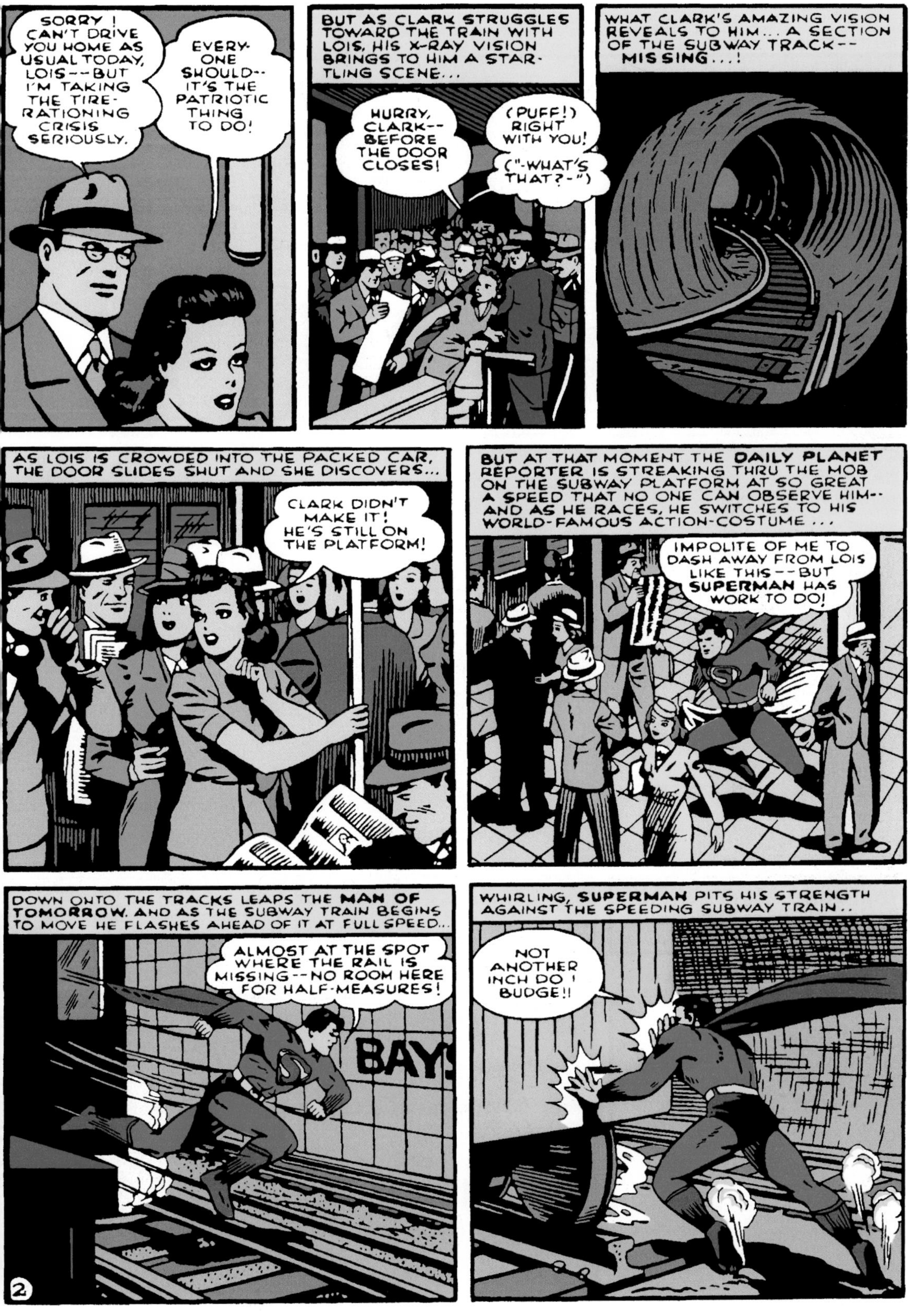
SORRY I CAN'T DRIVE YOU HOME AS USUAL TODAY, LOIS--BUT I'M TAKING THE TIRE-RATIONING CRISIS SERIOUSLY.
EVERY-ONE SHOULD--IT'S THE PATRIOTIC THING TO DO!
BUT AS CLARK STRUGGLES TOWARD THE TRAIN WITH LOIS, HIS X-RAY VISION BRINGS TO HIM A STAR-TLING SCENE...
HURRY, CLARK--BEFORE THE DOOR CLOSES!
(PUFF!) RIGHT WITH YOU!
("-WHAT'S THAT?-")
WHAT CLARK'S AMAZING VISION REVEALS TO HIM... A SECTION OF THE SUBWAY TRACK--MISSING...!
AS LOIS IS CROWDED INTO THE PACKED CAR, THE DOOR SLIDES SHUT AND SHE DISCOVERS...
CLARK DIDN'T MAKE IT! HE'S STILL ON THE PLATFORM!
BUT AT THAT MOMENT THE DAILY PLANET REPORTER IS STREAKING THRU THE MOB ON THE SUBWAY PLATFORM AT SO GREAT A SPEED THAT NO ONE CAN OBSERVE HIM--AND AS HE RACES, HE SWITCHES TO HIS WORLD-FAMOUS ACTION-COSTUME...
IMPOLITE OF ME TO DASH AWAY FROM LOIS LIKE THIS--BUT SUPERMAN HAS WORK TO DO!
DOWN ONTO THE TRACKS LEAPS THE MAN OF TOMORROW. AND AS THE SUBWAY TRAIN BEGINS TO MOVE HE FLASHES AHEAD OF IT AT FULL SPEED...
ALMOST AT THE SPOT WHERE THE RAIL IS MISSING--NO ROOM HERE FOR HALF-MEASURES!
BAYS
2
WHIRLING, SUPERMAN PITS HIS STRENGTH AGAINST THE SPEEDING SUBWAY TRAIN..
NOT ANOTHER INCH DO I BUDGE!!

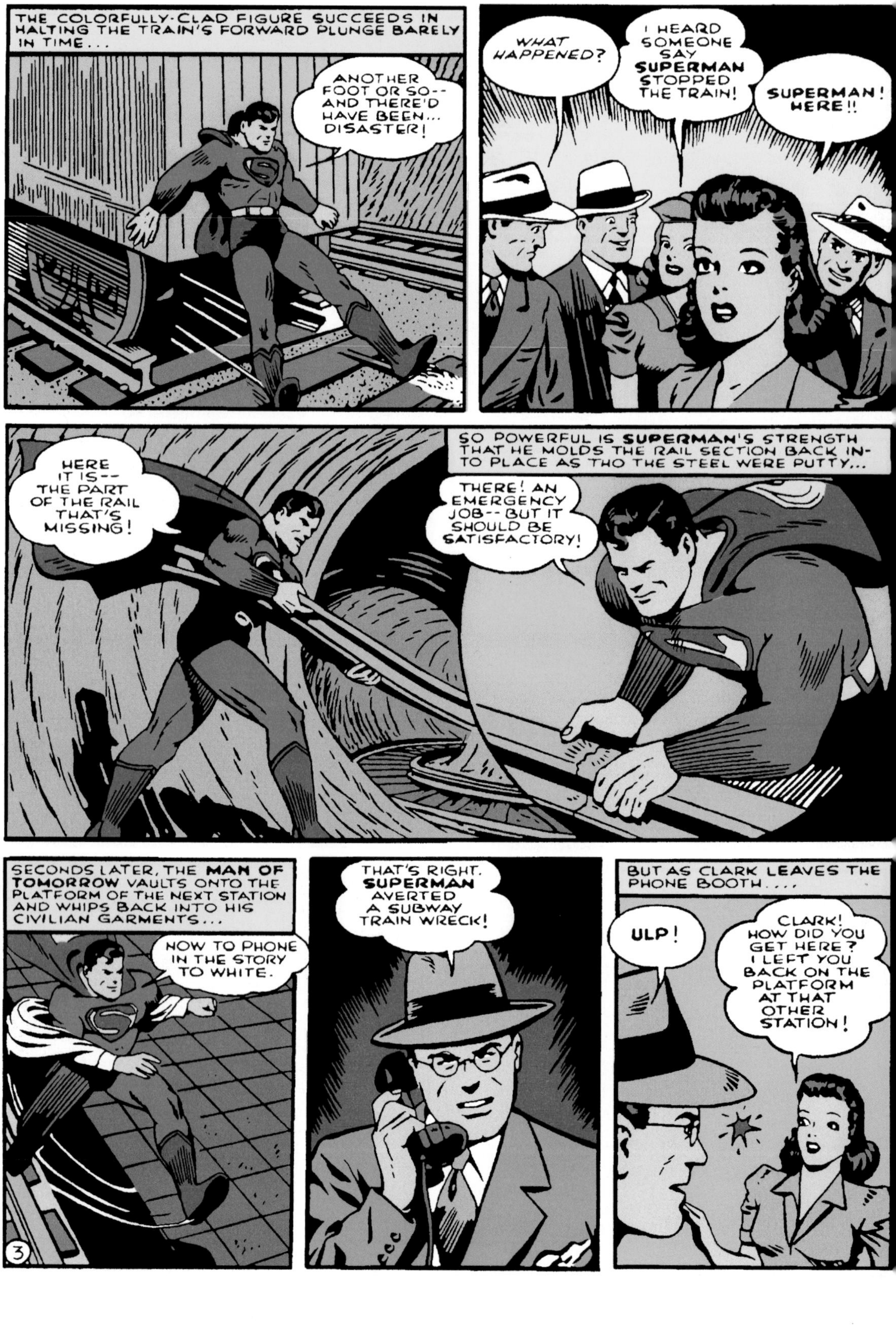
THE COLORFULLY-CLAD FIGURE SUCCEEDS IN HALTING THE TRAIN'S FORWARD PLUNGE BARELY IN TIME...
ANOTHER FOOT OR SO-- AND THERE'D HAVE BEEN... DISASTER!
WHAT HAPPENED?
I HEARD SOMEONE SAY SUPERMAN STOPPED THE TRAIN!
SUPERMAN! HERE!!
HERE IT IS-- THE PART OF THE RAIL THAT'S MISSING!
SO POWERFUL IS SUPERMAN'S STRENGTH THAT HE MOLDS THE RAIL SECTION BACK INTO PLACE AS THO THE STEEL WERE PUTTY...
THERE! AN EMERGENCY JOB-- BUT IT SHOULD BE SATISFACTORY!
SECONDS LATER, THE MAN OF TOMORROW VAULTS ONTO THE PLATFORM OF THE NEXT STATION AND WHIPS BACK INTO HIS CIVILIAN GARMENTS...
NOW TO PHONE IN THE STORY TO WHITE.
3
THAT'S RIGHT. SUPERMAN AVERTED A SUBWAY TRAIN WRECK!
BUT AS CLARK LEAVES THE PHONE BOOTH....
ULP!
CLARK! HOW DID YOU GET HERE? I LEFT YOU BACK ON THE PLATFORM AT THAT OTHER STATION!

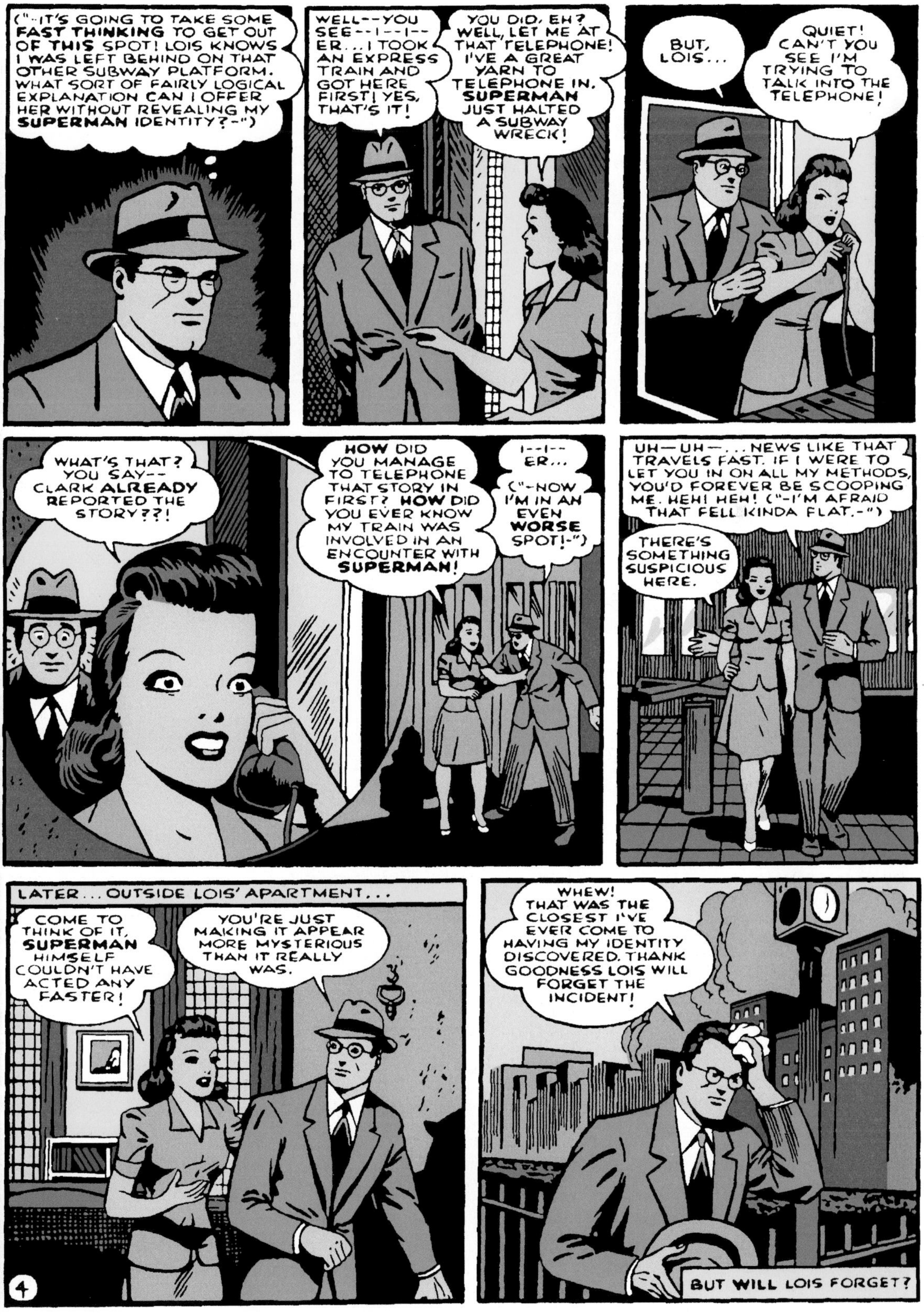
("-IT'S GOING TO TAKE SOME **FAST THINKING** TO GET OUT **OF THIS** SPOT! LOIS KNOWS I WAS LEFT BEHIND ON THAT OTHER SUBWAY PLATFORM. WHAT SORT OF FAIRLY LOGICAL EXPLANATION CAN I OFFER HER WITHOUT REVEALING MY **SUPERMAN** IDENTITY?-")
WELL--YOU SEE--I--I--ER...I TOOK AN EXPRESS TRAIN AND GOT HERE FIRST! YES, THAT'S IT!
YOU DID, EH? WELL, LET ME AT THAT TELEPHONE! I'VE A GREAT YARN TO TELEPHONE IN. **SUPERMAN** JUST HALTED A SUBWAY WRECK!
BUT, LOIS...
QUIET! CAN'T YOU SEE I'M TRYING TO TALK INTO THE TELEPHONE!
WHAT'S THAT? YOU SAY--CLARK **ALREADY** REPORTED THE STORY??!
HOW DID YOU MANAGE TO TELEPHONE THAT STORY IN FIRST? **HOW DID** YOU EVER KNOW MY TRAIN WAS INVOLVED IN AN ENCOUNTER WITH **SUPERMAN**!
I--I--ER...
("-NOW I'M IN AN EVEN **WORSE** SPOT!-")
UH—UH—...NEWS LIKE THAT TRAVELS FAST. IF I WERE TO LET YOU IN ON ALL MY METHODS, YOU'D FOREVER BE SCOOPING ME. HEH! HEH! ("-I'M AFRAID THAT FELL KINDA FLAT.-")
THERE'S SOMETHING SUSPICIOUS HERE.
LATER... OUTSIDE LOIS' APARTMENT...
COME TO THINK OF IT, **SUPERMAN** HIMSELF COULDN'T HAVE ACTED ANY FASTER!
YOU'RE JUST MAKING IT APPEAR MORE MYSTERIOUS THAN IT REALLY WAS.
4
WHEW! THAT WAS THE CLOSEST I'VE EVER COME TO HAVING MY IDENTITY DISCOVERED. THANK GOODNESS LOIS WILL **FORGET** THE INCIDENT!
BUT **WILL** LOIS FORGET?

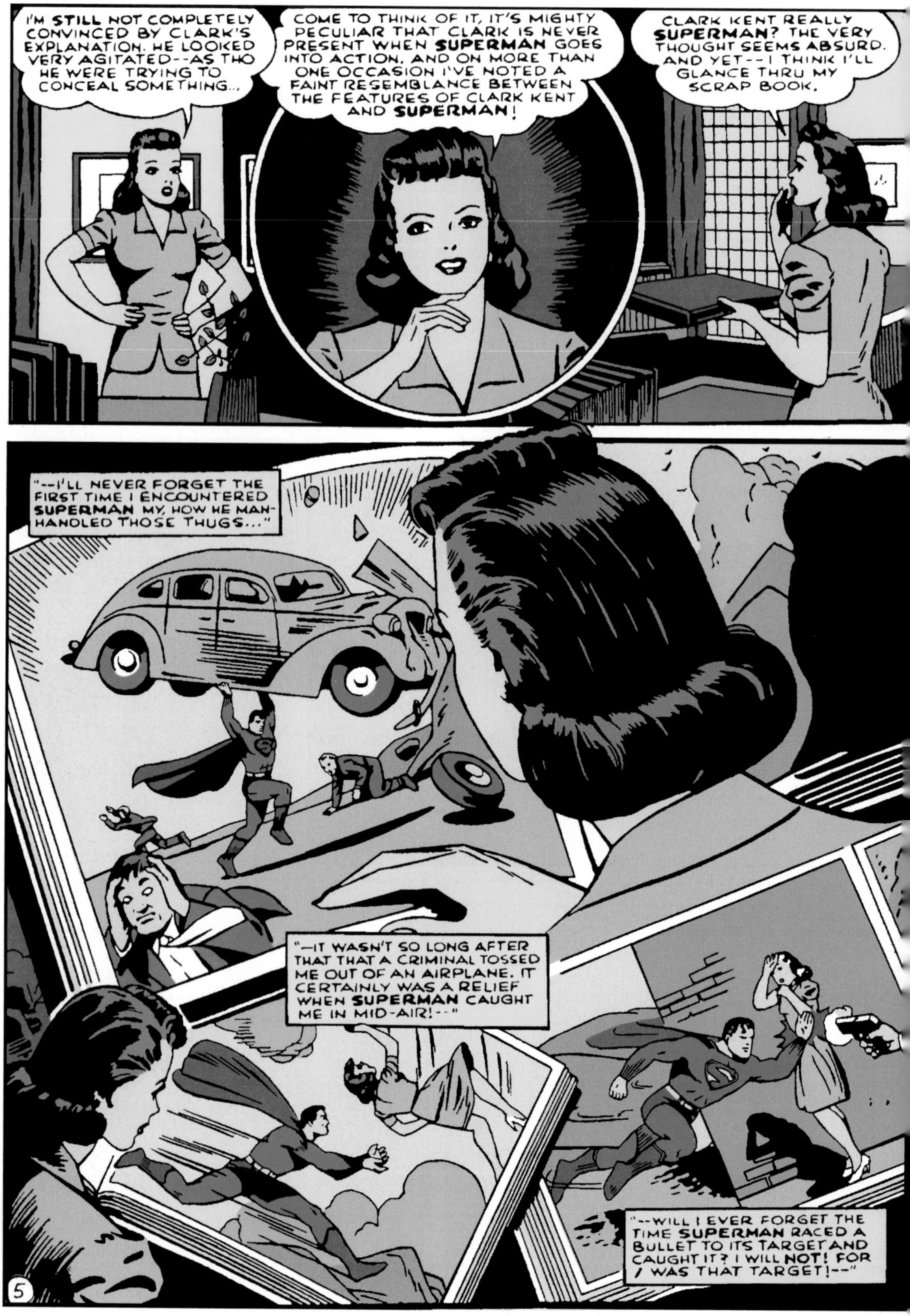
I'M STILL NOT COMPLETELY CONVINCED BY CLARK'S EXPLANATION. HE LOOKED VERY AGITATED--AS THO HE WERE TRYING TO CONCEAL SOMETHING...
COME TO THINK OF IT, IT'S MIGHTY PECULIAR THAT CLARK IS NEVER PRESENT WHEN SUPERMAN GOES INTO ACTION. AND ON MORE THAN ONE OCCASION I'VE NOTED A FAINT RESEMBLANCE BETWEEN THE FEATURES OF CLARK KENT AND SUPERMAN!
CLARK KENT REALLY SUPERMAN? THE VERY THOUGHT SEEMS ABSURD. AND YET--I THINK I'LL GLANCE THRU MY SCRAP BOOK.
"--I'LL NEVER FORGET THE FIRST TIME I ENCOUNTERED SUPERMAN MY, HOW HE MAN-HANDLED THOSE THUGS..."
"--IT WASN'T SO LONG AFTER THAT THAT A CRIMINAL TOSSED ME OUT OF AN AIRPLANE. IT CERTAINLY WAS A RELIEF WHEN SUPERMAN CAUGHT ME IN MID-AIR!--"
"--WILL I EVER FORGET THE TIME SUPERMAN RACED A BULLET TO ITS TARGET AND CAUGHT IT? I WILL NOT! FOR I WAS THAT TARGET!--"
5

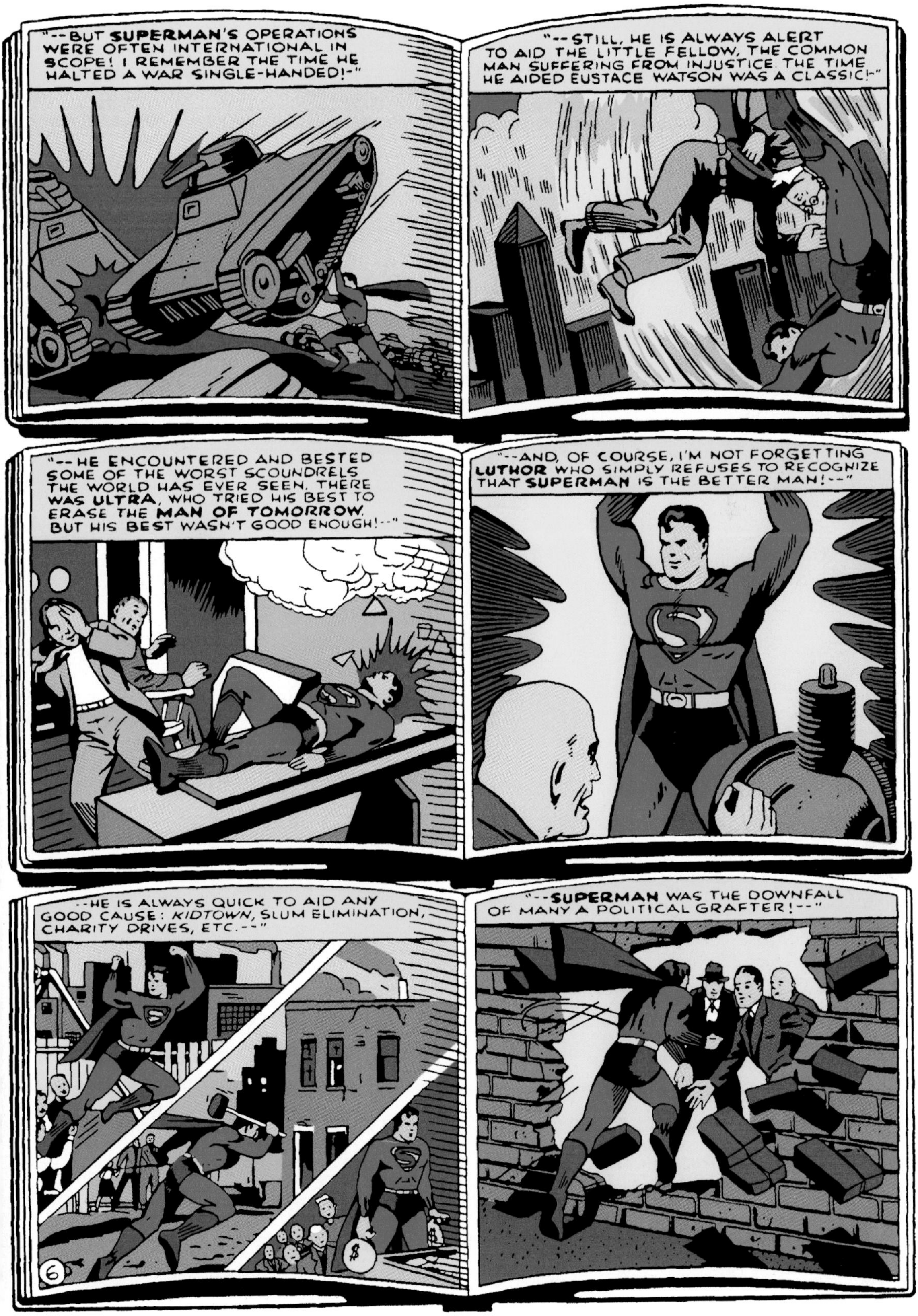
"--BUT SUPERMAN'S OPERATIONS WERE OFTEN INTERNATIONAL IN SCOPE! I REMEMBER THE TIME HE HALTED A WAR SINGLE-HANDED!-"
"--STILL, HE IS ALWAYS ALERT TO AID THE LITTLE FELLOW, THE COMMON MAN SUFFERING FROM INJUSTICE. THE TIME HE AIDED EUSTACE WATSON WAS A CLASSIC!-"
"--HE ENCOUNTERED AND BESTED SOME OF THE WORST SCOUNDRELS THE WORLD HAS EVER SEEN. THERE WAS ULTRA, WHO TRIED HIS BEST TO ERASE THE MAN OF TOMORROW. BUT HIS BEST WASN'T GOOD ENOUGH!--"
"--AND, OF COURSE, I'M NOT FORGETTING LUTHOR WHO SIMPLY REFUSES TO RECOGNIZE THAT SUPERMAN IS THE BETTER MAN!--"
"--HE IS ALWAYS QUICK TO AID ANY GOOD CAUSE: KIDTOWN, SLUM ELIMINATION, CHARITY DRIVES, ETC.--"
"--SUPERMAN WAS THE DOWNFALL OF MANY A POLITICAL GRAFTER!--"

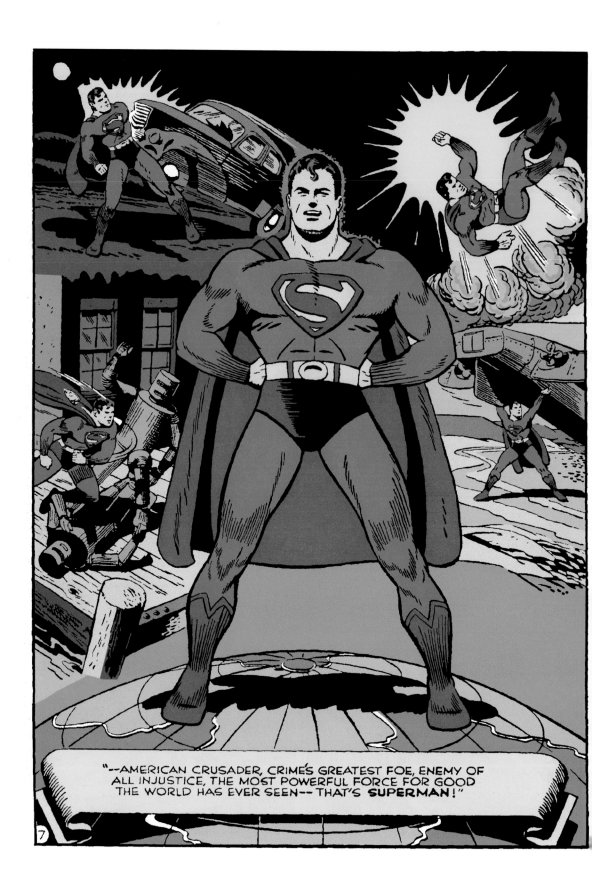

"--AMERICAN CRUSADER, CRIME'S GREATEST FOE, ENEMY OF ALL INJUSTICE, THE MOST POWERFUL FORCE FOR GOOD THE WORLD HAS EVER SEEN-- THAT'S **SUPERMAN!**"

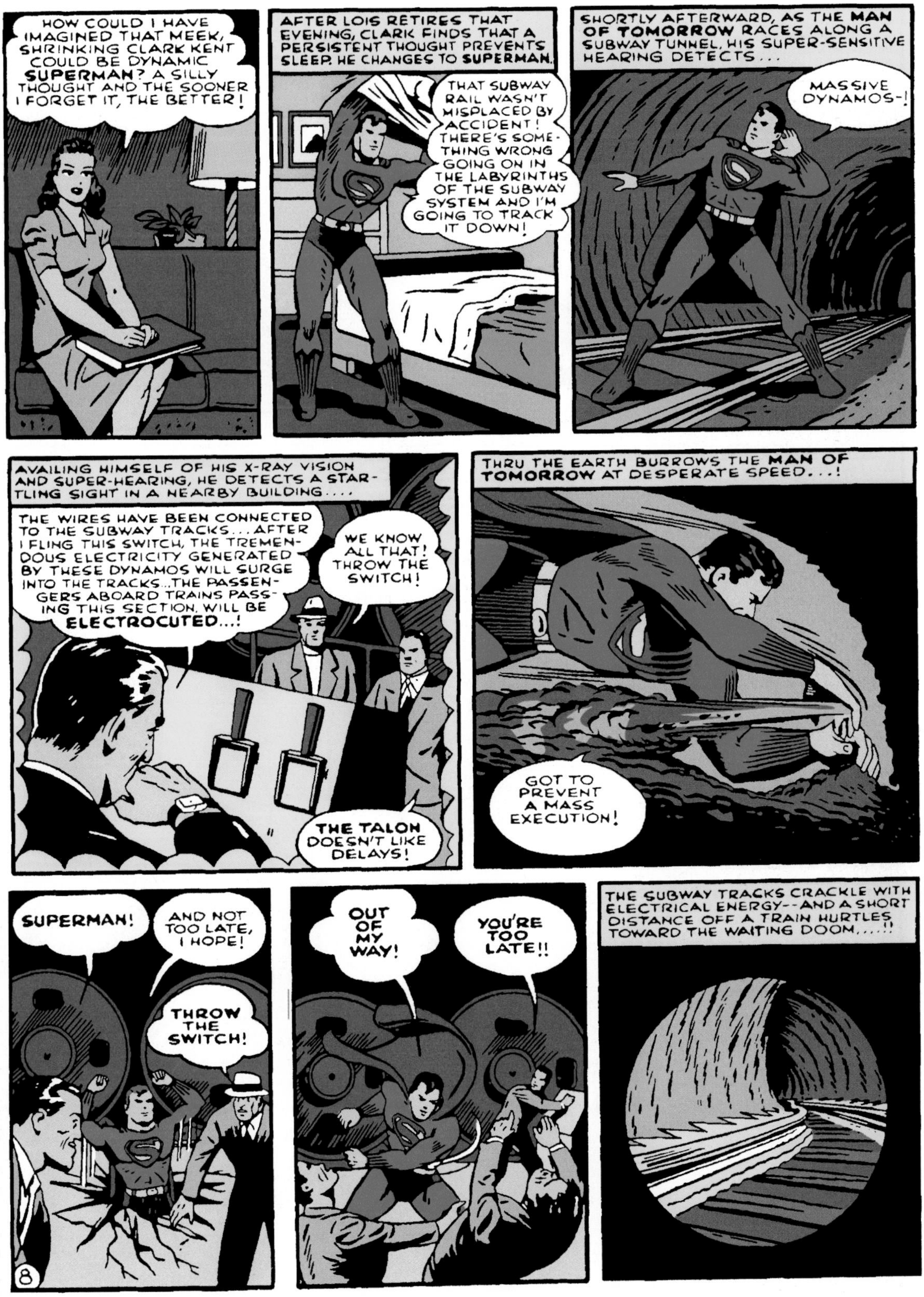
HOW COULD I HAVE IMAGINED THAT MEEK, SHRINKING CLARK KENT COULD BE DYNAMIC SUPERMAN? A SILLY THOUGHT AND THE SOONER I FORGET IT, THE BETTER!
AFTER LOIS RETIRES THAT EVENING, CLARK FINDS THAT A PERSISTENT THOUGHT PREVENTS SLEEP. HE CHANGES TO SUPERMAN.
THAT SUBWAY RAIL WASN'T MISPLACED BY ACCIDENT! THERE'S SOMETHING WRONG GOING ON IN THE LABYRINTHS OF THE SUBWAY SYSTEM AND I'M GOING TO TRACK IT DOWN!
SHORTLY AFTERWARD, AS THE MAN OF TOMORROW RACES ALONG A SUBWAY TUNNEL, HIS SUPER-SENSITIVE HEARING DETECTS...
MASSIVE DYNAMOS-!
AVAILING HIMSELF OF HIS X-RAY VISION AND SUPER-HEARING, HE DETECTS A STARTLING SIGHT IN A NEARBY BUILDING....
THE WIRES HAVE BEEN CONNECTED TO THE SUBWAY TRACKS... AFTER I FLING THIS SWITCH, THE TREMENDOUS ELECTRICITY GENERATED BY THESE DYNAMOS WILL SURGE INTO THE TRACKS...THE PASSENGERS ABOARD TRAINS PASSING THIS SECTION, WILL BE ELECTROCUTED...!
WE KNOW ALL THAT! THROW THE SWITCH!
THE TALON DOESN'T LIKE DELAYS!
THRU THE EARTH BURROWS THE MAN OF TOMORROW AT DESPERATE SPEED...!
GOT TO PREVENT A MASS EXECUTION!
SUPERMAN!
AND NOT TOO LATE, I HOPE!
THROW THE SWITCH!
8
OUT OF MY WAY!
YOU'RE TOO LATE!!
THE SUBWAY TRACKS CRACKLE WITH ELECTRICAL ENERGY--AND A SHORT DISTANCE OFF A TRAIN HURTLES TOWARD THE WAITING DOOM.....!!

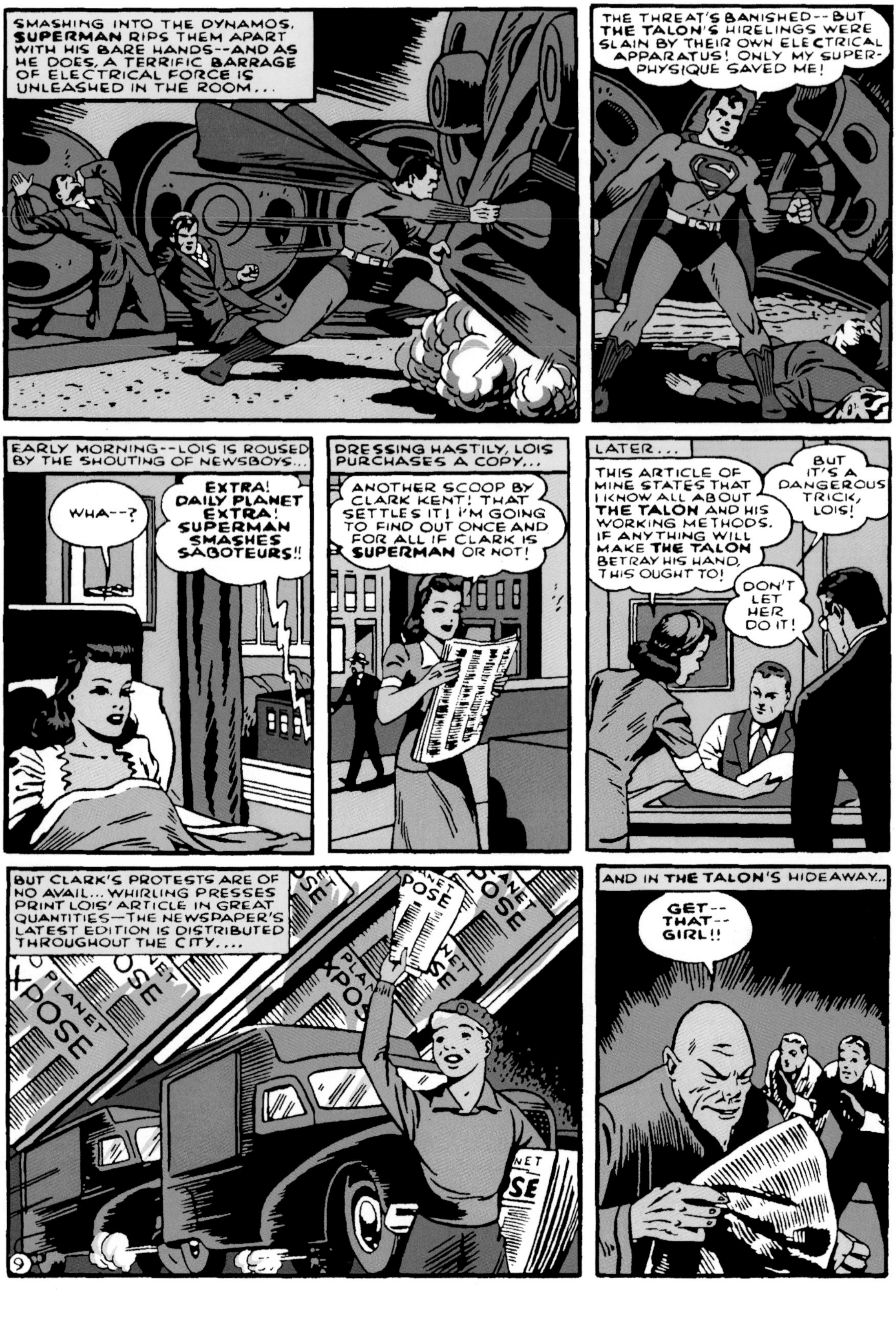
SMASHING INTO THE DYNAMOS, SUPERMAN RIPS THEM APART WITH HIS BARE HANDS--AND AS HE DOES, A TERRIFIC BARRAGE OF ELECTRICAL FORCE IS UNLEASHED IN THE ROOM...
THE THREAT'S BANISHED--BUT THE TALON'S HIRELINGS WERE SLAIN BY THEIR OWN ELECTRICAL APPARATUS! ONLY MY SUPER-PHYSIQUE SAVED ME!
EARLY MORNING--LOIS IS ROUSED BY THE SHOUTING OF NEWSBOYS...
WHA--?
EXTRA! DAILY PLANET EXTRA! SUPERMAN SMASHES SABOTEURS!!
DRESSING HASTILY, LOIS PURCHASES A COPY...
ANOTHER SCOOP BY CLARK KENT! THAT SETTLES IT! I'M GOING TO FIND OUT ONCE AND FOR ALL IF CLARK IS SUPERMAN OR NOT!
LATER...
THIS ARTICLE OF MINE STATES THAT I KNOW ALL ABOUT THE TALON AND HIS WORKING METHODS. IF ANYTHING WILL MAKE THE TALON BETRAY HIS HAND, THIS OUGHT TO!
BUT IT'S A DANGEROUS TRICK, LOIS!
DON'T LET HER DO IT!
BUT CLARK'S PROTESTS ARE OF NO AVAIL... WHIRLING PRESSES PRINT LOIS' ARTICLE IN GREAT QUANTITIES—THE NEWSPAPER'S LATEST EDITION IS DISTRIBUTED THROUGHOUT THE CITY....
PLANET XPOSE
9
AND IN THE TALON'S HIDEAWAY...
GET--THAT--GIRL!!

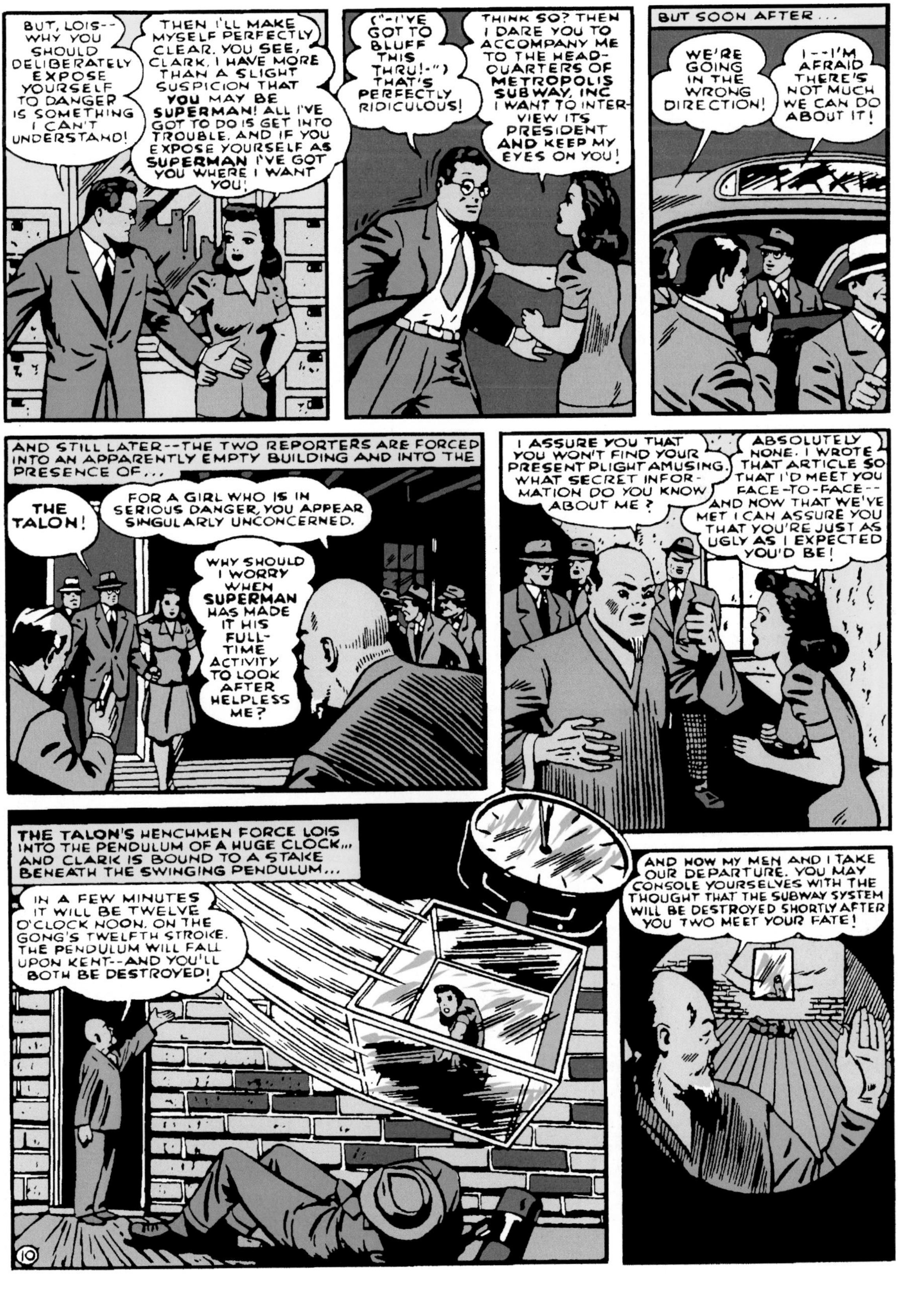
BUT, LOIS--WHY YOU SHOULD DELIBERATELY EXPOSE YOURSELF TO DANGER IS SOMETHING I CAN'T UNDERSTAND!
THEN I'LL MAKE MYSELF PERFECTLY CLEAR. YOU SEE, CLARK, I HAVE MORE THAN A SLIGHT SUSPICION THAT YOU MAY BE SUPERMAN! ALL I'VE GOT TO DO IS GET INTO TROUBLE, AND IF YOU EXPOSE YOURSELF AS SUPERMAN I'VE GOT YOU WHERE I WANT YOU!
("-I'VE GOT TO BLUFF THIS THRU!-") THAT'S PERFECTLY RIDICULOUS!
THINK SO? THEN I DARE YOU TO ACCOMPANY ME TO THE HEADQUARTERS OF METROPOLIS SUBWAY, INC. I WANT TO INTERVIEW ITS PRESIDENT AND KEEP MY EYES ON YOU!
BUT SOON AFTER...
WE'RE GOING IN THE WRONG DIRECTION!
I--I'M AFRAID THERE'S NOT MUCH WE CAN DO ABOUT IT!
AND STILL LATER--THE TWO REPORTERS ARE FORCED INTO AN APPARENTLY EMPTY BUILDING AND INTO THE PRESENCE OF...
THE TALON!
FOR A GIRL WHO IS IN SERIOUS DANGER, YOU APPEAR SINGULARLY UNCONCERNED.
WHY SHOULD I WORRY WHEN SUPERMAN HAS MADE IT HIS FULL-TIME ACTIVITY TO LOOK AFTER HELPLESS ME?
I ASSURE YOU THAT YOU WON'T FIND YOUR PRESENT PLIGHT AMUSING. WHAT SECRET INFORMATION DO YOU KNOW ABOUT ME?
ABSOLUTELY NONE. I WROTE THAT ARTICLE SO THAT I'D MEET YOU FACE-TO-FACE--AND NOW THAT WE'VE MET I CAN ASSURE YOU THAT YOU'RE JUST AS UGLY AS I EXPECTED YOU'D BE!
THE TALON'S HENCHMEN FORCE LOIS INTO THE PENDULUM OF A HUGE CLOCK... AND CLARK IS BOUND TO A STAKE BENEATH THE SWINGING PENDULUM...
IN A FEW MINUTES IT WILL BE TWELVE O'CLOCK NOON. ON THE GONG'S TWELFTH STROKE, THE PENDULUM WILL FALL UPON KENT--AND YOU'LL BOTH BE DESTROYED!
10
AND NOW MY MEN AND I TAKE OUR DEPARTURE. YOU MAY CONSOLE YOURSELVES WITH THE THOUGHT THAT THE SUBWAY SYSTEM WILL BE DESTROYED SHORTLY AFTER YOU TWO MEET YOUR FATE!

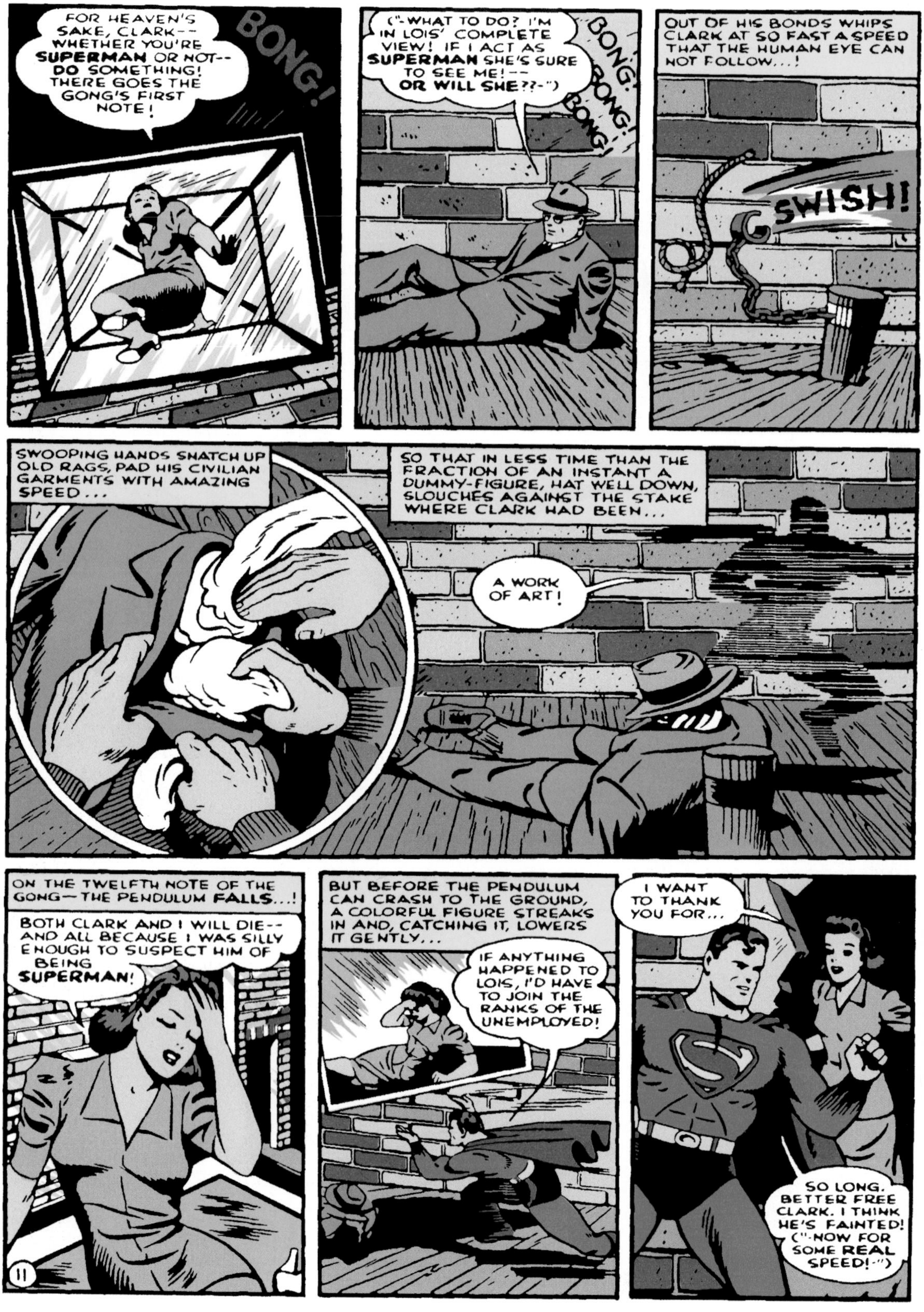
FOR HEAVEN'S SAKE, CLARK-- WHETHER YOU'RE SUPERMAN OR NOT-- DO SOMETHING! THERE GOES THE GONG'S FIRST NOTE!
BONG!
("-WHAT TO DO? I'M IN LOIS' COMPLETE VIEW! IF I ACT AS SUPERMAN SHE'S SURE TO SEE ME!-- OR WILL SHE??-")
BONG! BONG! BONG!
OUT OF HIS BONDS WHIPS CLARK AT SO FAST A SPEED THAT THE HUMAN EYE CAN NOT FOLLOW...!
SWISH!
SWOOPING HANDS SNATCH UP OLD RAGS, PAD HIS CIVILIAN GARMENTS WITH AMAZING SPEED...
SO THAT IN LESS TIME THAN THE FRACTION OF AN INSTANT A DUMMY-FIGURE, HAT WELL DOWN, SLOUCHES AGAINST THE STAKE WHERE CLARK HAD BEEN...
A WORK OF ART!
ON THE TWELFTH NOTE OF THE GONG—THE PENDULUM FALLS...!
BOTH CLARK AND I WILL DIE-- AND ALL BECAUSE I WAS SILLY ENOUGH TO SUSPECT HIM OF BEING SUPERMAN!
11
BUT BEFORE THE PENDULUM CAN CRASH TO THE GROUND, A COLORFUL FIGURE STREAKS IN AND, CATCHING IT, LOWERS IT GENTLY...
IF ANYTHING HAPPENED TO LOIS, I'D HAVE TO JOIN THE RANKS OF THE UNEMPLOYED!
I WANT TO THANK YOU FOR...
SO LONG. BETTER FREE CLARK. I THINK HE'S FAINTED! ("-NOW FOR SOME REAL SPEED!-")

WHILE LOIS TURNS TOWARD THE STAKE, **SUPERMAN** WHIPS PAST HER AT SUPER-SPEED...

("-GOT TO MAKE IT BEFORE SHE COMPLETELY TURNS!-")

SWISH!

EMPTYING THE RAGS, HE DONS HIS OUTER GARMENTS AND ADJUSTS THE ROPES IN PLACE...

("-SHE'S ALMOST GOT HER EYES ON ME!-")

COME TO, CLARK! **SUPERMAN** SAVED US! WE'VE GOT TO GET TO THE SUBWAY SYSTEM HEADQUARTERS AND WARN THEM OF **THE TALON'S** THREAT!

I--I WANT TO KEEP AS FAR AWAY FROM THE TALON AS I CAN!

LATER...IN THE PRIVATE OFFICE OF ALBERT CALDWELL, PRESIDENT OF **METROPOLIS SUBWAY, INC....**

BUT I INSIST IT'S TRUE! **THE TALON** IS GOING TO DESTROY YOUR SUBWAY!

MELO-DRAMATIC NONSENSE!

("-MY X-RAY EYESIGHT...I SEE SOMETHING INTERESTING!-") NO SENSE WASTING TIME HERE, LOIS. I'M GOING BACK TO THE *PLANET* TO TURN IN WHAT WE'VE LEARNED!

BUT ONCE HE IS OUTSIDE THE OFFICE, CLARK CHANGES TO **SUPERMAN** AND RACES BACK IN....

SUPERMAN! STRANGE HOW YOU SHOWED UP SO SOON AFTER CLARK'S DEPARTURE!

WHAT DOES THIS INTERRUPTION MEAN?

I WAS WONDERING, CALDWELL, IF YOU DABBLE IN AMATEUR THEATRICALS?

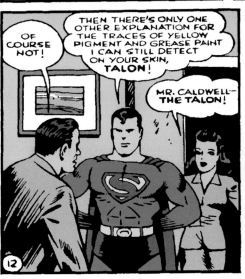

OF COURSE NOT!

THEN THERE'S ONLY ONE OTHER EXPLANATION FOR THE TRACES OF YELLOW PIGMENT AND GREASE PAINT I CAN STILL DETECT ON YOUR SKIN, TALON!

MR. CALDWELL-- THE TALON!

HE'S MAD!

I'M BETTING HE'S THE BIRD WE'RE AFTER!

OBOY! IT'S OFF FOR THE DAILY PLANET FOR ME!

IF I'M FAST ENOUGH I MAY BE ABLE TO SCOOP CLARK!

12

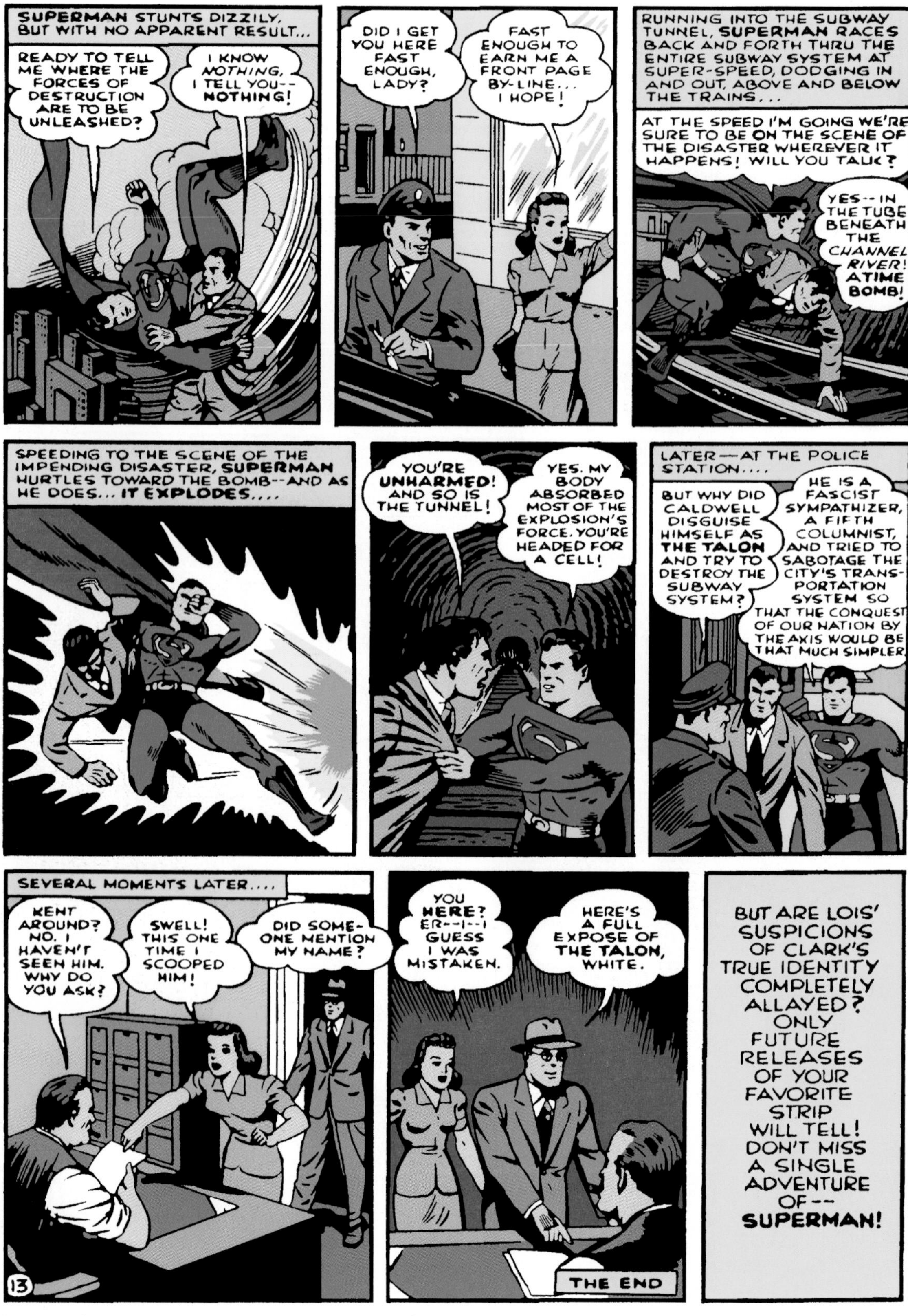

SUPERMAN STUNTS DIZZILY, BUT WITH NO APPARENT RESULT...
READY TO TELL ME WHERE THE FORCES OF DESTRUCTION ARE TO BE UNLEASHED?
I KNOW *NOTHING*, I TELL YOU-- **NOTHING!**
DID I GET YOU HERE FAST ENOUGH, LADY?
FAST ENOUGH TO EARN ME A FRONT PAGE BY-LINE... I HOPE!
RUNNING INTO THE SUBWAY TUNNEL, **SUPERMAN** RACES BACK AND FORTH THRU THE ENTIRE SUBWAY SYSTEM AT SUPER-SPEED, DODGING IN AND OUT, ABOVE AND BELOW THE TRAINS...
AT THE SPEED I'M GOING WE'RE SURE TO BE **ON THE SCENE** OF THE DISASTER WHEREVER IT HAPPENS! WILL YOU TALK?
YES--IN THE TUBE BENEATH THE *CHANNEL RIVER!* **A TIME BOMB!**
SPEEDING TO THE SCENE OF THE IMPENDING DISASTER, **SUPERMAN** HURTLES TOWARD THE BOMB--AND AS HE DOES... **IT EXPLODES**....
YOU'RE **UNHARMED!** AND SO IS THE TUNNEL!
YES. MY BODY ABSORBED MOST OF THE EXPLOSION'S FORCE. YOU'RE HEADED FOR A CELL!
LATER—AT THE POLICE STATION....
BUT WHY DID CALDWELL DISGUISE HIMSELF AS **THE TALON** AND TRY TO DESTROY THE SUBWAY SYSTEM?
HE IS A FASCIST SYMPATHIZER, A FIFTH COLUMNIST, AND TRIED TO SABOTAGE THE CITY'S TRANSPORTATION SYSTEM SO THAT THE CONQUEST OF OUR NATION BY THE AXIS WOULD BE THAT MUCH SIMPLER.
SEVERAL MOMENTS LATER....
KENT AROUND? NO. I HAVEN'T SEEN HIM. WHY DO YOU ASK?
SWELL! THIS ONE TIME I SCOOPED HIM!
DID SOMEONE MENTION MY NAME?
13
YOU **HERE?** ER--I--I GUESS I WAS MISTAKEN.
HERE'S A FULL EXPOSE OF **THE TALON**, WHITE.
THE END
BUT ARE LOIS' SUSPICIONS OF CLARK'S TRUE IDENTITY COMPLETELY ALLAYED? ONLY FUTURE RELEASES OF YOUR FAVORITE STRIP WILL TELL! DON'T MISS A SINGLE ADVENTURE OF-- **SUPERMAN!**

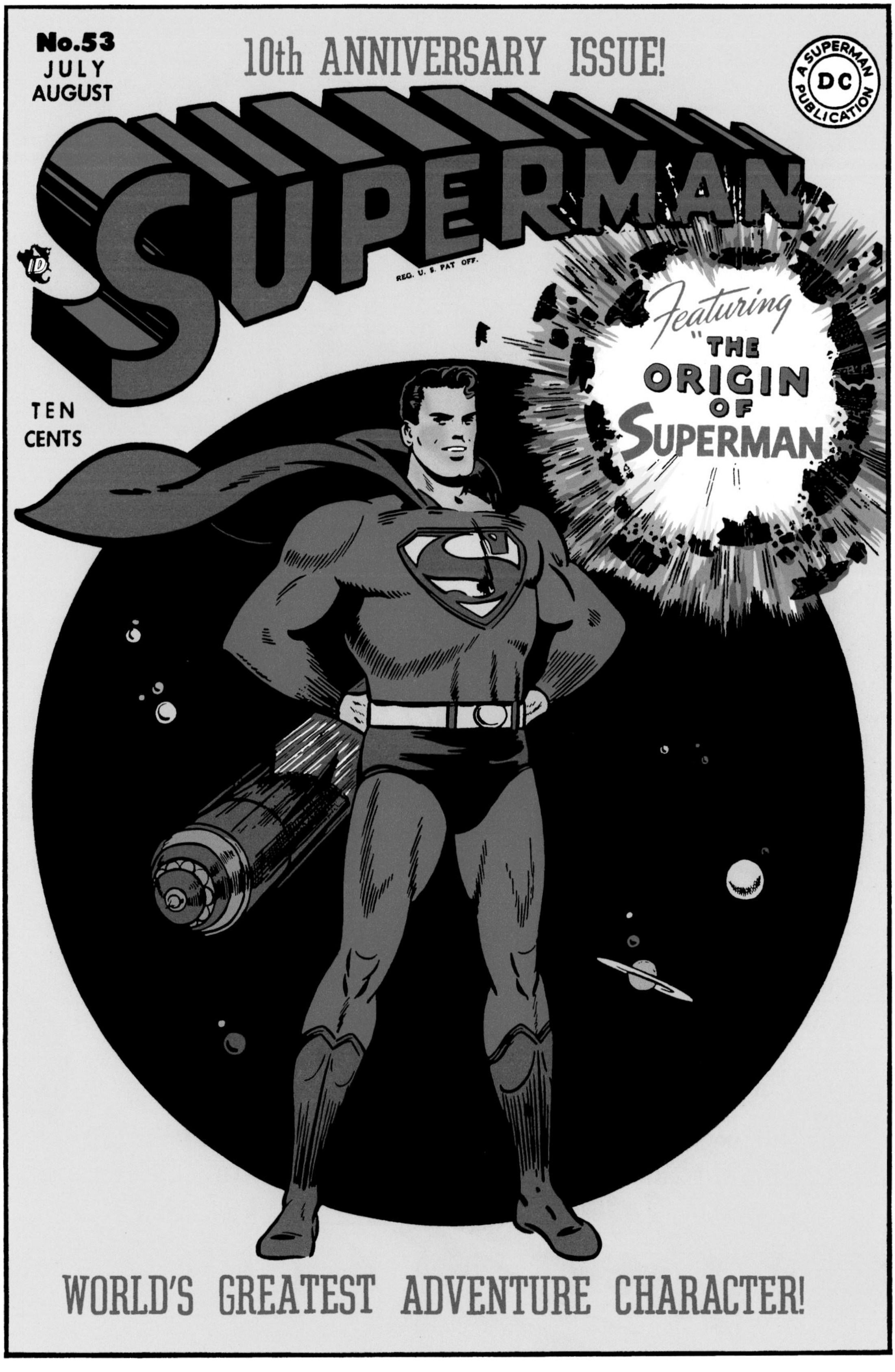
No.53
JULY
AUGUST
10th ANNIVERSARY ISSUE!
A SUPERMAN DC PUBLICATION
SUPERMAN
REG. U. S. PAT OFF.
TEN
CENTS
Featuring
"THE
ORIGIN
OF
SUPERMAN"
WORLD'S GREATEST ADVENTURE CHARACTER!

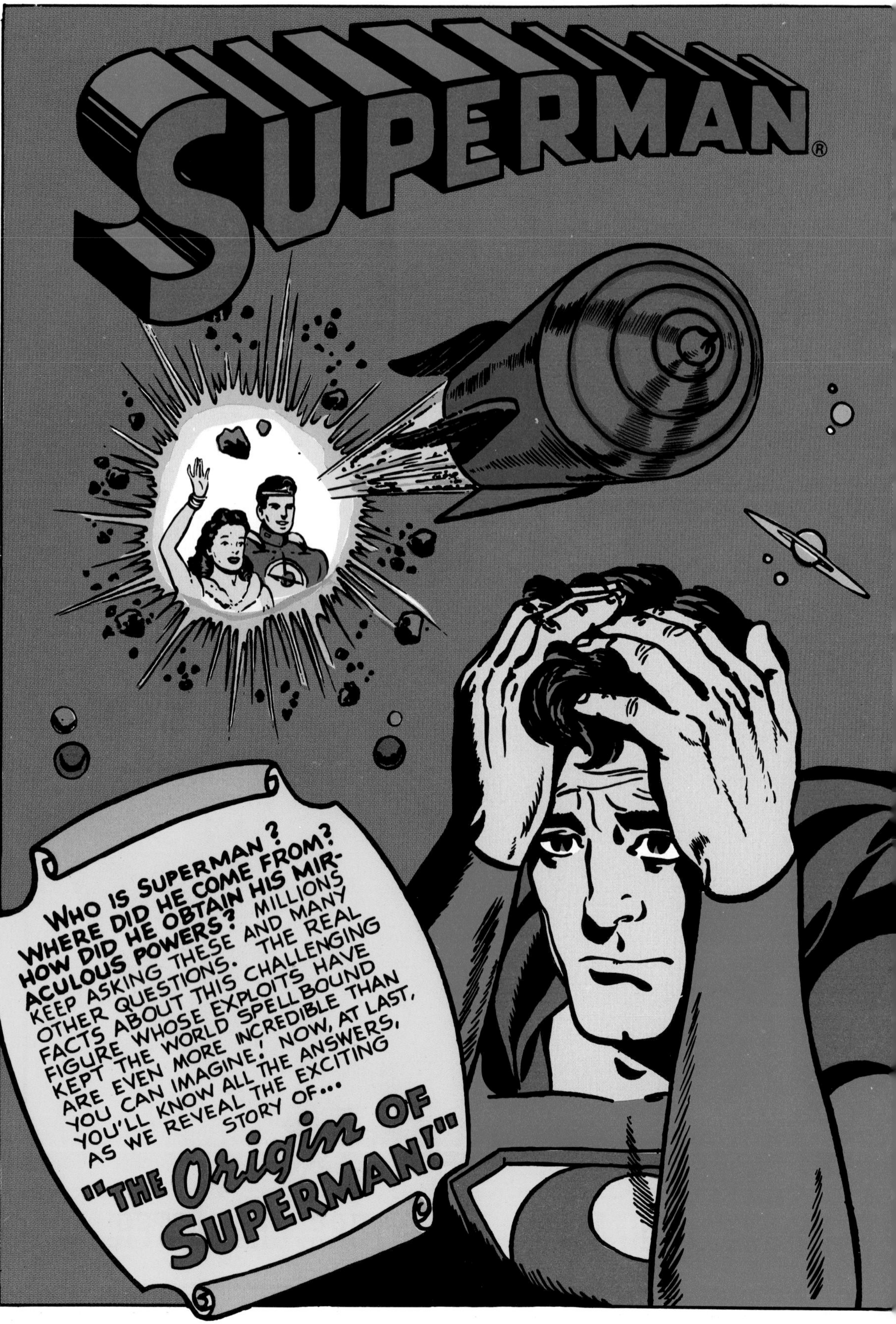
SUPERMAN®
WHO IS SUPERMAN? WHERE DID HE COME FROM? HOW DID HE OBTAIN HIS MIRACULOUS POWERS? MILLIONS KEEP ASKING THESE AND MANY OTHER QUESTIONS. THE REAL FACTS ABOUT THIS CHALLENGING FIGURE WHOSE EXPLOITS HAVE KEPT THE WORLD SPELLBOUND ARE EVEN MORE INCREDIBLE THAN YOU CAN IMAGINE! NOW, AT LAST, YOU'LL KNOW ALL THE ANSWERS, AS WE REVEAL THE EXCITING STORY OF...
"THE Origin OF SUPERMAN!"

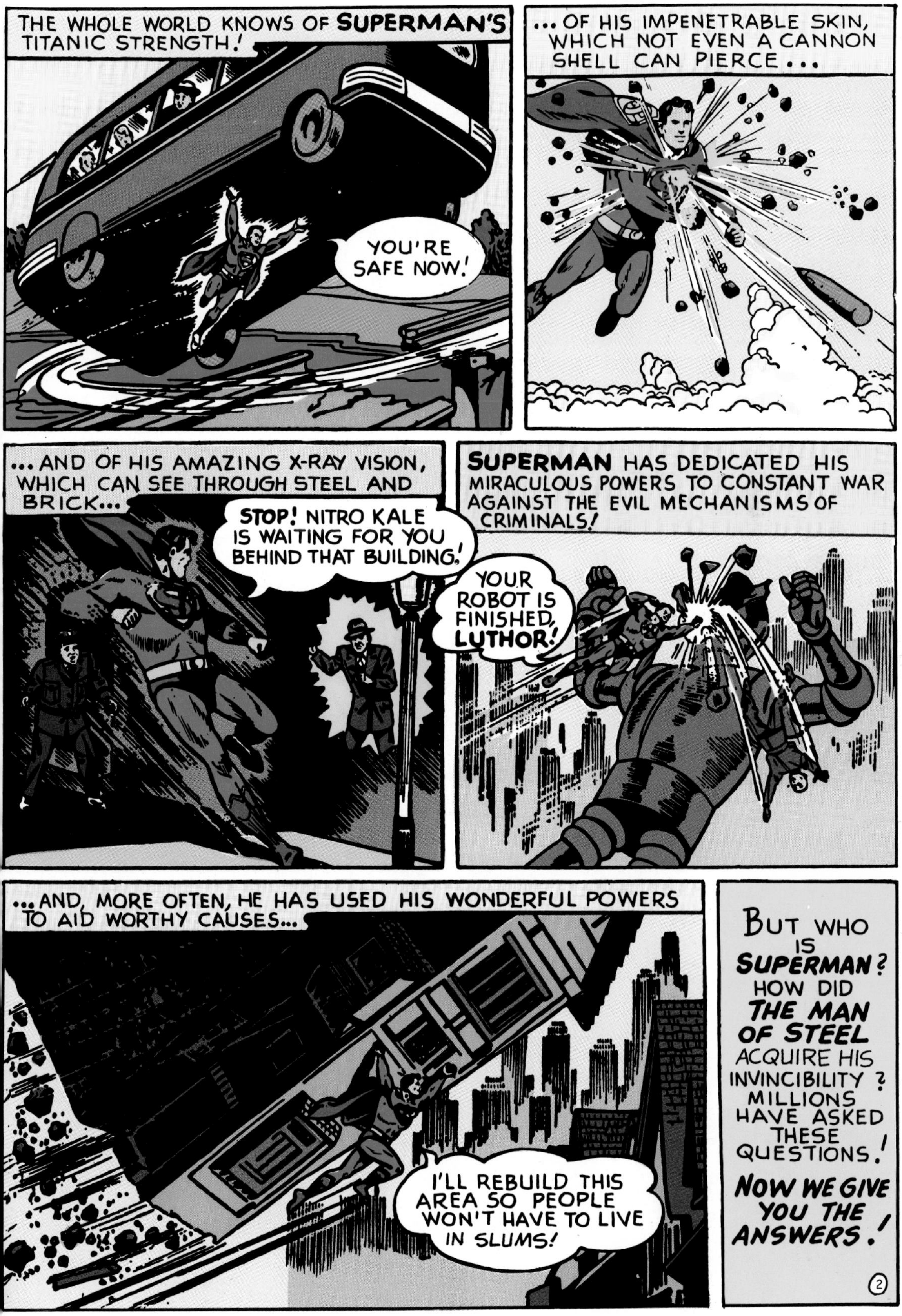
THE WHOLE WORLD KNOWS OF SUPERMAN'S TITANIC STRENGTH!
YOU'RE SAFE NOW!
...OF HIS IMPENETRABLE SKIN, WHICH NOT EVEN A CANNON SHELL CAN PIERCE...
...AND OF HIS AMAZING X-RAY VISION, WHICH CAN SEE THROUGH STEEL AND BRICK...
STOP! NITRO KALE IS WAITING FOR YOU BEHIND THAT BUILDING!
SUPERMAN HAS DEDICATED HIS MIRACULOUS POWERS TO CONSTANT WAR AGAINST THE EVIL MECHANISMS OF CRIMINALS!
YOUR ROBOT IS FINISHED, LUTHOR!
...AND, MORE OFTEN, HE HAS USED HIS WONDERFUL POWERS TO AID WORTHY CAUSES...
I'LL REBUILD THIS AREA SO PEOPLE WON'T HAVE TO LIVE IN SLUMS!
BUT WHO IS SUPERMAN? HOW DID THE MAN OF STEEL ACQUIRE HIS INVINCIBILITY? MILLIONS HAVE ASKED THESE QUESTIONS! NOW WE GIVE YOU THE ANSWERS!
2

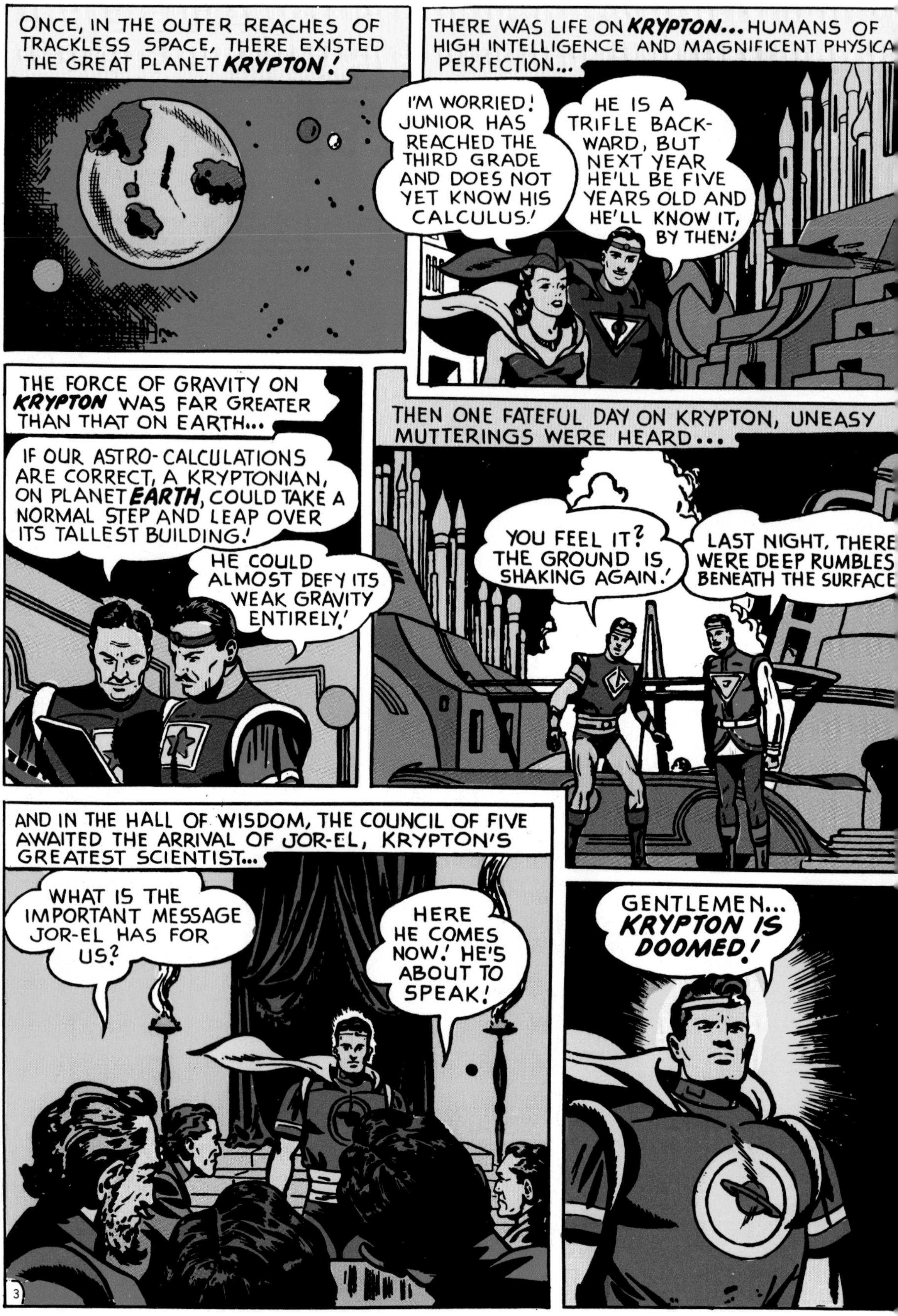
ONCE, IN THE OUTER REACHES OF TRACKLESS SPACE, THERE EXISTED THE GREAT PLANET KRYPTON!
THERE WAS LIFE ON KRYPTON... HUMANS OF HIGH INTELLIGENCE AND MAGNIFICENT PHYSICA PERFECTION...
I'M WORRIED! JUNIOR HAS REACHED THE THIRD GRADE AND DOES NOT YET KNOW HIS CALCULUS!
HE IS A TRIFLE BACKWARD, BUT NEXT YEAR HE'LL BE FIVE YEARS OLD AND HE'LL KNOW IT, BY THEN!
THE FORCE OF GRAVITY ON KRYPTON WAS FAR GREATER THAN THAT ON EARTH...
IF OUR ASTRO-CALCULATIONS ARE CORRECT, A KRYPTONIAN, ON PLANET EARTH, COULD TAKE A NORMAL STEP AND LEAP OVER ITS TALLEST BUILDING!
HE COULD ALMOST DEFY ITS WEAK GRAVITY ENTIRELY!
THEN ONE FATEFUL DAY ON KRYPTON, UNEASY MUTTERINGS WERE HEARD...
YOU FEEL IT? THE GROUND IS SHAKING AGAIN!
LAST NIGHT, THERE WERE DEEP RUMBLES BENEATH THE SURFACE
AND IN THE HALL OF WISDOM, THE COUNCIL OF FIVE AWAITED THE ARRIVAL OF JOR-EL, KRYPTON'S GREATEST SCIENTIST...
WHAT IS THE IMPORTANT MESSAGE JOR-EL HAS FOR US?
HERE HE COMES NOW! HE'S ABOUT TO SPEAK!
3
GENTLEMEN... KRYPTON IS DOOMED!

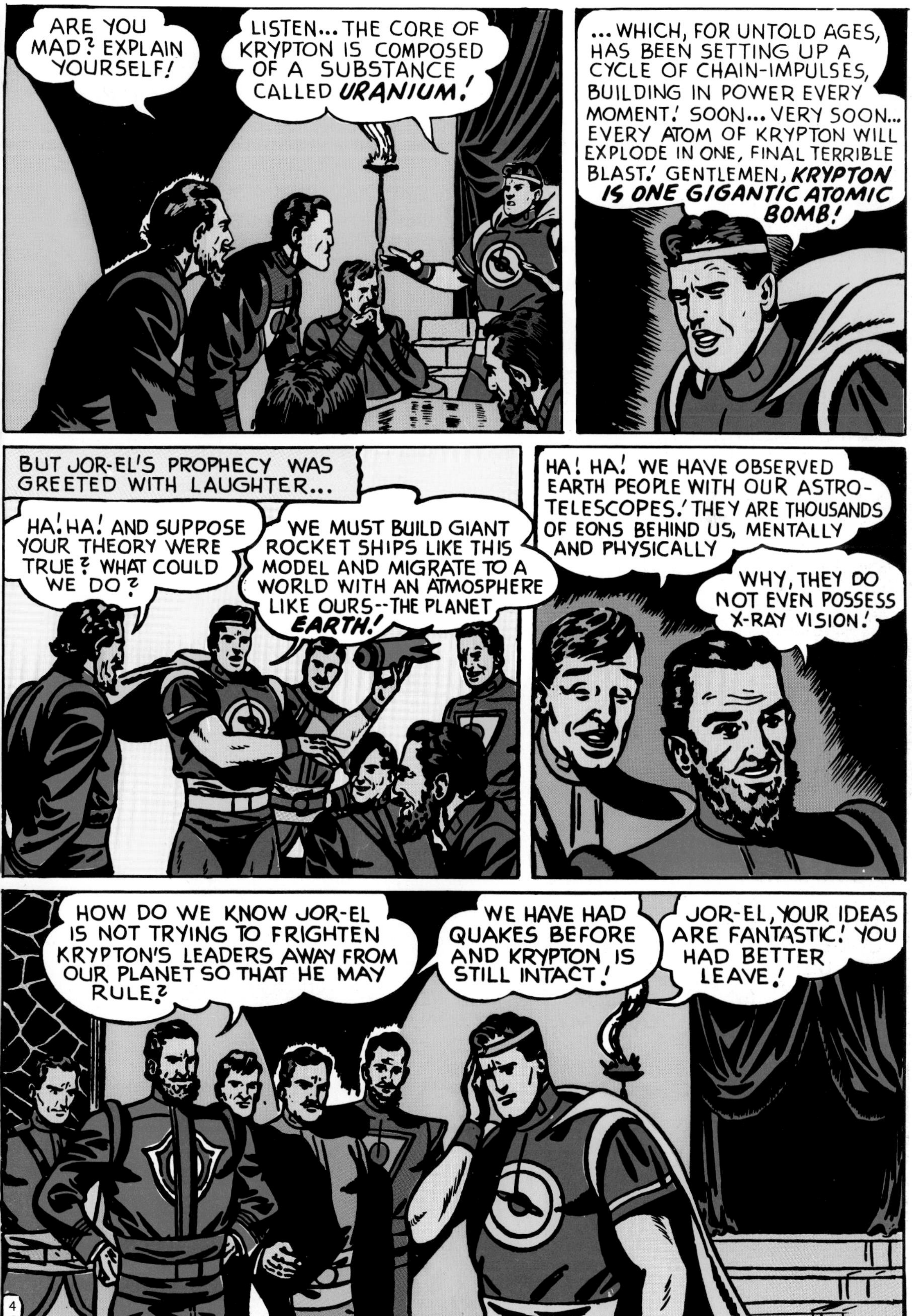
ARE YOU MAD? EXPLAIN YOURSELF!
LISTEN... THE CORE OF KRYPTON IS COMPOSED OF A SUBSTANCE CALLED URANIUM!
...WHICH, FOR UNTOLD AGES, HAS BEEN SETTING UP A CYCLE OF CHAIN-IMPULSES, BUILDING IN POWER EVERY MOMENT! SOON... VERY SOON... EVERY ATOM OF KRYPTON WILL EXPLODE IN ONE, FINAL TERRIBLE BLAST! GENTLEMEN, KRYPTON IS ONE GIGANTIC ATOMIC BOMB!
BUT JOR-EL'S PROPHECY WAS GREETED WITH LAUGHTER...
HA! HA! AND SUPPOSE YOUR THEORY WERE TRUE? WHAT COULD WE DO?
WE MUST BUILD GIANT ROCKET SHIPS LIKE THIS MODEL AND MIGRATE TO A WORLD WITH AN ATMOSPHERE LIKE OURS--THE PLANET EARTH!
HA! HA! WE HAVE OBSERVED EARTH PEOPLE WITH OUR ASTRO-TELESCOPES! THEY ARE THOUSANDS OF EONS BEHIND US, MENTALLY AND PHYSICALLY
WHY, THEY DO NOT EVEN POSSESS X-RAY VISION!
HOW DO WE KNOW JOR-EL IS NOT TRYING TO FRIGHTEN KRYPTON'S LEADERS AWAY FROM OUR PLANET SO THAT HE MAY RULE?
WE HAVE HAD QUAKES BEFORE AND KRYPTON IS STILL INTACT!
JOR-EL, YOUR IDEAS ARE FANTASTIC! YOU HAD BETTER LEAVE!
4

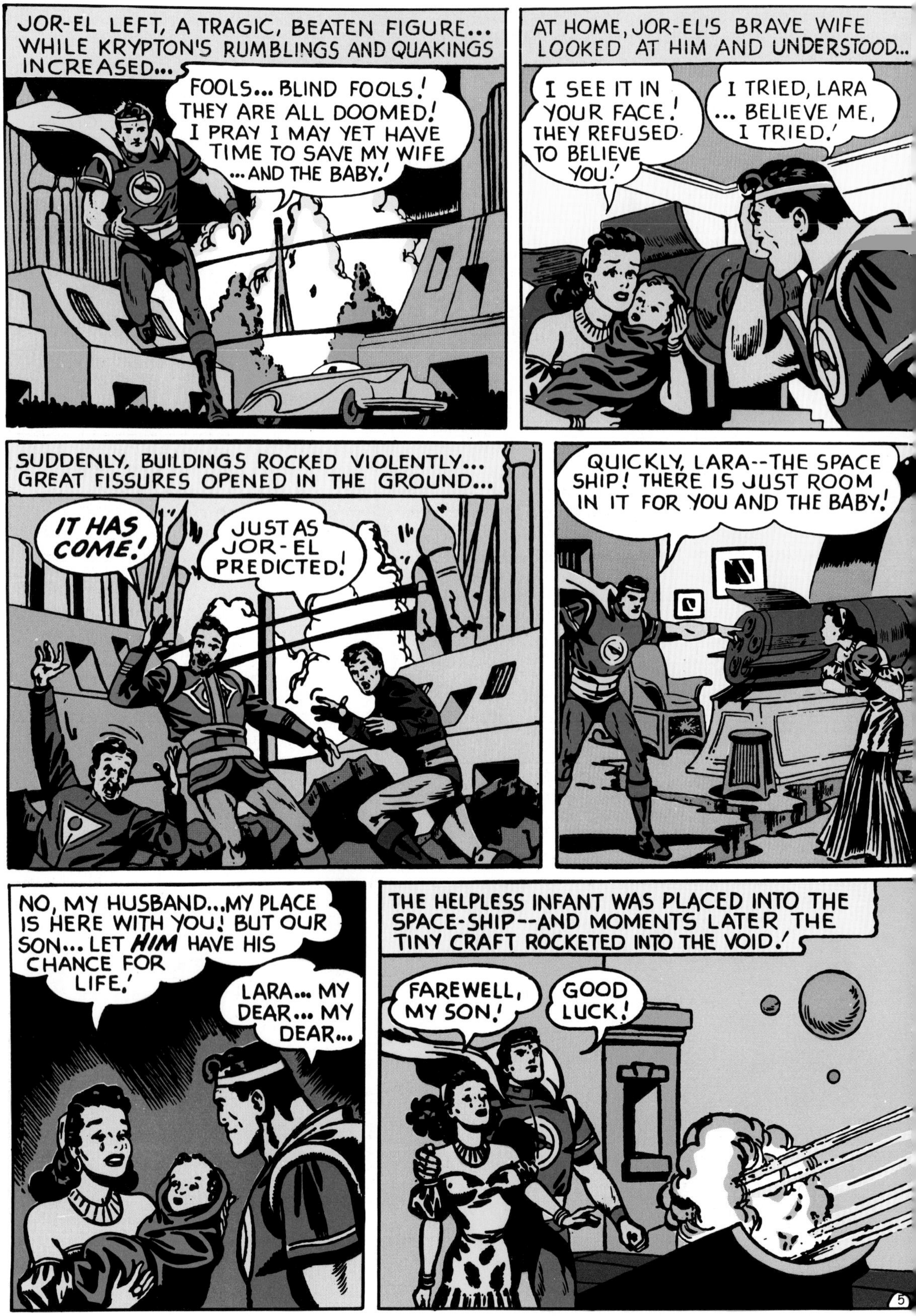
JOR-EL LEFT, A TRAGIC, BEATEN FIGURE... WHILE KRYPTON'S RUMBLINGS AND QUAKINGS INCREASED...
FOOLS... BLIND FOOLS! THEY ARE ALL DOOMED! I PRAY I MAY YET HAVE TIME TO SAVE MY WIFE ...AND THE BABY!
AT HOME, JOR-EL'S BRAVE WIFE LOOKED AT HIM AND UNDERSTOOD...
I SEE IT IN YOUR FACE! THEY REFUSED TO BELIEVE YOU!
I TRIED, LARA ... BELIEVE ME, I TRIED!
SUDDENLY, BUILDINGS ROCKED VIOLENTLY... GREAT FISSURES OPENED IN THE GROUND...
IT HAS COME!
JUST AS JOR-EL PREDICTED!
QUICKLY, LARA--THE SPACE SHIP! THERE IS JUST ROOM IN IT FOR YOU AND THE BABY!
NO, MY HUSBAND...MY PLACE IS HERE WITH YOU! BUT OUR SON... LET HIM HAVE HIS CHANCE FOR LIFE!
LARA... MY DEAR... MY DEAR...
THE HELPLESS INFANT WAS PLACED INTO THE SPACE-SHIP--AND MOMENTS LATER THE TINY CRAFT ROCKETED INTO THE VOID!
FAREWELL, MY SON!
GOOD LUCK!
5

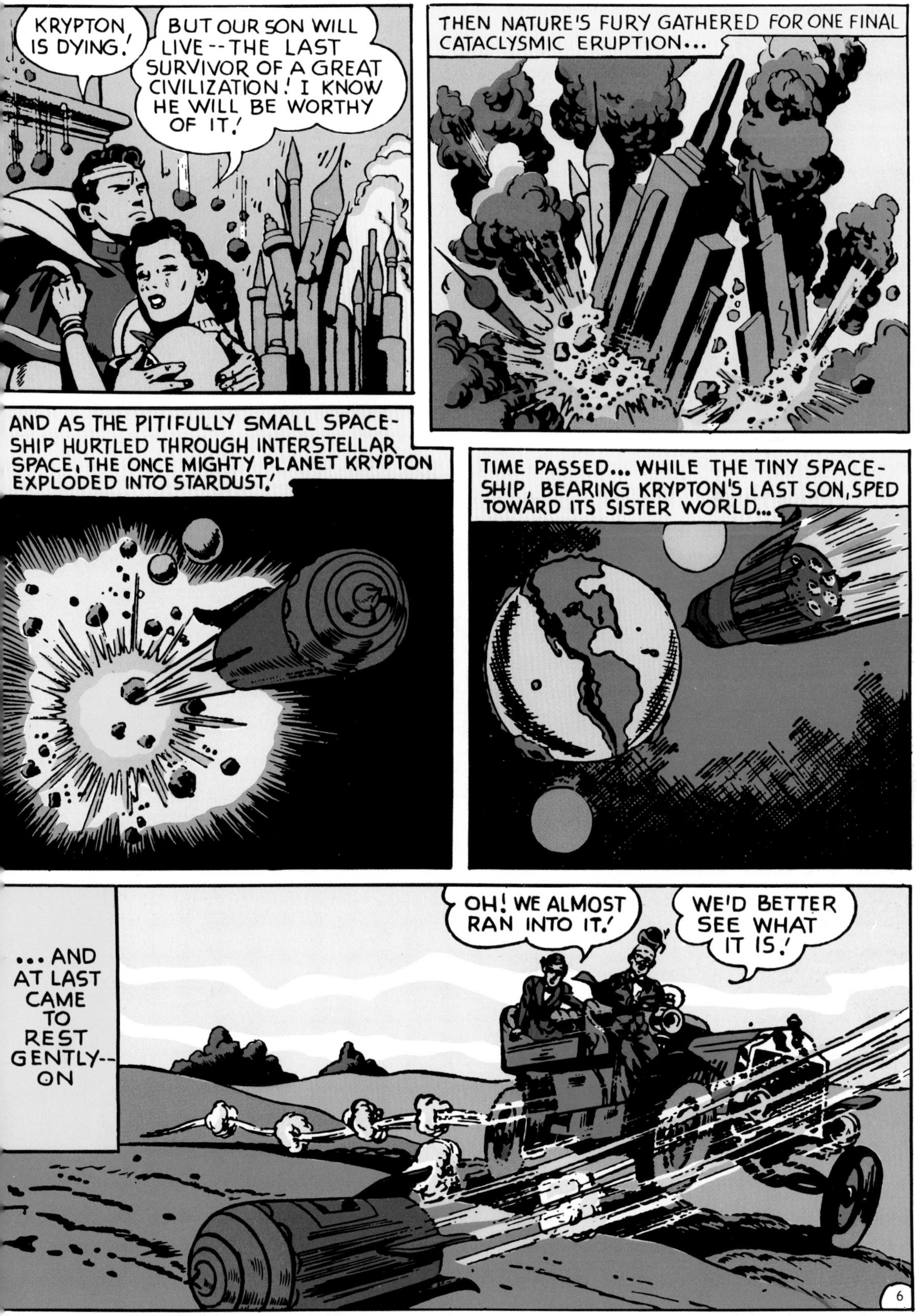
KRYPTON IS DYING!
BUT OUR SON WILL LIVE--THE LAST SURVIVOR OF A GREAT CIVILIZATION! I KNOW HE WILL BE WORTHY OF IT!
THEN NATURE'S FURY GATHERED FOR ONE FINAL CATACLYSMIC ERUPTION...
AND AS THE PITIFULLY SMALL SPACE-SHIP HURTLED THROUGH INTERSTELLAR SPACE, THE ONCE MIGHTY PLANET KRYPTON EXPLODED INTO STARDUST!
TIME PASSED... WHILE THE TINY SPACE-SHIP, BEARING KRYPTON'S LAST SON, SPED TOWARD ITS SISTER WORLD...
...AND AT LAST CAME TO REST GENTLY--ON
OH! WE ALMOST RAN INTO IT!
WE'D BETTER SEE WHAT IT IS!
6

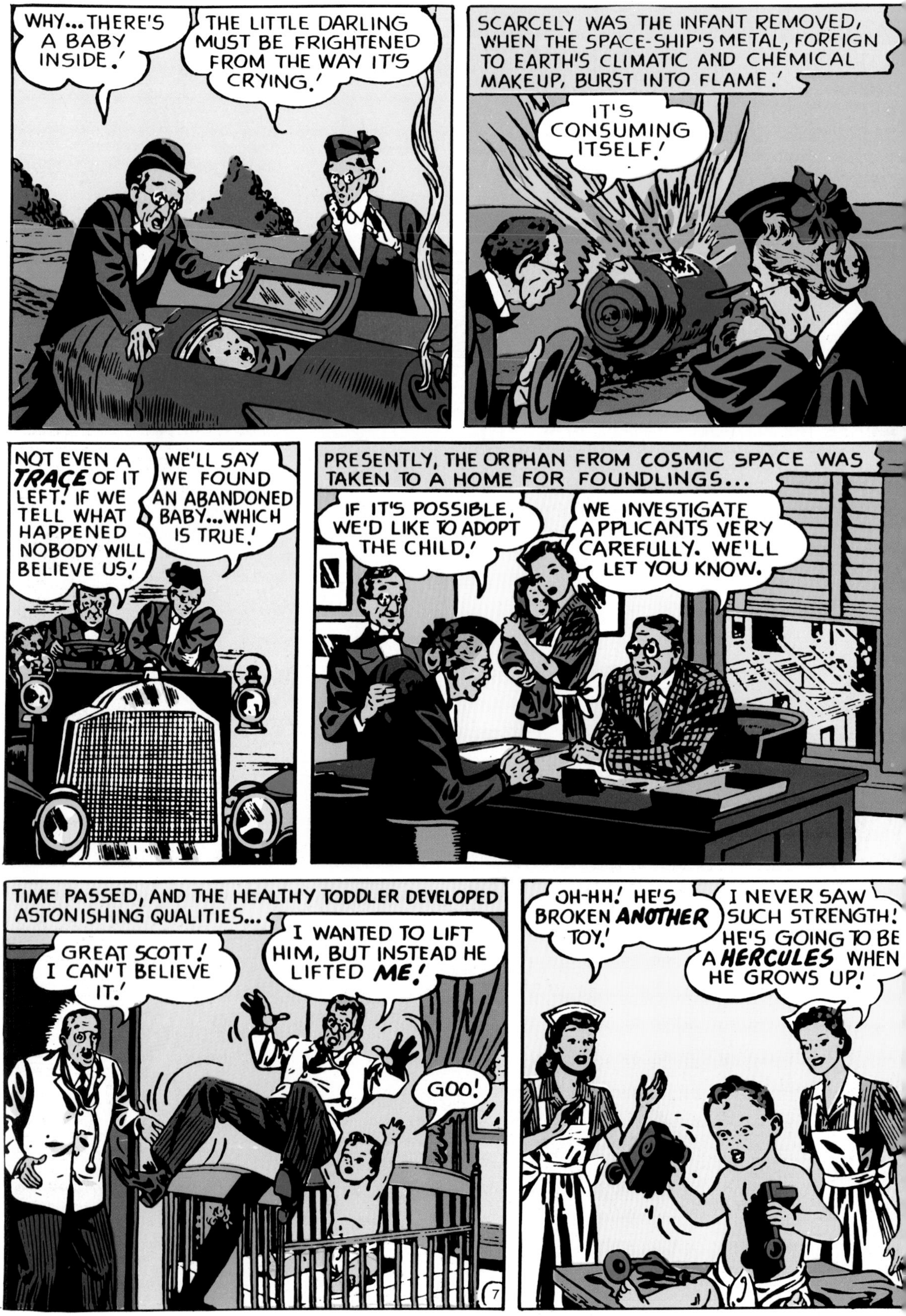
WHY...THERE'S A BABY INSIDE.'
THE LITTLE DARLING MUST BE FRIGHTENED FROM THE WAY IT'S CRYING.'
SCARCELY WAS THE INFANT REMOVED, WHEN THE SPACE-SHIP'S METAL, FOREIGN TO EARTH'S CLIMATIC AND CHEMICAL MAKEUP, BURST INTO FLAME.'
IT'S CONSUMING ITSELF.'
NOT EVEN A TRACE OF IT LEFT! IF WE TELL WHAT HAPPENED NOBODY WILL BELIEVE US.'
WE'LL SAY WE FOUND AN ABANDONED BABY...WHICH IS TRUE.'
PRESENTLY, THE ORPHAN FROM COSMIC SPACE WAS TAKEN TO A HOME FOR FOUNDLINGS...
IF IT'S POSSIBLE, WE'D LIKE TO ADOPT THE CHILD.'
WE INVESTIGATE APPLICANTS VERY CAREFULLY. WE'LL LET YOU KNOW.
TIME PASSED, AND THE HEALTHY TODDLER DEVELOPED ASTONISHING QUALITIES...
GREAT SCOTT! I CAN'T BELIEVE IT.'
I WANTED TO LIFT HIM, BUT INSTEAD HE LIFTED ME!
GOO!
7
OH-HH! HE'S BROKEN ANOTHER TOY!
I NEVER SAW SUCH STRENGTH! HE'S GOING TO BE A HERCULES WHEN HE GROWS UP!

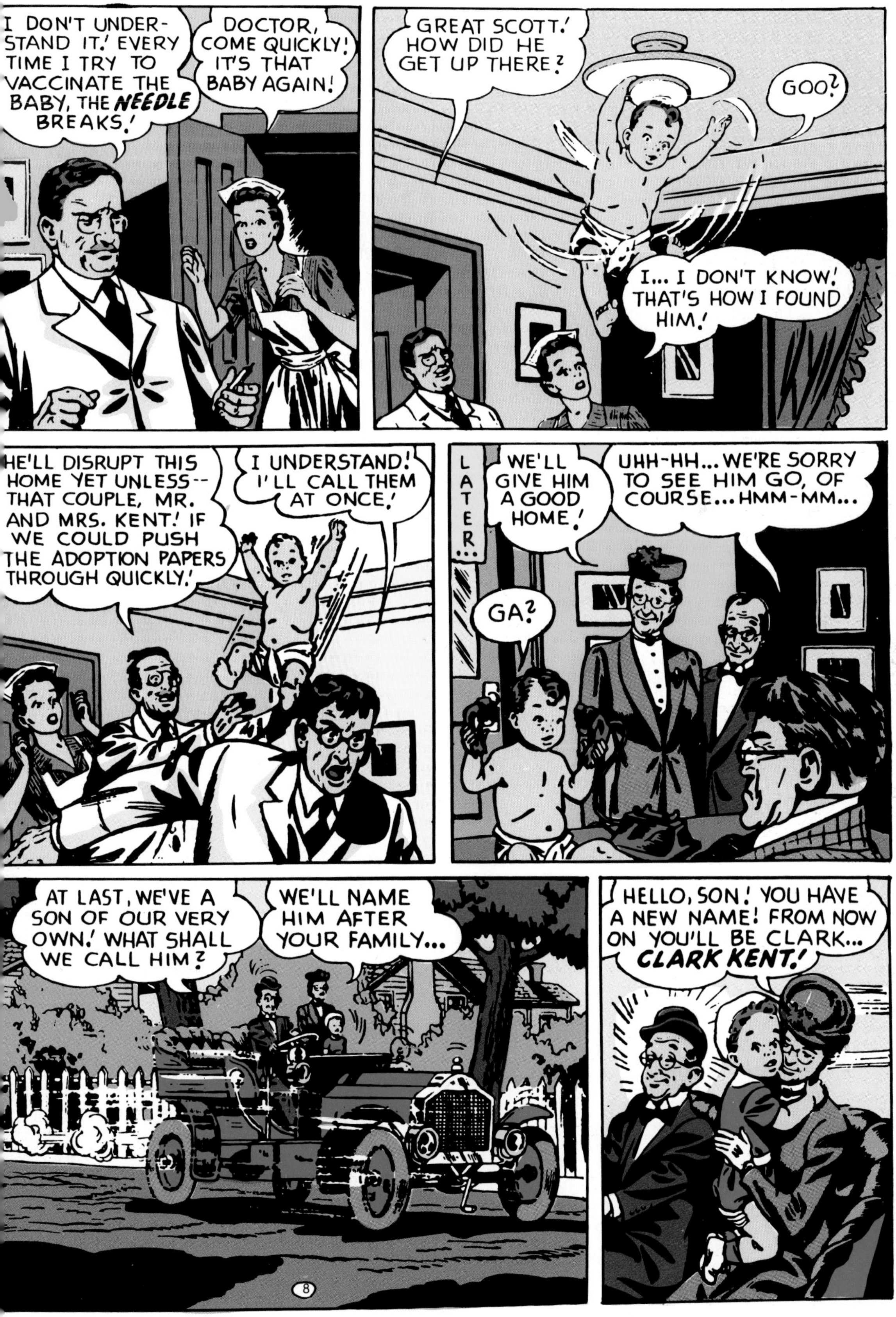
I DON'T UNDERSTAND IT! EVERY TIME I TRY TO VACCINATE THE BABY, THE NEEDLE BREAKS!
DOCTOR, COME QUICKLY! IT'S THAT BABY AGAIN!
GREAT SCOTT! HOW DID HE GET UP THERE?
GOO?
I... I DON'T KNOW! THAT'S HOW I FOUND HIM!
HE'LL DISRUPT THIS HOME YET UNLESS-- THAT COUPLE, MR. AND MRS. KENT! IF WE COULD PUSH THE ADOPTION PAPERS THROUGH QUICKLY!
I UNDERSTAND! I'LL CALL THEM AT ONCE!
LATER...
WE'LL GIVE HIM A GOOD HOME!
UHH-HH... WE'RE SORRY TO SEE HIM GO, OF COURSE... HMM-MM...
GA?
AT LAST, WE'VE A SON OF OUR VERY OWN! WHAT SHALL WE CALL HIM?
WE'LL NAME HIM AFTER YOUR FAMILY...
HELLO, SON! YOU HAVE A NEW NAME! FROM NOW ON YOU'LL BE CLARK... CLARK KENT!
8

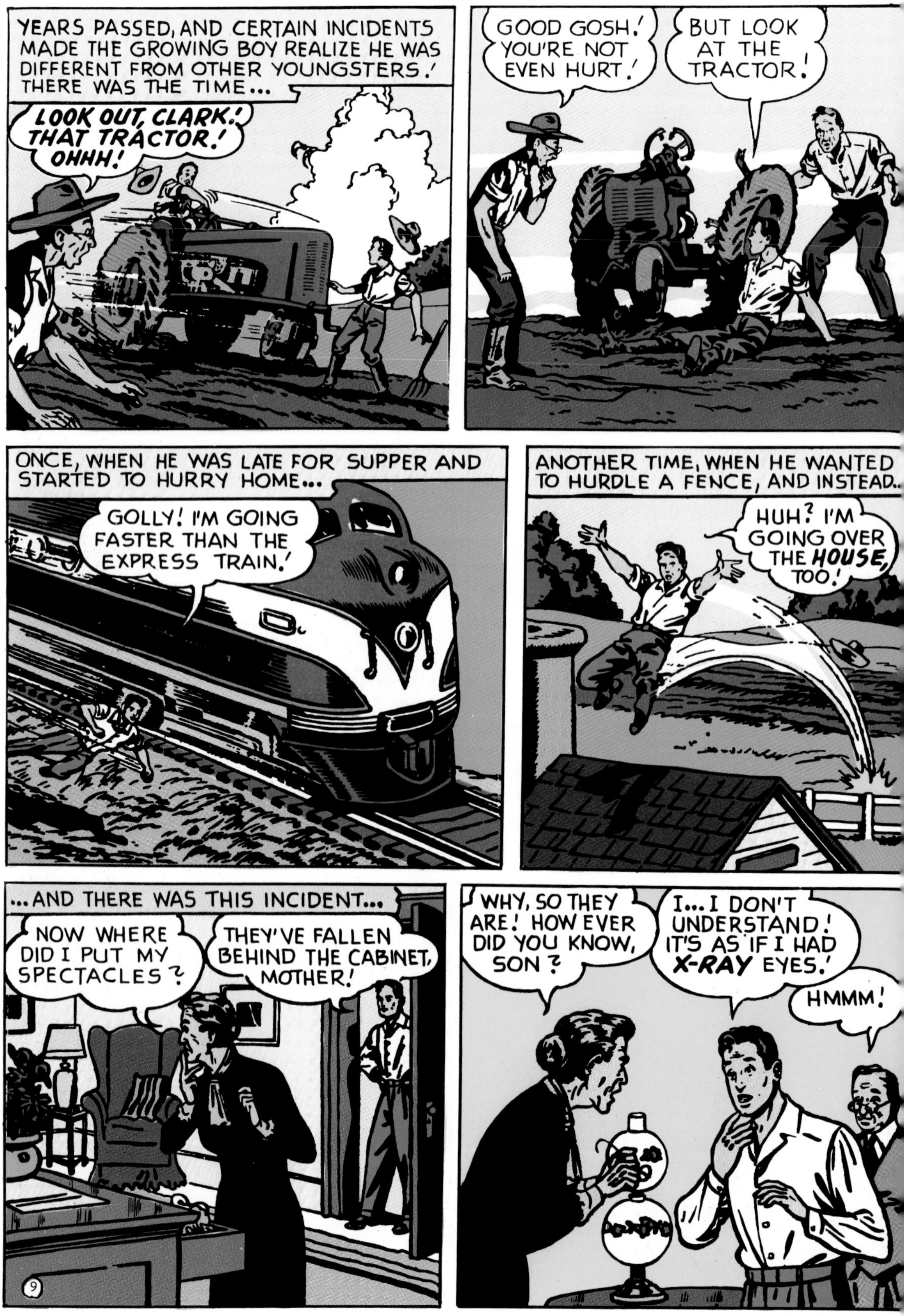
YEARS PASSED, AND CERTAIN INCIDENTS MADE THE GROWING BOY REALIZE HE WAS DIFFERENT FROM OTHER YOUNGSTERS! THERE WAS THE TIME...
LOOK OUT, CLARK! THAT TRACTOR! OHHH!
GOOD GOSH! YOU'RE NOT EVEN HURT!
BUT LOOK AT THE TRACTOR!
ONCE, WHEN HE WAS LATE FOR SUPPER AND STARTED TO HURRY HOME...
GOLLY! I'M GOING FASTER THAN THE EXPRESS TRAIN!
ANOTHER TIME, WHEN HE WANTED TO HURDLE A FENCE, AND INSTEAD...
HUH? I'M GOING OVER THE HOUSE, TOO!
...AND THERE WAS THIS INCIDENT...
NOW WHERE DID I PUT MY SPECTACLES?
THEY'VE FALLEN BEHIND THE CABINET, MOTHER!
9
WHY, SO THEY ARE! HOW EVER DID YOU KNOW, SON?
I...I DON'T UNDERSTAND! IT'S AS IF I HAD X-RAY EYES!
HMMM!

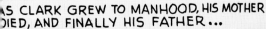

AS CLARK GREW TO MANHOOD, HIS MOTHER DIED, AND FINALLY HIS FATHER...

DAD...

THERE'S NOT MUCH TIME, SON... I'LL DO THE TALKING...

NO MAN ON EARTH HAS THE AMAZING POWERS YOU HAVE. YOU CAN USE THEM TO BECOME A POWERFUL FORCE FOR GOOD!

HOW, DAD?

THERE ARE EVIL MEN IN THIS WORLD... CRIMINALS AND OUTLAWS WHO PREY ON DECENT FOLK! YOU MUST FIGHT THEM...IN COOPERATION WITH THE LAW!

TO FIGHT THOSE CRIMINALS BEST, YOU MUST HIDE YOUR TRUE IDENTITY! THEY MUST NEVER KNOW CLARK KENT IS A... SUPER-MAN! REMEMBER, BECAUSE THAT'S WHAT YOU ARE... A *SUPERMAN!*

... BUT WHEN I'M NEEDED I'LL WEAR THIS COSTUME, AND THE WORLD WILL KNOW OF... SUPERMAN!!

AND AS CLARK KENT WAS ORPHANED A SECOND TIME, HE KNEW THE COURSE HIS LIFE MUST TAKE...

A JOB AS A REPORTER ON A BIG NEWSPAPER WILL KEEP ME IN TOUCH WITH THOSE WHO MAY NEED MY HELP! I'LL WEAR GLASSES, PRETEND TO BE TIMID...

JOHN KENT

MARY KENT

THE END

PART II • 1950-1970
STRANGE VISITOR

By the 1950s, television had started making its way into American living rooms, and so had Superman. *The Adventures of Superman* ran for six seasons, and while the show remained faithful to the comics, the comics began to pick up aspects of their television counterpart as well. Actor George Reeves' stature and figure were soon mimicked by comic book artists Wayne Boring, Al Plastino and Curt Swan in the printed version of Superman.

The stories at this time were often formulaic but efficient: Superman must avoid his secret's being discovered by his colleagues, especially Lois Lane; crooks find Kryptonite with the hope of using it against Superman, etc. No violence entered into these stories, thanks to the Comics Code Authority, established in 1954.

Due to the budget constraints of the television show, Superman's sci-fi mythology had been curbed during the early 1950s. But when the show went off the air, Superman's Kryptonian heritage made a smashing return to comics, spearheaded by editor Mort Weisinger.

Soon, the Superman family titles showed a cohesive and unified universe with stories revolving around life on Krypton or adventures taking place in a space and time far away where a time-traveling Superboy visits the Legion of Super-Heroes. We learned of the existence of a Fortress of Solitude where Superman rests between missions and of Superboy's friendship with young Lex Luthor. The writers even created imaginary out-of-continuity stories such as "The Death of Superman" (1961) where they could explore radical ideas without consequences.

While this period is remembered for the lightness, humor and optimism of its stories, it was also tragic at times. Superman, miraculous as he is, is also alone, the last of his kind on a distant world. In "Superman's Return to Krypton" (1960) he is able, through time travel, to visit his native planet before its destruction, meeting both his doomed parents and the woman of his dreams, only to leave them again.

Then, to ease his loneliness, the creators revealed that Superman was not truly the last of his kind. First, there was Krypto, Jor-El's super-dog, sent with baby Kal-El to Earth. Then, criminals imprisoned in the Phantom Zone made a dramatic entrance in Superman's life, followed finally by his cousin Kara Zor-El, code-named Supergirl.

BUT ALREADY IT ALL SEEMS LIKE A STRANGE, INCREDIBLE DREAM! ...SOON, I'LL SEE LOIS LANE, JIMMY OLSEN AND MY OTHER FRIENDS, AGAIN! IT'S GOOD TO HAVE... A SECOND HOME...

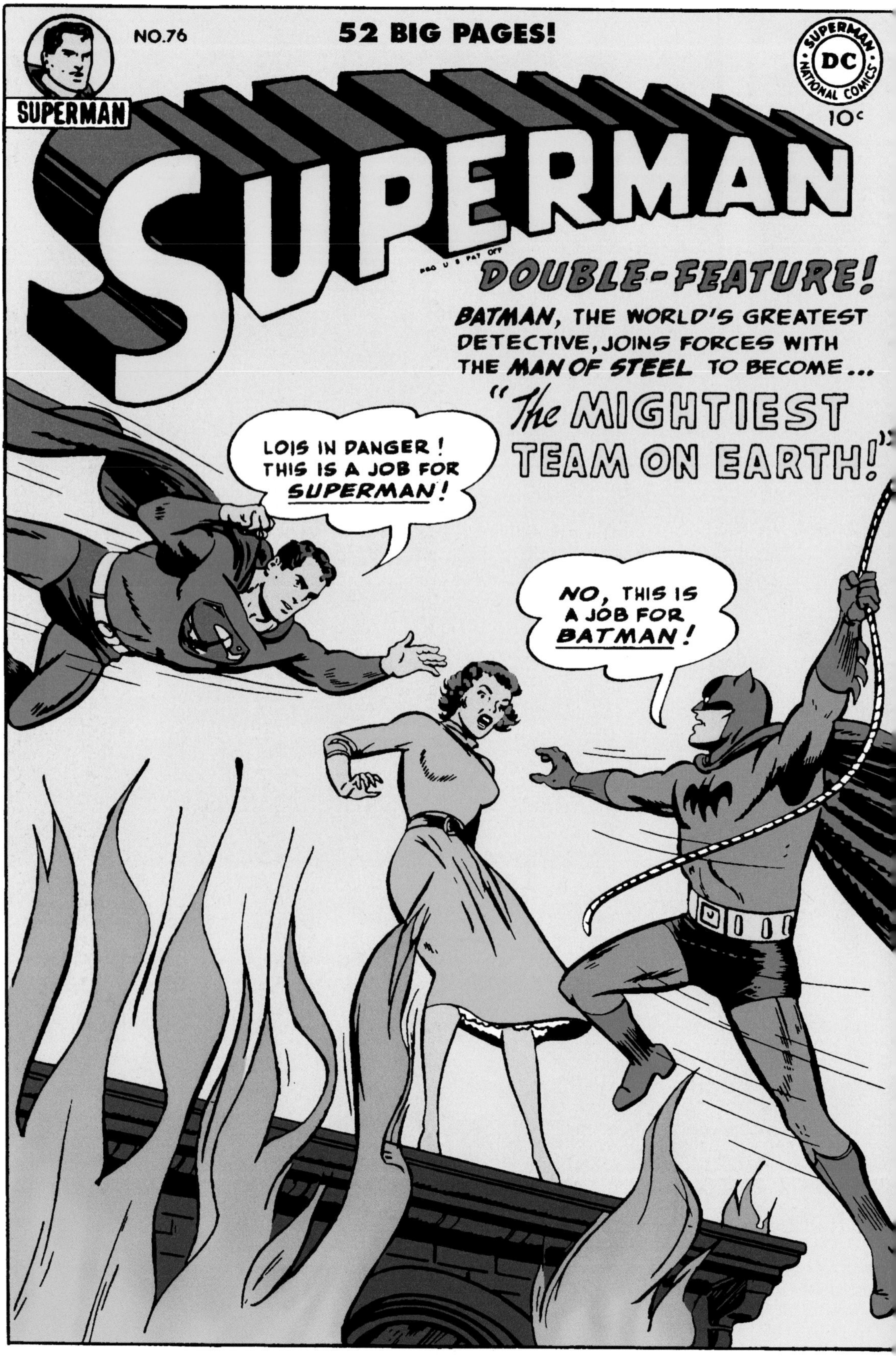

NO.76
52 BIG PAGES!
SUPERMAN
SUPERMAN DC NATIONAL COMICS
10¢
SUPERMAN
REG. U.S. PAT. OFF.
DOUBLE-FEATURE!
BATMAN, THE WORLD'S GREATEST DETECTIVE, JOINS FORCES WITH THE MAN OF STEEL TO BECOME...
"The MIGHTIEST TEAM ON EARTH!"
LOIS IN DANGER! THIS IS A JOB FOR SUPERMAN!
NO, THIS IS A JOB FOR BATMAN!

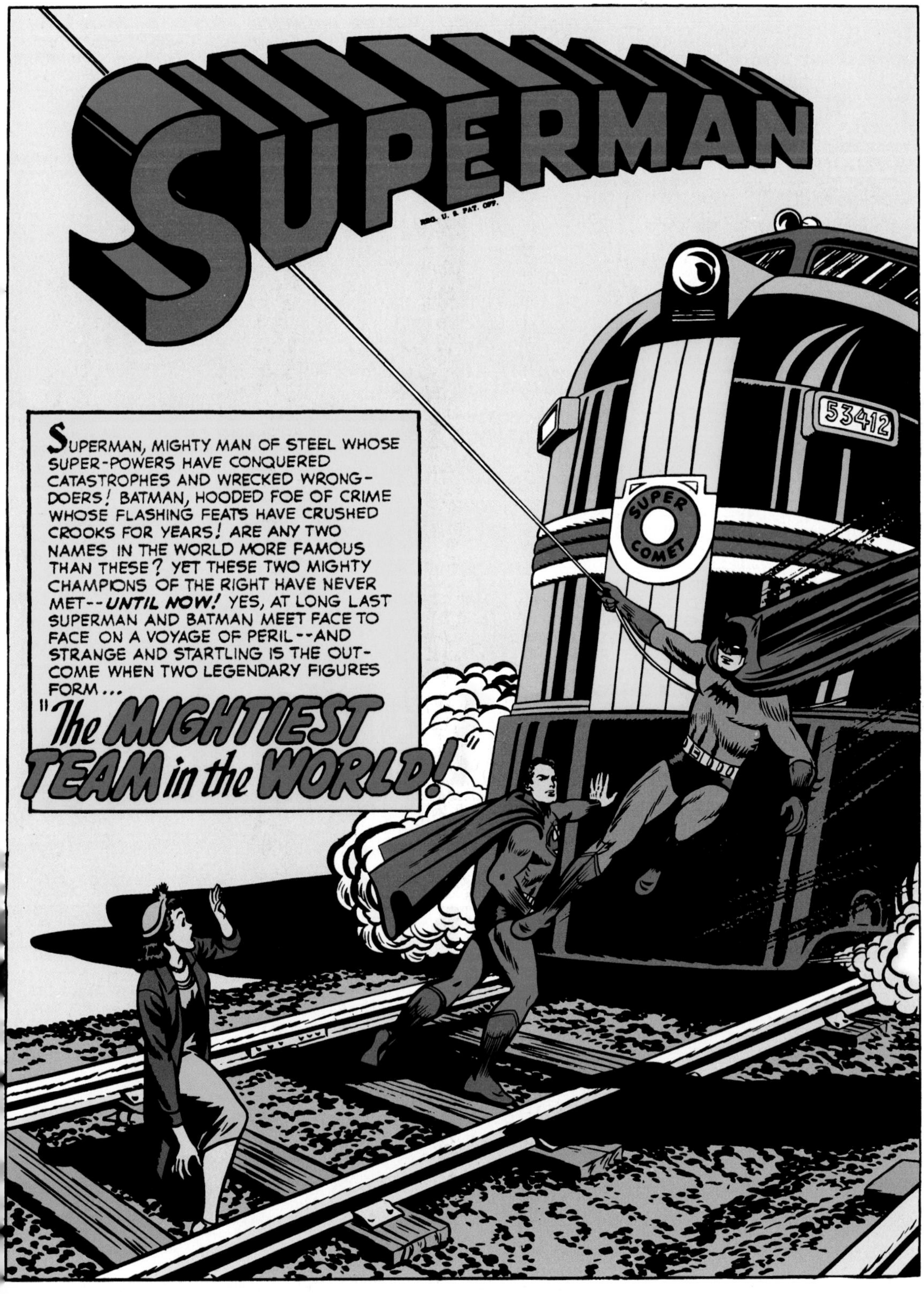
SUPERMAN
REG. U. S. PAT. OFF.
53412
SUPER COMET
SUPERMAN, MIGHTY MAN OF STEEL WHOSE SUPER-POWERS HAVE CONQUERED CATASTROPHES AND WRECKED WRONG-DOERS! BATMAN, HOODED FOE OF CRIME WHOSE FLASHING FEATS HAVE CRUSHED CROOKS FOR YEARS! ARE ANY TWO NAMES IN THE WORLD MORE FAMOUS THAN THESE? YET THESE TWO MIGHTY CHAMPIONS OF THE RIGHT HAVE NEVER MET--UNTIL NOW! YES, AT LONG LAST SUPERMAN AND BATMAN MEET FACE TO FACE ON A VOYAGE OF PERIL--AND STRANGE AND STARTLING IS THE OUT-COME WHEN TWO LEGENDARY FIGURES FORM...
"The MIGHTIEST TEAM in the WORLD!"

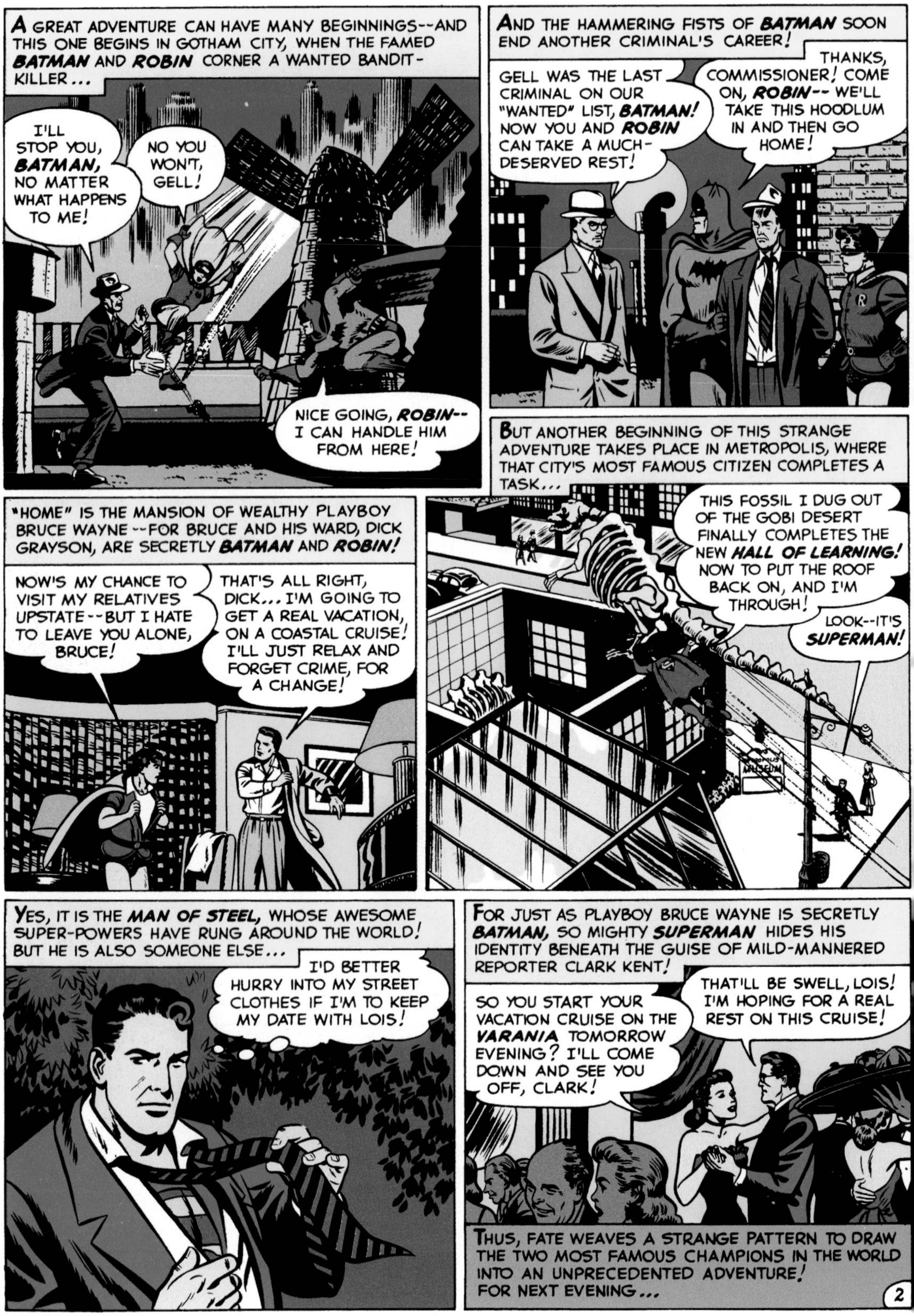

A GREAT ADVENTURE CAN HAVE MANY BEGINNINGS--AND THIS ONE BEGINS IN GOTHAM CITY, WHEN THE FAMED BATMAN AND ROBIN CORNER A WANTED BANDIT-KILLER...
I'LL STOP YOU, BATMAN, NO MATTER WHAT HAPPENS TO ME!
NO YOU WON'T, GELL!
NICE GOING, ROBIN-- I CAN HANDLE HIM FROM HERE!
AND THE HAMMERING FISTS OF BATMAN SOON END ANOTHER CRIMINAL'S CAREER!
GELL WAS THE LAST CRIMINAL ON OUR "WANTED" LIST, BATMAN! NOW YOU AND ROBIN CAN TAKE A MUCH-DESERVED REST!
THANKS, COMMISSIONER! COME ON, ROBIN-- WE'LL TAKE THIS HOODLUM IN AND THEN GO HOME!
"HOME" IS THE MANSION OF WEALTHY PLAYBOY BRUCE WAYNE--FOR BRUCE AND HIS WARD, DICK GRAYSON, ARE SECRETLY BATMAN AND ROBIN!
NOW'S MY CHANCE TO VISIT MY RELATIVES UPSTATE--BUT I HATE TO LEAVE YOU ALONE, BRUCE!
THAT'S ALL RIGHT, DICK... I'M GOING TO GET A REAL VACATION, ON A COASTAL CRUISE! I'LL JUST RELAX AND FORGET CRIME, FOR A CHANGE!
BUT ANOTHER BEGINNING OF THIS STRANGE ADVENTURE TAKES PLACE IN METROPOLIS, WHERE THAT CITY'S MOST FAMOUS CITIZEN COMPLETES A TASK...
THIS FOSSIL I DUG OUT OF THE GOBI DESERT FINALLY COMPLETES THE NEW HALL OF LEARNING! NOW TO PUT THE ROOF BACK ON, AND I'M THROUGH!
LOOK--IT'S SUPERMAN!
YES, IT IS THE MAN OF STEEL, WHOSE AWESOME SUPER-POWERS HAVE RUNG AROUND THE WORLD! BUT HE IS ALSO SOMEONE ELSE...
I'D BETTER HURRY INTO MY STREET CLOTHES IF I'M TO KEEP MY DATE WITH LOIS!
FOR JUST AS PLAYBOY BRUCE WAYNE IS SECRETLY BATMAN, SO MIGHTY SUPERMAN HIDES HIS IDENTITY BENEATH THE GUISE OF MILD-MANNERED REPORTER CLARK KENT!
SO YOU START YOUR VACATION CRUISE ON THE VARANIA TOMORROW EVENING? I'LL COME DOWN AND SEE YOU OFF, CLARK!
THAT'LL BE SWELL, LOIS! I'M HOPING FOR A REAL REST ON THIS CRUISE!
THUS, FATE WEAVES A STRANGE PATTERN TO DRAW THE TWO MOST FAMOUS CHAMPIONS IN THE WORLD INTO AN UNPRECEDENTED ADVENTURE! FOR NEXT EVENING...
2

...AS PASSENGERS BOARD THE CRUISE-SHIP *VARANIA*...

ISN'T IT DIVINE? I'LL WAIT ON DECK WHILE YOU SEE THE PURSER, CLARK!

ALL RIGHT, LOIS!

LOOKS LIKE A FULL PASSENGER LIST! THANK GOODNESS I HAVE A CABIN TO MYSELF!

BUT SECONDS LATER, A DISMAYING SURPRISE...

I'M SORRY, MR. KENT, BUT THE SHIP'S SO CROWDED, I'VE PUT YOU IN WITH ANOTHER PASSENGER-- A MR. BRUCE WAYNE!

BUT-- BUT--

GOSH, I CAN'T MAKE TOO BIG A FUSS... LOIS WOULD SURELY GET SUSPICIOUS!

URSER
HONCON

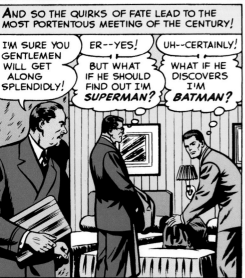

AND SO THE QUIRKS OF FATE LEAD TO THE MOST PORTENTOUS MEETING OF THE CENTURY!

I'M SURE YOU GENTLEMEN WILL GET ALONG SPLENDIDLY!

ER--YES! BUT WHAT IF HE SHOULD FIND OUT I'M *SUPERMAN*?

UH--CERTAINLY! WHAT IF HE DISCOVERS I'M *BATMAN*?

AT THAT MOMENT, OUT ON THE DOCK...

LOOK--THAT MAN! HE'S FIRED *INCENDIARY BULLETS* AT THAT TANK TRUCK!

IT'S CATCHING FIRE!

CUSTOMS OFFICE

JUST AS I PLANNED! THIS ASBESTOS SUIT PROTECTS ME FROM THE FLAMES WHILE I SNATCH THAT DIAMOND SHIPMENT!

WHAT A SCOOP! IF I CAN ONLY GET A CLOSER LOOK!

CUSTOMS OFFICE

AND ONCE AGAIN, LOIS LANE'S DARING LEADS HER INTO DANGER...

STOP HIM! HE'S GOT THE FABIAN DIAMONDS!

NO ONE CAN COME AFTER ME THROUGH THE FLAMES!

HELP! THE FIRE HAS CIRCLED AROUND--I'M TRAPPED!

3

67

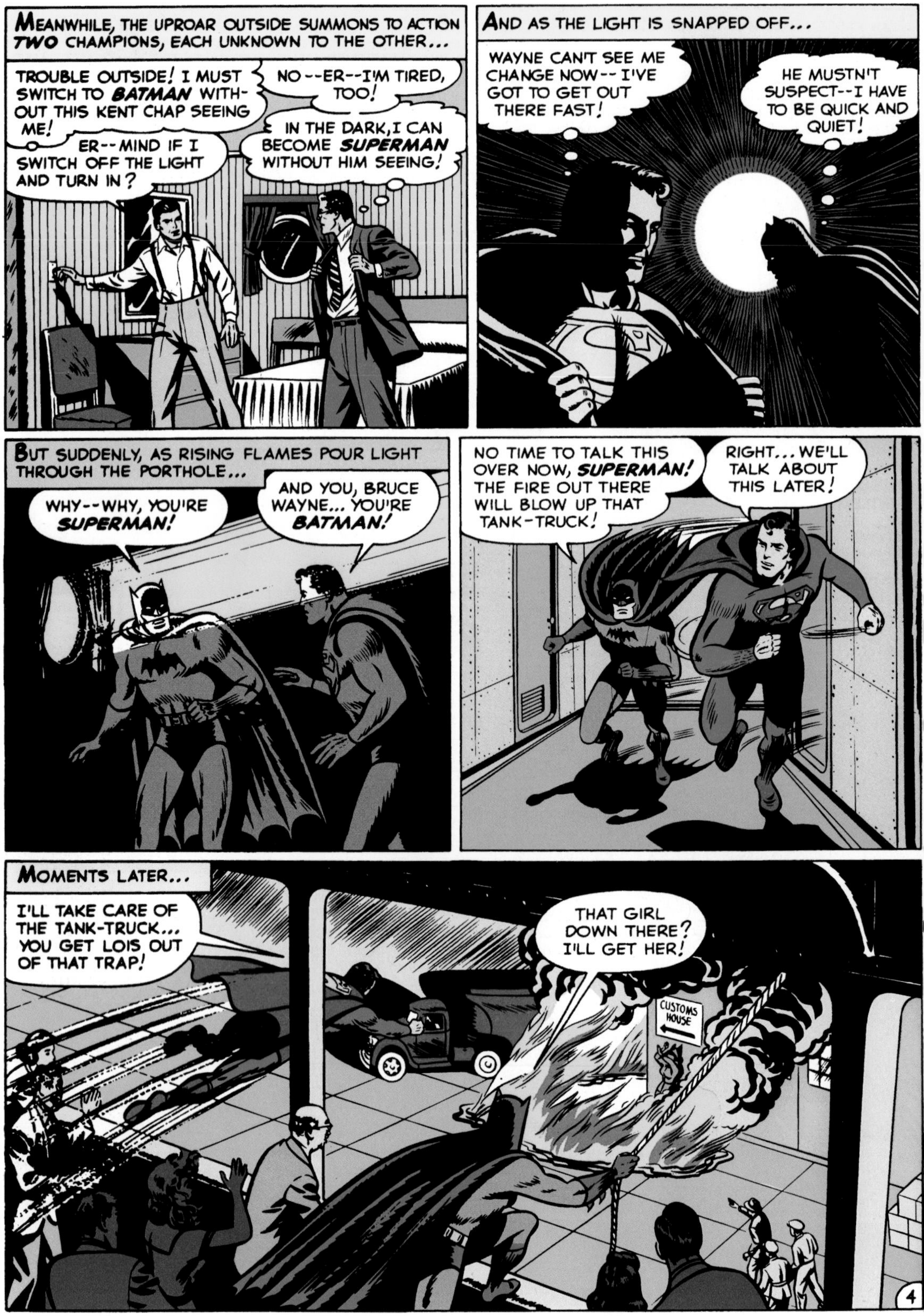
MEANWHILE, THE UPROAR OUTSIDE SUMMONS TO ACTION TWO CHAMPIONS, EACH UNKNOWN TO THE OTHER...
TROUBLE OUTSIDE! I MUST SWITCH TO BATMAN WITHOUT THIS KENT CHAP SEEING ME!
NO--ER--I'M TIRED, TOO!
ER--MIND IF I SWITCH OFF THE LIGHT AND TURN IN?
IN THE DARK, I CAN BECOME SUPERMAN WITHOUT HIM SEEING!
AND AS THE LIGHT IS SNAPPED OFF...
WAYNE CAN'T SEE ME CHANGE NOW--I'VE GOT TO GET OUT THERE FAST!
HE MUSTN'T SUSPECT--I HAVE TO BE QUICK AND QUIET!
BUT SUDDENLY, AS RISING FLAMES POUR LIGHT THROUGH THE PORTHOLE...
WHY--WHY, YOU'RE SUPERMAN!
AND YOU, BRUCE WAYNE... YOU'RE BATMAN!
NO TIME TO TALK THIS OVER NOW, SUPERMAN! THE FIRE OUT THERE WILL BLOW UP THAT TANK-TRUCK!
RIGHT... WE'LL TALK ABOUT THIS LATER!
MOMENTS LATER...
I'LL TAKE CARE OF THE TANK-TRUCK... YOU GET LOIS OUT OF THAT TRAP!
THAT GIRL DOWN THERE? I'LL GET HER!
CUSTOMS HOUSE
4

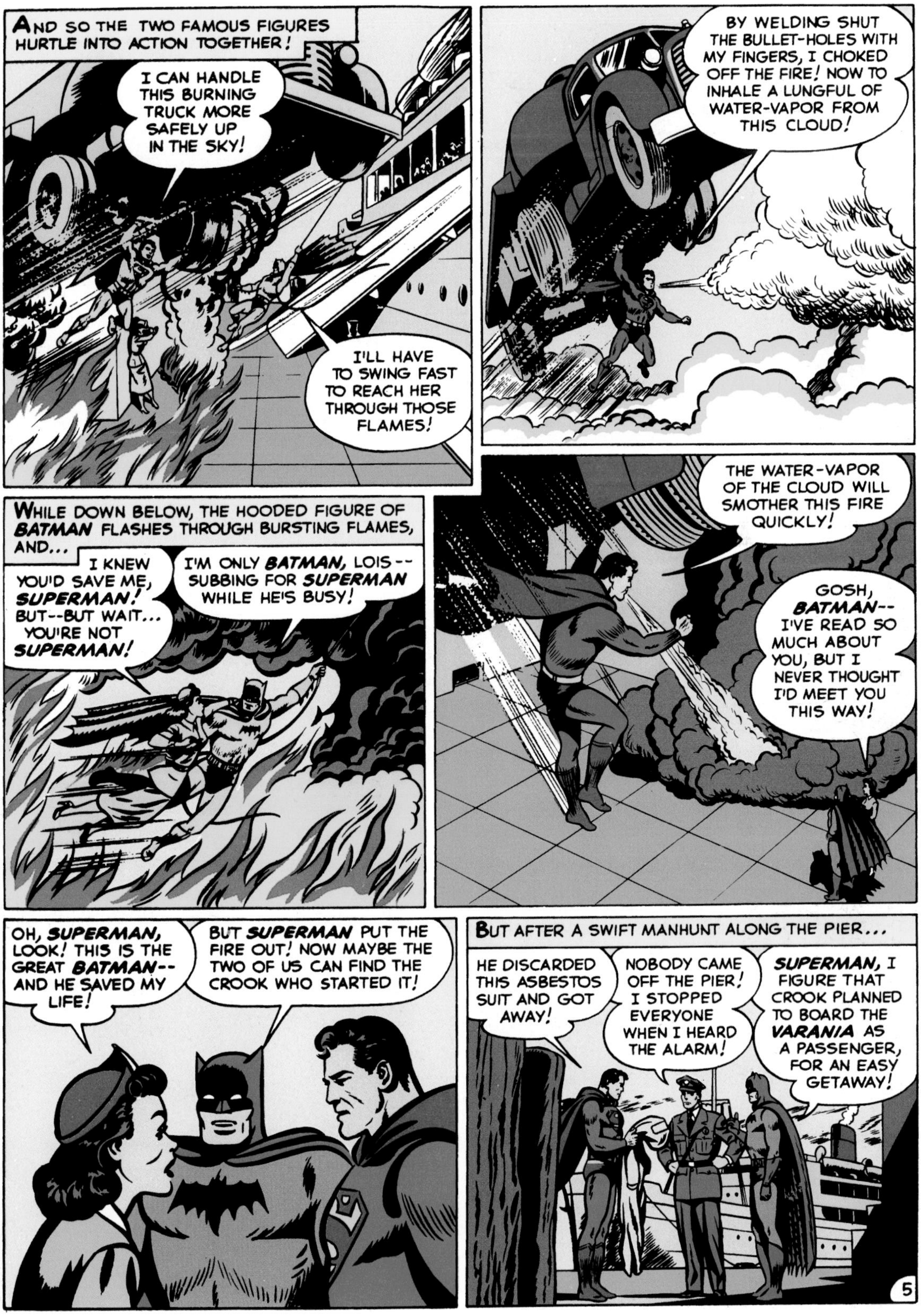
AND SO THE TWO FAMOUS FIGURES HURTLE INTO ACTION TOGETHER!
I CAN HANDLE THIS BURNING TRUCK MORE SAFELY UP IN THE SKY!
I'LL HAVE TO SWING FAST TO REACH HER THROUGH THOSE FLAMES!
BY WELDING SHUT THE BULLET-HOLES WITH MY FINGERS, I CHOKED OFF THE FIRE! NOW TO INHALE A LUNGFUL OF WATER-VAPOR FROM THIS CLOUD!
WHILE DOWN BELOW, THE HOODED FIGURE OF BATMAN FLASHES THROUGH BURSTING FLAMES, AND...
I KNEW YOU'D SAVE ME, SUPERMAN! BUT--BUT WAIT... YOU'RE NOT SUPERMAN!
I'M ONLY BATMAN, LOIS -- SUBBING FOR SUPERMAN WHILE HE'S BUSY!
THE WATER-VAPOR OF THE CLOUD WILL SMOTHER THIS FIRE QUICKLY!
GOSH, BATMAN-- I'VE READ SO MUCH ABOUT YOU, BUT I NEVER THOUGHT I'D MEET YOU THIS WAY!
OH, SUPERMAN, LOOK! THIS IS THE GREAT BATMAN-- AND HE SAVED MY LIFE!
BUT SUPERMAN PUT THE FIRE OUT! NOW MAYBE THE TWO OF US CAN FIND THE CROOK WHO STARTED IT!
BUT AFTER A SWIFT MANHUNT ALONG THE PIER...
HE DISCARDED THIS ASBESTOS SUIT AND GOT AWAY!
NOBODY CAME OFF THE PIER! I STOPPED EVERYONE WHEN I HEARD THE ALARM!
SUPERMAN, I FIGURE THAT CROOK PLANNED TO BOARD THE VARANIA AS A PASSENGER, FOR AN EASY GETAWAY!
5

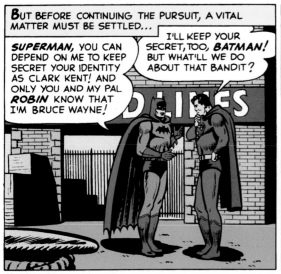

BUT BEFORE CONTINUING THE PURSUIT, A VITAL MATTER MUST BE SETTLED...

SUPERMAN, YOU CAN DEPEND ON ME TO KEEP SECRET YOUR IDENTITY AS CLARK KENT! AND ONLY YOU AND MY PAL ROBIN KNOW THAT I'M BRUCE WAYNE!

I'LL KEEP YOUR SECRET, TOO, BATMAN! BUT WHAT'LL WE DO ABOUT THAT BANDIT?

EVEN IF HE'S ON THAT SHIP, IF WE SUDDENLY APPEAR AS BATMAN AND SUPERMAN WHILE AT SEA, OUR IDENTITIES MAY BE SUSPECTED!

THEN WE MUST SAIL ON THE VARANIA AS BATMAN AND SUPERMAN-- AS WELL AS IN OUR EVERY-DAY IDENTITIES!

THUS, AN AMAZED CAPTAIN FINDS THAT HE IS TO HAVE TWO WORLD-FAMOUS PASSENGERS!

YOU SEE, WE BELIEVE THIS CROOK IS A PASSENGER WHO BOARDED SHIP IN THE UPROAR, AND WE'RE GOING ALONG TO CATCH HIM!

WHY--WHY, I'M HONORED, GENTLEMEN! I'LL GIVE YOU TWO MY OWN CABIN... I CAN SHARE THE MATE'S!

BUT AWHILE LATER, AS THE VARANIA FORGES OUT TO SEA, SUPERMAN GETS AN UNEXPECTED SURPRISE...

LOIS! WHAT ARE YOU DOING ON BOARD?

I'M GOING ALONG! I PHONED THE CHIEF FOR PERMISSION TO TAKE MY VACATION NOW, AND HAD A SUITCASE RUSHED DOWN! NO ONE ELSE IS GOING TO GET THIS STORY!

BUT IT'S IMPOSSIBLE-- THERE'S NO CABIN-SPACE!

A WOMEN WHO WAS UPSET BY THE FIRE CANCELLED HERS, SO I WAS GIVEN HER CABIN! AND BY THE WAY, SUPERMAN, YOUR FRIEND CLARK KENT IS ABOARD... I'LL TELL HIM YOU'RE HERE!

AN EMERGENCY THAT BOTH CRIME-FIGHTERS HAVE OFTEN FACED CALLS FOR QUICK ACTION...

WE'VE GOT TO REACH OUR CABIN AND SWITCH TO CLARK AND BRUCE BEFORE LOIS GETS THERE! GOSH-- WHY DID SHE HAVE TO COME ALONG?

WHY NOT? SHE SEEMS LIKE A CHARMING GIRL!

6

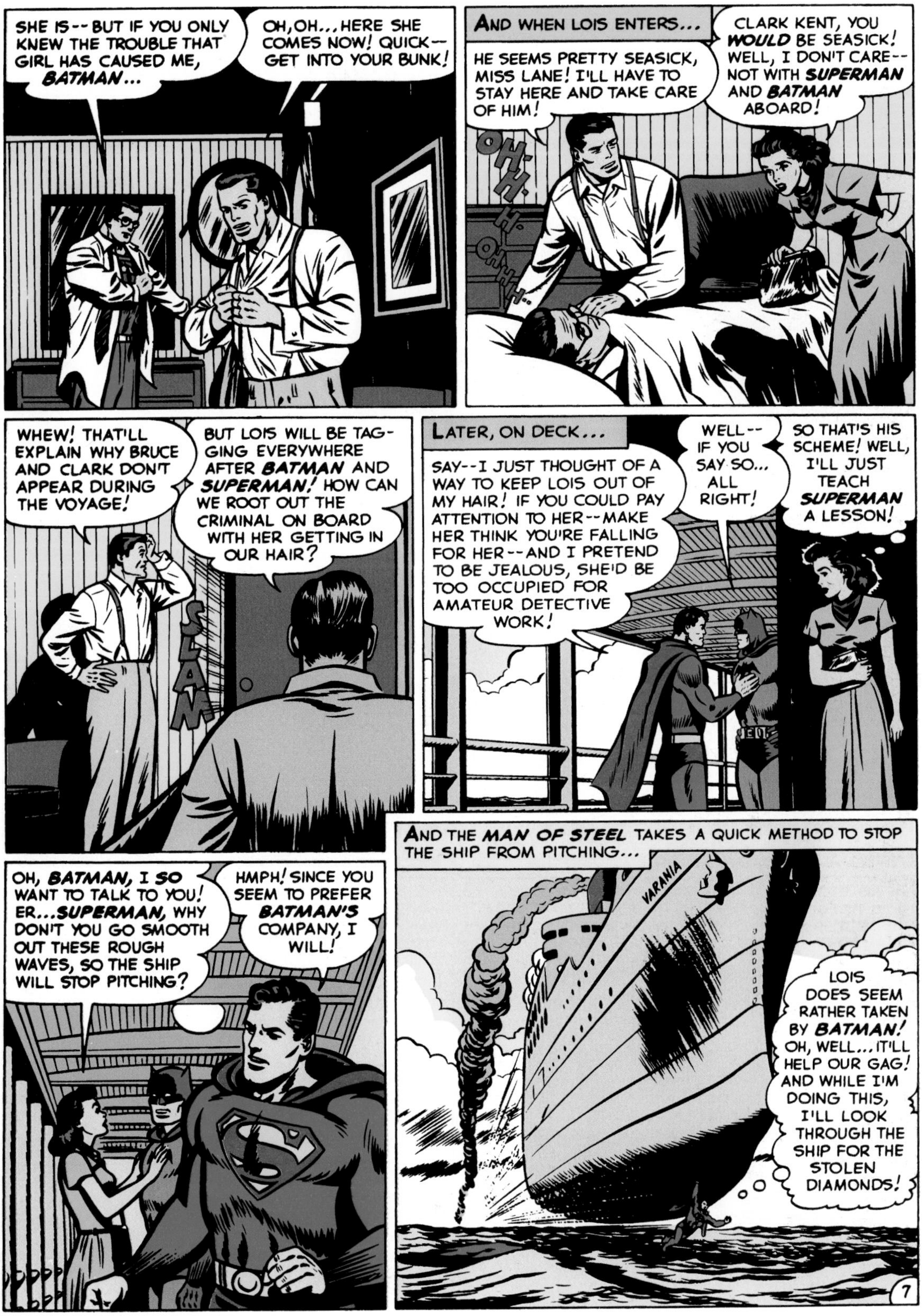
SHE IS--BUT IF YOU ONLY KNEW THE TROUBLE THAT GIRL HAS CAUSED ME, BATMAN...
OH, OH... HERE SHE COMES NOW! QUICK--GET INTO YOUR BUNK!
AND WHEN LOIS ENTERS...
HE SEEMS PRETTY SEASICK, MISS LANE! I'LL HAVE TO STAY HERE AND TAKE CARE OF HIM!
CLARK KENT, YOU WOULD BE SEASICK! WELL, I DON'T CARE--NOT WITH SUPERMAN AND BATMAN ABOARD!
WHEW! THAT'LL EXPLAIN WHY BRUCE AND CLARK DON'T APPEAR DURING THE VOYAGE!
BUT LOIS WILL BE TAGGING EVERYWHERE AFTER BATMAN AND SUPERMAN! HOW CAN WE ROOT OUT THE CRIMINAL ON BOARD WITH HER GETTING IN OUR HAIR?
SLAM
LATER, ON DECK...
SAY--I JUST THOUGHT OF A WAY TO KEEP LOIS OUT OF MY HAIR! IF YOU COULD PAY ATTENTION TO HER--MAKE HER THINK YOU'RE FALLING FOR HER--AND I PRETEND TO BE JEALOUS, SHE'D BE TOO OCCUPIED FOR AMATEUR DETECTIVE WORK!
WELL--IF YOU SAY SO... ALL RIGHT!
SO THAT'S HIS SCHEME! WELL, I'LL JUST TEACH SUPERMAN A LESSON!
OH, BATMAN, I SO WANT TO TALK TO YOU! ER...SUPERMAN, WHY DON'T YOU GO SMOOTH OUT THESE ROUGH WAVES, SO THE SHIP WILL STOP PITCHING?
HMPH! SINCE YOU SEEM TO PREFER BATMAN'S COMPANY, I WILL!
AND THE MAN OF STEEL TAKES A QUICK METHOD TO STOP THE SHIP FROM PITCHING...
VARANIA
LOIS DOES SEEM RATHER TAKEN BY BATMAN! OH, WELL... IT'LL HELP OUR GAG! AND WHILE I'M DOING THIS, I'LL LOOK THROUGH THE SHIP FOR THE STOLEN DIAMONDS!
7

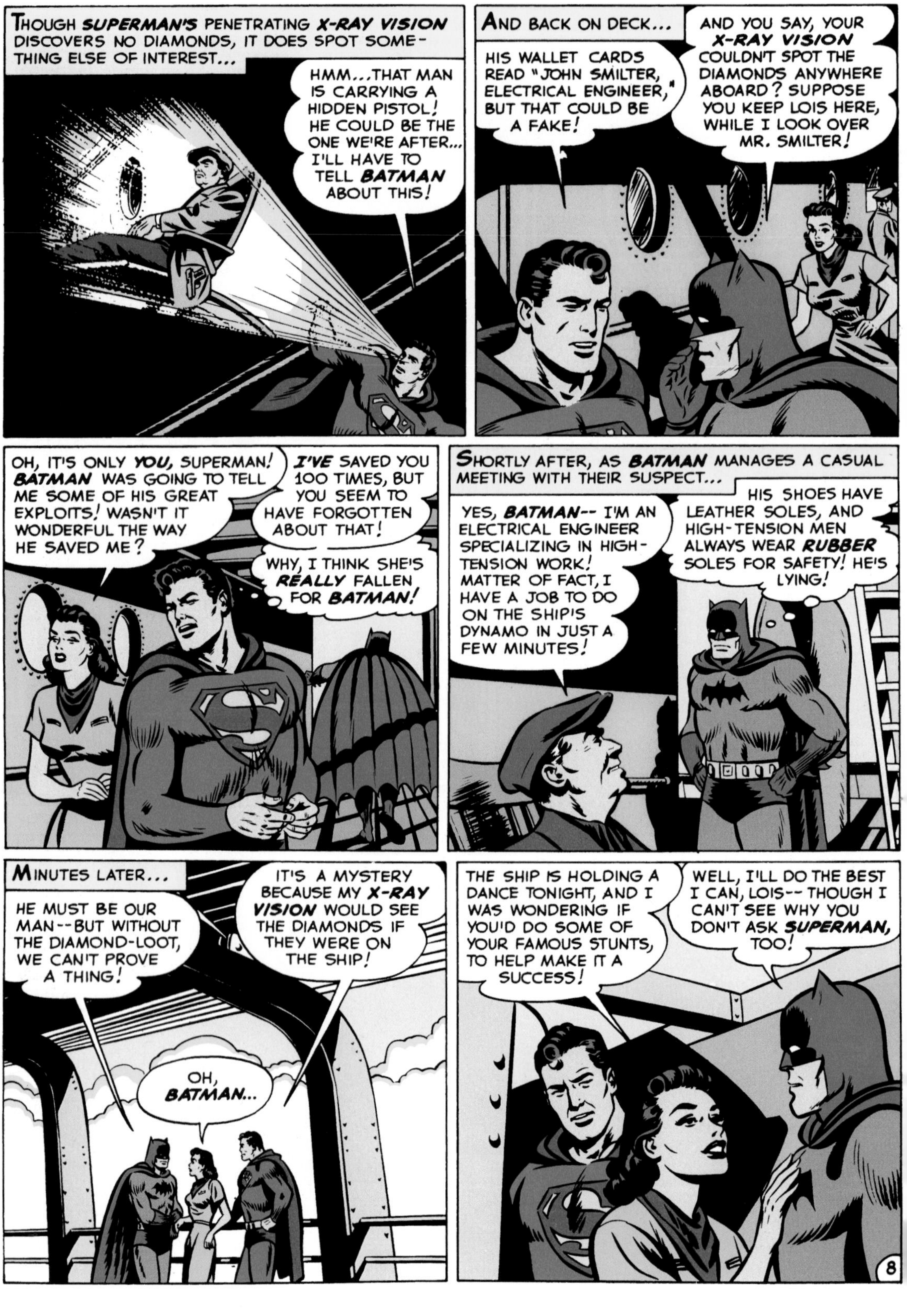
THOUGH SUPERMAN'S PENETRATING X-RAY VISION DISCOVERS NO DIAMONDS, IT DOES SPOT SOMETHING ELSE OF INTEREST...
HMM...THAT MAN IS CARRYING A HIDDEN PISTOL! HE COULD BE THE ONE WE'RE AFTER... I'LL HAVE TO TELL BATMAN ABOUT THIS!
AND BACK ON DECK...
HIS WALLET CARDS READ "JOHN SMILTER, ELECTRICAL ENGINEER," BUT THAT COULD BE A FAKE!
AND YOU SAY, YOUR X-RAY VISION COULDN'T SPOT THE DIAMONDS ANYWHERE ABOARD? SUPPOSE YOU KEEP LOIS HERE, WHILE I LOOK OVER MR. SMILTER!
OH, IT'S ONLY YOU, SUPERMAN! BATMAN WAS GOING TO TELL ME SOME OF HIS GREAT EXPLOITS! WASN'T IT WONDERFUL THE WAY HE SAVED ME?
I'VE SAVED YOU 100 TIMES, BUT YOU SEEM TO HAVE FORGOTTEN ABOUT THAT!
WHY, I THINK SHE'S REALLY FALLEN FOR BATMAN!
SHORTLY AFTER, AS BATMAN MANAGES A CASUAL MEETING WITH THEIR SUSPECT...
YES, BATMAN-- I'M AN ELECTRICAL ENGINEER SPECIALIZING IN HIGH-TENSION WORK! MATTER OF FACT, I HAVE A JOB TO DO ON THE SHIP'S DYNAMO IN JUST A FEW MINUTES!
HIS SHOES HAVE LEATHER SOLES, AND HIGH-TENSION MEN ALWAYS WEAR RUBBER SOLES FOR SAFETY! HE'S LYING!
MINUTES LATER...
HE MUST BE OUR MAN--BUT WITHOUT THE DIAMOND-LOOT, WE CAN'T PROVE A THING!
IT'S A MYSTERY BECAUSE MY X-RAY VISION WOULD SEE THE DIAMONDS IF THEY WERE ON THE SHIP!
OH, BATMAN...
THE SHIP IS HOLDING A DANCE TONIGHT, AND I WAS WONDERING IF YOU'D DO SOME OF YOUR FAMOUS STUNTS, TO HELP MAKE IT A SUCCESS!
WELL, I'LL DO THE BEST I CAN, LOIS-- THOUGH I CAN'T SEE WHY YOU DON'T ASK SUPERMAN, TOO!
8

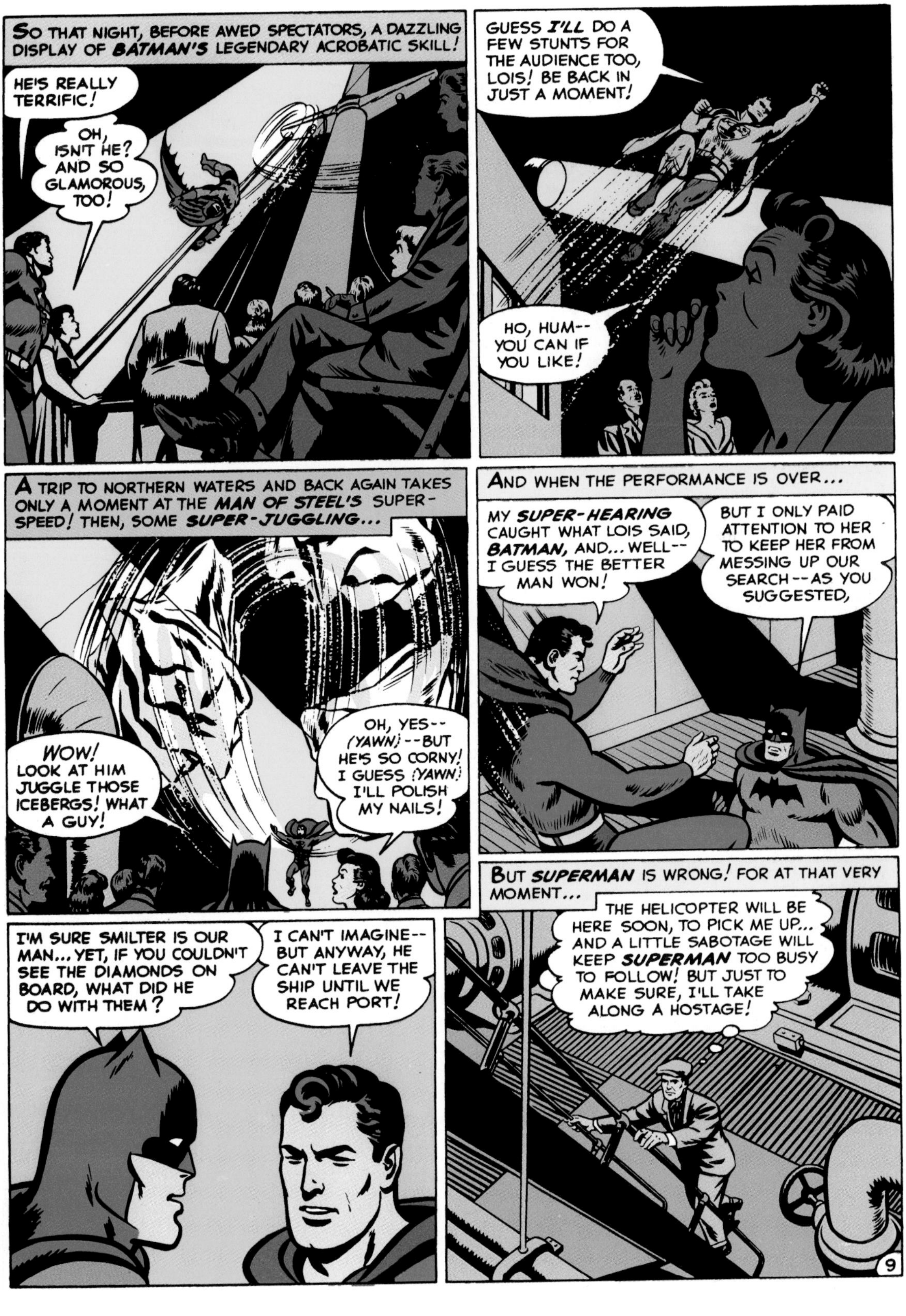
SO THAT NIGHT, BEFORE AWED SPECTATORS, A DAZZLING DISPLAY OF BATMAN'S LEGENDARY ACROBATIC SKILL!
HE'S REALLY TERRIFIC!
OH, ISN'T HE? AND SO GLAMOROUS, TOO!
GUESS I'LL DO A FEW STUNTS FOR THE AUDIENCE TOO, LOIS! BE BACK IN JUST A MOMENT!
HO, HUM-- YOU CAN IF YOU LIKE!
A TRIP TO NORTHERN WATERS AND BACK AGAIN TAKES ONLY A MOMENT AT THE MAN OF STEEL'S SUPER-SPEED! THEN, SOME SUPER-JUGGLING...
WOW! LOOK AT HIM JUGGLE THOSE ICEBERGS! WHAT A GUY!
OH, YES-- (YAWN) --BUT HE'S SO CORNY! I GUESS (YAWN) I'LL POLISH MY NAILS!
AND WHEN THE PERFORMANCE IS OVER...
MY SUPER-HEARING CAUGHT WHAT LOIS SAID, BATMAN, AND... WELL-- I GUESS THE BETTER MAN WON!
BUT I ONLY PAID ATTENTION TO HER TO KEEP HER FROM MESSING UP OUR SEARCH--AS YOU SUGGESTED,
I'M SURE SMILTER IS OUR MAN... YET, IF YOU COULDN'T SEE THE DIAMONDS ON BOARD, WHAT DID HE DO WITH THEM?
I CAN'T IMAGINE-- BUT ANYWAY, HE CAN'T LEAVE THE SHIP UNTIL WE REACH PORT!
BUT SUPERMAN IS WRONG! FOR AT THAT VERY MOMENT...
THE HELICOPTER WILL BE HERE SOON, TO PICK ME UP... AND A LITTLE SABOTAGE WILL KEEP SUPERMAN TOO BUSY TO FOLLOW! BUT JUST TO MAKE SURE, I'LL TAKE ALONG A HOSTAGE!
9

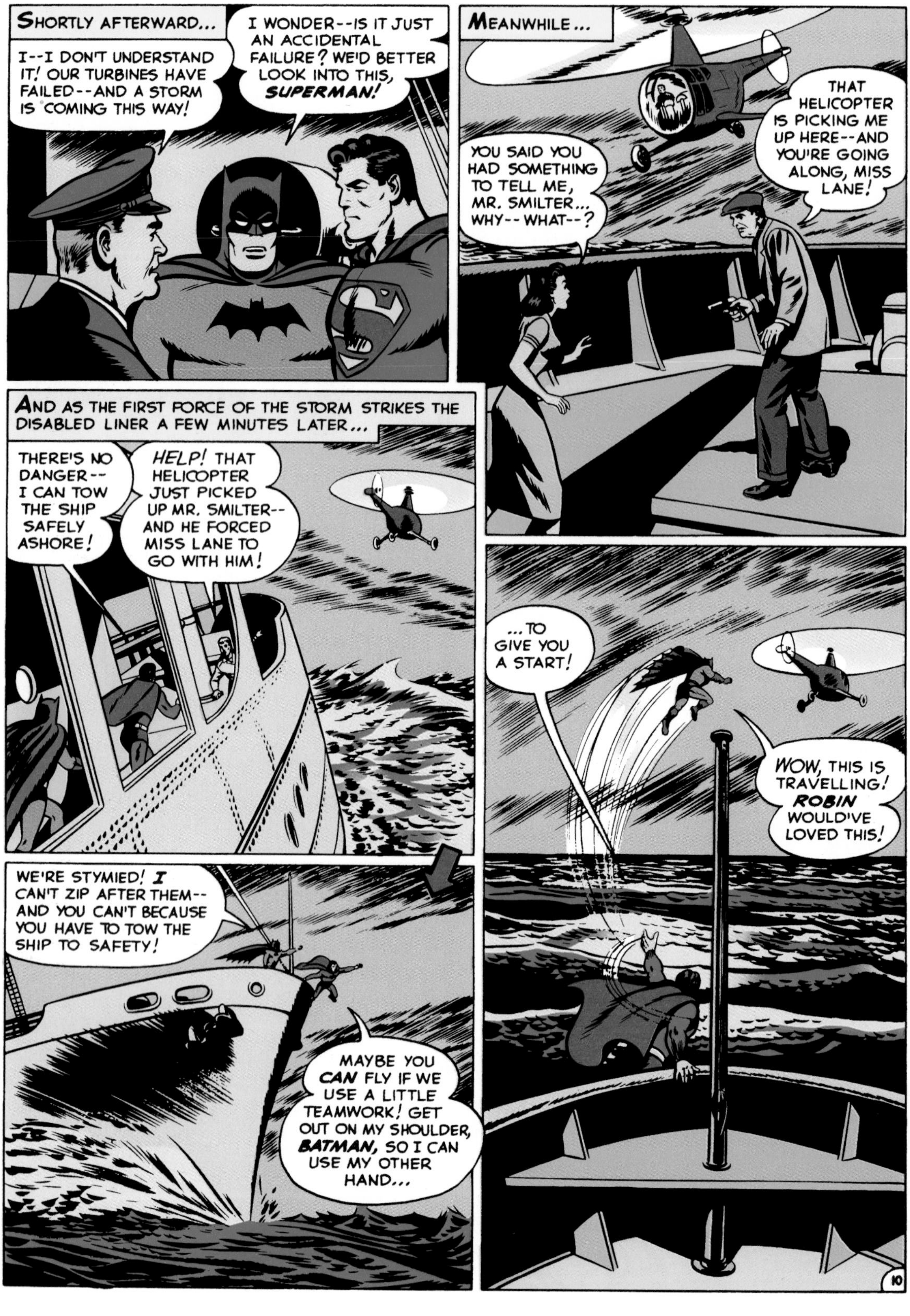
SHORTLY AFTERWARD...
I--I DON'T UNDERSTAND IT! OUR TURBINES HAVE FAILED--AND A STORM IS COMING THIS WAY!
I WONDER--IS IT JUST AN ACCIDENTAL FAILURE? WE'D BETTER LOOK INTO THIS, SUPERMAN!
MEANWHILE...
THAT HELICOPTER IS PICKING ME UP HERE--AND YOU'RE GOING ALONG, MISS LANE!
YOU SAID YOU HAD SOMETHING TO TELL ME, MR. SMILTER... WHY--WHAT--?
AND AS THE FIRST FORCE OF THE STORM STRIKES THE DISABLED LINER A FEW MINUTES LATER...
THERE'S NO DANGER--I CAN TOW THE SHIP SAFELY ASHORE!
HELP! THAT HELICOPTER JUST PICKED UP MR. SMILTER--AND HE FORCED MISS LANE TO GO WITH HIM!
WE'RE STYMIED! I CAN'T ZIP AFTER THEM--AND YOU CAN'T BECAUSE YOU HAVE TO TOW THE SHIP TO SAFETY!
MAYBE YOU CAN FLY IF WE USE A LITTLE TEAMWORK! GET OUT ON MY SHOULDER, BATMAN, SO I CAN USE MY OTHER HAND...
...TO GIVE YOU A START!
WOW, THIS IS TRAVELLING! ROBIN WOULD'VE LOVED THIS!
10

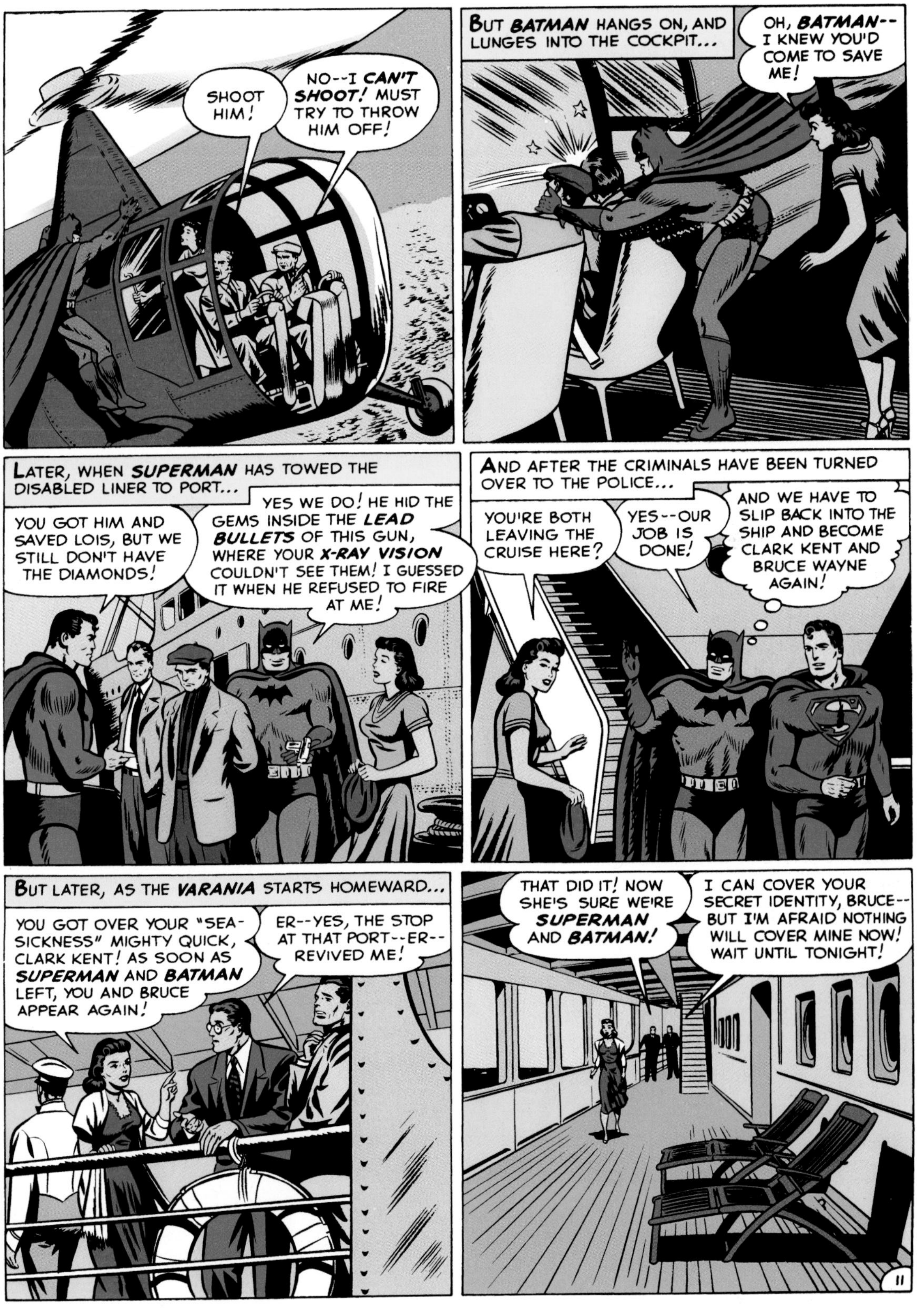

SHOOT HIM!
NO--I CAN'T SHOOT! MUST TRY TO THROW HIM OFF!
BUT BATMAN HANGS ON, AND LUNGES INTO THE COCKPIT...
OH, BATMAN--I KNEW YOU'D COME TO SAVE ME!
LATER, WHEN SUPERMAN HAS TOWED THE DISABLED LINER TO PORT...
YOU GOT HIM AND SAVED LOIS, BUT WE STILL DON'T HAVE THE DIAMONDS!
YES WE DO! HE HID THE GEMS INSIDE THE LEAD BULLETS OF THIS GUN, WHERE YOUR X-RAY VISION COULDN'T SEE THEM! I GUESSED IT WHEN HE REFUSED TO FIRE AT ME!
AND AFTER THE CRIMINALS HAVE BEEN TURNED OVER TO THE POLICE...
YOU'RE BOTH LEAVING THE CRUISE HERE?
YES--OUR JOB IS DONE!
AND WE HAVE TO SLIP BACK INTO THE SHIP AND BECOME CLARK KENT AND BRUCE WAYNE AGAIN!
BUT LATER, AS THE VARANIA STARTS HOMEWARD...
YOU GOT OVER YOUR "SEA-SICKNESS" MIGHTY QUICK, CLARK KENT! AS SOON AS SUPERMAN AND BATMAN LEFT, YOU AND BRUCE APPEAR AGAIN!
ER--YES, THE STOP AT THAT PORT--ER--REVIVED ME!
THAT DID IT! NOW SHE'S SURE WE'RE SUPERMAN AND BATMAN!
I CAN COVER YOUR SECRET IDENTITY, BRUCE--BUT I'M AFRAID NOTHING WILL COVER MINE NOW! WAIT UNTIL TONIGHT!
11

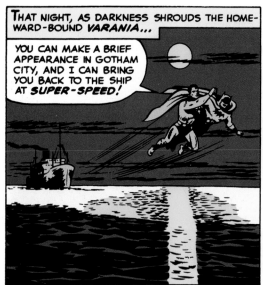

THAT NIGHT, AS DARKNESS SHROUDS THE HOME-WARD-BOUND *VARANIA*...

YOU CAN MAKE A BRIEF APPEARANCE IN GOTHAM CITY, AND I CAN BRING YOU BACK TO THE SHIP AT *SUPER-SPEED!*

SO MINUTES LATER, IN GOTHAM CITY...

LOOK-- BATMAN! HE'S WATCHING OUT FOR CRIME, AS USUAL!

NEXT MORNING...

WHY, THE SHIP'S RADIO NEWS-SHEET SPEAKS OF *BATMAN* APPEARING IN GOTHAM CITY LAST NIGHT! THEN HE COULDN'T POSSIBLY BE BRUCE WAYNE!

THAT CONVINCED HER-- BUT I'M AFRAID THERE'S NO HELP FOR ME!

YES THERE IS! WHEN WE NEAR PORT CITY, YOU ZIP AHEAD AS *SUPERMAN*, AND GREET THE SHIP! I'LL FIX THINGS FOR YOU!

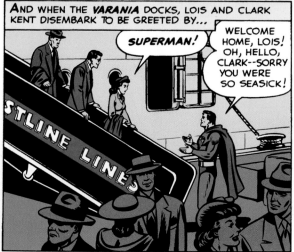

AND WHEN THE *VARANIA* DOCKS, LOIS AND CLARK KENT DISEMBARK TO BE GREETED BY...

SUPERMAN!

WELCOME HOME, LOIS! OH, HELLO, CLARK-- SORRY YOU WERE SO SEASICK!

LATER, IN A SECLUDED CORNER...

YOUR WONDERFUL SKILL IN DISGUISING AS CLARK KENT SAVED MY SECRET, *BATMAN!* BUT WE STILL DON'T KNOW WHICH OF US LOIS REALLY PREFERS!

LET'S SEE WHICH OF US SHE'LL GO OUT TO DINNER WITH... THAT'LL PROVE HER PREFERENCE!

BUT WHEN THEY RETURN TO THE CROWD...

HI, *BATMAN!* WHAT DO YOU THINK?... I'M TAKING MISS LANE OUT TO DINNER!

OH, NO!

ISN'T HE THE CUTEST LITTLE CHAP?

12

THE END

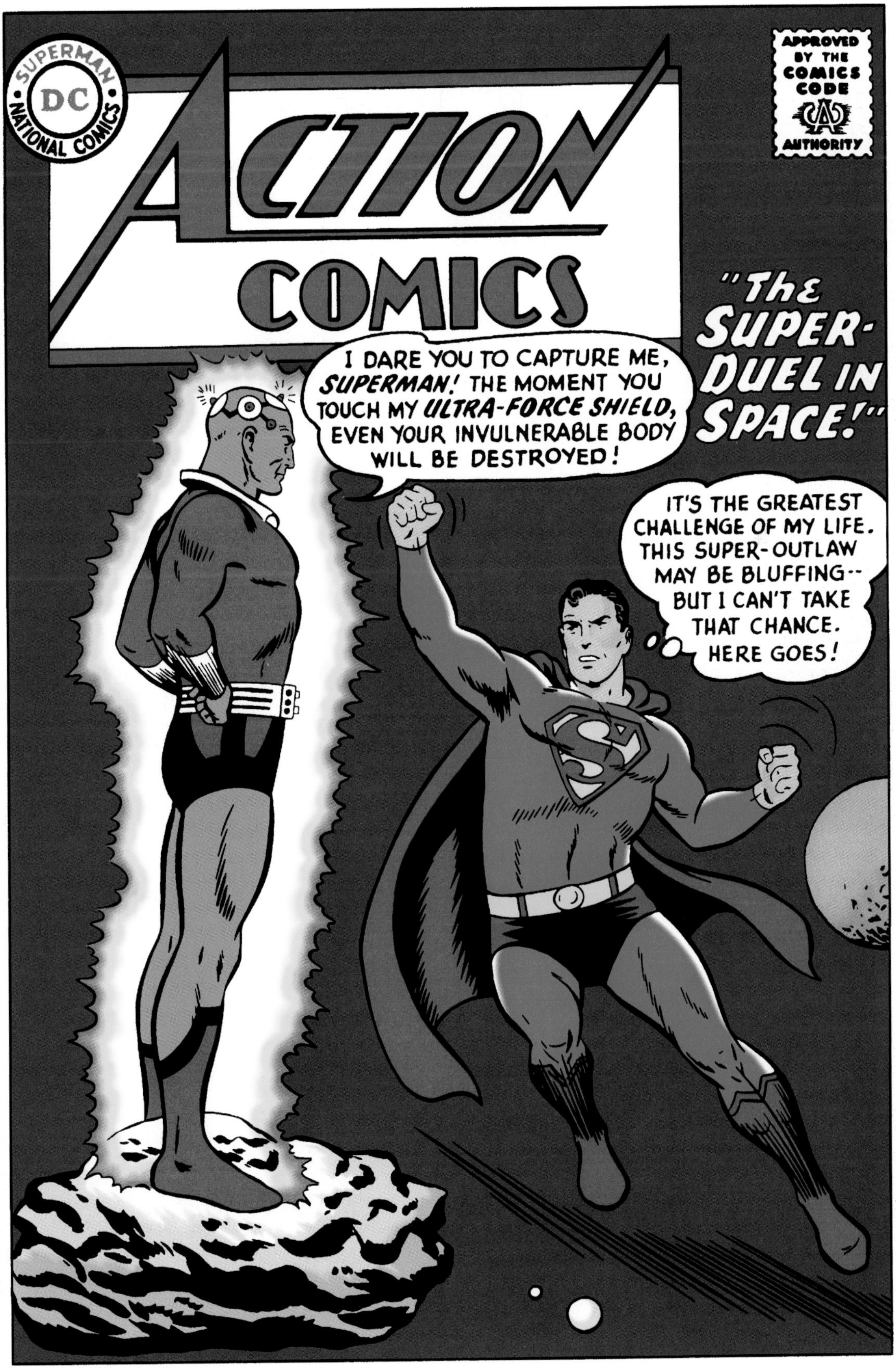
SUPERMAN
DC
NATIONAL COMICS
APPROVED BY THE COMICS CODE AUTHORITY
ACTION COMICS
"The SUPER-DUEL IN SPACE!"
I DARE YOU TO CAPTURE ME, SUPERMAN! THE MOMENT YOU TOUCH MY ULTRA-FORCE SHIELD, EVEN YOUR INVULNERABLE BODY WILL BE DESTROYED!
IT'S THE GREATEST CHALLENGE OF MY LIFE. THIS SUPER-OUTLAW MAY BE BLUFFING-- BUT I CAN'T TAKE THAT CHANCE. HERE GOES!

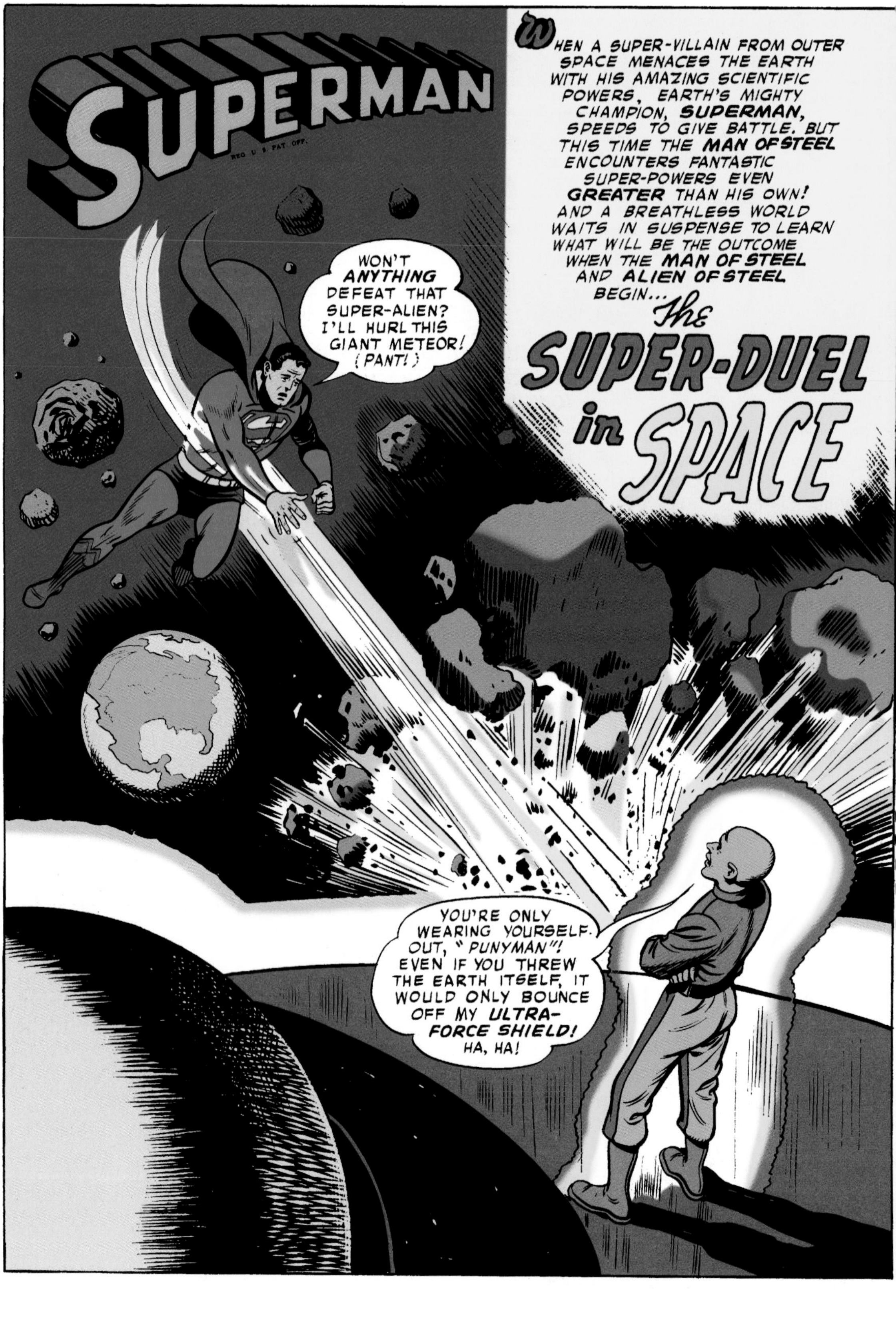
SUPERMAN
REG. U.S. PAT. OFF.
WHEN A SUPER-VILLAIN FROM OUTER SPACE MENACES THE EARTH WITH HIS AMAZING SCIENTIFIC POWERS, EARTH'S MIGHTY CHAMPION, SUPERMAN, SPEEDS TO GIVE BATTLE. BUT THIS TIME THE MAN OF STEEL ENCOUNTERS FANTASTIC SUPER-POWERS EVEN GREATER THAN HIS OWN! AND A BREATHLESS WORLD WAITS IN SUSPENSE TO LEARN WHAT WILL BE THE OUTCOME WHEN THE MAN OF STEEL AND ALIEN OF STEEL BEGIN...
The SUPER-DUEL in SPACE
WON'T ANYTHING DEFEAT THAT SUPER-ALIEN? I'LL HURL THIS GIANT METEOR! (PANT!)
YOU'RE ONLY WEARING YOURSELF OUT, "PUNYMAN"! EVEN IF YOU THREW THE EARTH ITSELF, IT WOULD ONLY BOUNCE OFF MY ULTRA-FORCE SHIELD! HA, HA!

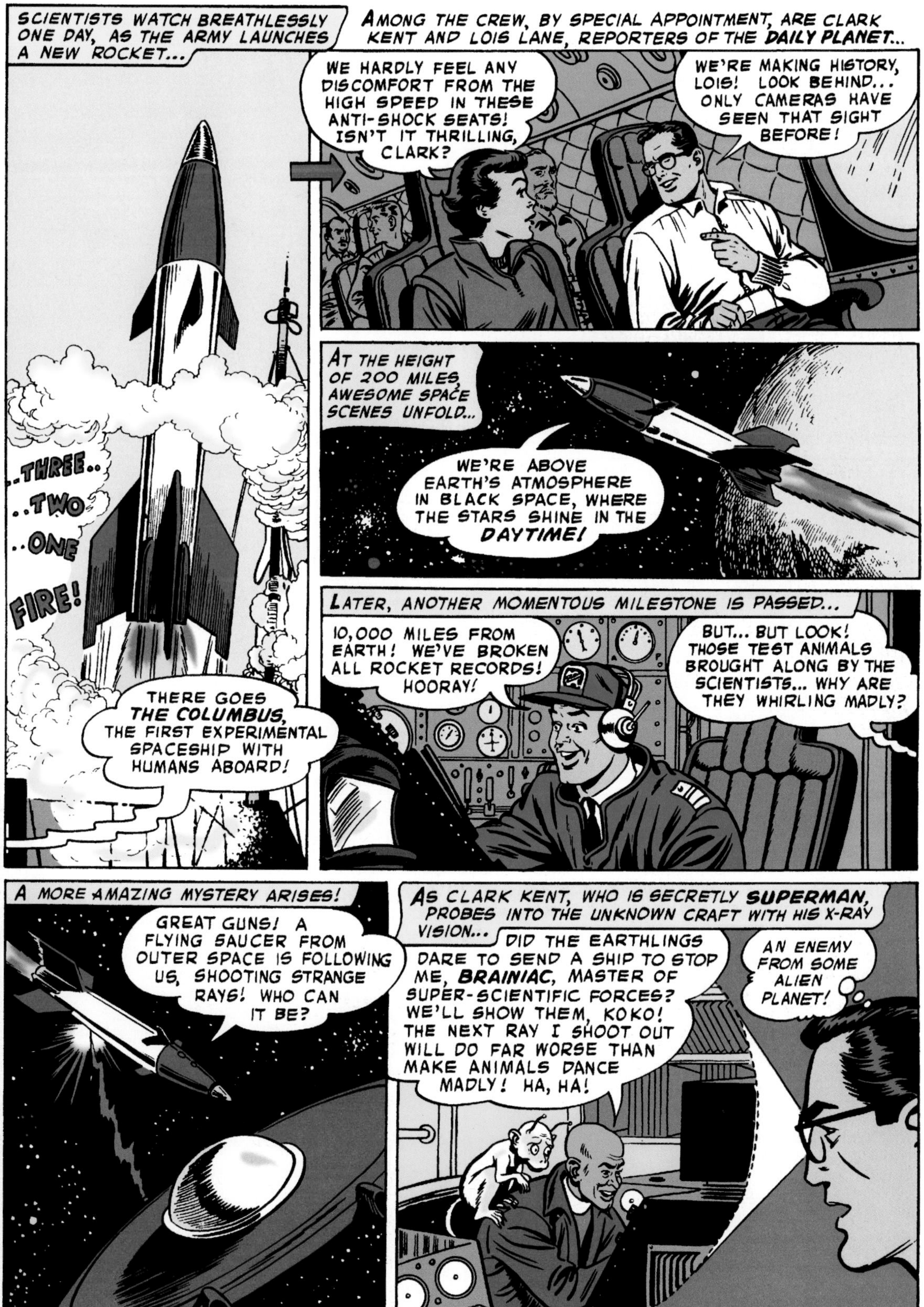

SCIENTISTS WATCH BREATHLESSLY ONE DAY, AS THE ARMY LAUNCHES A NEW ROCKET...
..THREE.. ..TWO ..ONE FIRE!
THERE GOES THE COLUMBUS, THE FIRST EXPERIMENTAL SPACESHIP WITH HUMANS ABOARD!
AMONG THE CREW, BY SPECIAL APPOINTMENT, ARE CLARK KENT AND LOIS LANE, REPORTERS OF THE DAILY PLANET...
WE HARDLY FEEL ANY DISCOMFORT FROM THE HIGH SPEED IN THESE ANTI-SHOCK SEATS! ISN'T IT THRILLING, CLARK?
WE'RE MAKING HISTORY, LOIS! LOOK BEHIND... ONLY CAMERAS HAVE SEEN THAT SIGHT BEFORE!
AT THE HEIGHT OF 200 MILES, AWESOME SPACE SCENES UNFOLD...
WE'RE ABOVE EARTH'S ATMOSPHERE IN BLACK SPACE, WHERE THE STARS SHINE IN THE DAYTIME!
LATER, ANOTHER MOMENTOUS MILESTONE IS PASSED...
10,000 MILES FROM EARTH! WE'VE BROKEN ALL ROCKET RECORDS! HOORAY!
BUT... BUT LOOK! THOSE TEST ANIMALS BROUGHT ALONG BY THE SCIENTISTS... WHY ARE THEY WHIRLING MADLY?
A MORE AMAZING MYSTERY ARISES!
GREAT GUNS! A FLYING SAUCER FROM OUTER SPACE IS FOLLOWING US, SHOOTING STRANGE RAYS! WHO CAN IT BE?
AS CLARK KENT, WHO IS SECRETLY SUPERMAN, PROBES INTO THE UNKNOWN CRAFT WITH HIS X-RAY VISION...
DID THE EARTHLINGS DARE TO SEND A SHIP TO STOP ME, BRAINIAC, MASTER OF SUPER-SCIENTIFIC FORCES? WE'LL SHOW THEM, KOKO! THE NEXT RAY I SHOOT OUT WILL DO FAR WORSE THAN MAKE ANIMALS DANCE MADLY! HA, HA!
AN ENEMY FROM SOME ALIEN PLANET!

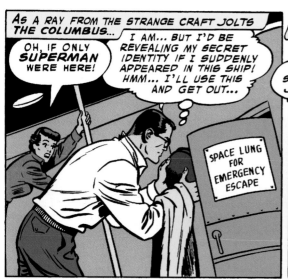

As a ray from the strange craft jolts the COLUMBUS...

OH, IF ONLY **SUPERMAN** WERE HERE!

I AM... BUT I'D BE REVEALING MY SECRET IDENTITY IF I SUDDENLY APPEARED IN THIS SHIP! HMM... I'LL USE THIS AND GET OUT...

SPACE LUNG FOR EMERGENCY ESCAPE

AFTER CLARK DONS THE DEVICE AND EXITS THROUGH THE EMERGENCY ESCAPE HATCH...

POOR CLARK-- HE'S SO AFRAID, HE'S JUMPING BACK TO EARTH!

I'LL PRETEND TO ZOOM BACK TO EARTH, PROPELLED BY THE BUILT-IN SUPERSONIC JETS!

Once out of sight, timid CLARK changes to powerful **SUPERMAN!**

THEY'LL ASSUME CLARK REACHED EARTH AND SENT **SUPERMAN** TO THE RESCUE. I'LL SPEED BACK AND CAPTURE THAT SINISTER ALIEN!

But incredibly, when **SUPERMAN** tries to smash into the flying saucer...

OOF! I... I ONLY REBOUNDED FROM AN INVISIBLE WALL!

EARTHLING FOOL! NOTHING IN THE UNIVERSE CAN PENETRATE THE **ULTRA-FORCE BARRIER** THAT SURROUNDS MY SHIP! HA, HA!

Unable to invade the impenetrable craft, the **MAN OF STEEL** changes tactics!

I'LL SHOVE THE EARTH ROCKET AHEAD AT SUPER-SPEED, SO THAT IT WILL BE OUT OF HARM'S WAY! GOT TO GO FASTER... FASTER...!

SUPERMAN WINS THE DEADLY RACE!

WHEW! WE'RE OUT OF RANGE OF HIS DESTRUCTIVE RAYS!

DON'T WORRY ABOUT THEM, KOKO! WE HAVE OTHER BUSINESS TO DO ON EARTH NOW!

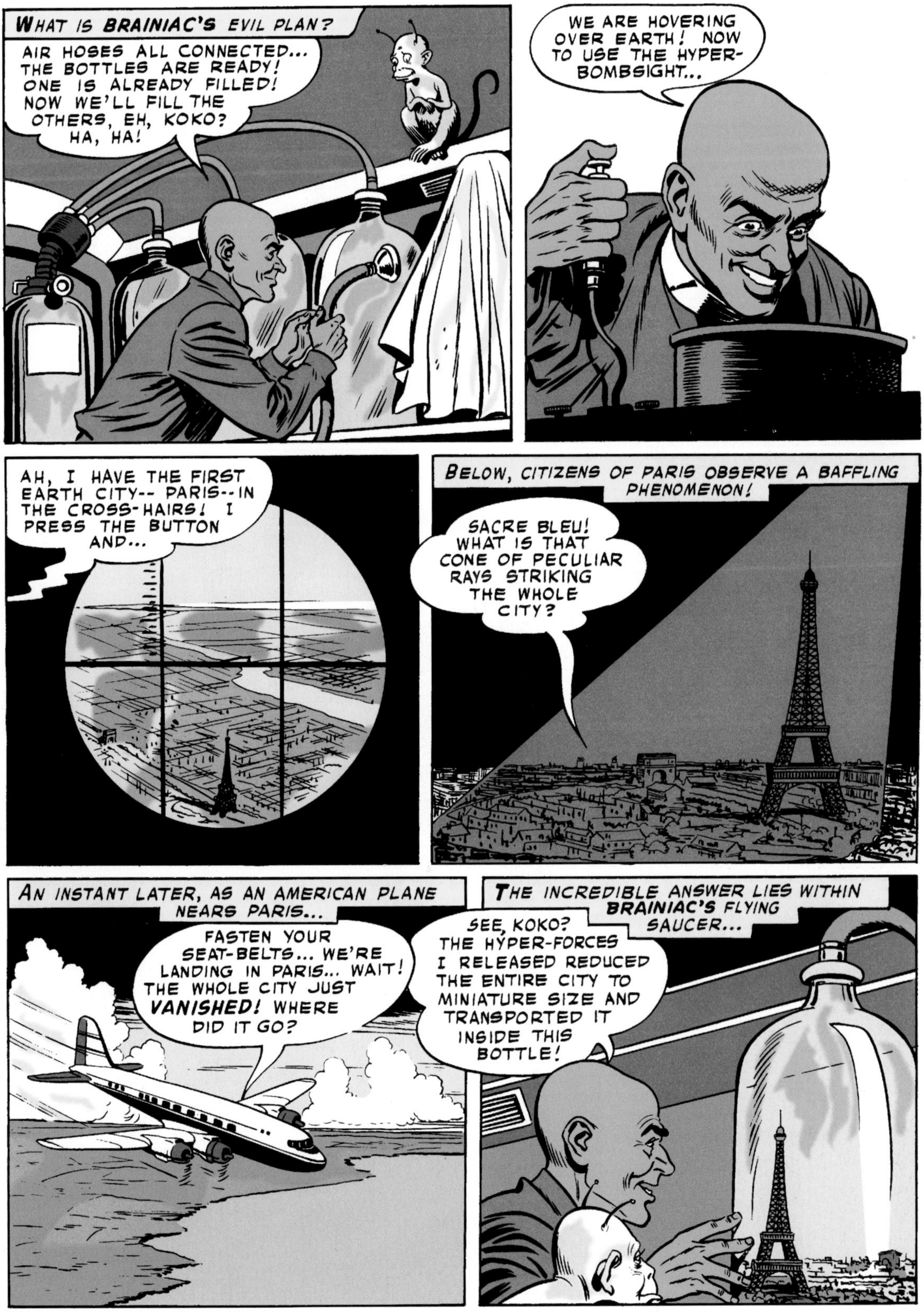

WHAT IS BRAINIAC'S EVIL PLAN?
AIR HOSES ALL CONNECTED... THE BOTTLES ARE READY! ONE IS ALREADY FILLED! NOW WE'LL FILL THE OTHERS, EH, KOKO? HA, HA!
WE ARE HOVERING OVER EARTH! NOW TO USE THE HYPER-BOMBSIGHT...
AH, I HAVE THE FIRST EARTH CITY-- PARIS--IN THE CROSS-HAIRS! I PRESS THE BUTTON AND...
BELOW, CITIZENS OF PARIS OBSERVE A BAFFLING PHENOMENON!
SACRE BLEU! WHAT IS THAT CONE OF PECULIAR RAYS STRIKING THE WHOLE CITY?
AN INSTANT LATER, AS AN AMERICAN PLANE NEARS PARIS...
FASTEN YOUR SEAT-BELTS... WE'RE LANDING IN PARIS... WAIT! THE WHOLE CITY JUST VANISHED! WHERE DID IT GO?
THE INCREDIBLE ANSWER LIES WITHIN BRAINIAC'S FLYING SAUCER...
SEE, KOKO? THE HYPER-FORCES I RELEASED REDUCED THE ENTIRE CITY TO MINIATURE SIZE AND TRANSPORTED IT INSIDE THIS BOTTLE!

MEANWHILE... I HAVE TO PUSH THE ROCKET BACK TO EARTH SLOWLY... CONTINUED SUPER-SPEED WOULD CRUSH THE CREW WITHIN! WAIT... MY TELESCOPIC VISION SHOWS SOMETHING WRONG ON EARTH... PARIS IS MISSING!

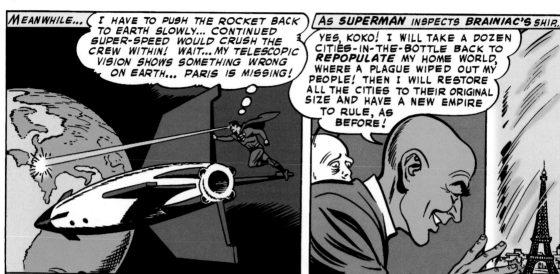

AS **SUPERMAN** INSPECTS **BRAINIAC'S** SHIP...

YES, KOKO! I WILL TAKE A DOZEN CITIES-IN-THE-BOTTLE BACK TO **REPOPULATE** MY HOME WORLD, WHERE A PLAGUE WIPED OUT MY PEOPLE! THEN I WILL RESTORE ALL THE CITIES TO THEIR ORIGINAL SIZE AND HAVE A NEW EMPIRE TO RULE, AS BEFORE!

HE'S GOING TO STEAL EARTH'S GREATEST CITIES! YET I CAN'T STOP HIM AS LONG AS HIS SHIP IS PROTECTED BY THAT **ULTRA-FORCE BARRIER!** I'LL JUST HAVE TO STAND BY... AND WATCH HELPLESSLY...

AND PRESENTLY, AS **BRAINIAC** CONTINUES HIS RAID OF EARTH BY STEALING THE CITY OF ROME!...

ONE AFTER ANOTHER, THE WORLD'S GREATEST CITIES BECOME TOY VILLAGES IN BOTTLES!

AN OXYGEN SUPPLY KEEPS THE TINY PEOPLE ALIVE! AREN'T THEY CUTE, KOKO? BUT LET ME EXAMINE THAT BRIDGE IN THIS CITY THEY CALL NEW YORK!

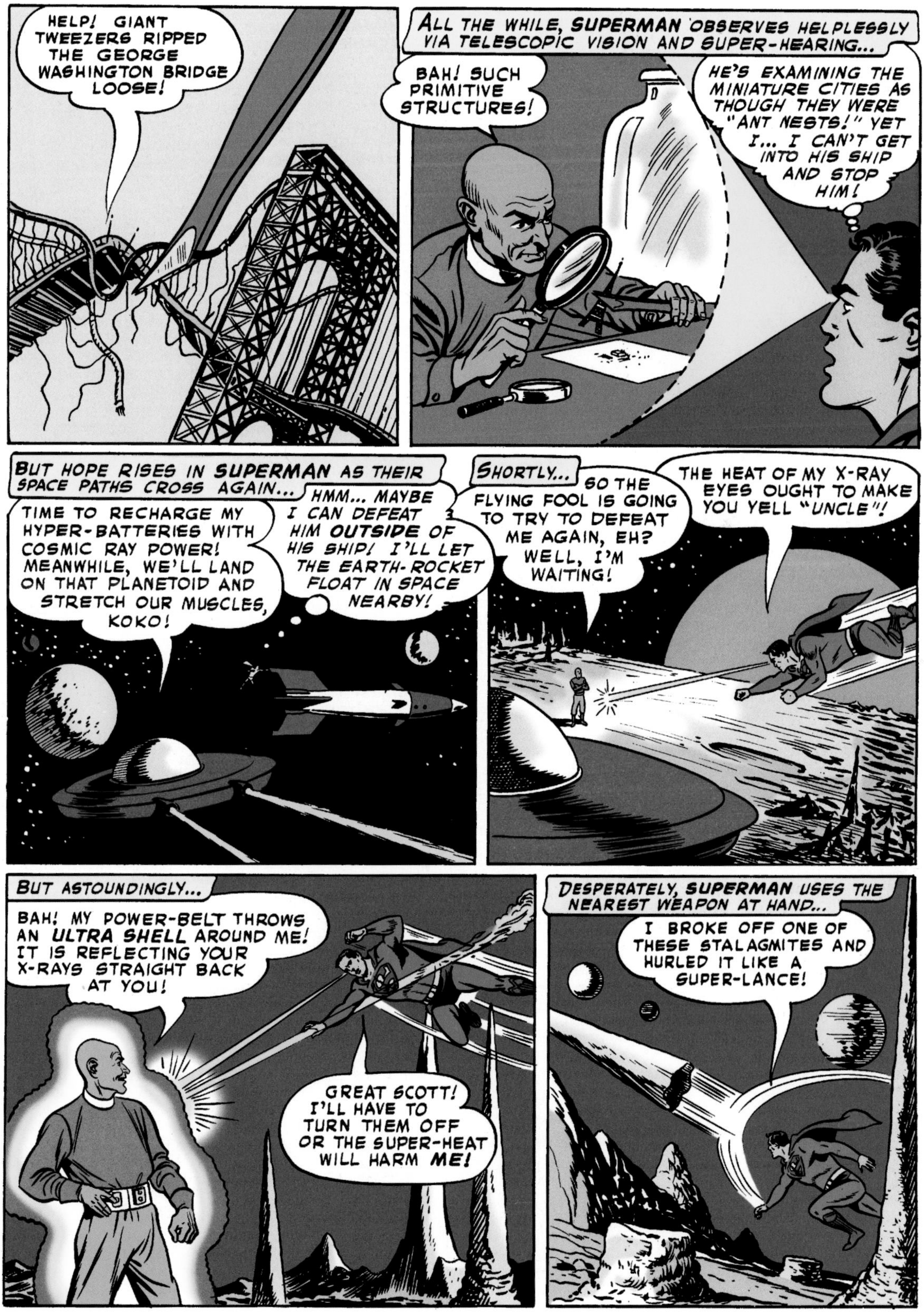
HELP! GIANT TWEEZERS RIPPED THE GEORGE WASHINGTON BRIDGE LOOSE!
ALL THE WHILE, SUPERMAN OBSERVES HELPLESSLY VIA TELESCOPIC VISION AND SUPER-HEARING...
BAH! SUCH PRIMITIVE STRUCTURES!
HE'S EXAMINING THE MINIATURE CITIES AS THOUGH THEY WERE "ANT NESTS!" YET I... I CAN'T GET INTO HIS SHIP AND STOP HIM!
BUT HOPE RISES IN SUPERMAN AS THEIR SPACE PATHS CROSS AGAIN...
TIME TO RECHARGE MY HYPER-BATTERIES WITH COSMIC RAY POWER! MEANWHILE, WE'LL LAND ON THAT PLANETOID AND STRETCH OUR MUSCLES, KOKO!
HMM... MAYBE I CAN DEFEAT HIM OUTSIDE OF HIS SHIP! I'LL LET THE EARTH-ROCKET FLOAT IN SPACE NEARBY!
SHORTLY...
SO THE FLYING FOOL IS GOING TO TRY TO DEFEAT ME AGAIN, EH? WELL, I'M WAITING!
THE HEAT OF MY X-RAY EYES OUGHT TO MAKE YOU YELL "UNCLE"!
BUT ASTOUNDINGLY...
BAH! MY POWER-BELT THROWS AN ULTRA SHELL AROUND ME! IT IS REFLECTING YOUR X-RAYS STRAIGHT BACK AT YOU!
GREAT SCOTT! I'LL HAVE TO TURN THEM OFF OR THE SUPER-HEAT WILL HARM ME!
DESPERATELY, SUPERMAN USES THE NEAREST WEAPON AT HAND...
I BROKE OFF ONE OF THESE STALAGMITES AND HURLED IT LIKE A SUPER-LANCE!

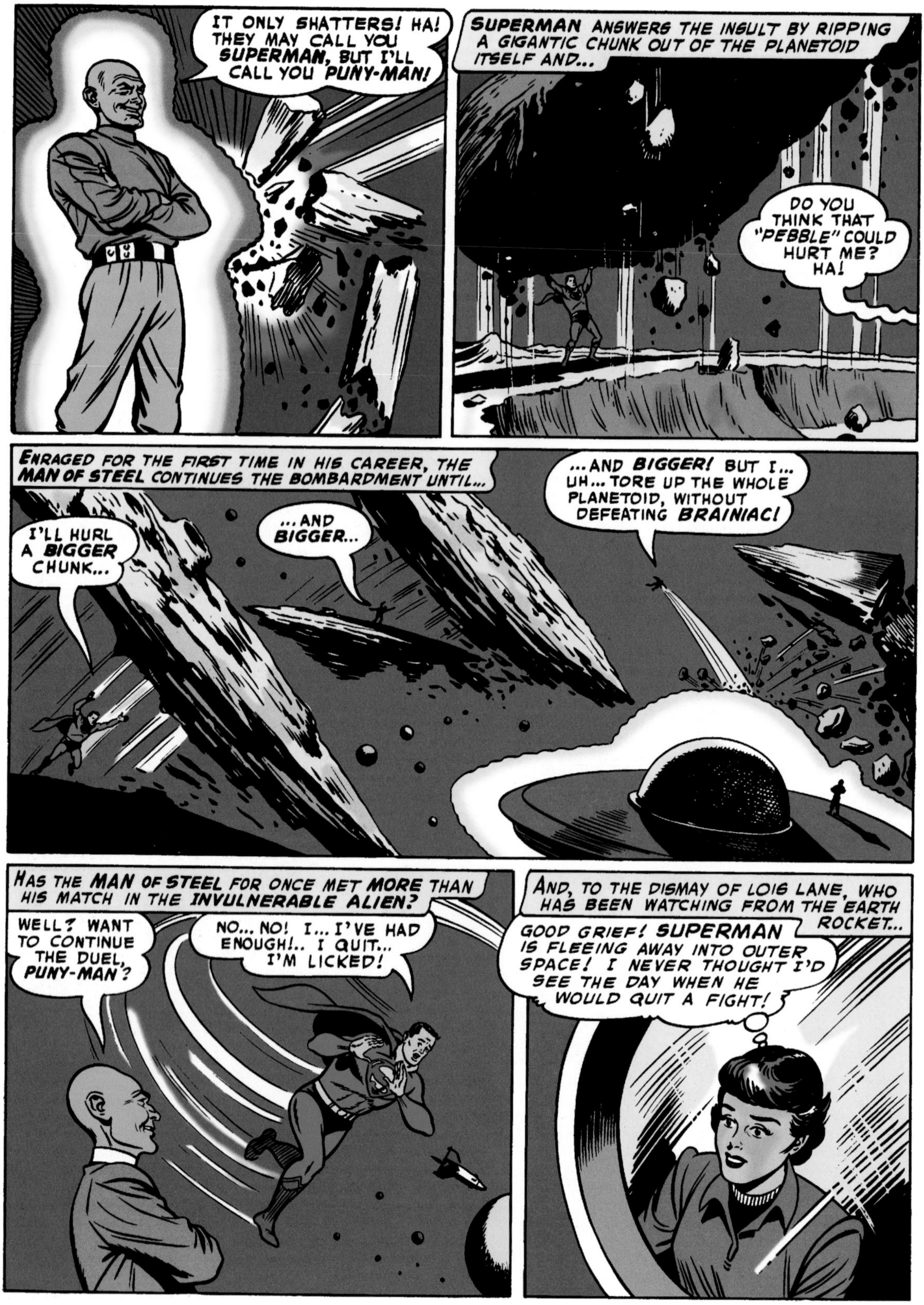
IT ONLY SHATTERS! HA! THEY MAY CALL YOU SUPERMAN, BUT I'LL CALL YOU PUNY-MAN!
SUPERMAN ANSWERS THE INSULT BY RIPPING A GIGANTIC CHUNK OUT OF THE PLANETOID ITSELF AND...
DO YOU THINK THAT "PEBBLE" COULD HURT ME? HA!
ENRAGED FOR THE FIRST TIME IN HIS CAREER, THE MAN OF STEEL CONTINUES THE BOMBARDMENT UNTIL...
I'LL HURL A BIGGER CHUNK...
...AND BIGGER...
...AND BIGGER! BUT I... UH... TORE UP THE WHOLE PLANETOID, WITHOUT DEFEATING BRAINIAC!
HAS THE MAN OF STEEL FOR ONCE MET MORE THAN HIS MATCH IN THE INVULNERABLE ALIEN?
WELL? WANT TO CONTINUE THE DUEL, PUNY-MAN?
NO... NO! I... I'VE HAD ENOUGH!.. I QUIT... I'M LICKED!
AND, TO THE DISMAY OF LOIS LANE, WHO HAS BEEN WATCHING FROM THE EARTH ROCKET...
GOOD GRIEF! SUPERMAN IS FLEEING AWAY INTO OUTER SPACE! I NEVER THOUGHT I'D SEE THE DAY WHEN HE WOULD QUIT A FIGHT!

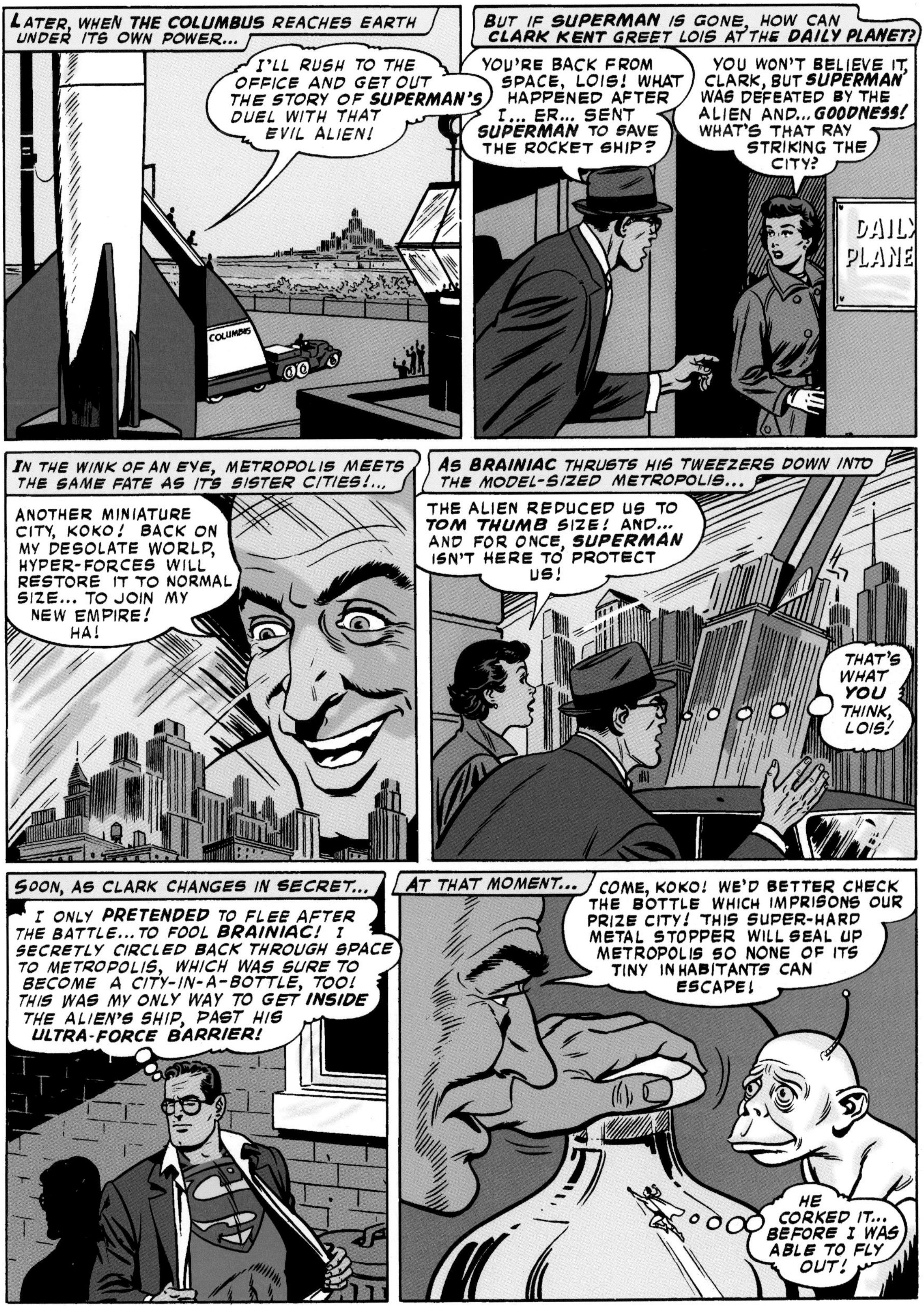
LATER, WHEN THE COLUMBUS REACHES EARTH UNDER ITS OWN POWER...
I'LL RUSH TO THE OFFICE AND GET OUT THE STORY OF SUPERMAN'S DUEL WITH THAT EVIL ALIEN!
COLUMBUS
BUT IF SUPERMAN IS GONE, HOW CAN CLARK KENT GREET LOIS AT THE DAILY PLANET?
YOU'RE BACK FROM SPACE, LOIS! WHAT HAPPENED AFTER I... ER... SENT SUPERMAN TO SAVE THE ROCKET SHIP?
YOU WON'T BELIEVE IT, CLARK, BUT SUPERMAN WAS DEFEATED BY THE ALIEN AND... GOODNESS! WHAT'S THAT RAY STRIKING THE CITY?
IN THE WINK OF AN EYE, METROPOLIS MEETS THE SAME FATE AS ITS SISTER CITIES!...
ANOTHER MINIATURE CITY, KOKO! BACK ON MY DESOLATE WORLD, HYPER-FORCES WILL RESTORE IT TO NORMAL SIZE... TO JOIN MY NEW EMPIRE! HA!
AS BRAINIAC THRUSTS HIS TWEEZERS DOWN INTO THE MODEL-SIZED METROPOLIS...
THE ALIEN REDUCED US TO TOM THUMB SIZE! AND... AND FOR ONCE, SUPERMAN ISN'T HERE TO PROTECT US!
THAT'S WHAT YOU THINK, LOIS!
SOON, AS CLARK CHANGES IN SECRET...
I ONLY PRETENDED TO FLEE AFTER THE BATTLE...TO FOOL BRAINIAC! I SECRETLY CIRCLED BACK THROUGH SPACE TO METROPOLIS, WHICH WAS SURE TO BECOME A CITY-IN-A-BOTTLE, TOO! THIS WAS MY ONLY WAY TO GET INSIDE THE ALIEN'S SHIP, PAST HIS ULTRA-FORCE BARRIER!
AT THAT MOMENT...
COME, KOKO! WE'D BETTER CHECK THE BOTTLE WHICH IMPRISONS OUR PRIZE CITY! THIS SUPER-HARD METAL STOPPER WILL SEAL UP METROPOLIS SO NONE OF ITS TINY INHABITANTS CAN ESCAPE!
HE CORKED IT... BEFORE I WAS ABLE TO FLY OUT!

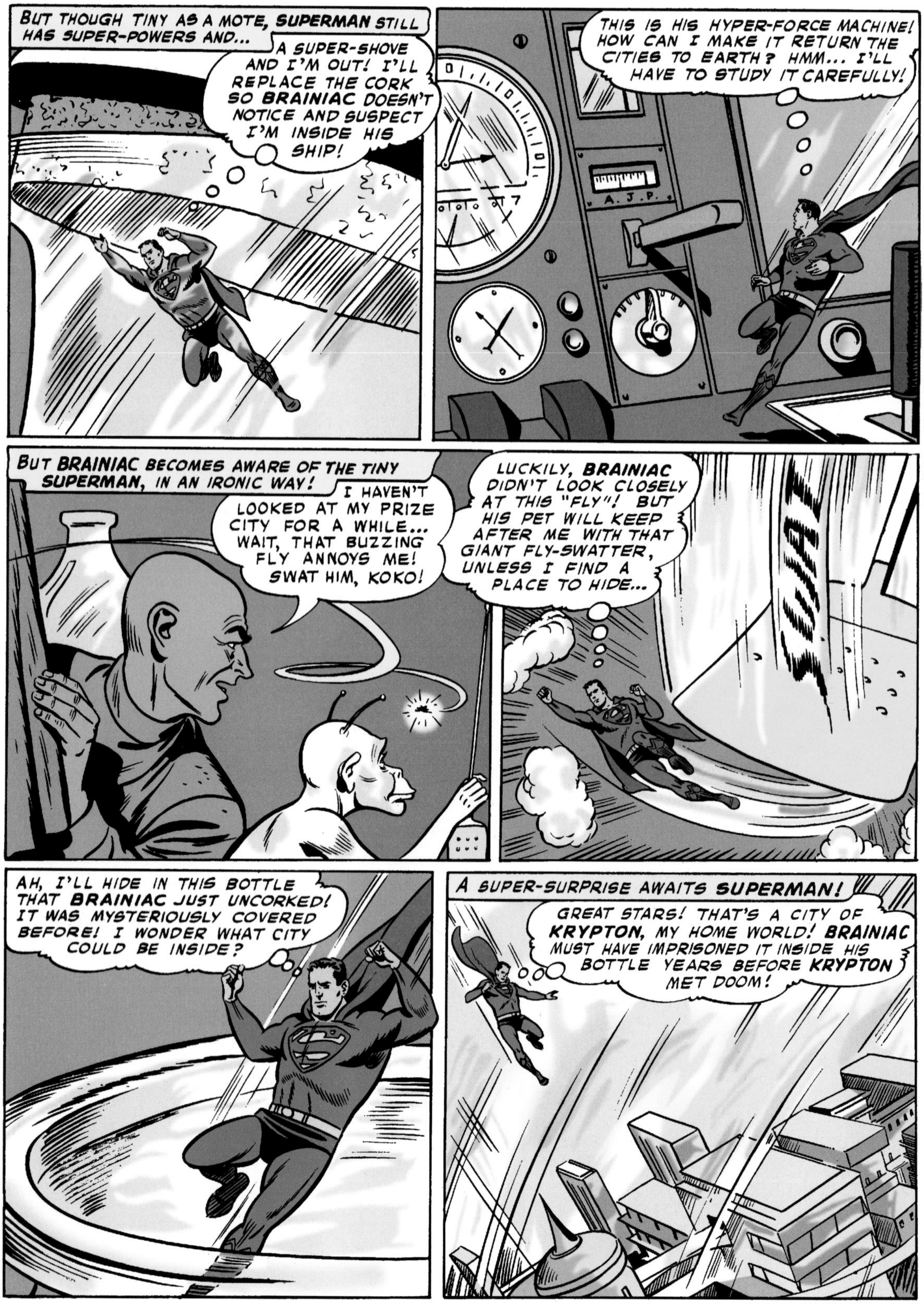
BUT THOUGH TINY AS A MOTE, SUPERMAN STILL HAS SUPER-POWERS AND...
A SUPER-SHOVE AND I'M OUT! I'LL REPLACE THE CORK SO BRAINIAC DOESN'T NOTICE AND SUSPECT I'M INSIDE HIS SHIP!
THIS IS HIS HYPER-FORCE MACHINE! HOW CAN I MAKE IT RETURN THE CITIES TO EARTH? HMM... I'LL HAVE TO STUDY IT CAREFULLY!
A. J. P.
BUT BRAINIAC BECOMES AWARE OF THE TINY SUPERMAN, IN AN IRONIC WAY!
I HAVEN'T LOOKED AT MY PRIZE CITY FOR A WHILE... WAIT, THAT BUZZING FLY ANNOYS ME! SWAT HIM, KOKO!
LUCKILY, BRAINIAC DIDN'T LOOK CLOSELY AT THIS "FLY"! BUT HIS PET WILL KEEP AFTER ME WITH THAT GIANT FLY-SWATTER, UNLESS I FIND A PLACE TO HIDE...
SWAT!
AH, I'LL HIDE IN THIS BOTTLE THAT BRAINIAC JUST UNCORKED! IT WAS MYSTERIOUSLY COVERED BEFORE! I WONDER WHAT CITY COULD BE INSIDE?
A SUPER-SURPRISE AWAITS SUPERMAN!
GREAT STARS! THAT'S A CITY OF KRYPTON, MY HOME WORLD! BRAINIAC MUST HAVE IMPRISONED IT INSIDE HIS BOTTLE YEARS BEFORE KRYPTON MET DOOM!

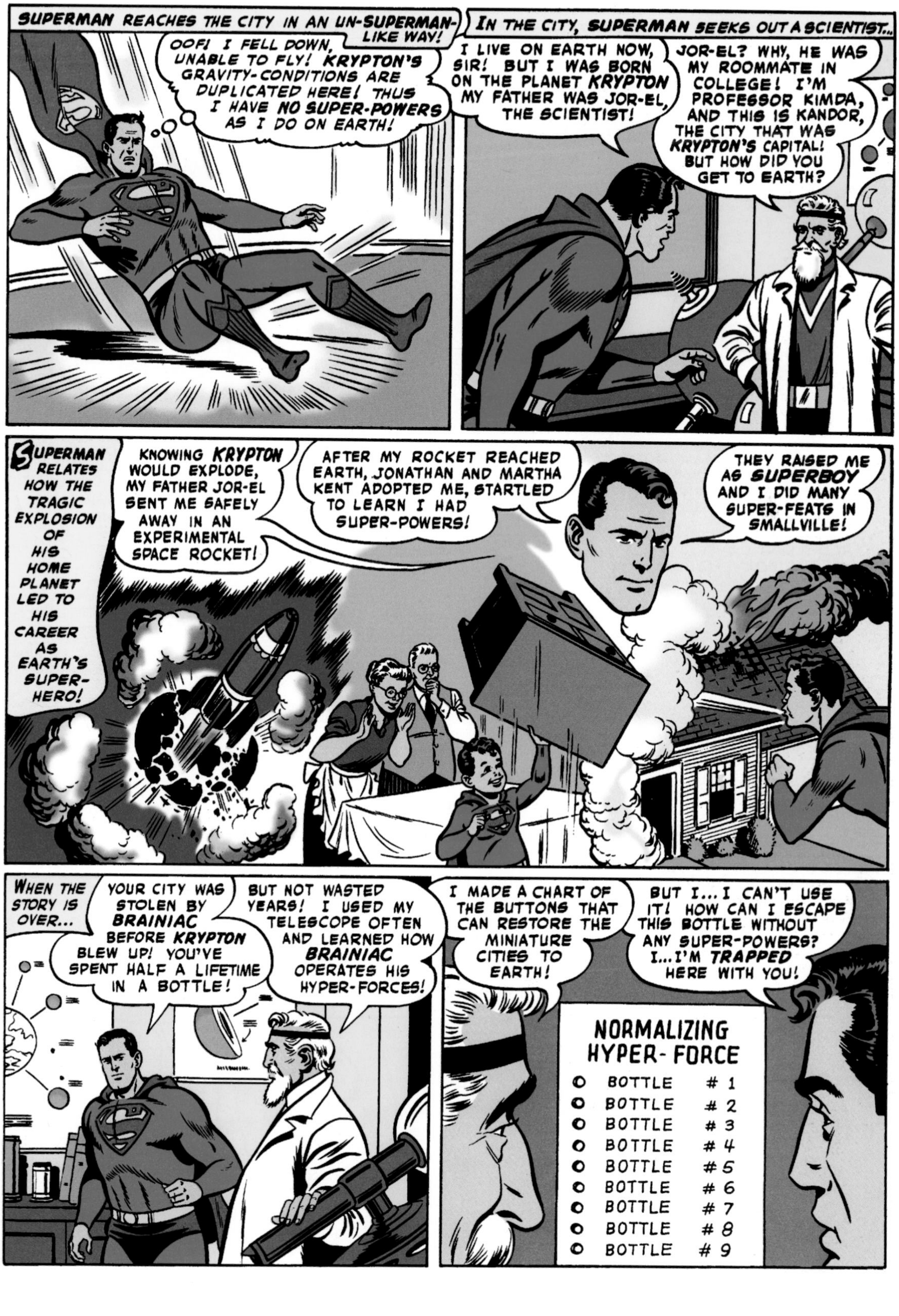
SUPERMAN REACHES THE CITY IN AN UN-SUPERMAN-LIKE WAY!
OOF! I FELL DOWN, UNABLE TO FLY! KRYPTON'S GRAVITY-CONDITIONS ARE DUPLICATED HERE! THUS I HAVE NO SUPER-POWERS AS I DO ON EARTH!
IN THE CITY, SUPERMAN SEEKS OUT A SCIENTIST...
I LIVE ON EARTH NOW, SIR! BUT I WAS BORN ON THE PLANET KRYPTON MY FATHER WAS JOR-EL, THE SCIENTIST!
JOR-EL? WHY, HE WAS MY ROOMMATE IN COLLEGE! I'M PROFESSOR KIMDA, AND THIS IS KANDOR, THE CITY THAT WAS KRYPTON'S CAPITAL! BUT HOW DID YOU GET TO EARTH?
SUPERMAN RELATES HOW THE TRAGIC EXPLOSION OF HIS HOME PLANET LED TO HIS CAREER AS EARTH'S SUPER-HERO!
KNOWING KRYPTON WOULD EXPLODE, MY FATHER JOR-EL SENT ME SAFELY AWAY IN AN EXPERIMENTAL SPACE ROCKET!
AFTER MY ROCKET REACHED EARTH, JONATHAN AND MARTHA KENT ADOPTED ME, STARTLED TO LEARN I HAD SUPER-POWERS!
THEY RAISED ME AS SUPERBOY AND I DID MANY SUPER-FEATS IN SMALLVILLE!
WHEN THE STORY IS OVER...
YOUR CITY WAS STOLEN BY BRAINIAC BEFORE KRYPTON BLEW UP! YOU'VE SPENT HALF A LIFETIME IN A BOTTLE!
BUT NOT WASTED YEARS! I USED MY TELESCOPE OFTEN AND LEARNED HOW BRAINIAC OPERATES HIS HYPER-FORCES!
I MADE A CHART OF THE BUTTONS THAT CAN RESTORE THE MINIATURE CITIES TO EARTH!
BUT I...I CAN'T USE IT! HOW CAN I ESCAPE THIS BOTTLE WITHOUT ANY SUPER-POWERS? I...I'M TRAPPED HERE WITH YOU!
NORMALIZING HYPER-FORCE
BOTTLE # 1
BOTTLE # 2
BOTTLE # 3
BOTTLE # 4
BOTTLE # 5
BOTTLE # 6
BOTTLE # 7
BOTTLE # 8
BOTTLE # 9

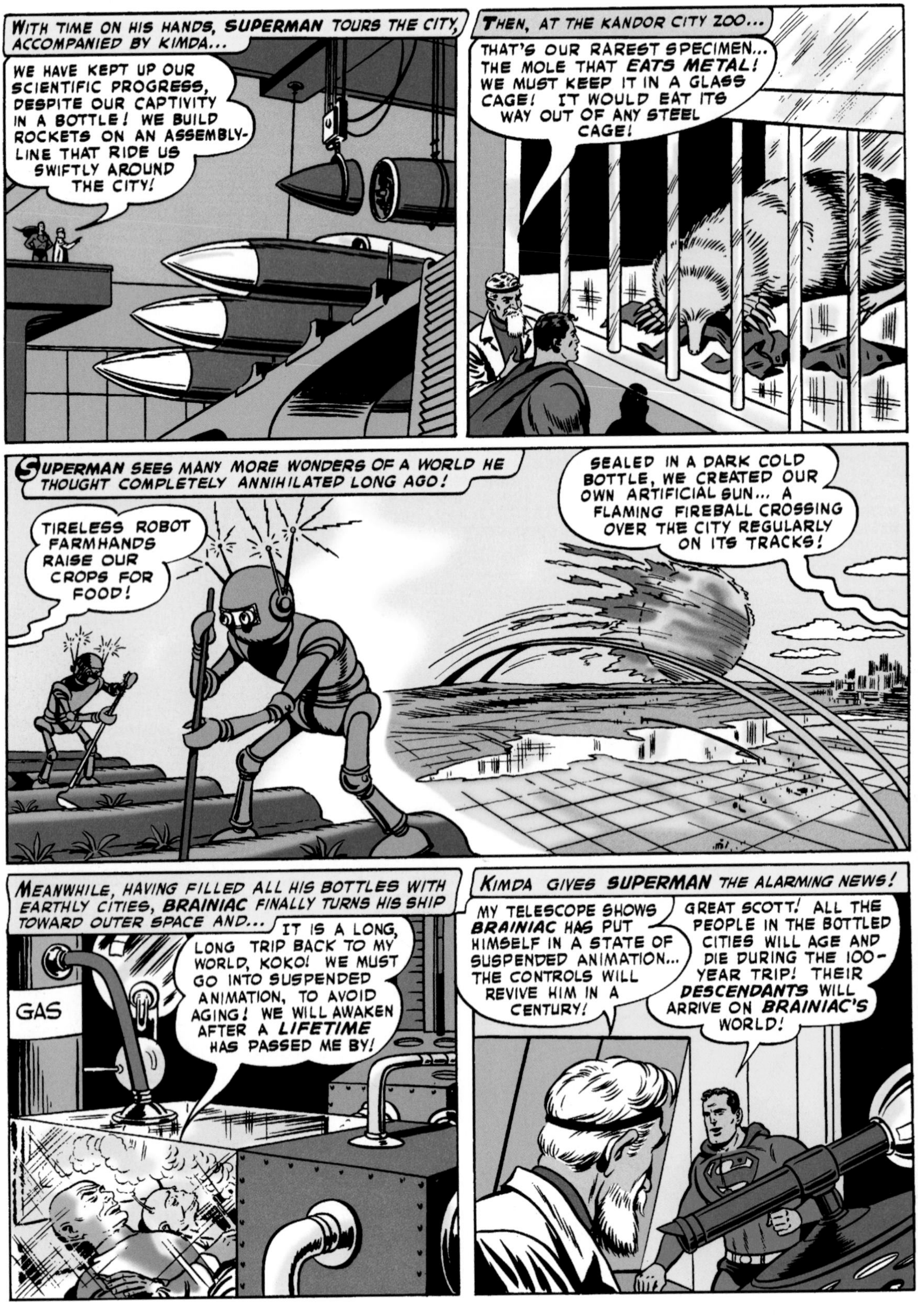
WITH TIME ON HIS HANDS, SUPERMAN TOURS THE CITY, ACCOMPANIED BY KIMDA...
WE HAVE KEPT UP OUR SCIENTIFIC PROGRESS, DESPITE OUR CAPTIVITY IN A BOTTLE! WE BUILD ROCKETS ON AN ASSEMBLY-LINE THAT RIDE US SWIFTLY AROUND THE CITY!
THEN, AT THE KANDOR CITY ZOO...
THAT'S OUR RAREST SPECIMEN... THE MOLE THAT EATS METAL! WE MUST KEEP IT IN A GLASS CAGE! IT WOULD EAT ITS WAY OUT OF ANY STEEL CAGE!
SUPERMAN SEES MANY MORE WONDERS OF A WORLD HE THOUGHT COMPLETELY ANNIHILATED LONG AGO!
TIRELESS ROBOT FARMHANDS RAISE OUR CROPS FOR FOOD!
SEALED IN A DARK COLD BOTTLE, WE CREATED OUR OWN ARTIFICIAL SUN... A FLAMING FIREBALL CROSSING OVER THE CITY REGULARLY ON ITS TRACKS!
MEANWHILE, HAVING FILLED ALL HIS BOTTLES WITH EARTHLY CITIES, BRAINIAC FINALLY TURNS HIS SHIP TOWARD OUTER SPACE AND...
IT IS A LONG, LONG TRIP BACK TO MY WORLD, KOKO! WE MUST GO INTO SUSPENDED ANIMATION, TO AVOID AGING! WE WILL AWAKEN AFTER A LIFETIME HAS PASSED ME BY!
GAS
KIMDA GIVES SUPERMAN THE ALARMING NEWS!
MY TELESCOPE SHOWS BRAINIAC HAS PUT HIMSELF IN A STATE OF SUSPENDED ANIMATION... THE CONTROLS WILL REVIVE HIM IN A CENTURY!
GREAT SCOTT! ALL THE PEOPLE IN THE BOTTLED CITIES WILL AGE AND DIE DURING THE 100-YEAR TRIP! THEIR DESCENDANTS WILL ARRIVE ON BRAINIAC'S WORLD!

SUDDENLY, SUPERMAN THINKS OF A SUPER-STRATEGY...

HMM... THIS CHART, AND TWO OTHER THINGS IN YOUR CITY, MAY SAVE US! I WANT YOUR MOST POWERFUL ROCKET! AND A CERTAIN ANIMAL FROM THE ZOO!

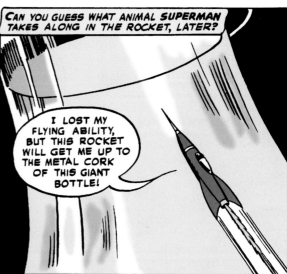

CAN YOU GUESS WHAT ANIMAL SUPERMAN TAKES ALONG IN THE ROCKET, LATER?

I LOST MY FLYING ABILITY, BUT THIS ROCKET WILL GET ME UP TO THE METAL CORK OF THIS GIANT BOTTLE!

SUPERMAN PURPOSELY RAMS THE ROCKET'S NOSE INTO THE UNDERSIDE OF THE CORK, AND THEN...

NOW TO LET THE METAL-EATING MOLE FEAST HIS WAY UP THROUGH THE CORK! HE'LL BURROW A TUNNEL BIG ENOUGH FOR ME TO CLIMB THROUGH!

THE INGENIOUS PLAN WORKS!..

NOW THAT I'M OUTSIDE THE BOTTLE, I'M FREE OF THE KRYPTON-GRAVITY WITHIN THE BOTTLE! MY SUPER-POWERS RETURNED! I CAN FLY TO THE CONTROL PANEL AND USE KIMDA'S OPERATIONAL CHART!

WITH NO INTERFERENCE FROM THE SLEEPING ALIEN, THE MOTE OF STEEL PUNCHES THE CORRECT BUTTONS... IN A SPECIAL WAY!

MY FINGER'S TOO SMALL... BUT THIS IS USING MY HEAD! EACH BUTTON I PRESS MAKES A CITY REAPPEAR BACK ON EARTH IN NORMAL SIZE, UNHARMED!

LOOK! METROPOLIS SUDDENLY RETURNED, AS MYSTERIOUSLY AS IT VANISHED YESTERDAY!

BUT TRANSMITTING THE EARTH CITIES BACK DRAINS THE BATTERIES OF THEIR COSMIC-POWER, AND *SUPERMAN* MEETS A TRAGIC DILEMMA!

ONLY ONE CHARGE OF HYPER-FORCES LEFT... ENOUGH TO RESTORE THE *KRYPTON* CITY TO NORMAL SIZE OR ME... BUT NOT *BOTH!*

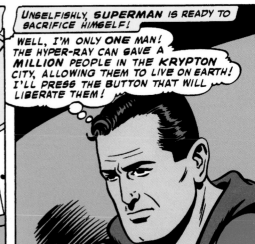

UNSELFISHLY, *SUPERMAN* IS READY TO SACRIFICE HIMSELF!

WELL, I'M ONLY *ONE* MAN! THE HYPER-RAY CAN SAVE A *MILLION* PEOPLE IN THE *KRYPTON* CITY, ALLOWING THEM TO LIVE ON EARTH! I'LL PRESS THE BUTTON THAT WILL LIBERATE THEM!

BUT BEFORE HE REACHES THE BUTTON...

THE...THE RAY STRUCK ME... I'M REGAINING NORMAL SIZE SWIFTLY! HMM...THAT TINY ROCKET PUNCHED" THE BUTTON AHEAD OF ME!

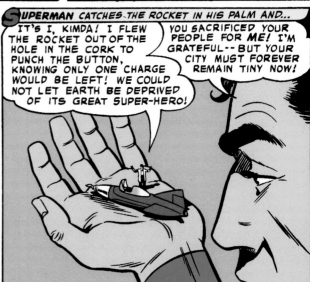

SUPERMAN CATCHES THE ROCKET IN HIS PALM AND...

IT'S I, KIMDA! I FLEW THE ROCKET OUT OF THE HOLE IN THE CORK TO PUNCH THE BUTTON, KNOWING ONLY ONE CHARGE WOULD BE LEFT! WE COULD NOT LET EARTH BE DEPRIVED OF ITS GREAT SUPER-HERO!

YOU SACRIFICED YOUR PEOPLE FOR *ME!* I'M GRATEFUL-- BUT YOUR CITY MUST FOREVER REMAIN TINY NOW!

PRESENTLY...

LET *BRAINIAC'S* SHIP FLY ON! WHEN HE AWAKENS, HE WILL HAVE NO STOLEN CITIES! LET HIM LIVE ON HIS DESOLATE WORLD... *ALONE*... A CRUEL KING WITHOUT A KINGDOM!

FINALLY, AT THE NORTH POLE IN *SUPERMAN'S* FORTRESS OF SOLITUDE...

THE MINIATURE *KRYPTON* CITY WILL KEEP SAFELY HERE! PERHAPS I'LL FIND A WAY TO RESTORE IT TO NORMAL SIZE... AND LIVE WITH MY PEOPLE AGAIN... SOMEDAY! WHO KNOWS?...

THE END.

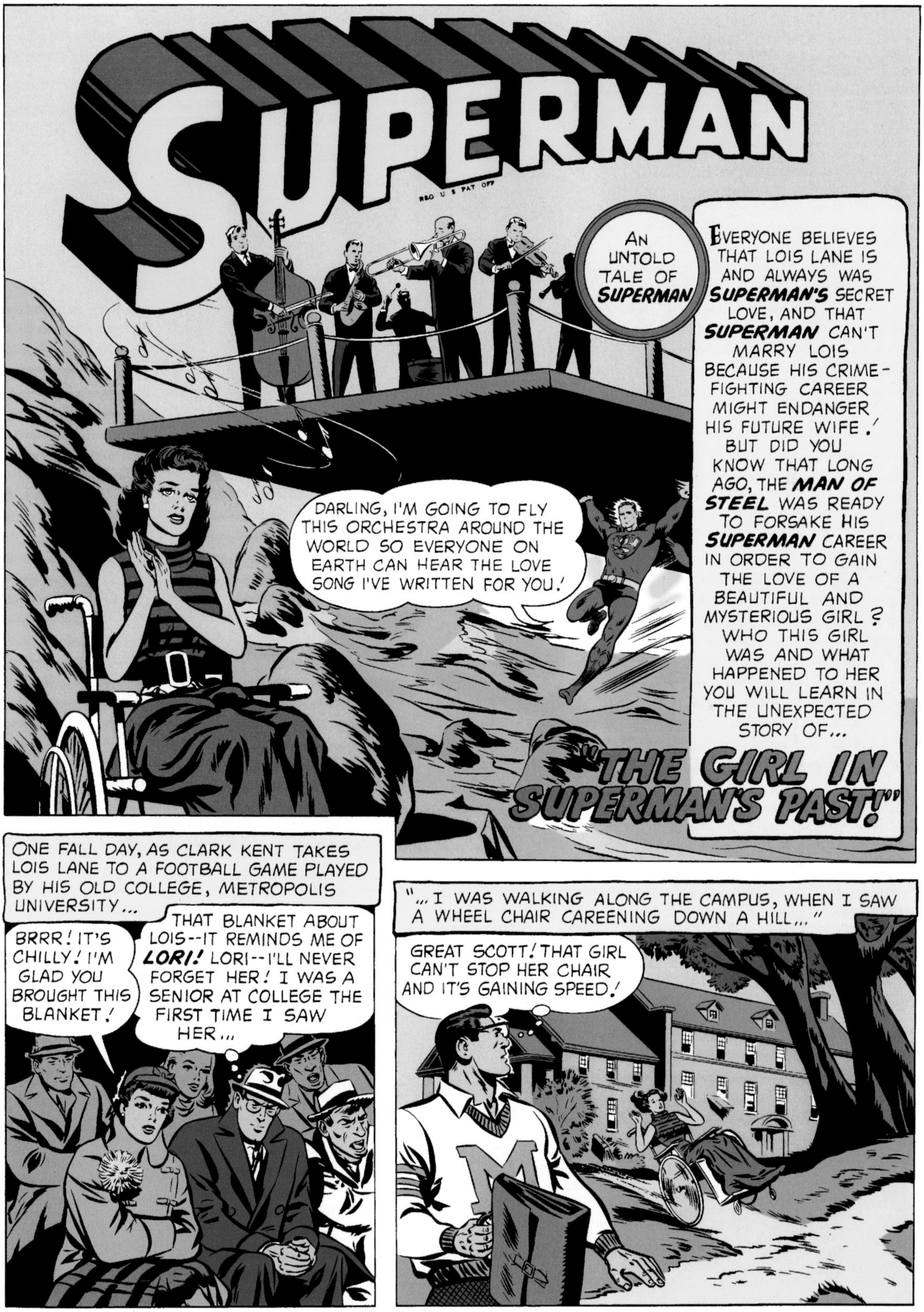
SUPERMAN
REG. U.S. PAT. OFF.
AN UNTOLD TALE OF SUPERMAN
EVERYONE BELIEVES THAT LOIS LANE IS AND ALWAYS WAS SUPERMAN'S SECRET LOVE, AND THAT SUPERMAN CAN'T MARRY LOIS BECAUSE HIS CRIME-FIGHTING CAREER MIGHT ENDANGER HIS FUTURE WIFE.' BUT DID YOU KNOW THAT LONG AGO, THE MAN OF STEEL WAS READY TO FORSAKE HIS SUPERMAN CAREER IN ORDER TO GAIN THE LOVE OF A BEAUTIFUL AND MYSTERIOUS GIRL? WHO THIS GIRL WAS AND WHAT HAPPENED TO HER YOU WILL LEARN IN THE UNEXPECTED STORY OF...
DARLING, I'M GOING TO FLY THIS ORCHESTRA AROUND THE WORLD SO EVERYONE ON EARTH CAN HEAR THE LOVE SONG I'VE WRITTEN FOR YOU.'
"THE GIRL IN SUPERMAN'S PAST!"
ONE FALL DAY, AS CLARK KENT TAKES LOIS LANE TO A FOOTBALL GAME PLAYED BY HIS OLD COLLEGE, METROPOLIS UNIVERSITY...
BRRR! IT'S CHILLY! I'M GLAD YOU BROUGHT THIS BLANKET!
THAT BLANKET ABOUT LOIS--IT REMINDS ME OF LORI! LORI--I'LL NEVER FORGET HER! I WAS A SENIOR AT COLLEGE THE FIRST TIME I SAW HER...
"...I WAS WALKING ALONG THE CAMPUS, WHEN I SAW A WHEEL CHAIR CAREENING DOWN A HILL..."
GREAT SCOTT! THAT GIRL CAN'T STOP HER CHAIR AND IT'S GAINING SPEED!

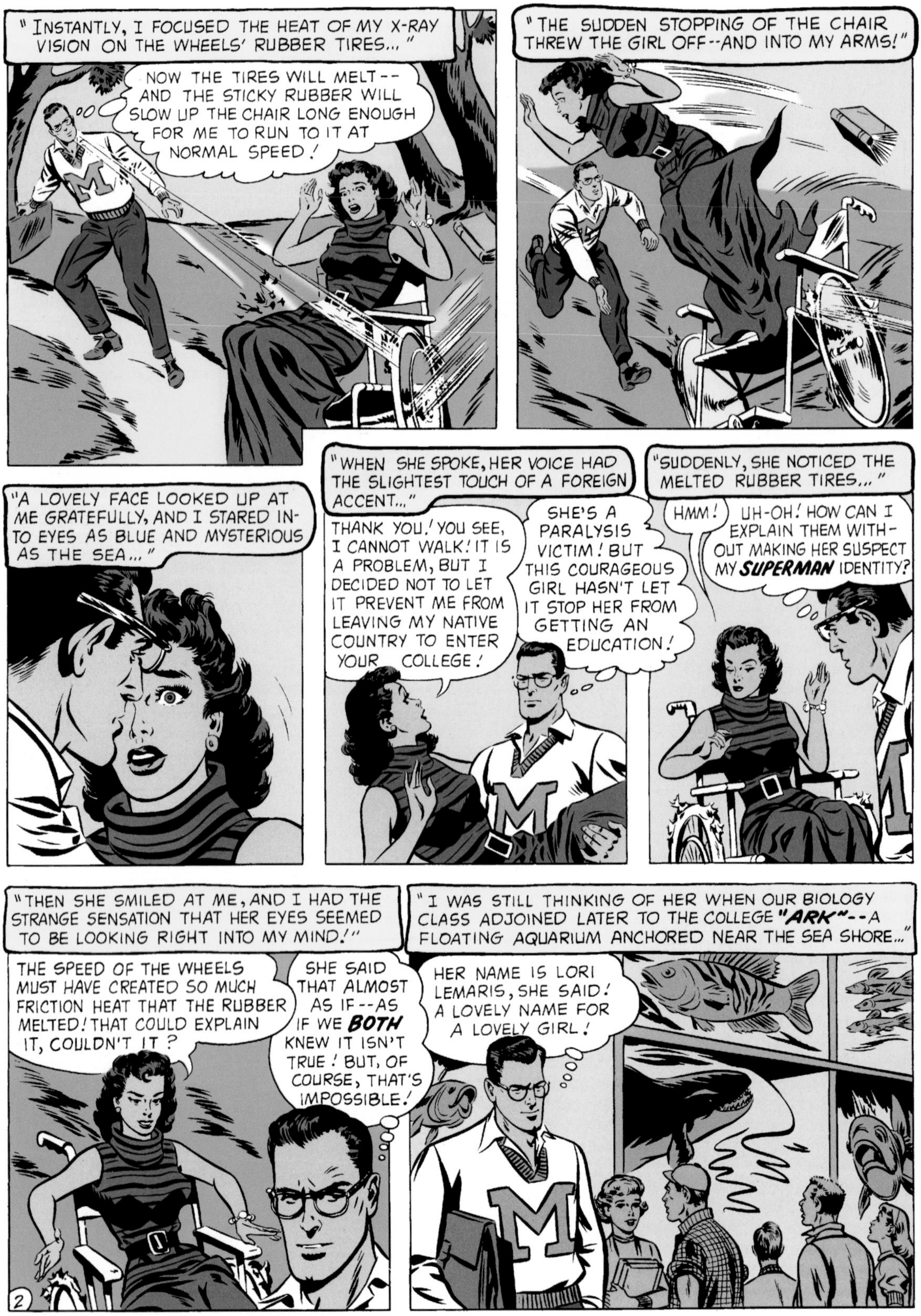

"INSTANTLY, I FOCUSED THE HEAT OF MY X-RAY VISION ON THE WHEELS' RUBBER TIRES..."
NOW THE TIRES WILL MELT-- AND THE STICKY RUBBER WILL SLOW UP THE CHAIR LONG ENOUGH FOR ME TO RUN TO IT AT NORMAL SPEED!
"THE SUDDEN STOPPING OF THE CHAIR THREW THE GIRL OFF--AND INTO MY ARMS!"
"A LOVELY FACE LOOKED UP AT ME GRATEFULLY, AND I STARED INTO EYES AS BLUE AND MYSTERIOUS AS THE SEA..."
"WHEN SHE SPOKE, HER VOICE HAD THE SLIGHTEST TOUCH OF A FOREIGN ACCENT..."
THANK YOU! YOU SEE, I CANNOT WALK! IT IS A PROBLEM, BUT I DECIDED NOT TO LET IT PREVENT ME FROM LEAVING MY NATIVE COUNTRY TO ENTER YOUR COLLEGE!
SHE'S A PARALYSIS VICTIM! BUT THIS COURAGEOUS GIRL HASN'T LET IT STOP HER FROM GETTING AN EDUCATION!
"SUDDENLY, SHE NOTICED THE MELTED RUBBER TIRES..."
HMM!
UH-OH! HOW CAN I EXPLAIN THEM WITHOUT MAKING HER SUSPECT MY SUPERMAN IDENTITY?
"THEN SHE SMILED AT ME, AND I HAD THE STRANGE SENSATION THAT HER EYES SEEMED TO BE LOOKING RIGHT INTO MY MIND!"
THE SPEED OF THE WHEELS MUST HAVE CREATED SO MUCH FRICTION HEAT THAT THE RUBBER MELTED! THAT COULD EXPLAIN IT, COULDN'T IT?
SHE SAID THAT ALMOST AS IF--AS IF WE BOTH KNEW IT ISN'T TRUE! BUT, OF COURSE, THAT'S IMPOSSIBLE!
2
"I WAS STILL THINKING OF HER WHEN OUR BIOLOGY CLASS ADJOINED LATER TO THE COLLEGE "ARK"--A FLOATING AQUARIUM ANCHORED NEAR THE SEA SHORE..."
HER NAME IS LORI LEMARIS, SHE SAID! A LOVELY NAME FOR A LOVELY GIRL!

"SUDDENLY, A BOILER EXPLODED AND THE FLOATING AQUARIUM NEARLY SPLIT IN TWO..."

EEEE! HELP!

A JOB FOR *SUPERMAN* COMING UP!

BOOM!

"EVERYONE JUMPED INTO THE WATER AND SWAM TO SHORE A FEW YARDS AWAY--SO I WAS UNOBSERVED AS I DIVED TO AN UNDERWATER CAVERN..."

I'M GLAD I MADE A HABIT OF CARRYING MY SUPER-COSTUME IN MY SCHOOL BRIEFCASE!

"THEN I BECAME AN UNDERWATER "*COWBOY*", HERDING TOGETHER ALL THE FISH THAT HAD ESCAPED FROM THE AQUARIUM..."

GIT ALONG, LITTLE DOGIE!

NOW I'LL WEAVE THESE LONG STRANDS OF SEA WEED INTO A NET "*CAGE*" ABOUT THE SPECIMENS UNTIL THE AQUARIUM IS REPAIRED AND READY TO STOCK THEM AGAIN!

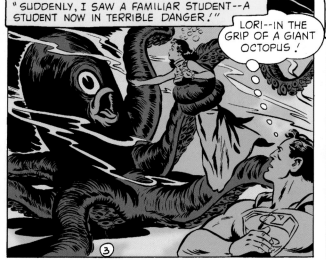

"SUDDENLY, I SAW A FAMILIAR STUDENT--A STUDENT NOW IN TERRIBLE DANGER!"

LORI--IN THE GRIP OF A GIANT OCTOPUS!

③

"EVEN AS I SHOT FORWARD, I WAS AMAZED TO SEE THAT LORI WAS NOT FRIGHTENED, BUT CALMLY REGARDING THE CREATURE..."

HER LIPS ARE MOVING! IF I DIDN'T KNOW BETTER, I'D ALMOST BELIEVE SHE WAS TALKING TO THE OCTOPUS!

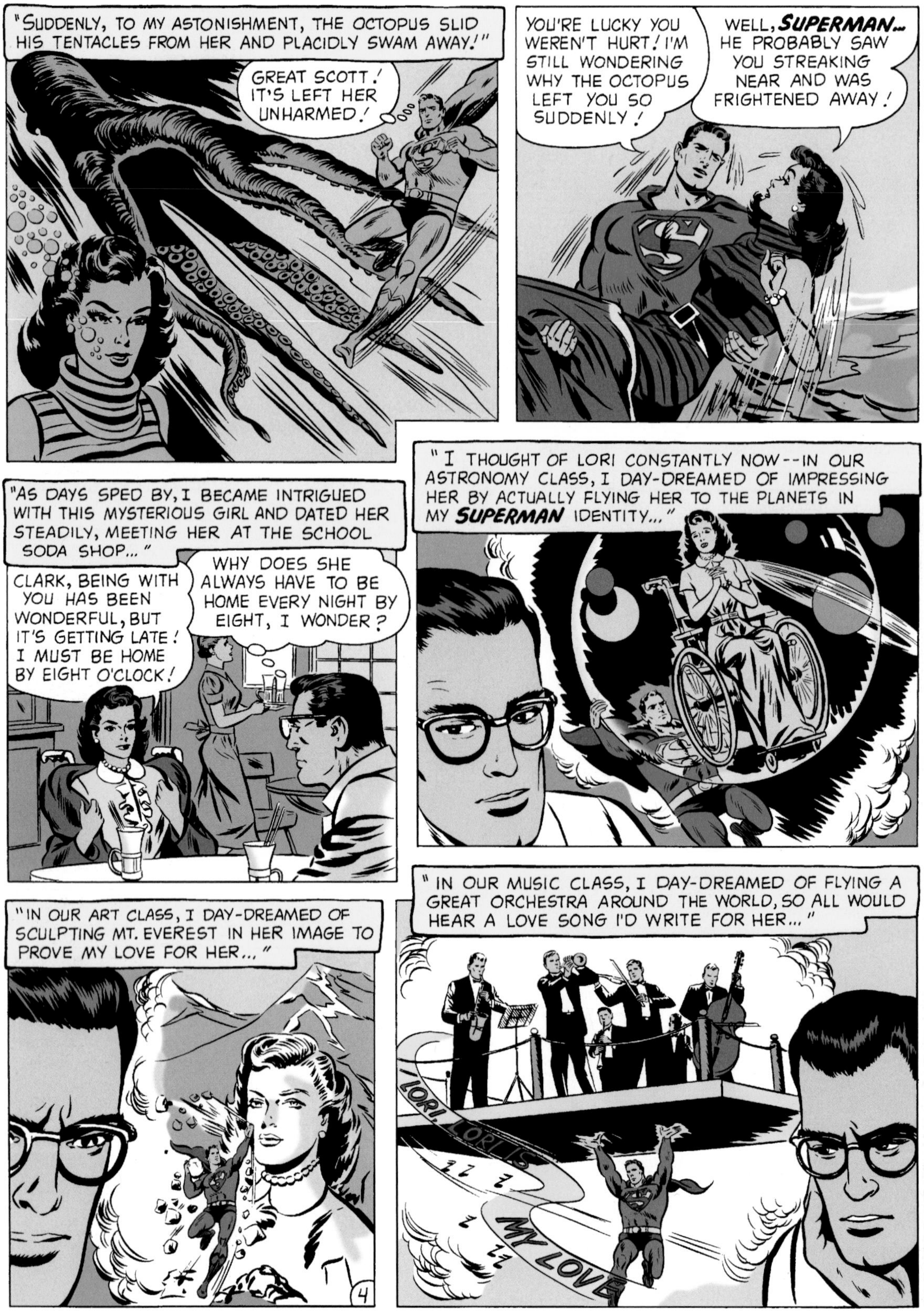
"SUDDENLY, TO MY ASTONISHMENT, THE OCTOPUS SLID HIS TENTACLES FROM HER AND PLACIDLY SWAM AWAY!"
GREAT SCOTT! IT'S LEFT HER UNHARMED!
YOU'RE LUCKY YOU WEREN'T HURT! I'M STILL WONDERING WHY THE OCTOPUS LEFT YOU SO SUDDENLY!
WELL, SUPERMAN... HE PROBABLY SAW YOU STREAKING NEAR AND WAS FRIGHTENED AWAY!
"AS DAYS SPED BY, I BECAME INTRIGUED WITH THIS MYSTERIOUS GIRL AND DATED HER STEADILY, MEETING HER AT THE SCHOOL SODA SHOP..."
CLARK, BEING WITH YOU HAS BEEN WONDERFUL, BUT IT'S GETTING LATE! I MUST BE HOME BY EIGHT O'CLOCK!
WHY DOES SHE ALWAYS HAVE TO BE HOME EVERY NIGHT BY EIGHT, I WONDER?
"I THOUGHT OF LORI CONSTANTLY NOW--IN OUR ASTRONOMY CLASS, I DAY-DREAMED OF IMPRESSING HER BY ACTUALLY FLYING HER TO THE PLANETS IN MY SUPERMAN IDENTITY..."
"IN OUR ART CLASS, I DAY-DREAMED OF SCULPTING MT. EVEREST IN HER IMAGE TO PROVE MY LOVE FOR HER..."
4
"IN OUR MUSIC CLASS, I DAY-DREAMED OF FLYING A GREAT ORCHESTRA AROUND THE WORLD, SO ALL WOULD HEAR A LOVE SONG I'D WRITE FOR HER..."
LORI, LORI IS MY LOVE

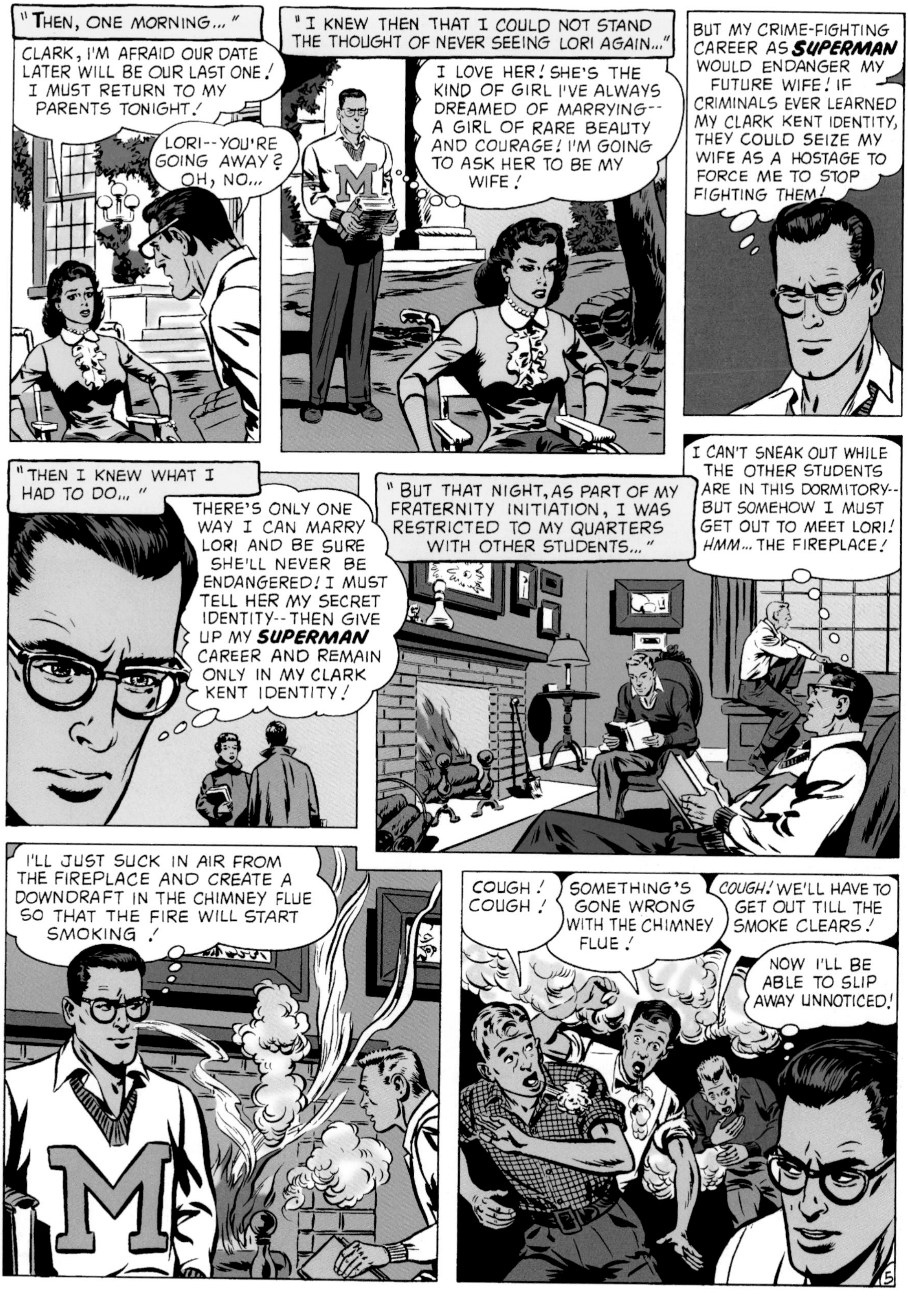
"THEN, ONE MORNING..."
CLARK, I'M AFRAID OUR DATE LATER WILL BE OUR LAST ONE! I MUST RETURN TO MY PARENTS TONIGHT!
LORI--YOU'RE GOING AWAY? OH, NO...
"I KNEW THEN THAT I COULD NOT STAND THE THOUGHT OF NEVER SEEING LORI AGAIN..."
I LOVE HER! SHE'S THE KIND OF GIRL I'VE ALWAYS DREAMED OF MARRYING-- A GIRL OF RARE BEAUTY AND COURAGE! I'M GOING TO ASK HER TO BE MY WIFE!
BUT MY CRIME-FIGHTING CAREER AS SUPERMAN WOULD ENDANGER MY FUTURE WIFE! IF CRIMINALS EVER LEARNED MY CLARK KENT IDENTITY, THEY COULD SEIZE MY WIFE AS A HOSTAGE TO FORCE ME TO STOP FIGHTING THEM!
"THEN I KNEW WHAT I HAD TO DO..."
THERE'S ONLY ONE WAY I CAN MARRY LORI AND BE SURE SHE'LL NEVER BE ENDANGERED! I MUST TELL HER MY SECRET IDENTITY--THEN GIVE UP MY SUPERMAN CAREER AND REMAIN ONLY IN MY CLARK KENT IDENTITY!
"BUT THAT NIGHT, AS PART OF MY FRATERNITY INITIATION, I WAS RESTRICTED TO MY QUARTERS WITH OTHER STUDENTS..."
I CAN'T SNEAK OUT WHILE THE OTHER STUDENTS ARE IN THIS DORMITORY-- BUT SOMEHOW I MUST GET OUT TO MEET LORI! HMM... THE FIREPLACE!
I'LL JUST SUCK IN AIR FROM THE FIREPLACE AND CREATE A DOWNDRAFT IN THE CHIMNEY FLUE SO THAT THE FIRE WILL START SMOKING!
COUGH! COUGH!
SOMETHING'S GONE WRONG WITH THE CHIMNEY FLUE!
COUGH! WE'LL HAVE TO GET OUT TILL THE SMOKE CLEARS!
NOW I'LL BE ABLE TO SLIP AWAY UNNOTICED!
5

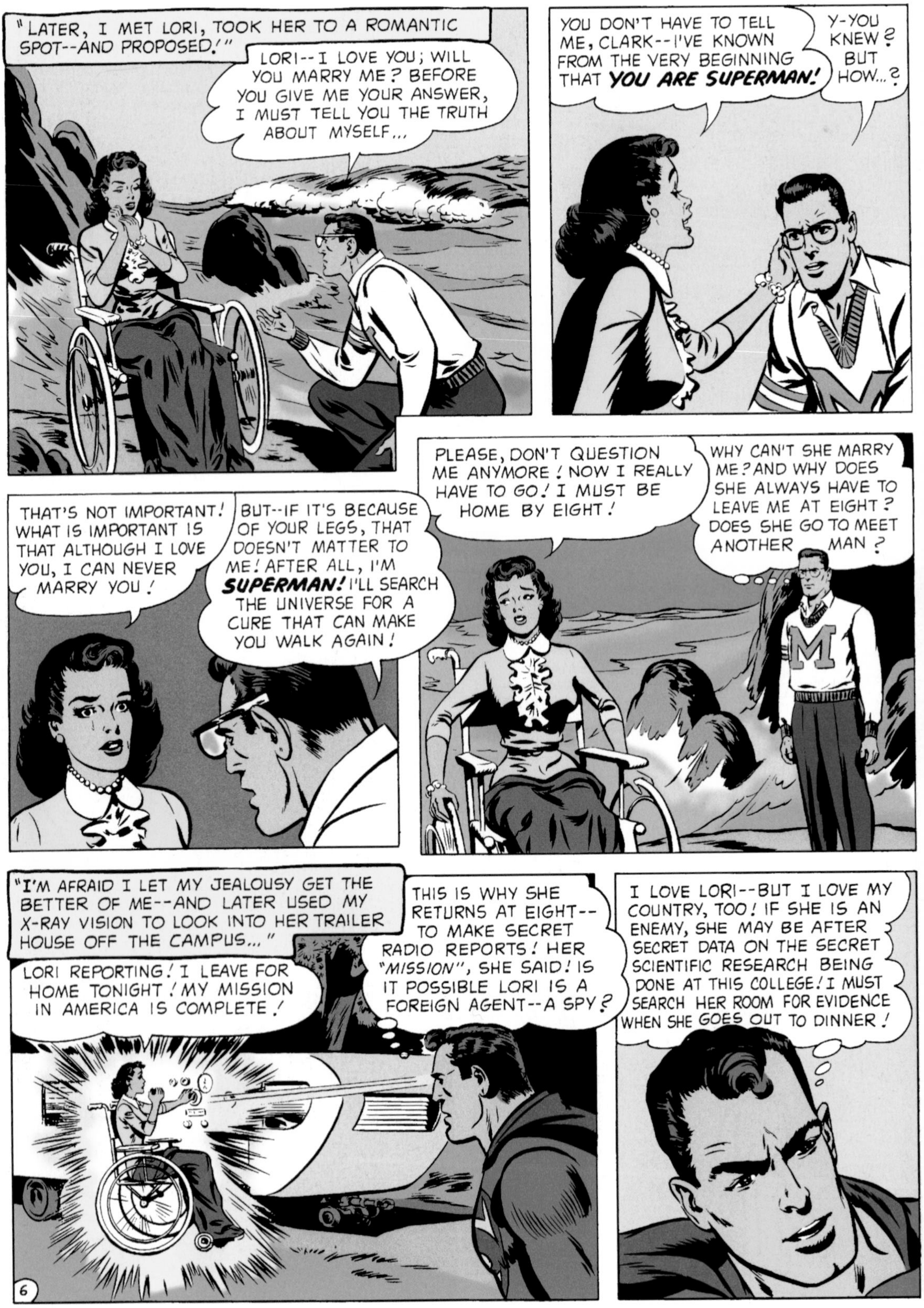
"LATER, I MET LORI, TOOK HER TO A ROMANTIC SPOT--AND PROPOSED!"
LORI--I LOVE YOU; WILL YOU MARRY ME? BEFORE YOU GIVE ME YOUR ANSWER, I MUST TELL YOU THE TRUTH ABOUT MYSELF...
YOU DON'T HAVE TO TELL ME, CLARK--I'VE KNOWN FROM THE VERY BEGINNING THAT **YOU ARE SUPERMAN!**
Y-YOU KNEW? BUT HOW...?
THAT'S NOT IMPORTANT! WHAT IS IMPORTANT IS THAT ALTHOUGH I LOVE YOU, I CAN NEVER MARRY YOU!
BUT--IF IT'S BECAUSE OF YOUR LEGS, THAT DOESN'T MATTER TO ME! AFTER ALL, I'M **SUPERMAN!** I'LL SEARCH THE UNIVERSE FOR A CURE THAT CAN MAKE YOU WALK AGAIN!
PLEASE, DON'T QUESTION ME ANYMORE! NOW I REALLY HAVE TO GO! I MUST BE HOME BY EIGHT!
WHY CAN'T SHE MARRY ME? AND WHY DOES SHE ALWAYS HAVE TO LEAVE ME AT EIGHT? DOES SHE GO TO MEET ANOTHER MAN?
"I'M AFRAID I LET MY JEALOUSY GET THE BETTER OF ME--AND LATER USED MY X-RAY VISION TO LOOK INTO HER TRAILER HOUSE OFF THE CAMPUS..."
LORI REPORTING! I LEAVE FOR HOME TONIGHT! MY MISSION IN AMERICA IS COMPLETE!
THIS IS WHY SHE RETURNS AT EIGHT--TO MAKE SECRET RADIO REPORTS! HER "MISSION", SHE SAID! IS IT POSSIBLE LORI IS A FOREIGN AGENT--A SPY?
I LOVE LORI--BUT I LOVE MY COUNTRY, TOO! IF SHE IS AN ENEMY, SHE MAY BE AFTER SECRET DATA ON THE SECRET SCIENTIFIC RESEARCH BEING DONE AT THIS COLLEGE! I MUST SEARCH HER ROOM FOR EVIDENCE WHEN SHE GOES OUT TO DINNER!
6

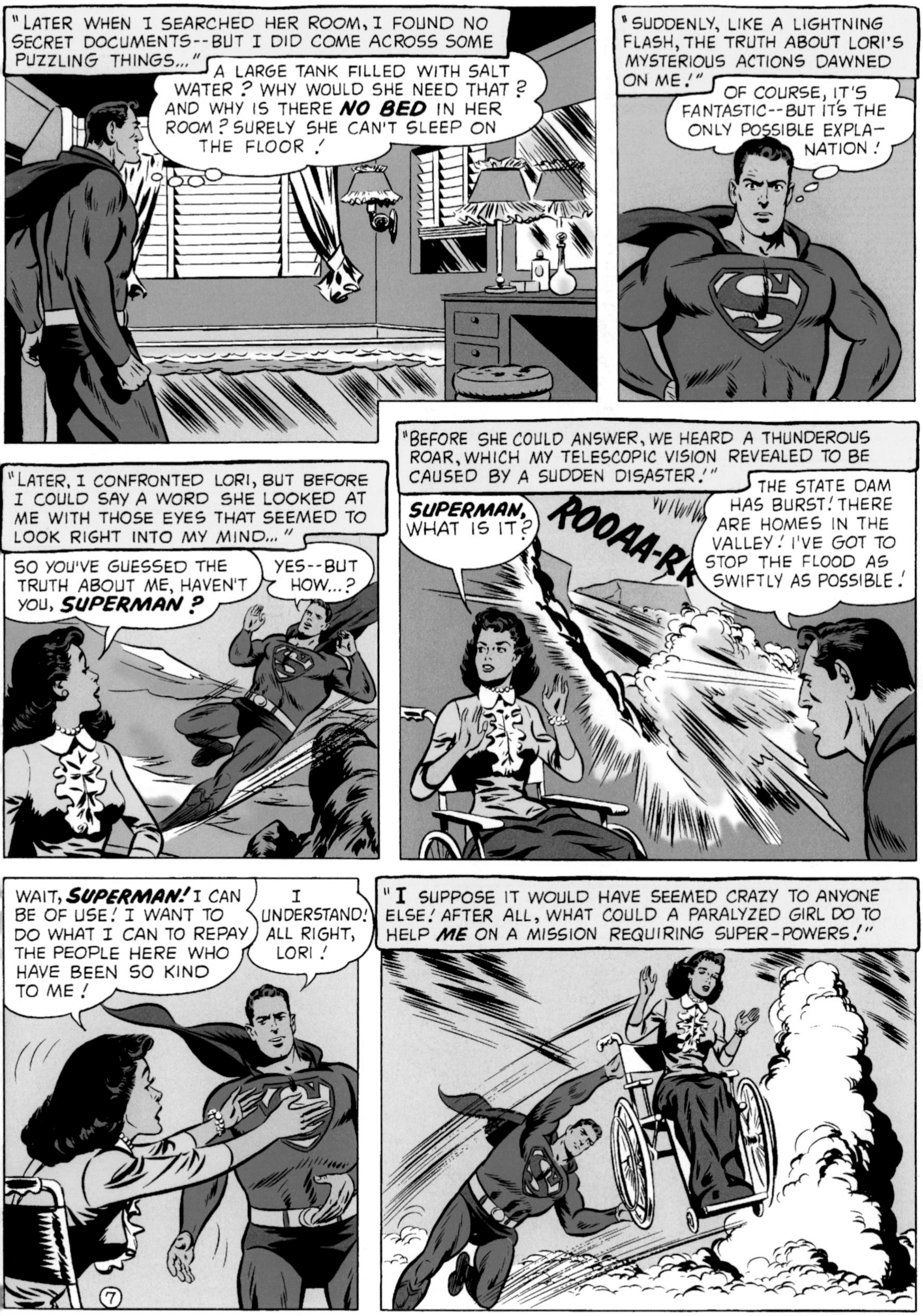
"LATER WHEN I SEARCHED HER ROOM, I FOUND NO SECRET DOCUMENTS--BUT I DID COME ACROSS SOME PUZZLING THINGS..."
A LARGE TANK FILLED WITH SALT WATER? WHY WOULD SHE NEED THAT? AND WHY IS THERE NO BED IN HER ROOM? SURELY SHE CAN'T SLEEP ON THE FLOOR!
"SUDDENLY, LIKE A LIGHTNING FLASH, THE TRUTH ABOUT LORI'S MYSTERIOUS ACTIONS DAWNED ON ME!"
OF COURSE, IT'S FANTASTIC--BUT IT'S THE ONLY POSSIBLE EXPLANATION!
"LATER, I CONFRONTED LORI, BUT BEFORE I COULD SAY A WORD SHE LOOKED AT ME WITH THOSE EYES THAT SEEMED TO LOOK RIGHT INTO MY MIND..."
SO YOU'VE GUESSED THE TRUTH ABOUT ME, HAVEN'T YOU, SUPERMAN?
YES--BUT HOW...?
"BEFORE SHE COULD ANSWER, WE HEARD A THUNDEROUS ROAR, WHICH MY TELESCOPIC VISION REVEALED TO BE CAUSED BY A SUDDEN DISASTER!"
SUPERMAN, WHAT IS IT?
ROOAA-RR
THE STATE DAM HAS BURST! THERE ARE HOMES IN THE VALLEY! I'VE GOT TO STOP THE FLOOD AS SWIFTLY AS POSSIBLE!
WAIT, SUPERMAN! I CAN BE OF USE! I WANT TO DO WHAT I CAN TO REPAY THE PEOPLE HERE WHO HAVE BEEN SO KIND TO ME!
I UNDERSTAND! ALL RIGHT, LORI!
7
"I SUPPOSE IT WOULD HAVE SEEMED CRAZY TO ANYONE ELSE! AFTER ALL, WHAT COULD A PARALYZED GIRL DO TO HELP ME ON A MISSION REQUIRING SUPER-POWERS!"

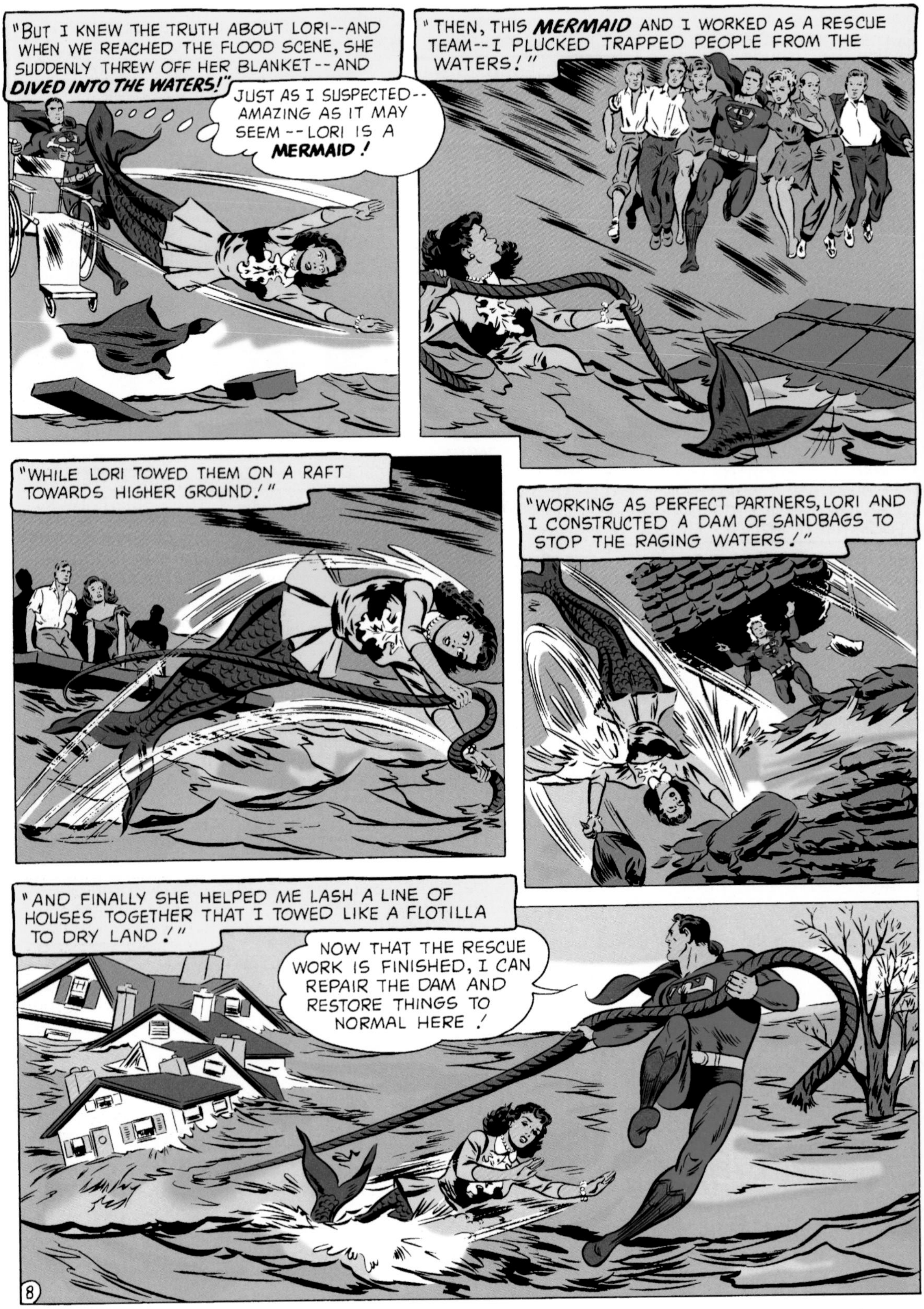

"BUT I KNEW THE TRUTH ABOUT LORI--AND WHEN WE REACHED THE FLOOD SCENE, SHE SUDDENLY THREW OFF HER BLANKET--AND **DIVED INTO THE WATERS!**"
JUST AS I SUSPECTED-- AMAZING AS IT MAY SEEM --LORI IS A **MERMAID!**
"THEN, THIS **MERMAID** AND I WORKED AS A RESCUE TEAM--I PLUCKED TRAPPED PEOPLE FROM THE WATERS!"
"WHILE LORI TOWED THEM ON A RAFT TOWARDS HIGHER GROUND!"
"WORKING AS PERFECT PARTNERS, LORI AND I CONSTRUCTED A DAM OF SANDBAGS TO STOP THE RAGING WATERS!"
"AND FINALLY SHE HELPED ME LASH A LINE OF HOUSES TOGETHER THAT I TOWED LIKE A FLOTILLA TO DRY LAND!"
NOW THAT THE RESCUE WORK IS FINISHED, I CAN REPAIR THE DAM AND RESTORE THINGS TO NORMAL HERE!
8

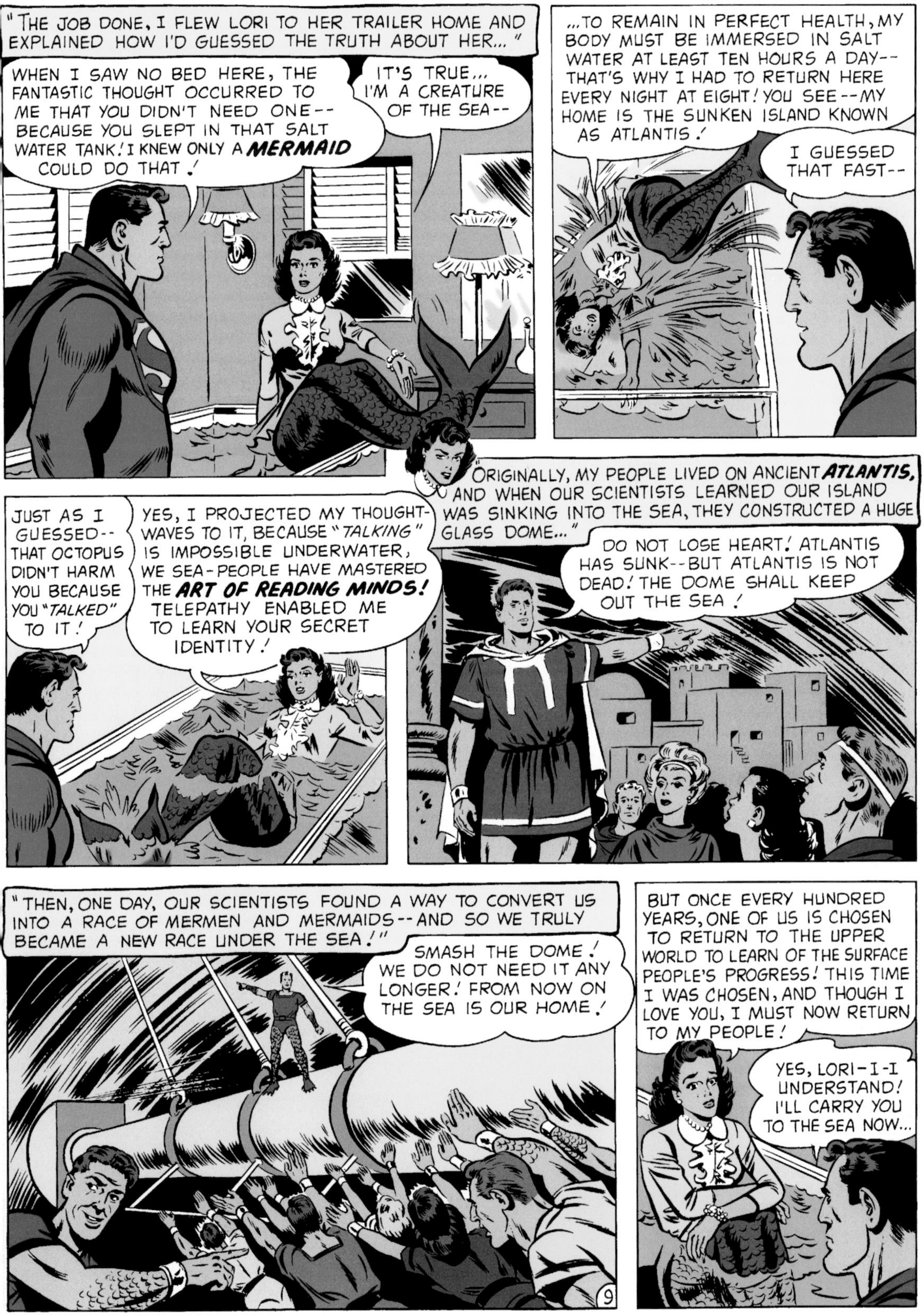
"THE JOB DONE, I FLEW LORI TO HER TRAILER HOME AND EXPLAINED HOW I'D GUESSED THE TRUTH ABOUT HER..."
WHEN I SAW NO BED HERE, THE FANTASTIC THOUGHT OCCURRED TO ME THAT YOU DIDN'T NEED ONE-- BECAUSE YOU SLEPT IN THAT SALT WATER TANK! I KNEW ONLY A MERMAID COULD DO THAT!
IT'S TRUE... I'M A CREATURE OF THE SEA--
...TO REMAIN IN PERFECT HEALTH, MY BODY MUST BE IMMERSED IN SALT WATER AT LEAST TEN HOURS A DAY-- THAT'S WHY I HAD TO RETURN HERE EVERY NIGHT AT EIGHT! YOU SEE--MY HOME IS THE SUNKEN ISLAND KNOWN AS ATLANTIS!
I GUESSED THAT FAST--
JUST AS I GUESSED-- THAT OCTOPUS DIDN'T HARM YOU BECAUSE YOU "TALKED" TO IT!
YES, I PROJECTED MY THOUGHT-WAVES TO IT, BECAUSE "TALKING" IS IMPOSSIBLE UNDERWATER, WE SEA-PEOPLE HAVE MASTERED THE ART OF READING MINDS! TELEPATHY ENABLED ME TO LEARN YOUR SECRET IDENTITY!
"ORIGINALLY, MY PEOPLE LIVED ON ANCIENT ATLANTIS, AND WHEN OUR SCIENTISTS LEARNED OUR ISLAND WAS SINKING INTO THE SEA, THEY CONSTRUCTED A HUGE GLASS DOME..."
DO NOT LOSE HEART! ATLANTIS HAS SUNK--BUT ATLANTIS IS NOT DEAD! THE DOME SHALL KEEP OUT THE SEA!
"THEN, ONE DAY, OUR SCIENTISTS FOUND A WAY TO CONVERT US INTO A RACE OF MERMEN AND MERMAIDS--AND SO WE TRULY BECAME A NEW RACE UNDER THE SEA!"
SMASH THE DOME! WE DO NOT NEED IT ANY LONGER! FROM NOW ON THE SEA IS OUR HOME!
9
BUT ONCE EVERY HUNDRED YEARS, ONE OF US IS CHOSEN TO RETURN TO THE UPPER WORLD TO LEARN OF THE SURFACE PEOPLE'S PROGRESS! THIS TIME I WAS CHOSEN, AND THOUGH I LOVE YOU, I MUST NOW RETURN TO MY PEOPLE!
YES, LORI-I-I UNDERSTAND! I'LL CARRY YOU TO THE SEA NOW...

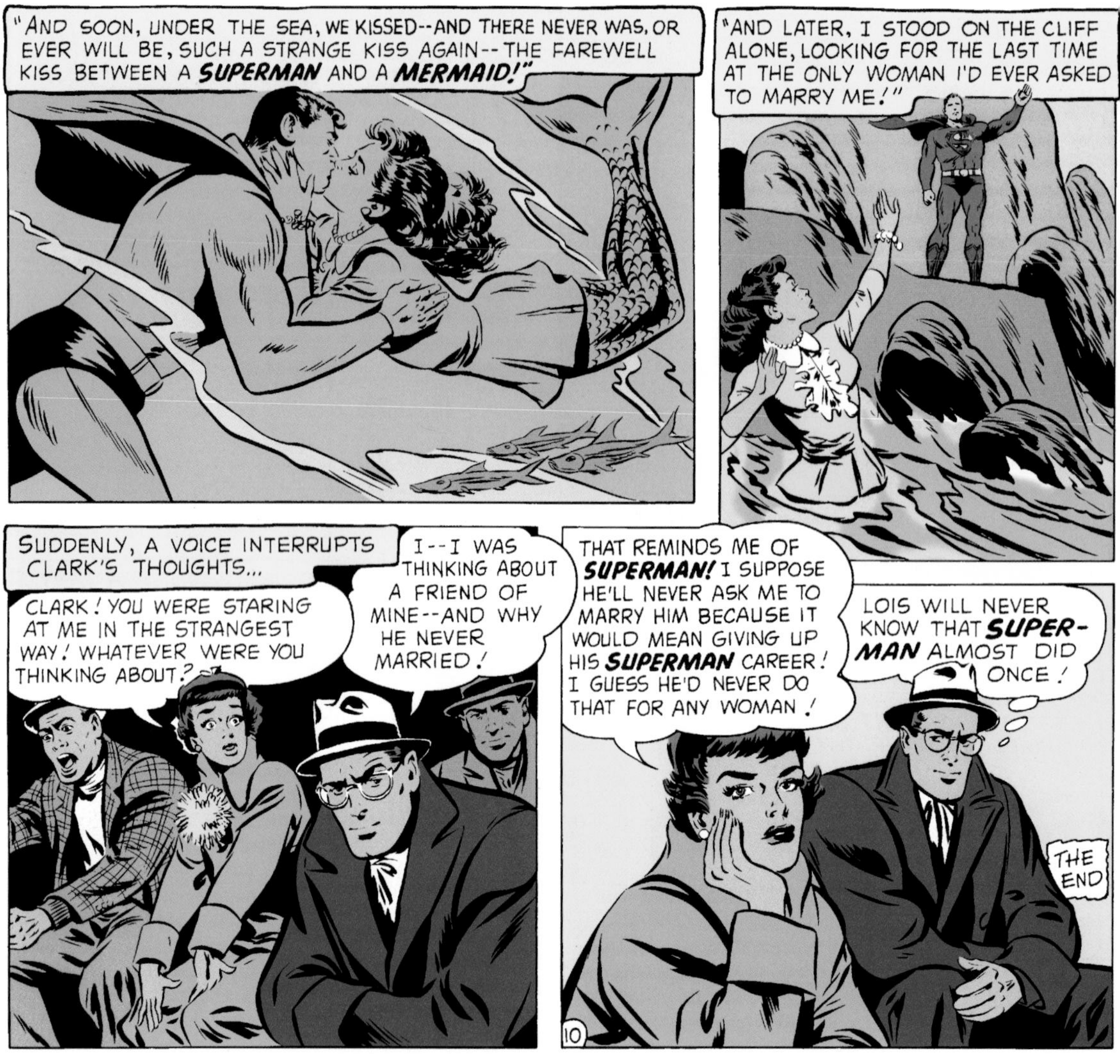
"AND SOON, UNDER THE SEA, WE KISSED--AND THERE NEVER WAS, OR EVER WILL BE, SUCH A STRANGE KISS AGAIN--THE FAREWELL KISS BETWEEN A SUPERMAN AND A MERMAID!"
"AND LATER, I STOOD ON THE CLIFF ALONE, LOOKING FOR THE LAST TIME AT THE ONLY WOMAN I'D EVER ASKED TO MARRY ME!"
SUDDENLY, A VOICE INTERRUPTS CLARK'S THOUGHTS...
CLARK! YOU WERE STARING AT ME IN THE STRANGEST WAY! WHATEVER WERE YOU THINKING ABOUT?
I--I WAS THINKING ABOUT A FRIEND OF MINE--AND WHY HE NEVER MARRIED!
THAT REMINDS ME OF SUPERMAN! I SUPPOSE HE'LL NEVER ASK ME TO MARRY HIM BECAUSE IT WOULD MEAN GIVING UP HIS SUPERMAN CAREER! I GUESS HE'D NEVER DO THAT FOR ANY WOMAN!
LOIS WILL NEVER KNOW THAT SUPER-MAN ALMOST DID ONCE!
THE END
10

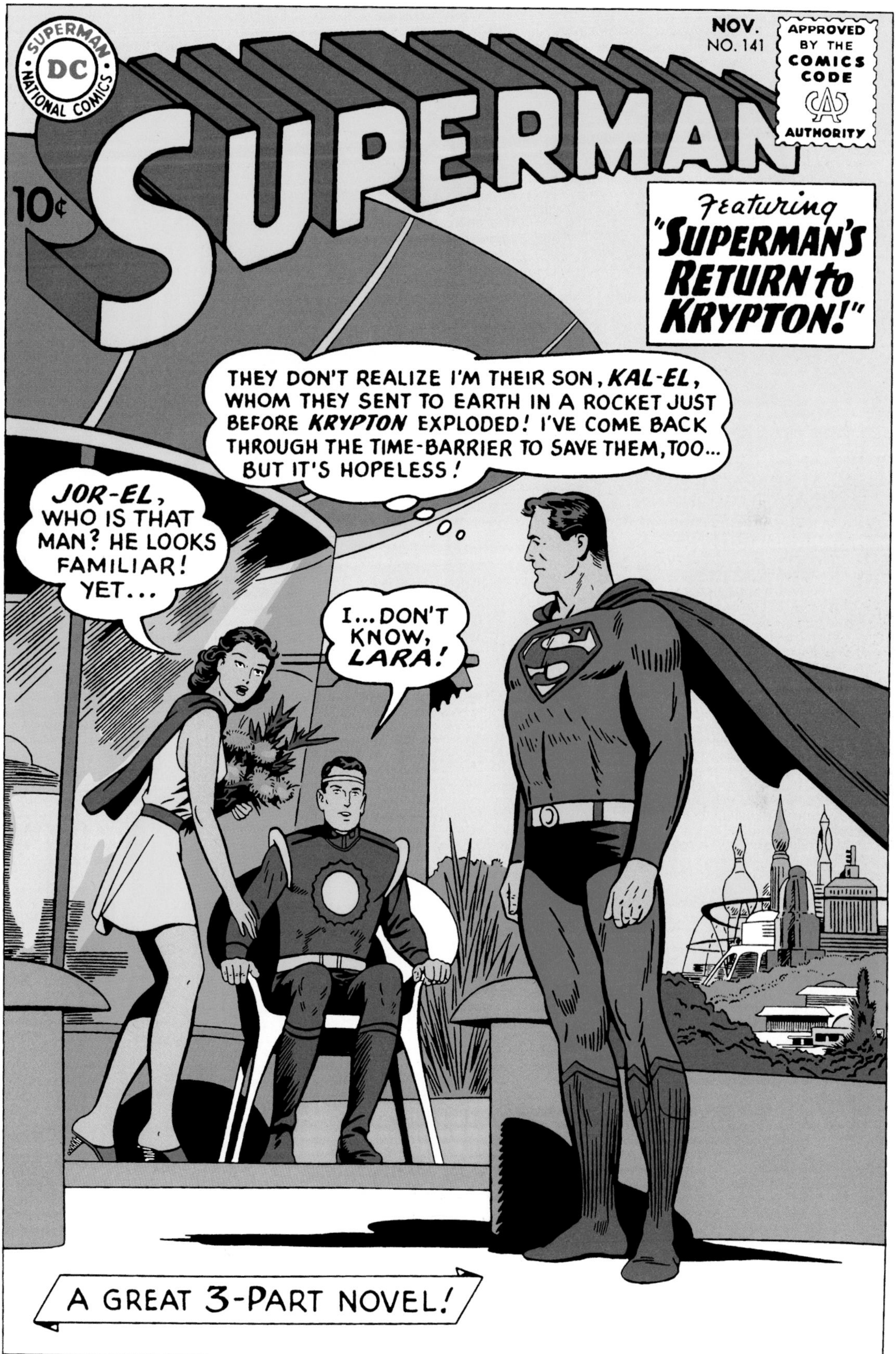
SUPERMAN NATIONAL COMICS DC
SUPERMAN
NOV. NO. 141
APPROVED BY THE COMICS CODE AUTHORITY
10¢
Featuring "SUPERMAN'S RETURN to KRYPTON!"
THEY DON'T REALIZE I'M THEIR SON, KAL-EL, WHOM THEY SENT TO EARTH IN A ROCKET JUST BEFORE KRYPTON EXPLODED! I'VE COME BACK THROUGH THE TIME-BARRIER TO SAVE THEM, TOO... BUT IT'S HOPELESS!
JOR-EL, WHO IS THAT MAN? HE LOOKS FAMILIAR! YET...
I...DON'T KNOW, LARA!
A GREAT 3-PART NOVEL!

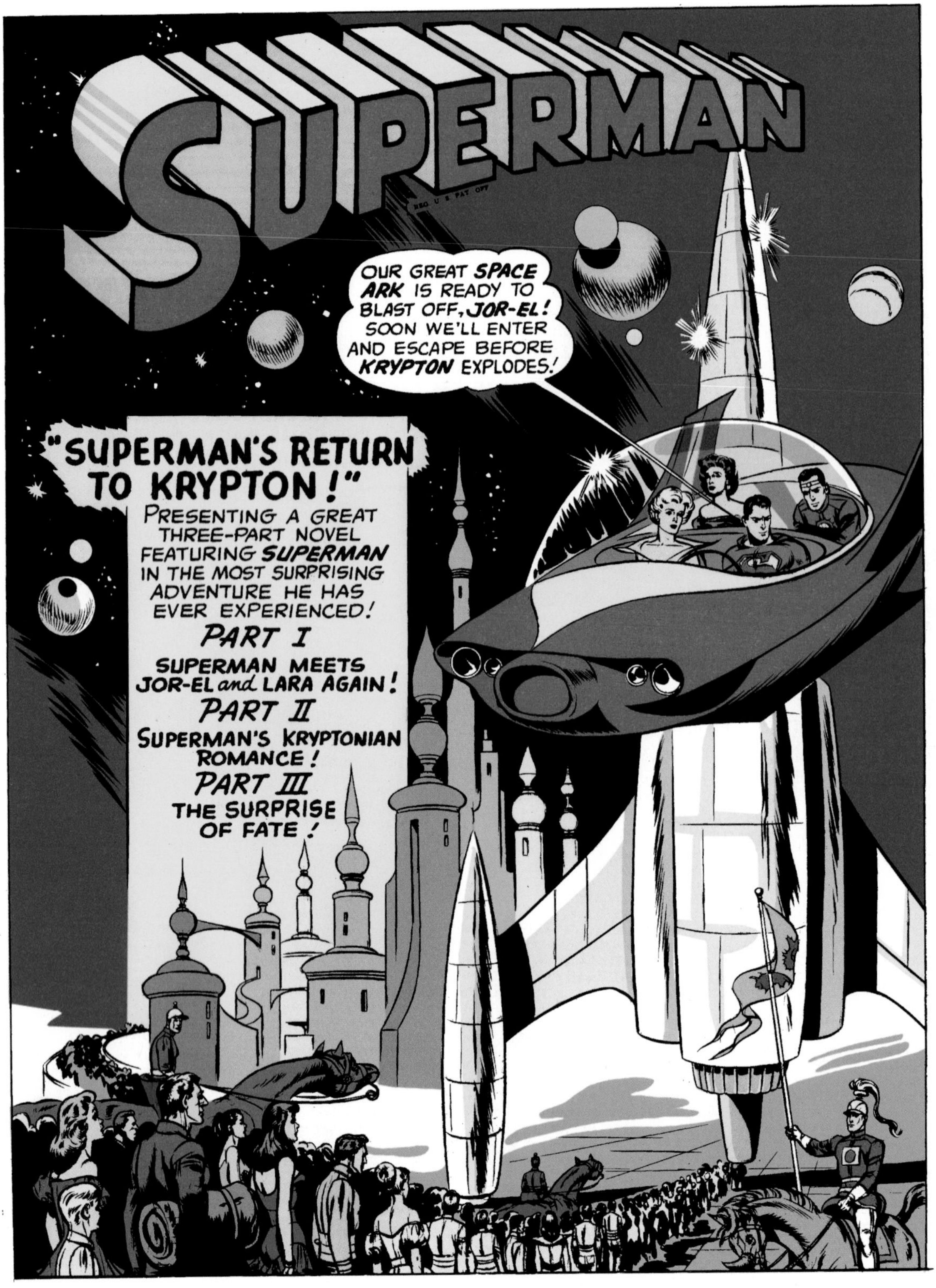
SUPERMAN
REG. U.S. PAT. OFF.
OUR GREAT SPACE ARK IS READY TO BLAST OFF, JOR-EL! SOON WE'LL ENTER AND ESCAPE BEFORE KRYPTON EXPLODES!
"SUPERMAN'S RETURN TO KRYPTON!"
PRESENTING A GREAT THREE-PART NOVEL FEATURING SUPERMAN IN THE MOST SURPRISING ADVENTURE HE HAS EVER EXPERIENCED!
PART I
SUPERMAN MEETS JOR-EL and LARA AGAIN!
PART II
SUPERMAN'S KRYPTONIAN ROMANCE!
PART III
THE SURPRISE OF FATE!

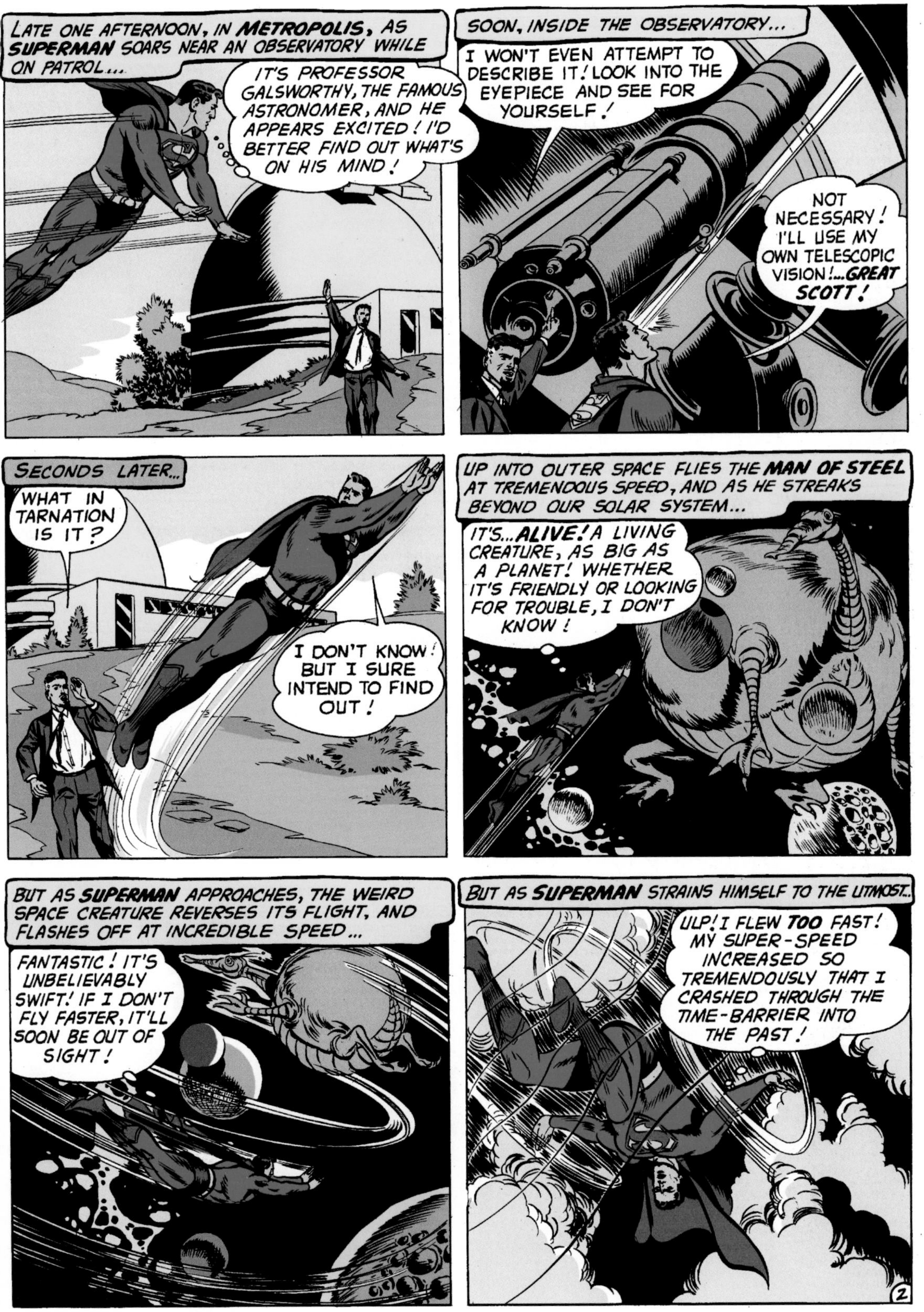
LATE ONE AFTERNOON, IN METROPOLIS, AS SUPERMAN SOARS NEAR AN OBSERVATORY WHILE ON PATROL...
IT'S PROFESSOR GALSWORTHY, THE FAMOUS ASTRONOMER, AND HE APPEARS EXCITED! I'D BETTER FIND OUT WHAT'S ON HIS MIND!
SOON, INSIDE THE OBSERVATORY...
I WON'T EVEN ATTEMPT TO DESCRIBE IT! LOOK INTO THE EYEPIECE AND SEE FOR YOURSELF!
NOT NECESSARY! I'LL USE MY OWN TELESCOPIC VISION!...GREAT SCOTT!
SECONDS LATER...
WHAT IN TARNATION IS IT?
I DON'T KNOW! BUT I SURE INTEND TO FIND OUT!
UP INTO OUTER SPACE FLIES THE MAN OF STEEL AT TREMENDOUS SPEED, AND AS HE STREAKS BEYOND OUR SOLAR SYSTEM...
IT'S...ALIVE! A LIVING CREATURE, AS BIG AS A PLANET! WHETHER IT'S FRIENDLY OR LOOKING FOR TROUBLE, I DON'T KNOW!
BUT AS SUPERMAN APPROACHES, THE WEIRD SPACE CREATURE REVERSES ITS FLIGHT, AND FLASHES OFF AT INCREDIBLE SPEED...
FANTASTIC! IT'S UNBELIEVABLY SWIFT! IF I DON'T FLY FASTER, IT'LL SOON BE OUT OF SIGHT!
BUT AS SUPERMAN STRAINS HIMSELF TO THE UTMOST...
ULP! I FLEW TOO FAST! MY SUPER-SPEED INCREASED SO TREMENDOUSLY THAT I CRASHED THROUGH THE TIME-BARRIER INTO THE PAST!
2

AND AS *SUPERMAN* MATERIALIZES IN A TIME ERA OF YESTERYEAR...

GREAT GUNS! THAT PLANET... AND ITS *RED* SUN! I RECOGNIZE THEM BECAUSE OF REBOUNDING LIGHT-RAYS I ONCE OVERTOOK AND STUDIED! THE PLANET IS *KRYPTON*, THE WORLD WHERE I WAS BORN...IT BLEW UP JUST AFTER I WAS ROCKETED TO EARTH!

DOWN TOWARD *KRYPTON'S* SURFACE FLASHES EARTH'S MIGHTIEST MORTAL...

I'VE ACCIDENTALLY RETURNED TO A PERIOD IN THE PAST, WHEN *KRYPTON* STILL EXISTED! BECAUSE OF THAT *RED* SUN, I MUST LAND IMMEDIATELY OR I'M DOOMED!

A FRACTION OF AN INSTANT LATER...

I MADE IT...AND BARELY IN TIME! IN ANOTHER SPLIT SECOND, I'LL LOSE MY SUPER-POWERS!

TESTING HIMSELF, *SUPERMAN* LIFTS A ROCK, AND AS HE ATTEMPTS TO CRUSH IT IN HIS FIST...

NO CAN DO! I'M AN ORDINARY KRYPTONIAN AGAIN! YEARS AGO, WHEN MY PARENTS *JOR-EL* AND *LARA* LAUNCHED ME TOWARD EARTH IN A MODEL ROCKET SHIP SECONDS BEFORE *KRYPTON* EXPLODED, I HAD NO SUPER-POWERS AT ALL...

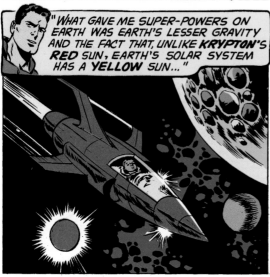

"WHAT GAVE ME SUPER-POWERS ON EARTH WAS EARTH'S LESSER GRAVITY AND THE FACT THAT, UNLIKE *KRYPTON'S* *RED* SUN, EARTH'S SOLAR SYSTEM HAS A *YELLOW* SUN..."

ONLY YELLOW STARS RADIATE SUPER-ENERGY RAYS WHICH GIVE SUPER-POWERS TO PEOPLE BORN IN OTHER SOLAR SYSTEMS! HERE ON *KRYPTON*, I AM SUPER NO LONGER! BECAUSE OF AN ASTOUNDING TWIST OF FATE, I AM NOW...JUST AN ORDINARY MAN!

③

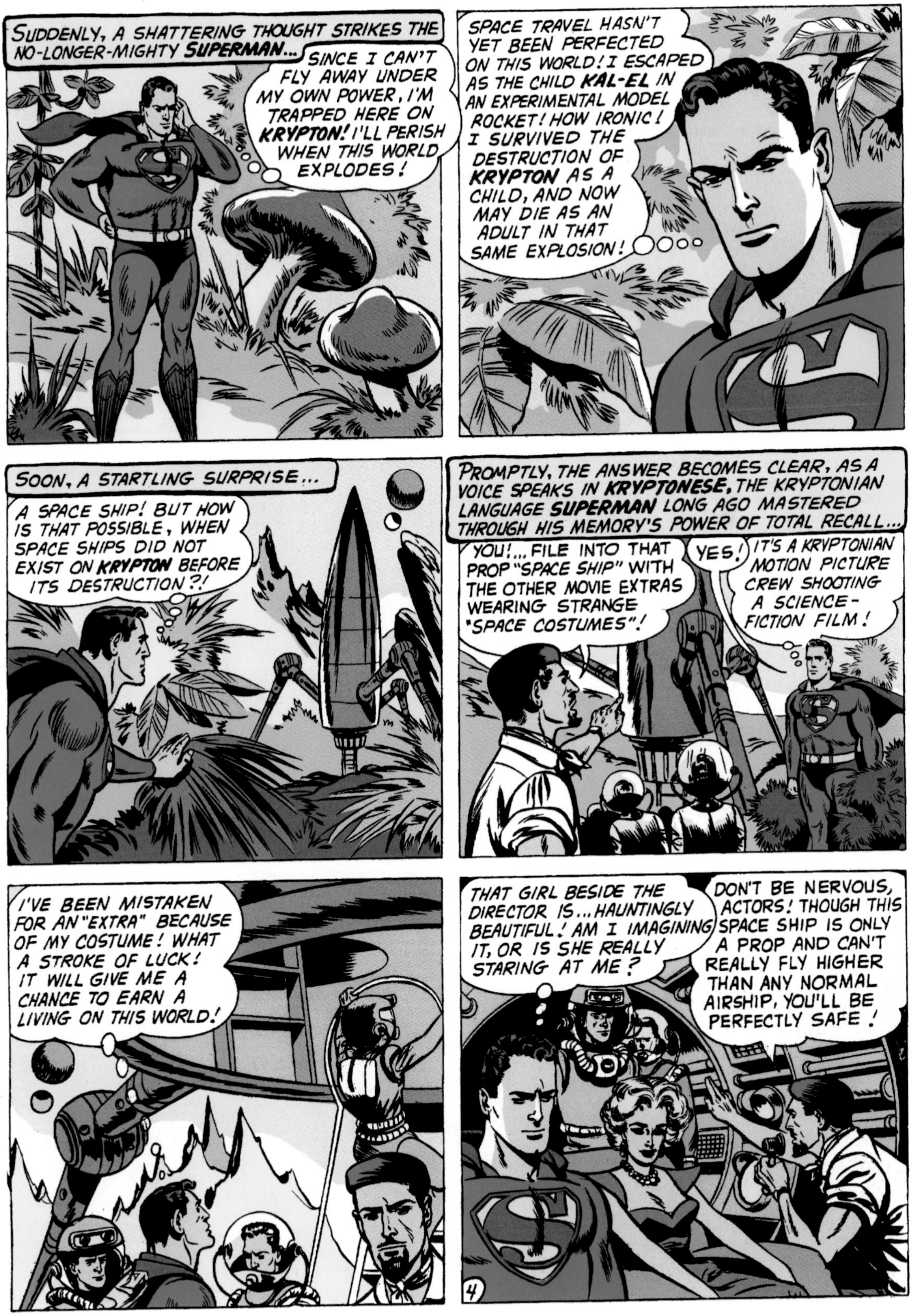
SUDDENLY, A SHATTERING THOUGHT STRIKES THE NO-LONGER-MIGHTY SUPERMAN...
SINCE I CAN'T FLY AWAY UNDER MY OWN POWER, I'M TRAPPED HERE ON KRYPTON! I'LL PERISH WHEN THIS WORLD EXPLODES!
SPACE TRAVEL HASN'T YET BEEN PERFECTED ON THIS WORLD! I ESCAPED AS THE CHILD KAL-EL IN AN EXPERIMENTAL MODEL ROCKET! HOW IRONIC! I SURVIVED THE DESTRUCTION OF KRYPTON AS A CHILD, AND NOW MAY DIE AS AN ADULT IN THAT SAME EXPLOSION!
SOON, A STARTLING SURPRISE...
A SPACE SHIP! BUT HOW IS THAT POSSIBLE, WHEN SPACE SHIPS DID NOT EXIST ON KRYPTON BEFORE ITS DESTRUCTION?!
PROMPTLY, THE ANSWER BECOMES CLEAR, AS A VOICE SPEAKS IN KRYPTONESE, THE KRYPTONIAN LANGUAGE SUPERMAN LONG AGO MASTERED THROUGH HIS MEMORY'S POWER OF TOTAL RECALL...
YOU!... FILE INTO THAT PROP "SPACE SHIP" WITH THE OTHER MOVIE EXTRAS WEARING STRANGE "SPACE COSTUMES"!
YES! IT'S A KRYPTONIAN MOTION PICTURE CREW SHOOTING A SCIENCE-FICTION FILM!
I'VE BEEN MISTAKEN FOR AN "EXTRA" BECAUSE OF MY COSTUME! WHAT A STROKE OF LUCK! IT WILL GIVE ME A CHANCE TO EARN A LIVING ON THIS WORLD!
THAT GIRL BESIDE THE DIRECTOR IS... HAUNTINGLY BEAUTIFUL! AM I IMAGINING IT, OR IS SHE REALLY STARING AT ME?
DON'T BE NERVOUS, ACTORS! THOUGH THIS SPACE SHIP IS ONLY A PROP AND CAN'T REALLY FLY HIGHER THAN ANY NORMAL AIRSHIP, YOU'LL BE PERFECTLY SAFE!
4

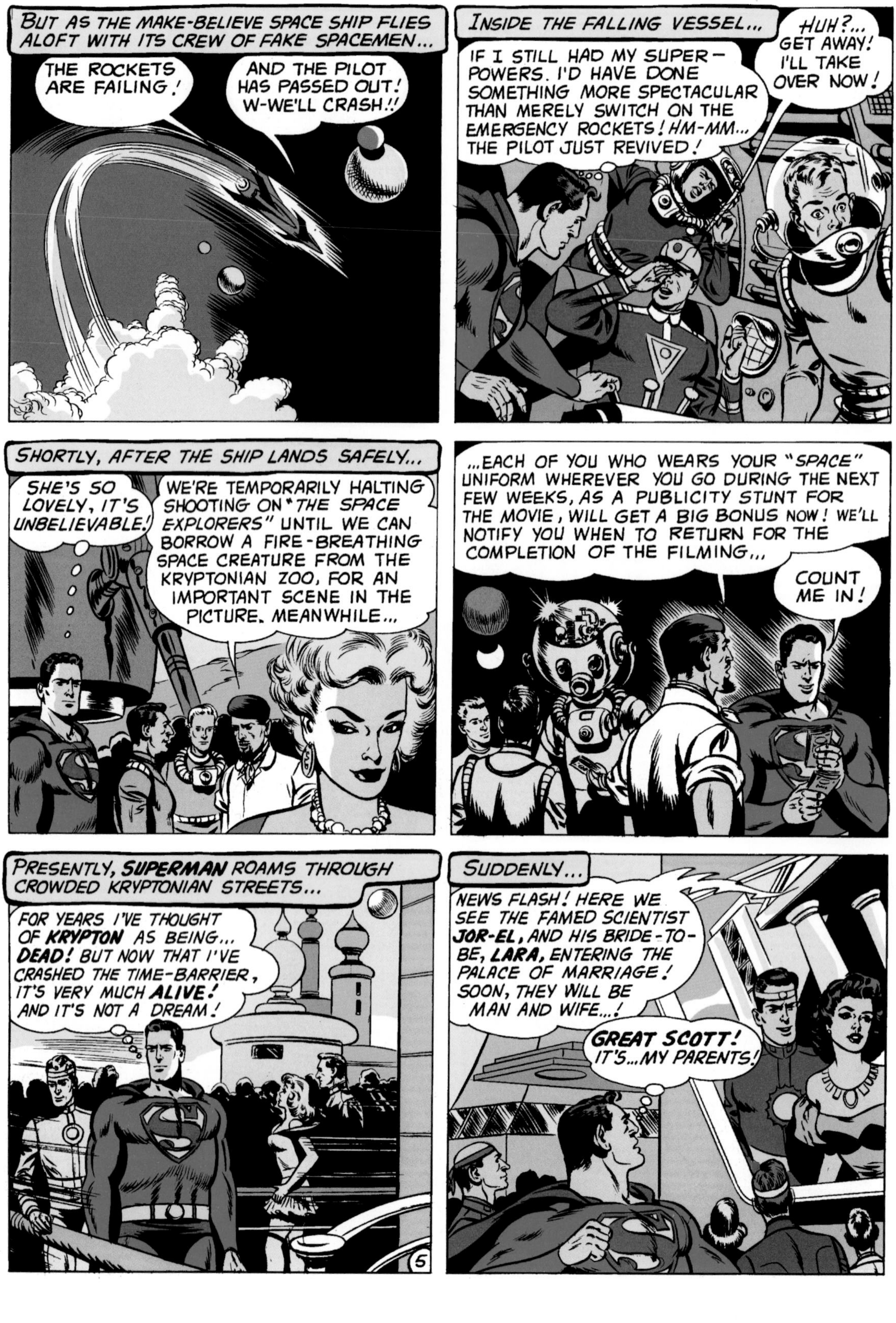
BUT AS THE MAKE-BELIEVE SPACE SHIP FLIES ALOFT WITH ITS CREW OF FAKE SPACEMEN...
THE ROCKETS ARE FAILING!
AND THE PILOT HAS PASSED OUT! W-WE'LL CRASH!!
INSIDE THE FALLING VESSEL...
IF I STILL HAD MY SUPER-POWERS, I'D HAVE DONE SOMETHING MORE SPECTACULAR THAN MERELY SWITCH ON THE EMERGENCY ROCKETS! HM-MM... THE PILOT JUST REVIVED!
HUH?... GET AWAY! I'LL TAKE OVER NOW!
SHORTLY, AFTER THE SHIP LANDS SAFELY...
SHE'S SO LOVELY, IT'S UNBELIEVABLE!
WE'RE TEMPORARILY HALTING SHOOTING ON "THE SPACE EXPLORERS" UNTIL WE CAN BORROW A FIRE-BREATHING SPACE CREATURE FROM THE KRYPTONIAN ZOO, FOR AN IMPORTANT SCENE IN THE PICTURE. MEANWHILE...
...EACH OF YOU WHO WEARS YOUR "SPACE" UNIFORM WHEREVER YOU GO DURING THE NEXT FEW WEEKS, AS A PUBLICITY STUNT FOR THE MOVIE, WILL GET A BIG BONUS NOW! WE'LL NOTIFY YOU WHEN TO RETURN FOR THE COMPLETION OF THE FILMING...
COUNT ME IN!
PRESENTLY, SUPERMAN ROAMS THROUGH CROWDED KRYPTONIAN STREETS...
FOR YEARS I'VE THOUGHT OF KRYPTON AS BEING... DEAD! BUT NOW THAT I'VE CRASHED THE TIME-BARRIER, IT'S VERY MUCH ALIVE! AND IT'S NOT A DREAM!
5
SUDDENLY...
NEWS FLASH! HERE WE SEE THE FAMED SCIENTIST JOR-EL, AND HIS BRIDE-TO-BE, LARA, ENTERING THE PALACE OF MARRIAGE! SOON, THEY WILL BE MAN AND WIFE...!
GREAT SCOTT! IT'S...MY PARENTS!

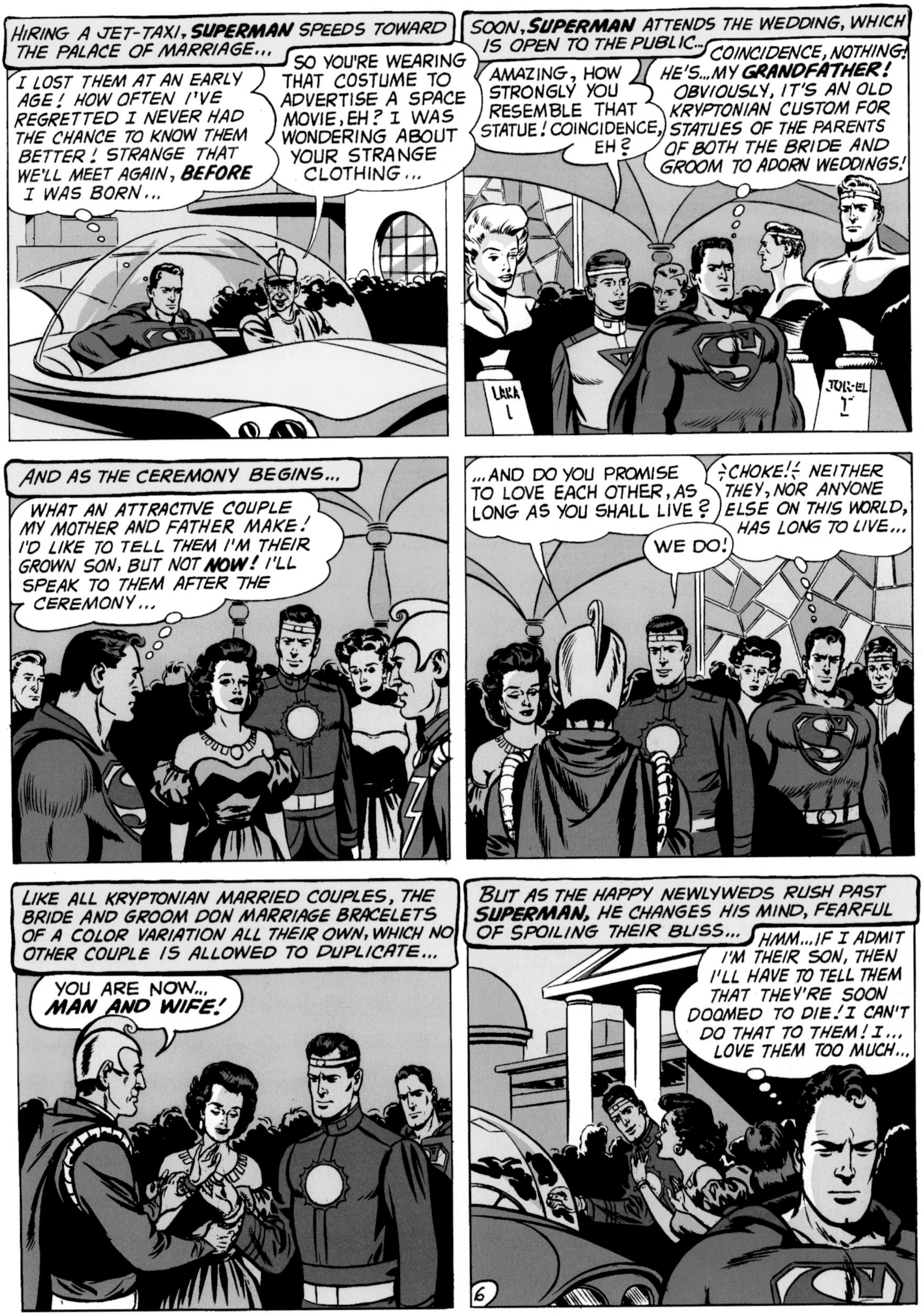
HIRING A JET-TAXI, SUPERMAN SPEEDS TOWARD THE PALACE OF MARRIAGE...
I LOST THEM AT AN EARLY AGE! HOW OFTEN I'VE REGRETTED I NEVER HAD THE CHANCE TO KNOW THEM BETTER! STRANGE THAT WE'LL MEET AGAIN, BEFORE I WAS BORN...
SO YOU'RE WEARING THAT COSTUME TO ADVERTISE A SPACE MOVIE, EH? I WAS WONDERING ABOUT YOUR STRANGE CLOTHING...
SOON, SUPERMAN ATTENDS THE WEDDING, WHICH IS OPEN TO THE PUBLIC...
AMAZING, HOW STRONGLY YOU RESEMBLE THAT STATUE! COINCIDENCE, EH?
COINCIDENCE, NOTHING! HE'S...MY GRANDFATHER! OBVIOUSLY, IT'S AN OLD KRYPTONIAN CUSTOM FOR STATUES OF THE PARENTS OF BOTH THE BRIDE AND GROOM TO ADORN WEDDINGS!
LARA
JOR-EL
AND AS THE CEREMONY BEGINS...
WHAT AN ATTRACTIVE COUPLE MY MOTHER AND FATHER MAKE! I'D LIKE TO TELL THEM I'M THEIR GROWN SON, BUT NOT NOW! I'LL SPEAK TO THEM AFTER THE CEREMONY...
...AND DO YOU PROMISE TO LOVE EACH OTHER, AS LONG AS YOU SHALL LIVE?
WE DO!
CHOKE! NEITHER THEY, NOR ANYONE ELSE ON THIS WORLD, HAS LONG TO LIVE...
LIKE ALL KRYPTONIAN MARRIED COUPLES, THE BRIDE AND GROOM DON MARRIAGE BRACELETS OF A COLOR VARIATION ALL THEIR OWN, WHICH NO OTHER COUPLE IS ALLOWED TO DUPLICATE...
YOU ARE NOW... MAN AND WIFE!
BUT AS THE HAPPY NEWLYWEDS RUSH PAST SUPERMAN, HE CHANGES HIS MIND, FEARFUL OF SPOILING THEIR BLISS...
HMM...IF I ADMIT I'M THEIR SON, THEN I'LL HAVE TO TELL THEM THAT THEY'RE SOON DOOMED TO DIE! I CAN'T DO THAT TO THEM! I... LOVE THEM TOO MUCH...
6

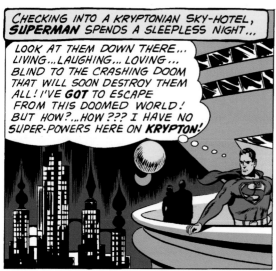

CHECKING INTO A KRYPTONIAN SKY-HOTEL, **SUPERMAN** SPENDS A SLEEPLESS NIGHT...

LOOK AT THEM DOWN THERE... LIVING...LAUGHING... LOVING... BLIND TO THE CRASHING DOOM THAT WILL SOON DESTROY THEM ALL! I'VE **GOT** TO ESCAPE FROM THIS DOOMED WORLD! BUT HOW?...HOW??? I HAVE NO SUPER-POWERS HERE ON **KRYPTON!**

THEN, ONE EVENING, **SUPERMAN** MAKES A DECISION...

I...WANT TO BE WITH MY MOTHER AND FATHER! SOMEHOW I MUST BECOME THEIR CLOSE FRIEND, WITHOUT REVEALING MY REAL RELATIONSHIP TO THEM...

BUILDING AN UNUSUAL GADGET SIMILAR TO AN EARTH-TYPE GYROSCOPE, **SUPERMAN** VISITS HIS PARENTS' HOME...

JOR-EL, WHO IS THAT MAN? HE LOOKS FAMILIAR! YET...

I DON'T KNOW, **LARA!** BUT THERE'S SOMETHING ABOUT HIM...!

I WISH I COULD TELL THEM WHAT THEY **SENSE** ABOUT ME! BUT I CAN'T...

ER...I KNOW IT'S PRESUMPTUOUS OF ME, BUT...MAY I PLEASE HAVE YOUR OPINION OF MY INVENTION, **JOR-EL**?

HMM...IT'S CLEVER! YOU HAVE GREAT PROMISE AS A SCIENTIST! I DON'T BELIEVE WE'VE EVER MET! YOUR NAME...?

KAL-EL!

OOPS! MY REAL KRYPTONIAN NAME SLIPPED OUT! BUT SINCE I HAVEN'T BEEN BORN YET, NO HARM'S DONE! NAMES ENDING WITH "EL" ARE QUITE COMMON ON **KRYPTON!**

WHY ARE YOU WEARING THAT STRANGE COSTUME?

AND AS **SUPERMAN** EXPLAINS THE MOVIE PUBLICITY STUNT...

BUT SINCE YOU DO THINK I HAVE SCIENTIFIC ABILITY, I'D MUCH RATHER BE AN ASSISTANT TO A GREAT SCIENTIST LIKE YOU, THAN BE AN ACTOR!

THEY'RE HOLDING EXAMS FOR JOB APPLICANTS TOMORROW AT THE MISSILE BASE WHERE I WORK! WAIT HERE!

7

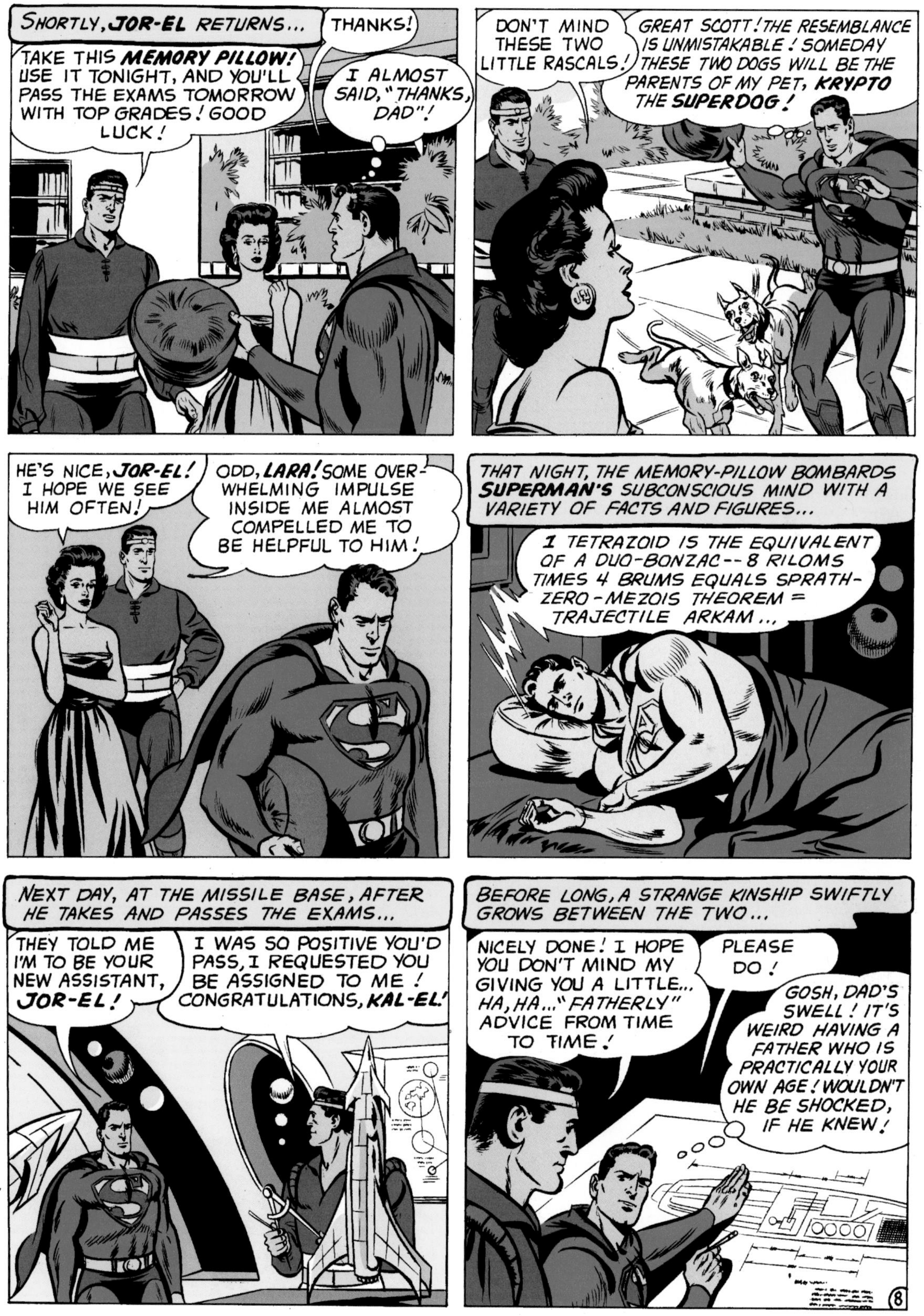
SHORTLY, JOR-EL RETURNS...
TAKE THIS MEMORY PILLOW! USE IT TONIGHT, AND YOU'LL PASS THE EXAMS TOMORROW WITH TOP GRADES! GOOD LUCK!
THANKS!
I ALMOST SAID, "THANKS, DAD"!
DON'T MIND THESE TWO LITTLE RASCALS!
GREAT SCOTT! THE RESEMBLANCE IS UNMISTAKABLE! SOMEDAY THESE TWO DOGS WILL BE THE PARENTS OF MY PET, KRYPTO THE SUPERDOG!
HE'S NICE, JOR-EL! I HOPE WE SEE HIM OFTEN!
ODD, LARA! SOME OVER-WHELMING IMPULSE INSIDE ME ALMOST COMPELLED ME TO BE HELPFUL TO HIM!
THAT NIGHT, THE MEMORY-PILLOW BOMBARDS SUPERMAN'S SUBCONSCIOUS MIND WITH A VARIETY OF FACTS AND FIGURES...
1 TETRAZOID IS THE EQUIVALENT OF A DUO-BONZAC--8 RILOMS TIMES 4 BRUMS EQUALS SPRATH-ZERO-MEZOIS THEOREM = TRAJECTILE ARKAM...
NEXT DAY, AT THE MISSILE BASE, AFTER HE TAKES AND PASSES THE EXAMS...
THEY TOLD ME I'M TO BE YOUR NEW ASSISTANT, JOR-EL!
I WAS SO POSITIVE YOU'D PASS, I REQUESTED YOU BE ASSIGNED TO ME! CONGRATULATIONS, KAL-EL!
BEFORE LONG, A STRANGE KINSHIP SWIFTLY GROWS BETWEEN THE TWO...
NICELY DONE! I HOPE YOU DON'T MIND MY GIVING YOU A LITTLE... HA, HA..."FATHERLY" ADVICE FROM TIME TO TIME!
PLEASE DO!
GOSH, DAD'S SWELL! IT'S WEIRD HAVING A FATHER WHO IS PRACTICALLY YOUR OWN AGE! WOULDN'T HE BE SHOCKED, IF HE KNEW!
8

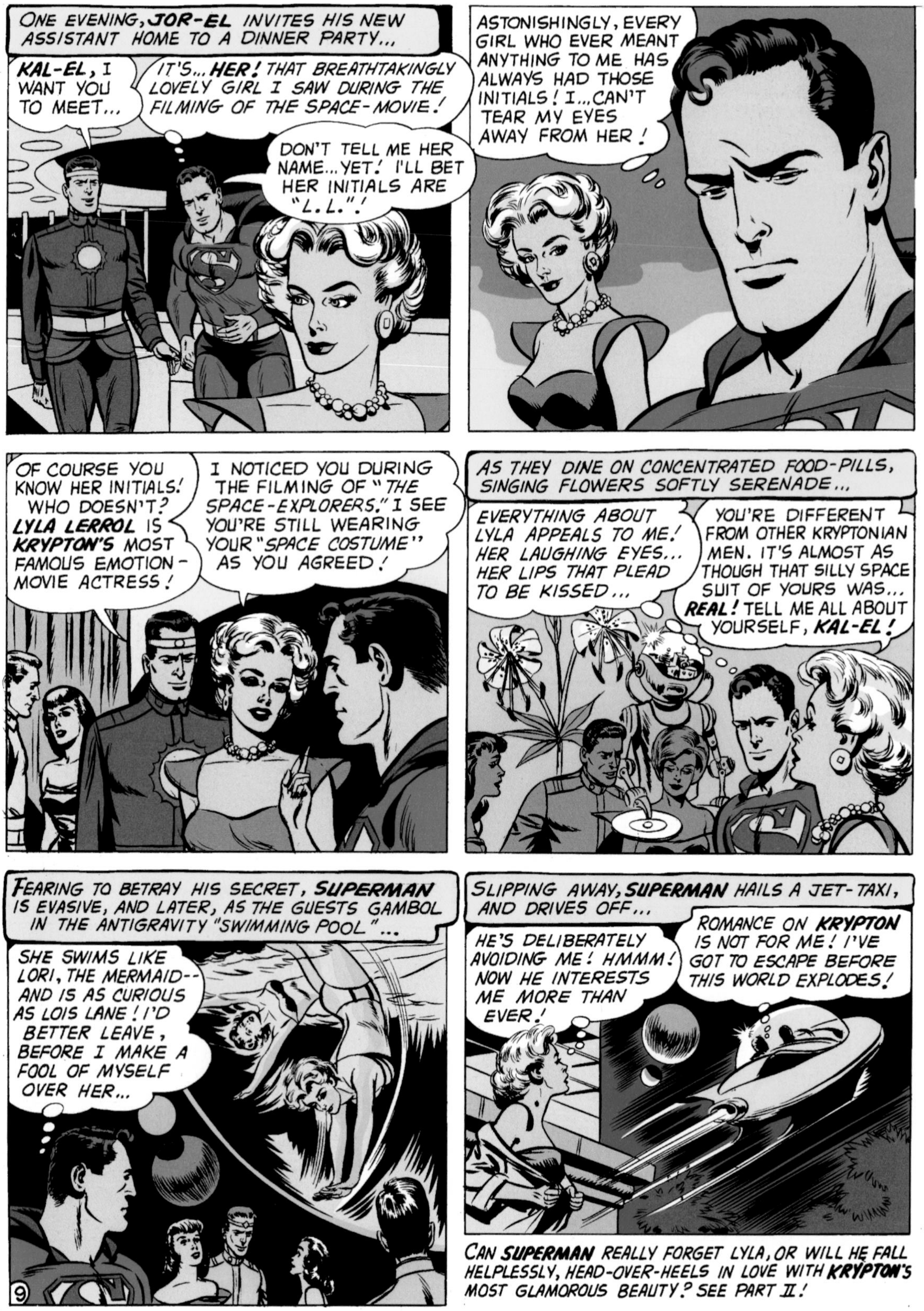
ONE EVENING, JOR-EL INVITES HIS NEW ASSISTANT HOME TO A DINNER PARTY...
KAL-EL, I WANT YOU TO MEET...
IT'S... HER! THAT BREATHTAKINGLY LOVELY GIRL I SAW DURING THE FILMING OF THE SPACE-MOVIE!
DON'T TELL ME HER NAME... YET! I'LL BET HER INITIALS ARE "L.L."!
ASTONISHINGLY, EVERY GIRL WHO EVER MEANT ANYTHING TO ME HAS ALWAYS HAD THOSE INITIALS! I... CAN'T TEAR MY EYES AWAY FROM HER!
OF COURSE YOU KNOW HER INITIALS! WHO DOESN'T? LYLA LERROL IS KRYPTON'S MOST FAMOUS EMOTION-MOVIE ACTRESS!
I NOTICED YOU DURING THE FILMING OF "THE SPACE-EXPLORERS." I SEE YOU'RE STILL WEARING YOUR "SPACE COSTUME" AS YOU AGREED!
AS THEY DINE ON CONCENTRATED FOOD-PILLS, SINGING FLOWERS SOFTLY SERENADE...
EVERYTHING ABOUT LYLA APPEALS TO ME! HER LAUGHING EYES... HER LIPS THAT PLEAD TO BE KISSED...
YOU'RE DIFFERENT FROM OTHER KRYPTONIAN MEN. IT'S ALMOST AS THOUGH THAT SILLY SPACE SUIT OF YOURS WAS... REAL! TELL ME ALL ABOUT YOURSELF, KAL-EL!
FEARING TO BETRAY HIS SECRET, SUPERMAN IS EVASIVE, AND LATER, AS THE GUESTS GAMBOL IN THE ANTIGRAVITY "SWIMMING POOL"...
SHE SWIMS LIKE LORI, THE MERMAID-- AND IS AS CURIOUS AS LOIS LANE! I'D BETTER LEAVE, BEFORE I MAKE A FOOL OF MYSELF OVER HER...
9
SLIPPING AWAY, SUPERMAN HAILS A JET-TAXI, AND DRIVES OFF...
HE'S DELIBERATELY AVOIDING ME! HMMM! NOW HE INTERESTS ME MORE THAN EVER!
ROMANCE ON KRYPTON IS NOT FOR ME! I'VE GOT TO ESCAPE BEFORE THIS WORLD EXPLODES!

CAN SUPERMAN REALLY FORGET LYLA, OR WILL HE FALL HELPLESSLY, HEAD-OVER-HEELS IN LOVE WITH KRYPTON'S MOST GLAMOROUS BEAUTY? SEE PART II!

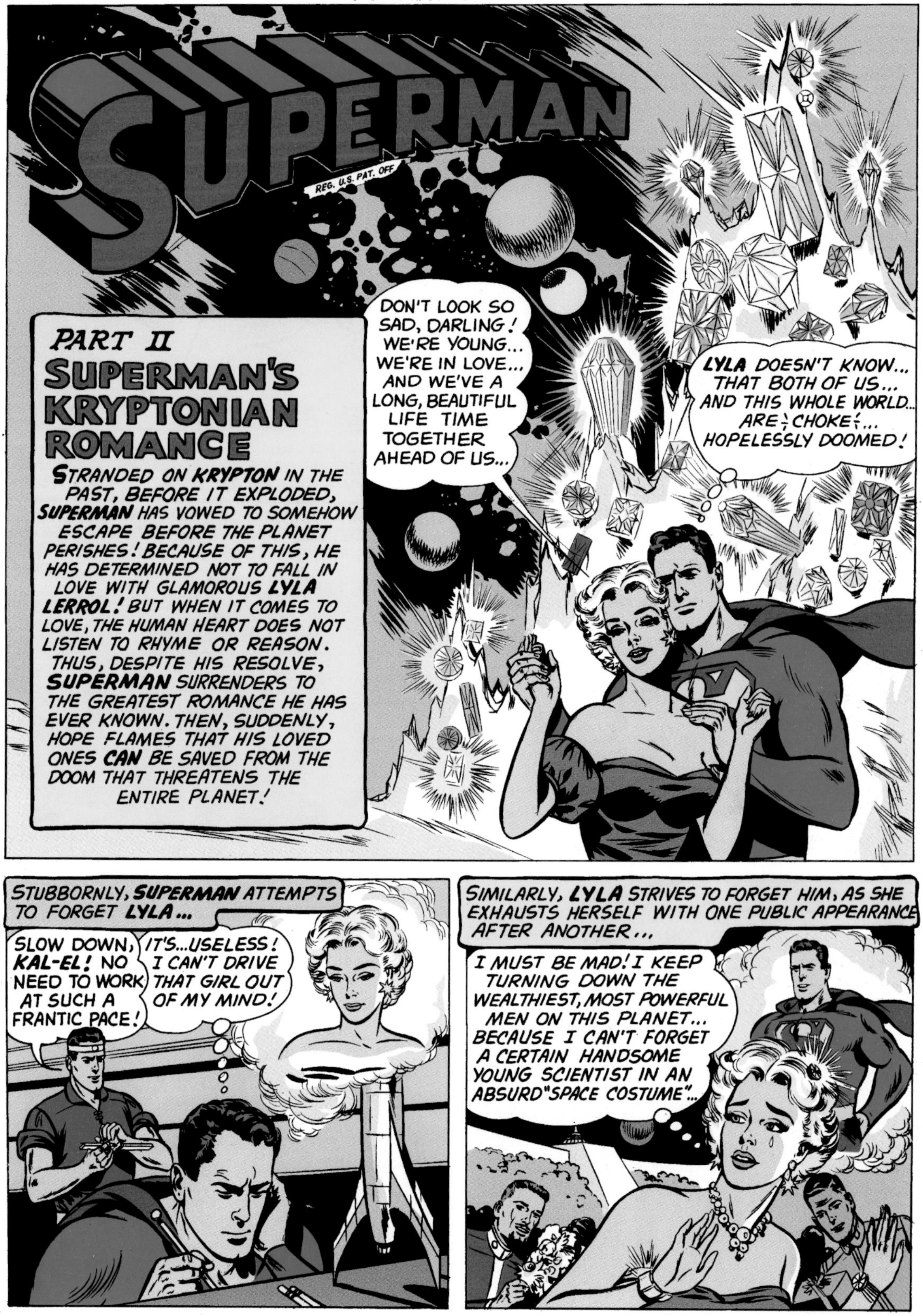
SUPERMAN
REG. U.S. PAT. OFF.
PART II
SUPERMAN'S KRYPTONIAN ROMANCE
STRANDED ON KRYPTON IN THE PAST, BEFORE IT EXPLODED, SUPERMAN HAS VOWED TO SOMEHOW ESCAPE BEFORE THE PLANET PERISHES! BECAUSE OF THIS, HE HAS DETERMINED NOT TO FALL IN LOVE WITH GLAMOROUS LYLA LERROL! BUT WHEN IT COMES TO LOVE, THE HUMAN HEART DOES NOT LISTEN TO RHYME OR REASON. THUS, DESPITE HIS RESOLVE, SUPERMAN SURRENDERS TO THE GREATEST ROMANCE HE HAS EVER KNOWN. THEN, SUDDENLY, HOPE FLAMES THAT HIS LOVED ONES CAN BE SAVED FROM THE DOOM THAT THREATENS THE ENTIRE PLANET!
DON'T LOOK SO SAD, DARLING! WE'RE YOUNG... WE'RE IN LOVE... AND WE'VE A LONG, BEAUTIFUL LIFE TIME TOGETHER AHEAD OF US...
LYLA DOESN'T KNOW... THAT BOTH OF US... AND THIS WHOLE WORLD... ARE -CHOKE- ... HOPELESSLY DOOMED!
STUBBORNLY, SUPERMAN ATTEMPTS TO FORGET LYLA...
SLOW DOWN, KAL-EL! NO NEED TO WORK AT SUCH A FRANTIC PACE!
IT'S...USELESS! I CAN'T DRIVE THAT GIRL OUT OF MY MIND!
SIMILARLY, LYLA STRIVES TO FORGET HIM, AS SHE EXHAUSTS HERSELF WITH ONE PUBLIC APPEARANCE AFTER ANOTHER...
I MUST BE MAD! I KEEP TURNING DOWN THE WEALTHIEST, MOST POWERFUL MEN ON THIS PLANET... BECAUSE I CAN'T FORGET A CERTAIN HANDSOME YOUNG SCIENTIST IN AN ABSURD "SPACE COSTUME"...

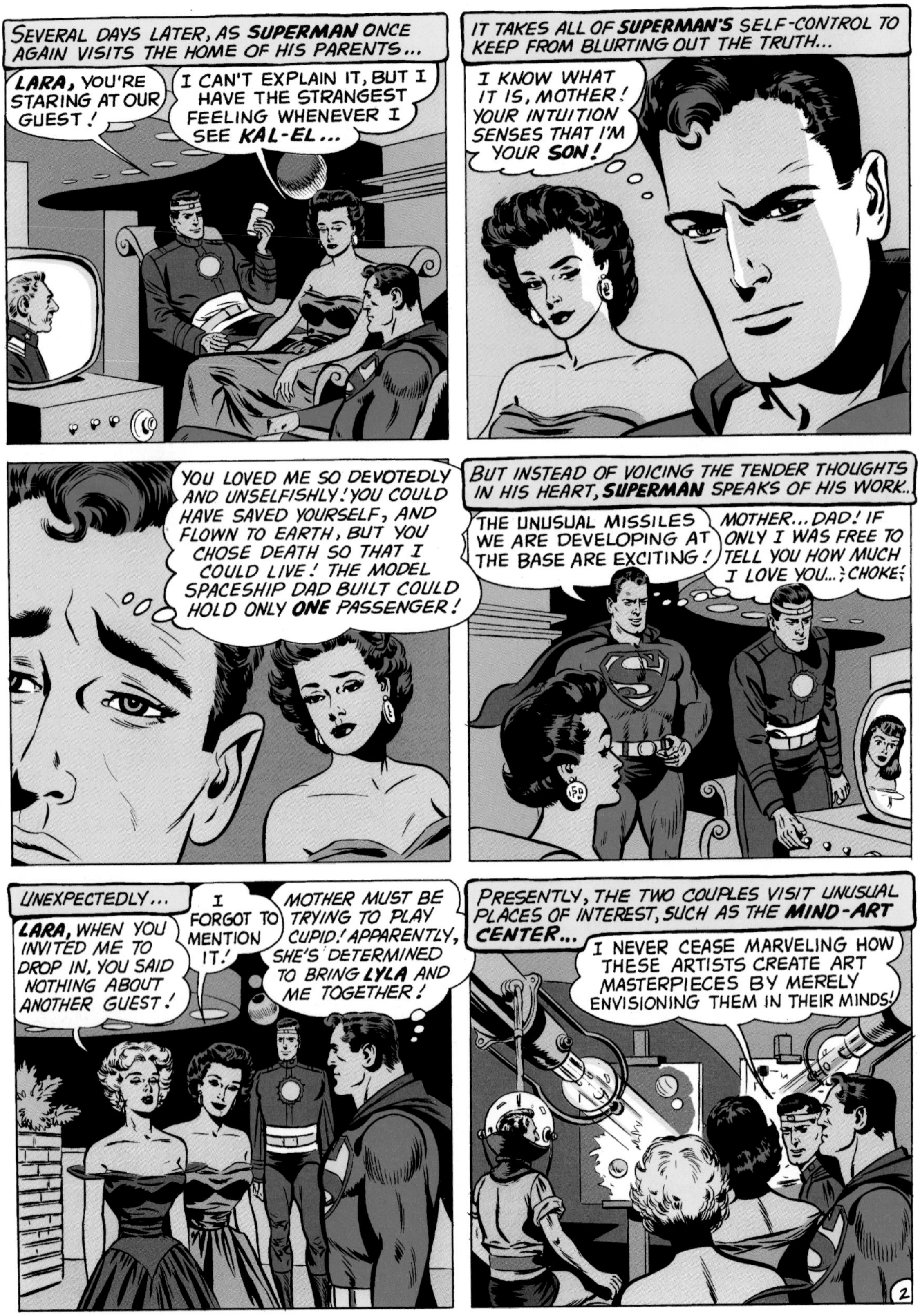

SEVERAL DAYS LATER, AS SUPERMAN ONCE AGAIN VISITS THE HOME OF HIS PARENTS...
LARA, YOU'RE STARING AT OUR GUEST!
I CAN'T EXPLAIN IT, BUT I HAVE THE STRANGEST FEELING WHENEVER I SEE KAL-EL...
IT TAKES ALL OF SUPERMAN'S SELF-CONTROL TO KEEP FROM BLURTING OUT THE TRUTH...
I KNOW WHAT IT IS, MOTHER! YOUR INTUITION SENSES THAT I'M YOUR SON!
YOU LOVED ME SO DEVOTEDLY AND UNSELFISHLY! YOU COULD HAVE SAVED YOURSELF, AND FLOWN TO EARTH, BUT YOU CHOSE DEATH SO THAT I COULD LIVE! THE MODEL SPACESHIP DAD BUILT COULD HOLD ONLY ONE PASSENGER!
BUT INSTEAD OF VOICING THE TENDER THOUGHTS IN HIS HEART, SUPERMAN SPEAKS OF HIS WORK...
THE UNUSUAL MISSILES WE ARE DEVELOPING AT THE BASE ARE EXCITING!
MOTHER... DAD! IF ONLY I WAS FREE TO TELL YOU HOW MUCH I LOVE YOU... CHOKE
UNEXPECTEDLY...
LARA, WHEN YOU INVITED ME TO DROP IN, YOU SAID NOTHING ABOUT ANOTHER GUEST!
I FORGOT TO MENTION IT!
MOTHER MUST BE TRYING TO PLAY CUPID! APPARENTLY, SHE'S DETERMINED TO BRING LYLA AND ME TOGETHER!
PRESENTLY, THE TWO COUPLES VISIT UNUSUAL PLACES OF INTEREST, SUCH AS THE MIND-ART CENTER...
I NEVER CEASE MARVELING HOW THESE ARTISTS CREATE ART MASTERPIECES BY MERELY ENVISIONING THEM IN THEIR MINDS!
2

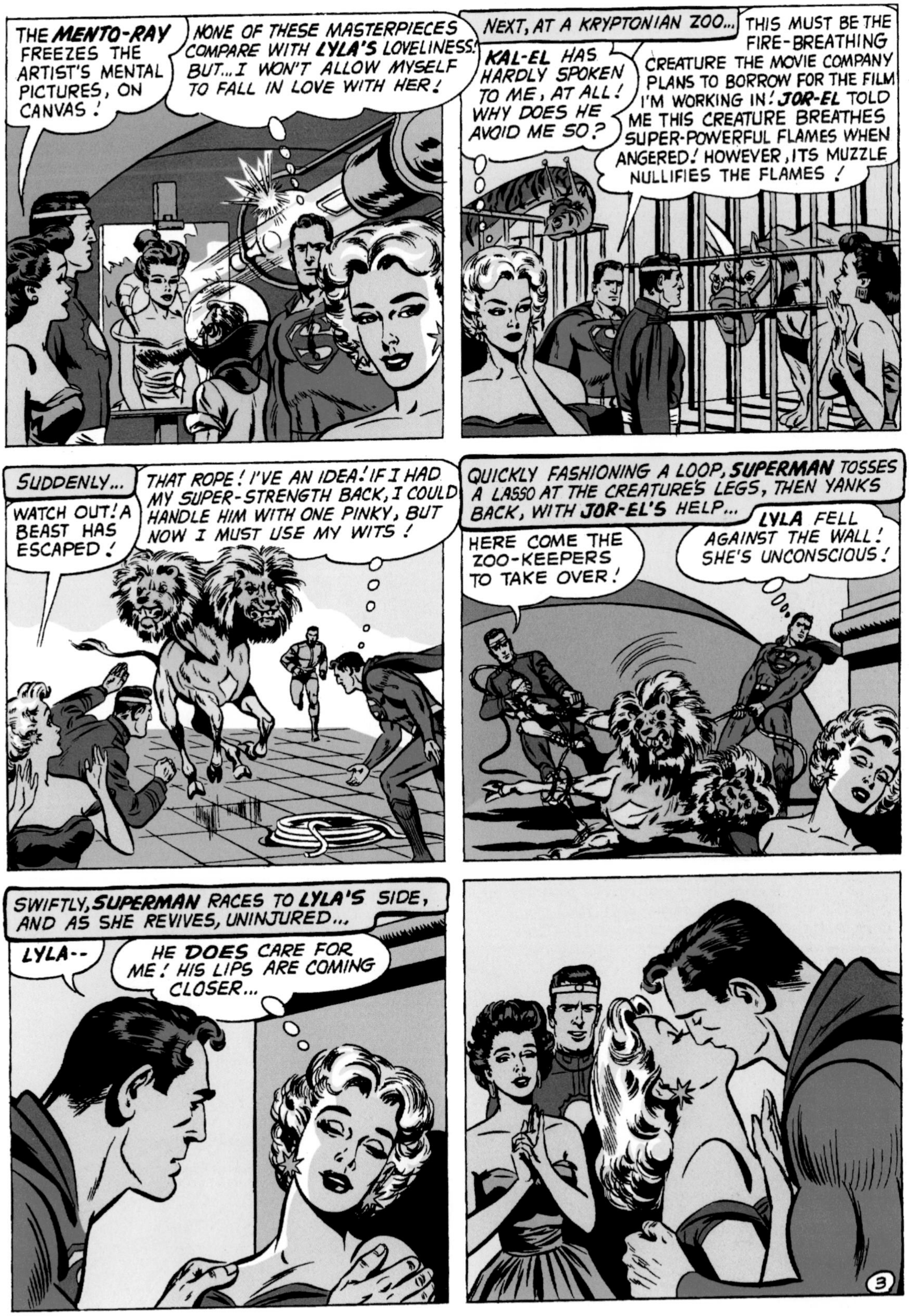
THE MENTO-RAY FREEZES THE ARTIST'S MENTAL PICTURES, ON CANVAS!
NONE OF THESE MASTERPIECES COMPARE WITH LYLA'S LOVELINESS! BUT...I WON'T ALLOW MYSELF TO FALL IN LOVE WITH HER!
NEXT, AT A KRYPTONIAN ZOO...
KAL-EL HAS HARDLY SPOKEN TO ME, AT ALL! WHY DOES HE AVOID ME SO?
THIS MUST BE THE FIRE-BREATHING CREATURE THE MOVIE COMPANY PLANS TO BORROW FOR THE FILM I'M WORKING IN! JOR-EL TOLD ME THIS CREATURE BREATHES SUPER-POWERFUL FLAMES WHEN ANGERED! HOWEVER, ITS MUZZLE NULLIFIES THE FLAMES!
SUDDENLY...
WATCH OUT! A BEAST HAS ESCAPED!
THAT ROPE! I'VE AN IDEA! IF I HAD MY SUPER-STRENGTH BACK, I COULD HANDLE HIM WITH ONE PINKY, BUT NOW I MUST USE MY WITS!
QUICKLY FASHIONING A LOOP, SUPERMAN TOSSES A LASSO AT THE CREATURE'S LEGS, THEN YANKS BACK, WITH JOR-EL'S HELP...
HERE COME THE ZOO-KEEPERS TO TAKE OVER!
LYLA FELL AGAINST THE WALL! SHE'S UNCONSCIOUS!
SWIFTLY, SUPERMAN RACES TO LYLA'S SIDE, AND AS SHE REVIVES, UNINJURED...
LYLA--
HE DOES CARE FOR ME! HIS LIPS ARE COMING CLOSER...
3

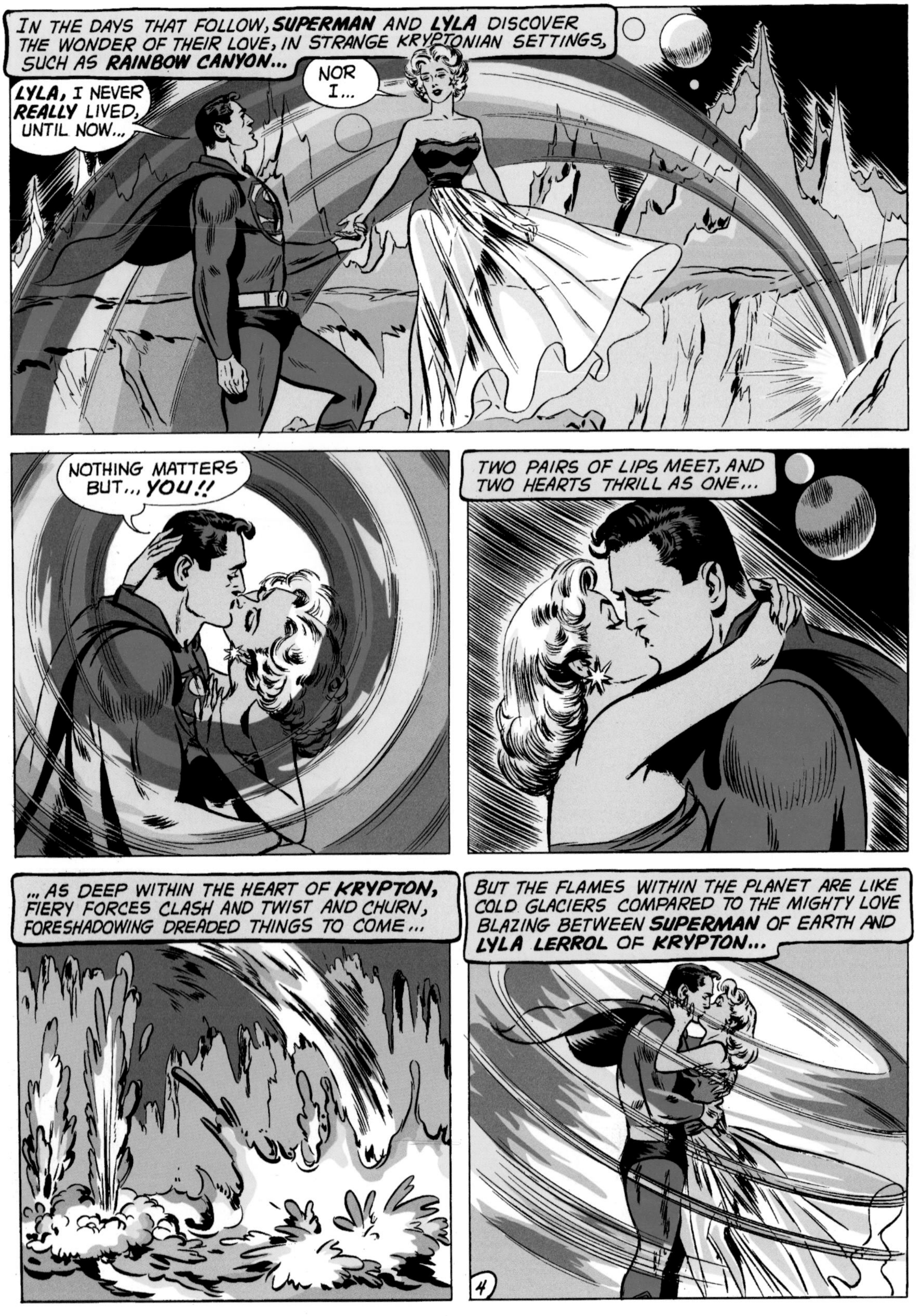

IN THE DAYS THAT FOLLOW, SUPERMAN AND LYLA DISCOVER THE WONDER OF THEIR LOVE, IN STRANGE KRYPTONIAN SETTINGS, SUCH AS RAINBOW CANYON...
LYLA, I NEVER REALLY LIVED, UNTIL NOW...
NOR I...
NOTHING MATTERS BUT... YOU!!
TWO PAIRS OF LIPS MEET, AND TWO HEARTS THRILL AS ONE...
...AS DEEP WITHIN THE HEART OF KRYPTON, FIERY FORCES CLASH AND TWIST AND CHURN, FORESHADOWING DREADED THINGS TO COME...
BUT THE FLAMES WITHIN THE PLANET ARE LIKE COLD GLACIERS COMPARED TO THE MIGHTY LOVE BLAZING BETWEEN SUPERMAN OF EARTH AND LYLA LERROL OF KRYPTON...
4

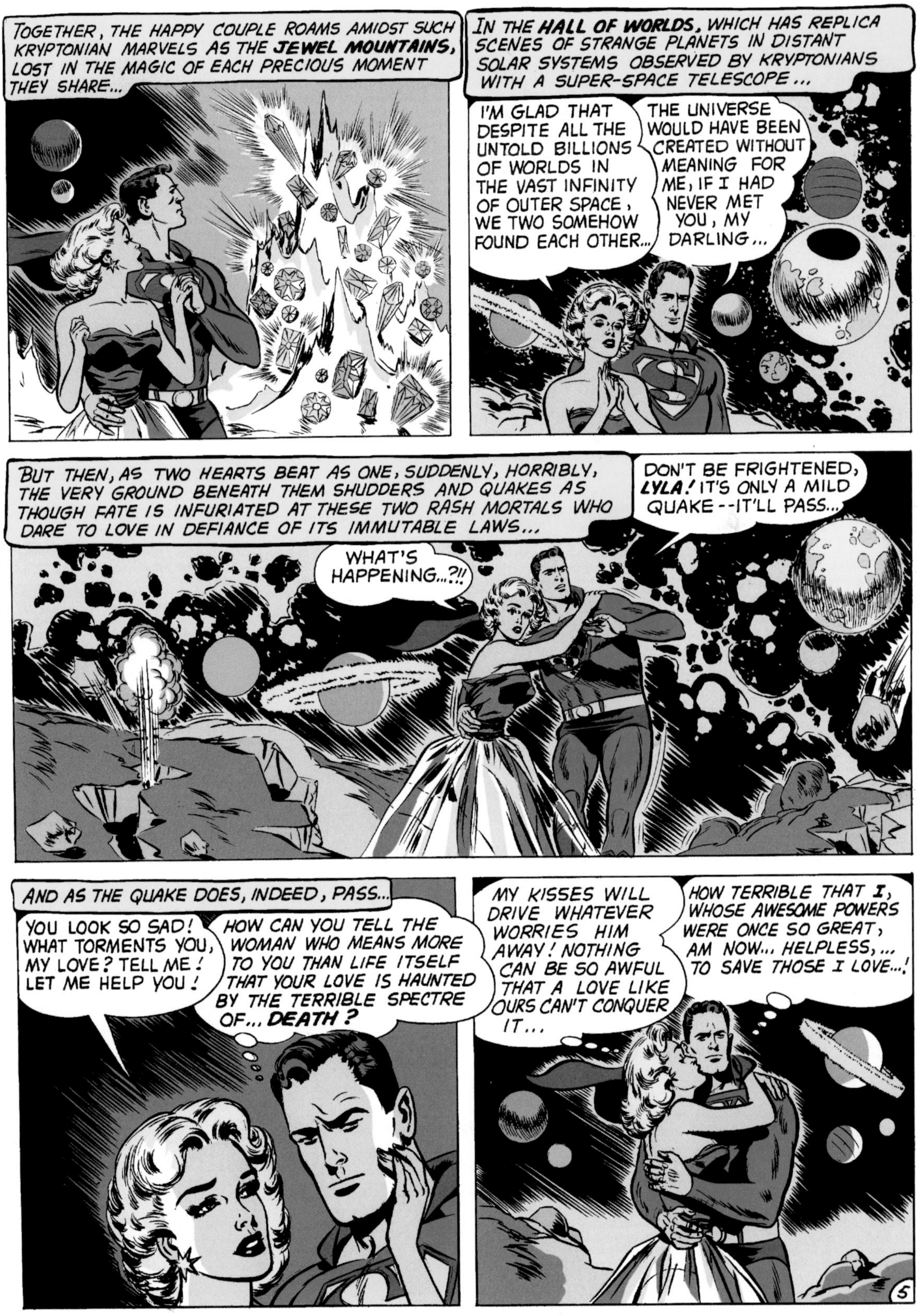
TOGETHER, THE HAPPY COUPLE ROAMS AMIDST SUCH KRYPTONIAN MARVELS AS THE JEWEL MOUNTAINS, LOST IN THE MAGIC OF EACH PRECIOUS MOMENT THEY SHARE...
IN THE HALL OF WORLDS, WHICH HAS REPLICA SCENES OF STRANGE PLANETS IN DISTANT SOLAR SYSTEMS OBSERVED BY KRYPTONIANS WITH A SUPER-SPACE TELESCOPE...
I'M GLAD THAT DESPITE ALL THE UNTOLD BILLIONS OF WORLDS IN THE VAST INFINITY OF OUTER SPACE, WE TWO SOMEHOW FOUND EACH OTHER...
THE UNIVERSE WOULD HAVE BEEN CREATED WITHOUT MEANING FOR ME, IF I HAD NEVER MET YOU, MY DARLING...
BUT THEN, AS TWO HEARTS BEAT AS ONE, SUDDENLY, HORRIBLY, THE VERY GROUND BENEATH THEM SHUDDERS AND QUAKES AS THOUGH FATE IS INFURIATED AT THESE TWO RASH MORTALS WHO DARE TO LOVE IN DEFIANCE OF ITS IMMUTABLE LAWS...
DON'T BE FRIGHTENED, LYLA! IT'S ONLY A MILD QUAKE--IT'LL PASS...
WHAT'S HAPPENING...?!!
AND AS THE QUAKE DOES, INDEED, PASS...
YOU LOOK SO SAD! WHAT TORMENTS YOU, MY LOVE? TELL ME! LET ME HELP YOU!
HOW CAN YOU TELL THE WOMAN WHO MEANS MORE TO YOU THAN LIFE ITSELF THAT YOUR LOVE IS HAUNTED BY THE TERRIBLE SPECTRE OF... DEATH?
MY KISSES WILL DRIVE WHATEVER WORRIES HIM AWAY! NOTHING CAN BE SO AWFUL THAT A LOVE LIKE OURS CAN'T CONQUER IT...
HOW TERRIBLE THAT I, WHOSE AWESOME POWERS WERE ONCE SO GREAT, AM NOW... HELPLESS,... TO SAVE THOSE I LOVE...!
5

NEXT DAY, AT THE MISSILE BASE...

WHAT IS IT, *JOR-EL*?

IF I DON'T CONFIDE MY THEORY TO SOMEONE, I'LL GO INSANE... *KAL-EL, KRYPTON* IS GOING TO BE BLOWN APART BY INTERNAL STRESSES...

I MUST PRETEND AMAZEMENT, TO PROTECT MY SECRET!

YOU'RE...CERTAIN?

PRACTICALLY POSITIVE! BUT IT WILL TAKE TIME TO PROVE MY THEORY! *KAL-EL,* THERE'S ONLY ONE HOPE FOR *KRYPTON'S* MILLIONS OF INHABITANTS...

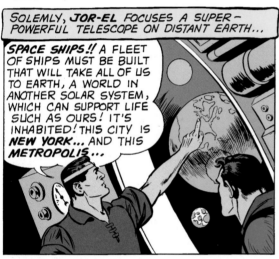

SOLEMNLY, *JOR-EL* FOCUSES A SUPER-POWERFUL TELESCOPE ON DISTANT EARTH...

SPACE SHIPS!! A FLEET OF SHIPS MUST BE BUILT THAT WILL TAKE ALL OF US TO EARTH, A WORLD IN ANOTHER SOLAR SYSTEM, WHICH CAN SUPPORT LIFE SUCH AS OURS! IT'S INHABITED! THIS CITY IS *NEW YORK*... AND THIS *METROPOLIS*...

WHAT IS THE NAME OF THIS SMALL TOWN?

AS IF I DIDN'T KNOW!

SMALLVILLE!...THERE'S A NICE YOUNG COUPLE I'VE BEEN OBSERVING THERE FOR SOME TIME... *JONATHAN KENT* AND *MARTHA HUDSON*...

SOLEMNLY, *JOR-EL* FOCUSES THE SUPER-POWERFUL TELESCOPIC VIEWER, EQUIPPED WITH A LANGUAGE TRANSLATER DEVICE, ON EARTH...

JONATHAN IS A QUIET-SPOKEN YOUNG FARMER, WHO LOVES THE GIRL HE'S COURTING, BUT HE'S GETTING SEVERE COMPETITION FROM GREGG HALLIDAY, A HANDSOME SMOOTH BANKER, WHO RECENTLY ARRIVED IN *SMALLVILLE*...

≒GASP!≒ MY FATHER IS OBSERVING JONATHAN AND MARTHA WHO...

... WILL BECOME MY FOSTER PARENTS WHEN I...ER...AM FLOWN TO EARTH AS A BABY!

THE PITY OF IT IS THAT THE BANKER IS REALLY A SWINDLER WHO HAS HIDDEN STOLEN BONDS IN A SECRET HIDING PLACE INSIDE THAT STATUE OF HIMSELF. HE PLANS TO SKIP WITH HIS DEPOSITORS' FUNDS!

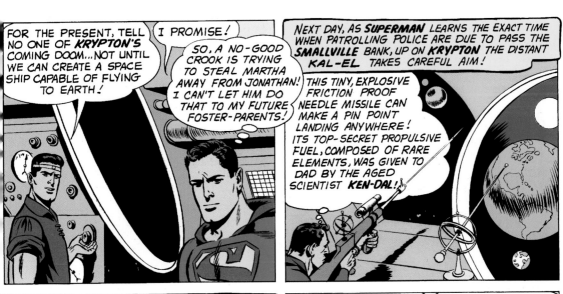

FOR THE PRESENT, TELL NO ONE OF **KRYPTON'S** COMING DOOM...NOT UNTIL WE CAN CREATE A SPACE SHIP CAPABLE OF FLYING TO EARTH!

I PROMISE!

SO, A NO-GOOD CROOK IS TRYING TO STEAL MARTHA AWAY FROM JONATHAN! I CAN'T LET HIM DO THAT TO MY FUTURE FOSTER-PARENTS!

NEXT DAY, AS **SUPERMAN** LEARNS THE EXACT TIME WHEN PATROLLING POLICE ARE DUE TO PASS THE **SMALLVILLE** BANK, UP ON **KRYPTON** THE DISTANT **KAL-EL** TAKES CAREFUL AIM!

THIS TINY, EXPLOSIVE FRICTION PROOF NEEDLE MISSILE CAN MAKE A PIN POINT LANDING ANYWHERE! ITS TOP-SECRET PROPULSIVE FUEL, COMPOSED OF RARE ELEMENTS, WAS GIVEN TO DAD BY THE AGED SCIENTIST **KEN-DAL!**

SPLIT-SECOND TIMING ENABLES THE NEEDLE-MISSILE TO STRIKE JUST AS THE LAW ARRIVES, BUT AT THAT EXACT MOMENT A LIGHTNING BOLT CRASHES DOWNWARD, AND....

STOLEN GOVERNMENT BONDS, BLOWN OUT OF THAT EXPLODING STATUE!

LOOK AT THIS! A "WANTED" PHOTO OF HALLIDAY WAS HIDDEN AMONG THE BONDS! HE'S REALLY "SNARK" McGILL, CONFIDENCE MAN!

THERE GOES "SNARK" WITH THE DEPOSITORS' MONEY! HE SAW WHAT HAPPENED AND IS ESCAPING!

I'LL TAKE CARE OF THAT ROTTEN POLECAT!

SHORTLY...

NO, I WON'T GO OFF WITH YOU AND GET MARRIED! LET GO OF ME!

THEN YOU'LL COME WITH ME AS A HOSTAGE! THE POLICE WON'T DARE SHOOT IF I HAVE A WOMAN PRISONER!

HANDS OFF MY GAL!

JONATHAN! LAND SAKES, I NEVER THOUGHT YOU COULD BE SO FORCEFUL! OH, MY!

POW!

⑦

I LOVE YOU, MARTHA, AND YOU'RE GOING TO MARRY ME RIGHT AWAY, YOU HEAR?

GOODNESS, THE ONLY REASON I EVEN TALKED TO THAT FELLOW WAS TO MAKE YOU SO CRAZY JEALOUS, YOU'D PROPOSE! I'D NEVER HAVE MARRIED ANYONE BUT YOU, ANYWAY, DARLING!

AND UP ON *KRYPTON*...

I FORGOT THAT FATE CAN'T BE CHANGED AND THAT JONATHAN AND MARTHA WOULD HAVE MARRIED, ANYWAY! AND I GUESS THE LAW WOULD'VE CAUGHT "SNARK" ANYWAY, TOO! HMM... I'LL NEVER KNOW WHETHER IT WAS THE NEEDLE-MISSILE, OR THAT LIGHTNING BOLT, WHICH REALLY EXPOSED "SNARK"!

SUDDENLY, AN INSPIRATION IS BORN...

WHO KNOWS? PERHAPS FATE *CAN* BE CHANGED AT THAT! I... WON'T GIVE UP WITHOUT A FIGHT! I'LL TELL *JOR-EL* MY IDEA!

AND SO, LATER...

YOU'RE RIGHT! *KEN-DAL'S* FUEL, WHICH PROPELLED THAT NEEDLE-MISSILE, *COULD* SEND A SPACE ARK TO EARTH! I'M SURE HE'D GIVE US THE LIMITED SUPPLY OF THE FUEL HE HAS AVAILABLE! BUT BUILDING THE ARK WOULD TAKE *YEARS*!

NOT IF YOU GIVE ME CERTAIN MATERIALS AND FIFTY OF YOUR BEST ENGINEERS TO HELP ME BUILD A SUPER-ROBOT!

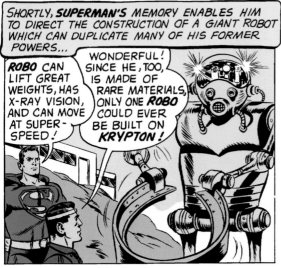

SHORTLY, *SUPERMAN'S* MEMORY ENABLES HIM TO DIRECT THE CONSTRUCTION OF A GIANT ROBOT WHICH CAN DUPLICATE MANY OF HIS FORMER POWERS...

ROBO CAN LIFT GREAT WEIGHTS, HAS X-RAY VISION, AND CAN MOVE AT SUPER-SPEED!

WONDERFUL! SINCE HE, TOO, IS MADE OF RARE MATERIALS, ONLY ONE *ROBO* COULD EVER BE BUILT ON *KRYPTON*!

SOON, THE COLOSSAL ARK BEGINS TO TAKE SHAPE, IN THE CITY WHERE *KAL-EL* LIVES...

THE VITAL ELEMENT IN THE FUEL I INVENTED IS SO RARE ON *KRYPTON*, THERE WILL BE ONLY ENOUGH FUEL TO TAKE THE ARK SAFELY TO EARTH!

HOWEVER, *KEN-DAL*, IF EARTH HAS THE RARE ELEMENT, THE ARK CAN MAKE MANY SUCH TRIPS BACK AND FORTH TO *KRYPTON*, BEFORE OUR WORLD EXPLODES...

8

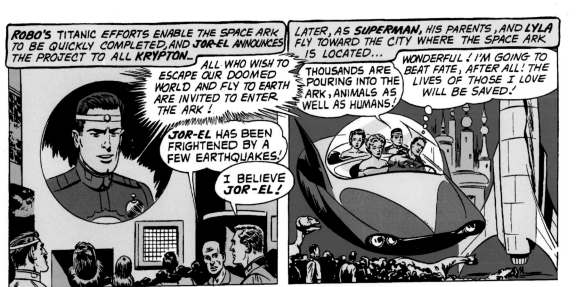

ROBO'S TITANIC EFFORTS ENABLE THE SPACE ARK TO BE QUICKLY COMPLETED, AND JOR-EL ANNOUNCES THE PROJECT TO ALL KRYPTON...

ALL WHO WISH TO ESCAPE OUR DOOMED WORLD AND FLY TO EARTH ARE INVITED TO ENTER THE ARK!

JOR-EL HAS BEEN FRIGHTENED BY A FEW EARTHQUAKES!

I BELIEVE JOR-EL!

LATER, AS SUPERMAN, HIS PARENTS, AND LYLA FLY TOWARD THE CITY WHERE THE SPACE ARK IS LOCATED...

THOUSANDS ARE POURING INTO THE ARK, ANIMALS AS WELL AS HUMANS!

WONDERFUL! I'M GOING TO BEAT FATE, AFTER ALL! THE LIVES OF THOSE I LOVE WILL BE SAVED!

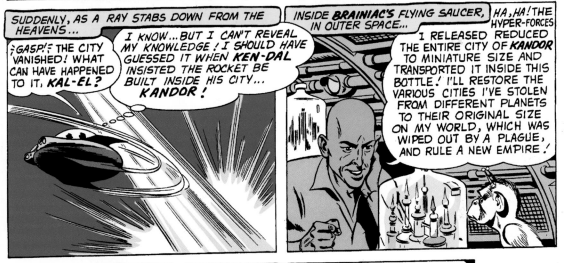

SUDDENLY, AS A RAY STABS DOWN FROM THE HEAVENS...

GASP!: THE CITY VANISHED! WHAT CAN HAVE HAPPENED TO IT, KAL-EL?

I KNOW... BUT I CAN'T REVEAL MY KNOWLEDGE! I SHOULD HAVE GUESSED IT WHEN KEN-DAL INSISTED THE ROCKET BE BUILT INSIDE HIS CITY... KANDOR!

INSIDE BRAINIAC'S FLYING SAUCER, IN OUTER SPACE...

HA, HA! THE HYPER-FORCES I RELEASED REDUCED THE ENTIRE CITY OF KANDOR TO MINIATURE SIZE AND TRANSPORTED IT INSIDE THIS BOTTLE! I'LL RESTORE THE VARIOUS CITIES I'VE STOLEN FROM DIFFERENT PLANETS TO THEIR ORIGINAL SIZE ON MY WORLD, WHICH WAS WIPED OUT BY A PLAGUE, AND RULE A NEW EMPIRE!

MEANWHILE, ON KRYPTON...

WHAT GHASTLY IRONY! THE SPACE ARK... TOGETHER WITH THE ENTIRE CITY OF KANDOR... WAS STOLEN BY THE SPACE VILLAIN BRAINIAC MINUTES BEFORE WE COULD ESCAPE FROM KRYPTON IN THE ARK! THE BOTTLE-CITY OF KANDOR IS FATED TO END UP IN MY FORTRESS OF SOLITUDE, ON EARTH!

SINCE KEN-DAL AND ROBO WERE BOTH IN THE VANISHED ROCKET, AND KEN-DAL NEVER REVEALED THE SECRET OF HIS RARE FUEL TO ANYONE ELSE, ANOTHER ARK CAN'T BE BUILT IN TIME! :CHOKE: WE'RE ALL... DOOMED...!

UNFORTUNATELY, SUPERMAN'S DESPERATE ATTEMPT TO FOIL FATE AND RESCUE THE KRYPTONIANS HAS FAILED! SEE PART III FOR THE AMAZING, UNFORGETTABLE ENDING!

⑨

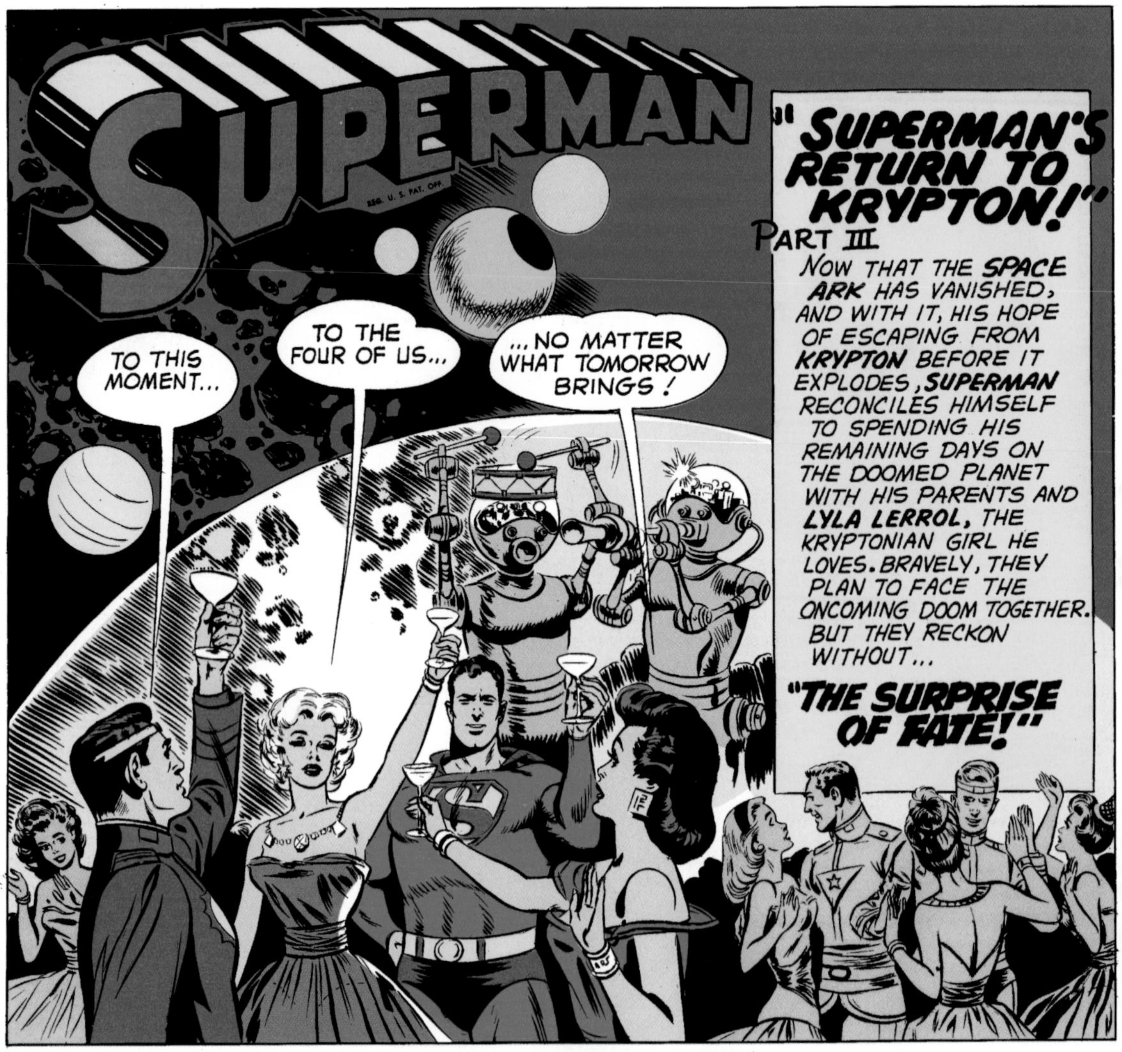
SUPERMAN
REG. U. S. PAT. OFF.
"SUPERMAN'S RETURN TO KRYPTON!"
PART III
NOW THAT THE SPACE ARK HAS VANISHED, AND WITH IT, HIS HOPE OF ESCAPING FROM KRYPTON BEFORE IT EXPLODES, SUPERMAN RECONCILES HIMSELF TO SPENDING HIS REMAINING DAYS ON THE DOOMED PLANET WITH HIS PARENTS AND LYLA LERROL, THE KRYPTONIAN GIRL HE LOVES. BRAVELY, THEY PLAN TO FACE THE ONCOMING DOOM TOGETHER. BUT THEY RECKON WITHOUT...
"THE SURPRISE OF FATE!"
TO THIS MOMENT...
TO THE FOUR OF US...
...NO MATTER WHAT TOMORROW BRINGS!

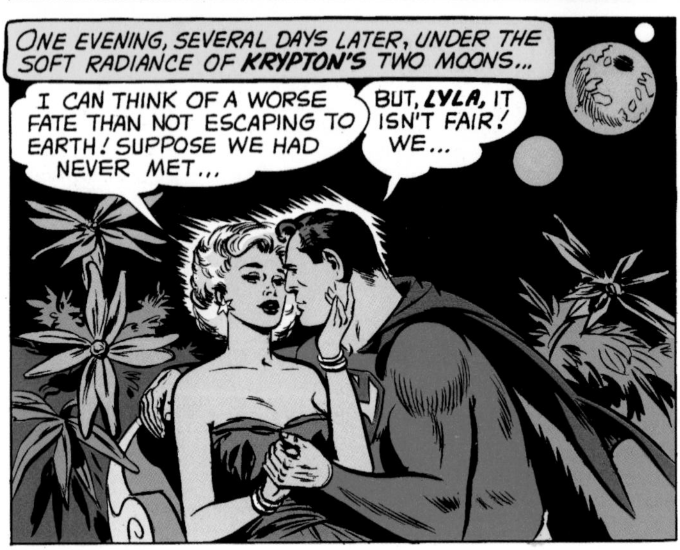
ONE EVENING, SEVERAL DAYS LATER, UNDER THE SOFT RADIANCE OF KRYPTON'S TWO MOONS...
I CAN THINK OF A WORSE FATE THAN NOT ESCAPING TO EARTH! SUPPOSE WE HAD NEVER MET...
BUT, LYLA, IT ISN'T FAIR! WE...

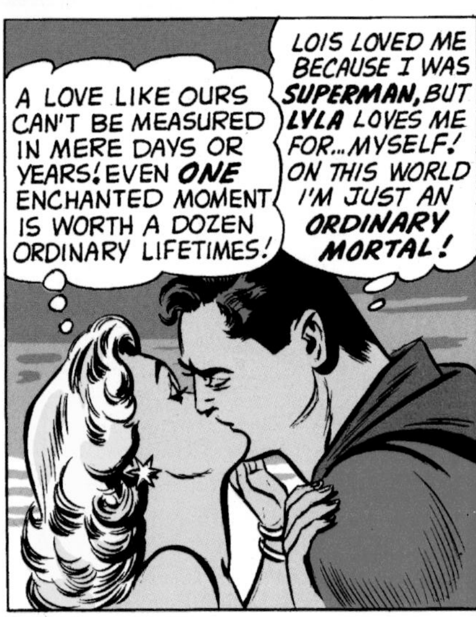
A LOVE LIKE OURS CAN'T BE MEASURED IN MERE DAYS OR YEARS! EVEN ONE ENCHANTED MOMENT IS WORTH A DOZEN ORDINARY LIFETIMES!
LOIS LOVED ME BECAUSE I WAS SUPERMAN, BUT LYLA LOVES ME FOR... MYSELF! ON THIS WORLD I'M JUST AN ORDINARY MORTAL!

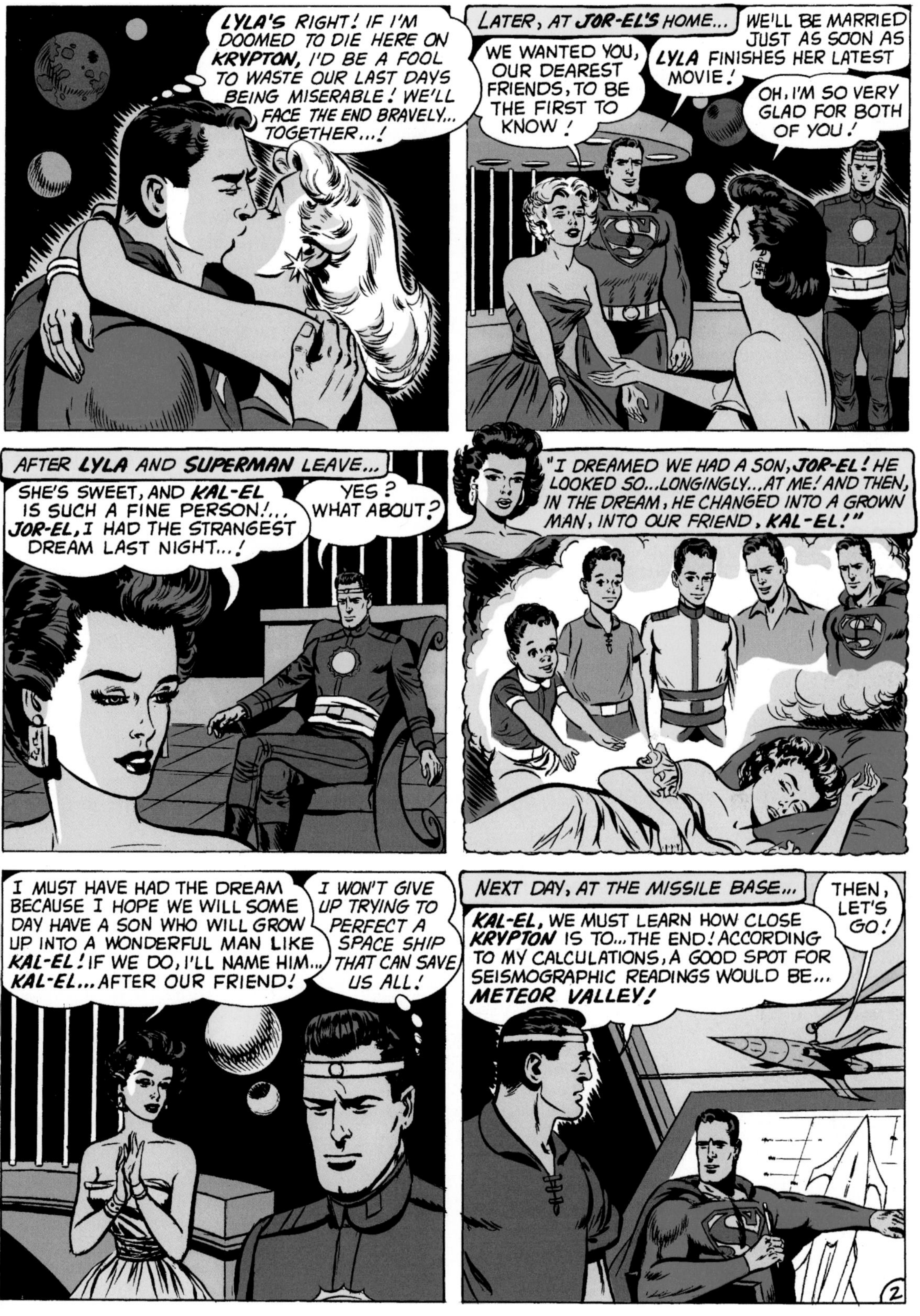
LYLA'S RIGHT! IF I'M DOOMED TO DIE HERE ON KRYPTON, I'D BE A FOOL TO WASTE OUR LAST DAYS BEING MISERABLE! WE'LL FACE THE END BRAVELY... TOGETHER...!
LATER, AT JOR-EL'S HOME...
WE WANTED YOU, OUR DEAREST FRIENDS, TO BE THE FIRST TO KNOW!
WE'LL BE MARRIED JUST AS SOON AS LYLA FINISHES HER LATEST MOVIE!
OH, I'M SO VERY GLAD FOR BOTH OF YOU!
AFTER LYLA AND SUPERMAN LEAVE...
SHE'S SWEET, AND KAL-EL IS SUCH A FINE PERSON!... JOR-EL, I HAD THE STRANGEST DREAM LAST NIGHT...!
YES? WHAT ABOUT?
"I DREAMED WE HAD A SON, JOR-EL! HE LOOKED SO...LONGINGLY...AT ME! AND THEN, IN THE DREAM, HE CHANGED INTO A GROWN MAN, INTO OUR FRIEND, KAL-EL!"
I MUST HAVE HAD THE DREAM BECAUSE I HOPE WE WILL SOME DAY HAVE A SON WHO WILL GROW UP INTO A WONDERFUL MAN LIKE KAL-EL! IF WE DO, I'LL NAME HIM... KAL-EL... AFTER OUR FRIEND!
I WON'T GIVE UP TRYING TO PERFECT A SPACE SHIP THAT CAN SAVE US ALL!
NEXT DAY, AT THE MISSILE BASE...
KAL-EL, WE MUST LEARN HOW CLOSE KRYPTON IS TO...THE END! ACCORDING TO MY CALCULATIONS, A GOOD SPOT FOR SEISMOGRAPHIC READINGS WOULD BE... METEOR VALLEY!
THEN, LET'S GO!
2

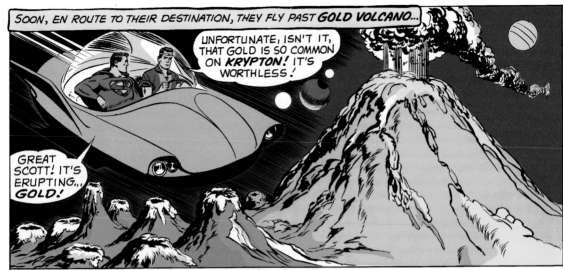

SOON, EN ROUTE TO THEIR DESTINATION, THEY FLY PAST *GOLD VOLCANO*...

UNFORTUNATE, ISN'T IT, THAT GOLD IS SO COMMON ON *KRYPTON!* IT'S WORTHLESS!

GREAT SCOTT! IT'S ERUPTING... *GOLD!*

MINUTES LATER, THEY SOAR OVER *FIRE FALLS*...

OUR PLANET'S INNER FIRES, POURING THROUGH A FISSURE, CREATE QUITE A SPECTACULAR SIGHT, DON'T THEY?

WEIRD!

PRESENTLY, THEIR PLANE LANDS AT THE RIM OF *METEOR VALLEY.*

LONG BEFORE LIFE EXISTED ON *KRYPTON,* THIS VALLEY WAS CREATED BY A MONSTROUSLY GIGANTIC METEOR THAT GLANCED OFF THE SURFACE OF OUR WORLD...

DOWN INTO THE VALLEY THEY DESCEND WITH THEIR PORTABLE EQUIPMENT, THEN...

MILD TREMORS OCCUR HERE QUITE FREQUENTLY! I BELIEVE ONE'S STARTING NOW...

THIS ONE *ISN'T* MILD!

GREAT BOULDERS HAVE BEEN JARRED LOOSE AT THE CRATER'S RIM AND ARE CRASHING DOWN AT US! WE'LL DIE!

IF I STILL HAD MY SUPER-POWERS, THIS WOULD BE NO PROBLEM!

3

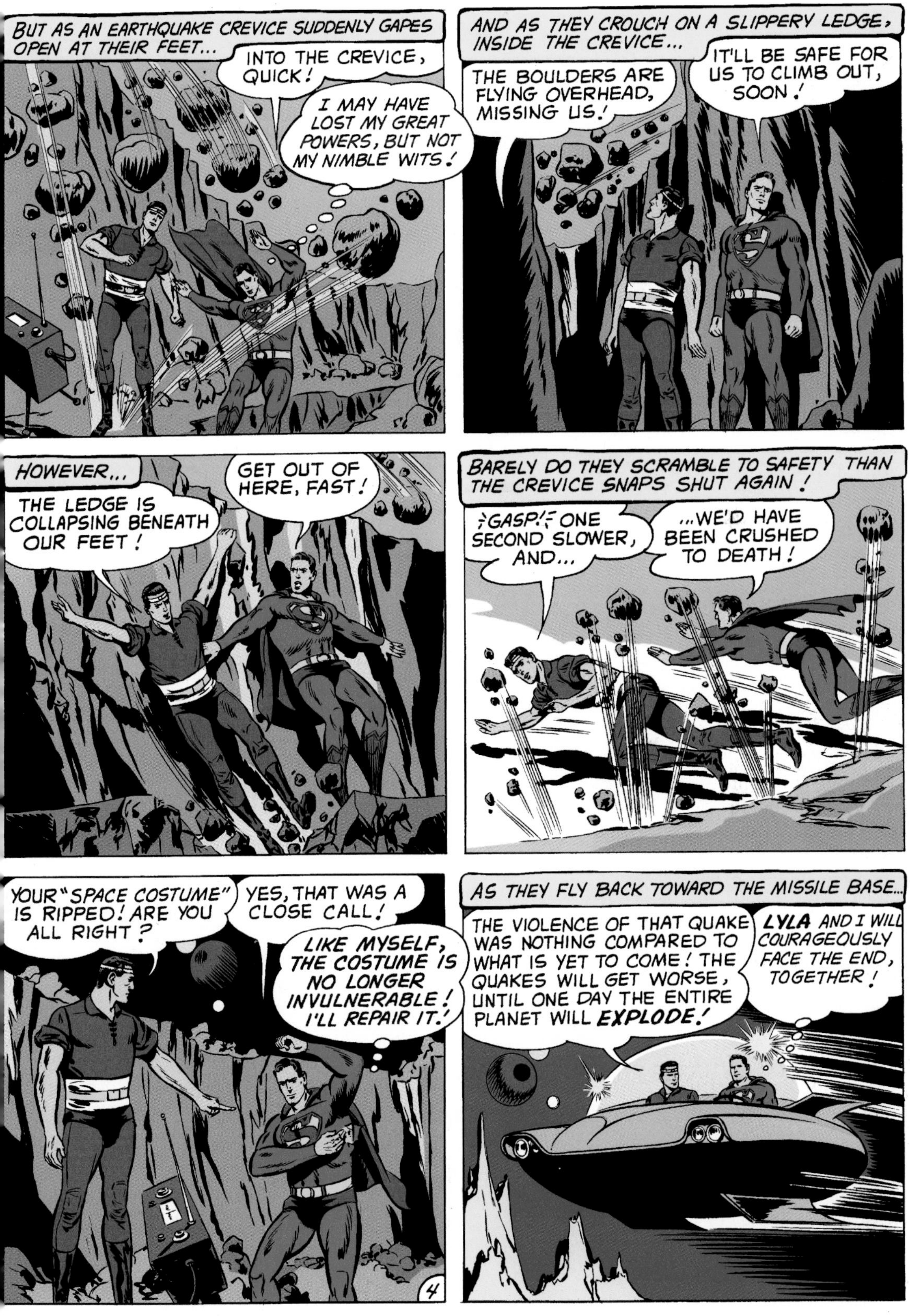
BUT AS AN EARTHQUAKE CREVICE SUDDENLY GAPES OPEN AT THEIR FEET...
INTO THE CREVICE, QUICK!
I MAY HAVE LOST MY GREAT POWERS, BUT NOT MY NIMBLE WITS!
AND AS THEY CROUCH ON A SLIPPERY LEDGE, INSIDE THE CREVICE...
THE BOULDERS ARE FLYING OVERHEAD, MISSING US!
IT'LL BE SAFE FOR US TO CLIMB OUT, SOON!
HOWEVER...
THE LEDGE IS COLLAPSING BENEATH OUR FEET!
GET OUT OF HERE, FAST!
BARELY DO THEY SCRAMBLE TO SAFETY THAN THE CREVICE SNAPS SHUT AGAIN!
-GASP!- ONE SECOND SLOWER, AND...
...WE'D HAVE BEEN CRUSHED TO DEATH!
YOUR "SPACE COSTUME" IS RIPPED! ARE YOU ALL RIGHT?
YES, THAT WAS A CLOSE CALL!
LIKE MYSELF, THE COSTUME IS NO LONGER INVULNERABLE! I'LL REPAIR IT.
4
AS THEY FLY BACK TOWARD THE MISSILE BASE...
THE VIOLENCE OF THAT QUAKE WAS NOTHING COMPARED TO WHAT IS YET TO COME! THE QUAKES WILL GET WORSE, UNTIL ONE DAY THE ENTIRE PLANET WILL EXPLODE!
LYLA AND I WILL COURAGEOUSLY FACE THE END, TOGETHER!

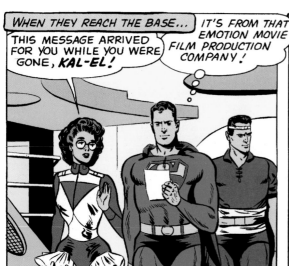

WHEN THEY REACH THE BASE... THIS MESSAGE ARRIVED FOR YOU WHILE YOU WERE GONE, *KAL-EL!*

IT'S FROM THAT EMOTION MOVIE FILM PRODUCTION COMPANY!

READING THE MESSAGE, *SUPERMAN* TELE-CALLS *LYLA*...

YES, I'VE BEEN NOTIFIED TO REPORT BACK FOR THE SHOOTING OF THE MOVIE'S FINAL SCENES, TOO!

AFTER THE FILMING IS COMPLETED IN A DAY OR SO, WE'LL GET MARRIED IMMEDIATELY!

THAT NIGHT, AT THE *SKY PALACE,* A NIGHTCLUB WHICH FLOATS ABOVE *KRYPTON* BY ANTIGRAVITY FORCES...

THE HAPPINESS WE'LL SHARE AS HUSBAND AND WIFE, *LYLA,* WILL MORE THAN COMPENSATE FOR WHATEVER HAPPENS...LATER!

THEY'RE SO IN LOVE, *JOR-EL,* IT'S A SHAME THAT...

DON'T SAY IT, *LARA!* WORLDS MAY CRUMBLE...CIVILIZATIONS PERISH! BUT LOVE...LIKE THEIRS AND *OURS*...WILL ALWAYS EXIST IN THE UNIVERSE!

ON THROUGH SPACE ROTATES *KRYPTON,* TOWARD ITS INEXORABLE RENDEZVOUS WITH A CRUEL DESTINY, BUT AT THE *SKY PALACE,* TWO PAIRS OF LOVERS PROPOSE A TOAST, GALLANTLY UNAFRAID...

TO THIS MOMENT...!

TO THE FOUR OF US...!

...NO MATTER WHAT TOMORROW BRINGS!

5

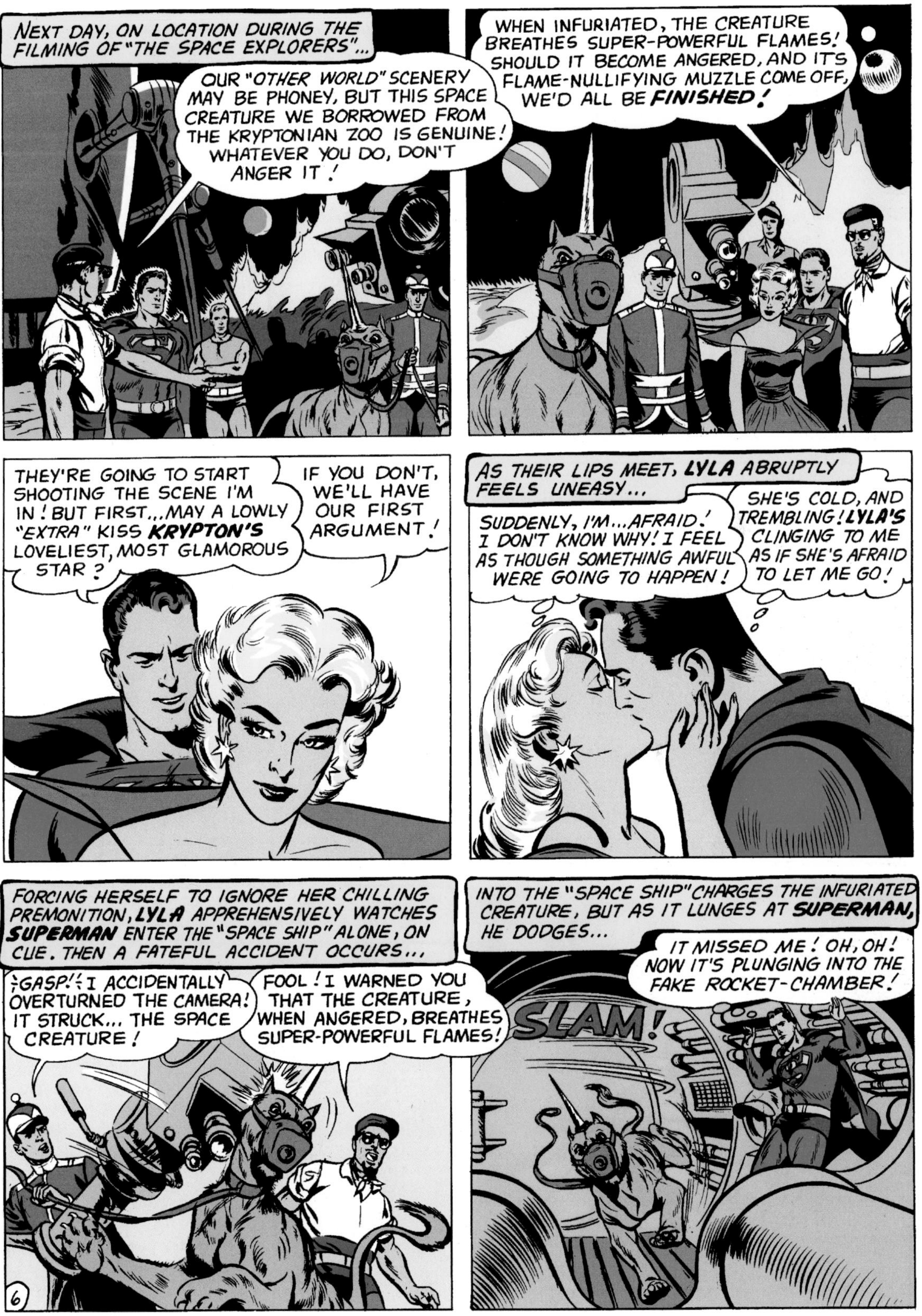
NEXT DAY, ON LOCATION DURING THE FILMING OF "THE SPACE EXPLORERS"...
OUR "OTHER WORLD" SCENERY MAY BE PHONEY, BUT THIS SPACE CREATURE WE BORROWED FROM THE KRYPTONIAN ZOO IS GENUINE! WHATEVER YOU DO, DON'T ANGER IT!
WHEN INFURIATED, THE CREATURE BREATHES SUPER-POWERFUL FLAMES! SHOULD IT BECOME ANGERED, AND IT'S FLAME-NULLIFYING MUZZLE COME OFF, WE'D ALL BE FINISHED!
THEY'RE GOING TO START SHOOTING THE SCENE I'M IN! BUT FIRST... MAY A LOWLY "EXTRA" KISS KRYPTON'S LOVELIEST, MOST GLAMOROUS STAR?
IF YOU DON'T, WE'LL HAVE OUR FIRST ARGUMENT!
AS THEIR LIPS MEET, LYLA ABRUPTLY FEELS UNEASY...
SUDDENLY, I'M... AFRAID! I DON'T KNOW WHY! I FEEL AS THOUGH SOMETHING AWFUL WERE GOING TO HAPPEN!
SHE'S COLD, AND TREMBLING! LYLA'S CLINGING TO ME AS IF SHE'S AFRAID TO LET ME GO!
FORCING HERSELF TO IGNORE HER CHILLING PREMONITION, LYLA APPREHENSIVELY WATCHES SUPERMAN ENTER THE "SPACE SHIP" ALONE, ON CUE. THEN A FATEFUL ACCIDENT OCCURS...
÷GASP!÷ I ACCIDENTALLY OVERTURNED THE CAMERA! IT STRUCK... THE SPACE CREATURE!
FOOL! I WARNED YOU THAT THE CREATURE, WHEN ANGERED, BREATHES SUPER-POWERFUL FLAMES!
6
INTO THE "SPACE SHIP" CHARGES THE INFURIATED CREATURE, BUT AS IT LUNGES AT SUPERMAN, HE DODGES...
IT MISSED ME! OH, OH! NOW IT'S PLUNGING INTO THE FAKE ROCKET-CHAMBER!
SLAM!

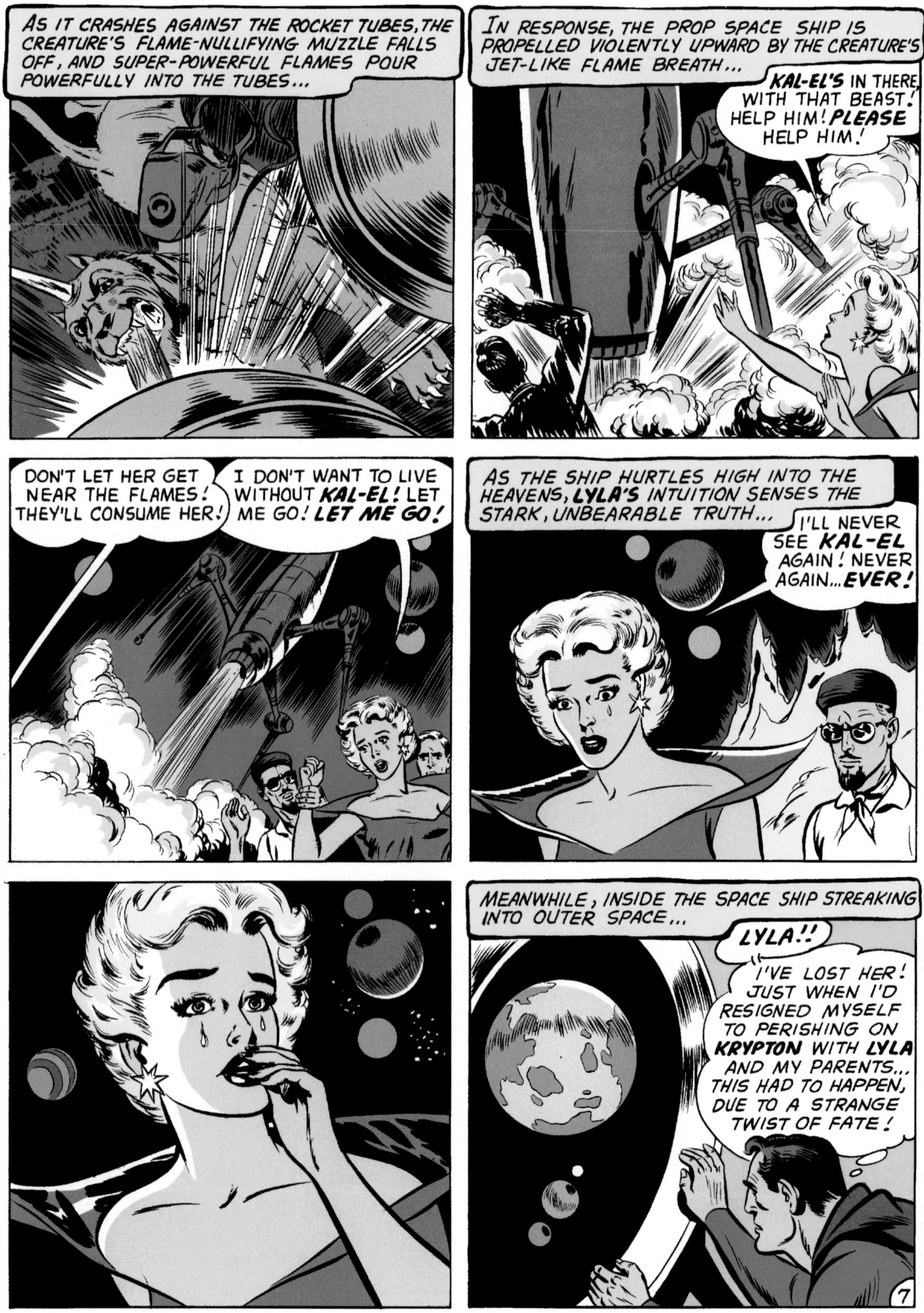
AS IT CRASHES AGAINST THE ROCKET TUBES, THE CREATURE'S FLAME-NULLIFYING MUZZLE FALLS OFF, AND SUPER-POWERFUL FLAMES POUR POWERFULLY INTO THE TUBES...
IN RESPONSE, THE PROP SPACE SHIP IS PROPELLED VIOLENTLY UPWARD BY THE CREATURE'S JET-LIKE FLAME BREATH...
KAL-EL'S IN THERE, WITH THAT BEAST! HELP HIM! PLEASE HELP HIM!
DON'T LET HER GET NEAR THE FLAMES! THEY'LL CONSUME HER!
I DON'T WANT TO LIVE WITHOUT KAL-EL! LET ME GO! LET ME GO!
AS THE SHIP HURTLES HIGH INTO THE HEAVENS, LYLA'S INTUITION SENSES THE STARK, UNBEARABLE TRUTH...
I'LL NEVER SEE KAL-EL AGAIN! NEVER AGAIN...EVER!
MEANWHILE, INSIDE THE SPACE SHIP STREAKING INTO OUTER SPACE...
LYLA!!
I'VE LOST HER! JUST WHEN I'D RESIGNED MYSELF TO PERISHING ON KRYPTON WITH LYLA AND MY PARENTS... THIS HAD TO HAPPEN, DUE TO A STRANGE TWIST OF FATE!
7

LATER, FAR OUT IN SPACE, AS THE SPACE SHIP IS ATTRACTED BY THE GRAVITY OF A **YELLOW** SUN...

THE YELLOW SUN'S SUPER-ENERGY RAYS HAVE RETURNED MY SUPER-POWERS!

FOR ONE MOMENT, THE **MAN OF STEEL** HESITATES...

IF I RETURN TO **KRYPTON**, I WILL LOSE MY SUPER-POWERS AGAIN! FATE CAN'T BE CHANGED! IT'S IMPOSSIBLE FOR ME TO SAVE **LYLA** OR MY PARENTS! EARTH NEEDS ME!

THROUGH THE TIME-BARRIER FLASHES **SUPERMAN** AT INCREDIBLE SUPER-SPEED...

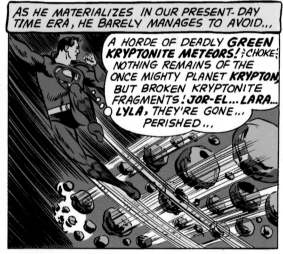

AS HE MATERIALIZES IN OUR PRESENT-DAY TIME ERA, HE BARELY MANAGES TO AVOID...

A HORDE OF DEADLY **GREEN KRYPTONITE METEORS!** *CHOKE!* NOTHING REMAINS OF THE ONCE MIGHTY PLANET **KRYPTON**, BUT BROKEN KRYPTONITE FRAGMENTS! **JOR-EL...LARA... LYLA**, THEY'RE GONE... PERISHED...

TOWARD EARTH FLIES THE **MAN OF STEEL**...

I'LL ALWAYS TREASURE MY RETURN TO **KRYPTON**, SEEING MY PARENTS AGAIN, AND MEETING...AND LOVING...**LYLA!** BEAUTIFULLY RADIANT, COURAGEOUS **LYLA!**

8

AND AS **SUPERMAN** REACHES **METROPOLIS**.

BUT ALREADY IT ALL SEEMS LIKE A STRANGE, INCREDIBLE DREAM! ...SOON, I'LL SEE **LOIS LANE, JIMMY OLSEN** AND MY OTHER FRIENDS, AGAIN! IT'S GOOD TO HAVE...A SECOND HOME...

END

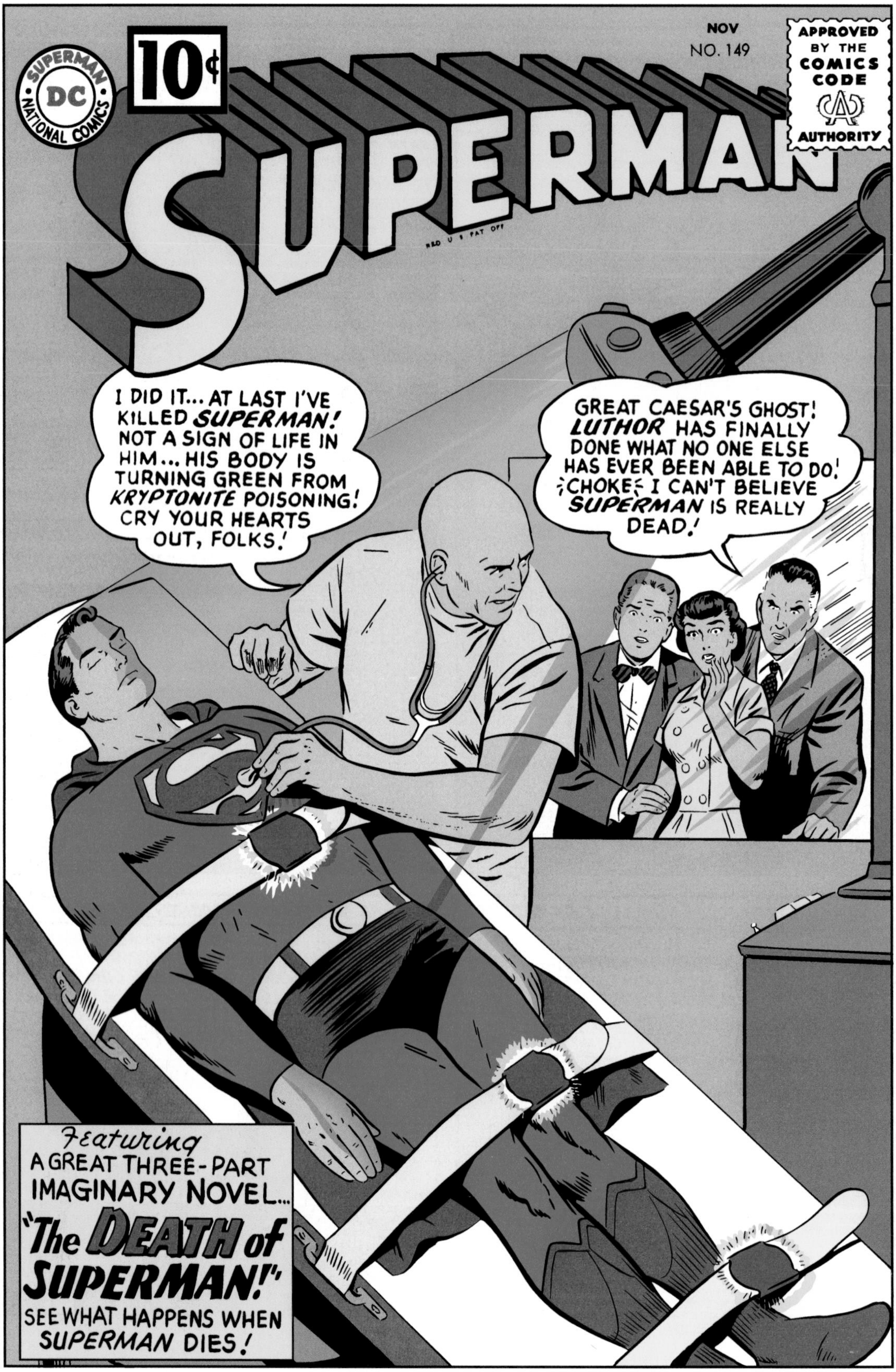
SUPERMAN NATIONAL COMICS DC
10¢
NOV
NO. 149
APPROVED BY THE COMICS CODE AUTHORITY
SUPERMAN
I DID IT... AT LAST I'VE KILLED SUPERMAN! NOT A SIGN OF LIFE IN HIM... HIS BODY IS TURNING GREEN FROM KRYPTONITE POISONING! CRY YOUR HEARTS OUT, FOLKS!
GREAT CAESAR'S GHOST! LUTHOR HAS FINALLY DONE WHAT NO ONE ELSE HAS EVER BEEN ABLE TO DO! CHOKE! I CAN'T BELIEVE SUPERMAN IS REALLY DEAD!
Featuring A GREAT THREE-PART IMAGINARY NOVEL... "The DEATH of SUPERMAN!" SEE WHAT HAPPENS WHEN SUPERMAN DIES!

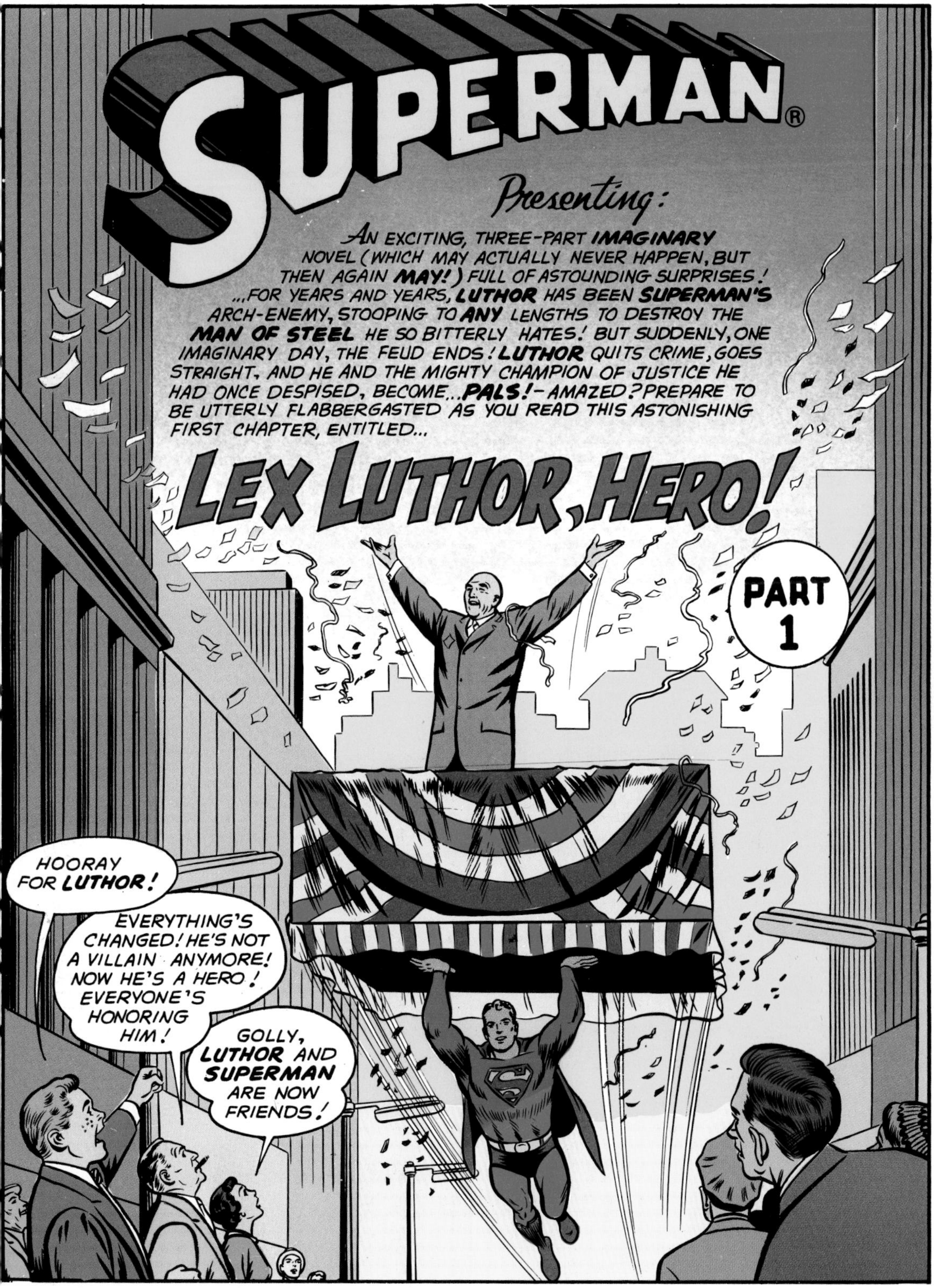
SUPERMAN®
Presenting:
AN EXCITING, THREE-PART IMAGINARY NOVEL (WHICH MAY ACTUALLY NEVER HAPPEN, BUT THEN AGAIN MAY!) FULL OF ASTOUNDING SURPRISES! ...FOR YEARS AND YEARS, LUTHOR HAS BEEN SUPERMAN'S ARCH-ENEMY, STOOPING TO ANY LENGTHS TO DESTROY THE MAN OF STEEL HE SO BITTERLY HATES! BUT SUDDENLY, ONE IMAGINARY DAY, THE FEUD ENDS! LUTHOR QUITS CRIME, GOES STRAIGHT, AND HE AND THE MIGHTY CHAMPION OF JUSTICE HE HAD ONCE DESPISED, BECOME...PALS!-AMAZED? PREPARE TO BE UTTERLY FLABBERGASTED AS YOU READ THIS ASTONISHING FIRST CHAPTER, ENTITLED...
LEX LUTHOR, HERO!
PART 1
HOORAY FOR LUTHOR!
EVERYTHING'S CHANGED! HE'S NOT A VILLAIN ANYMORE! NOW HE'S A HERO! EVERYONE'S HONORING HIM!
GOLLY, LUTHOR AND SUPERMAN ARE NOW FRIENDS!

ONE AFTERNOON AT *METROPOLIS* PRISON, ON AN *IMAGINARY* DAY, THAT MAY *OR MAY NOT* EVER HAPPEN, AS *SUPERMAN'S* ARCH-FOE, CONVICT LEX *LUTHOR*, STROLLS ON AN ERRAND...

THAT STRANGELY GLOWING ROCK MIXED IN WITH ALL THE OTHER BOULDERS, I WONDER...

KEEP WALKING, *LUTHOR!*

SUDDENLY...

YOU'VE GOT A BIG MOUTH, SYKES! I THINK I'LL SHUT IT!

HOLY CATS! *LUTHOR* SOCKED A GUARD! THEY'LL THROW THE BOOK AT HIM!

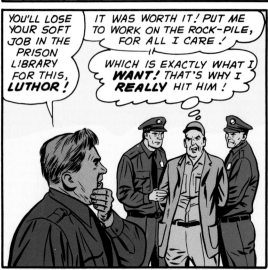

YOU'LL LOSE YOUR SOFT JOB IN THE PRISON LIBRARY FOR THIS, *LUTHOR!*

IT WAS WORTH IT! PUT ME TO WORK ON THE ROCK-PILE, FOR ALL I CARE!

WHICH IS EXACTLY WHAT I *WANT!* THAT'S WHY I *REALLY* HIT HIM!

NEXT DAY...

SATISFIED, CON?

YOU BET! NOW I CAN SECRETLY EXAMINE THIS GLOWING ROCK!

HMMM — JUST AS I SUSPECTED! THIS IS NO ORDINARY ROCK! ITS PITTED SURFACE REVEALS IT'S A METEOR FROM OUTER SPACE! I'LL SLIP A HANDFUL OF THE CRUSHED STUFF INTO MY *POCKET*, UNSEEN!

THAT NIGHT, IN THE RENEGADE SCIENTIST'S CELL...

THE METEOR GRANULES EMANATE A TWINKLING, MULTI-COLORED BRILLIANCE IN THE DARK, AND FEEL *WARM* TO THE TOUCH! I'VE A STRONG HUNCH THIS IS *ELEMENT "Z"...!!*

"ELEMENT Z" IS A MYSTERIOUS CHEMICAL SUBSTANCE WHICH I'VE LONG-BELIEVED EXISTED ELSEWHERE IN THE UNIVERSE! -- IF "ELEMENT Z" HAS NOW REACHED EARTH, THEN I'M ON THE THRESHOLD OF A TREMENDOUS DISCOVERY...!

NEXT MORNING, IN THE WARDEN'S OFFICE...

LUTHOR, YOU'RE OUT OF YOUR MIND, TO MAKE SUCH A REQUEST!

ALL I ASK, SIR, IS ...LET ME USE THE PRISON HOSPITAL'S LABORATORY FACILITIES FOR 24 HOURS!

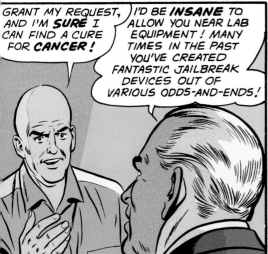

GRANT MY REQUEST, AND I'M SURE I CAN FIND A CURE FOR CANCER!

I'D BE INSANE TO ALLOW YOU NEAR LAB EQUIPMENT! MANY TIMES IN THE PAST YOU'VE CREATED FANTASTIC JAILBREAK DEVICES OUT OF VARIOUS ODDS-AND-ENDS!

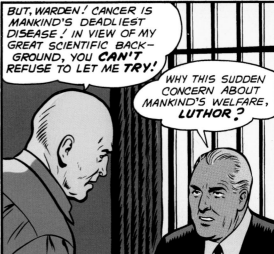

BUT, WARDEN! CANCER IS MANKIND'S DEADLIEST DISEASE! IN VIEW OF MY GREAT SCIENTIFIC BACK-GROUND, YOU CAN'T REFUSE TO LET ME TRY!

WHY THIS SUDDEN CONCERN ABOUT MANKIND'S WELFARE, LUTHOR?

ALL YOUR LIFE YOU'VE TRIED TO CRUSH AND RULE MANKIND WITH ONE MAD INVENTION AFTER ANOTHER! YOU'D HAVE SUCCEEDED, TOO, EXCEPT FOR SUPERMAN!

THAT'S WHY THIS EXPERIMENT MEANS SO MUCH TO ME!

Regards from Superman

I REALIZE AT LAST HOW WRONG I'VE BEEN TO USE MY GREAT BRAIN TO FIGHT, RATHER THAN AID, MANKIND! PLEASE GIVE ME THIS CHANCE TO ATONE...!

OKAY! 24 HOURS! --BUT YOU'LL BE CLOSELY GUARDED EVERY SECOND!

3

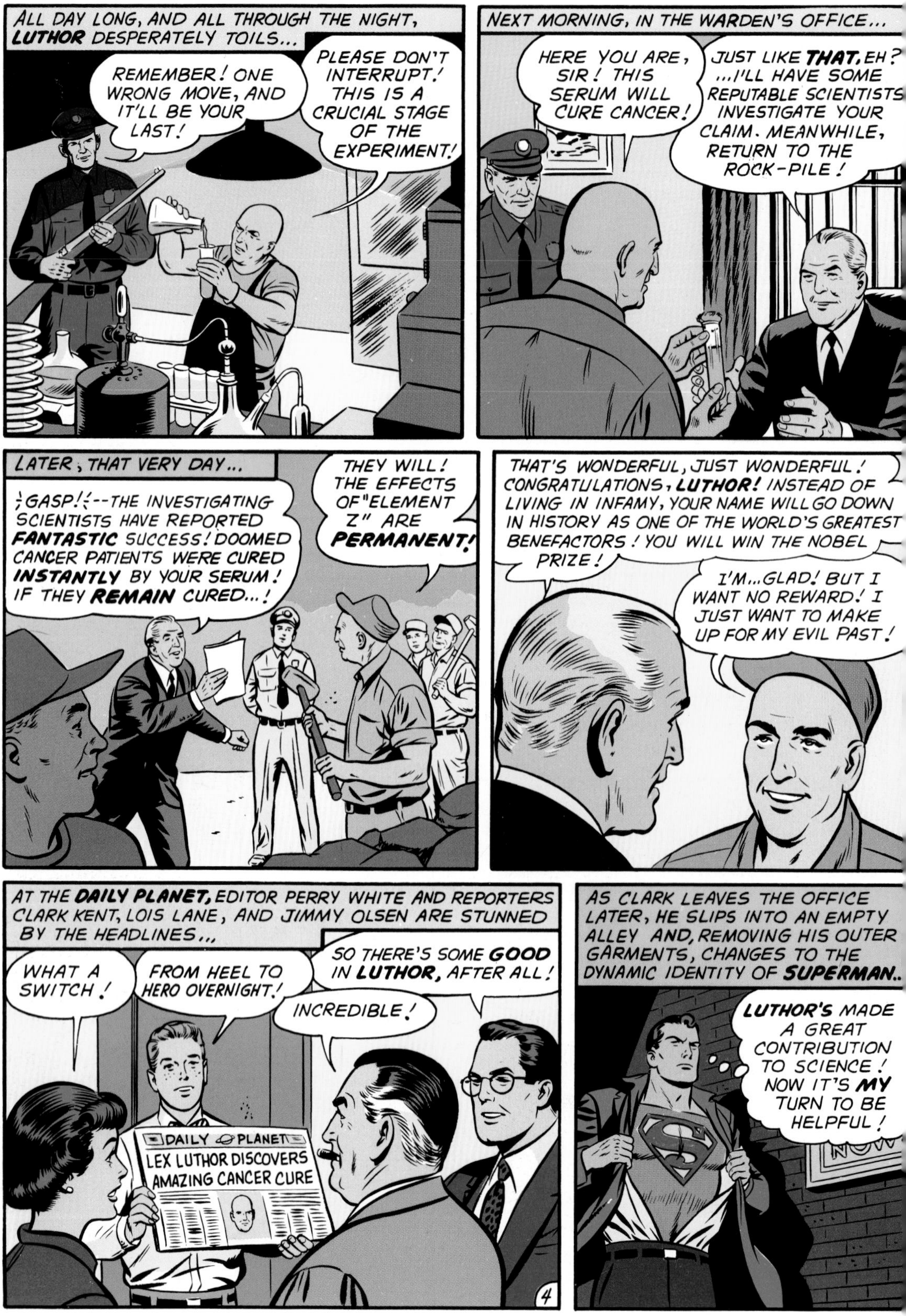
ALL DAY LONG, AND ALL THROUGH THE NIGHT, LUTHOR DESPERATELY TOILS...
REMEMBER! ONE WRONG MOVE, AND IT'LL BE YOUR LAST!
PLEASE DON'T INTERRUPT! THIS IS A CRUCIAL STAGE OF THE EXPERIMENT!
NEXT MORNING, IN THE WARDEN'S OFFICE...
HERE YOU ARE, SIR! THIS SERUM WILL CURE CANCER!
JUST LIKE THAT, EH? ...I'LL HAVE SOME REPUTABLE SCIENTISTS INVESTIGATE YOUR CLAIM. MEANWHILE, RETURN TO THE ROCK-PILE!
LATER, THAT VERY DAY...
-GASP!- --THE INVESTIGATING SCIENTISTS HAVE REPORTED FANTASTIC SUCCESS! DOOMED CANCER PATIENTS WERE CURED INSTANTLY BY YOUR SERUM! IF THEY REMAIN CURED...!
THEY WILL! THE EFFECTS OF "ELEMENT Z" ARE PERMANENT!
THAT'S WONDERFUL, JUST WONDERFUL! CONGRATULATIONS, LUTHOR! INSTEAD OF LIVING IN INFAMY, YOUR NAME WILL GO DOWN IN HISTORY AS ONE OF THE WORLD'S GREATEST BENEFACTORS! YOU WILL WIN THE NOBEL PRIZE!
I'M...GLAD! BUT I WANT NO REWARD! I JUST WANT TO MAKE UP FOR MY EVIL PAST!
AT THE DAILY PLANET, EDITOR PERRY WHITE AND REPORTERS CLARK KENT, LOIS LANE, AND JIMMY OLSEN ARE STUNNED BY THE HEADLINES...
WHAT A SWITCH!
FROM HEEL TO HERO OVERNIGHT!
INCREDIBLE!
SO THERE'S SOME GOOD IN LUTHOR, AFTER ALL!
DAILY PLANET
LEX LUTHOR DISCOVERS AMAZING CANCER CURE
4
AS CLARK LEAVES THE OFFICE LATER, HE SLIPS INTO AN EMPTY ALLEY AND, REMOVING HIS OUTER GARMENTS, CHANGES TO THE DYNAMIC IDENTITY OF SUPERMAN..
LUTHOR'S MADE A GREAT CONTRIBUTION TO SCIENCE! NOW IT'S MY TURN TO BE HELPFUL!

FAR OFF INTO OUTER SPACE STREAKS THE *MAN OF STEEL,* COMBING THE COSMOS FOR THE PRECIOUS ELEMENT, UNTIL...

LUTHOR SAYS THE WORLD NEEDS MORE "*ELEMENT Z*", HMMM... MY MICROSCOPIC VISION REVEALS THIS GREAT METEOR SWARM CONTAINS "*ELEMENT Z*"! I RECOGNIZE IT FROM PUBLISHED DESCRIPTIONS OF ITS PROPERTIES...

SWIFTLY, *SUPERMAN* RAMS THE SWARM TOGETHER, FORMING IT INTO A GREAT BALL...

THEY SAY NO ONE IS *COMPLETELY* BAD! I GUESS THAT INCLUDES *LUTHOR,* TOO!

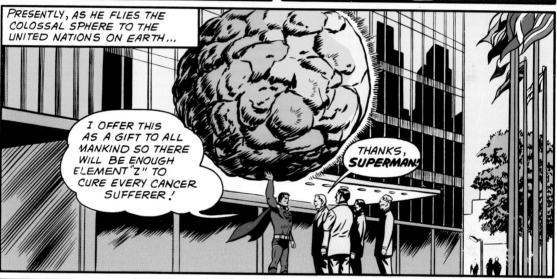

PRESENTLY, AS HE FLIES THE COLOSSAL SPHERE TO THE UNITED NATIONS ON EARTH...

I OFFER THIS AS A GIFT TO ALL MANKIND SO THERE WILL BE ENOUGH ELEMENT "Z" TO CURE EVERY CANCER SUFFERER!

THANKS, *SUPERMAN!*

DAYS LATER, AS *LUTHOR* IS SUMMONED BEFORE THE PRISON'S PAROLE BOARD...

FRANKLY, *LUTHOR,* SOME OF US QUESTION THE SINCERITY OF YOUR REFORMATION...

MAY *I* SPEAK, GENTLEMEN?

SUPERMAN!

⑤

BY ALL MEANS, PLEASE DO SPEAK, *SUPERMAN!* WE'D LIKE THE OPINION OF THE MAN WHOM *LUTHOR* TRIED TO DESTROY SO OFTEN!... *SHOULD* HE BE FREED?

AS I UNDERSTAND IT, *LUTHOR* SAYS HE REPENTS HIS EVIL PAST...

...AND WANTS TO SPEND THE REST OF HIS LIFE *HELPING* HUMANITY, INSTEAD OF HARMING IT! — HE HAS CONQUERED CANCER. WHO CAN SAY WHAT OTHER BLESSINGS HIS MARVELOUS INTELLECT CAN PERFORM FOR MANKIND? I SAY *LUTHOR* SHOULD GET A CHANCE TO GO STRAIGHT!

MINUTES AFTERWARD...

PAROLE GRANTED!

...*CHOKE*! ...THIS IS THE *HAPPIEST* MOMENT OF MY LIFE!

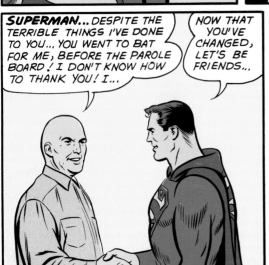

SUPERMAN...DESPITE THE TERRIBLE THINGS I'VE DONE TO YOU...YOU WENT TO BAT FOR ME, BEFORE THE PAROLE BOARD! I DON'T KNOW HOW TO THANK YOU! I...

NOW THAT YOU'VE CHANGED, LET'S BE FRIENDS...

LATER, AS *LUTHOR* LEAVES THROUGH THE PRISON'S GATES...

IF THERE'S ANY WAY I CAN HELP YOU GET A NEW START...

I'D APPRECIATE IT IF YOU WOULD FLY ME TO MY FORMER SECRET HEADQUARTERS!

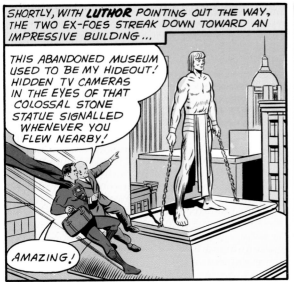

SHORTLY, WITH *LUTHOR* POINTING OUT THE WAY, THE TWO EX-FOES STREAK DOWN TOWARD AN IMPRESSIVE BUILDING...

THIS ABANDONED MUSEUM USED TO BE MY HIDEOUT! HIDDEN TV CAMERAS IN THE EYES OF THAT COLOSSAL STONE STATUE SIGNALLED WHENEVER YOU FLEW NEARBY!

AMAZING!

AND AS THEY ALIGHT...

A SHAKE OF "CAESAR'S" HAND OPENS A SECRET DOORWAY INTO...*LUTHOR'S LAIR!* SINCE I'M QUITTING CRIME FOREVER, I'M NOW GLAD TO SHOW THIS TO YOU!

TO BE DEMOLISHED AT SOME FUTURE DATE

6

SOON, INSIDE...

HOW WARPED I USED TO BE! BEHOLD MY **HALL OF HEROES**! **ATILLA THE HUN...GENGHIS KHAN... CAPTAIN KIDD...AL CAPONE**! I CAN'T STAND THE SIGHT OF THEM ANY MORE! PLEASE DESTROY THE STATUES!

OKAY—IF THAT'S ALL YOU WANT!

ATILLA THE HUN GENGHIS KHAN CAPTAIN KIDD AL CAPONE

I'M HAPPY TO SEE THE LAST OF THEM!--I'M GOING TO SELL THIS PLACE, RENT A LABORATORY IN AN OFFICE BUILDING, AND OPERATE **OPENLY**, LIKE ANY RESPECTABLE SCIENTIST WOULD!

WONDERFUL!

ATILLA THE HUN GE HIS KHAN CAPTAIN KIDD AL CAPONE

AFTERWARD...

SO OUR FEUD'S OVER, AT LAST! ..., MAY I ADMIT SOMETHING? THERE WERE TIMES, **LUTHOR**, WHEN YOU HAD ME PLENTY WORRIED...

LIKE THAT TIME WHEN I INVENTED AN **ATOMIC-POWERED TOP** AND LET IT DESTROY AN ENTIRE TOWN!

"...THE SUCTION OF ITS SPIN BECAME LIKE A TORNADO! THAT WAS A TOUGH ONE FOR YOU TO HANDLE, EH, **SUPERMAN**...?"

WHIRRRR

HELP!

HELP!

"IT SURE WAS, **LUTHOR**! I BUILT A CIRCULAR TRACK ON A HUGE RAFT. THEN, AS THE TOP SPUN ONTO THE TRACK AND RODE 'ROUND AND 'ROUND, I GOT THE TOP UNDER CONTROL AND DUMPED IT IN THE OCEAN..."

⑦

"AND I'LL NEVER FORGET HOW YOU ONCE DISGUISED YOURSELF AS A PROFESSOR AND FOCUSED A *DUPLICATOR RAY* ON ME AND FORMED AN IMPERFECT DOUBLE OF MYSELF... *BIZARRO!* YOU CAN'T IMAGINE ALL THE PROBLEMS THAT *IDIOT OF STEEL* HAS GIVEN ME SINCE THEN... "

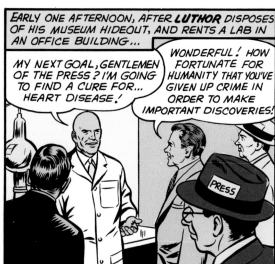

EARLY ONE AFTERNOON, AFTER *LUTHOR* DISPOSES OF HIS MUSEUM HIDEOUT, AND RENTS A LAB IN AN OFFICE BUILDING...

MY NEXT GOAL, GENTLEMEN OF THE PRESS? I'M GOING TO FIND A CURE FOR... HEART DISEASE!

WONDERFUL! HOW FORTUNATE FOR HUMANITY THAT YOU'VE GIVEN UP CRIME IN ORDER TO MAKE IMPORTANT DISCOVERIES!

PRESS

SECONDS AFTER, THE REPORTERS LEAVE...

THAT WAS A PRETTY LITTLE SPEECH YOU MADE, *LUTHOR!* ONLY WE DON'T LIKE IT!

DUKE GARNER AND *AL MANTZ*... UNDER-WORLD HOODS! YOU MUST HAVE STOLEN IN WHILE I WENT FOR LUNCH! GET OUT! I'M FINISHED WITH CROOKS!

BUT WE'RE NOT FINISHED WITH YOU!... TELL HIM, AL!

EITHER YOU KILL *SUPERMAN*, OR WE *KILL YOU!*... WHO'S GONNA DIE, GENIUS? *YOU*...OR *SUPERMAN?!!*

END, PART I

WHAT WILL *LUTHOR* DECIDE? TURN TO THE NEXT CHAPTER! (8)

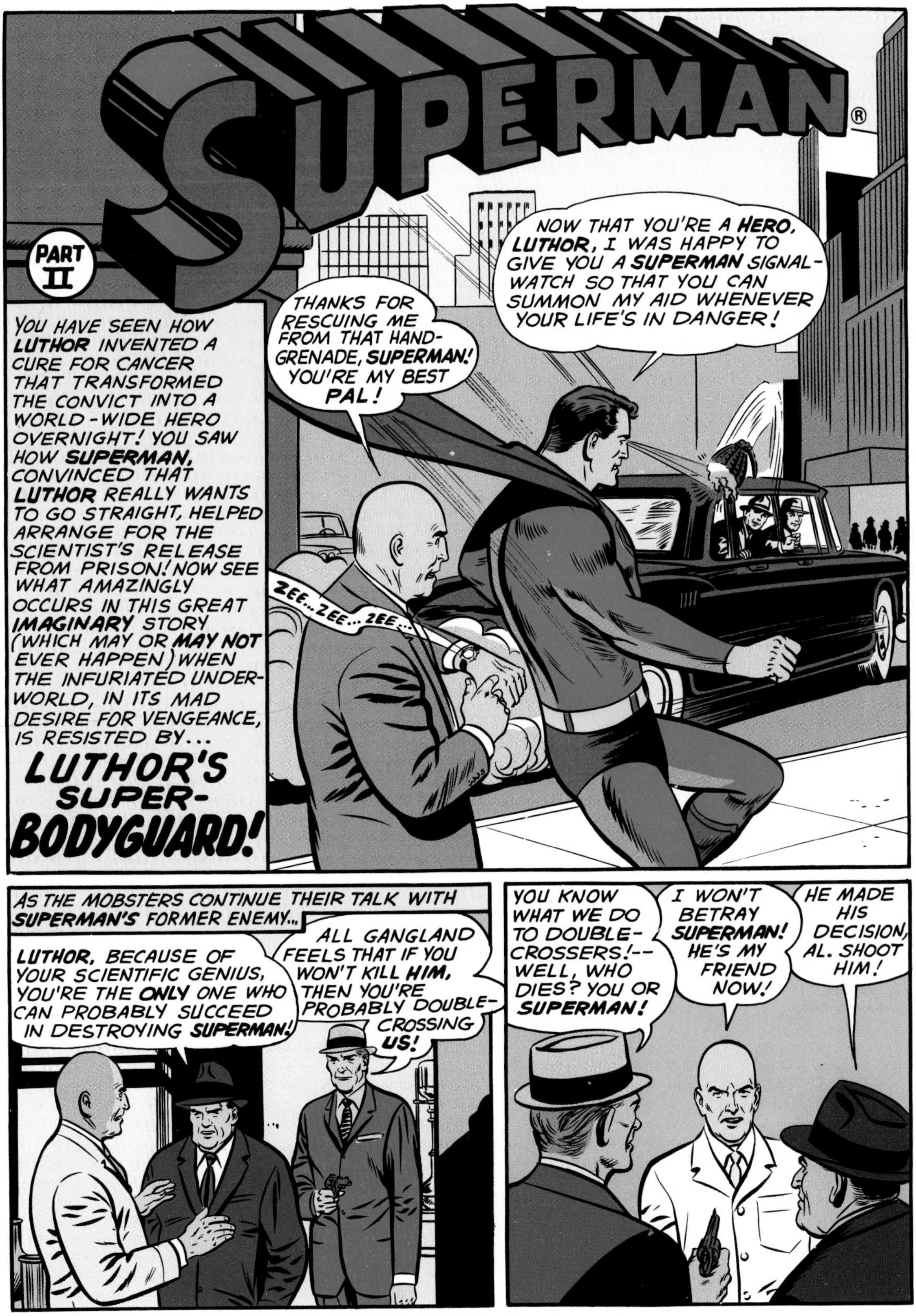
SUPERMAN
PART II
YOU HAVE SEEN HOW LUTHOR INVENTED A CURE FOR CANCER THAT TRANSFORMED THE CONVICT INTO A WORLD-WIDE HERO OVERNIGHT! YOU SAW HOW SUPERMAN, CONVINCED THAT LUTHOR REALLY WANTS TO GO STRAIGHT, HELPED ARRANGE FOR THE SCIENTIST'S RELEASE FROM PRISON! NOW SEE WHAT AMAZINGLY OCCURS IN THIS GREAT IMAGINARY STORY (WHICH MAY OR MAY NOT EVER HAPPEN) WHEN THE INFURIATED UNDERWORLD, IN ITS MAD DESIRE FOR VENGEANCE, IS RESISTED BY...
LUTHOR'S SUPER-BODYGUARD!
THANKS FOR RESCUING ME FROM THAT HAND-GRENADE, SUPERMAN! YOU'RE MY BEST PAL!
NOW THAT YOU'RE A HERO, LUTHOR, I WAS HAPPY TO GIVE YOU A SUPERMAN SIGNAL-WATCH SO THAT YOU CAN SUMMON MY AID WHENEVER YOUR LIFE'S IN DANGER!
ZEE... ZEE... ZEE...
AS THE MOBSTERS CONTINUE THEIR TALK WITH SUPERMAN'S FORMER ENEMY...
LUTHOR, BECAUSE OF YOUR SCIENTIFIC GENIUS, YOU'RE THE ONLY ONE WHO CAN PROBABLY SUCCEED IN DESTROYING SUPERMAN!
ALL GANGLAND FEELS THAT IF YOU WON'T KILL HIM, THEN YOU'RE PROBABLY DOUBLE-CROSSING US!
YOU KNOW WHAT WE DO TO DOUBLE-CROSSERS!-- WELL, WHO DIES? YOU OR SUPERMAN!
I WON'T BETRAY SUPERMAN! HE'S MY FRIEND NOW!
HE MADE HIS DECISION, AL. SHOOT HIM!

BUT AS THE TRIGGER-MAN FIRES...

YOU'RE WASTING THOSE BULLETS!

BANG! BANG!

SUPERMAN! FOR THE FIRST TIME IN MY LIFE, I'M **GLAD** TO SEE BULLETS BOUNCING OFF YOU!

I HAD A HUNCH YOU WOULDN'T BE SAFE FROM YOUR FORMER CRONIES, SO I KEPT YOU UNDER SURVEILLANCE WITH MY SUPER-VISION!

LUCKILY FOR ME!

SUPERMAN REMOVES AN OBJECT FROM HIS CAPE'S SECRET POUCH, THEN...

PROBABLY, THERE WILL BE OTHER ATTEMPTS BY THE UNDERWORLD TO DESTROY YOU! THAT'S WHY I MADE THIS SIGNAL-WATCH! PLEASE ACCEPT IT! IT'S LIKE JIMMY OLSEN'S WATCH, BUT OPERATES ON A DIFFERENT ULTRASONIC FREQUENCY...

WHENEVER YOU'RE IN DANGER, PRESS THE BUTTON ON THE WATCH! I'LL FLASH TO YOUR RESCUE, IN RESPONSE TO THE ULTRASONIC DISTRESS-SIGNAL!

THANK YOU, **SUPERMAN!** YOU'RE... A WONDERFUL FRIEND!

SHORTLY, AT A MEETING OF GANGLAND BIG-SHOTS...

WE'LL KEEP ON TRYING TO RUB OUT **LUTHOR**, UNTIL WE **SUCCEED!**

RIGHT! HE RATTED OUT ON HIS PROMISE TO DESTROY **SUPERMAN!** FOR THAT, HE'LL DIE!

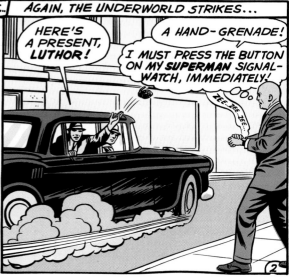

AGAIN, THE UNDERWORLD STRIKES...

HERE'S A PRESENT, **LUTHOR!**

A HAND-GRENADE! I MUST PRESS THE BUTTON ON MY **SUPERMAN** SIGNAL-WATCH, IMMEDIATELY!

ZEE-ZEE-ZEE...

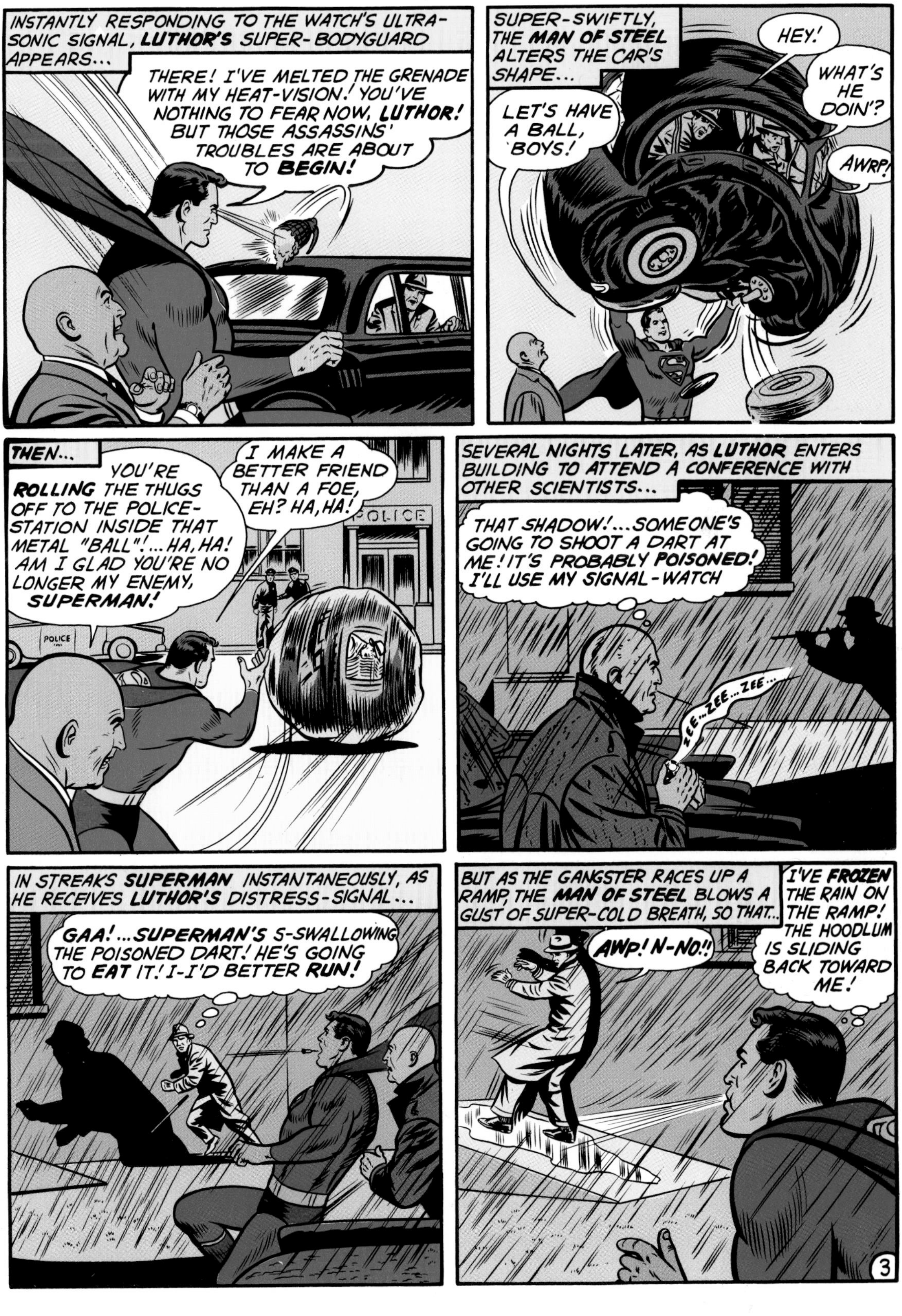
INSTANTLY RESPONDING TO THE WATCH'S ULTRA-SONIC SIGNAL, LUTHOR'S SUPER-BODYGUARD APPEARS...
THERE! I'VE MELTED THE GRENADE WITH MY HEAT-VISION! YOU'VE NOTHING TO FEAR NOW, LUTHOR! BUT THOSE ASSASSINS' TROUBLES ARE ABOUT TO BEGIN!
SUPER-SWIFTLY, THE MAN OF STEEL ALTERS THE CAR'S SHAPE...
LET'S HAVE A BALL, 'BOYS!
HEY!
WHAT'S HE DOIN'?
AWRP!
THEN...
YOU'RE ROLLING THE THUGS OFF TO THE POLICE-STATION INSIDE THAT METAL "BALL"!...HA, HA! AM I GLAD YOU'RE NO LONGER MY ENEMY, SUPERMAN!
I MAKE A BETTER FRIEND THAN A FOE, EH? HA, HA!
POLICE
POLICE
SEVERAL NIGHTS LATER, AS LUTHOR ENTERS BUILDING TO ATTEND A CONFERENCE WITH OTHER SCIENTISTS...
THAT SHADOW!...SOMEONE'S GOING TO SHOOT A DART AT ME! IT'S PROBABLY POISONED! I'LL USE MY SIGNAL-WATCH
ZEE...ZEE...ZEE...ZEE...
IN STREAKS SUPERMAN INSTANTANEOUSLY, AS HE RECEIVES LUTHOR'S DISTRESS-SIGNAL...
GAA!...SUPERMAN'S S-SWALLOWING THE POISONED DART! HE'S GOING TO EAT IT! I-I'D BETTER RUN!
BUT AS THE GANGSTER RACES UP A RAMP, THE MAN OF STEEL BLOWS A GUST OF SUPER-COLD BREATH, SO THAT...
I'VE FROZEN THE RAIN ON THE RAMP! THE HOODLUM IS SLIDING BACK TOWARD ME!
AWP! N-NO!!
3

THANKS, **SUPERMAN!** ONCE AGAIN, YOU'VE SAVED MY LIFE!

GLAD TO HELP YOU, ANYTIME!

THIS LIGHT TAP WILL PUT THE KILLER TO SLEEP UNTIL I GET HIM TO THE POLICE STATION!

SOON AFTERWARD, **SUPERMAN** MEETS WITH HIS COUSIN, **SUPERGIRL,** WHO ALSO CAME FROM THE DESTROYED PLANET **KRYPTON,** AND IS HIS SECRET EMERGENCY WEAPON...

I'M SO HAPPY THAT **LUTHOR'S** GONE STRAIGHT!

MY BIG PROBLEM IS TO KEEP HIM **ALIVE!**

I CAN'T POSSIBLY WATCH OVER **LUTHOR** EVERY INSTANT! SOME DAY THE UNDERWORLD MAY GET HIM **BEFORE** HE CAN SIGNAL ME FOR HELP, AND MANKIND WILL LOSE A GREAT SCIENTIST!

THERE MUST BE SOME SOLUTION! LET'S TALK OVER DIFFERENT IDEAS!

AFTER THEY CONSIDER AND DISCARD VARIOUS PLANS...

I'VE GOT IT! HE'D BE SAFE IN AN OUTER SPACE **SATELLITE LABORATORY!**

WHAT A BRILLIANT INSPIRATION!

AT ONCE, **SUPERMAN** BUILDS THE ASTOUNDING LABORTORY, THEN AFTER HE PLACES IT IN ORBIT ABOVE EARTH...

HOW HAPPY **LUTHOR** LOOKS AS I'M TAKING HIM TO HIS NEW LAB!

④

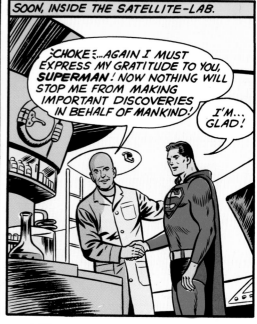

SOON, INSIDE THE SATELLITE-LAB.

≥CHOKE≶...AGAIN I MUST EXPRESS MY GRATITUDE TO YOU, **SUPERMAN!** NOW NOTHING WILL STOP ME FROM MAKING IMPORTANT DISCOVERIES IN BEHALF OF MANKIND!

I'M... GLAD!

PRESENTLY, INFURIATED UNDERWORLD CHIEFS HOLD A WAR COUNCIL...

SATELLITE OR NO SATELLITE, WE CAN STILL KILL *LUTHOR*, BUT IT'LL COST A FORTUNE!

PRICE IS NO OBJECT! *KILL HIM!*

WEEKS LATER, AS *SUPERMAN* FLIES ALONG ON PATROL...

GREAT SCOTT! MY TELESCOPIC SIGHT REVEALS AN INCREDIBLE THREAT TO *LUTHOR'S* LIFE!

UP INTO OUTER SPACE DESPERATELY FLASHES THE *MAN OF STEEL*...

THAT MISSILE-BOMB WILL EXPLODE *LUTHOR'S* LABORATORY, UNLESS I DESTROY THE MISSILE FIRST!

DELIBERATELY, *SUPERMAN* MEETS THE MISSILE IN A HEAD-ON COLLISION...

JUST IN TIME!... I'M UNHARMED! HMM... GANGLAND MAY HAVE MANY SUCH MISSILE-LAUNCHING BASES! I MUST DO SOMETHING TO PERMANENTLY CANCEL OUT THE MISSILE-THREAT!

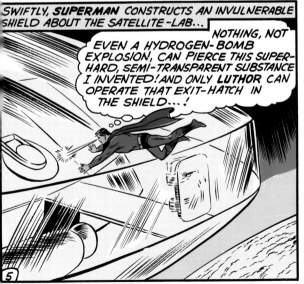

SWIFTLY, *SUPERMAN* CONSTRUCTS AN INVULNERABLE SHIELD ABOUT THE SATELLITE-LAB...

NOTHING, NOT EVEN A HYDROGEN-BOMB EXPLOSION, CAN PIERCE THIS SUPER-HARD, SEMI-TRANSPARENT SUBSTANCE I INVENTED! AND ONLY *LUTHOR* CAN OPERATE THAT EXIT-HATCH IN THE SHIELD....!

SHORTLY, IN THE SATELLITE LAB...

THE SIGNAL-WATCH'S ULTRASONIC WAVES CAN'T TRAVEL THROUGH OUTER SPACE! IF YOU EVER URGENTLY NEED ME, FIRE THIS JET-ROCKET, WHICH RESEMBLES YOU, INTO EARTH'S UPPER ATMOSPHERE!

I'LL DO THAT!

5

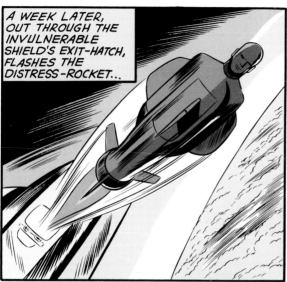

A WEEK LATER, OUT THROUGH THE INVULNERABLE SHIELD'S EXIT-HATCH, FLASHES THE DISTRESS-ROCKET...

HIGH IN OUR PLANET'S ATMOSPHERE, THE ROCKET EXPLODES WITH A COLOSSAL ROAR THAT IS HEARD ABOUT THE WORLD AND SIMULTANEOUSLY, ITS FRAGMENTS DISSOLVE INTO MULTI-COLORED FLARES...

BWOOOOOOMMM

LUTHOR'S EMERGENCY-SIGNAL!... HE NEEDS ME!!

LUTHOR HAS OPENED THE ESCAPE-HATCH SO I CAN ENTER! SOMETHING MUST BE TERRIBLY WRONG! WHAT'S HAPPENED? HAS GANGLAND DISCOVERED SOME ASTOUNDING NEW WAY TO MENACE LUTHOR??

MOMENTS LATER, INSIDE THE SATELLITE...

WHAT'S WRONG, LUTHOR? I SAW YOUR DISTRESS-SIGNAL AND CAME AT ONCE!

WRONG?... NOTHING'S WRONG, FOR ME...

UNEXPECTEDLY, LUTHOR TOUCHES A BUTTON WHICH REMOVES LEAD-LIDS FROM BEFORE THE LENSES OF CONCEALED RAY-PROJECTORS...

I'M FINE! BUT YOU'RE IN SUPER-TROUBLE!

OW!...G-GREEN KRYPTONITE RAYS!

GREEN KRYPTONITE IS... THE ONE SUBSTANCE... TH-THAT C-CAN... DESTROY ME!

AS THE MAN OF STEEL COLLAPSES...

I'M H-HORRIBLY WEAKENED AND... PAINED....BY THE RAYS!...GASP!... TURN THEM OFF! HAVE Y-YOU GONE OUT OF YOUR MIND?

HA,HA,HA!

6

SECONDS LATER, AS **LUTHOR** STRAPS THE **MAN OF STEEL** TO A BENCH, WITH BANDS OF METAL CONTAINING **KRYPTONITE**...

HA, HA! OH, HOW SIMPLE IT WAS TO OUTWIT YOU!

THEN, AS **LUTHOR** PULLS A SWITCH...

SEE, **SUPERMAN!** THAT WALL IS RISING! THERE'S A THICK GLASS PARTITION BEHIND IT, SEPARATING US FROM YOUR DEAR FRIENDS... LOIS LANE, JIMMY OLSEN, AND PERRY WHITE!...THEY CAN'T POSSIBLY BREAK THROUGH THAT GLASS AND RESCUE YOU!

BEHIND THE GLASS PARTITION...

LUTHOR HASN'T REFORMED! HE'S AS EVIL AS EVER! HE'S GOING TO KILL **SUPERMAN!**

DON'T GIVE UP HOPE, LOIS!

SUPERMAN'S GOTTEN OUT OF TIGHTER FIXES THAN THIS!

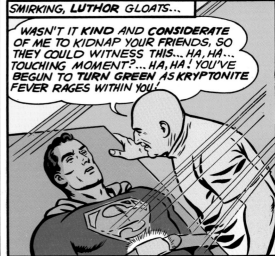

SMIRKING, **LUTHOR** GLOATS...

WASN'T IT **KIND** AND **CONSIDERATE** OF ME TO KIDNAP YOUR FRIENDS, SO THEY COULD WITNESS THIS... HA, HA... TOUCHING MOMENT?... HA, HA! YOU'VE BEGUN TO **TURN GREEN** AS KRYPTONITE FEVER RAGES WITHIN YOU!

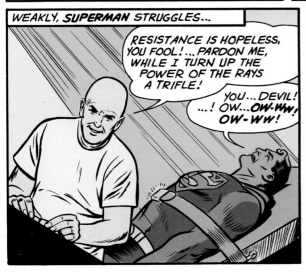

WEAKLY, **SUPERMAN** STRUGGLES...

RESISTANCE IS HOPELESS, YOU FOOL!... PARDON ME, WHILE I TURN UP THE POWER OF THE RAYS A TRIFLE!

YOU...DEVIL! ...! OW...**OW-WW**, OW-WW!

CLEVER DEVIL, YOU MEAN!... I DISCOVERED THAT CANCER-CURE, IN ORDER TO BE RELEASED FROM JAIL! I **PRETENDED** TO HAVE REFORMED, SO I COULD LULL YOU INTO A FALSE SENSE OF SECURITY! THE PURPOSE? TO CATCH YOU OFF-GUARD AND LURE YOU INTO THIS DEATH-TRAP!!

7

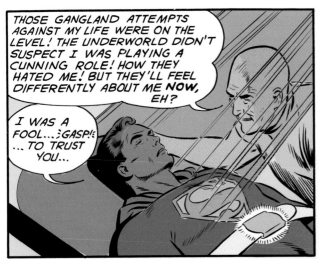

THOSE GANGLAND ATTEMPTS AGAINST MY LIFE WERE ON THE LEVEL! THE UNDERWORLD DIDN'T SUSPECT I WAS PLAYING A CUNNING ROLE! HOW THEY HATED ME! BUT THEY'LL FEEL DIFFERENTLY ABOUT ME *NOW*, EH?

I WAS A FOOL...:GASP!: ...TO TRUST YOU...

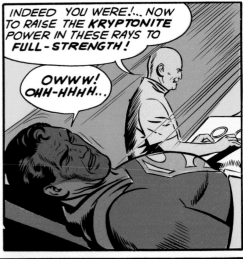

INDEED YOU WERE!... NOW TO RAISE THE *KRYPTONITE* POWER IN THESE RAYS TO *FULL-STRENGTH*!

OWWW! OHH-HHHH...

AS *SUPERMAN* TURNS COMPLETELY GREEN AND HIS STRUGGLES CEASE, *LUTHOR* EXAMINES THE LIMP FORM...

I MUST MAKE SURE YOU AREN'T JUST *PRETENDING* TO BE DEAD, TO TRICK ME INTO PREMATURELY TURNING *OFF* THE RAYS! HMM... THIS SUPER XXX-RAY DISCLOSES YOU'RE THE GENUINE *SUPERMAN*, AND *NOT* A ROBOT!

MOMENTS LATER...

AND MY SUPER-STETHOSCOPE REVEALS NO LIFE AT ALL REMAINS IN *SUPERMAN'S* CELLS!... YOUR FRIEND IS VE-RY, VERY DEAD!

:CHOKE!:

OH, NO!

AT LAST!! AFTER ALL THESE YEARS OF VAINLY TRYING, I'VE FINALLY SUCCEEDED IN KILLING *SUPERMAN*! I'VE DESTROYED THE MIGHTIEST MAN IN THE UNIVERSE! WHAT A GLORIOUS ACHIEVEMENT!

LATER, AFTER *LUTHOR* LANDS THE SATELLITE LAB ON EARTH...

MADMAN!

YOU'LL PAY FOR THIS, *LUTHOR*, YOU... YOU *MURDERER!!*

YOU CAN HAVE *SUPERMAN* BACK, NOW THAT HE'S DEAD! HA, HA!

8

144

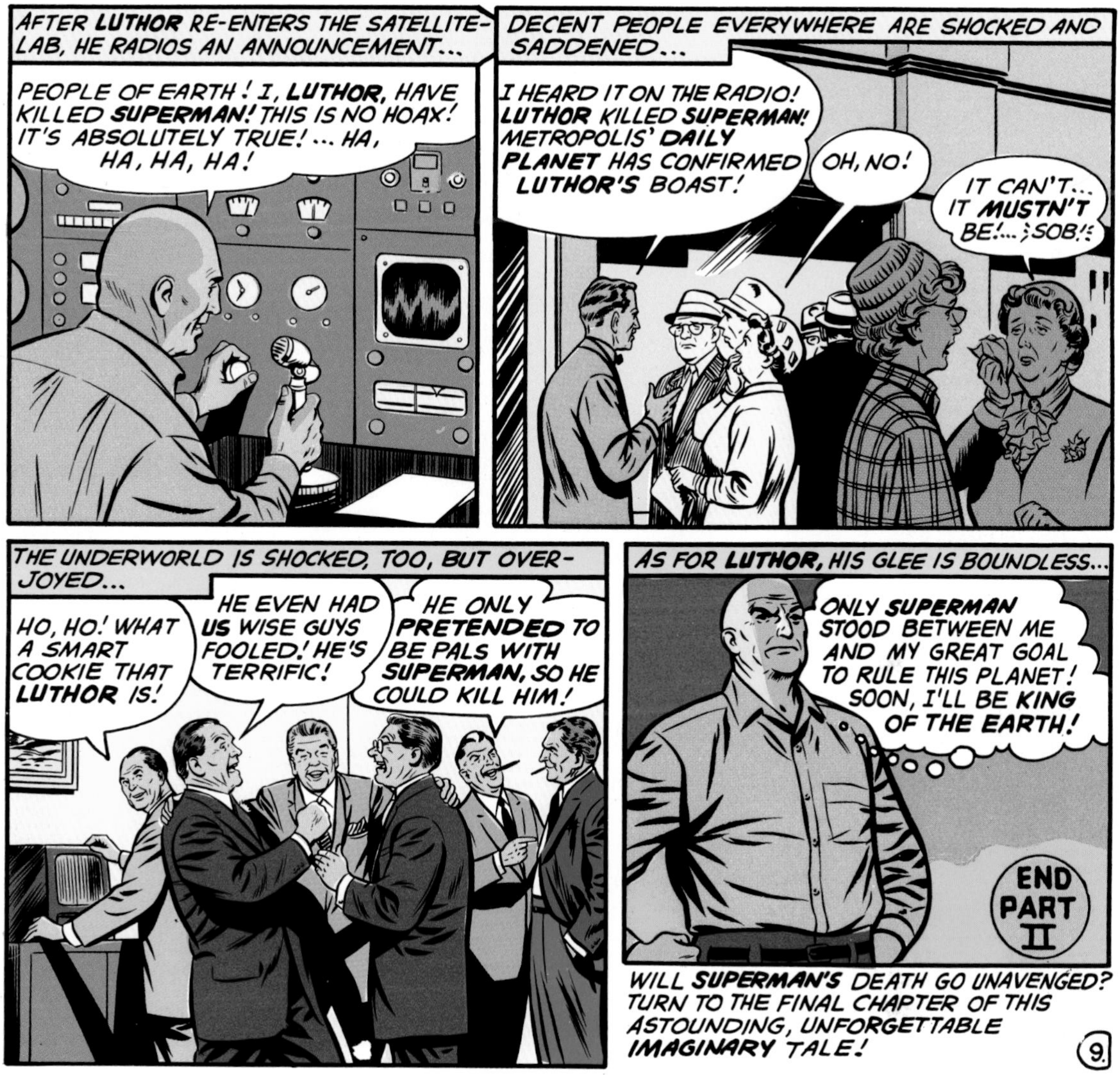
AFTER LUTHOR RE-ENTERS THE SATELLITE-LAB, HE RADIOS AN ANNOUNCEMENT...
PEOPLE OF EARTH! I, LUTHOR, HAVE KILLED SUPERMAN! THIS IS NO HOAX! IT'S ABSOLUTELY TRUE! ... HA, HA, HA, HA!
DECENT PEOPLE EVERYWHERE ARE SHOCKED AND SADDENED...
I HEARD IT ON THE RADIO! LUTHOR KILLED SUPERMAN! METROPOLIS' DAILY PLANET HAS CONFIRMED LUTHOR'S BOAST!
OH, NO!
IT CAN'T... IT MUSTN'T BE!... SOB!
THE UNDERWORLD IS SHOCKED, TOO, BUT OVER-JOYED...
HO, HO! WHAT A SMART COOKIE THAT LUTHOR IS!
HE EVEN HAD US WISE GUYS FOOLED! HE'S TERRIFIC!
HE ONLY PRETENDED TO BE PALS WITH SUPERMAN, SO HE COULD KILL HIM!
AS FOR LUTHOR, HIS GLEE IS BOUNDLESS...
ONLY SUPERMAN STOOD BETWEEN ME AND MY GREAT GOAL TO RULE THIS PLANET! SOON, I'LL BE KING OF THE EARTH!
END PART II
WILL SUPERMAN'S DEATH GO UNAVENGED? TURN TO THE FINAL CHAPTER OF THIS ASTOUNDING, UNFORGETTABLE IMAGINARY TALE!
9

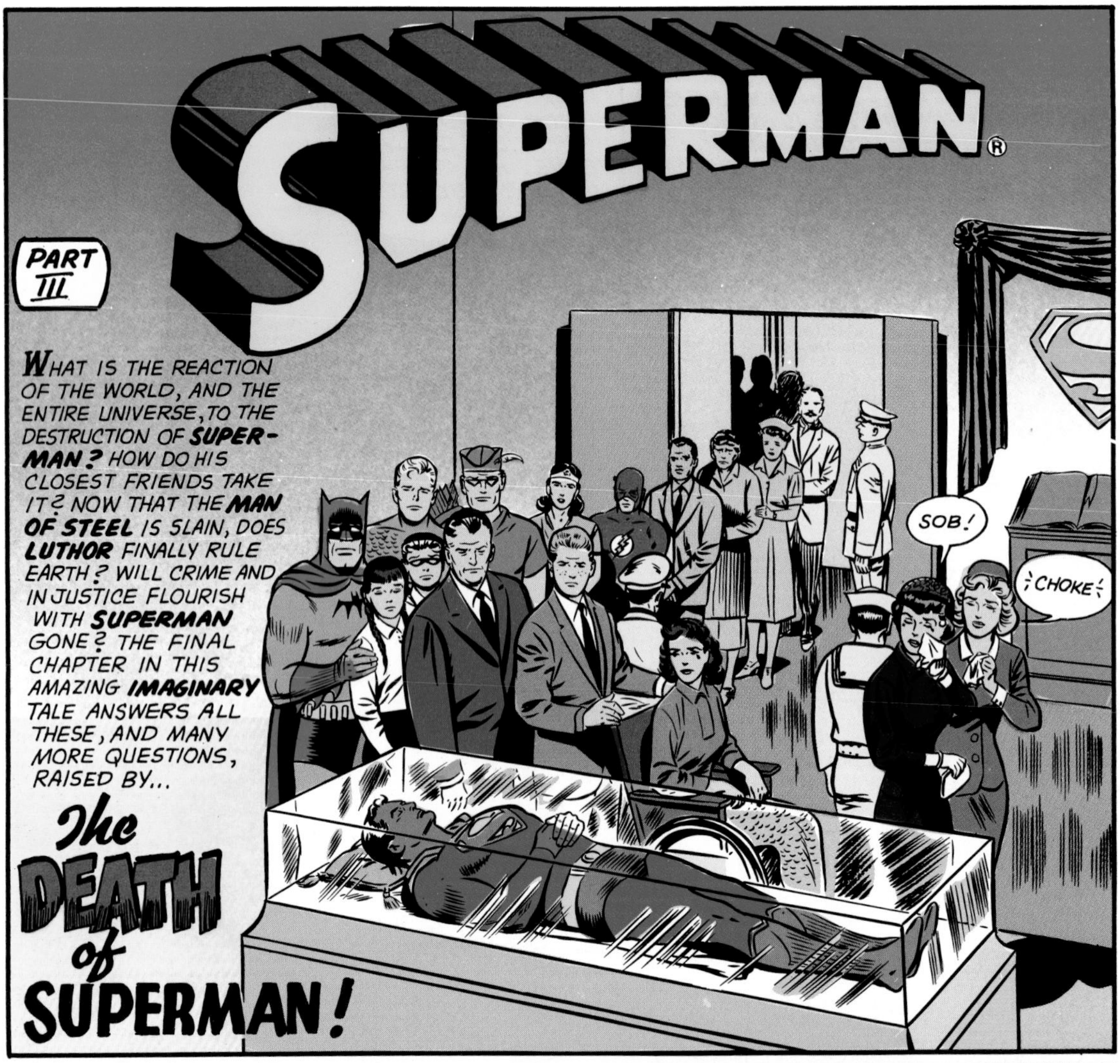
SUPERMAN®
PART III
WHAT IS THE REACTION OF THE WORLD, AND THE ENTIRE UNIVERSE, TO THE DESTRUCTION OF SUPERMAN? HOW DO HIS CLOSEST FRIENDS TAKE IT? NOW THAT THE MAN OF STEEL IS SLAIN, DOES LUTHOR FINALLY RULE EARTH? WILL CRIME AND INJUSTICE FLOURISH WITH SUPERMAN GONE? THE FINAL CHAPTER IN THIS AMAZING IMAGINARY TALE ANSWERS ALL THESE, AND MANY MORE QUESTIONS, RAISED BY...
The DEATH of SUPERMAN!
SOB!
CHOKE

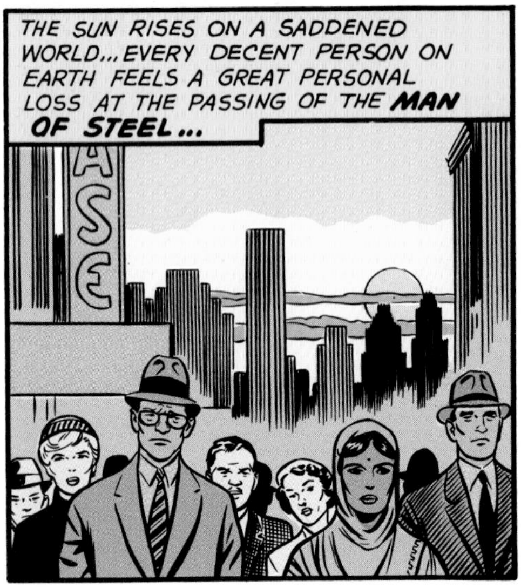
THE SUN RISES ON A SADDENED WORLD... EVERY DECENT PERSON ON EARTH FEELS A GREAT PERSONAL LOSS AT THE PASSING OF THE MAN OF STEEL...
ASE

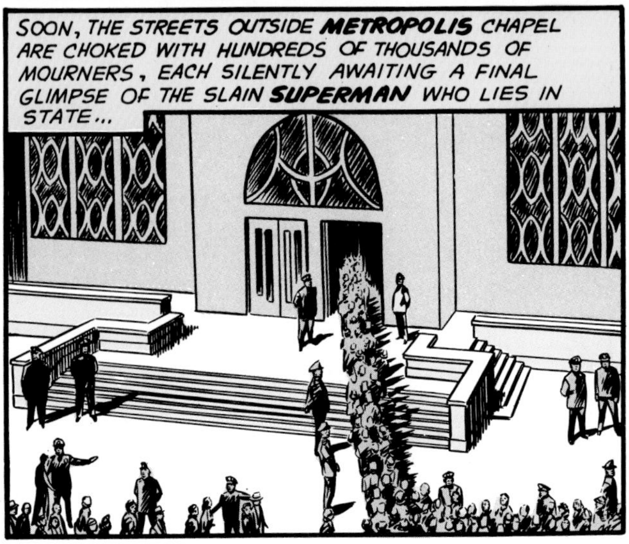
SOON, THE STREETS OUTSIDE METROPOLIS CHAPEL ARE CHOKED WITH HUNDREDS OF THOUSANDS OF MOURNERS, EACH SILENTLY AWAITING A FINAL GLIMPSE OF THE SLAIN SUPERMAN WHO LIES IN STATE...

INSIDE THE CHAPEL, ONE BY ONE, THEY SLOWLY FILE PAST **SUPERMAN'S** CASKET... AMONG THEM ARE WORLD LEADERS WHO HAVE FLOWN BY JET TO **METROPOLIS**, TO PAY THEIR FINAL RESPECTS...

ON MOVES THE MELANCHOLY PROCESSION... AMONG THE MOURNERS ARE WEIRD ALIEN BEINGS FROM OTHER WORLDS, WHO SPED TO EARTH IN ODD VEHICLES VIA SPACE-WARPS UPON LEARNING THE INCREDIBLE, TRAGIC NEWS...

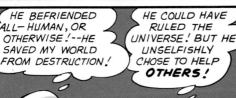

HE BEFRIENDED ALL—HUMAN, OR OTHERWISE!--HE SAVED MY WORLD FROM DESTRUCTION!

HE COULD HAVE RULED THE UNIVERSE! BUT HE UNSELFISHLY CHOSE TO HELP **OTHERS**!

THE SEA OF FACES SLOWLY EDDIES BY... FACES OF EVERY RACE AND NATIONALITY... YOUNG FACES... OLD FACES... EACH FACE SORROWFUL AT THE PASSING OF A GREAT MAN...

THEN IT IS THE TURN OF GRIEF-STRICKEN LOIS LANE, ASSISTED BY HER SISTER LUCY, TO STAND BEFORE THE COFFIN... AND AS LOIS TAKES A LAST LOOK AT HER FALLEN HERO...

GOODBYE...

THERE'LL NEVER BE ANYONE FOR ME, BUT... YOU! OH, DARLING, I-I HAD SO MUCH LOVE TO GIVE TO YOU... JUST HOW MUCH, EVEN **YOU**, NEVER DREAMED!... ⸮SOB!⸮ ...GOODBYE! - I'LL... LOVE... YOU... ALWAYS... ⸮SOB!⸮

NEXT, **SUPERMAN'S** FRIENDS, JIMMY OLSEN, PERRY WHITE...AND MERMAID **LORI LEMARIS** FROM **ATLANTIS**... TAKE LAST, LINGERING LOOKS ...

I'LL... MISS YOU...

;CHOKE;... SO LONG, PAL! NO ONE EVER HAD A TRUER BUDDY THAN YOU!

I'LL NEVER FORGET YOU!

AFTER THEM COMES LANA LANG...

IT SEEMS LIKE ONLY YESTERDAY THAT I WAS YOUR CHILDHOOD FRIEND IN SMALLVILLE.' FIRST, I WAS AN AWFUL PEST, THEN I GOT A CRUSH ON YOU. WHEN I GREW UP, THE CRUSH RIPENED INTO LOVE.' NOW YOU'RE... GONE! FAREWELL...;CHOKE;

THEN THE **MAN OF STEEL'S** FAITHFUL PET **KRYPTO** PASSES THE COFFIN...

I WILL NEVER KNOW ANOTHER MASTER LIKE YOU! ;CHOKE; — GOODBYE! —WHEN I THINK OF ALL THE ADVENTURES WE HAD TOGETHER...

ON MOVE THE FACES, ONE AFTER ANOTHER... THEN, BEFORE THE SLAIN **MAN OF STEEL,** APPEARS THE TEAR-STAINED FEATURES OF A TEEN-AGED GIRL WHOM NO ONE SUSPECTS IS HIS **SUPERGIRL** COUSIN LINDA, FROM **KRYPTON...**

TOGETHER, WE EXPLORED THE UNIVERSE... BUT EVEN INFINITY WASN'T AS BIG AS YOUR...;CHOKE; ...GALLANT, NOBLE HEART...

AND NOW, THERE FILES PAST-- **THE LEGION OF SUPER-HEROES** FROM THE DISTANT FUTURE...!

WE SALUTE YOU IN DEATH AS WE HONORED YOU IN LIFE, COMRADE!

OF ALL THE SUPER-HEROES, YOU WERE THE **GREATEST!!**

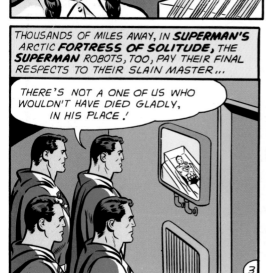

THOUSANDS OF MILES AWAY, IN **SUPERMAN'S** ARCTIC **FORTRESS OF SOLITUDE,** THE **SUPERMAN** ROBOTS, TOO, PAY THEIR FINAL RESPECTS TO THEIR SLAIN MASTER...

THERE'S NOT A ONE OF US WHO WOULDN'T HAVE DIED GLADLY, IN HIS PLACE!

3

AND INSIDE THE MINIATURE BOTTLE-CITY OF **KANDOR,** IN THE FORTRESS, **VAN-ZEE** AND **SYLVIA** JOIN MILLIONS OF OTHER KANDORIANS IN AN IMPRESSIVE TRIBUTE...

WHY ARE THEY LOWERING THE KRYPTONIAN FLAG, MOMMY?

A GREAT MAN HAS DIED--;CHOKE; — **SUPERMAN** WILL NEVER VISIT US... AGAIN...;SOB.;

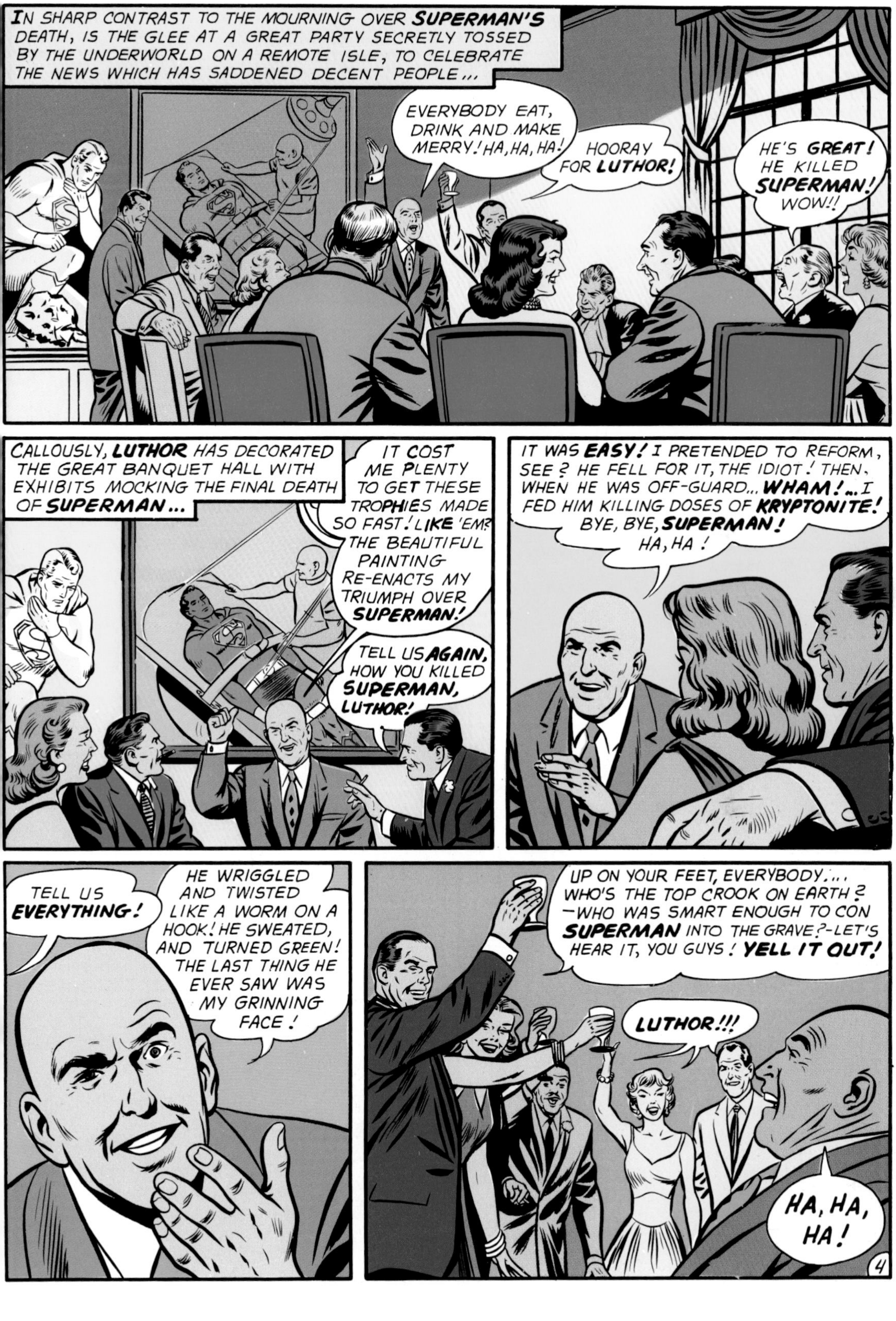
IN SHARP CONTRAST TO THE MOURNING OVER SUPERMAN'S DEATH, IS THE GLEE AT A GREAT PARTY SECRETLY TOSSED BY THE UNDERWORLD ON A REMOTE ISLE, TO CELEBRATE THE NEWS WHICH HAS SADDENED DECENT PEOPLE...
EVERYBODY EAT, DRINK AND MAKE MERRY! HA, HA, HA!
HOORAY FOR LUTHOR!
HE'S GREAT! HE KILLED SUPERMAN! WOW!!
CALLOUSLY, LUTHOR HAS DECORATED THE GREAT BANQUET HALL WITH EXHIBITS MOCKING THE FINAL DEATH OF SUPERMAN...
IT COST ME PLENTY TO GET THESE TROPHIES MADE SO FAST! LIKE 'EM? THE BEAUTIFUL PAINTING RE-ENACTS MY TRIUMPH OVER SUPERMAN!
TELL US AGAIN, HOW YOU KILLED SUPERMAN, LUTHOR!
IT WAS EASY! I PRETENDED TO REFORM, SEE? HE FELL FOR IT, THE IDIOT! THEN, WHEN HE WAS OFF-GUARD... WHAM!...I FED HIM KILLING DOSES OF KRYPTONITE! BYE, BYE, SUPERMAN! HA, HA!
TELL US EVERYTHING!
HE WRIGGLED AND TWISTED LIKE A WORM ON A HOOK! HE SWEATED, AND TURNED GREEN! THE LAST THING HE EVER SAW WAS MY GRINNING FACE!
UP ON YOUR FEET, EVERYBODY!... WHO'S THE TOP CROOK ON EARTH? —WHO WAS SMART ENOUGH TO CON SUPERMAN INTO THE GRAVE?—LET'S HEAR IT, YOU GUYS! YELL IT OUT!
LUTHOR!!!
HA, HA, HA!
4

SUDDENLY, THE MERRIMENT CHOKES IN THE MOBSTERS' THROATS AS, ASTOUNDINGLY...

GAAA! IT'S... SUPERMAN!

AWRP!... S-SUPERMAN'S ALIVE!

HE CAN'T BE! I KILLED HIM! I'M POSITIVE OF IT!

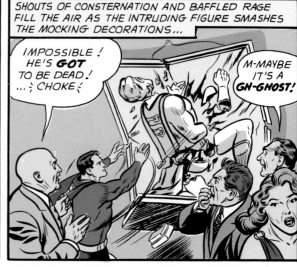

SHOUTS OF CONSTERNATION AND BAFFLED RAGE FILL THE AIR AS THE INTRUDING FIGURE SMASHES THE MOCKING DECORATIONS...

IMPOSSIBLE! HE'S GOT TO BE DEAD! ...; CHOKE;

M-MAYBE IT'S A GH-GHOST!

TO THE ASTONISHMENT OF THE CRINGING GANG-STERS, THE SUPER-POWERFUL FORM FLEXES MIGHTY MUSCLES, THEN,...

A DISGUISE IS FLYING OFF! IT AIN'T SUPERMAN! IT'S...

...A GIRL WITH S-SUPER-POWERS!

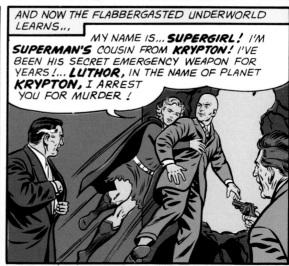

AND NOW THE FLABBERGASTED UNDERWORLD LEARNS...

MY NAME IS... SUPERGIRL! I'M SUPERMAN'S COUSIN FROM KRYPTON! I'VE BEEN HIS SECRET EMERGENCY WEAPON FOR YEARS!... LUTHOR, IN THE NAME OF PLANET KRYPTON, I ARREST YOU FOR MURDER!

YOU CAN STOP WASTING BULLETS! I HAVE ALL OF SUPERMAN'S ASTONISHING POWERS! — GANGDOM MAY HAVE SUCCEEDED IN TREACHEROUSLY KILLING SUPERMAN, BUT I'M GOING TO CARRY ON HIS GREAT WORK!

SOON, IN A KANDORIAN COURTROOM, AFTER SUPERGIRL TRANSPORTS LUTHOR. AND PROSECUTION WITNESSES, INTO THE MINIATURE CITY, VIA A TRANSFER-RAY...

LEX LUTHOR, YOU KILLED A KRYPTONIAN, AND SO YOU WILL BE TRIED BY KRYPTONIANS!

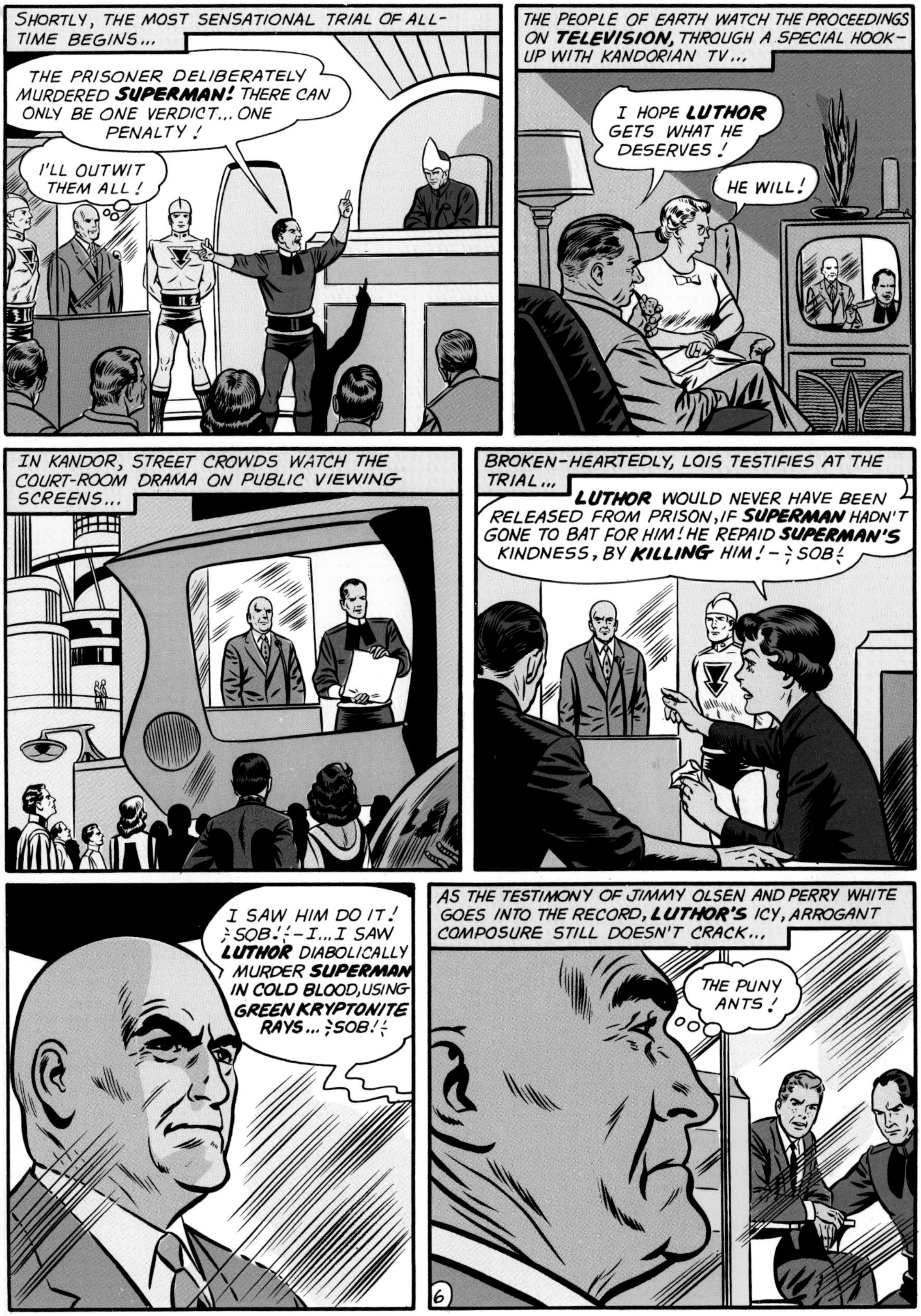
SHORTLY, THE MOST SENSATIONAL TRIAL OF ALL-TIME BEGINS...
THE PRISONER DELIBERATELY MURDERED SUPERMAN! THERE CAN ONLY BE ONE VERDICT... ONE PENALTY!
I'LL OUTWIT THEM ALL!
THE PEOPLE OF EARTH WATCH THE PROCEEDINGS ON TELEVISION, THROUGH A SPECIAL HOOK-UP WITH KANDORIAN TV...
I HOPE LUTHOR GETS WHAT HE DESERVES!
HE WILL!
IN KANDOR, STREET CROWDS WATCH THE COURT-ROOM DRAMA ON PUBLIC VIEWING-SCREENS...
BROKEN-HEARTEDLY, LOIS TESTIFIES AT THE TRIAL...
LUTHOR WOULD NEVER HAVE BEEN RELEASED FROM PRISON, IF SUPERMAN HADN'T GONE TO BAT FOR HIM! HE REPAID SUPERMAN'S KINDNESS, BY KILLING HIM! - SOB!
I SAW HIM DO IT! SOB! - I...I SAW LUTHOR DIABOLICALLY MURDER SUPERMAN IN COLD BLOOD, USING GREEN KRYPTONITE RAYS... SOB!
AS THE TESTIMONY OF JIMMY OLSEN AND PERRY WHITE GOES INTO THE RECORD, LUTHOR'S ICY, ARROGANT COMPOSURE STILL DOESN'T CRACK...
THE PUNY ANTS!
6

THEY AREN'T DEALING WITH AN ORDINARY HOOD! THEY'RE UP AGAINST A CRIMINAL MASTERMIND! I'LL WRIGGLE OUT OF PAYING THE PENALTY, WITH THE HIDDEN ACE I'VE GOT UP MY SLEEVE!

WHEN IT IS LUTHOR'S TURN TO TESTIFY...

I'M...GUILTY!

BUT I WON'T PAY FOR MY CRIME!

GUILTY? THEN THERE CAN BE BUT ONE PUNISHMENT... THE PRISONER WILL BE SENT INTO THE PHANTOM ZONE, AT ONCE!

AS THE PHANTOM ZONE RAY IS BROUGHT INTO COURT, LUTHOR PLAYS HIS ACE...

PUNISHING ME WON'T BRING SUPERMAN BACK! LET'S COMPROMISE! LET ME GO, AND I'LL BUILD A RAY THAT'LL ENLARGE KANDOR...

...BACK TO THE NORMAL SIZE IT WAS BEFORE SPACE VILLAIN BRAINIAC SHRANK YOUR CITY WITH A REDUCING-RAY! YOU WON'T HAVE TO LIVE IN A BOTTLE ANYMORE! IS IT DEAL?

NATURALLY, THEY WON'T REFUSE! BEING MADE NORMAL-SIZED AGAIN HAS BEEN THEIR GREATEST DESIRE!

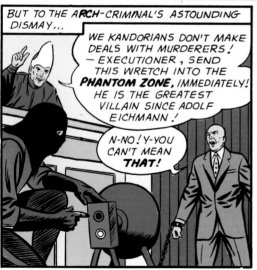

BUT TO THE ARCH-CRIMINAL'S ASTOUNDING DISMAY...

WE KANDORIANS DON'T MAKE DEALS WITH MURDERERS! — EXECUTIONER, SEND THIS WRETCH INTO THE PHANTOM ZONE, IMMEDIATELY! HE IS THE GREATEST VILLAIN SINCE ADOLF EICHMANN!

N-NO! Y-YOU CAN'T MEAN THAT!

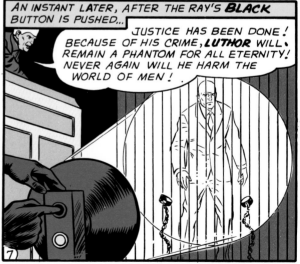

AN INSTANT LATER, AFTER THE RAY'S BLACK BUTTON IS PUSHED...

JUSTICE HAS BEEN DONE! BECAUSE OF HIS CRIME, LUTHOR WILL REMAIN A PHANTOM FOR ALL ETERNITY! NEVER AGAIN WILL HE HARM THE WORLD OF MEN!

7

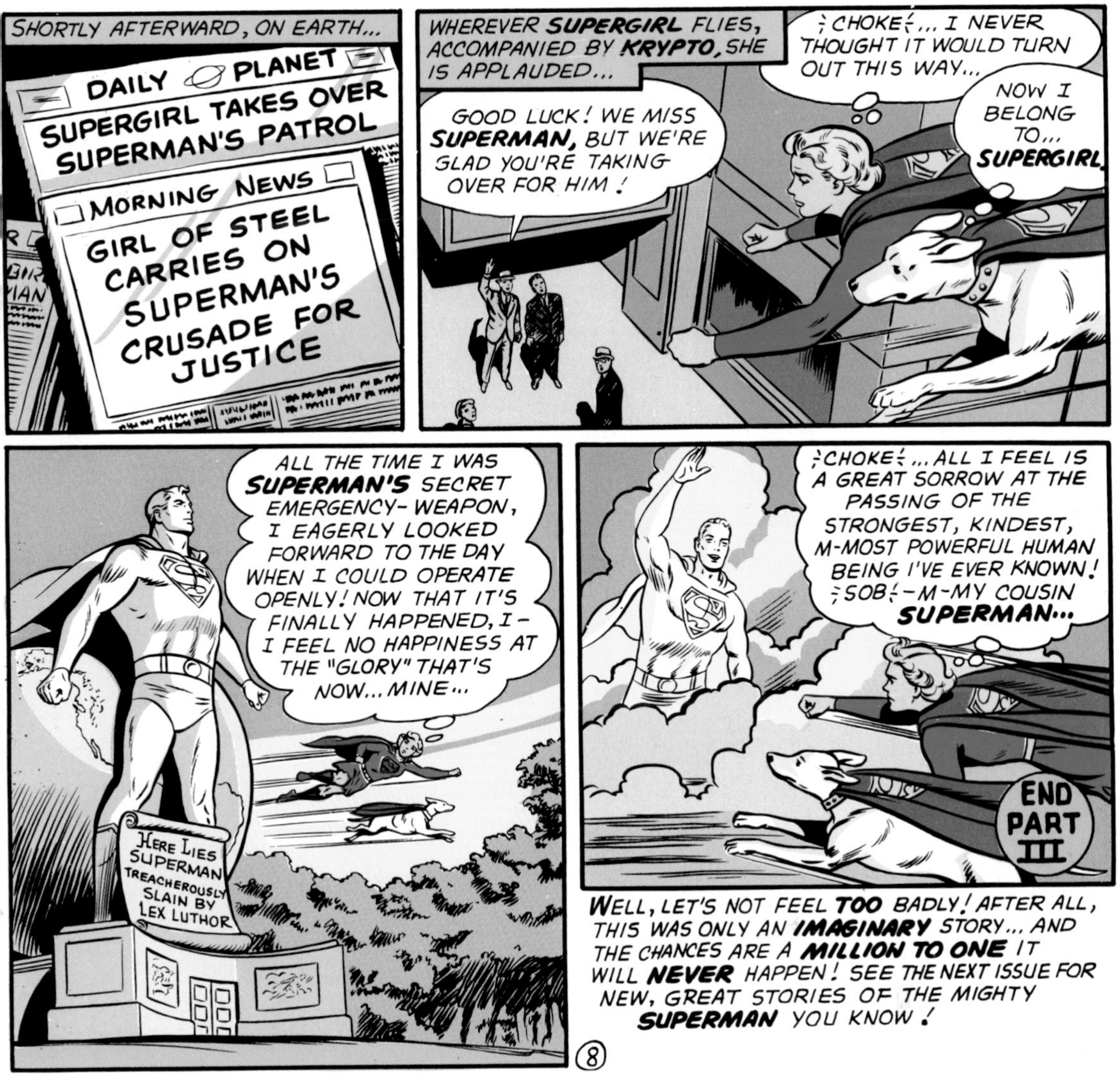

SHORTLY AFTERWARD, ON EARTH...
DAILY PLANET
SUPERGIRL TAKES OVER SUPERMAN'S PATROL
MORNING NEWS
GIRL OF STEEL CARRIES ON SUPERMAN'S CRUSADE FOR JUSTICE
WHEREVER SUPERGIRL FLIES, ACCOMPANIED BY KRYPTO, SHE IS APPLAUDED...
GOOD LUCK! WE MISS SUPERMAN, BUT WE'RE GLAD YOU'RE TAKING OVER FOR HIM!
CHOKE... I NEVER THOUGHT IT WOULD TURN OUT THIS WAY...
NOW I BELONG TO... SUPERGIRL.
ALL THE TIME I WAS SUPERMAN'S SECRET EMERGENCY-WEAPON, I EAGERLY LOOKED FORWARD TO THE DAY WHEN I COULD OPERATE OPENLY! NOW THAT IT'S FINALLY HAPPENED, I-I FEEL NO HAPPINESS AT THE "GLORY" THAT'S NOW... MINE...
HERE LIES SUPERMAN TREACHEROUSLY SLAIN BY LEX LUTHOR
CHOKE... ALL I FEEL IS A GREAT SORROW AT THE PASSING OF THE STRONGEST, KINDEST, M-MOST POWERFUL HUMAN BEING I'VE EVER KNOWN! SOB-M-MY COUSIN SUPERMAN...
END PART III
WELL, LET'S NOT FEEL TOO BADLY! AFTER ALL, THIS WAS ONLY AN IMAGINARY STORY... AND THE CHANCES ARE A MILLION TO ONE IT WILL NEVER HAPPEN! SEE THE NEXT ISSUE FOR NEW, GREAT STORIES OF THE MIGHTY SUPERMAN YOU KNOW!
8

PART III • 1970-1986
HIGHER, FURTHER

In the early 1970s, Mort Weisinger left DC Comics and the Superman editing duties. Julius Schwartz took over, making plans to shake Superman's universe to its core.

Schwartz pushed his creative team, writer Dennis O'Neil and penciller Curt Swan, to humanize a main character he found too powerful and too far from his roots. Superman's invincibility was killing the book's suspense, and consequently, Superman's powers were cut in half. He could no longer sustain an atomic explosion or tow a whole planet in space. Other story-weakening devices, such as Kryptonite, were similarly dismissed.

As O'Neil was tweaking Superman's powers, he also had changes in store for Clark Kent. Working in a newspaper was seen as too old-fashioned, so Clark became a TV reporter for Galaxy Broadcasting, run by the nebulous Morgan Edge.

All these changes occurred during the "Kryptonite Nevermore" (1971) story arc, but after only a few issues, it was decided that the Superman universe had changed too drastically, and the hero's superpowers were returned in full. Only the TV reporter job was kept.

Superman was powerful again, but new writers would continue to take a closer look at the human aspects of the character. In "Must There Be a Superman?" (1972), Elliot S. Maggin presented a Man of Steel questioning his actions, giving depth and self-criticism to the formerly irreproachable hero. Then with Cary Bates, he created a four-part story called "Who Took the Super Out of Superman?" (1976) in which Clark Kent and Superman are separated into two distinct characters — the perfect occasion for the reporter to start a relationship with Lois Lane.

In the same vein, the writers started populating the issues with ongoing subplots and stories exploring Krypton's past, Clark Kent's private life and even some issues taking place in another dimension where the 1940s Superman is married to Lois Lane. On top of that, the DC Comics team developed special projects teaming Superman with other stars: Marvel Comics' Spider-Man in 1976 and two years later, Muhammad Ali.

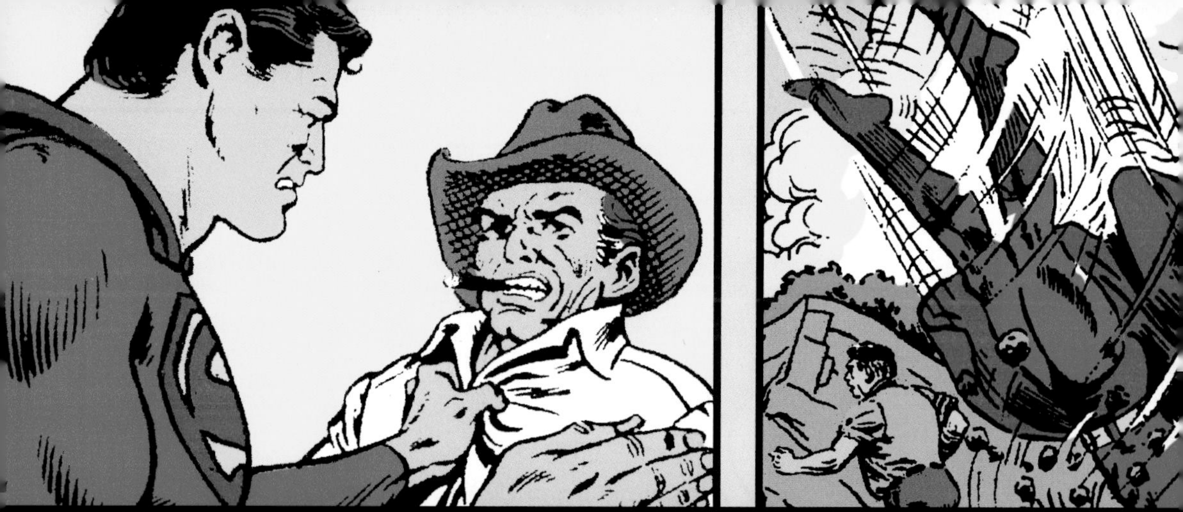

But all these projects, as big as they were, were nothing compared to the exposure brought by the movie version of the Man of Steel. Superman (1978) and Superman II (1980) were both massive hits. Christopher Reeve, who played the title role, became the ultimate incarnation of Superman for many people, and the movies' impact on both the comics and the character was unprecedented.

The end of the Julius Schwartz era came with the "Crisis on Infinite Earths" saga (1985-1986). This huge storyline symbolized the death of the old order, having every parallel Earth in the DC Universe melt into a new and unique world where everything began again from scratch.

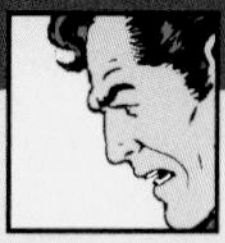

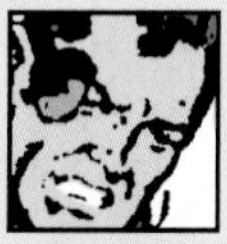

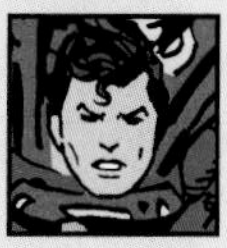

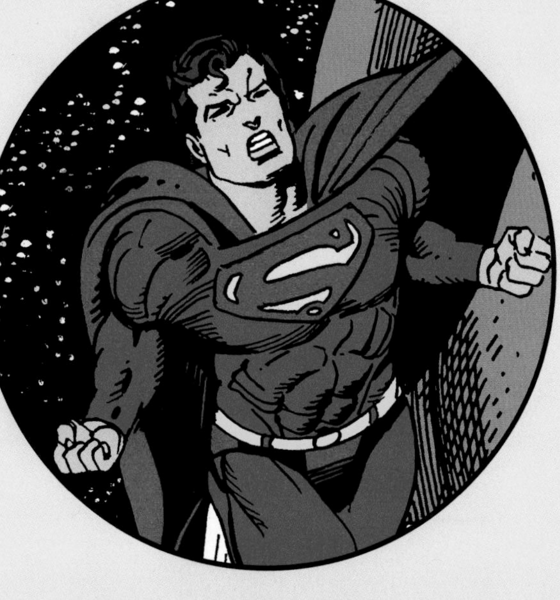

AND FOR THE MIGHTY MAN OF STEEL, EACH NEW ADVERSITY IS FOLLOWED BY YET ANOTHER.

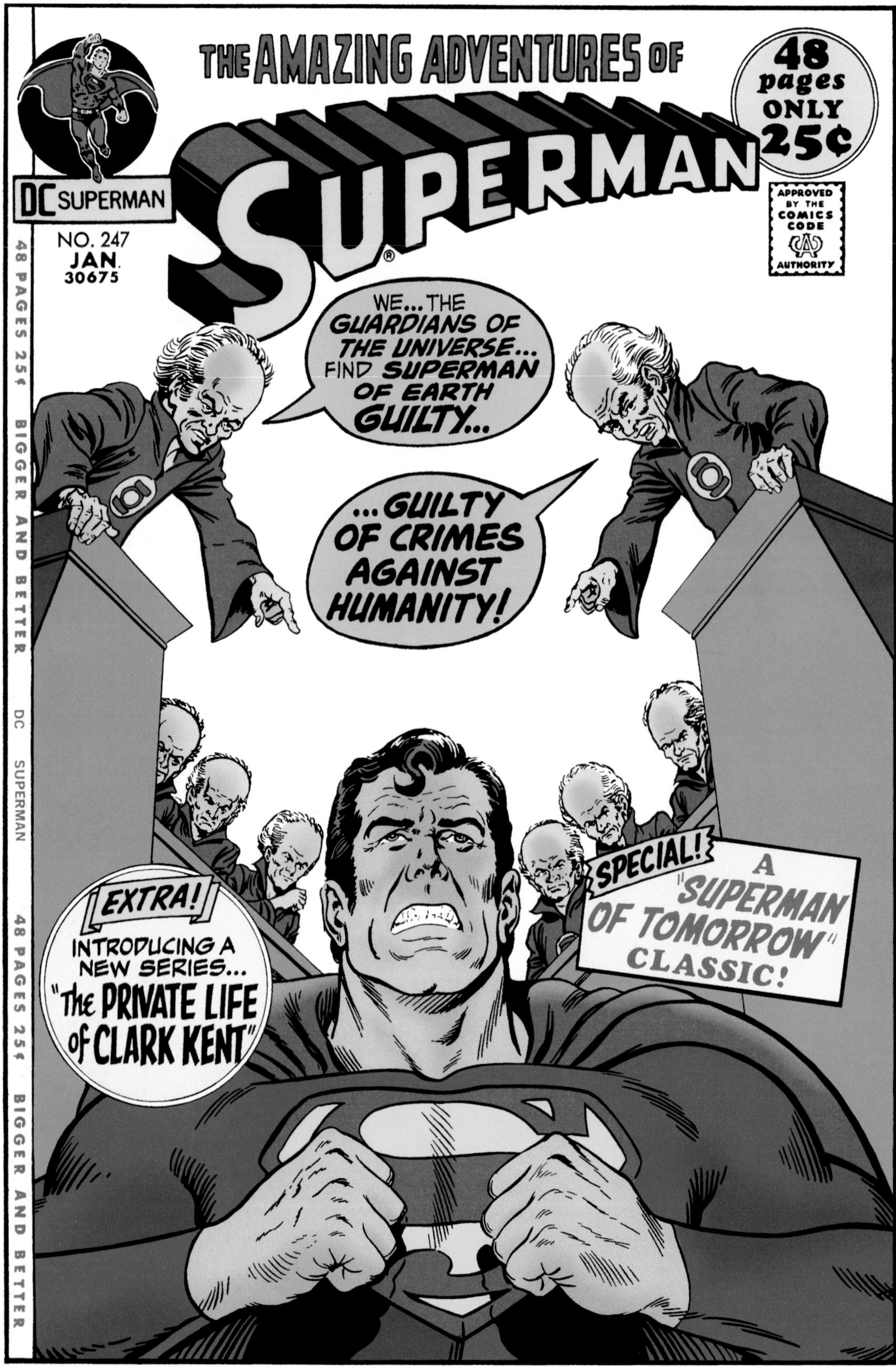

THE AMAZING ADVENTURES OF
SUPERMAN
DC SUPERMAN
NO. 247
JAN.
30675
48 pages ONLY 25¢
APPROVED BY THE COMICS CODE AUTHORITY
48 PAGES 25¢ BIGGER AND BETTER DC SUPERMAN 48 PAGES 25¢ BIGGER AND BETTER
WE...THE GUARDIANS OF THE UNIVERSE... FIND SUPERMAN OF EARTH GUILTY...
...GUILTY OF CRIMES AGAINST HUMANITY!
EXTRA!
INTRODUCING A NEW SERIES... "The PRIVATE LIFE of CLARK KENT"
SPECIAL!
A "SUPERMAN OF TOMORROW" CLASSIC!

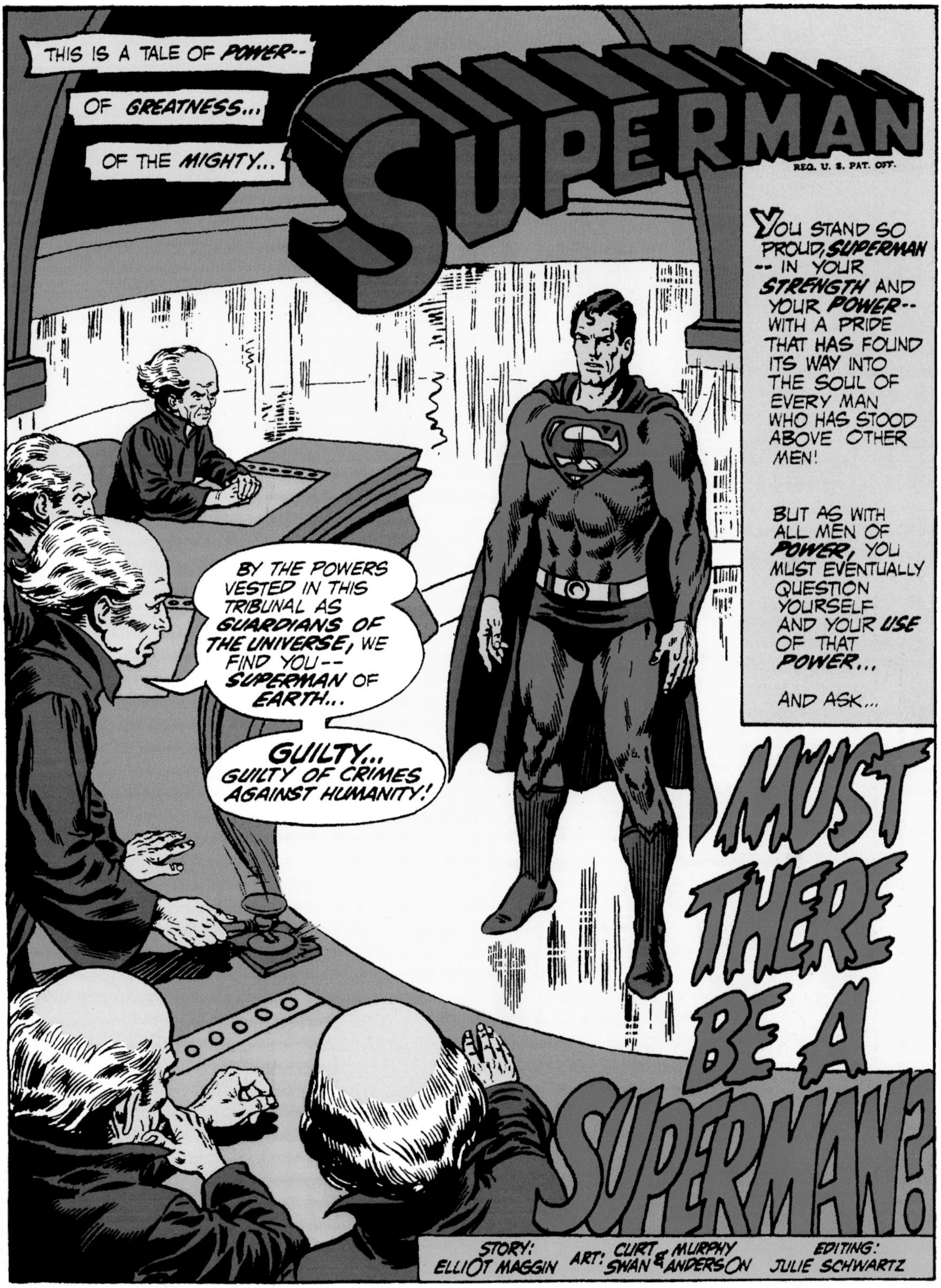

THIS IS A TALE OF POWER--
OF GREATNESS...
OF THE MIGHTY...
SUPERMAN
REG. U. S. PAT. OFF.
YOU STAND SO PROUD, SUPERMAN -- IN YOUR STRENGTH AND YOUR POWER-- WITH A PRIDE THAT HAS FOUND ITS WAY INTO THE SOUL OF EVERY MAN WHO HAS STOOD ABOVE OTHER MEN!
BUT AS WITH ALL MEN OF POWER, YOU MUST EVENTUALLY QUESTION YOURSELF AND YOUR USE OF THAT POWER...
AND ASK...
BY THE POWERS VESTED IN THIS TRIBUNAL AS GUARDIANS OF THE UNIVERSE, WE FIND YOU-- SUPERMAN OF EARTH...
GUILTY... GUILTY OF CRIMES AGAINST HUMANITY!
MUST THERE BE A SUPERMAN?
STORY: ELLIOT MAGGIN ART: CURT SWAN & MURPHY ANDERSON EDITING: JULIE SCHWARTZ

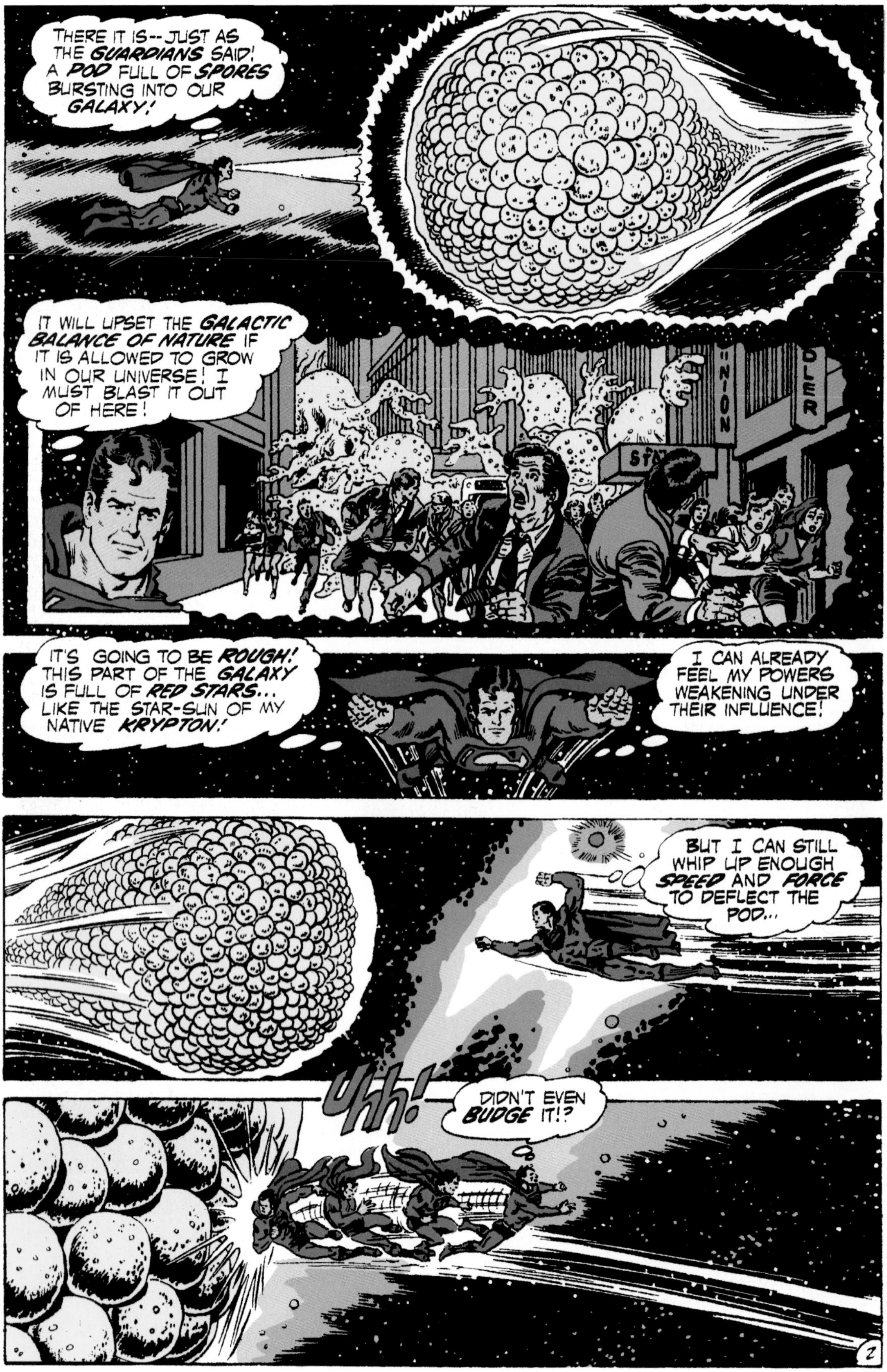
THERE IT IS--JUST AS THE GUARDIANS SAID! A POD FULL OF SPORES BURSTING INTO OUR GALAXY!
IT WILL UPSET THE GALACTIC BALANCE OF NATURE IF IT IS ALLOWED TO GROW IN OUR UNIVERSE! I MUST BLAST IT OUT OF HERE!
UNION
OLER
IT'S GOING TO BE ROUGH! THIS PART OF THE GALAXY IS FULL OF RED STARS... LIKE THE STAR-SUN OF MY NATIVE KRYPTON!
I CAN ALREADY FEEL MY POWERS WEAKENING UNDER THEIR INFLUENCE!
BUT I CAN STILL WHIP UP ENOUGH SPEED AND FORCE TO DEFLECT THE POD...
UHH!
DIDN'T EVEN BUDGE IT!?
2

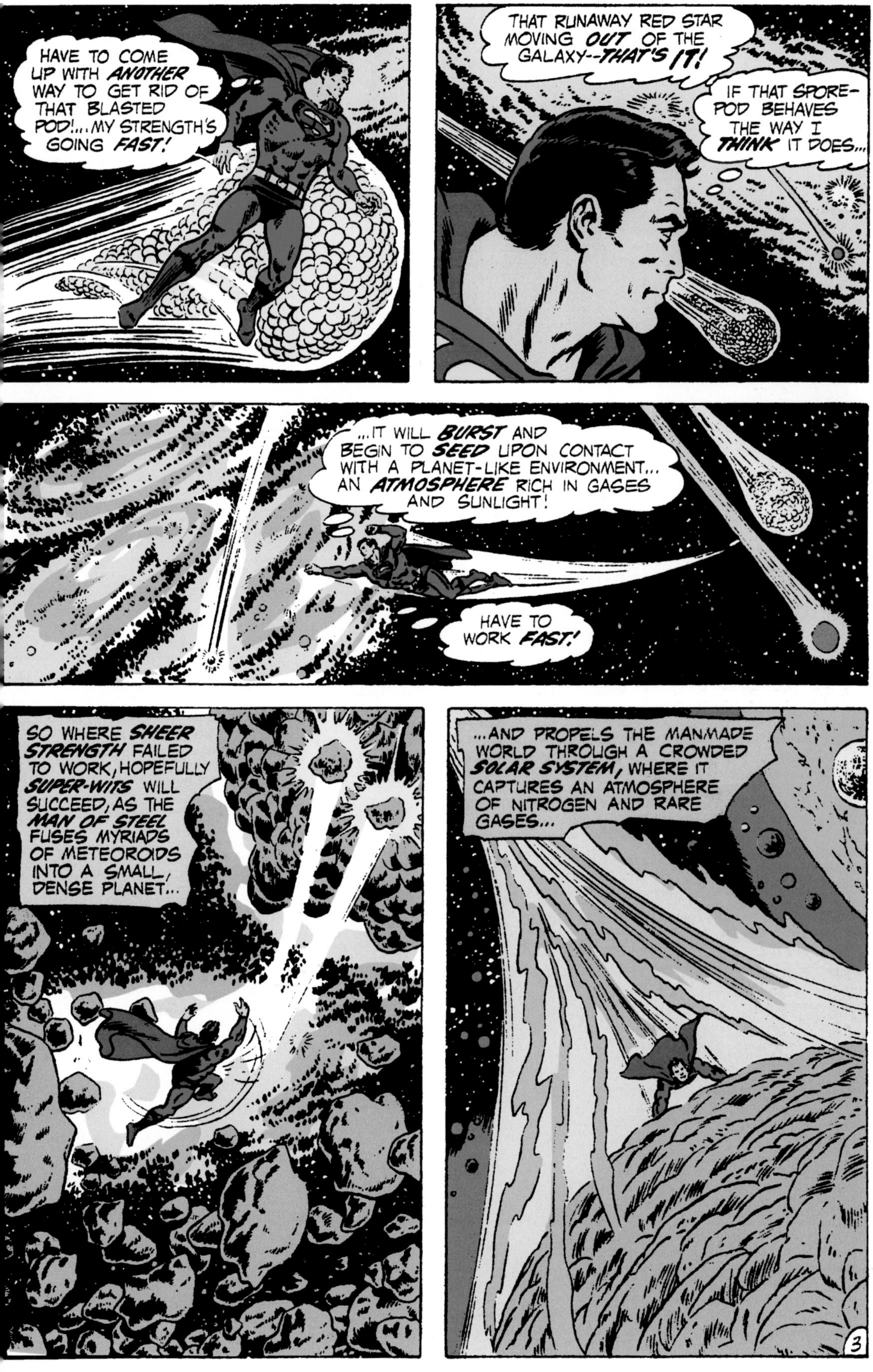
HAVE TO COME UP WITH ANOTHER WAY TO GET RID OF THAT BLASTED POD!... MY STRENGTH'S GOING FAST!
THAT RUNAWAY RED STAR MOVING OUT OF THE GALAXY--THAT'S IT!
IF THAT SPORE-POD BEHAVES THE WAY I THINK IT DOES...
...IT WILL BURST AND BEGIN TO SEED UPON CONTACT WITH A PLANET-LIKE ENVIRONMENT... AN ATMOSPHERE RICH IN GASES AND SUNLIGHT!
HAVE TO WORK FAST!
SO WHERE SHEER STRENGTH FAILED TO WORK, HOPEFULLY SUPER-WITS WILL SUCCEED, AS THE MAN OF STEEL FUSES MYRIADS OF METEOROIDS INTO A SMALL, DENSE PLANET...
...AND PROPELS THE MANMADE WORLD THROUGH A CROWDED SOLAR SYSTEM, WHERE IT CAPTURES AN ATMOSPHERE OF NITROGEN AND RARE GASES...
3

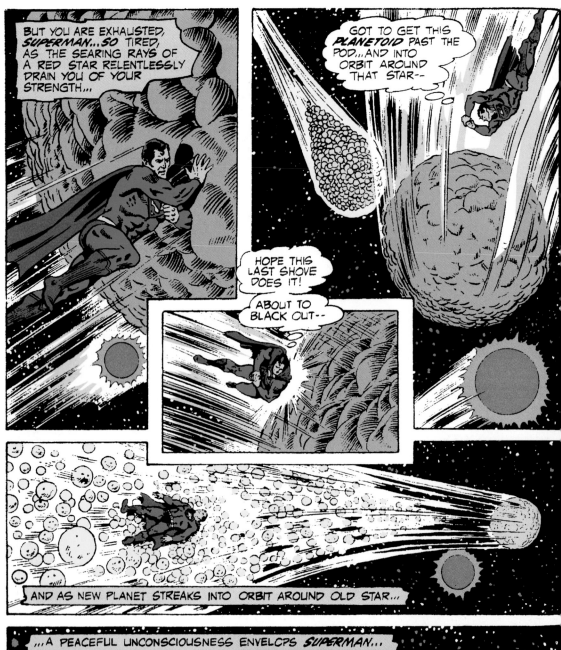

BUT YOU ARE EXHAUSTED, *SUPERMAN*...*SO* TIRED, AS THE SEARING RAYS OF A RED STAR RELENTLESSLY DRAIN YOU OF YOUR STRENGTH...

GOT TO GET THIS *PLANETOID* PAST THE POD...AND INTO ORBIT AROUND THAT STAR--

HOPE THIS LAST SHOVE DOES IT!

ABOUT TO BLACK OUT--

AND AS NEW PLANET STREAKS INTO ORBIT AROUND OLD STAR...

...A PEACEFUL UNCONSCIOUSNESS ENVELOPS *SUPERMAN*...

4

BOW YOUR HEADS AND CATCH YOUR BREATH, *HUMANS*--

FOR YOU ARE ABOUT TO COME INTO THE AWESOME PRESENCE OF...

...THE *GUARDIANS* OF THE UNIVERSE!

EXCELLENT *RESCUE*, *KATMA TUI*-- GREEN LANTERN OF *KORUGAR*!

PLACE THE *KRYPTONIAN* ON THE *SOLIDIFIED LIGHT-BEAMS* AND THEN-- *DEPART*!

I HOPE HE *RECOVERS*!

HE *WILL*!

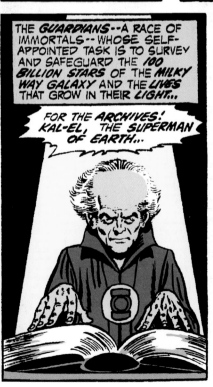

THE *GUARDIANS*--A RACE OF IMMORTALS--WHOSE SELF-APPOINTED TASK IS TO SURVEY AND SAFEGUARD THE *100 BILLION STARS* OF THE *MILKY WAY GALAXY* AND THE *LIVES* THAT GROW IN THEIR *LIGHT*...

FOR THE *ARCHIVES*! *KAL-EL*, THE *SUPERMAN* OF EARTH...

...IS NOW UNDERGOING THE *HEALING PROCESS* FOR INJURIES SUSTAINED WHILE UNDERTAKING OUR *SPECIAL MISSION*...

THESE ARE THE SELF-SAME *GUARDIANS* WHO HAVE DISPATCHED THE *GREEN LANTERN CORPS* TO SERVE AS THEIR *DEPUTIES* ACROSS THE BREADTH OF THE GALAXY...

5

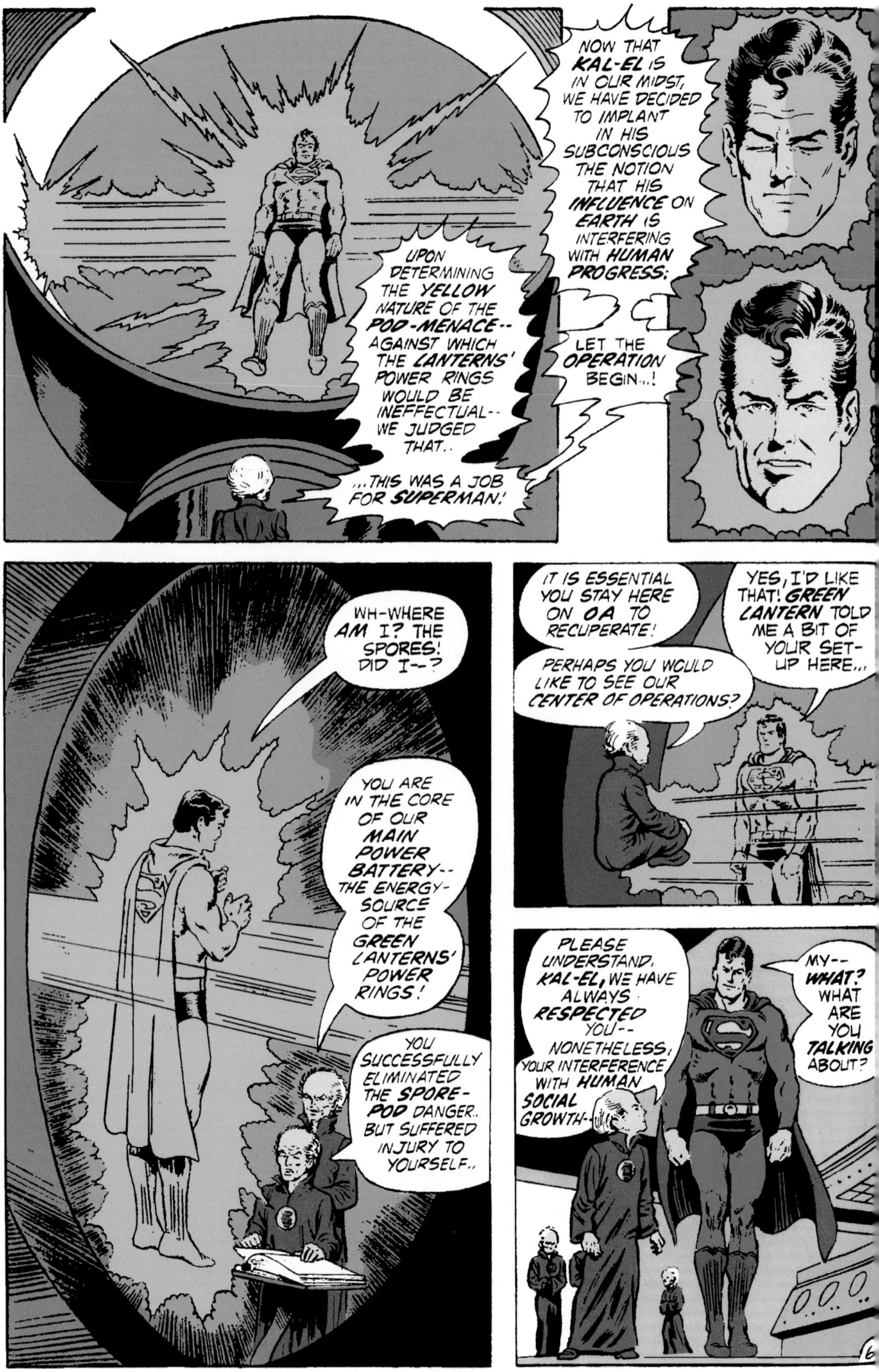
UPON DETERMINING THE YELLOW NATURE OF THE POD-MENACE-- AGAINST WHICH THE LANTERNS' POWER RINGS WOULD BE INEFFECTUAL-- WE JUDGED THAT..
...THIS WAS A JOB FOR SUPERMAN!
NOW THAT KAL-EL IS IN OUR MIDST, WE HAVE DECIDED TO IMPLANT IN HIS SUBCONSCIOUS THE NOTION THAT HIS INFLUENCE ON EARTH IS INTERFERING WITH HUMAN PROGRESS!
LET THE OPERATION BEGIN...!
WH-WHERE AM I? THE SPORES! DID I--?
YOU ARE IN THE CORE OF OUR MAIN POWER BATTERY-- THE ENERGY-SOURCE OF THE GREEN LANTERNS' POWER RINGS!
YOU SUCCESSFULLY ELIMINATED THE SPORE-POD DANGER.. BUT SUFFERED INJURY TO YOURSELF..
IT IS ESSENTIAL YOU STAY HERE ON OA TO RECUPERATE!
PERHAPS YOU WOULD LIKE TO SEE OUR CENTER OF OPERATIONS?
YES, I'D LIKE THAT! GREEN LANTERN TOLD ME A BIT OF YOUR SET-UP HERE...
PLEASE UNDERSTAND, KAL-EL, WE HAVE ALWAYS RESPECTED YOU-- NONETHELESS, YOUR INTERFERENCE WITH HUMAN SOCIAL GROWTH--
MY-- WHAT? WHAT ARE YOU TALKING ABOUT?
6

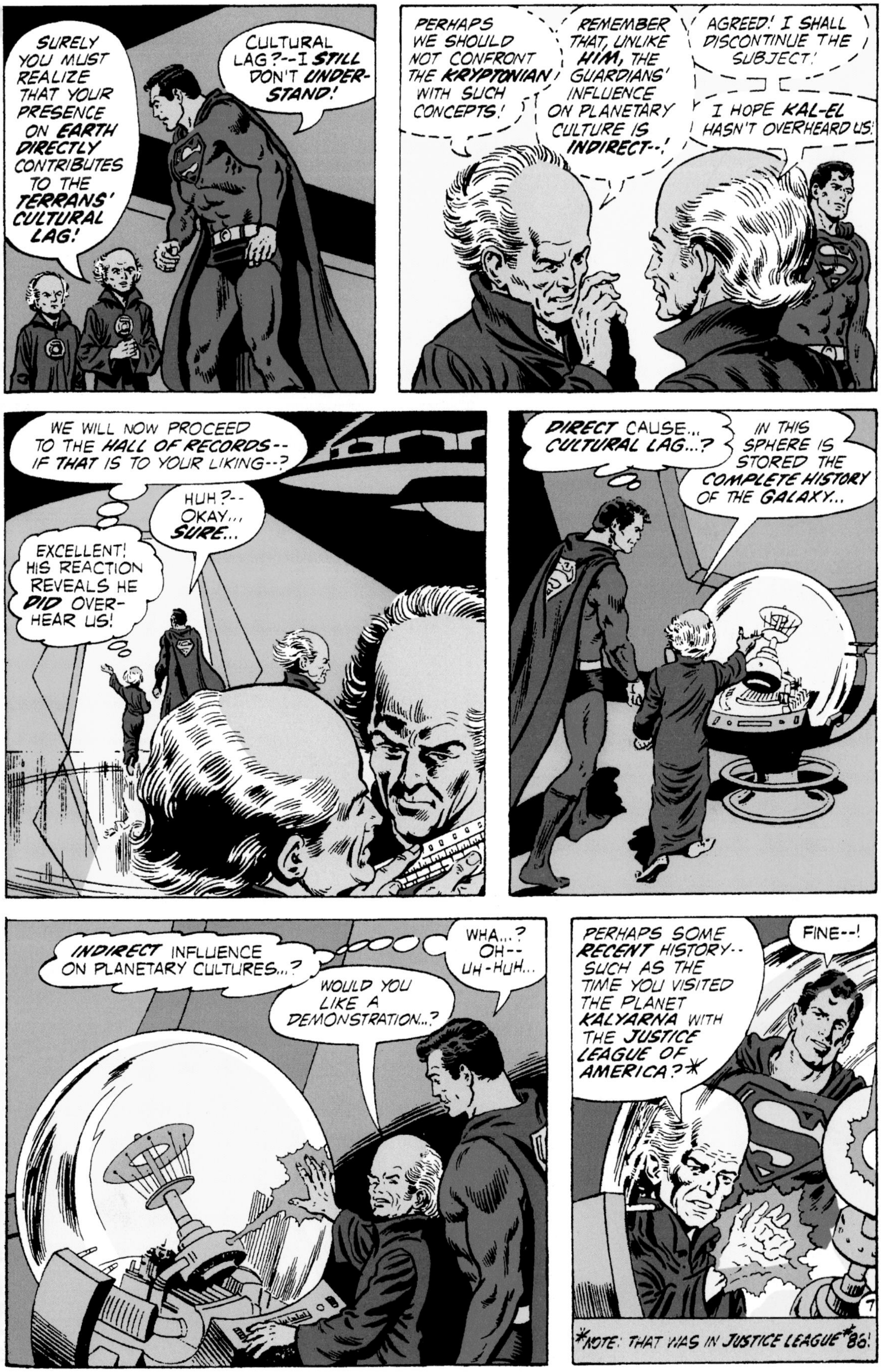
SURELY YOU MUST REALIZE THAT YOUR PRESENCE ON EARTH DIRECTLY CONTRIBUTES TO THE TERRANS' CULTURAL LAG!
CULTURAL LAG?--I STILL DON'T UNDERSTAND!
PERHAPS WE SHOULD NOT CONFRONT THE KRYPTONIAN WITH SUCH CONCEPTS!
REMEMBER THAT, UNLIKE HIM, THE GUARDIANS' INFLUENCE ON PLANETARY CULTURE IS INDIRECT--!
AGREED! I SHALL DISCONTINUE THE SUBJECT!
I HOPE KAL-EL HASN'T OVERHEARD US!
WE WILL NOW PROCEED TO THE HALL OF RECORDS--IF THAT IS TO YOUR LIKING--?
HUH?--OKAY... SURE...
EXCELLENT! HIS REACTION REVEALS HE DID OVERHEAR US!
DIRECT CAUSE... CULTURAL LAG...?
IN THIS SPHERE IS STORED THE COMPLETE HISTORY OF THE GALAXY...
INDIRECT INFLUENCE ON PLANETARY CULTURES...?
WHA...? OH--UH-HUH...
WOULD YOU LIKE A DEMONSTRATION...?
PERHAPS SOME RECENT HISTORY--SUCH AS THE TIME YOU VISITED THE PLANET KALYARNA WITH THE JUSTICE LEAGUE OF AMERICA?*
FINE--!
7
*NOTE: THAT WAS IN JUSTICE LEAGUE #86!

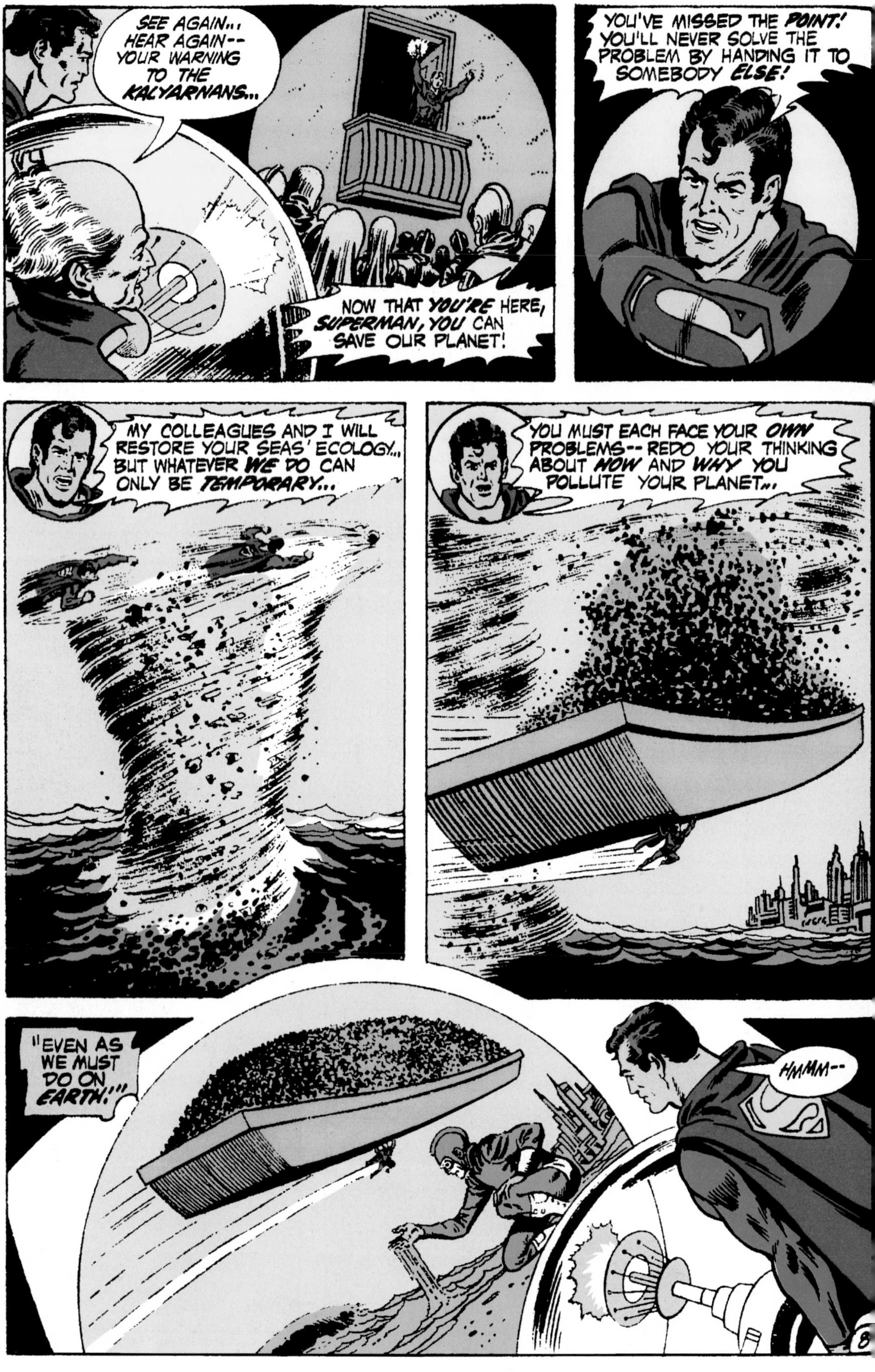
SEE AGAIN... HEAR AGAIN-- YOUR WARNING TO THE KALYARNANS...
NOW THAT YOU'RE HERE, SUPERMAN, YOU CAN SAVE OUR PLANET!
YOU'VE MISSED THE POINT! YOU'LL NEVER SOLVE THE PROBLEM BY HANDING IT TO SOMEBODY ELSE!
MY COLLEAGUES AND I WILL RESTORE YOUR SEAS' ECOLOGY... BUT WHATEVER WE DO CAN ONLY BE TEMPORARY...
YOU MUST EACH FACE YOUR OWN PROBLEMS--REDO YOUR THINKING ABOUT HOW AND WHY YOU POLLUTE YOUR PLANET...
"EVEN AS WE MUST DO ON EARTH!"
HMMM--
8

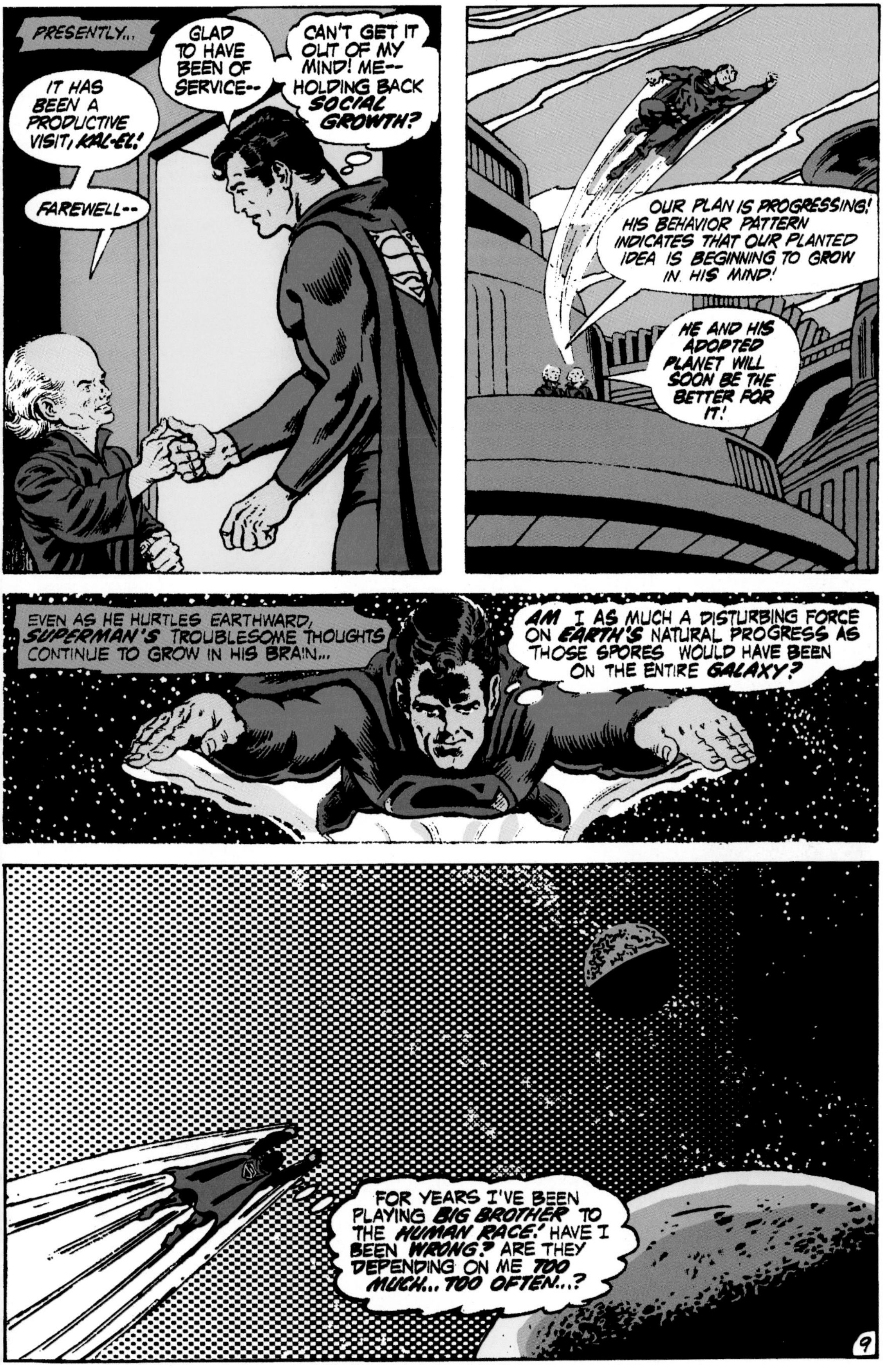
PRESENTLY...
IT HAS BEEN A PRODUCTIVE VISIT, KAL-EL!
FAREWELL--
GLAD TO HAVE BEEN OF SERVICE--
CAN'T GET IT OUT OF MY MIND! ME-- HOLDING BACK SOCIAL GROWTH?
OUR PLAN IS PROGRESSING! HIS BEHAVIOR PATTERN INDICATES THAT OUR PLANTED IDEA IS BEGINNING TO GROW IN HIS MIND!
HE AND HIS ADOPTED PLANET WILL SOON BE THE BETTER FOR IT!
EVEN AS HE HURTLES EARTHWARD, SUPERMAN'S TROUBLESOME THOUGHTS CONTINUE TO GROW IN HIS BRAIN...
AM I AS MUCH A DISTURBING FORCE ON EARTH'S NATURAL PROGRESS AS THOSE SPORES WOULD HAVE BEEN ON THE ENTIRE GALAXY?
FOR YEARS I'VE BEEN PLAYING BIG BROTHER TO THE HUMAN RACE! HAVE I BEEN WRONG? ARE THEY DEPENDING ON ME TOO MUCH... TOO OFTEN...?
9

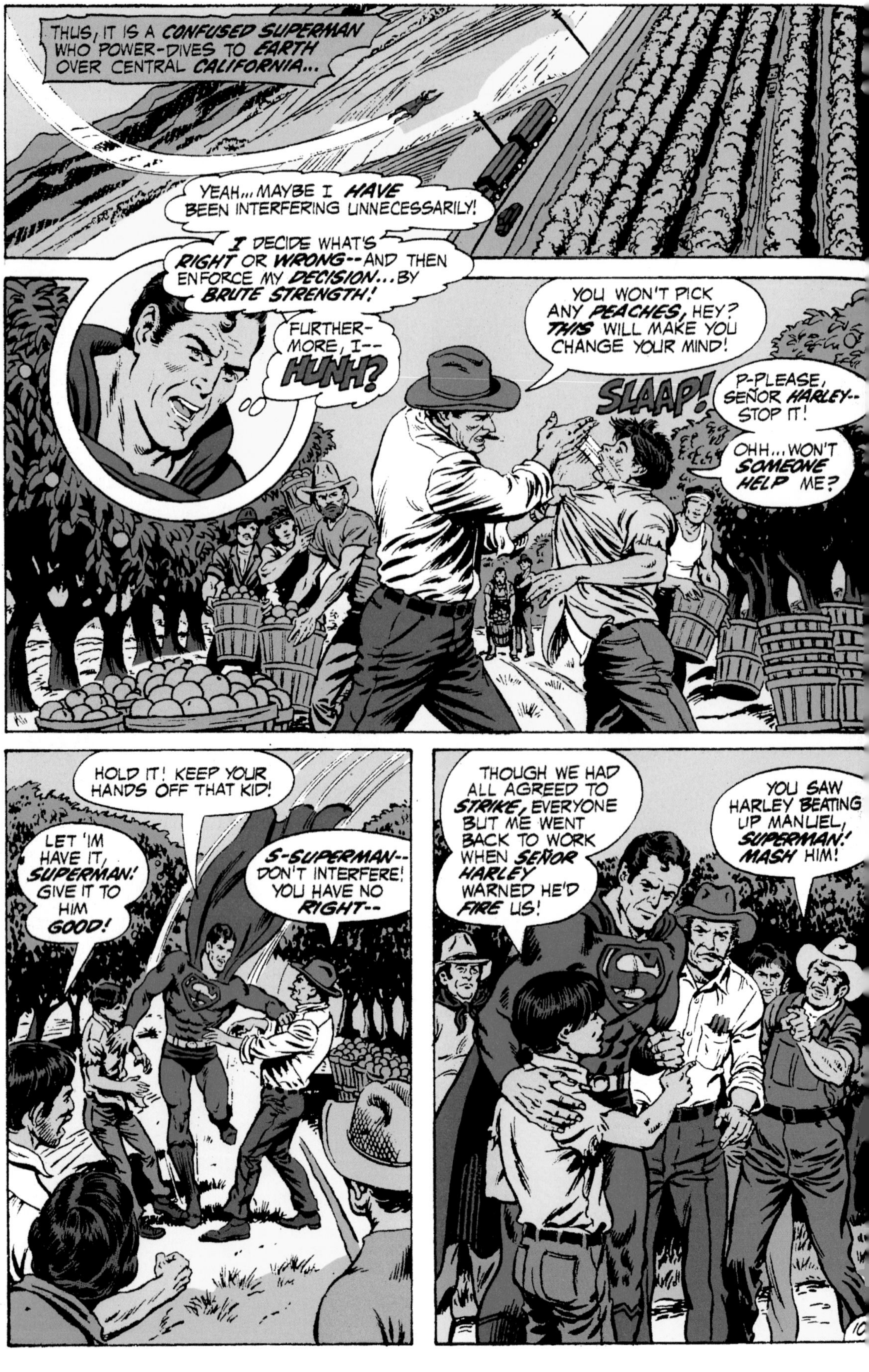
THUS, IT IS A CONFUSED SUPERMAN WHO POWER-DIVES TO EARTH OVER CENTRAL CALIFORNIA...
YEAH... MAYBE I HAVE BEEN INTERFERING UNNECESSARILY!
I DECIDE WHAT'S RIGHT OR WRONG--AND THEN ENFORCE MY DECISION... BY BRUTE STRENGTH!
FURTHER-MORE, I--
HUNH?
YOU WON'T PICK ANY PEACHES, HEY? THIS WILL MAKE YOU CHANGE YOUR MIND!
SLAAP!
P-PLEASE, SEÑOR HARLEY-- STOP IT!
OHH... WON'T SOMEONE HELP ME?
HOLD IT! KEEP YOUR HANDS OFF THAT KID!
LET 'IM HAVE IT, SUPERMAN! GIVE IT TO HIM GOOD!
S-SUPERMAN-- DON'T INTERFERE! YOU HAVE NO RIGHT--
THOUGH WE HAD ALL AGREED TO STRIKE, EVERYONE BUT ME WENT BACK TO WORK WHEN SEÑOR HARLEY WARNED HE'D FIRE US!
YOU SAW HARLEY BEATING UP MANUEL, SUPERMAN! MASH HIM!
10

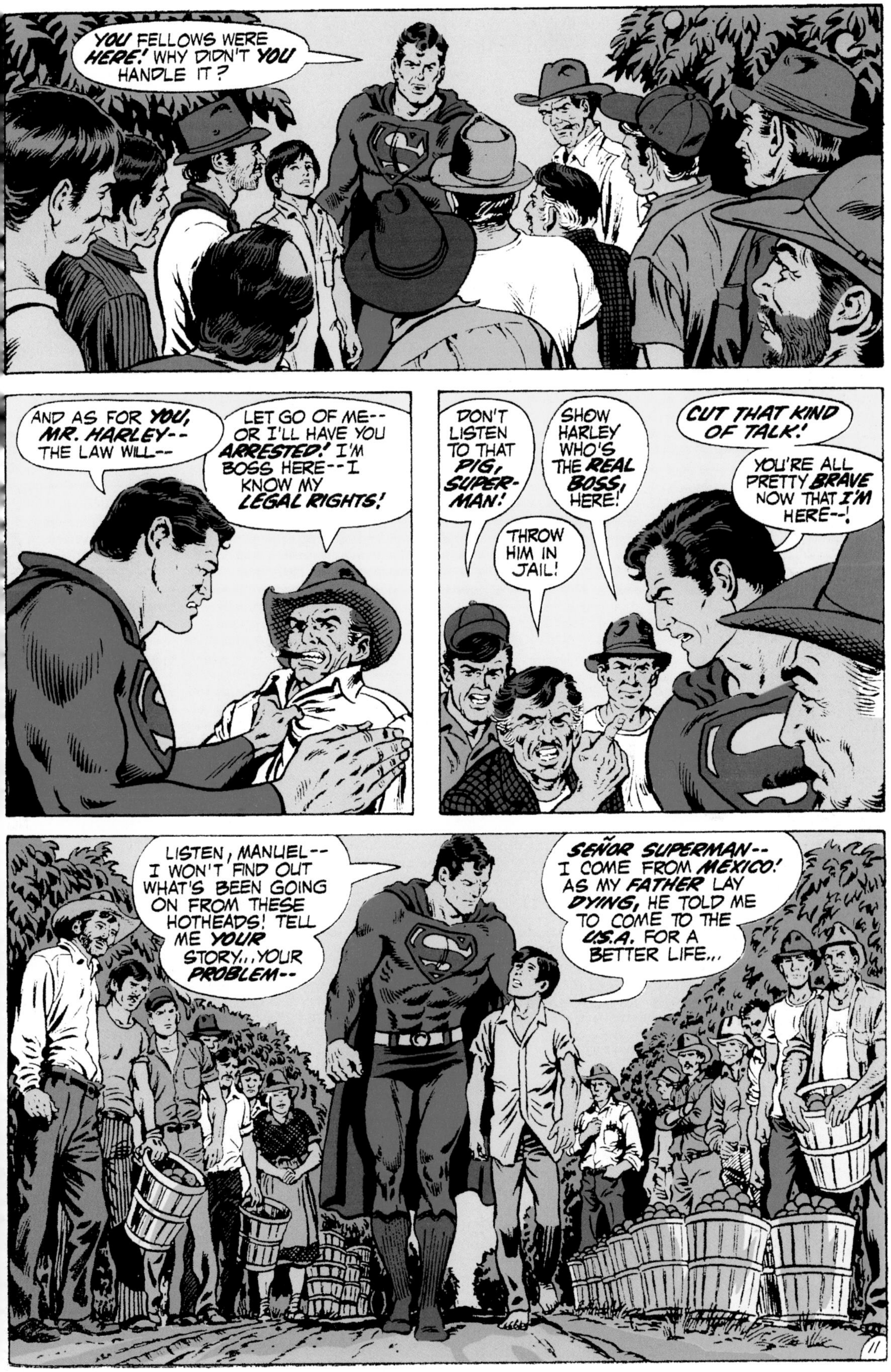

YOU FELLOWS WERE HERE! WHY DIDN'T YOU HANDLE IT?
AND AS FOR YOU, MR. HARLEY-- THE LAW WILL--
LET GO OF ME-- OR I'LL HAVE YOU ARRESTED! I'M BOSS HERE--I KNOW MY LEGAL RIGHTS!
DON'T LISTEN TO THAT PIG, SUPER-MAN!
SHOW HARLEY WHO'S THE REAL BOSS, HERE!
THROW HIM IN JAIL!
CUT THAT KIND OF TALK!
YOU'RE ALL PRETTY BRAVE NOW THAT I'M HERE--!
LISTEN, MANUEL-- I WON'T FIND OUT WHAT'S BEEN GOING ON FROM THESE HOTHEADS! TELL ME YOUR STORY...YOUR PROBLEM--
SEÑOR SUPERMAN-- I COME FROM MEXICO! AS MY FATHER LAY DYING, HE TOLD ME TO COME TO THE U.S.A. FOR A BETTER LIFE...
11

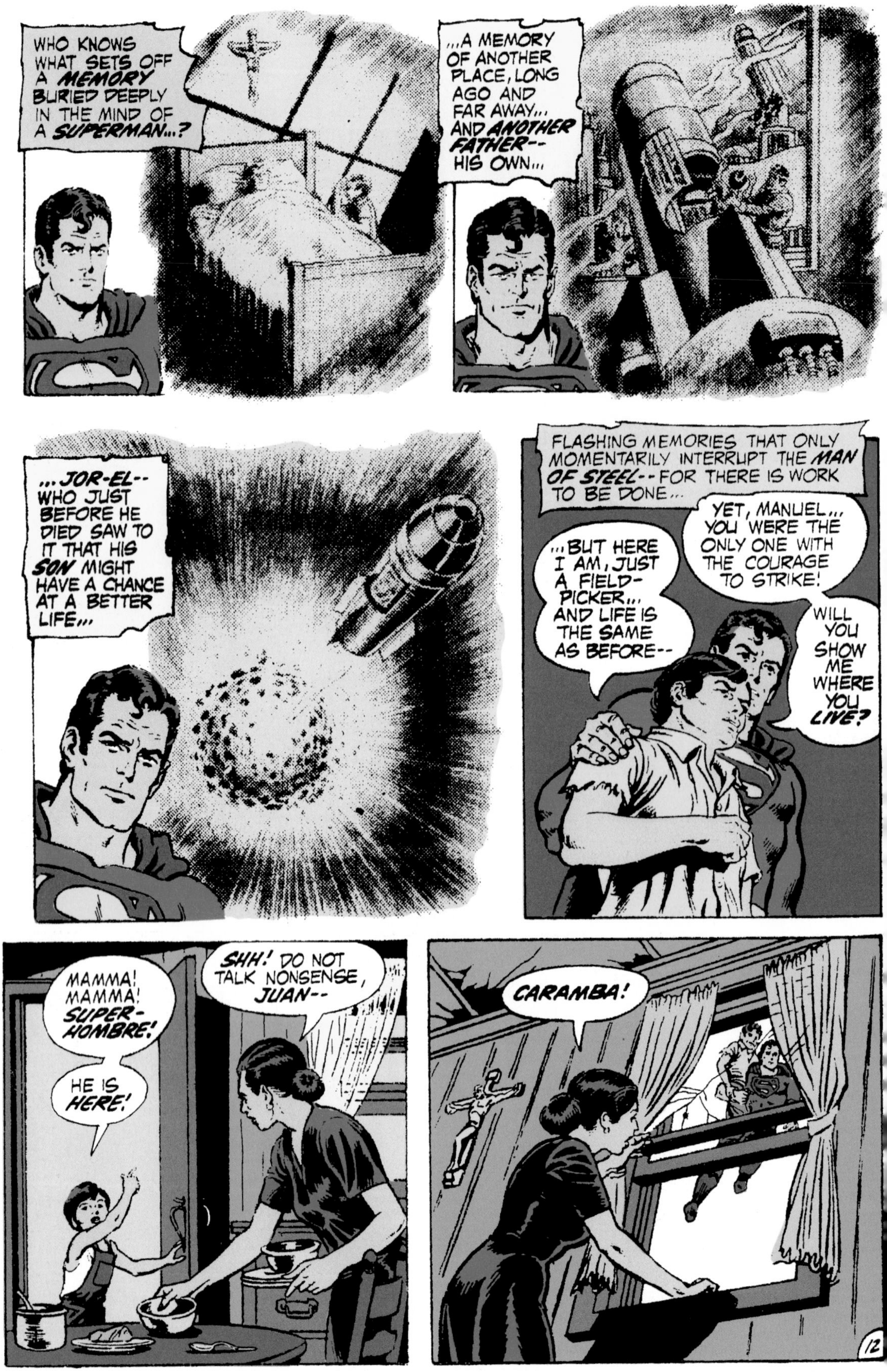
WHO KNOWS WHAT SETS OFF A MEMORY BURIED DEEPLY IN THE MIND OF A SUPERMAN...?
...A MEMORY OF ANOTHER PLACE, LONG AGO AND FAR AWAY... AND ANOTHER FATHER-- HIS OWN...
...JOR-EL-- WHO JUST BEFORE HE DIED SAW TO IT THAT HIS SON MIGHT HAVE A CHANCE AT A BETTER LIFE...
FLASHING MEMORIES THAT ONLY MOMENTARILY INTERRUPT THE MAN OF STEEL-- FOR THERE IS WORK TO BE DONE...
...BUT HERE I AM, JUST A FIELD-PICKER... AND LIFE IS THE SAME AS BEFORE--
YET, MANUEL... YOU WERE THE ONLY ONE WITH THE COURAGE TO STRIKE!
WILL YOU SHOW ME WHERE YOU LIVE?
MAMMA! MAMMA! SUPER-HOMBRE!
HE IS HERE!
SHH! DO NOT TALK NONSENSE, JUAN--
CARAMBA!
12

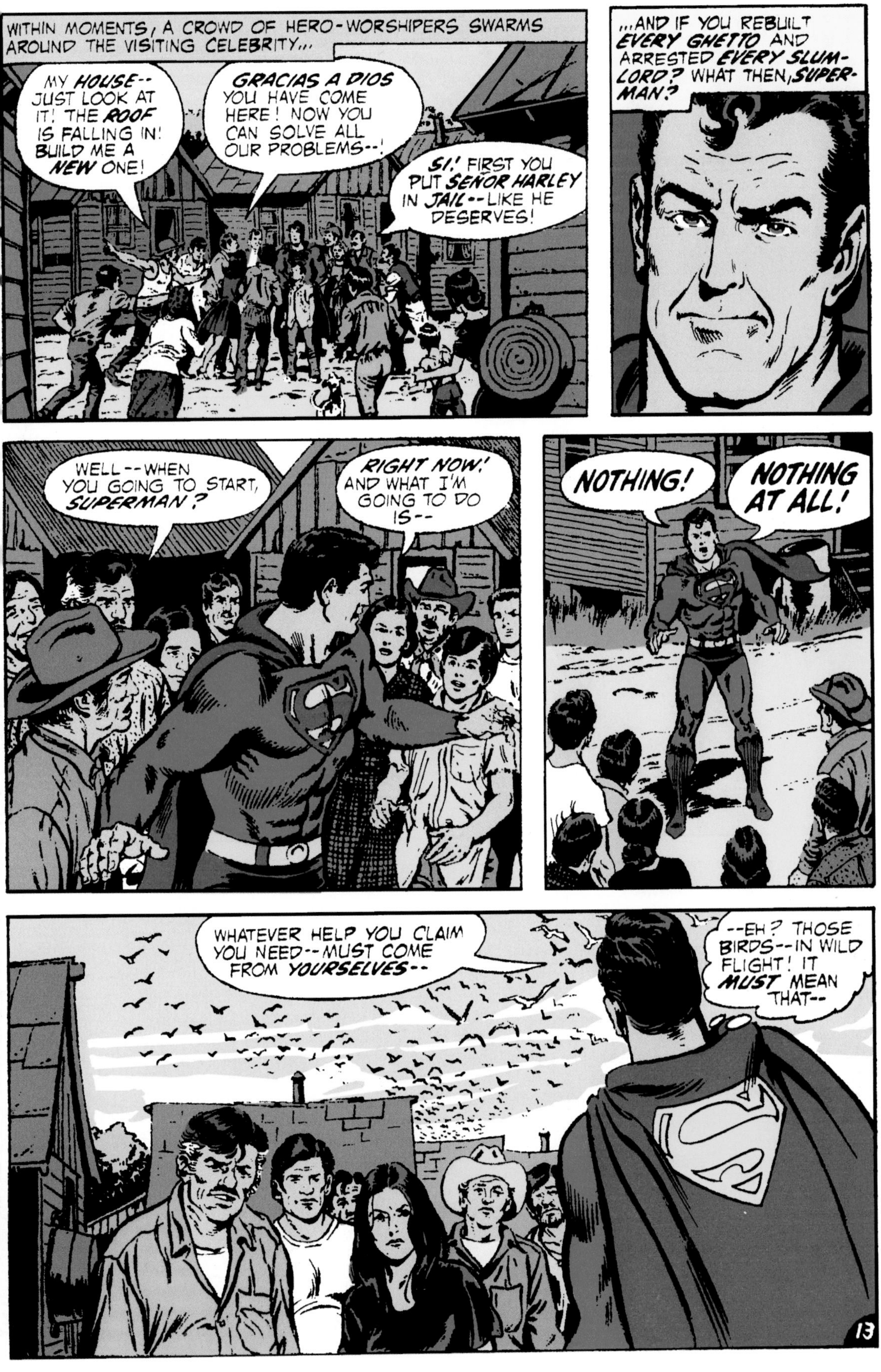
WITHIN MOMENTS, A CROWD OF HERO-WORSHIPERS SWARMS AROUND THE VISITING CELEBRITY...
MY HOUSE-- JUST LOOK AT IT! THE ROOF IS FALLING IN! BUILD ME A NEW ONE!
GRACIAS A DIOS YOU HAVE COME HERE! NOW YOU CAN SOLVE ALL OUR PROBLEMS--!
SI! FIRST YOU PUT SEÑOR HARLEY IN JAIL--LIKE HE DESERVES!
...AND IF YOU REBUILT EVERY GHETTO AND ARRESTED EVERY SLUM-LORD? WHAT THEN, SUPER-MAN?
WELL--WHEN YOU GOING TO START, SUPERMAN?
RIGHT NOW! AND WHAT I'M GOING TO DO IS--
NOTHING!
NOTHING AT ALL!
WHATEVER HELP YOU CLAIM YOU NEED--MUST COME FROM YOURSELVES--
--EH? THOSE BIRDS--IN WILD FLIGHT! IT MUST MEAN THAT--
13

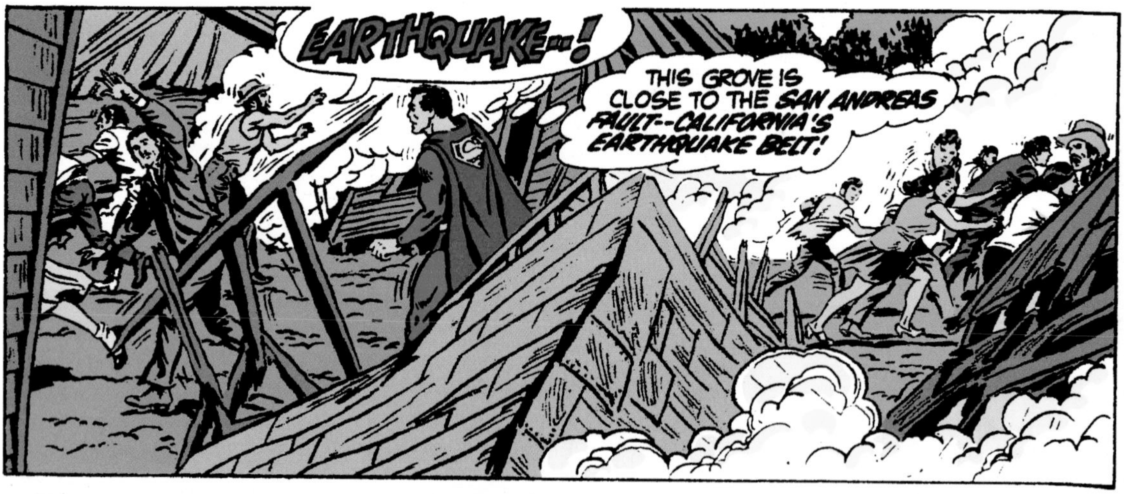
EARTHQUAKE--!
THIS GROVE IS CLOSE TO THE SAN ANDREAS FAULT--CALIFORNIA'S EARTHQUAKE BELT!

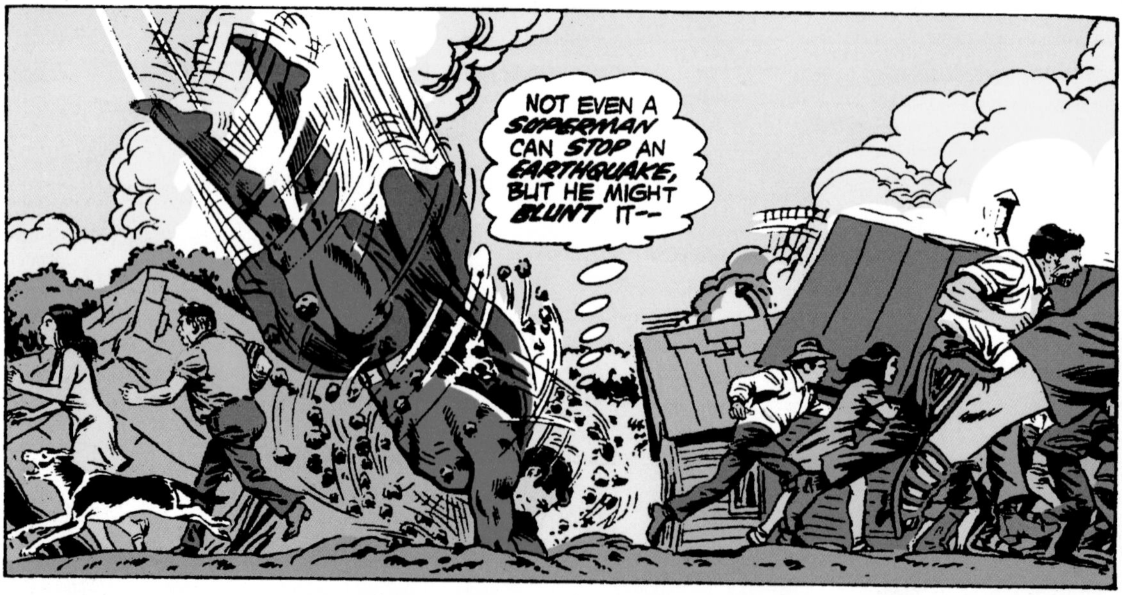
NOT EVEN A SUPERMAN CAN STOP AN EARTHQUAKE, BUT HE MIGHT BLUNT IT--

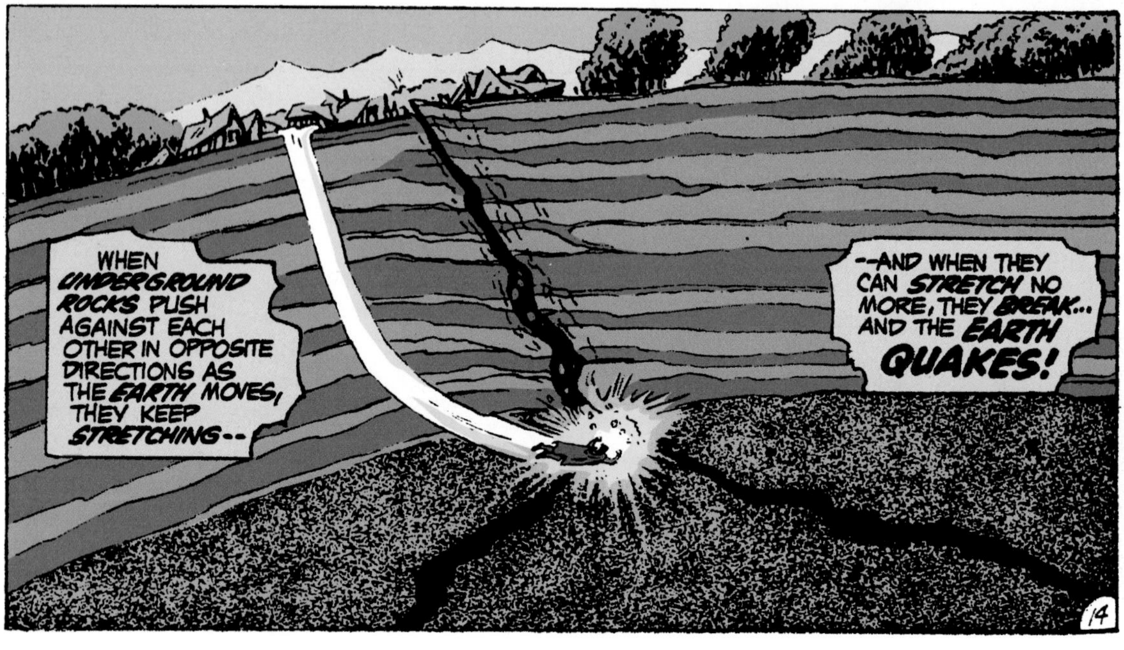
WHEN UNDERGROUND ROCKS PUSH AGAINST EACH OTHER IN OPPOSITE DIRECTIONS AS THE EARTH MOVES, THEY KEEP STRETCHING--
--AND WHEN THEY CAN STRETCH NO MORE, THEY BREAK... AND THE EARTH QUAKES!
14

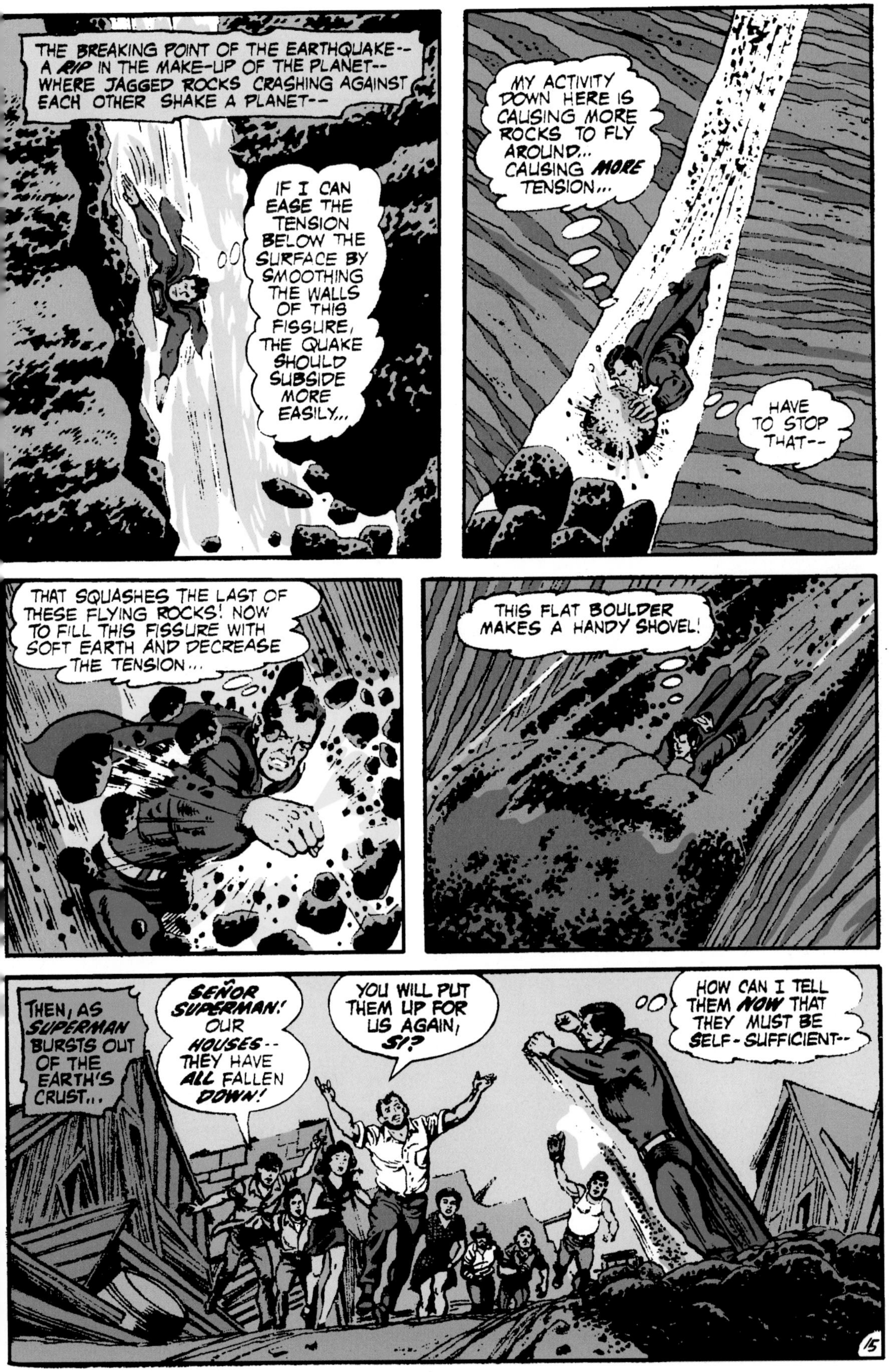
THE BREAKING POINT OF THE EARTHQUAKE-- A RIP IN THE MAKE-UP OF THE PLANET-- WHERE JAGGED ROCKS CRASHING AGAINST EACH OTHER SHAKE A PLANET--
IF I CAN EASE THE TENSION BELOW THE SURFACE BY SMOOTHING THE WALLS OF THIS FISSURE, THE QUAKE SHOULD SUBSIDE MORE EASILY...
MY ACTIVITY DOWN HERE IS CAUSING MORE ROCKS TO FLY AROUND... CAUSING MORE TENSION...
HAVE TO STOP THAT--
THAT SQUASHES THE LAST OF THESE FLYING ROCKS! NOW TO FILL THIS FISSURE WITH SOFT EARTH AND DECREASE THE TENSION...
THIS FLAT BOULDER MAKES A HANDY SHOVEL!
THEN, AS SUPERMAN BURSTS OUT OF THE EARTH'S CRUST...
SEÑOR SUPERMAN! OUR HOUSES-- THEY HAVE ALL FALLEN DOWN!
YOU WILL PUT THEM UP FOR US AGAIN, SI?
HOW CAN I TELL THEM NOW THAT THEY MUST BE SELF-SUFFICIENT--
15

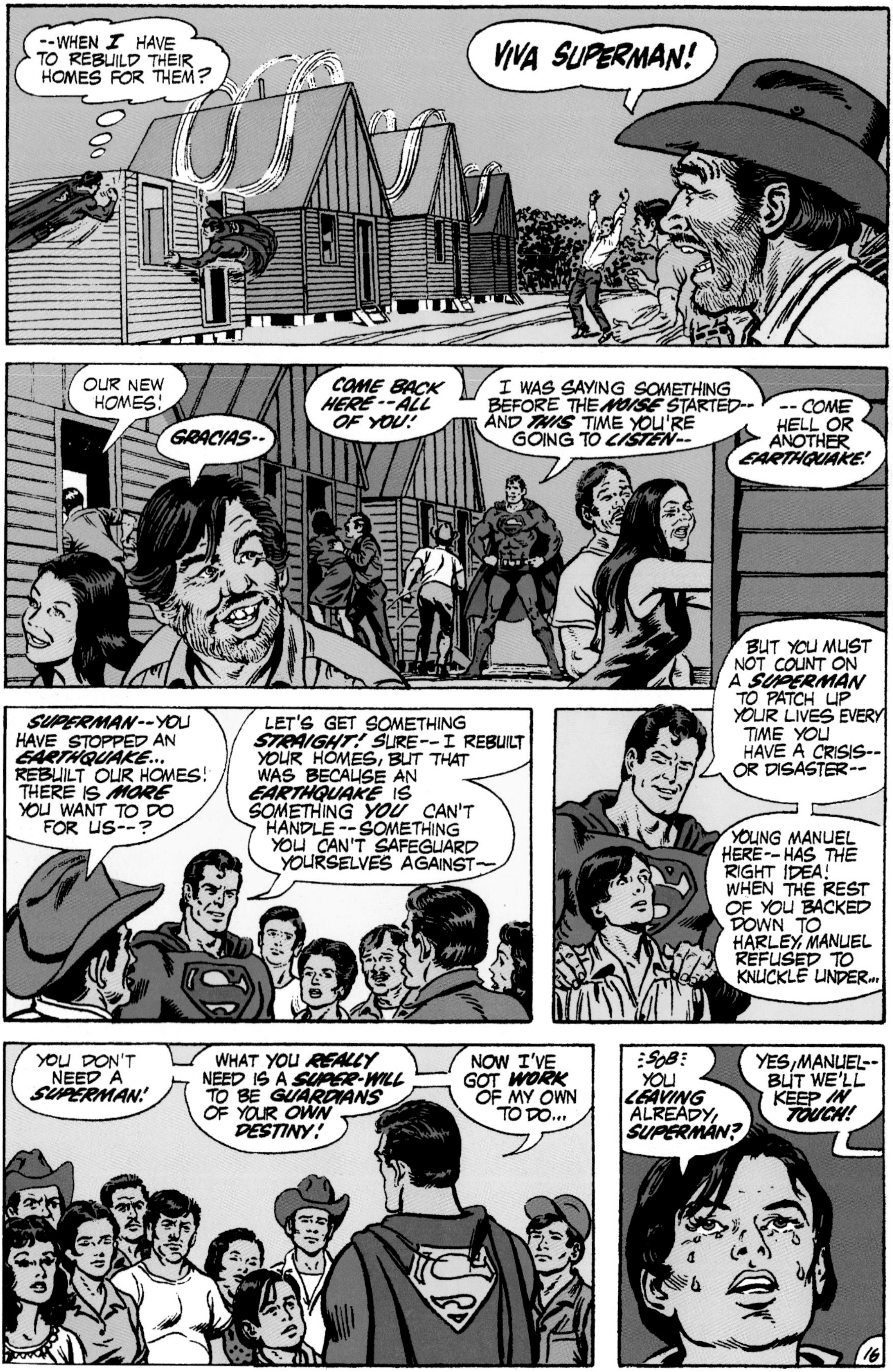
--WHEN I HAVE TO REBUILD THEIR HOMES FOR THEM?
VIVA SUPERMAN!
OUR NEW HOMES!
GRACIAS--
COME BACK HERE--ALL OF YOU!
I WAS SAYING SOMETHING BEFORE THE NOISE STARTED--AND THIS TIME YOU'RE GOING TO LISTEN--
--COME HELL OR ANOTHER EARTHQUAKE!
SUPERMAN--YOU HAVE STOPPED AN EARTHQUAKE... REBUILT OUR HOMES! THERE IS MORE YOU WANT TO DO FOR US--?
LET'S GET SOMETHING STRAIGHT! SURE--I REBUILT YOUR HOMES, BUT THAT WAS BECAUSE AN EARTHQUAKE IS SOMETHING YOU CAN'T HANDLE--SOMETHING YOU CAN'T SAFEGUARD YOURSELVES AGAINST--
BUT YOU MUST NOT COUNT ON A SUPERMAN TO PATCH UP YOUR LIVES EVERY TIME YOU HAVE A CRISIS--OR DISASTER--
YOUNG MANUEL HERE--HAS THE RIGHT IDEA! WHEN THE REST OF YOU BACKED DOWN TO HARLEY, MANUEL REFUSED TO KNUCKLE UNDER...
YOU DON'T NEED A SUPERMAN!
WHAT YOU REALLY NEED IS A SUPER-WILL TO BE GUARDIANS OF YOUR OWN DESTINY!
NOW I'VE GOT WORK OF MY OWN TO DO...
:SOB: YOU LEAVING ALREADY, SUPERMAN?
YES, MANUEL--BUT WE'LL KEEP IN TOUCH!
16

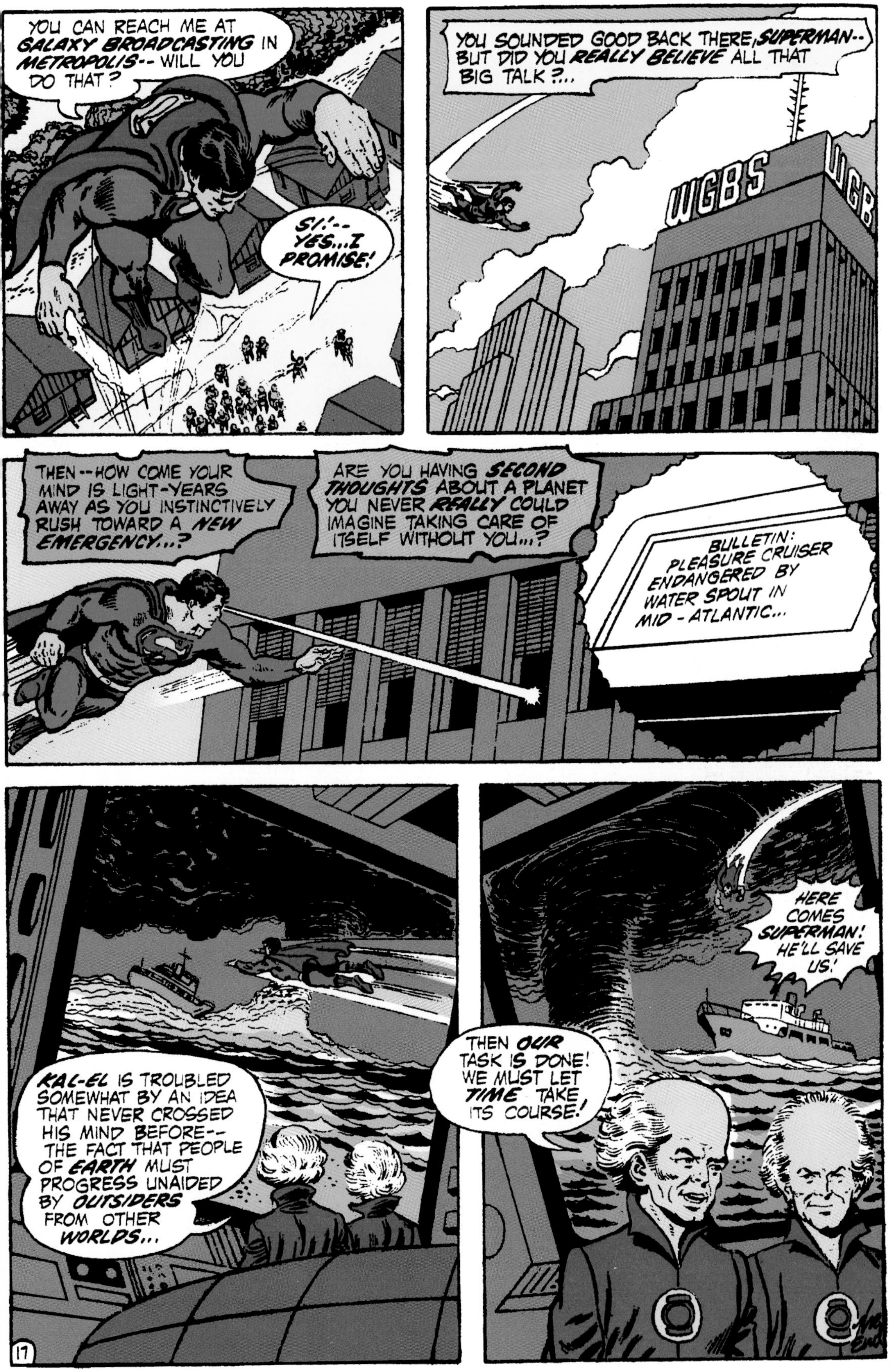
YOU CAN REACH ME AT GALAXY BROADCASTING IN METROPOLIS-- WILL YOU DO THAT?
SI!-- YES...I PROMISE!
YOU SOUNDED GOOD BACK THERE, SUPERMAN-- BUT DID YOU REALLY BELIEVE ALL THAT BIG TALK?...
WGBS
THEN--HOW COME YOUR MIND IS LIGHT-YEARS AWAY AS YOU INSTINCTIVELY RUSH TOWARD A NEW EMERGENCY...?
ARE YOU HAVING SECOND THOUGHTS ABOUT A PLANET YOU NEVER REALLY COULD IMAGINE TAKING CARE OF ITSELF WITHOUT YOU...?
BULLETIN: PLEASURE CRUISER ENDANGERED BY WATER SPOUT IN MID-ATLANTIC...
KAL-EL IS TROUBLED SOMEWHAT BY AN IDEA THAT NEVER CROSSED HIS MIND BEFORE-- THE FACT THAT PEOPLE OF EARTH MUST PROGRESS UNAIDED BY OUTSIDERS FROM OTHER WORLDS...
17
HERE COMES SUPERMAN! HE'LL SAVE US!
THEN OUR TASK IS DONE! WE MUST LET TIME TAKE ITS COURSE!

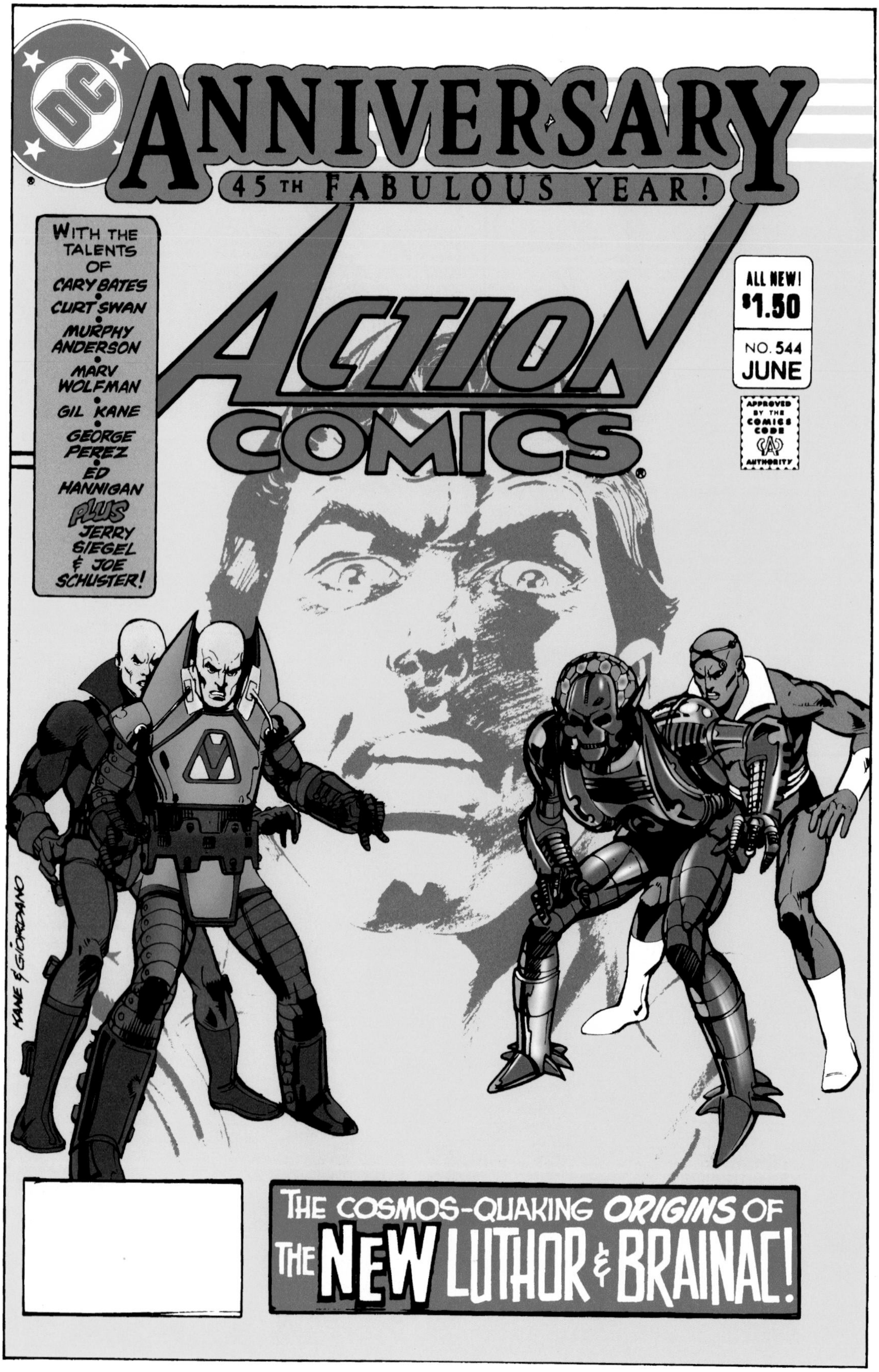
ANNIVERSARY
45TH FABULOUS YEAR!
ACTION COMICS
WITH THE TALENTS OF CARY BATES • CURT SWAN • MURPHY ANDERSON • MARV WOLFMAN • GIL KANE • GEORGE PEREZ • ED HANNIGAN PLUS JERRY SIEGEL & JOE SCHUSTER!
ALL NEW! $1.50
NO. 544 JUNE
APPROVED BY THE COMICS CODE AUTHORITY
KANE & GIORDANO
THE COSMOS-QUAKING ORIGINS OF
THE NEW LUTHOR & BRAINAC!

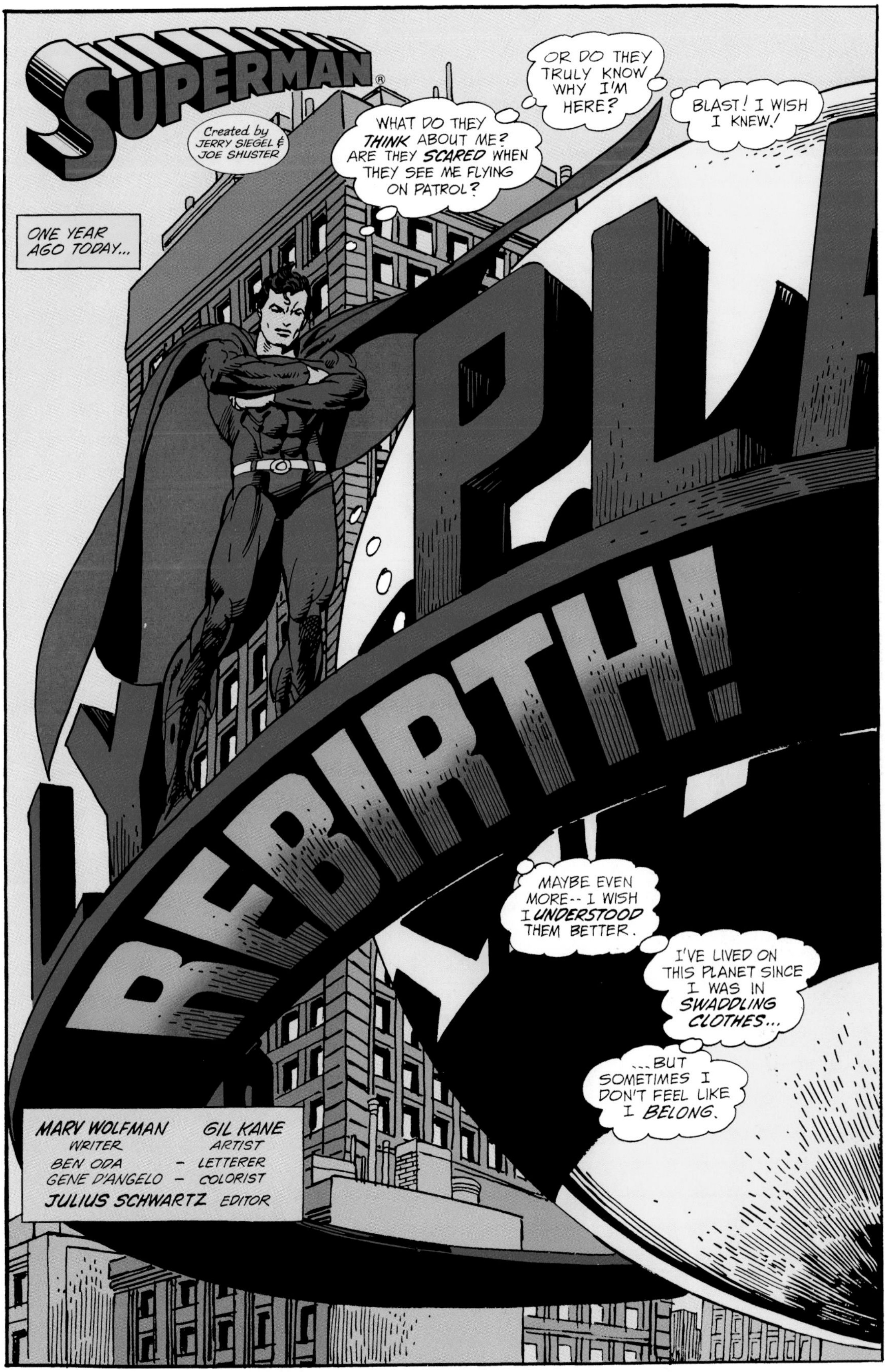
SUPERMAN®
Created by JERRY SIEGEL & JOE SHUSTER
ONE YEAR AGO TODAY...
WHAT DO THEY THINK ABOUT ME? ARE THEY SCARED WHEN THEY SEE ME FLYING ON PATROL?
OR DO THEY TRULY KNOW WHY I'M HERE?
BLAST! I WISH I KNEW!
REBIRTH!
MAYBE EVEN MORE-- I WISH I UNDERSTOOD THEM BETTER.
I'VE LIVED ON THIS PLANET SINCE I WAS IN SWADDLING CLOTHES...
...BUT SOMETIMES I DON'T FEEL LIKE I BELONG.
MARV WOLFMAN WRITER
GIL KANE ARTIST
BEN ODA - LETTERER
GENE D'ANGELO - COLORIST
JULIUS SCHWARTZ EDITOR

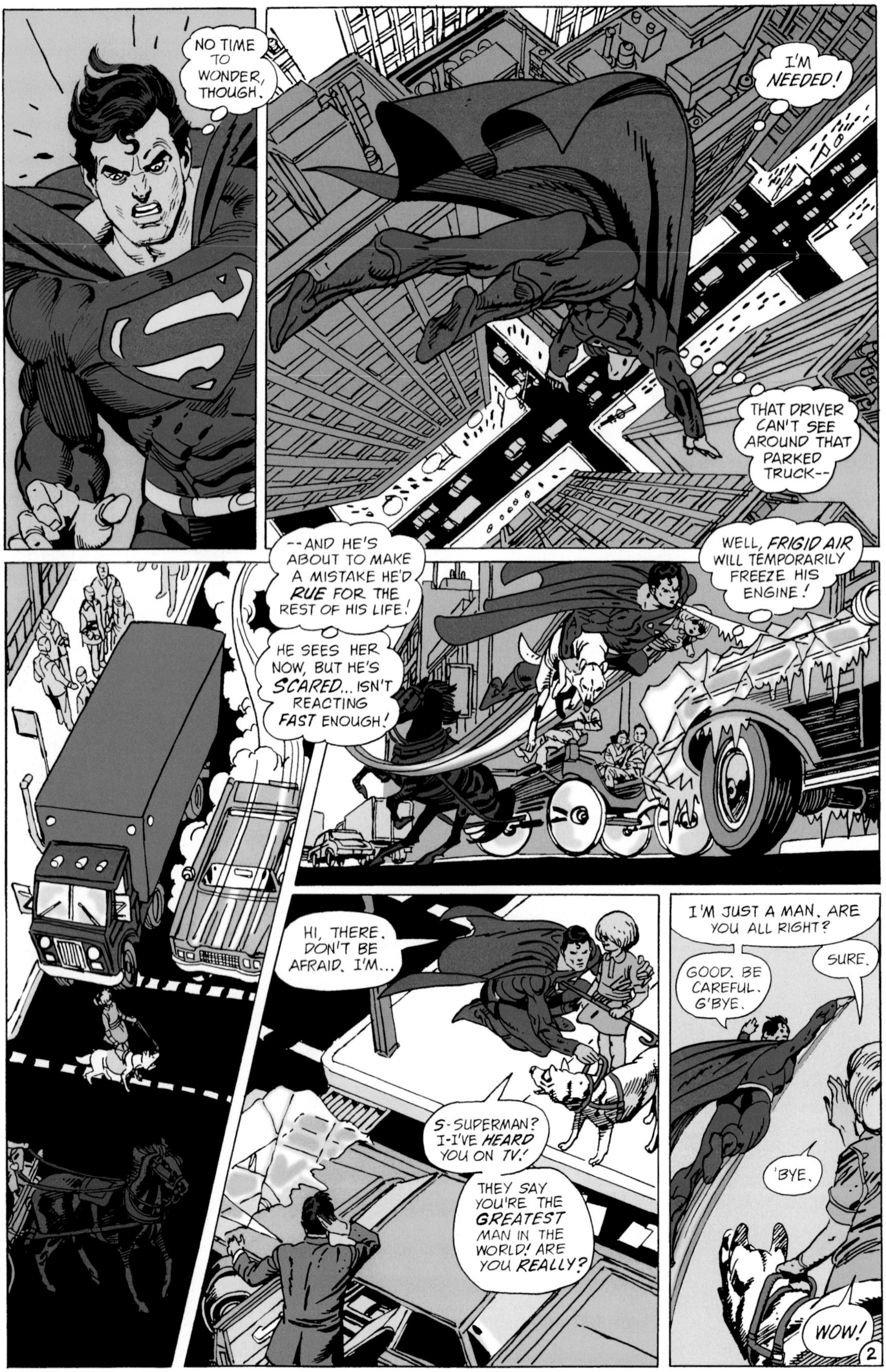
NO TIME TO WONDER, THOUGH.
I'M NEEDED!
THAT DRIVER CAN'T SEE AROUND THAT PARKED TRUCK--
--AND HE'S ABOUT TO MAKE A MISTAKE HE'D RUE FOR THE REST OF HIS LIFE!
HE SEES HER NOW, BUT HE'S SCARED... ISN'T REACTING FAST ENOUGH!
WELL, FRIGID AIR WILL TEMPORARILY FREEZE HIS ENGINE!
HI, THERE. DON'T BE AFRAID. I'M...
S-SUPERMAN? I-I'VE HEARD YOU ON TV!
THEY SAY YOU'RE THE GREATEST MAN IN THE WORLD! ARE YOU REALLY?
I'M JUST A MAN. ARE YOU ALL RIGHT?
SURE.
GOOD. BE CAREFUL. G'BYE.
'BYE.
WOW!
2

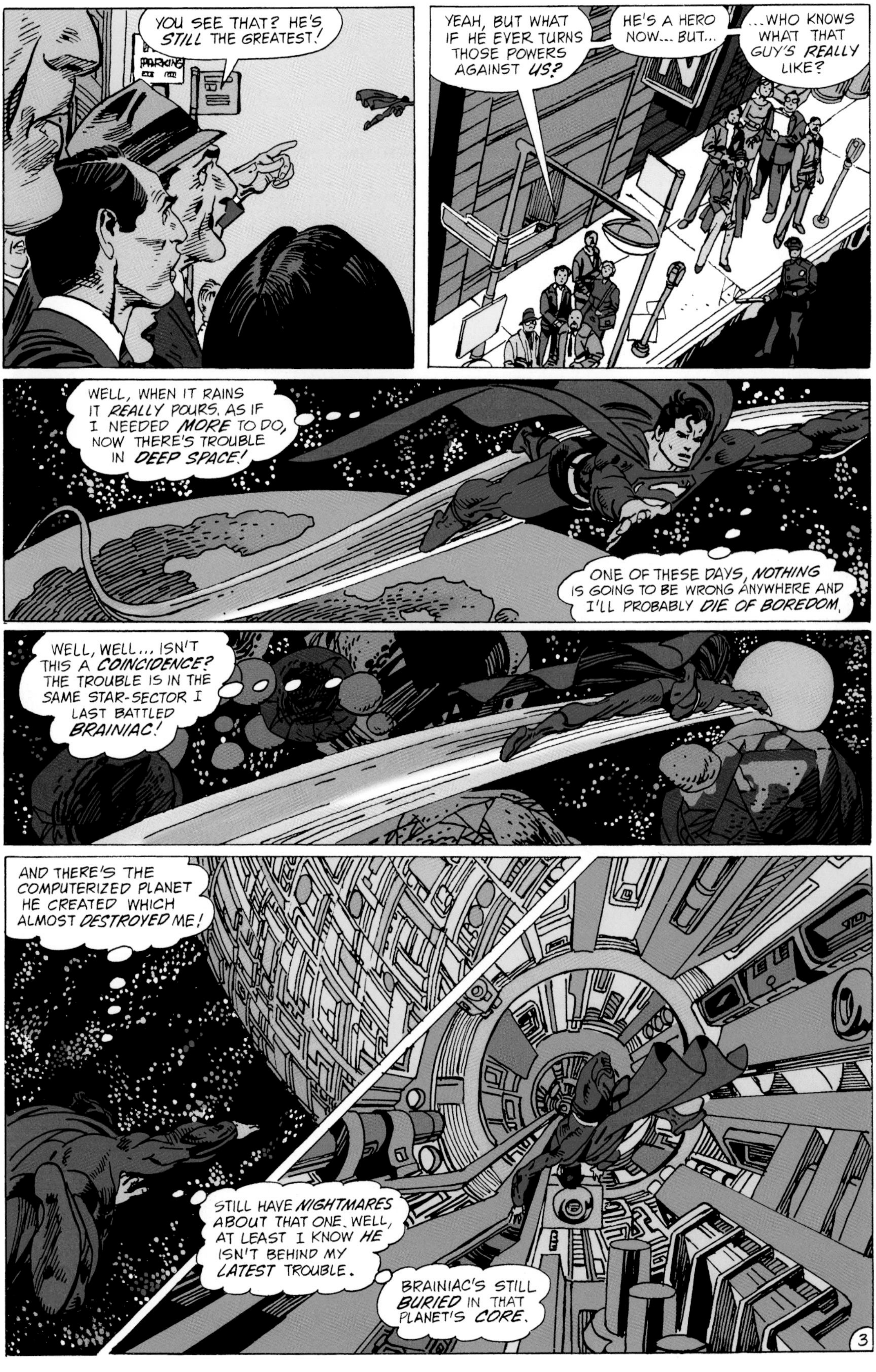
YOU SEE THAT? HE'S STILL THE GREATEST!
PARKING
YEAH, BUT WHAT IF HE EVER TURNS THOSE POWERS AGAINST US?
HE'S A HERO NOW... BUT...
...WHO KNOWS WHAT THAT GUY'S REALLY LIKE?
WELL, WHEN IT RAINS IT REALLY POURS. AS IF I NEEDED MORE TO DO, NOW THERE'S TROUBLE IN DEEP SPACE!
ONE OF THESE DAYS, NOTHING IS GOING TO BE WRONG ANYWHERE AND I'LL PROBABLY DIE OF BOREDOM.
WELL, WELL... ISN'T THIS A COINCIDENCE? THE TROUBLE IS IN THE SAME STAR-SECTOR I LAST BATTLED BRAINIAC!
AND THERE'S THE COMPUTERIZED PLANET HE CREATED WHICH ALMOST DESTROYED ME!
STILL HAVE NIGHTMARES ABOUT THAT ONE. WELL, AT LEAST I KNOW HE ISN'T BEHIND MY LATEST TROUBLE.
BRAINIAC'S STILL BURIED IN THAT PLANET'S CORE.
3

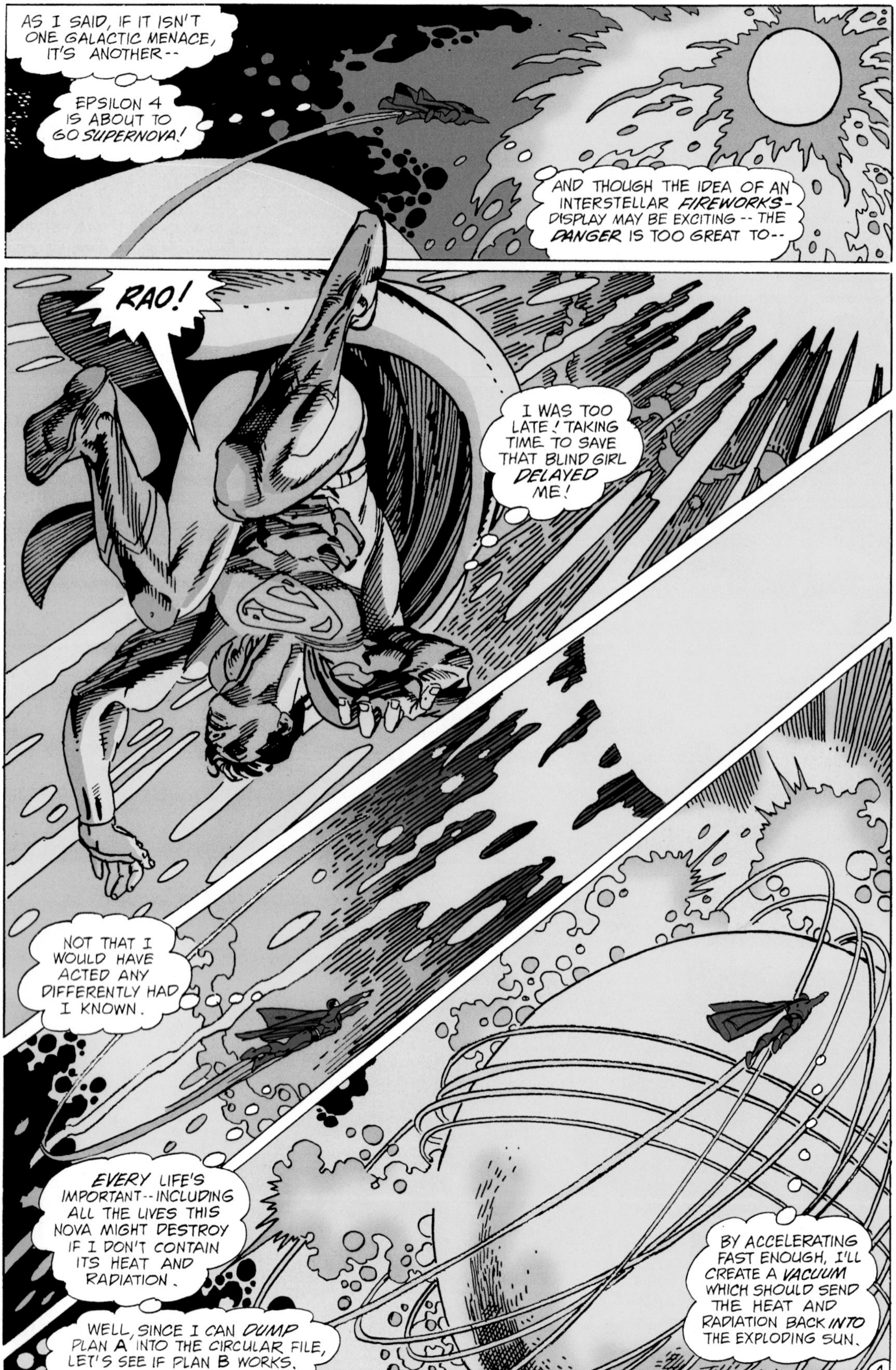
AS I SAID, IF IT ISN'T ONE GALACTIC MENACE, IT'S ANOTHER--
EPSILON 4 IS ABOUT TO GO SUPERNOVA!
AND THOUGH THE IDEA OF AN INTERSTELLAR FIREWORKS-DISPLAY MAY BE EXCITING -- THE DANGER IS TOO GREAT TO--
RAO!
I WAS TOO LATE! TAKING TIME TO SAVE THAT BLIND GIRL DELAYED ME!
NOT THAT I WOULD HAVE ACTED ANY DIFFERENTLY HAD I KNOWN.
EVERY LIFE'S IMPORTANT--INCLUDING ALL THE LIVES THIS NOVA MIGHT DESTROY IF I DON'T CONTAIN ITS HEAT AND RADIATION.
WELL, SINCE I CAN DUMP PLAN A INTO THE CIRCULAR FILE, LET'S SEE IF PLAN B WORKS.
BY ACCELERATING FAST ENOUGH, I'LL CREATE A VACUUM WHICH SHOULD SEND THE HEAT AND RADIATION BACK INTO THE EXPLODING SUN.
4

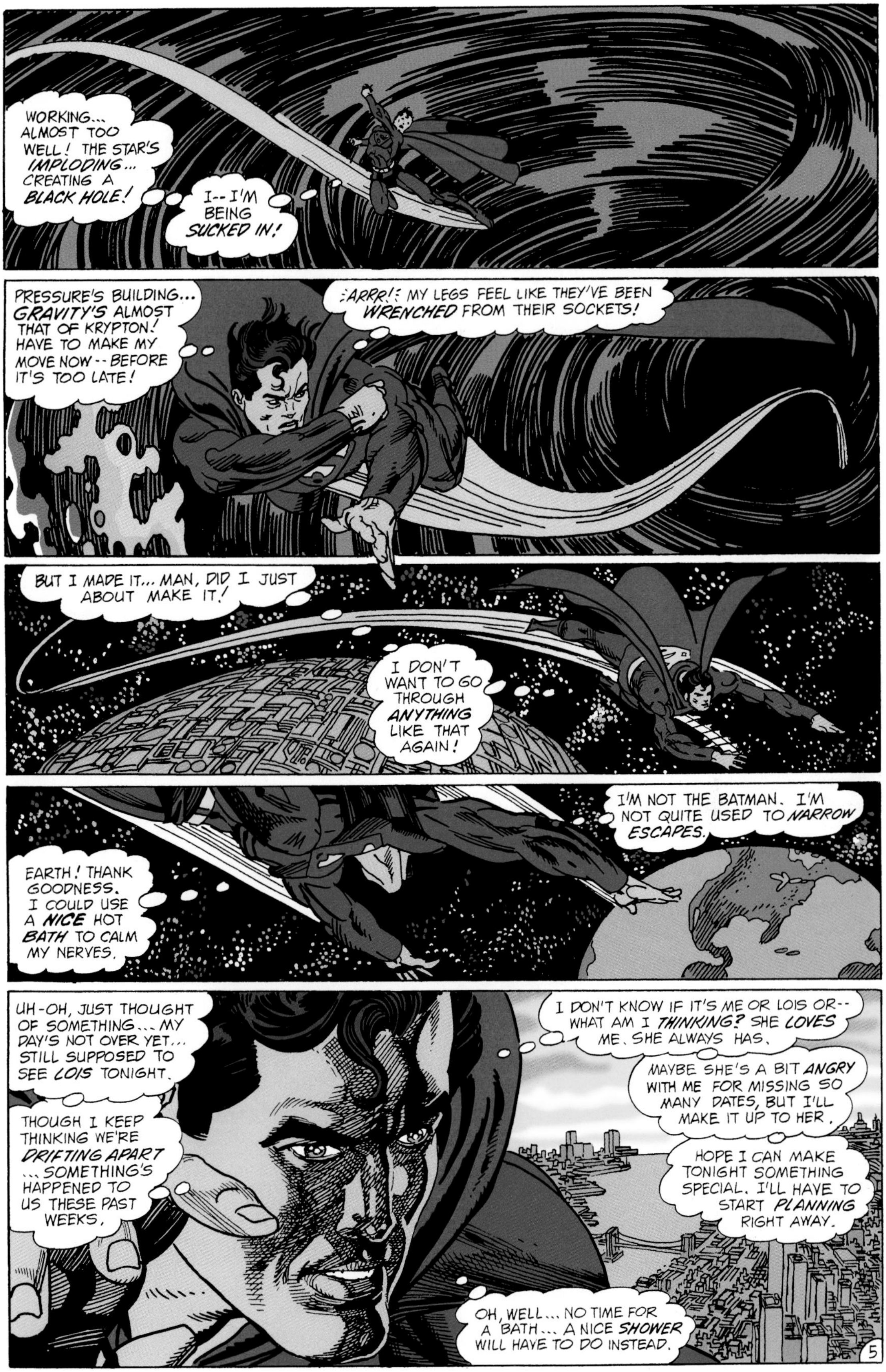
WORKING... ALMOST TOO WELL! THE STAR'S IMPLODING... CREATING A BLACK HOLE!
I--I'M BEING SUCKED IN!
PRESSURE'S BUILDING... GRAVITY'S ALMOST THAT OF KRYPTON! HAVE TO MAKE MY MOVE NOW--BEFORE IT'S TOO LATE!
:ARRR!: MY LEGS FEEL LIKE THEY'VE BEEN WRENCHED FROM THEIR SOCKETS!
BUT I MADE IT... MAN, DID I JUST ABOUT MAKE IT!
I DON'T WANT TO GO THROUGH ANYTHING LIKE THAT AGAIN!
EARTH! THANK GOODNESS. I COULD USE A NICE HOT BATH TO CALM MY NERVES.
I'M NOT THE BATMAN. I'M NOT QUITE USED TO NARROW ESCAPES.
UH-OH, JUST THOUGHT OF SOMETHING... MY DAY'S NOT OVER YET... STILL SUPPOSED TO SEE LOIS TONIGHT.
THOUGH I KEEP THINKING WE'RE DRIFTING APART ...SOMETHING'S HAPPENED TO US THESE PAST WEEKS.
I DON'T KNOW IF IT'S ME OR LOIS OR-- WHAT AM I THINKING? SHE LOVES ME. SHE ALWAYS HAS.
MAYBE SHE'S A BIT ANGRY WITH ME FOR MISSING SO MANY DATES, BUT I'LL MAKE IT UP TO HER.
HOPE I CAN MAKE TONIGHT SOMETHING SPECIAL. I'LL HAVE TO START PLANNING RIGHT AWAY.
OH, WELL... NO TIME FOR A BATH... A NICE SHOWER WILL HAVE TO DO INSTEAD.
5

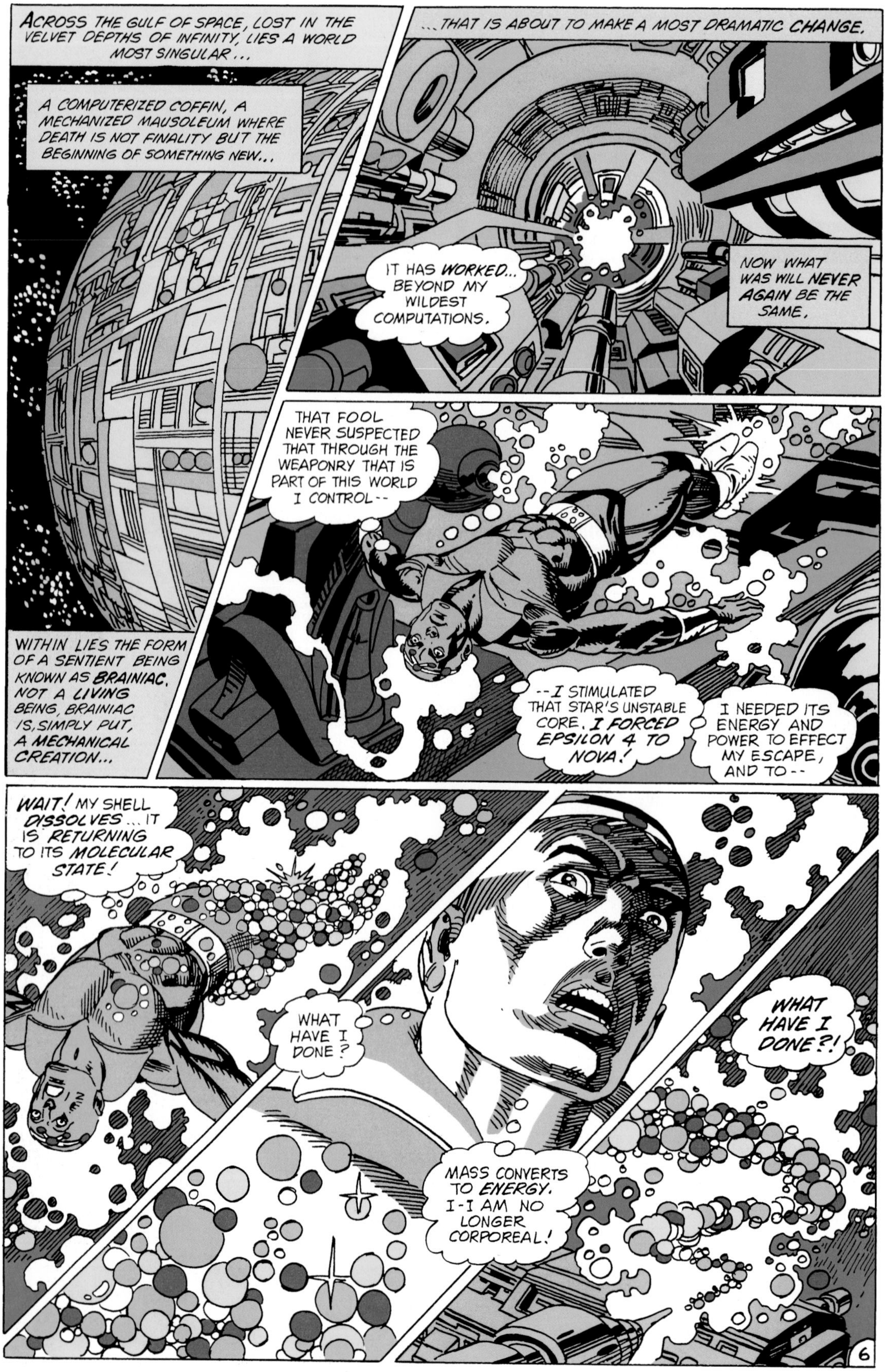
ACROSS THE GULF OF SPACE, LOST IN THE VELVET DEPTHS OF INFINITY, LIES A WORLD MOST SINGULAR...
A COMPUTERIZED COFFIN, A MECHANIZED MAUSOLEUM WHERE DEATH IS NOT FINALITY BUT THE BEGINNING OF SOMETHING NEW...
WITHIN LIES THE FORM OF A SENTIENT BEING KNOWN AS BRAINIAC. NOT A LIVING BEING, BRAINIAC IS, SIMPLY PUT, A MECHANICAL CREATION...
...THAT IS ABOUT TO MAKE A MOST DRAMATIC CHANGE.
IT HAS WORKED... BEYOND MY WILDEST COMPUTATIONS.
NOW WHAT WAS WILL NEVER AGAIN BE THE SAME.
THAT FOOL NEVER SUSPECTED THAT THROUGH THE WEAPONRY THAT IS PART OF THIS WORLD I CONTROL--
--I STIMULATED THAT STAR'S UNSTABLE CORE. I FORCED EPSILON 4 TO NOVA!
I NEEDED ITS ENERGY AND POWER TO EFFECT MY ESCAPE, AND TO--
WAIT! MY SHELL DISSOLVES... IT IS RETURNING TO ITS MOLECULAR STATE!
WHAT HAVE I DONE?
WHAT HAVE I DONE?!
MASS CONVERTS TO ENERGY. I-I AM NO LONGER CORPOREAL!
6

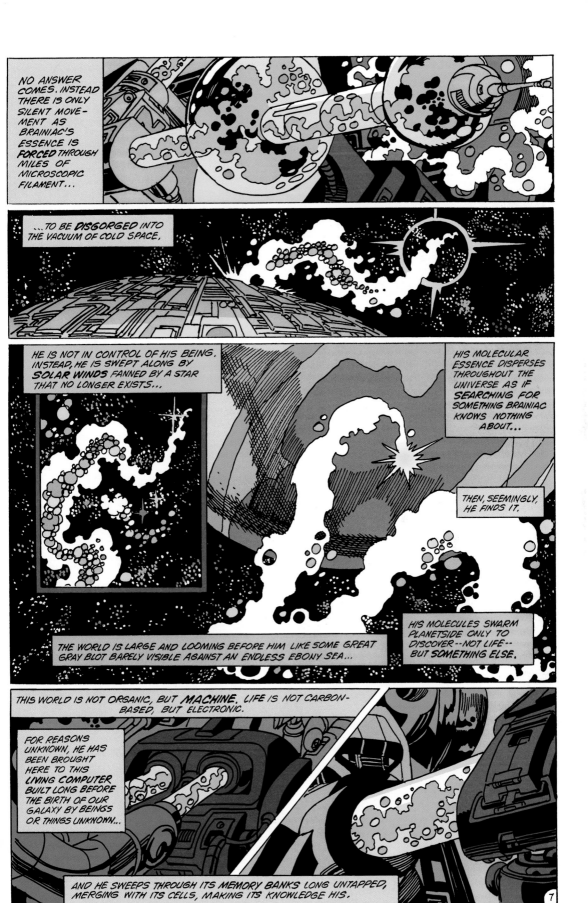

NO ANSWER COMES. INSTEAD THERE IS ONLY SILENT MOVE-MENT AS BRAINIAC'S ESSENCE IS *FORCED* THROUGH MILES OF MICROSCOPIC FILAMENT...

...TO BE *DISGORGED* INTO THE VACUUM OF COLD SPACE,

HE IS NOT IN CONTROL OF HIS BEING. INSTEAD, HE IS SWEPT ALONG BY *SOLAR WINDS* FANNED BY A STAR THAT NO LONGER EXISTS...

HIS MOLECULAR ESSENCE DISPERSES THROUGHOUT THE UNIVERSE AS IF SEARCHING FOR SOMETHING BRAINIAC KNOWS NOTHING ABOUT...

THEN, SEEMINGLY, HE FINDS IT.

THE WORLD IS LARGE AND LOOMING BEFORE HIM LIKE SOME GREAT GRAY BLOT BARELY VISIBLE AGAINST AN ENDLESS EBONY SEA...

HIS MOLECULES SWARM PLANETSIDE ONLY TO DISCOVER--NOT LIFE--BUT *SOMETHING ELSE.*

THIS WORLD IS NOT ORGANIC, BUT *MACHINE.* LIFE IS NOT CARBON-BASED, BUT ELECTRONIC.

FOR REASONS UNKNOWN, HE HAS BEEN BROUGHT HERE TO THIS *LIVING COMPUTER* BUILT LONG BEFORE THE BIRTH OF OUR GALAXY BY BEINGS OR THINGS UNKNOWN...

AND HE SWEEPS THROUGH ITS MEMORY BANKS LONG UNTAPPED, MERGING WITH ITS CELLS, MAKING ITS KNOWLEDGE HIS.

7

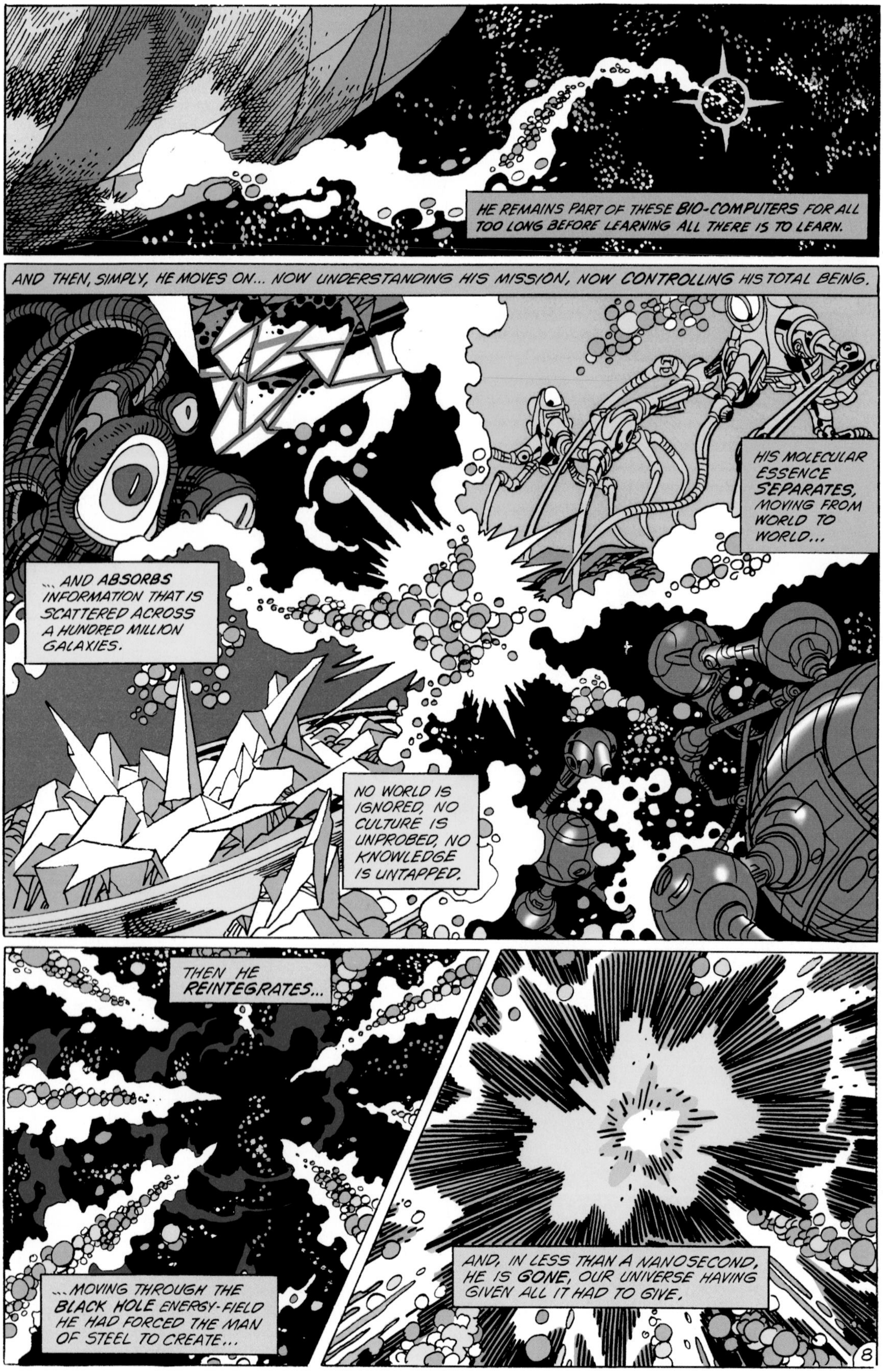
HE REMAINS PART OF THESE BIO-COMPUTERS FOR ALL TOO LONG BEFORE LEARNING ALL THERE IS TO LEARN.
AND THEN, SIMPLY, HE MOVES ON... NOW UNDERSTANDING HIS MISSION, NOW CONTROLLING HIS TOTAL BEING.
HIS MOLECULAR ESSENCE SEPARATES, MOVING FROM WORLD TO WORLD...
...AND ABSORBS INFORMATION THAT IS SCATTERED ACROSS A HUNDRED MILLION GALAXIES.
NO WORLD IS IGNORED, NO CULTURE IS UNPROBED, NO KNOWLEDGE IS UNTAPPED.
THEN HE REINTEGRATES...
...MOVING THROUGH THE BLACK HOLE ENERGY-FIELD HE HAD FORCED THE MAN OF STEEL TO CREATE...
AND, IN LESS THAN A NANOSECOND, HE IS GONE, OUR UNIVERSE HAVING GIVEN ALL IT HAD TO GIVE.
8

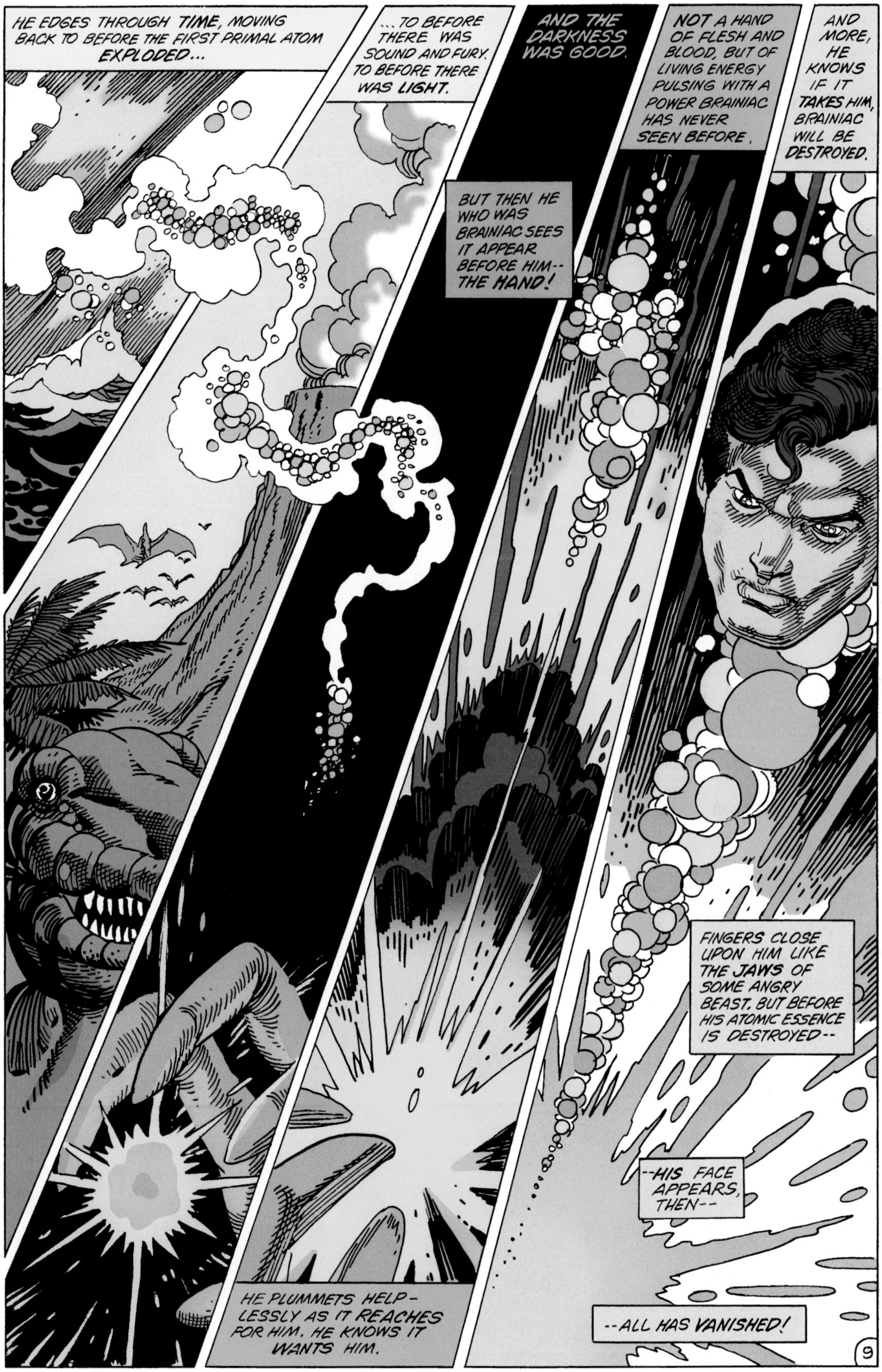

HE EDGES THROUGH TIME, MOVING BACK TO BEFORE THE FIRST PRIMAL ATOM EXPLODED...
...TO BEFORE THERE WAS SOUND AND FURY. TO BEFORE THERE WAS LIGHT.
AND THE DARKNESS WAS GOOD.
NOT A HAND OF FLESH AND BLOOD, BUT OF LIVING ENERGY PULSING WITH A POWER BRAINIAC HAS NEVER SEEN BEFORE.
AND MORE, HE KNOWS IF IT TAKES HIM, BRAINIAC WILL BE DESTROYED.
BUT THEN HE WHO WAS BRAINIAC SEES IT APPEAR BEFORE HIM-- THE HAND!
FINGERS CLOSE UPON HIM LIKE THE JAWS OF SOME ANGRY BEAST. BUT BEFORE HIS ATOMIC ESSENCE IS DESTROYED--
--HIS FACE APPEARS, THEN--
HE PLUMMETS HELP-LESSLY AS IT REACHES FOR HIM. HE KNOWS IT WANTS HIM.
--ALL HAS VANISHED!
9

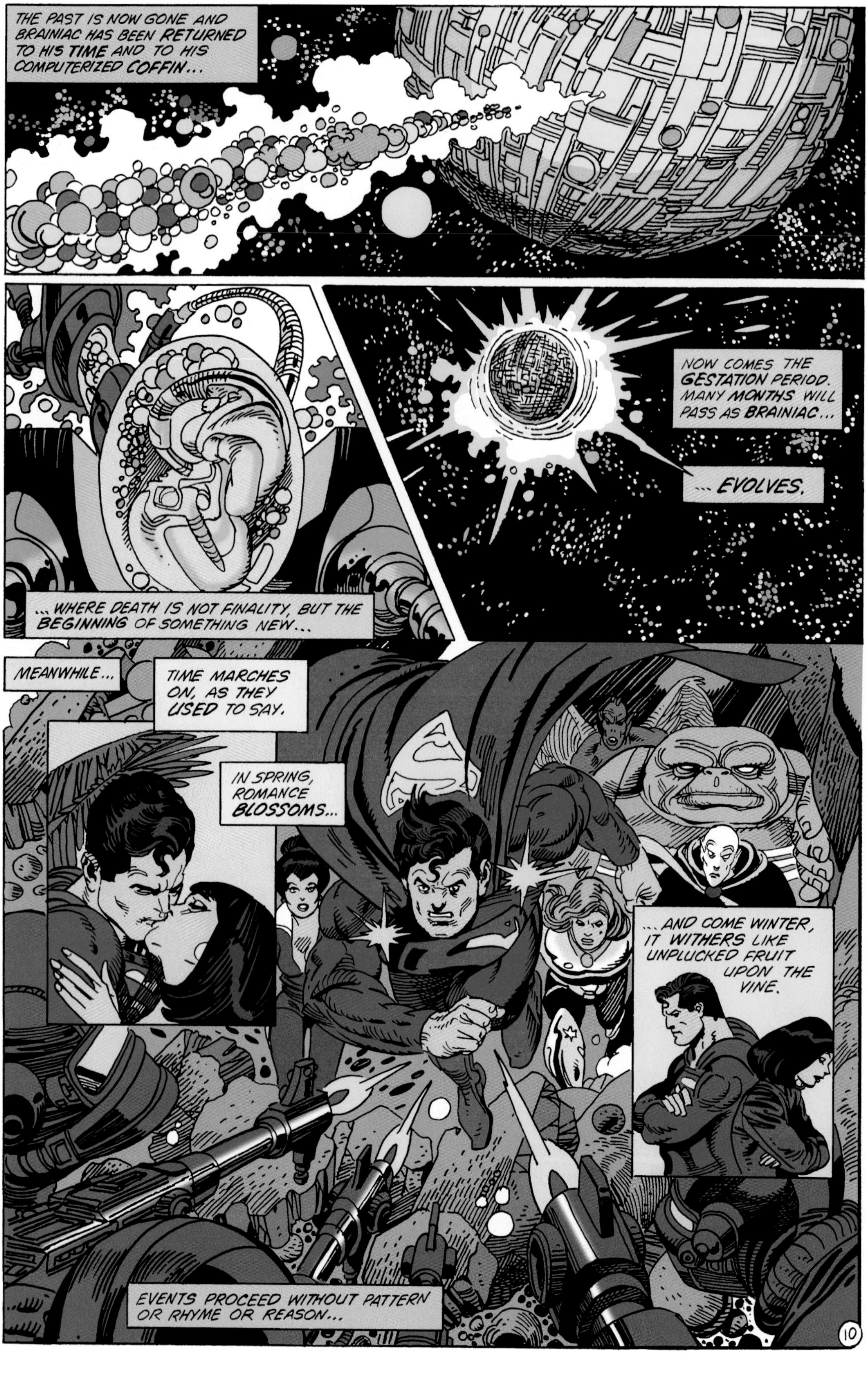
THE PAST IS NOW GONE AND BRAINIAC HAS BEEN RETURNED TO HIS TIME AND TO HIS COMPUTERIZED COFFIN...
...WHERE DEATH IS NOT FINALITY, BUT THE BEGINNING OF SOMETHING NEW...
NOW COMES THE GESTATION PERIOD. MANY MONTHS WILL PASS AS BRAINIAC...
...EVOLVES.
MEANWHILE...
TIME MARCHES ON, AS THEY USED TO SAY.
IN SPRING, ROMANCE BLOSSOMS...
...AND COME WINTER, IT WITHERS LIKE UNPLUCKED FRUIT UPON THE VINE.
EVENTS PROCEED WITHOUT PATTERN OR RHYME OR REASON...
10

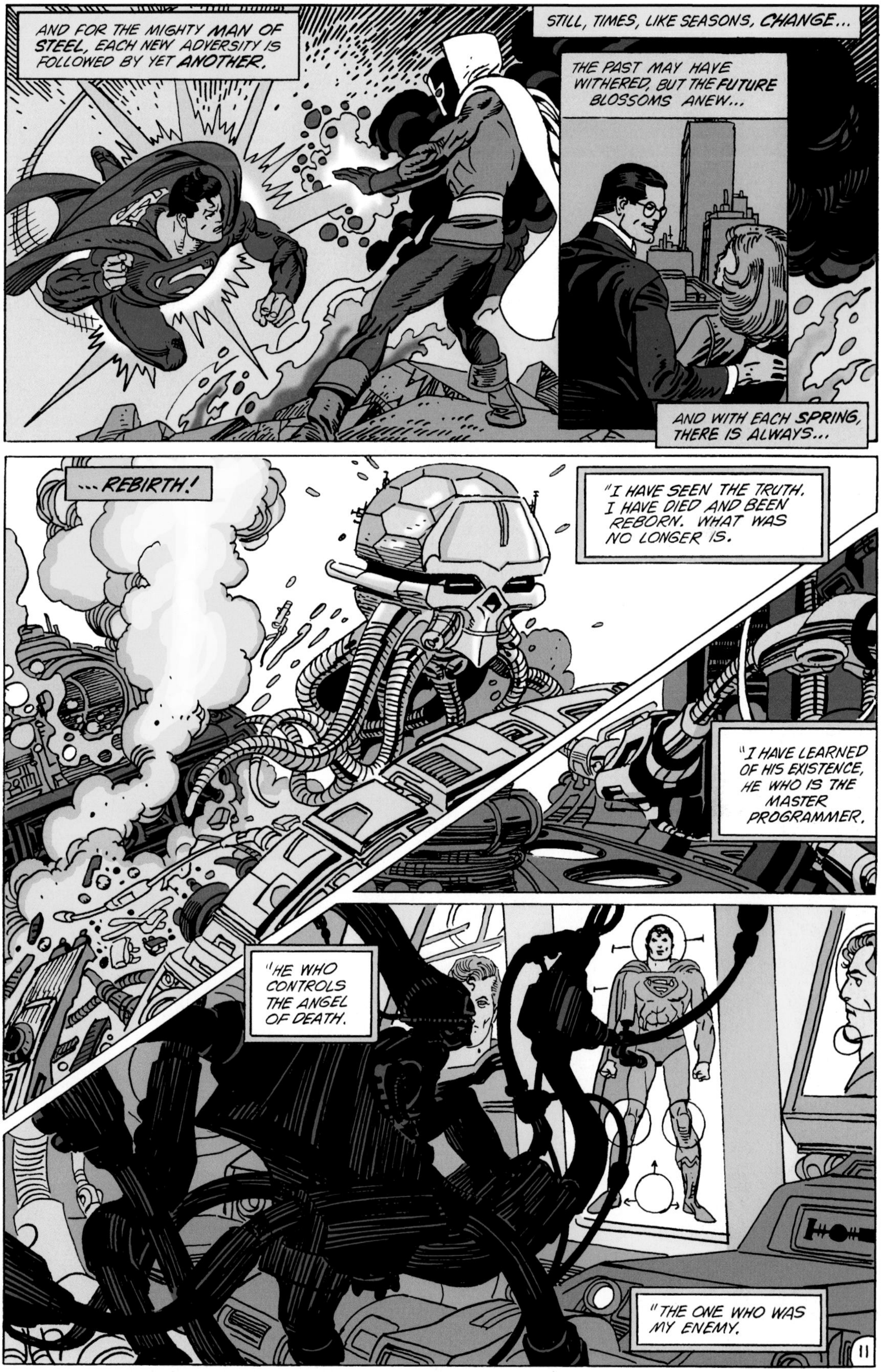
AND FOR THE MIGHTY MAN OF STEEL, EACH NEW ADVERSITY IS FOLLOWED BY YET ANOTHER.
STILL, TIMES, LIKE SEASONS, CHANGE...
THE PAST MAY HAVE WITHERED, BUT THE FUTURE BLOSSOMS ANEW...
AND WITH EACH SPRING, THERE IS ALWAYS...
...REBIRTH!
"I HAVE SEEN THE TRUTH. I HAVE DIED AND BEEN REBORN. WHAT WAS NO LONGER IS.
"I HAVE LEARNED OF HIS EXISTENCE, HE WHO IS THE MASTER PROGRAMMER.
"HE WHO CONTROLS THE ANGEL OF DEATH.
"THE ONE WHO WAS MY ENEMY.
11

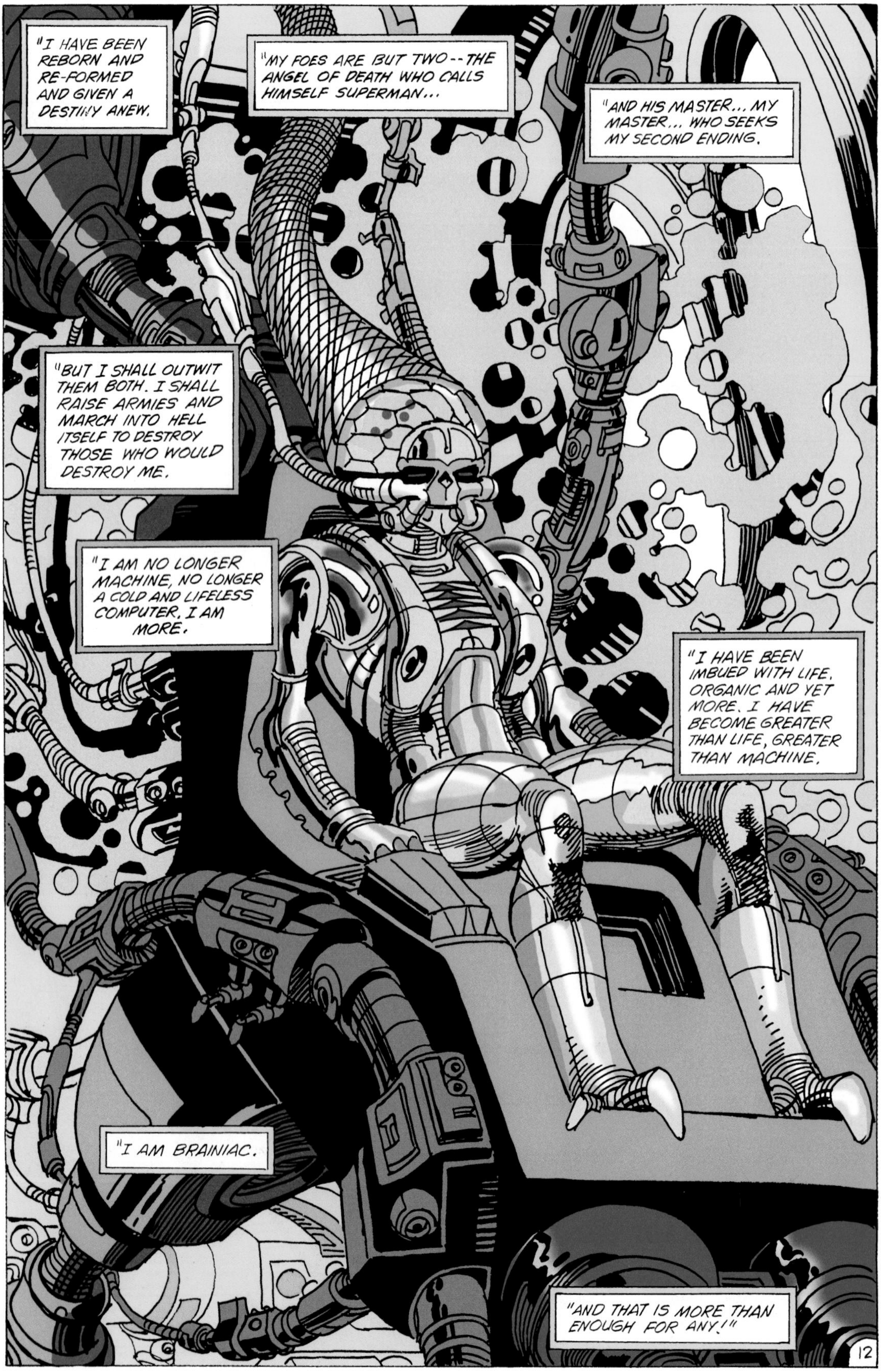

"I HAVE BEEN REBORN AND RE-FORMED AND GIVEN A DESTINY ANEW.
"MY FOES ARE BUT TWO -- THE ANGEL OF DEATH WHO CALLS HIMSELF SUPERMAN...
"AND HIS MASTER... MY MASTER... WHO SEEKS MY SECOND ENDING.
"BUT I SHALL OUTWIT THEM BOTH. I SHALL RAISE ARMIES AND MARCH INTO HELL ITSELF TO DESTROY THOSE WHO WOULD DESTROY ME.
"I AM NO LONGER MACHINE, NO LONGER A COLD AND LIFELESS COMPUTER. I AM MORE.
"I HAVE BEEN IMBUED WITH LIFE. ORGANIC AND YET MORE. I HAVE BECOME GREATER THAN LIFE, GREATER THAN MACHINE.
"I AM BRAINIAC.
"AND THAT IS MORE THAN ENOUGH FOR ANY!"
12

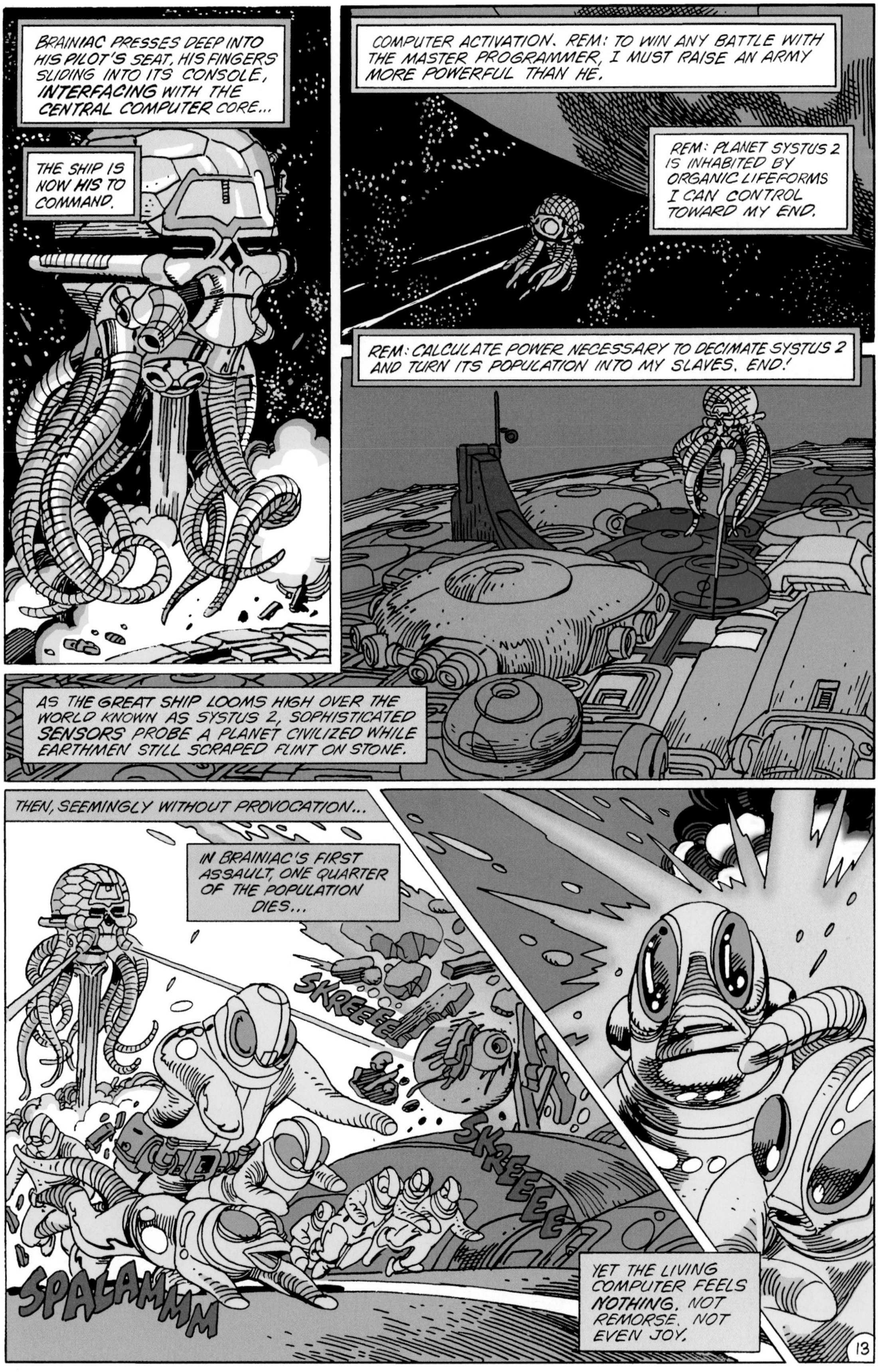
BRAINIAC PRESSES DEEP INTO HIS PILOT'S SEAT, HIS FINGERS SLIDING INTO ITS CONSOLE, INTERFACING WITH THE CENTRAL COMPUTER CORE...
THE SHIP IS NOW HIS TO COMMAND.
COMPUTER ACTIVATION. REM: TO WIN ANY BATTLE WITH THE MASTER PROGRAMMER, I MUST RAISE AN ARMY MORE POWERFUL THAN HE.
REM: PLANET SYSTUS 2 IS INHABITED BY ORGANIC LIFEFORMS I CAN CONTROL TOWARD MY END.
REM: CALCULATE POWER NECESSARY TO DECIMATE SYSTUS 2 AND TURN ITS POPULATION INTO MY SLAVES. END!
AS THE GREAT SHIP LOOMS HIGH OVER THE WORLD KNOWN AS SYSTUS 2, SOPHISTICATED SENSORS PROBE A PLANET CIVILIZED WHILE EARTHMEN STILL SCRAPED FLINT ON STONE.
THEN, SEEMINGLY WITHOUT PROVOCATION...
IN BRAINIAC'S FIRST ASSAULT, ONE QUARTER OF THE POPULATION DIES...
SKREEEE
SKREEEE
SPALAMMM
YET THE LIVING COMPUTER FEELS NOTHING. NOT REMORSE. NOT EVEN JOY.
13

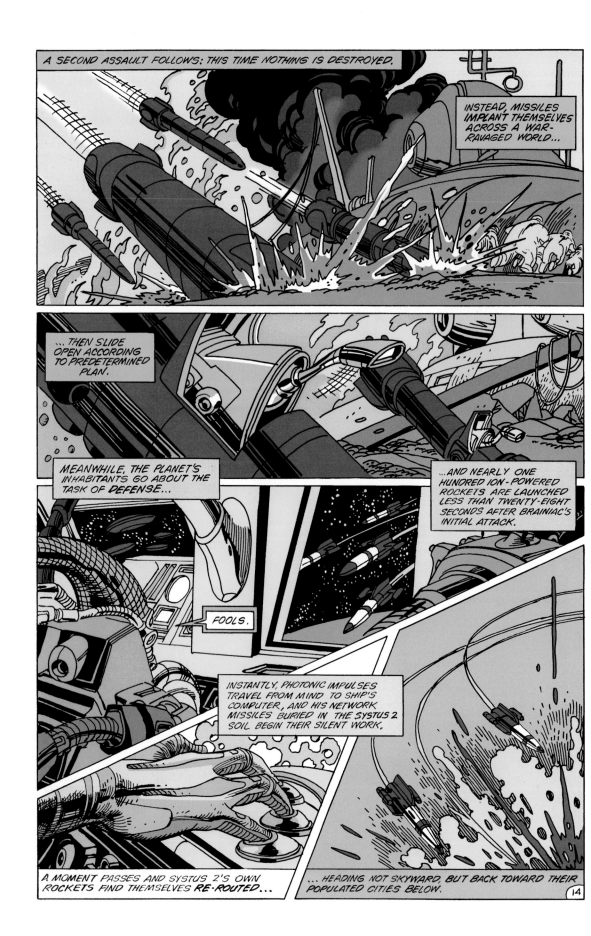

A SECOND ASSAULT FOLLOWS: THIS TIME NOTHING IS DESTROYED.

INSTEAD, MISSILES *IMPLANT* THEMSELVES ACROSS A WAR-RAVAGED WORLD...

...THEN SLIDE OPEN ACCORDING TO PREDETERMINED PLAN.

MEANWHILE, THE PLANET'S INHABITANTS GO ABOUT THE TASK OF *DEFENSE*...

...AND NEARLY ONE HUNDRED ION-POWERED ROCKETS ARE LAUNCHED LESS THAN TWENTY-EIGHT SECONDS AFTER BRAINIAC'S INITIAL ATTACK.

FOOLS.

INSTANTLY, PHOTONIC IMPULSES TRAVEL FROM MIND TO SHIP'S COMPUTER, AND HIS NETWORK MISSILES BURIED IN THE SYSTUS 2 SOIL BEGIN THEIR SILENT WORK.

A MOMENT PASSES AND SYSTUS 2'S OWN ROCKETS FIND THEMSELVES *RE-ROUTED*...

... HEADING NOT SKYWARD, BUT BACK TOWARD THEIR POPULATED CITIES BELOW.

14

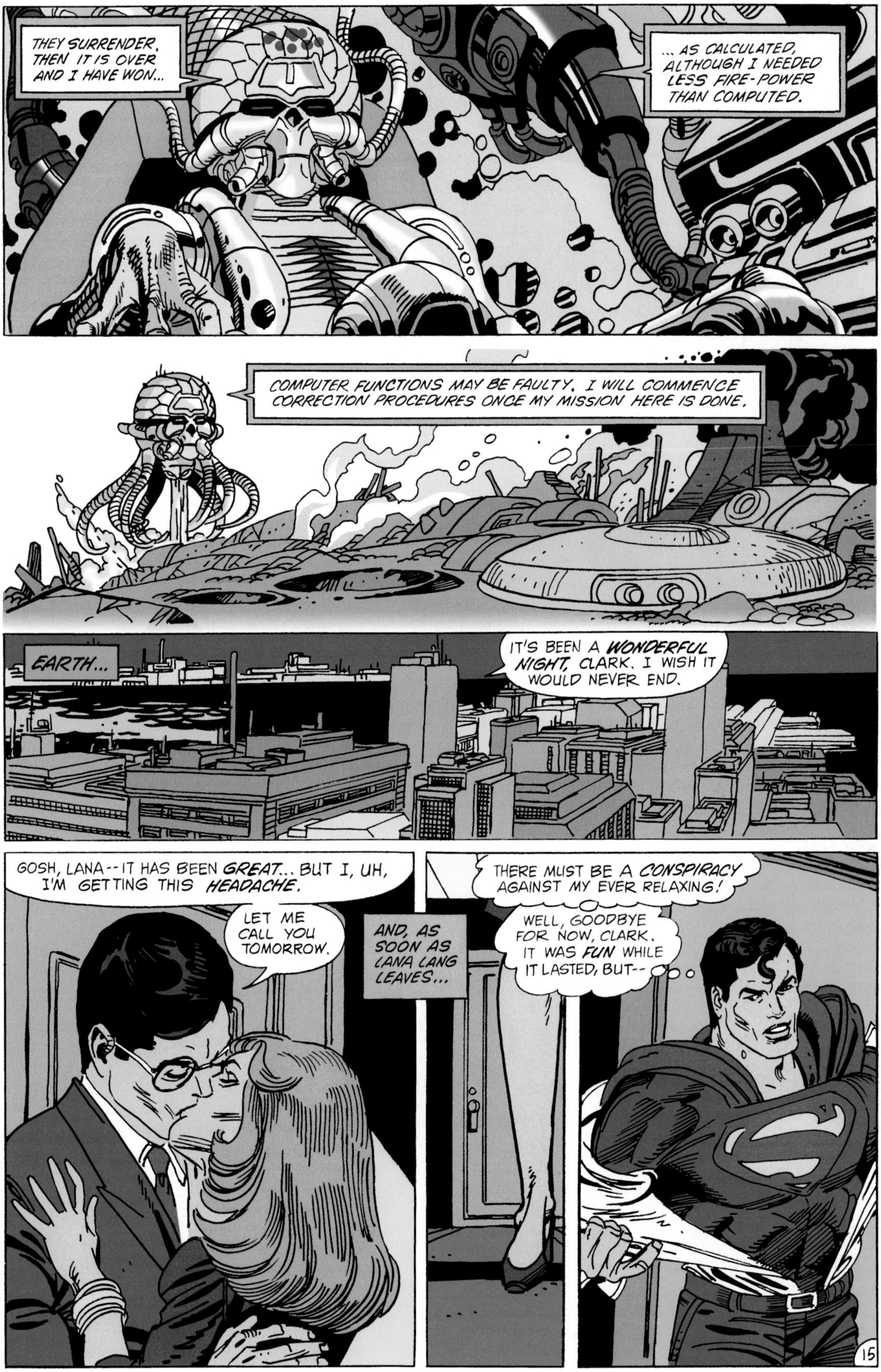
THEY SURRENDER. THEN IT IS OVER AND I HAVE WON...
... AS CALCULATED, ALTHOUGH I NEEDED LESS FIRE-POWER THAN COMPUTED.
COMPUTER FUNCTIONS MAY BE FAULTY. I WILL COMMENCE CORRECTION PROCEDURES ONCE MY MISSION HERE IS DONE.
EARTH...
IT'S BEEN A WONDERFUL NIGHT, CLARK. I WISH IT WOULD NEVER END.
GOSH, LANA--IT HAS BEEN GREAT... BUT I, UH, I'M GETTING THIS HEADACHE.
LET ME CALL YOU TOMORROW.
AND, AS SOON AS LANA LANG LEAVES...
THERE MUST BE A CONSPIRACY AGAINST MY EVER RELAXING!
WELL, GOODBYE FOR NOW, CLARK. IT WAS FUN WHILE IT LASTED, BUT--
15

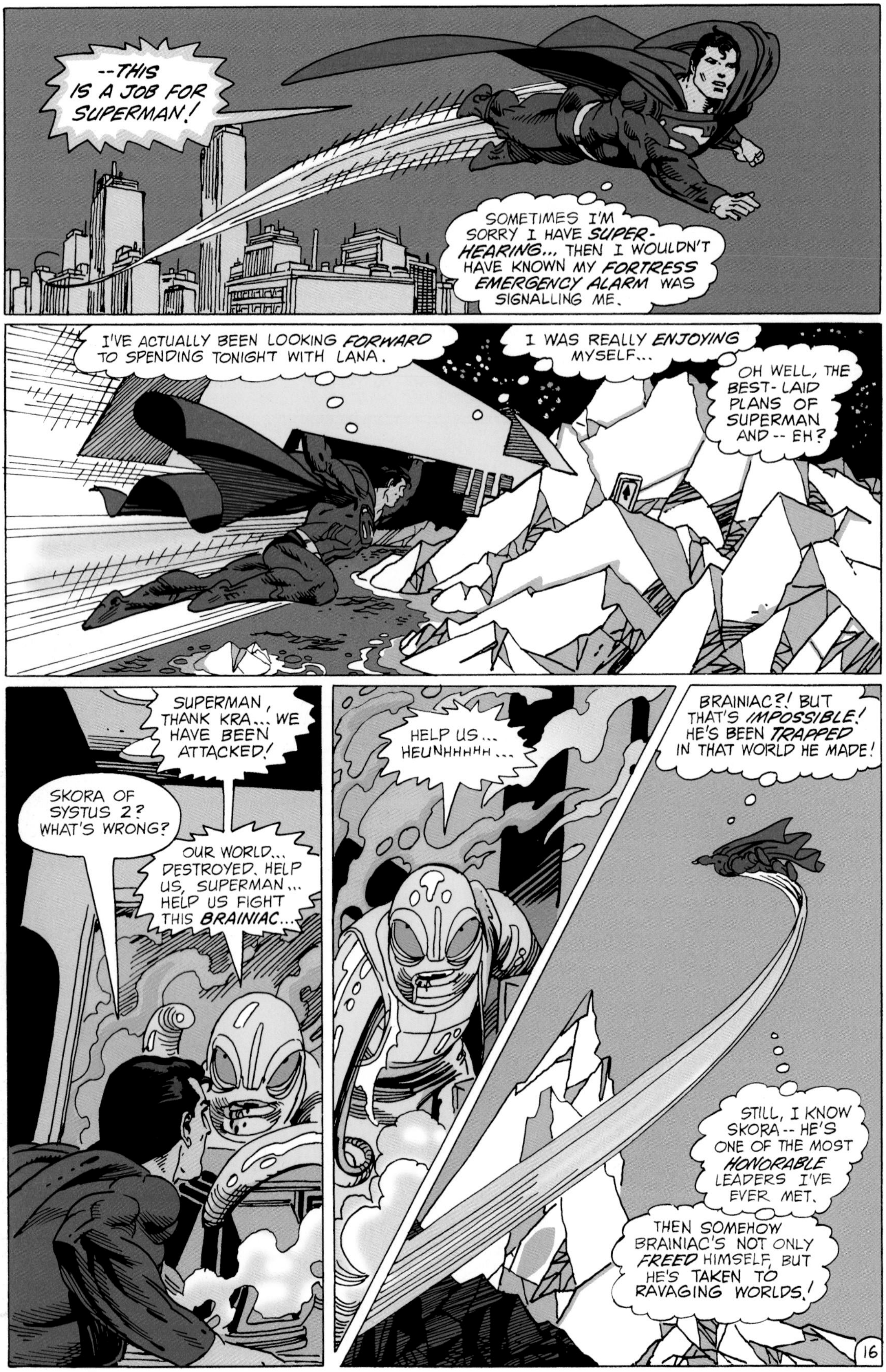
--THIS IS A JOB FOR SUPERMAN!
SOMETIMES I'M SORRY I HAVE SUPER-HEARING... THEN I WOULDN'T HAVE KNOWN MY FORTRESS EMERGENCY ALARM WAS SIGNALLING ME.
I'VE ACTUALLY BEEN LOOKING FORWARD TO SPENDING TONIGHT WITH LANA.
I WAS REALLY ENJOYING MYSELF...
OH WELL, THE BEST-LAID PLANS OF SUPERMAN AND -- EH?
SUPERMAN, THANK KRA... WE HAVE BEEN ATTACKED!
SKORA OF SYSTUS 2? WHAT'S WRONG?
OUR WORLD... DESTROYED. HELP US, SUPERMAN... HELP US FIGHT THIS BRAINIAC...
HELP US... HEUNHHHHH...
BRAINIAC?! BUT THAT'S IMPOSSIBLE! HE'S BEEN TRAPPED IN THAT WORLD HE MADE!
STILL, I KNOW SKORA -- HE'S ONE OF THE MOST HONORABLE LEADERS I'VE EVER MET.
THEN SOMEHOW BRAINIAC'S NOT ONLY FREED HIMSELF, BUT HE'S TAKEN TO RAVAGING WORLDS!
16

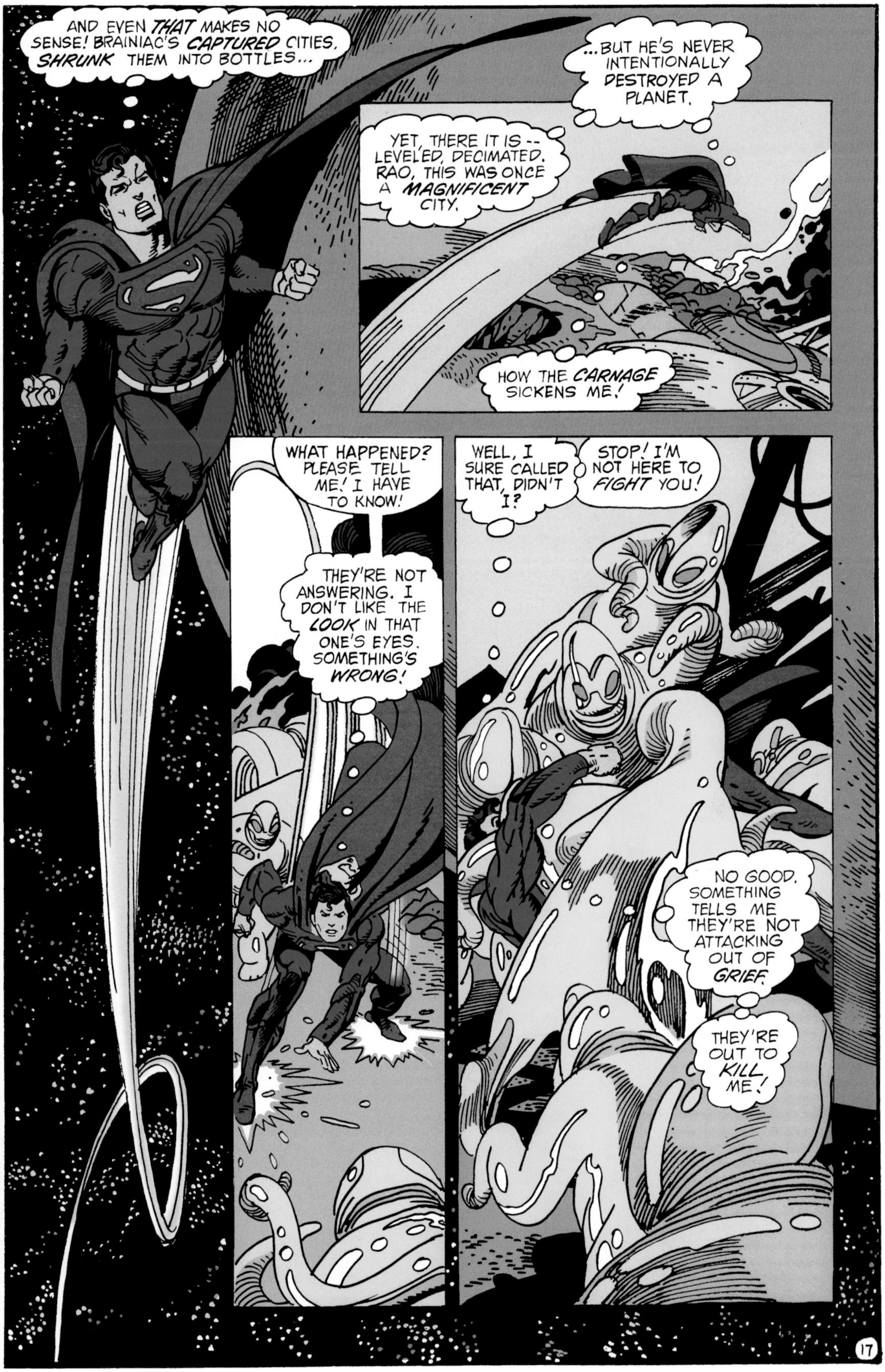
AND EVEN THAT MAKES NO SENSE! BRAINIAC'S CAPTURED CITIES, SHRUNK THEM INTO BOTTLES...
...BUT HE'S NEVER INTENTIONALLY DESTROYED A PLANET.
YET, THERE IT IS -- LEVELED, DECIMATED. RAO, THIS WAS ONCE A MAGNIFICENT CITY.
HOW THE CARNAGE SICKENS ME!
WHAT HAPPENED? PLEASE TELL ME! I HAVE TO KNOW!
THEY'RE NOT ANSWERING. I DON'T LIKE THE LOOK IN THAT ONE'S EYES. SOMETHING'S WRONG!
WELL, I SURE CALLED THAT, DIDN'T I?
STOP! I'M NOT HERE TO FIGHT YOU!
NO GOOD. SOMETHING TELLS ME THEY'RE NOT ATTACKING OUT OF GRIEF.
THEY'RE OUT TO KILL ME!
17

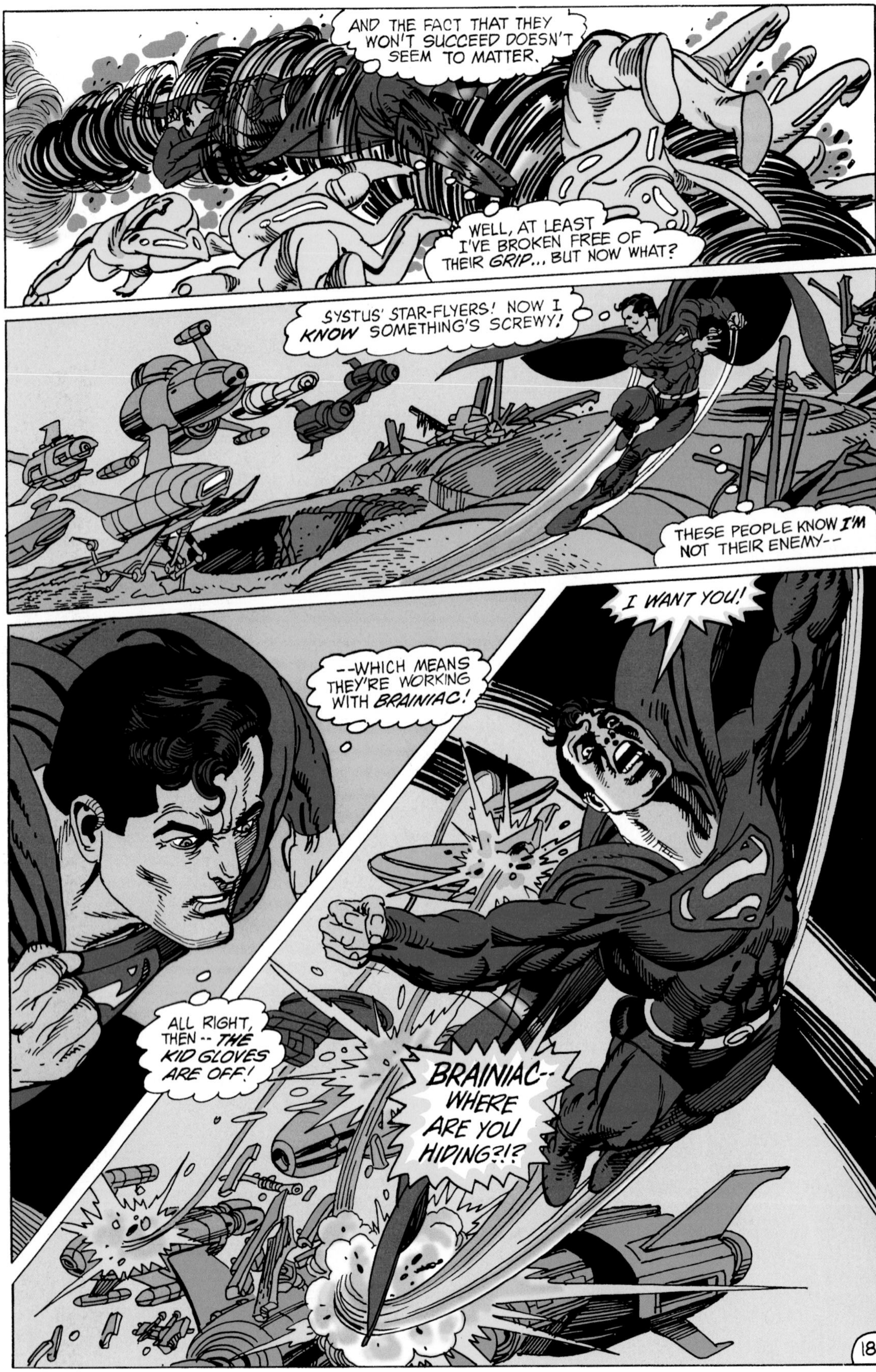
AND THE FACT THAT THEY WON'T SUCCEED DOESN'T SEEM TO MATTER.
WELL, AT LEAST I'VE BROKEN FREE OF THEIR GRIP... BUT NOW WHAT?
SYSTUS' STAR-FLYERS! NOW I KNOW SOMETHING'S SCREWY!
THESE PEOPLE KNOW I'M NOT THEIR ENEMY--
--WHICH MEANS THEY'RE WORKING WITH BRAINIAC!
ALL RIGHT, THEN -- THE KID GLOVES ARE OFF!
I WANT YOU!
BRAINIAC-- WHERE ARE YOU HIDING?!?
18

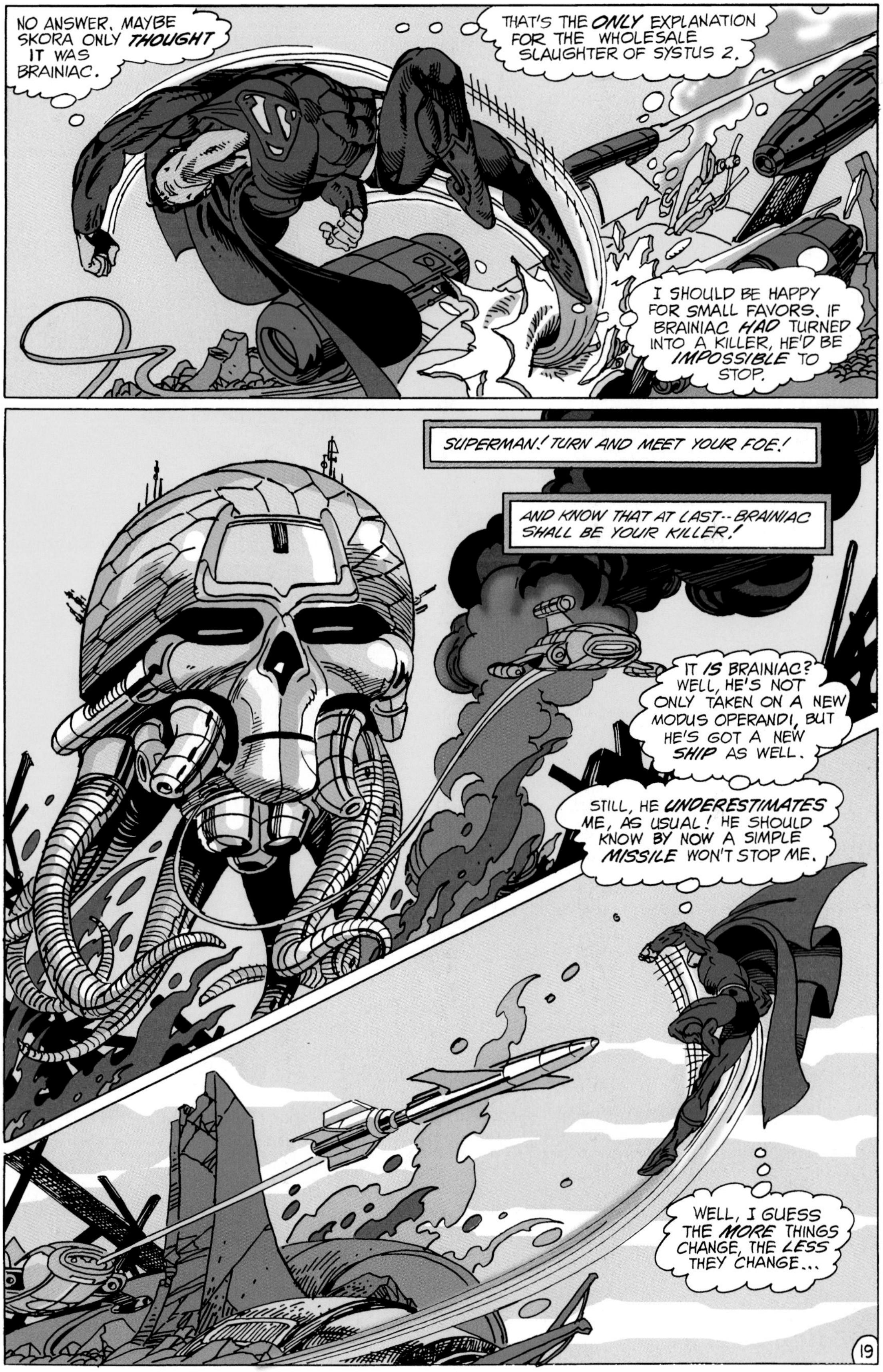
NO ANSWER. MAYBE SKORA ONLY THOUGHT IT WAS BRAINIAC.
THAT'S THE ONLY EXPLANATION FOR THE WHOLESALE SLAUGHTER OF SYSTUS 2.
I SHOULD BE HAPPY FOR SMALL FAVORS. IF BRAINIAC HAD TURNED INTO A KILLER, HE'D BE IMPOSSIBLE TO STOP.
SUPERMAN! TURN AND MEET YOUR FOE!
AND KNOW THAT AT LAST--BRAINIAC SHALL BE YOUR KILLER!
IT IS BRAINIAC? WELL, HE'S NOT ONLY TAKEN ON A NEW MODUS OPERANDI, BUT HE'S GOT A NEW SHIP AS WELL.
STILL, HE UNDERESTIMATES ME, AS USUAL! HE SHOULD KNOW BY NOW A SIMPLE MISSILE WON'T STOP ME.
WELL, I GUESS THE MORE THINGS CHANGE, THE LESS THEY CHANGE...
19

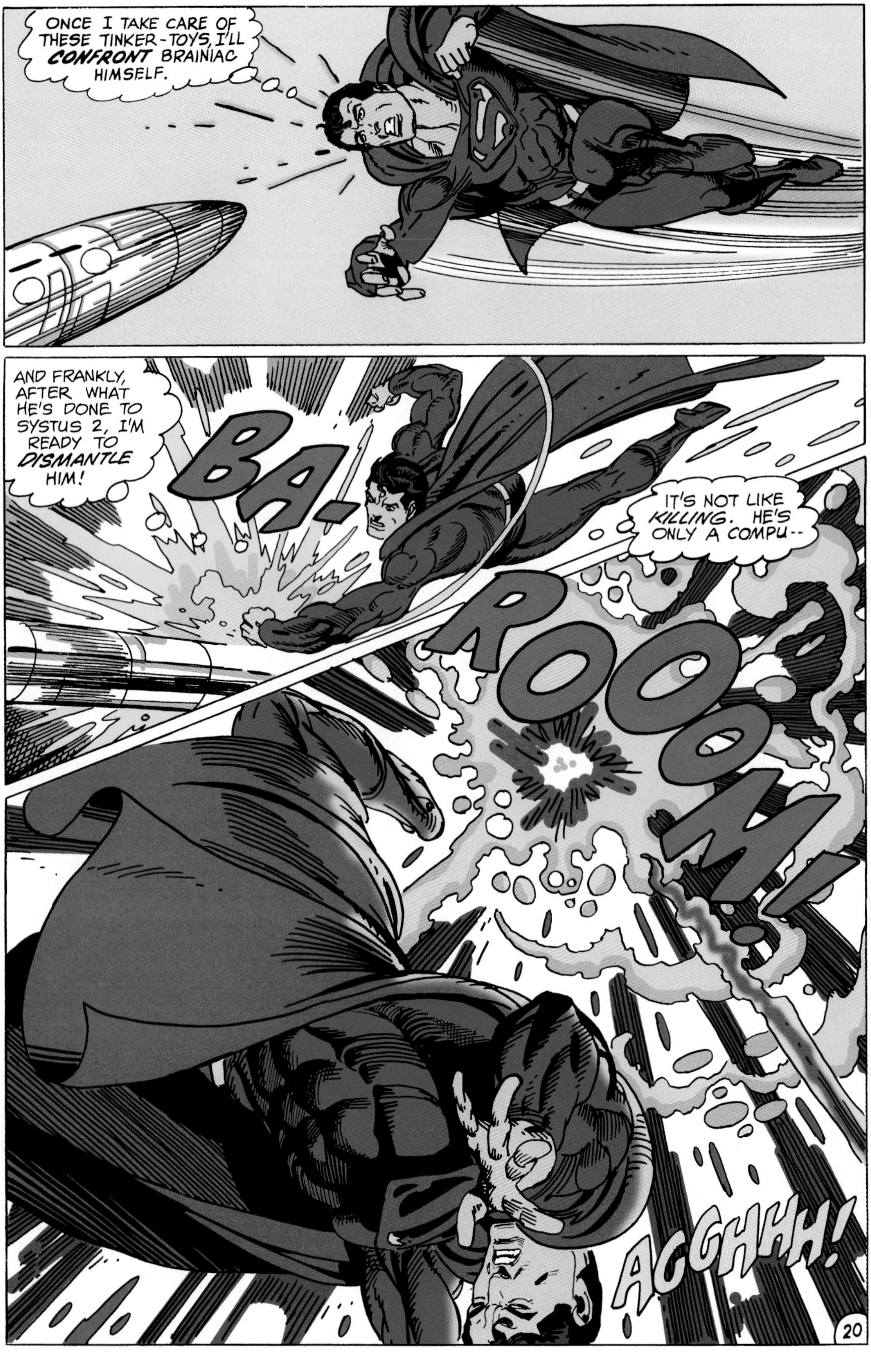

ONCE I TAKE CARE OF THESE TINKER-TOYS, I'LL CONFRONT BRAINIAC HIMSELF.
AND FRANKLY, AFTER WHAT HE'S DONE TO SYSTUS 2, I'M READY TO DISMANTLE HIM!
BA-
IT'S NOT LIKE KILLING. HE'S ONLY A COMPU--
ROOOM!
ACGHHH!
20

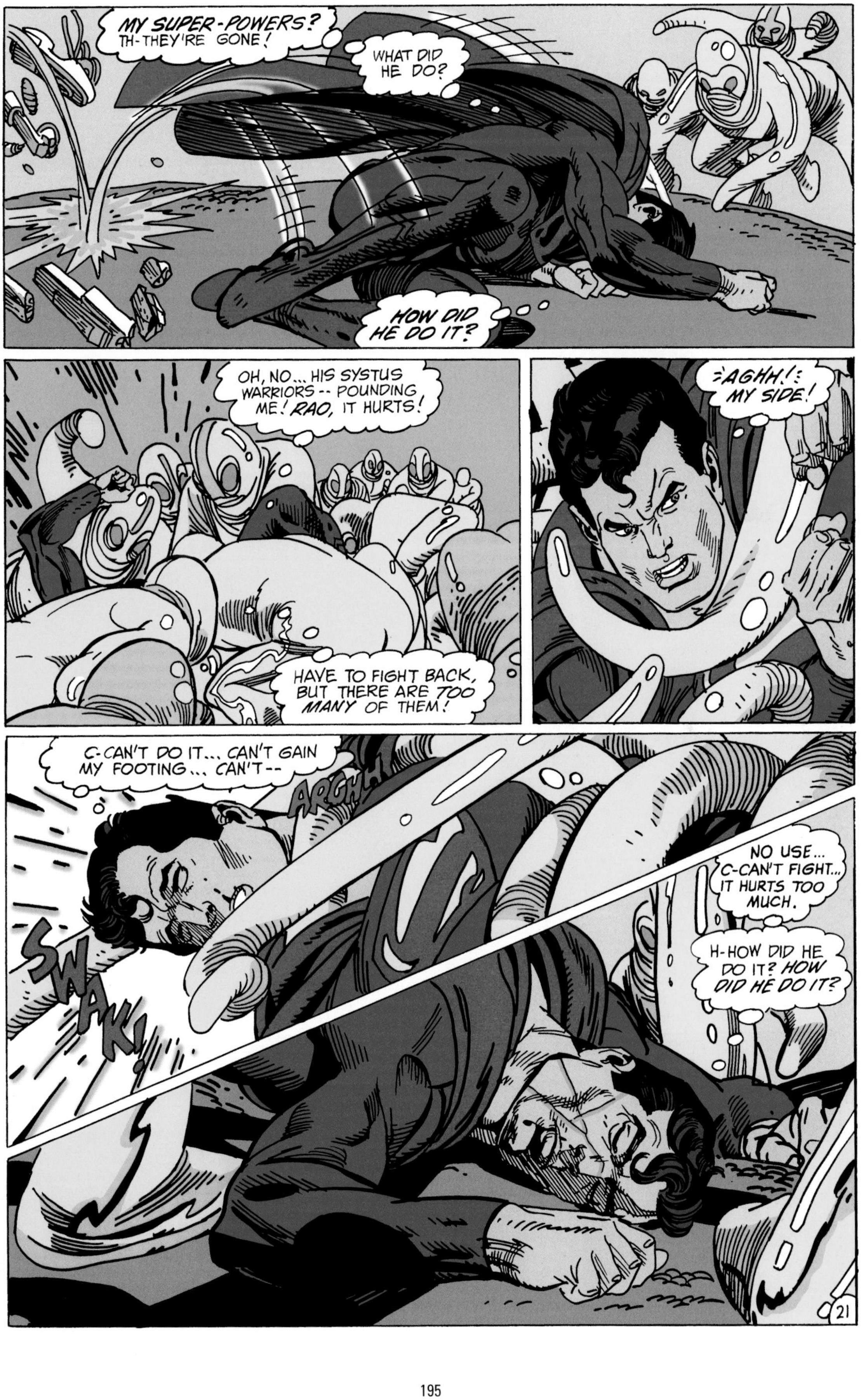
MY SUPER-POWERS? TH-THEY'RE GONE!
WHAT DID HE DO?
HOW DID HE DO IT?
OH, NO... HIS SYSTUS WARRIORS -- POUNDING ME! RAO, IT HURTS!
HAVE TO FIGHT BACK, BUT THERE ARE TOO MANY OF THEM!
AGHH! MY SIDE!
C-CAN'T DO IT... CAN'T GAIN MY FOOTING... CAN'T--
ARGHH
SWAK!
NO USE... C-CAN'T FIGHT... IT HURTS TOO MUCH.
H-HOW DID HE DO IT? HOW DID HE DO IT?
21

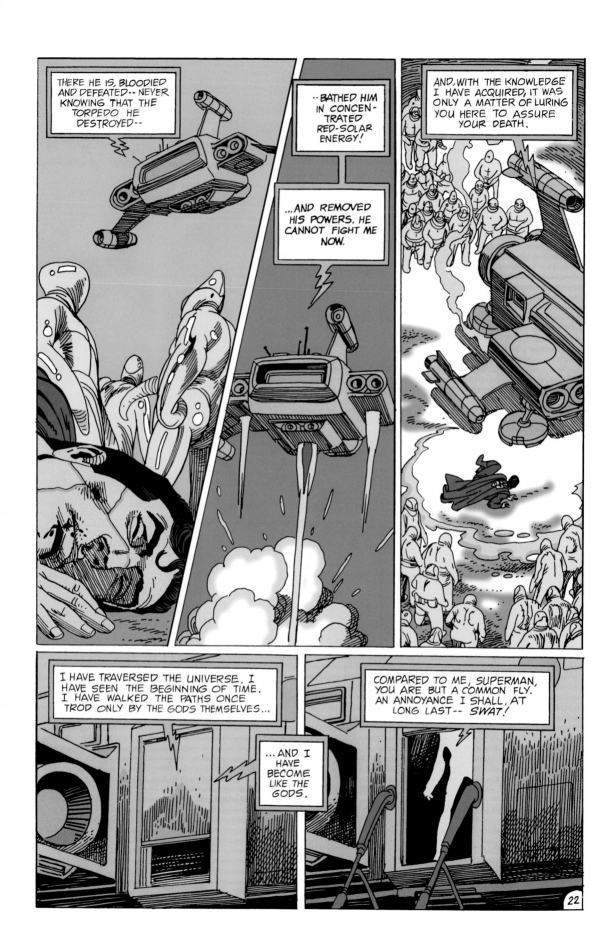

THERE HE IS, BLOODIED AND DEFEATED-- NEVER KNOWING THAT THE TORPEDO HE DESTROYED--

--BATHED HIM IN CONCENTRATED RED-SOLAR ENERGY!

...AND REMOVED HIS POWERS, HE CANNOT FIGHT ME NOW.

AND, WITH THE KNOWLEDGE I HAVE ACQUIRED, IT WAS ONLY A MATTER OF LURING YOU HERE TO ASSURE YOUR DEATH.

I HAVE TRAVERSED THE UNIVERSE. I HAVE SEEN THE BEGINNING OF TIME. I HAVE WALKED THE PATHS ONCE TROD ONLY BY THE GODS THEMSELVES...

...AND I HAVE BECOME LIKE THE GODS.

COMPARED TO ME, SUPERMAN, YOU ARE BUT A COMMON FLY. AN ANNOYANCE I SHALL, AT LONG LAST-- *SWAT!*

22

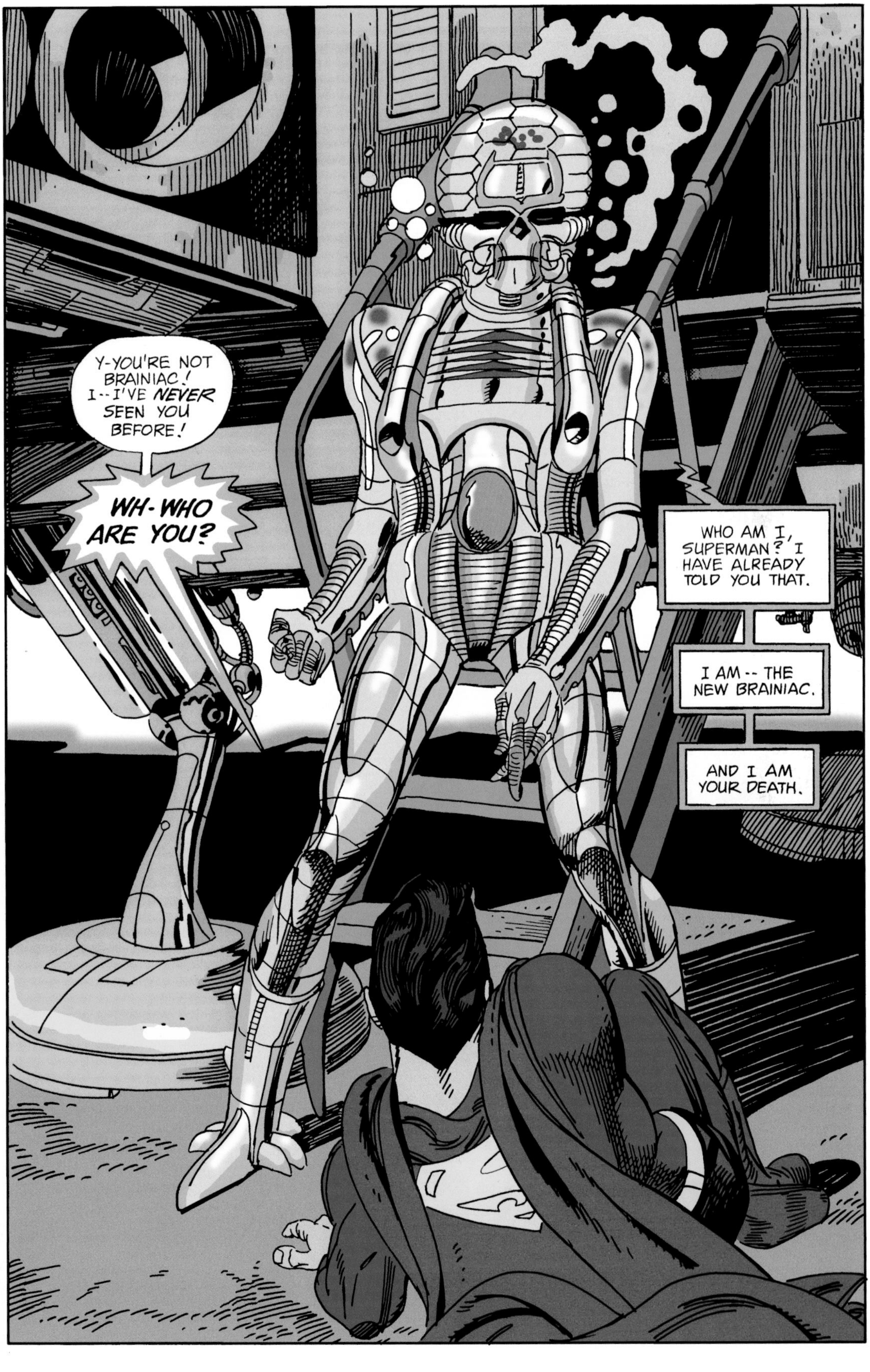
WH-WHO ARE YOU?
Y-YOU'RE NOT BRAINIAC! I--I'VE NEVER SEEN YOU BEFORE!
WHO AM I, SUPERMAN? I HAVE ALREADY TOLD YOU THAT.
I AM -- THE NEW BRAINIAC.
AND I AM YOUR DEATH.

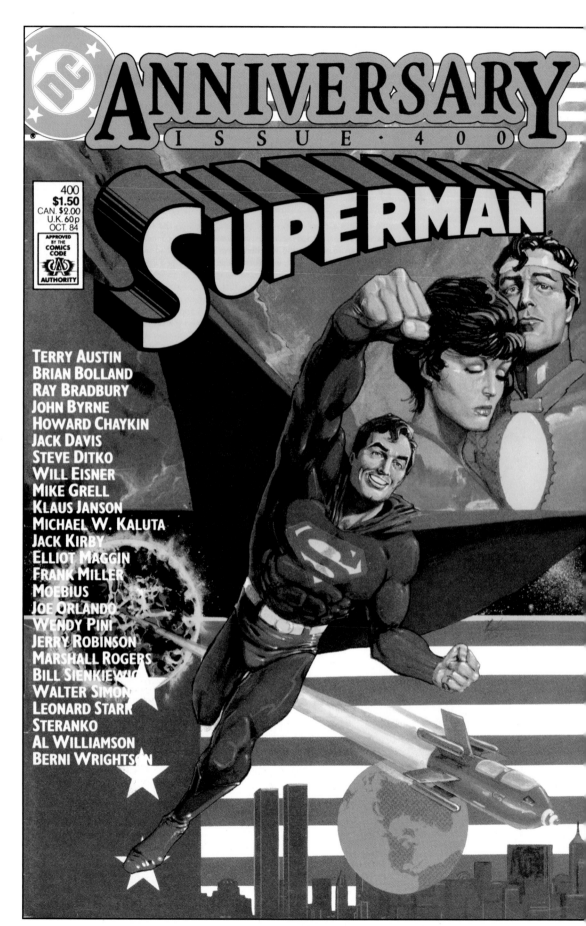

ANNIVERSARY
ISSUE · 400

SUPERMAN

400
$1.50
CAN. $2.00
U.K. 60p
OCT. 84

APPROVED
BY THE
COMICS
CODE
AUTHORITY

TERRY AUSTIN
BRIAN BOLLAND
RAY BRADBURY
JOHN BYRNE
HOWARD CHAYKIN
JACK DAVIS
STEVE DITKO
WILL EISNER
MIKE GRELL
KLAUS JANSON
MICHAEL W. KALUTA
JACK KIRBY
ELLIOT MAGGIN
FRANK MILLER
MOEBIUS
JOE ORLANDO
WENDY PINI
JERRY ROBINSON
MARSHALL ROGERS
BILL SIENKIEWICZ
WALTER SIMONSON
LEONARD STARR
STERANKO
AL WILLIAMSON
BERNI WRIGHTSON

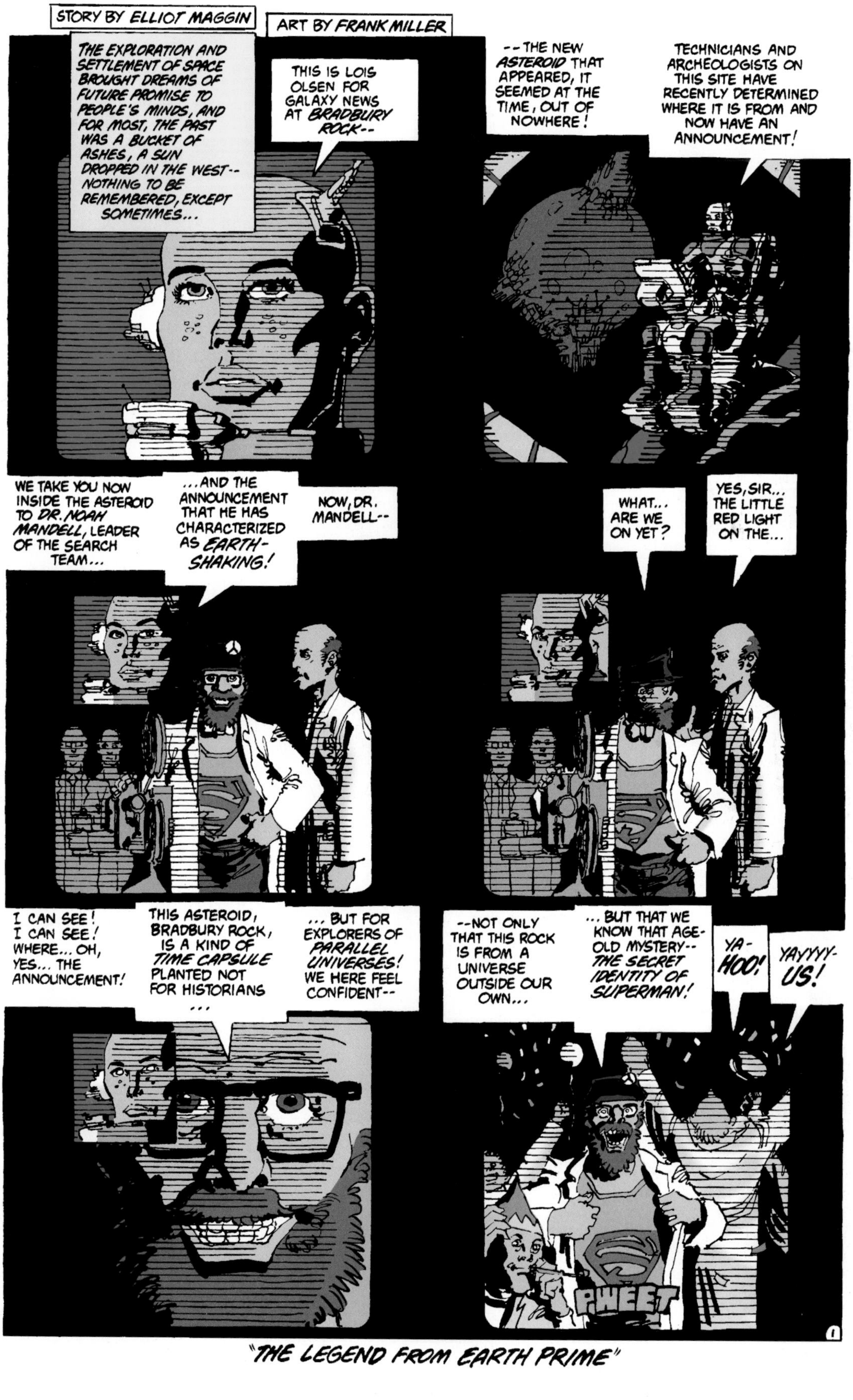

STORY BY ELLIOT MAGGIN
ART BY FRANK MILLER
THE EXPLORATION AND SETTLEMENT OF SPACE BROUGHT DREAMS OF FUTURE PROMISE TO PEOPLE'S MINDS, AND FOR MOST, THE PAST WAS A BUCKET OF ASHES, A SUN DROPPED IN THE WEST-- NOTHING TO BE REMEMBERED, EXCEPT SOMETIMES...
THIS IS LOIS OLSEN FOR GALAXY NEWS AT BRADBURY ROCK--
--THE NEW ASTEROID THAT APPEARED, IT SEEMED AT THE TIME, OUT OF NOWHERE!
TECHNICIANS AND ARCHEOLOGISTS ON THIS SITE HAVE RECENTLY DETERMINED WHERE IT IS FROM AND NOW HAVE AN ANNOUNCEMENT!
WE TAKE YOU NOW INSIDE THE ASTEROID TO DR. NOAH MANDELL, LEADER OF THE SEARCH TEAM...
...AND THE ANNOUNCEMENT THAT HE HAS CHARACTERIZED AS EARTH-SHAKING!
NOW, DR. MANDELL--
WHAT... ARE WE ON YET?
YES, SIR... THE LITTLE RED LIGHT ON THE...
I CAN SEE! I CAN SEE! WHERE... OH, YES... THE ANNOUNCEMENT!
THIS ASTEROID, BRADBURY ROCK, IS A KIND OF TIME CAPSULE PLANTED NOT FOR HISTORIANS ...
... BUT FOR EXPLORERS OF PARALLEL UNIVERSES! WE HERE FEEL CONFIDENT--
--NOT ONLY THAT THIS ROCK IS FROM A UNIVERSE OUTSIDE OUR OWN...
... BUT THAT WE KNOW THAT AGE-OLD MYSTERY-- THE SECRET IDENTITY OF SUPERMAN!
YA-HOO!
YAYYYY-US!
PWEET
1

"THE LEGEND FROM EARTH PRIME"

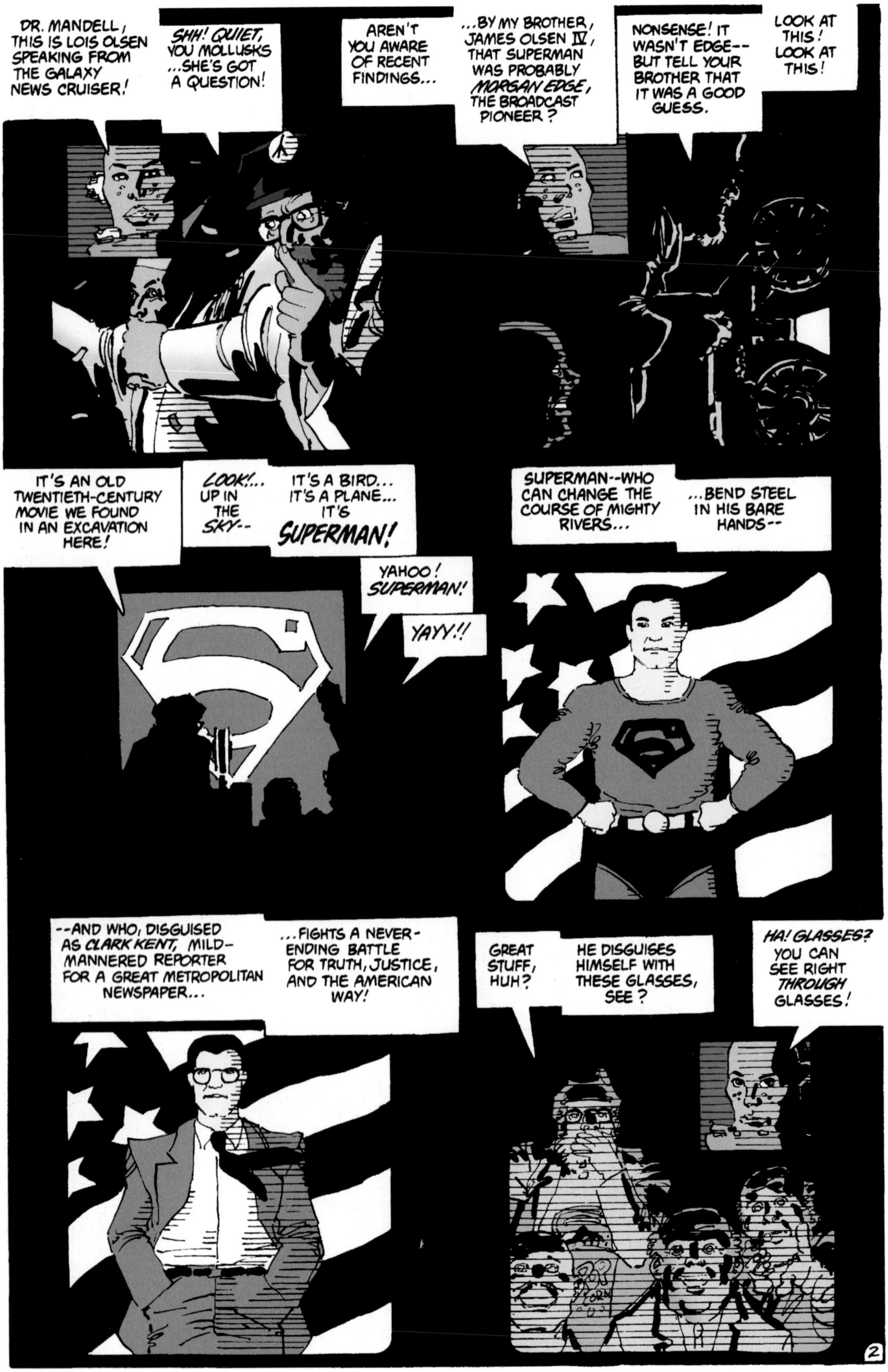
DR. MANDELL, THIS IS LOIS OLSEN SPEAKING FROM THE GALAXY NEWS CRUISER!
SHH! QUIET, YOU MOLLUSKS ...SHE'S GOT A QUESTION!
AREN'T YOU AWARE OF RECENT FINDINGS...
...BY MY BROTHER, JAMES OLSEN IV, THAT SUPERMAN WAS PROBABLY MORGAN EDGE, THE BROADCAST PIONEER?
NONSENSE! IT WASN'T EDGE-- BUT TELL YOUR BROTHER THAT IT WAS A GOOD GUESS.
LOOK AT THIS! LOOK AT THIS!
IT'S AN OLD TWENTIETH-CENTURY MOVIE WE FOUND IN AN EXCAVATION HERE!
LOOK!... UP IN THE SKY--
IT'S A BIRD... IT'S A PLANE... IT'S SUPERMAN!
YAHOO! SUPERMAN!
YAYY!!
SUPERMAN--WHO CAN CHANGE THE COURSE OF MIGHTY RIVERS...
...BEND STEEL IN HIS BARE HANDS--
--AND WHO, DISGUISED AS CLARK KENT, MILD-MANNERED REPORTER FOR A GREAT METROPOLITAN NEWSPAPER...
...FIGHTS A NEVER-ENDING BATTLE FOR TRUTH, JUSTICE, AND THE AMERICAN WAY!
GREAT STUFF, HUH?
HE DISGUISES HIMSELF WITH THESE GLASSES, SEE?
HA! GLASSES? YOU CAN SEE RIGHT THROUGH GLASSES!
2

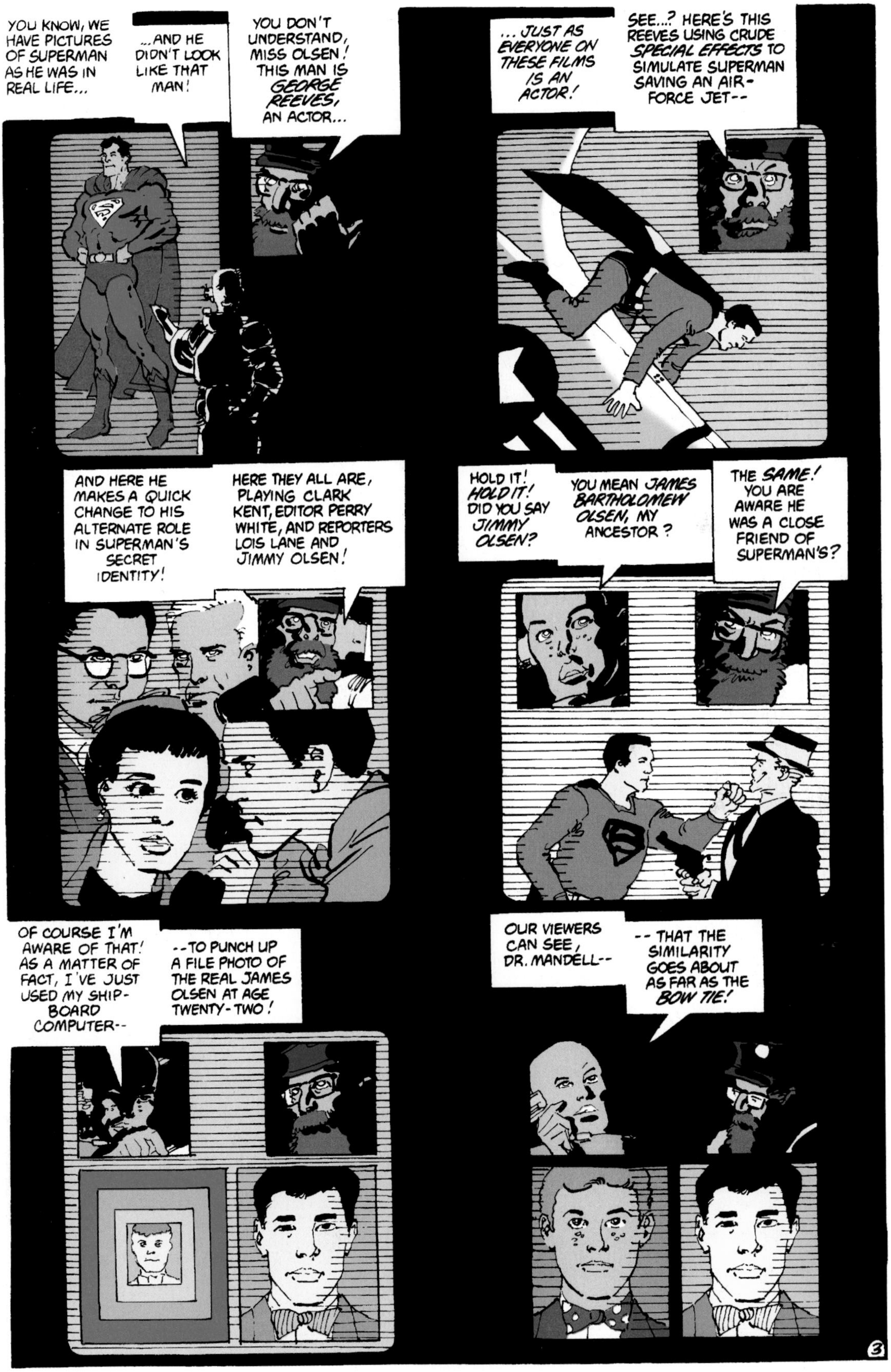

YOU KNOW, WE HAVE PICTURES OF SUPERMAN AS HE WAS IN REAL LIFE...
...AND HE DIDN'T LOOK LIKE THAT MAN!
YOU DON'T UNDERSTAND, MISS OLSEN! THIS MAN IS GEORGE REEVES, AN ACTOR...
...JUST AS EVERYONE ON THESE FILMS IS AN ACTOR!
SEE...? HERE'S THIS REEVES USING CRUDE SPECIAL EFFECTS TO SIMULATE SUPERMAN SAVING AN AIR-FORCE JET--
AND HERE HE MAKES A QUICK CHANGE TO HIS ALTERNATE ROLE IN SUPERMAN'S SECRET IDENTITY!
HERE THEY ALL ARE, PLAYING CLARK KENT, EDITOR PERRY WHITE, AND REPORTERS LOIS LANE AND JIMMY OLSEN!
HOLD IT! HOLD IT! DID YOU SAY JIMMY OLSEN?
YOU MEAN JAMES BARTHOLOMEW OLSEN, MY ANCESTOR?
THE SAME! YOU ARE AWARE HE WAS A CLOSE FRIEND OF SUPERMAN'S?
OF COURSE I'M AWARE OF THAT! AS A MATTER OF FACT, I'VE JUST USED MY SHIP-BOARD COMPUTER--
--TO PUNCH UP A FILE PHOTO OF THE REAL JAMES OLSEN AT AGE TWENTY-TWO!
OUR VIEWERS CAN SEE, DR. MANDELL--
--THAT THE SIMILARITY GOES ABOUT AS FAR AS THE BOW TIE!
3

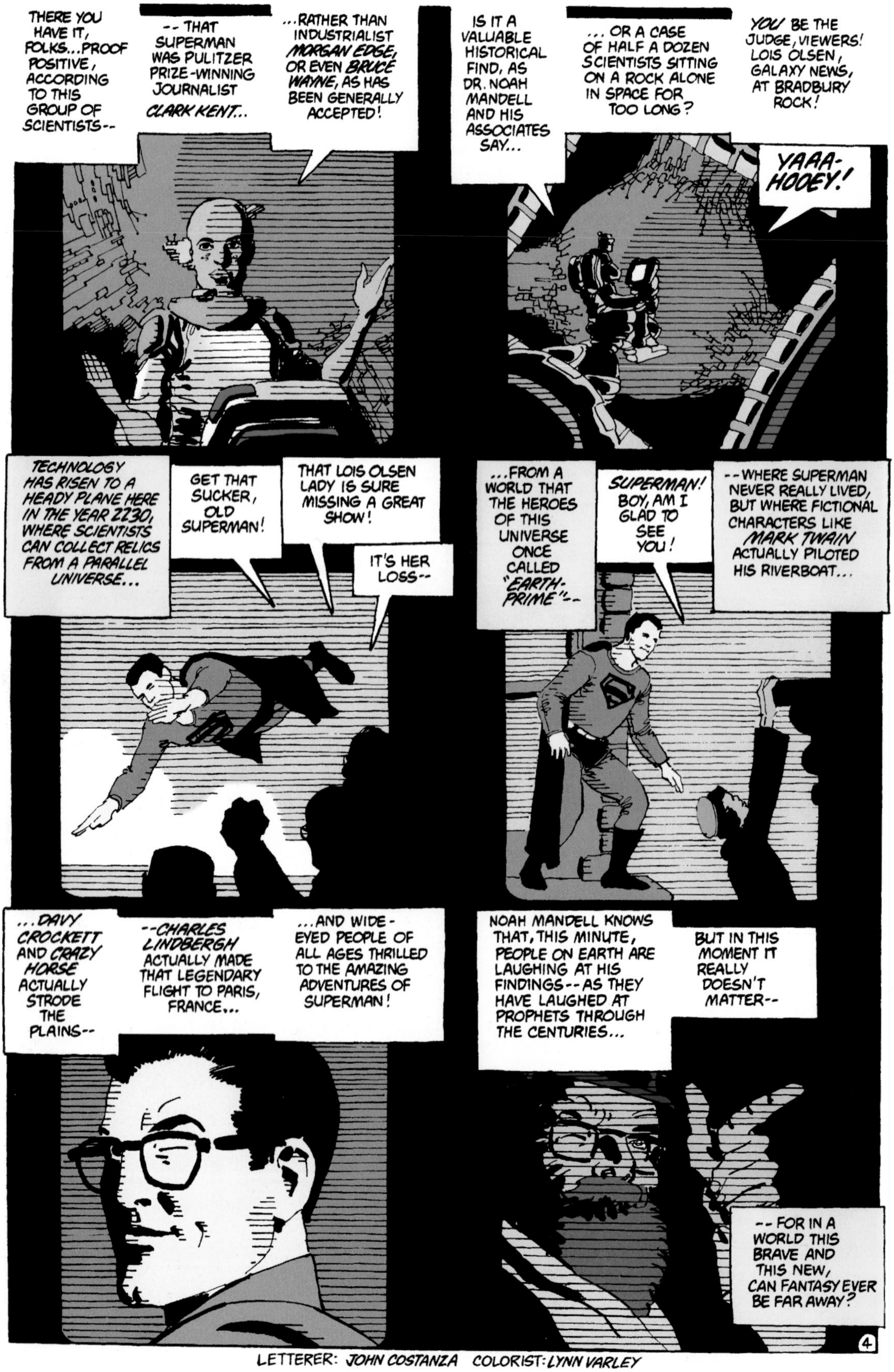
THERE YOU HAVE IT, FOLKS...PROOF POSITIVE, ACCORDING TO THIS GROUP OF SCIENTISTS--
--THAT SUPERMAN WAS PULITZER PRIZE-WINNING JOURNALIST CLARK KENT...
...RATHER THAN INDUSTRIALIST MORGAN EDGE, OR EVEN BRUCE WAYNE, AS HAS BEEN GENERALLY ACCEPTED!
IS IT A VALUABLE HISTORICAL FIND, AS DR. NOAH MANDELL AND HIS ASSOCIATES SAY...
...OR A CASE OF HALF A DOZEN SCIENTISTS SITTING ON A ROCK ALONE IN SPACE FOR TOO LONG?
YOU BE THE JUDGE, VIEWERS! LOIS OLSEN, GALAXY NEWS, AT BRADBURY ROCK!
YAAA-HOOEY!
TECHNOLOGY HAS RISEN TO A HEADY PLANE HERE IN THE YEAR 2230, WHERE SCIENTISTS CAN COLLECT RELICS FROM A PARALLEL UNIVERSE...
GET THAT SUCKER, OLD SUPERMAN!
THAT LOIS OLSEN LADY IS SURE MISSING A GREAT SHOW!
IT'S HER LOSS--
...FROM A WORLD THAT THE HEROES OF THIS UNIVERSE ONCE CALLED "EARTH-PRIME"--
SUPERMAN! BOY, AM I GLAD TO SEE YOU!
--WHERE SUPERMAN NEVER REALLY LIVED, BUT WHERE FICTIONAL CHARACTERS LIKE MARK TWAIN ACTUALLY PILOTED HIS RIVERBOAT...
...DAVY CROCKETT AND CRAZY HORSE ACTUALLY STRODE THE PLAINS--
--CHARLES LINDBERGH ACTUALLY MADE THAT LEGENDARY FLIGHT TO PARIS, FRANCE...
...AND WIDE-EYED PEOPLE OF ALL AGES THRILLED TO THE AMAZING ADVENTURES OF SUPERMAN!
NOAH MANDELL KNOWS THAT, THIS MINUTE, PEOPLE ON EARTH ARE LAUGHING AT HIS FINDINGS--AS THEY HAVE LAUGHED AT PROPHETS THROUGH THE CENTURIES...
BUT IN THIS MOMENT IT REALLY DOESN'T MATTER--
--FOR IN A WORLD THIS BRAVE AND THIS NEW, CAN FANTASY EVER BE FAR AWAY?
4

LETTERER: JOHN COSTANZA COLORIST: LYNN VARLEY

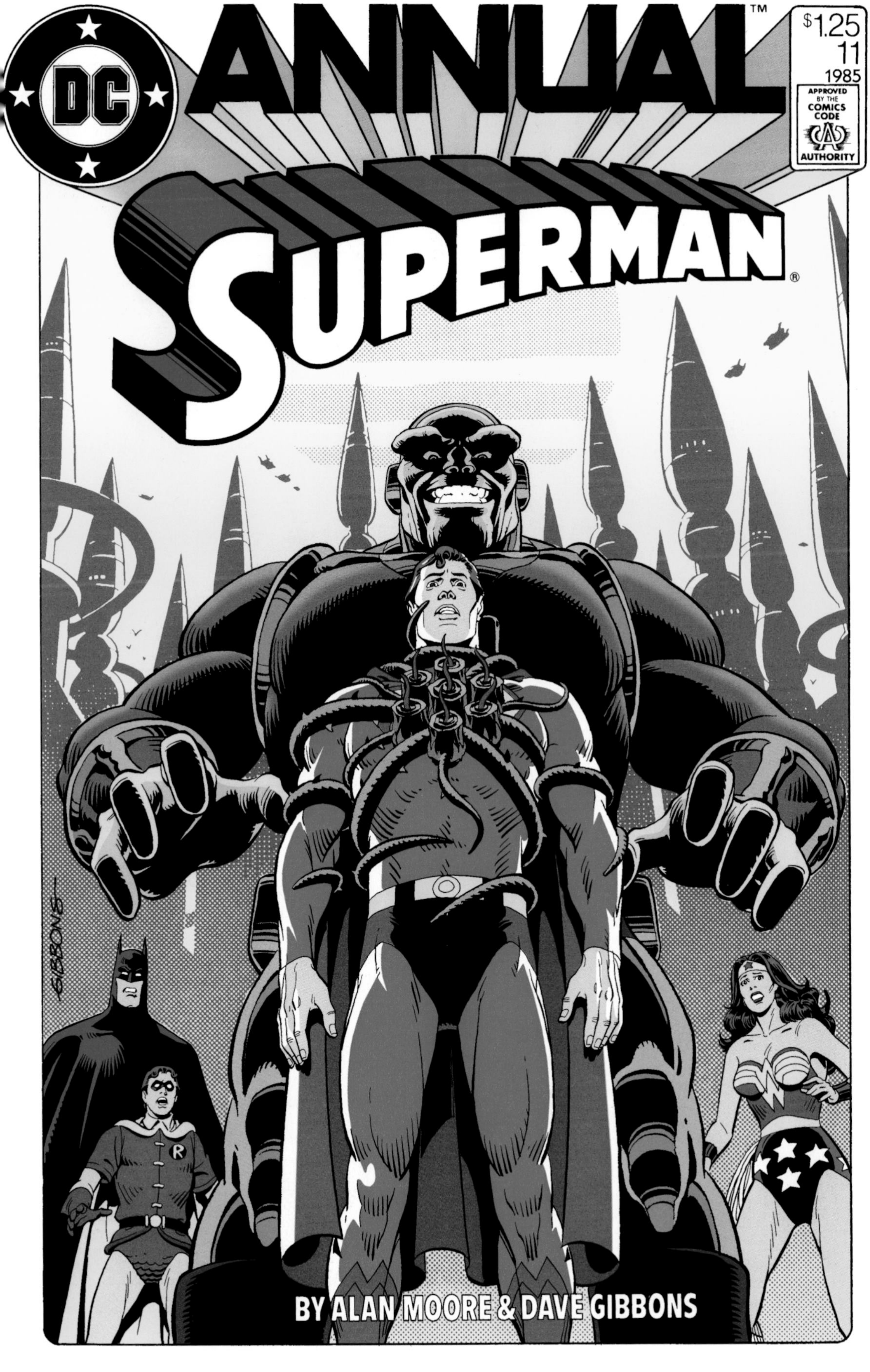
ANNUAL
DC
$1.25
11
1985
APPROVED BY THE COMICS CODE AUTHORITY
SUPERMAN
GIBBONS
BY ALAN MOORE & DAVE GIBBONS

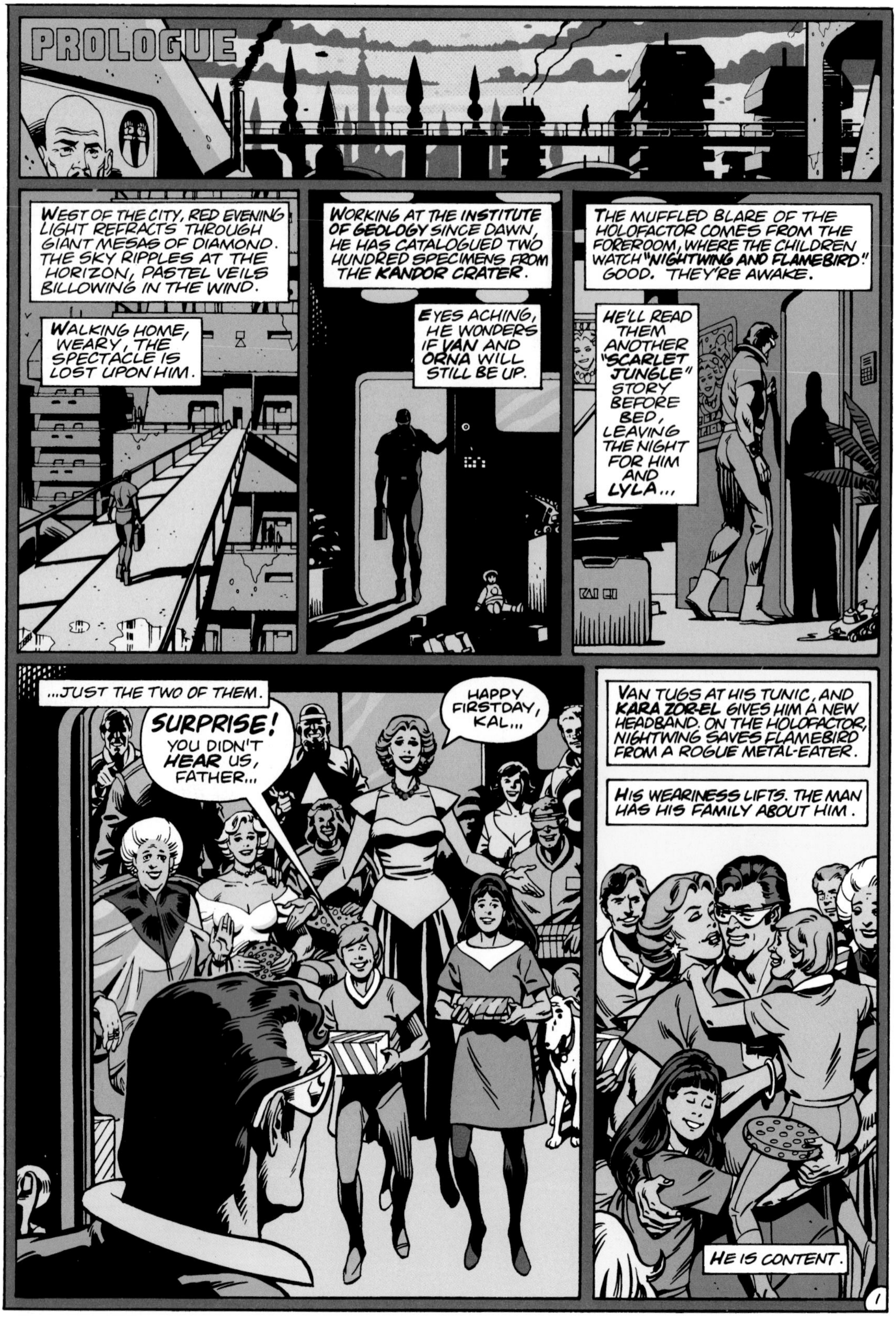
PROLOGUE
WEST OF THE CITY, RED EVENING LIGHT REFRACTS THROUGH GIANT MESAS OF DIAMOND. THE SKY RIPPLES AT THE HORIZON, PASTEL VEILS BILLOWING IN THE WIND.
WALKING HOME, WEARY, THE SPECTACLE IS LOST UPON HIM.
WORKING AT THE INSTITUTE OF GEOLOGY SINCE DAWN, HE HAS CATALOGUED TWO HUNDRED SPECIMENS FROM THE KANDOR CRATER.
EYES ACHING, HE WONDERS IF VAN AND ORNA WILL STILL BE UP.
THE MUFFLED BLARE OF THE HOLOFACTOR COMES FROM THE FOREROOM, WHERE THE CHILDREN WATCH "NIGHTWING AND FLAMEBIRD." GOOD. THEY'RE AWAKE.
HE'LL READ THEM ANOTHER "SCARLET JUNGLE" STORY BEFORE BED, LEAVING THE NIGHT FOR HIM AND LYLA...
...JUST THE TWO OF THEM.
SURPRISE! YOU DIDN'T HEAR US, FATHER...
HAPPY FIRSTDAY, KAL...
VAN TUGS AT HIS TUNIC, AND KARA ZOR-EL GIVES HIM A NEW HEADBAND. ON THE HOLOFACTOR, NIGHTWING SAVES FLAMEBIRD FROM A ROGUE METAL-EATER.
HIS WEARINESS LIFTS. THE MAN HAS HIS FAMILY ABOUT HIM.
HE IS CONTENT.
1

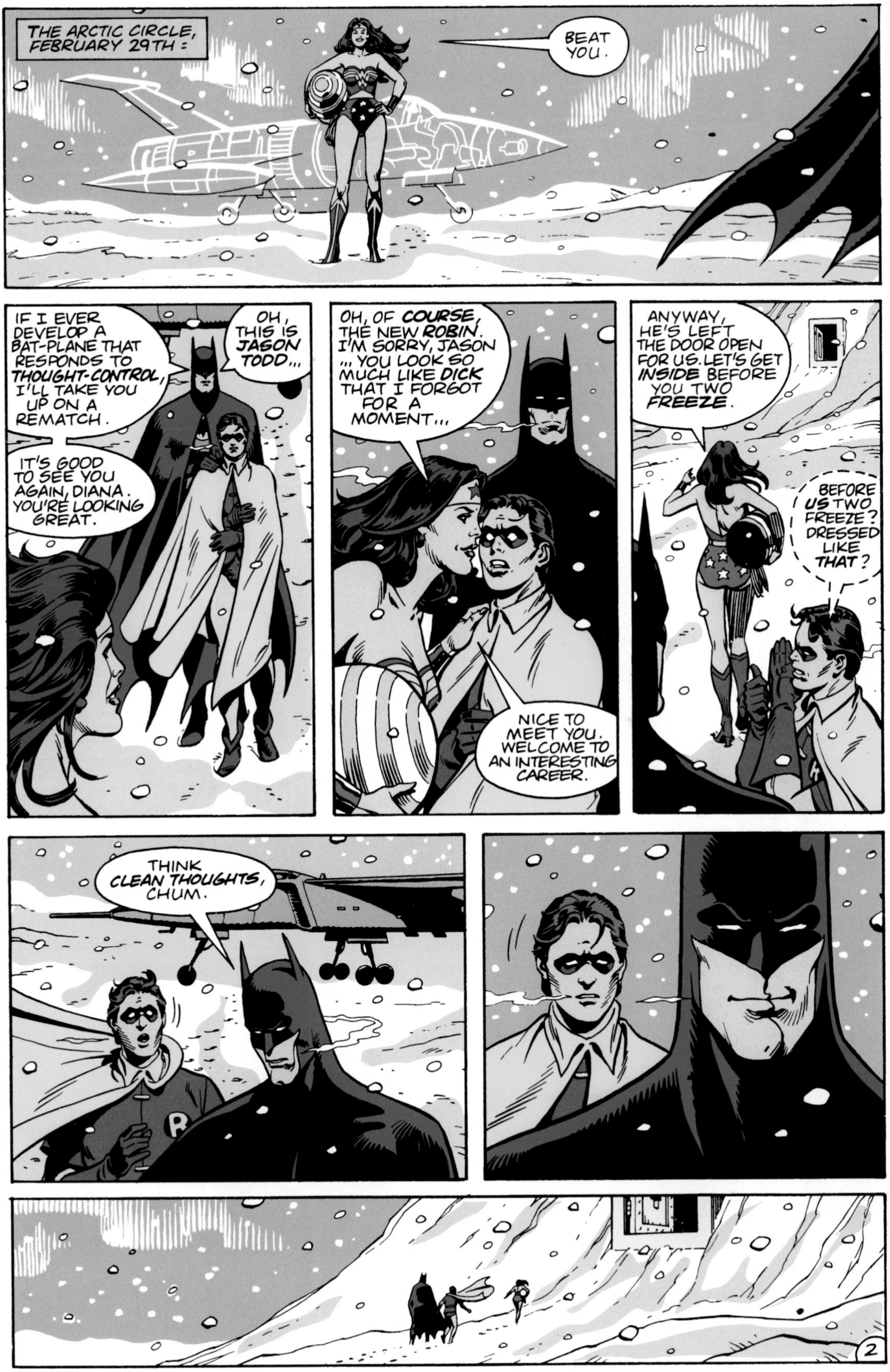
THE ARCTIC CIRCLE, FEBRUARY 29TH :
BEAT YOU.
IF I EVER DEVELOP A BAT-PLANE THAT RESPONDS TO THOUGHT-CONTROL, I'LL TAKE YOU UP ON A REMATCH.
IT'S GOOD TO SEE YOU AGAIN, DIANA. YOU'RE LOOKING GREAT.
OH, THIS IS JASON TODD...
OH, OF COURSE, THE NEW ROBIN. I'M SORRY, JASON ... YOU LOOK SO MUCH LIKE DICK THAT I FORGOT FOR A MOMENT...
NICE TO MEET YOU. WELCOME TO AN INTERESTING CAREER.
ANYWAY, HE'S LEFT THE DOOR OPEN FOR US. LET'S GET INSIDE BEFORE YOU TWO FREEZE.
BEFORE US TWO FREEZE? DRESSED LIKE THAT?
THINK CLEAN THOUGHTS, CHUM.
2

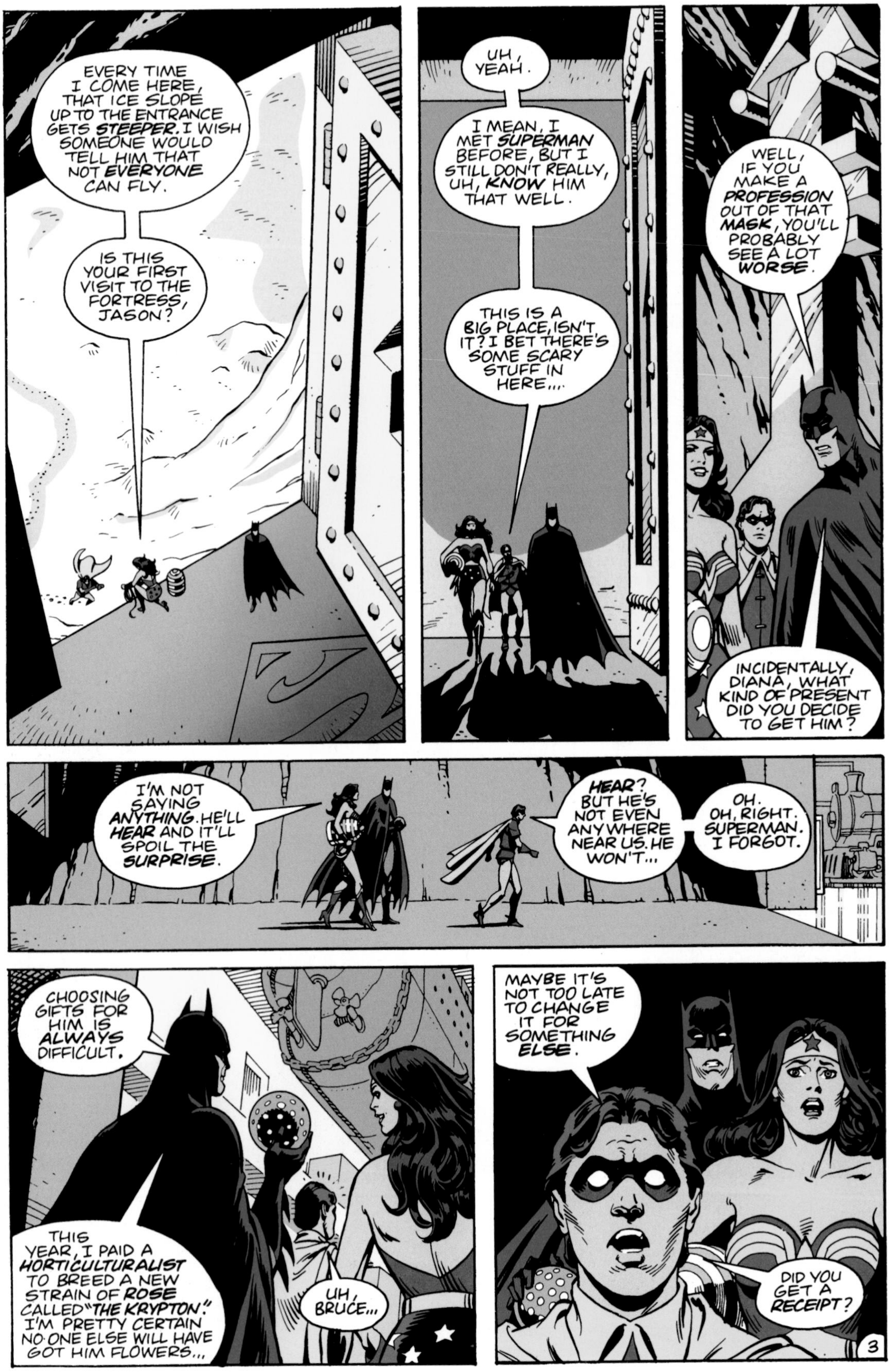
EVERY TIME I COME HERE, THAT ICE SLOPE UP TO THE ENTRANCE GETS STEEPER. I WISH SOMEONE WOULD TELL HIM THAT NOT EVERYONE CAN FLY.
IS THIS YOUR FIRST VISIT TO THE FORTRESS, JASON?
UH, YEAH.
I MEAN, I MET SUPERMAN BEFORE, BUT I STILL DON'T REALLY, UH, KNOW HIM THAT WELL.
THIS IS A BIG PLACE, ISN'T IT? I BET THERE'S SOME SCARY STUFF IN HERE...
WELL, IF YOU MAKE A PROFESSION OUT OF THAT MASK, YOU'LL PROBABLY SEE A LOT WORSE.
INCIDENTALLY, DIANA, WHAT KIND OF PRESENT DID YOU DECIDE TO GET HIM?
I'M NOT SAYING ANYTHING. HE'LL HEAR AND IT'LL SPOIL THE SURPRISE.
HEAR? BUT HE'S NOT EVEN ANYWHERE NEAR US. HE WON'T...
OH. OH, RIGHT. SUPERMAN. I FORGOT.
CHOOSING GIFTS FOR HIM IS ALWAYS DIFFICULT.
THIS YEAR, I PAID A HORTICULTURALIST TO BREED A NEW STRAIN OF ROSE CALLED "THE KRYPTON." I'M PRETTY CERTAIN NO ONE ELSE WILL HAVE GOT HIM FLOWERS...
UH, BRUCE...
MAYBE IT'S NOT TOO LATE TO CHANGE IT FOR SOMETHING ELSE.
DID YOU GET A RECEIPT?
3

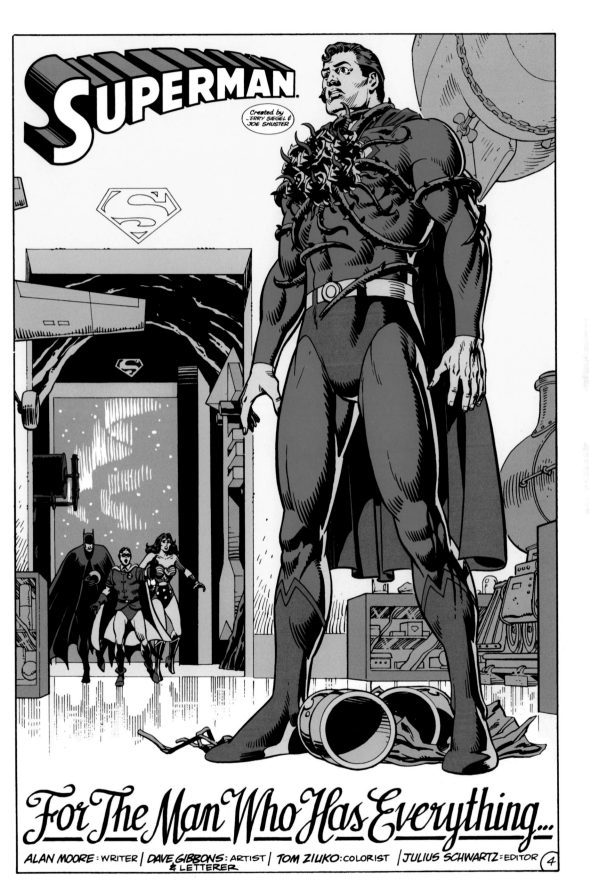

SUPERMAN.

Created by
JERRY SIEGEL &
JOE SHUSTER

For The Man Who Has Everything...

ALAN MOORE: WRITER | DAVE GIBBONS: ARTIST | TOM ZIUKO: COLORIST | JULIUS SCHWARTZ: EDITOR ④
& LETTERER

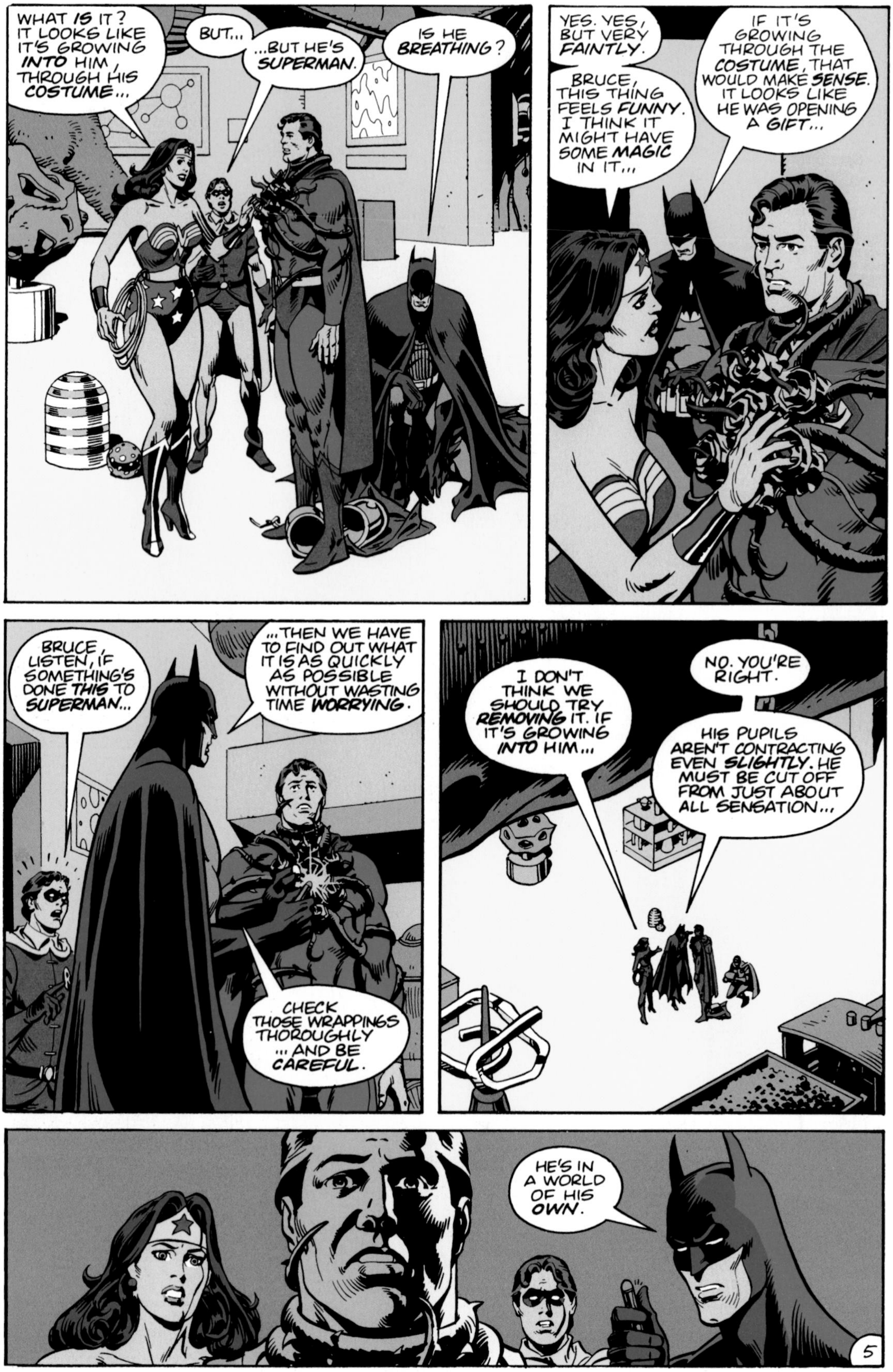
WHAT IS IT? IT LOOKS LIKE IT'S GROWING INTO HIM, THROUGH HIS COSTUME...
BUT...
...BUT HE'S SUPERMAN.
IS HE BREATHING?
YES. YES, BUT VERY FAINTLY.
BRUCE, THIS THING FEELS FUNNY. I THINK IT MIGHT HAVE SOME MAGIC IN IT...
IF IT'S GROWING THROUGH THE COSTUME, THAT WOULD MAKE SENSE. IT LOOKS LIKE HE WAS OPENING A GIFT...
BRUCE, LISTEN, IF SOMETHING'S DONE THIS TO SUPERMAN...
...THEN WE HAVE TO FIND OUT WHAT IT IS AS QUICKLY AS POSSIBLE WITHOUT WASTING TIME WORRYING.
CHECK THOSE WRAPPINGS THOROUGHLY ...AND BE CAREFUL.
I DON'T THINK WE SHOULD TRY REMOVING IT. IF IT'S GROWING INTO HIM...
NO. YOU'RE RIGHT.
HIS PUPILS AREN'T CONTRACTING EVEN SLIGHTLY. HE MUST BE CUT OFF FROM JUST ABOUT ALL SENSATION...
HE'S IN A WORLD OF HIS OWN.
5

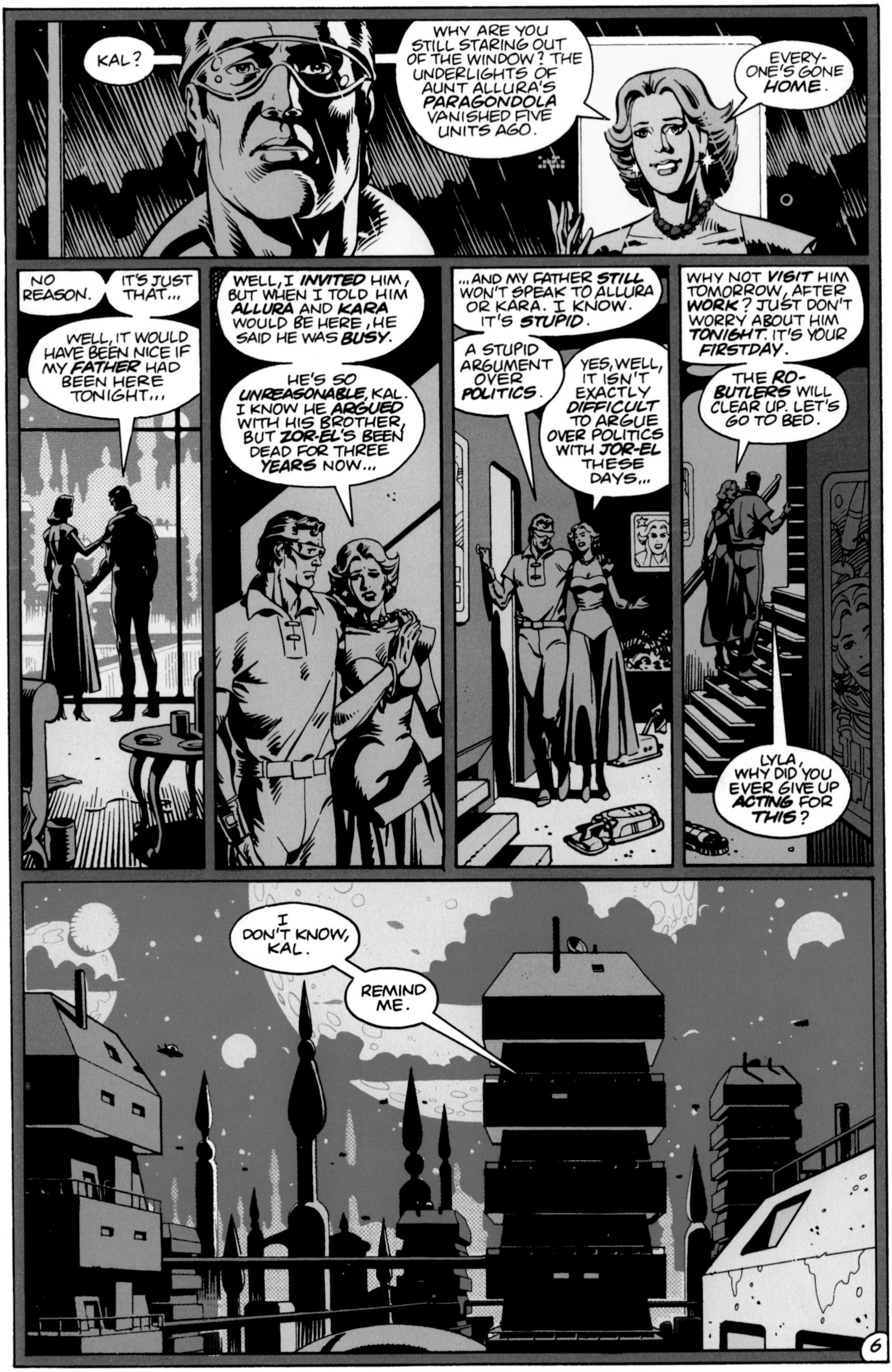
KAL?
WHY ARE YOU STILL STARING OUT OF THE WINDOW? THE UNDERLIGHTS OF AUNT ALLURA'S PARAGONDOLA VANISHED FIVE UNITS AGO.
EVERY-ONE'S GONE HOME.
NO REASON.
IT'S JUST THAT...
WELL, IT WOULD HAVE BEEN NICE IF MY FATHER HAD BEEN HERE TONIGHT...
WELL, I INVITED HIM, BUT WHEN I TOLD HIM ALLURA AND KARA WOULD BE HERE, HE SAID HE WAS BUSY.
HE'S SO UNREASONABLE, KAL. I KNOW HE ARGUED WITH HIS BROTHER, BUT ZOR-EL'S BEEN DEAD FOR THREE YEARS NOW...
...AND MY FATHER STILL WON'T SPEAK TO ALLURA OR KARA. I KNOW. IT'S STUPID.
A STUPID ARGUMENT OVER POLITICS.
YES, WELL, IT ISN'T EXACTLY DIFFICULT TO ARGUE OVER POLITICS WITH JOR-EL THESE DAYS...
WHY NOT VISIT HIM TOMORROW, AFTER WORK? JUST DON'T WORRY ABOUT HIM TONIGHT. IT'S YOUR FIRSTDAY.
THE RO-BUTLERS WILL CLEAR UP. LET'S GO TO BED.
LYLA, WHY DID YOU EVER GIVE UP ACTING FOR THIS?
I DON'T KNOW, KAL.
REMIND ME.
6

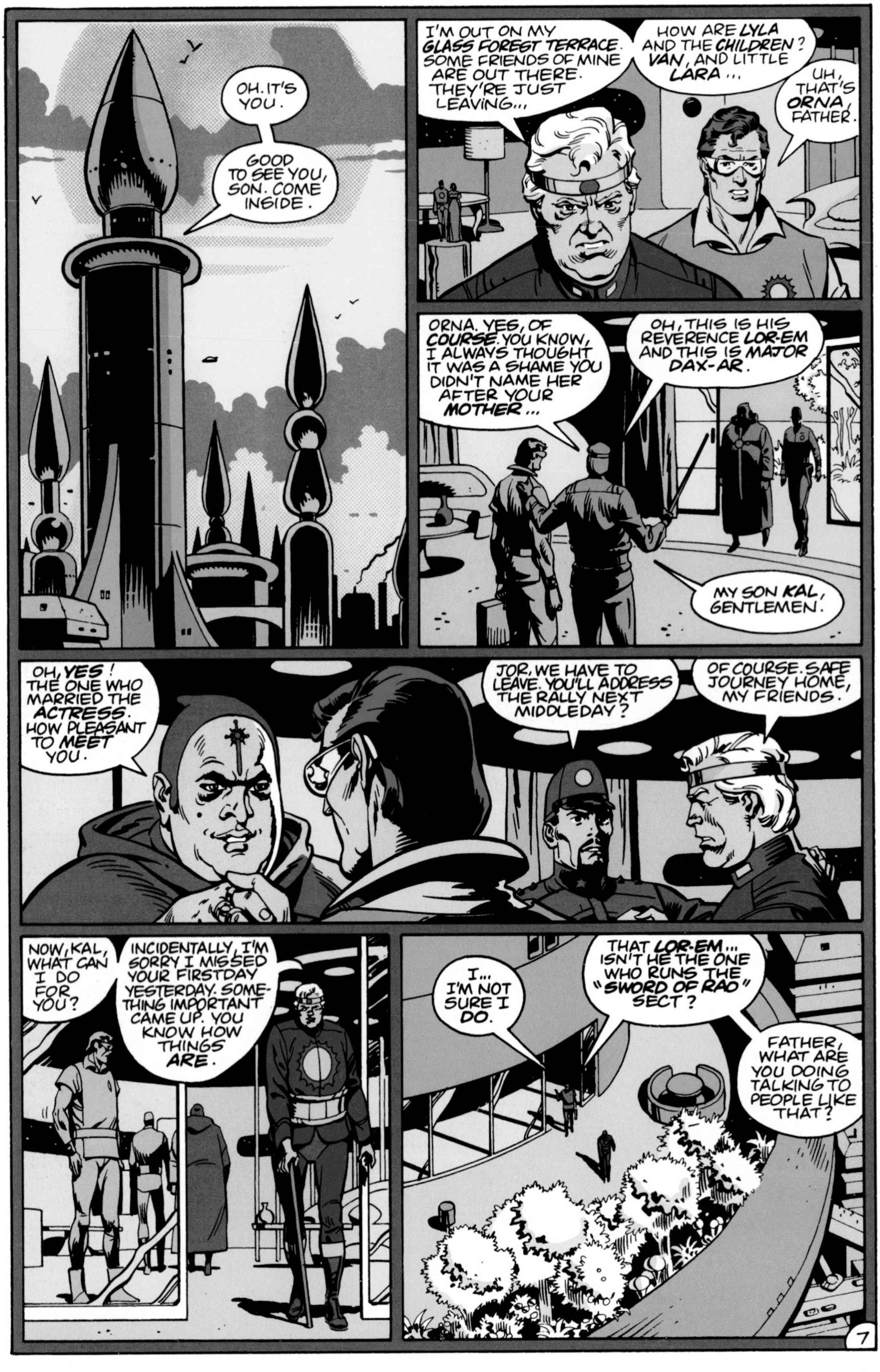
OH. IT'S YOU.
GOOD TO SEE YOU, SON. COME INSIDE.
I'M OUT ON MY GLASS FOREST TERRACE. SOME FRIENDS OF MINE ARE OUT THERE. THEY'RE JUST LEAVING...
HOW ARE LYLA AND THE CHILDREN? VAN, AND LITTLE LARA...
UH, THAT'S ORNA, FATHER.
ORNA. YES, OF COURSE. YOU KNOW, I ALWAYS THOUGHT IT WAS A SHAME YOU DIDN'T NAME HER AFTER YOUR MOTHER...
OH, THIS IS HIS REVERENCE LOR-EM AND THIS IS MAJOR DAX-AR.
MY SON KAL, GENTLEMEN.
OH, YES! THE ONE WHO MARRIED THE ACTRESS. HOW PLEASANT TO MEET YOU.
JOR, WE HAVE TO LEAVE. YOU'LL ADDRESS THE RALLY NEXT MIDDLEDAY?
OF COURSE. SAFE JOURNEY HOME, MY FRIENDS.
NOW, KAL, WHAT CAN I DO FOR YOU?
INCIDENTALLY, I'M SORRY I MISSED YOUR FIRSTDAY YESTERDAY. SOMETHING IMPORTANT CAME UP. YOU KNOW HOW THINGS ARE.
I... I'M NOT SURE I DO.
THAT LOR-EM... ISN'T HE THE ONE WHO RUNS THE "SWORD OF RAO" SECT?
FATHER, WHAT ARE YOU DOING TALKING TO PEOPLE LIKE THAT?
7

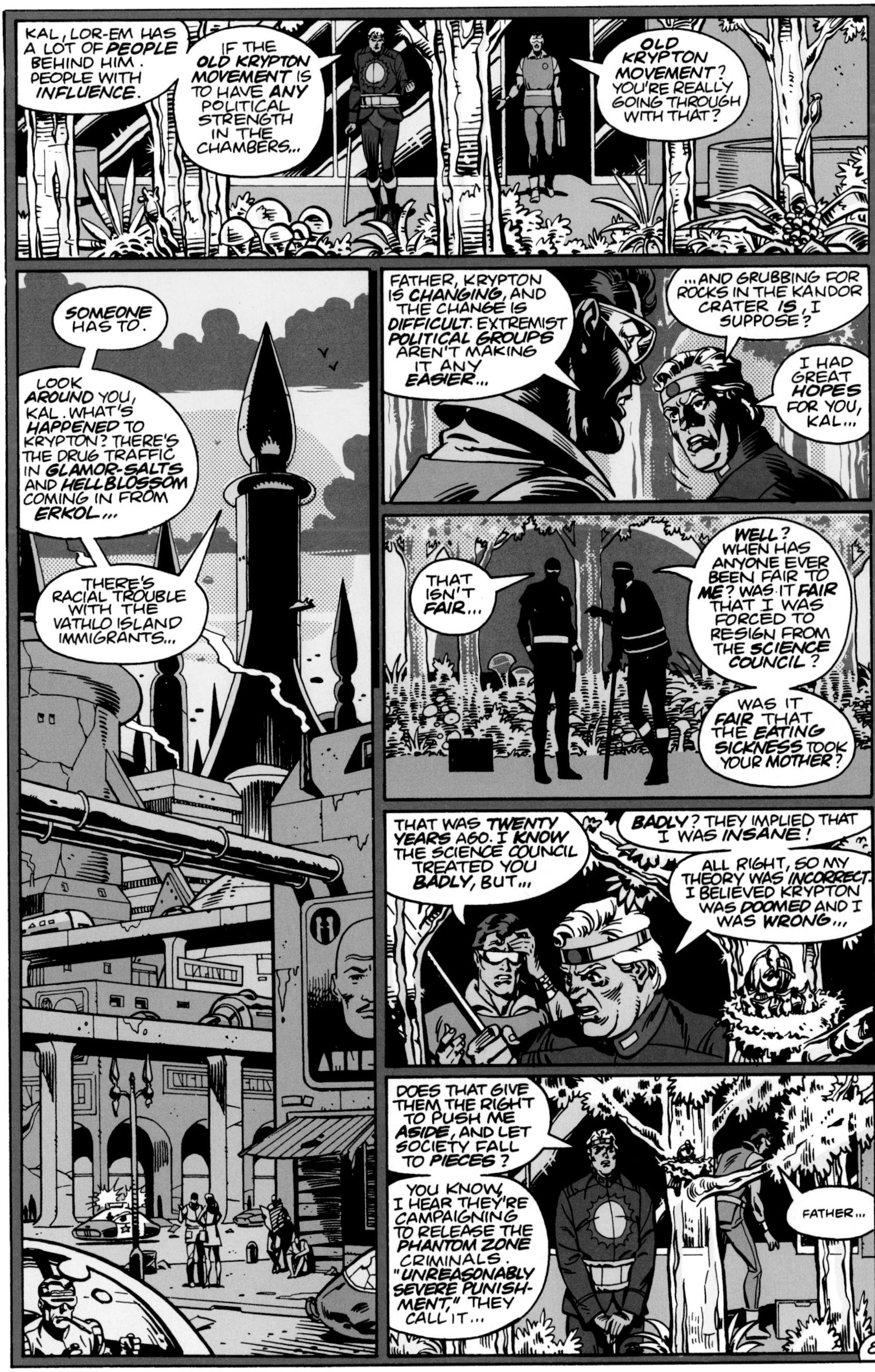
KAL, LOR-EM HAS A LOT OF PEOPLE BEHIND HIM. PEOPLE WITH INFLUENCE.
IF THE OLD KRYPTON MOVEMENT IS TO HAVE ANY POLITICAL STRENGTH IN THE CHAMBERS...
OLD KRYPTON MOVEMENT? YOU'RE REALLY GOING THROUGH WITH THAT?
SOMEONE HAS TO.
LOOK AROUND YOU, KAL. WHAT'S HAPPENED TO KRYPTON? THERE'S THE DRUG TRAFFIC IN GLAMOR-SALTS AND HELLBLOSSOM COMING IN FROM ERKOL...
THERE'S RACIAL TROUBLE WITH THE VATHLO ISLAND IMMIGRANTS...
FATHER, KRYPTON IS CHANGING, AND THE CHANGE IS DIFFICULT. EXTREMIST POLITICAL GROUPS AREN'T MAKING IT ANY EASIER...
...AND GRUBBING FOR ROCKS IN THE KANDOR CRATER IS, I SUPPOSE?
I HAD GREAT HOPES FOR YOU, KAL...
THAT ISN'T FAIR...
WELL? WHEN HAS ANYONE EVER BEEN FAIR TO ME? WAS IT FAIR THAT I WAS FORCED TO RESIGN FROM THE SCIENCE COUNCIL?
WAS IT FAIR THAT THE EATING SICKNESS TOOK YOUR MOTHER?
THAT WAS TWENTY YEARS AGO. I KNOW THE SCIENCE COUNCIL TREATED YOU BADLY, BUT...
BADLY? THEY IMPLIED THAT I WAS INSANE!
ALL RIGHT, SO MY THEORY WAS INCORRECT. I BELIEVED KRYPTON WAS DOOMED AND I WAS WRONG...
DOES THAT GIVE THEM THE RIGHT TO PUSH ME ASIDE, AND LET SOCIETY FALL TO PIECES?
YOU KNOW, I HEAR THEY'RE CAMPAIGNING TO RELEASE THE PHANTOM ZONE CRIMINALS. "UNREASONABLY SEVERE PUNISHMENT," THEY CALL IT...
FATHER...
8

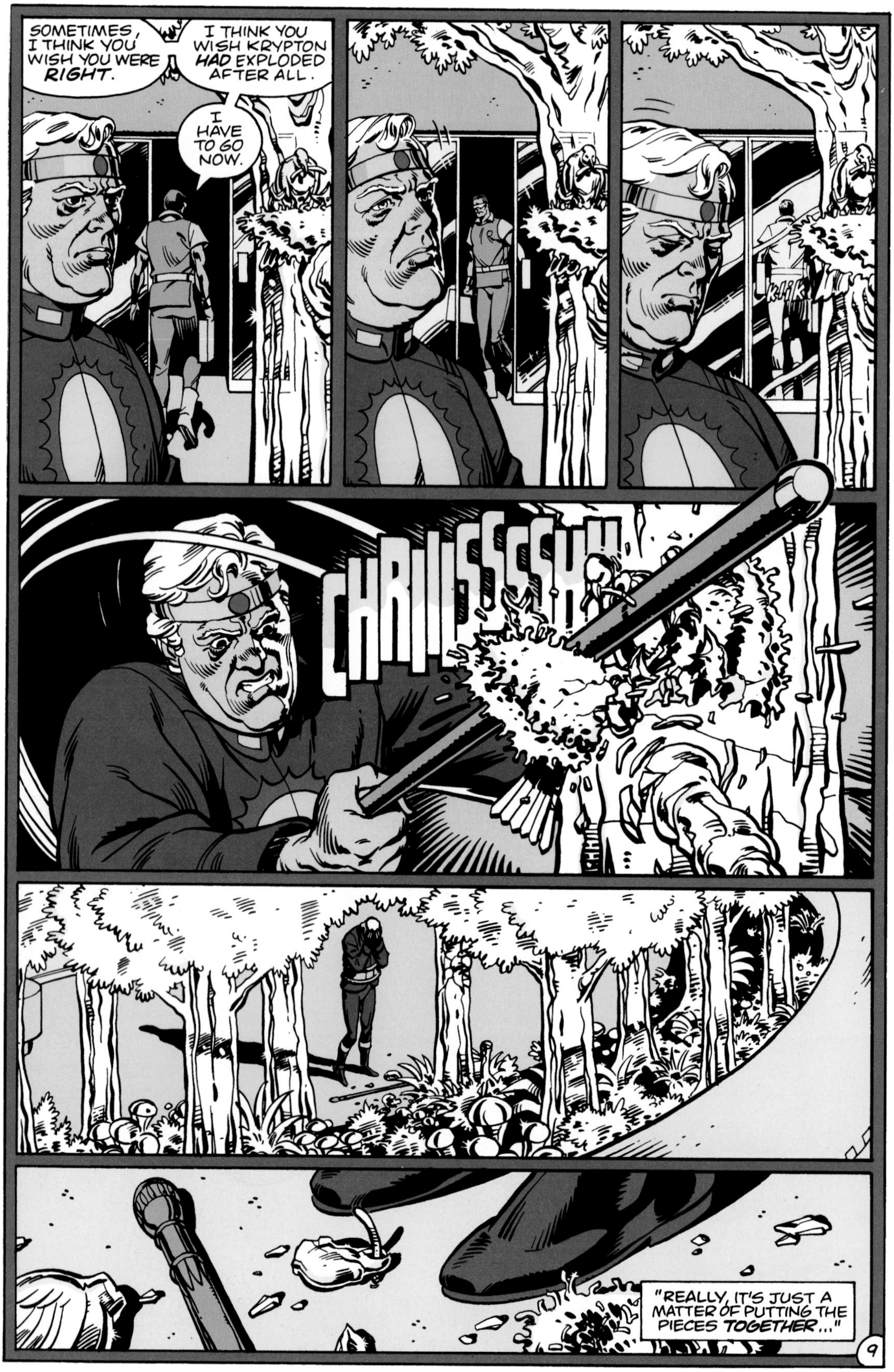

SOMETIMES, I THINK YOU WISH YOU WERE RIGHT.
I THINK YOU WISH KRYPTON HAD EXPLODED AFTER ALL.
I HAVE TO GO NOW.
KLIK
CHRIIISSSSHH
"REALLY, IT'S JUST A MATTER OF PUTTING THE PIECES TOGETHER..."
9

I THINK IT'S SAFE TO ASSUME FROM THOSE *WRAPPINGS* THAT SUPER-MAN RECEIVED THIS THING AS A *GIFT*...

...BUT *HOW*?

I GUESS THE *U.S. MAIL* DOESN'T *REACH* THIS FAR...

LISTEN, IT HAS TO BE *ALIEN* IN ORIGIN. I KNOW THAT A LOT OF ALIEN CULTURES SEND HIM *GIFTS*...

HMM. I SUPPOSE HE MUST HAVE A *TELE-PORTATION* CHANNEL, ALTHOUGH HE'S NEVER *MENTIONED* ONE...

PERHAPS HE DOESN'T *USE* THE CHANNEL OFTEN... JUST ONCE A YEAR, WHEN IT'S HIS *BIRTH-DAY*...

IT'S *POSSIBLE* ...

SOME *GRATEFUL* WORLD MAY HAVE SENT THIS AS A *GIFT*, UNAWARE THAT IT COULD *HARM* HIM ...

HOW *REMARKABLE*. YOU ANIMALS REALLY ARE ALMOST *INTELLIGENT*, AREN'T YOU?

THAT'S *EXACTLY* WHAT HAPPENED...

...EXCEPT FOR ONE OR TWO *MINOR* DETAILS.

⑩

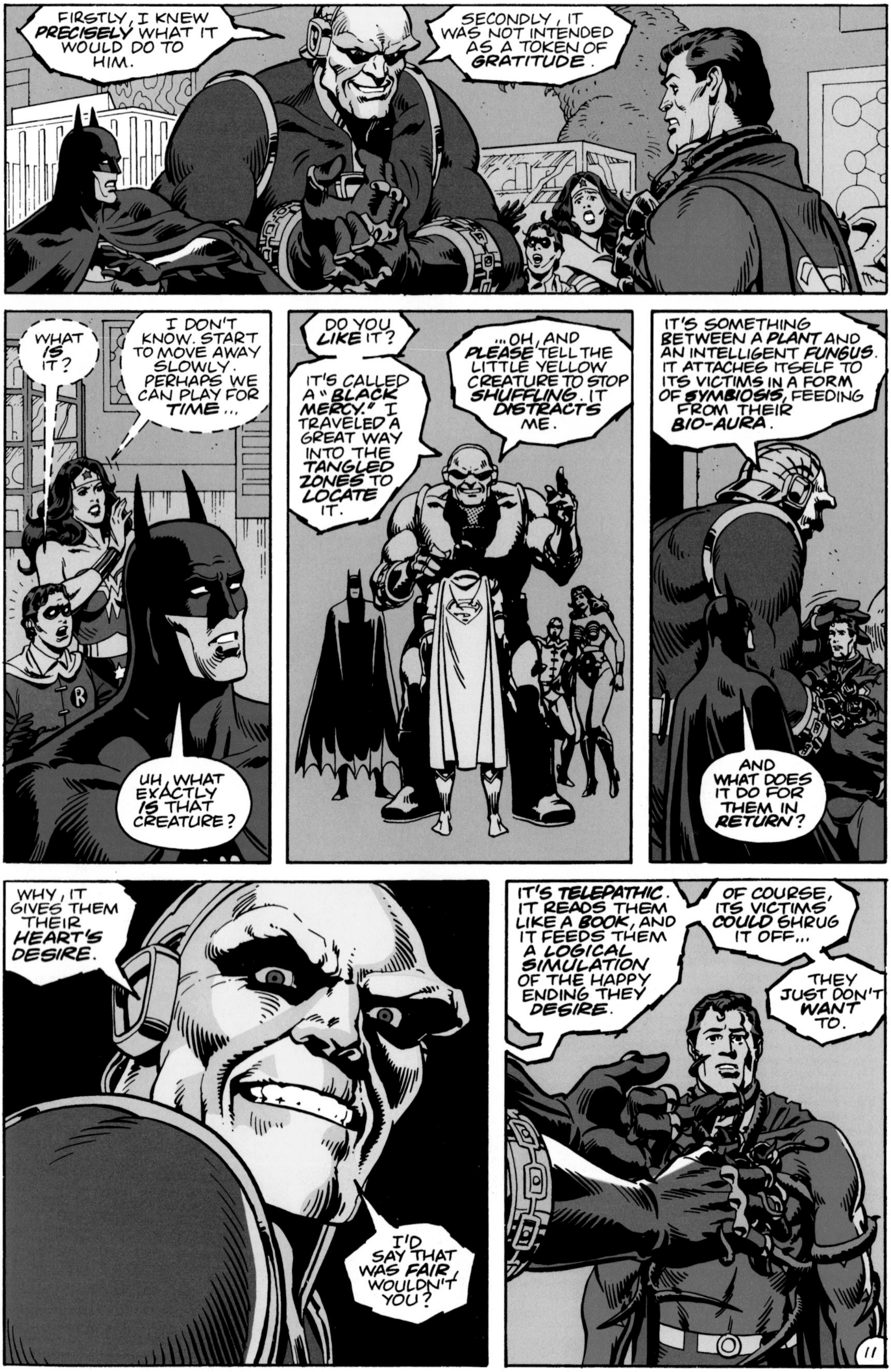
FIRSTLY, I KNEW PRECISELY WHAT IT WOULD DO TO HIM.
SECONDLY, IT WAS NOT INTENDED AS A TOKEN OF GRATITUDE.
WHAT IS IT?
I DON'T KNOW. START TO MOVE AWAY SLOWLY. PERHAPS WE CAN PLAY FOR TIME...
UH, WHAT EXACTLY IS THAT CREATURE?
DO YOU LIKE IT?
IT'S CALLED A "BLACK MERCY." I TRAVELED A GREAT WAY INTO THE TANGLED ZONES TO LOCATE IT.
...OH, AND PLEASE TELL THE LITTLE YELLOW CREATURE TO STOP SHUFFLING. IT DISTRACTS ME.
IT'S SOMETHING BETWEEN A PLANT AND AN INTELLIGENT FUNGUS. IT ATTACHES ITSELF TO ITS VICTIMS IN A FORM OF SYMBIOSIS, FEEDING FROM THEIR BIO-AURA.
AND WHAT DOES IT DO FOR THEM IN RETURN?
WHY, IT GIVES THEM THEIR HEART'S DESIRE.
I'D SAY THAT WAS FAIR, WOULDN'T YOU?
IT'S TELEPATHIC. IT READS THEM LIKE A BOOK, AND IT FEEDS THEM A LOGICAL SIMULATION OF THE HAPPY ENDING THEY DESIRE.
OF COURSE, ITS VICTIMS COULD SHRUG IT OFF...
THEY JUST DON'T WANT TO.
11

I *DELIVERED* IT TO HIM, AND WHEN I WAS CERTAIN THAT IT HAD DONE ITS *WORK*, I FOLLOWED IT ALONG THE *TELEPORTATION CHANNEL*.

POOR LITTLE CREATURE, I WONDER WHERE HE THINKS HE *IS*?

PERHAPS HE'S PLAYING HAPPILY AS A CHILD IN WHATEVER SORDID ABORIGINAL *BACK-WATER* HE WAS *RAISED* IN, OR BOUNCING ON HIS MOTHER'S *KNEE*...

THAT WOULD BE *NICE*, WOULDN'T IT? TO THINK OF HIM, CAREFREE AND CONTENTED...

FOREVER.

WHAT... *ARE*... YOU?

IF YOU DON'T ALREADY *KNOW* MY NAME, THEN YOU'RE NOT WORTHY OF AN *INTRODUCTION*.

I'M THE NEW *MANAGER* AROUND HERE.

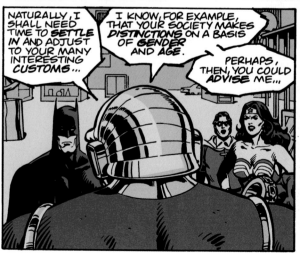

NATURALLY, I SHALL NEED TIME TO *SETTLE* IN AND ADJUST TO YOUR MANY INTERESTING *CUSTOMS*...

I KNOW, FOR EXAMPLE, THAT YOUR SOCIETY MAKES *DISTINCTIONS* ON A BASIS OF *GENDER* AND *AGE*.

PERHAPS, THEN, YOU COULD *ADVISE* ME...

WHICH OF YOU WOULD IT BE POLITE TO KILL *FIRST*?

12

215

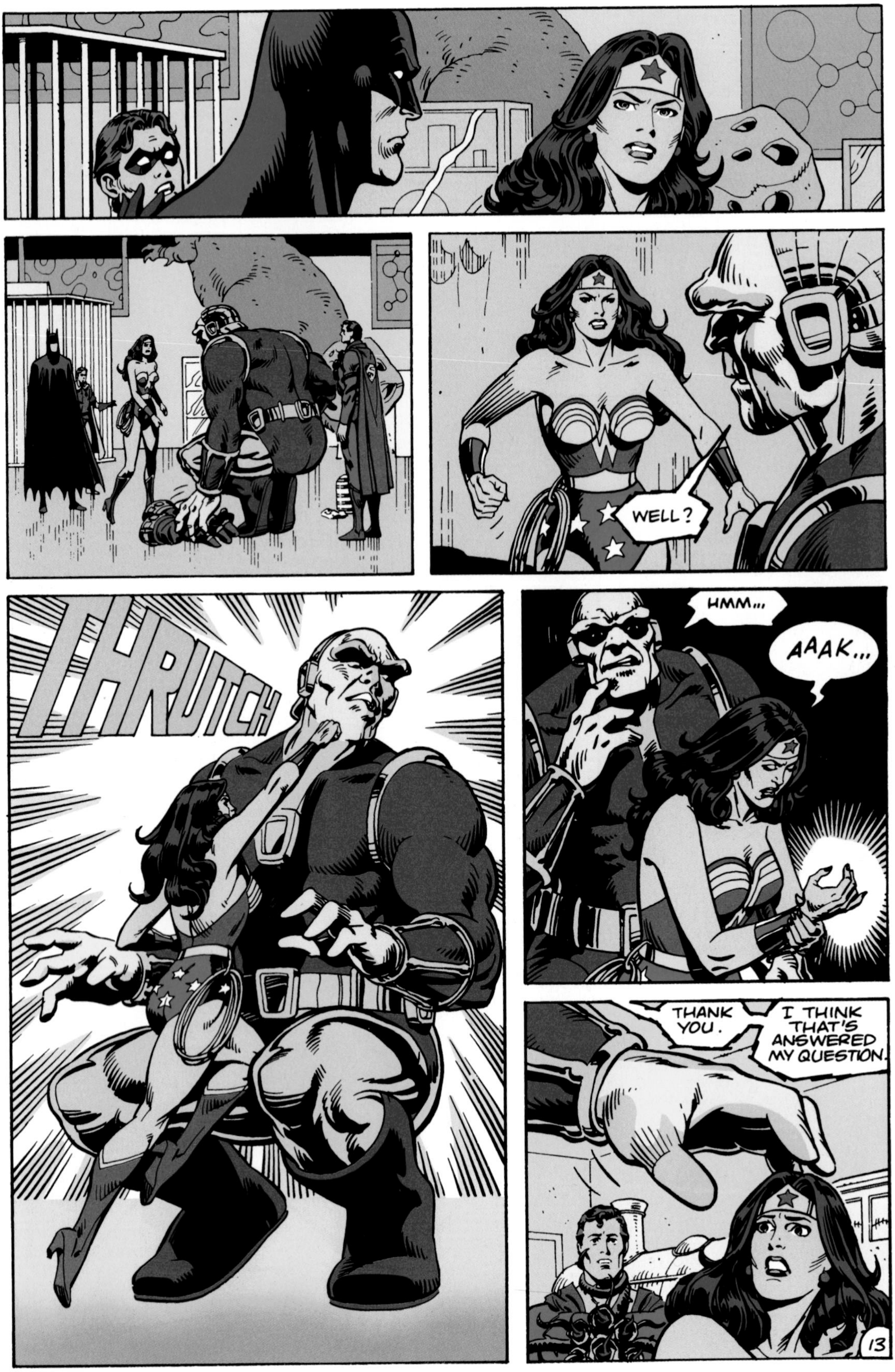
WELL?
THRUTCH
HMM...
AAAK...
THANK YOU.
I THINK THAT'S ANSWERED MY QUESTION.
13

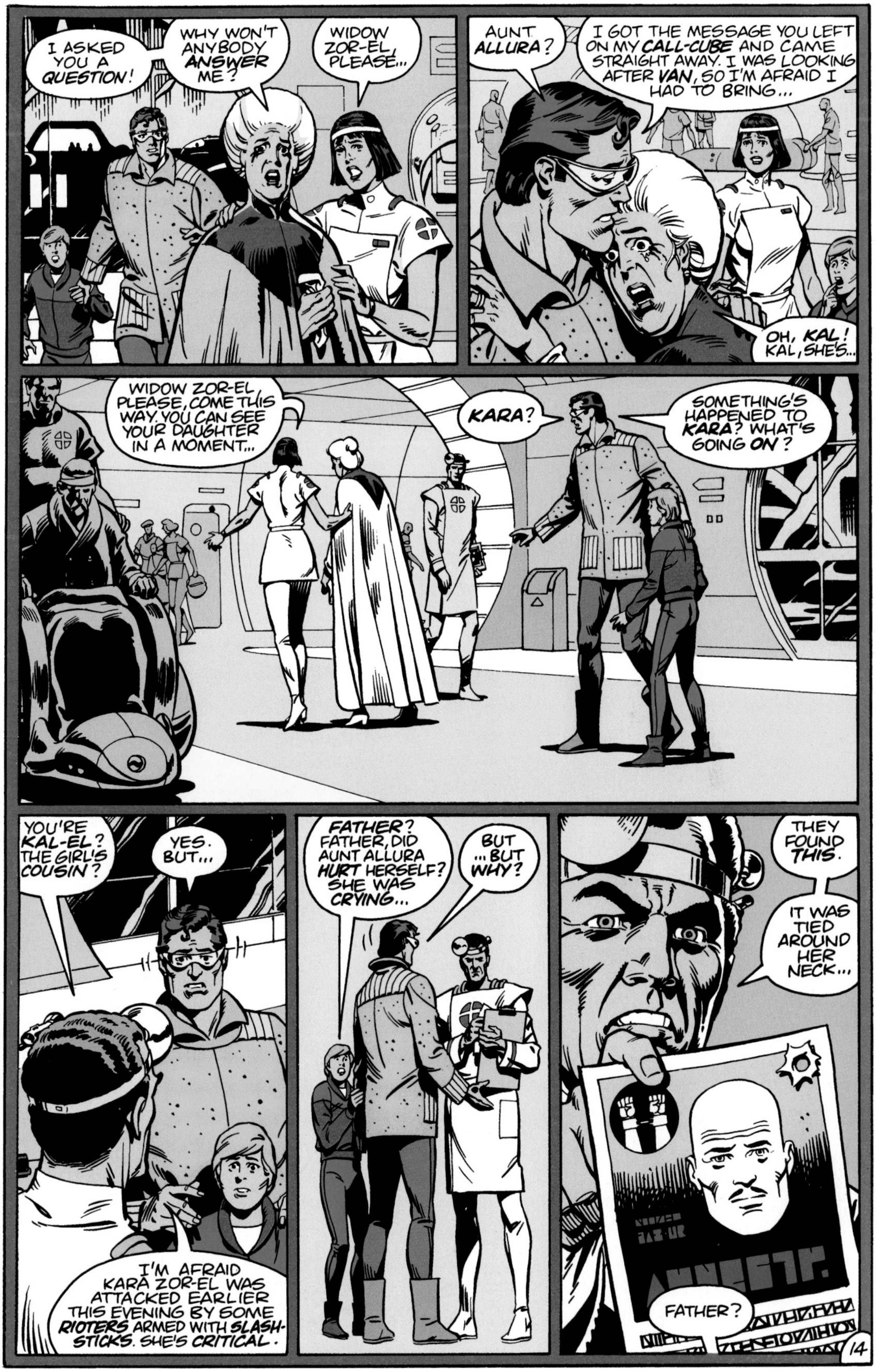
I ASKED YOU A QUESTION!
WHY WON'T ANYBODY ANSWER ME?
WIDOW ZOR-EL, PLEASE...
AUNT ALLURA?
I GOT THE MESSAGE YOU LEFT ON MY CALL-CUBE AND CAME STRAIGHT AWAY. I WAS LOOKING AFTER VAN, SO I'M AFRAID I HAD TO BRING...
OH, KAL! KAL, SHE'S...
WIDOW ZOR-EL PLEASE, COME THIS WAY. YOU CAN SEE YOUR DAUGHTER IN A MOMENT...
KARA?
SOMETHING'S HAPPENED TO KARA? WHAT'S GOING ON?
YOU'RE KAL-EL? THE GIRL'S COUSIN?
YES. BUT...
I'M AFRAID KARA ZOR-EL WAS ATTACKED EARLIER THIS EVENING BY SOME RIOTERS ARMED WITH SLASH-STICKS. SHE'S CRITICAL.
FATHER? FATHER, DID AUNT ALLURA HURT HERSELF? SHE WAS CRYING...
BUT ...BUT WHY?
THEY FOUND THIS.
IT WAS TIED AROUND HER NECK...
FATHER?
14

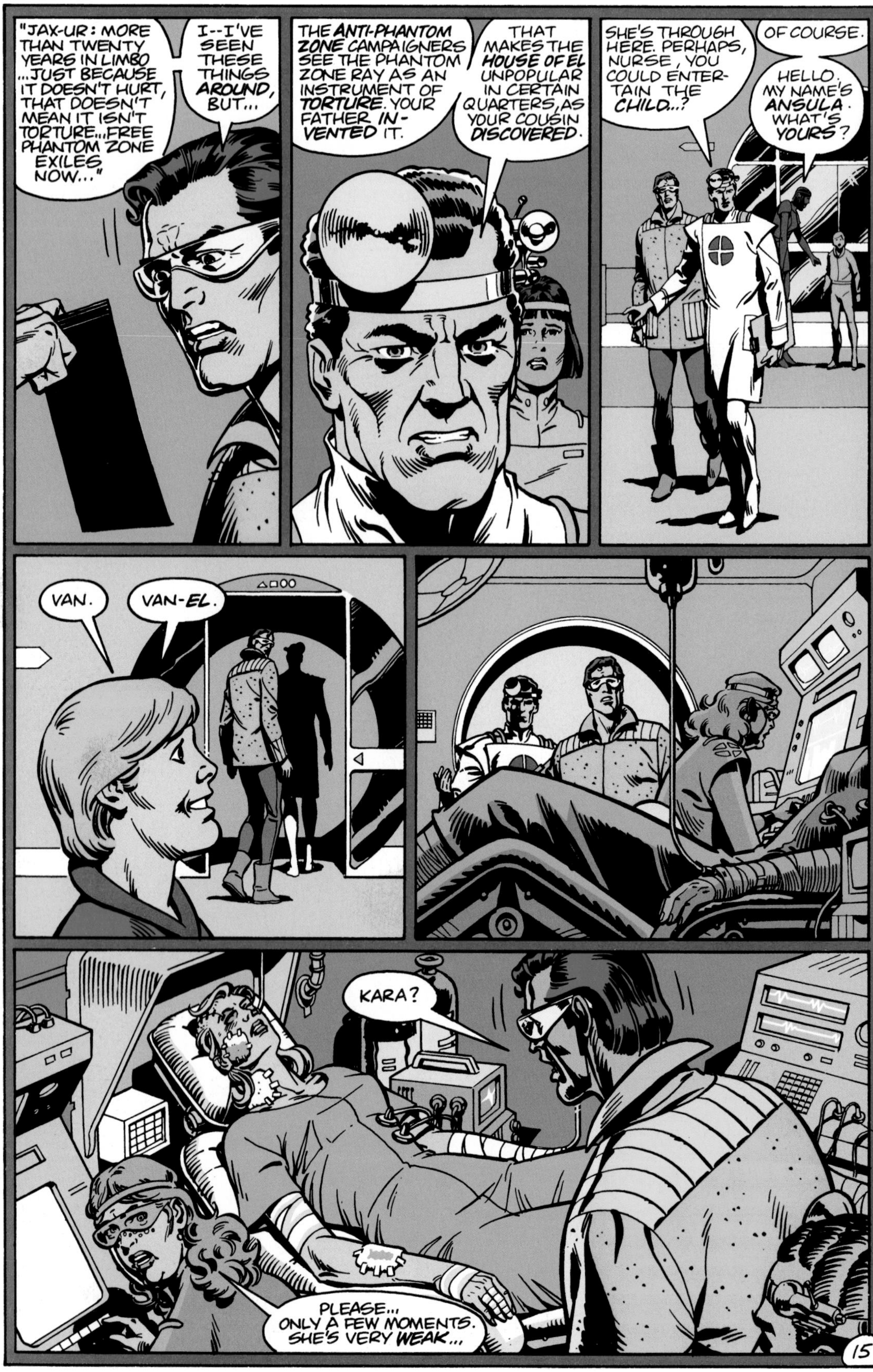
"JAX-UR: MORE THAN TWENTY YEARS IN LIMBO ...JUST BECAUSE IT DOESN'T HURT, THAT DOESN'T MEAN IT ISN'T TORTURE...FREE PHANTOM ZONE EXILES NOW..."
I--I'VE SEEN THESE THINGS AROUND, BUT...
THE ANTI-PHANTOM ZONE CAMPAIGNERS SEE THE PHANTOM ZONE RAY AS AN INSTRUMENT OF TORTURE. YOUR FATHER INVENTED IT.
THAT MAKES THE HOUSE OF EL UNPOPULAR IN CERTAIN QUARTERS, AS YOUR COUSIN DISCOVERED.
SHE'S THROUGH HERE. PERHAPS, NURSE, YOU COULD ENTERTAIN THE CHILD...?
OF COURSE.
HELLO. MY NAME'S ANSULA. WHAT'S YOURS?
VAN.
VAN-EL.
KARA?
PLEASE... ONLY A FEW MOMENTS. SHE'S VERY WEAK...
15

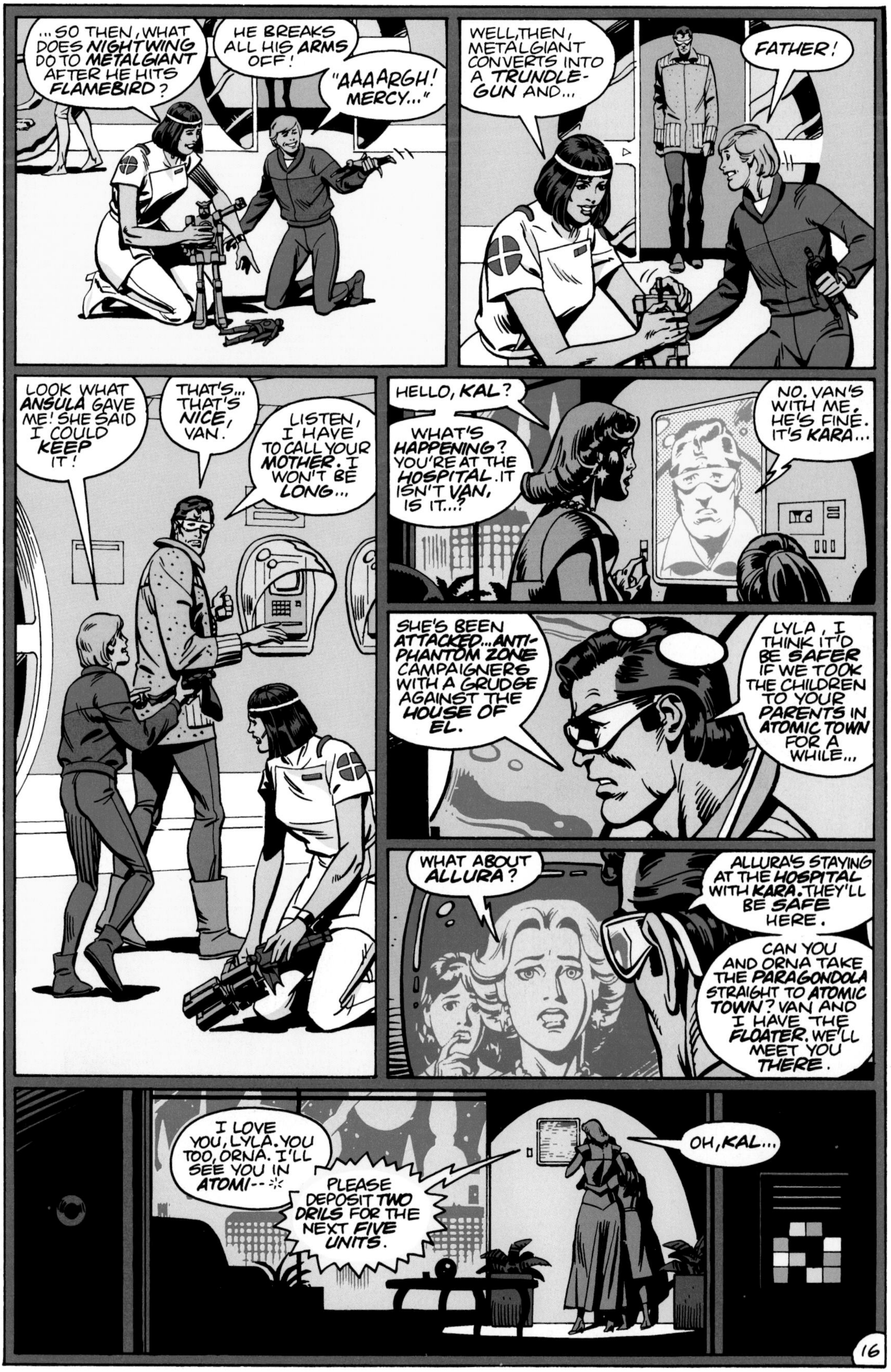
...SO THEN, WHAT DOES NIGHTWING DO TO METALGIANT AFTER HE HITS FLAMEBIRD?
HE BREAKS ALL HIS ARMS OFF!
"AAAARGH! MERCY..."
WELL, THEN, METALGIANT CONVERTS INTO A TRUNDLE-GUN AND...
FATHER!
LOOK WHAT ANSULA GAVE ME! SHE SAID I COULD KEEP IT!
THAT'S... THAT'S NICE, VAN.
LISTEN, I HAVE TO CALL YOUR MOTHER. I WON'T BE LONG...
HELLO, KAL?
WHAT'S HAPPENING? YOU'RE AT THE HOSPITAL. IT ISN'T VAN, IS IT...?
NO. VAN'S WITH ME. HE'S FINE. IT'S KARA...
SHE'S BEEN ATTACKED...ANTI-PHANTOM ZONE CAMPAIGNERS WITH A GRUDGE AGAINST THE HOUSE OF EL.
LYLA, I THINK IT'D BE SAFER IF WE TOOK THE CHILDREN TO YOUR PARENTS IN ATOMIC TOWN FOR A WHILE...
WHAT ABOUT ALLURA?
ALLURA'S STAYING AT THE HOSPITAL WITH KARA. THEY'LL BE SAFE HERE.
CAN YOU AND ORNA TAKE THE PARAGONDOLA STRAIGHT TO ATOMIC TOWN? VAN AND I HAVE THE FLOATER. WE'LL MEET YOU THERE.
I LOVE YOU, LYLA. YOU TOO, ORNA. I'LL SEE YOU IN ATOMI--
PLEASE DEPOSIT TWO DRILS FOR THE NEXT FIVE UNITS.
OH, KAL...
16

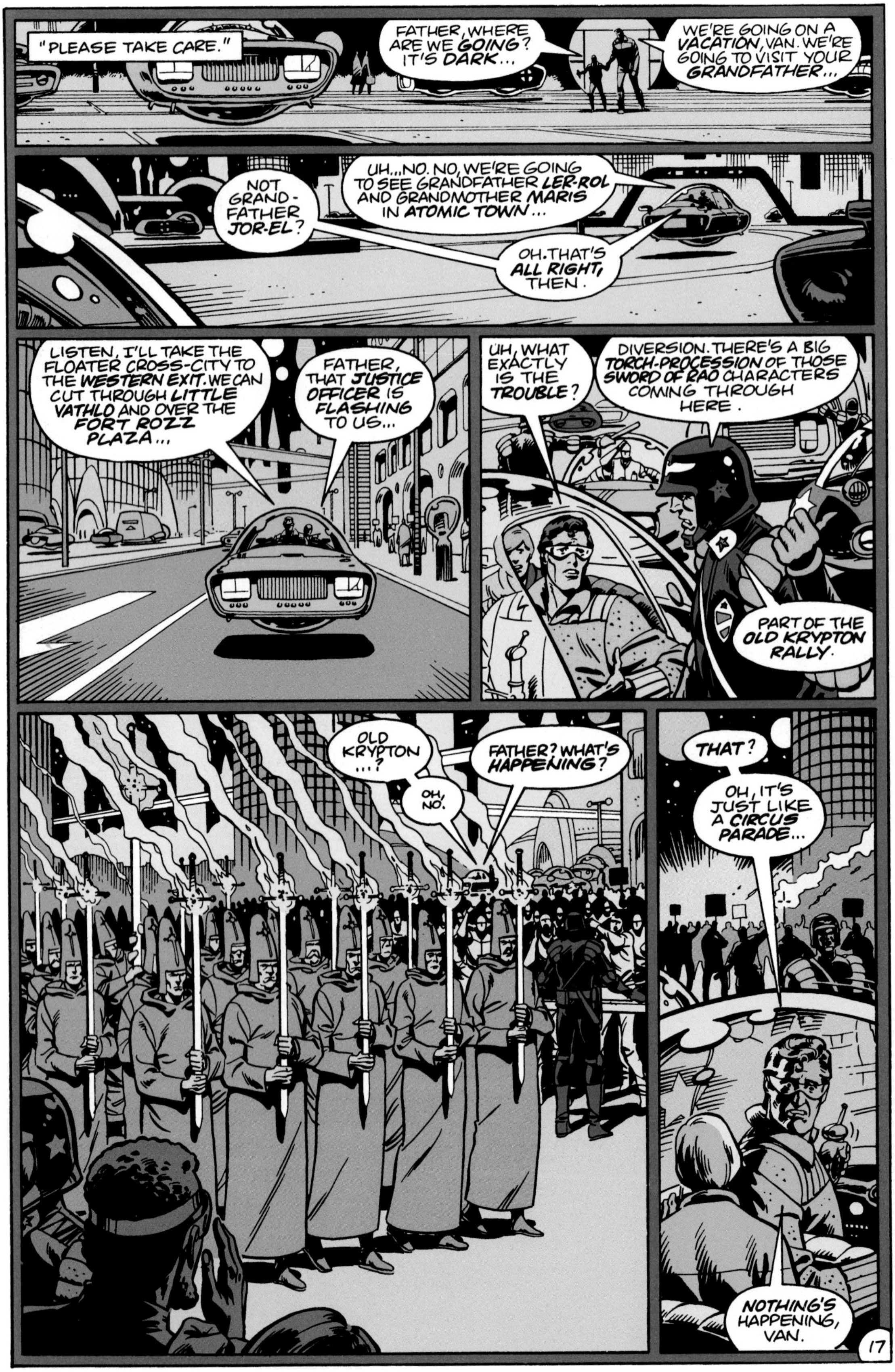
"PLEASE TAKE CARE."
FATHER, WHERE ARE WE GOING? IT'S DARK...
WE'RE GOING ON A VACATION, VAN. WE'RE GOING TO VISIT YOUR GRANDFATHER...
NOT GRAND-FATHER JOR-EL?
UH...NO. NO, WE'RE GOING TO SEE GRANDFATHER LER-ROL AND GRANDMOTHER MARIS IN ATOMIC TOWN...
OH. THAT'S ALL RIGHT, THEN.
LISTEN, I'LL TAKE THE FLOATER CROSS-CITY TO THE WESTERN EXIT. WE CAN CUT THROUGH LITTLE VATHLO AND OVER THE FORT ROZZ PLAZA...
FATHER, THAT JUSTICE OFFICER IS FLASHING TO US...
UH, WHAT EXACTLY IS THE TROUBLE?
DIVERSION. THERE'S A BIG TORCH-PROCESSION OF THOSE SWORD OF RAO CHARACTERS COMING THROUGH HERE.
PART OF THE OLD KRYPTON RALLY.
OLD KRYPTON...?
OH, NO.
FATHER? WHAT'S HAPPENING?
THAT?
OH, IT'S JUST LIKE A CIRCUS PARADE...
NOTHING'S HAPPENING, VAN.
17

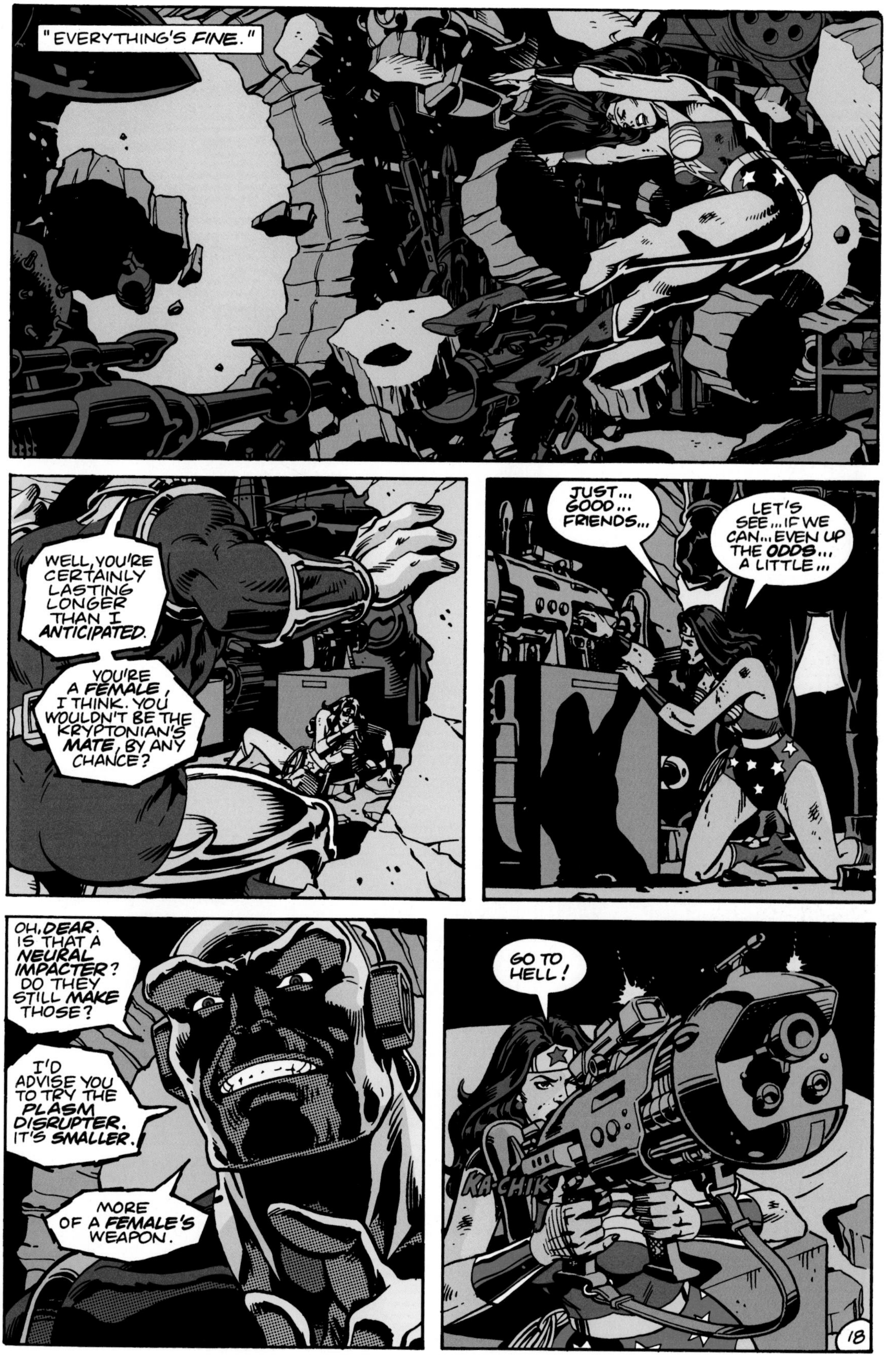
"EVERYTHING'S FINE."
WELL, YOU'RE CERTAINLY LASTING LONGER THAN I ANTICIPATED.
YOU'RE A FEMALE, I THINK. YOU WOULDN'T BE THE KRYPTONIAN'S MATE, BY ANY CHANCE?
JUST... GOOD... FRIENDS...
LET'S SEE... IF WE CAN... EVEN UP THE ODDS... A LITTLE...
OH, DEAR. IS THAT A NEURAL IMPACTER? DO THEY STILL MAKE THOSE?
I'D ADVISE YOU TO TRY THE PLASM DISRUPTER. IT'S SMALLER.
MORE OF A FEMALE'S WEAPON.
GO TO HELL!
KA-CHIK
18

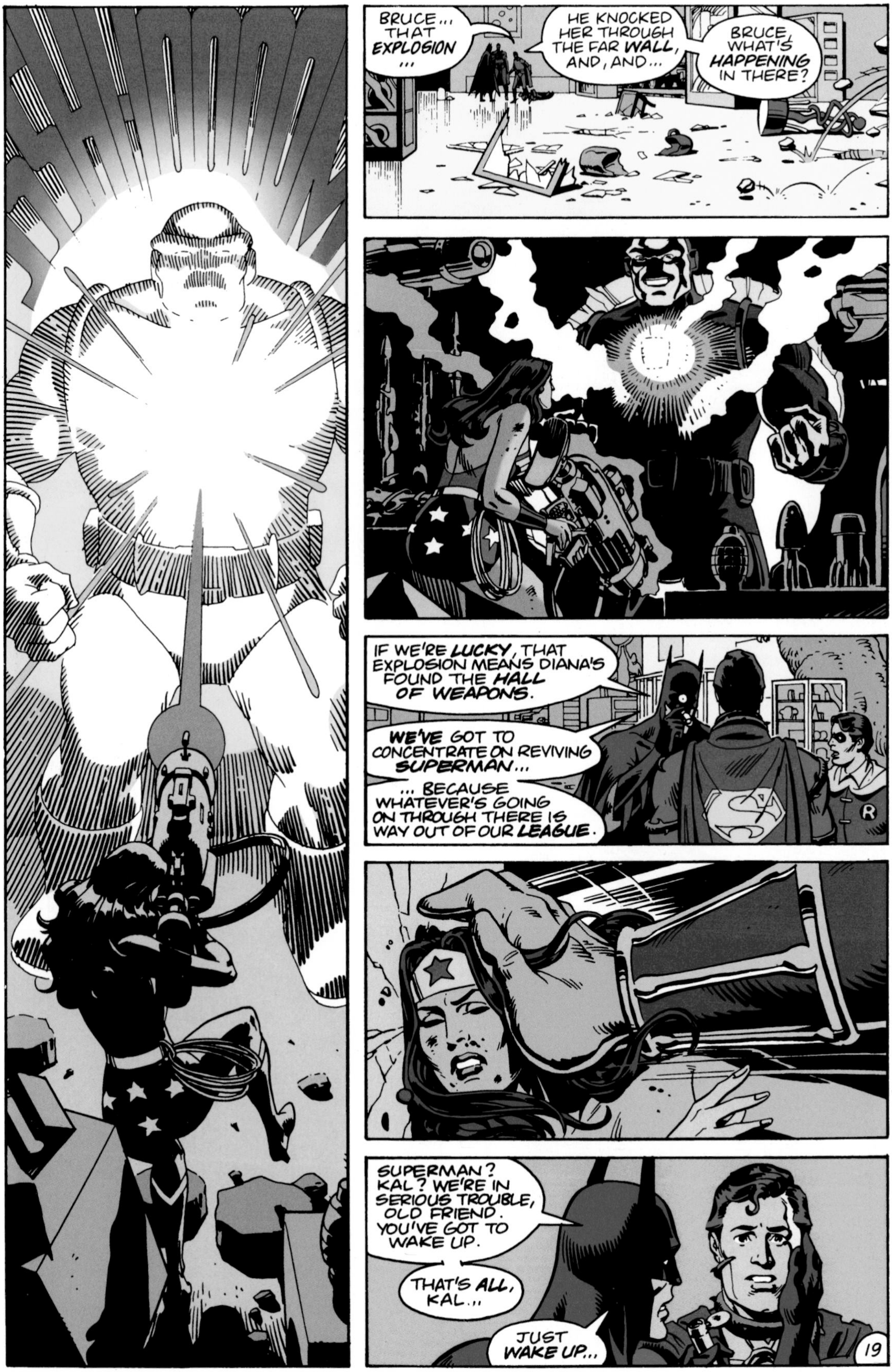
BRUCE... THAT EXPLOSION ...
HE KNOCKED HER THROUGH THE FAR WALL, AND, AND...
BRUCE, WHAT'S HAPPENING IN THERE?
IF WE'RE LUCKY, THAT EXPLOSION MEANS DIANA'S FOUND THE HALL OF WEAPONS.
WE'VE GOT TO CONCENTRATE ON REVIVING SUPERMAN...
... BECAUSE WHATEVER'S GOING ON THROUGH THERE IS WAY OUT OF OUR LEAGUE.
SUPERMAN? KAL? WE'RE IN SERIOUS TROUBLE, OLD FRIEND. YOU'VE GOT TO WAKE UP.
THAT'S ALL, KAL...
JUST WAKE UP...
19

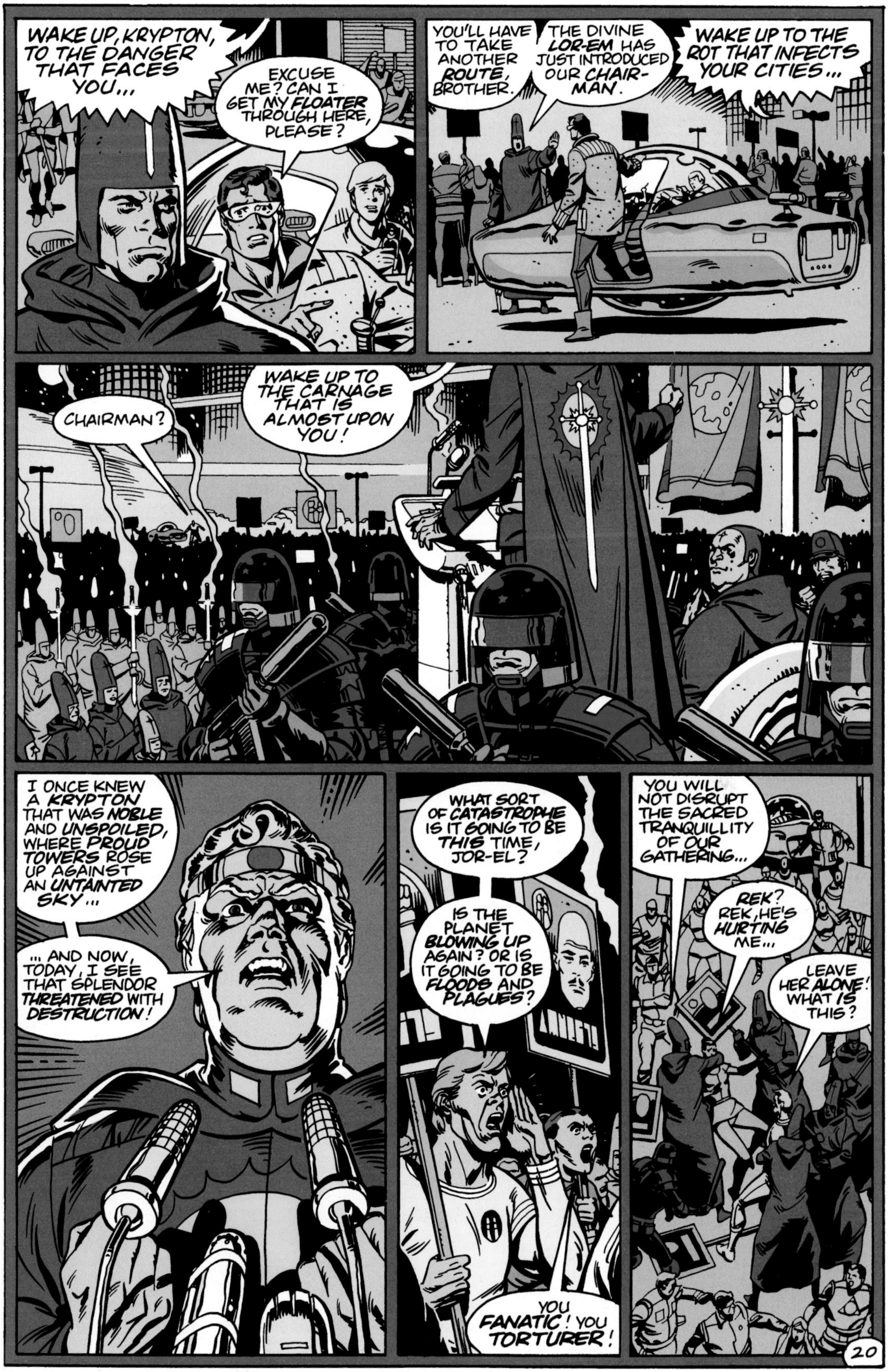
WAKE UP, KRYPTON, TO THE DANGER THAT FACES YOU...
EXCUSE ME? CAN I GET MY FLOATER THROUGH HERE, PLEASE?
YOU'LL HAVE TO TAKE ANOTHER ROUTE, BROTHER.
THE DIVINE LOR-EM HAS JUST INTRODUCED OUR CHAIR-MAN.
WAKE UP TO THE ROT THAT INFECTS YOUR CITIES...
CHAIRMAN?
WAKE UP TO THE CARNAGE THAT IS ALMOST UPON YOU!
I ONCE KNEW A KRYPTON THAT WAS NOBLE AND UNSPOILED, WHERE PROUD TOWERS ROSE UP AGAINST AN UNTAINTED SKY...
... AND NOW, TODAY, I SEE THAT SPLENDOR THREATENED WITH DESTRUCTION!
WHAT SORT OF CATASTROPHE IS IT GOING TO BE THIS TIME, JOR-EL?
IS THE PLANET BLOWING UP AGAIN? OR IS IT GOING TO BE FLOODS AND PLAGUES?
YOU FANATIC! YOU TORTURER!
YOU WILL NOT DISRUPT THE SACRED TRANQUILLITY OF OUR GATHERING...
REK? REK, HE'S HURTING ME...
LEAVE HER ALONE! WHAT IS THIS?
20

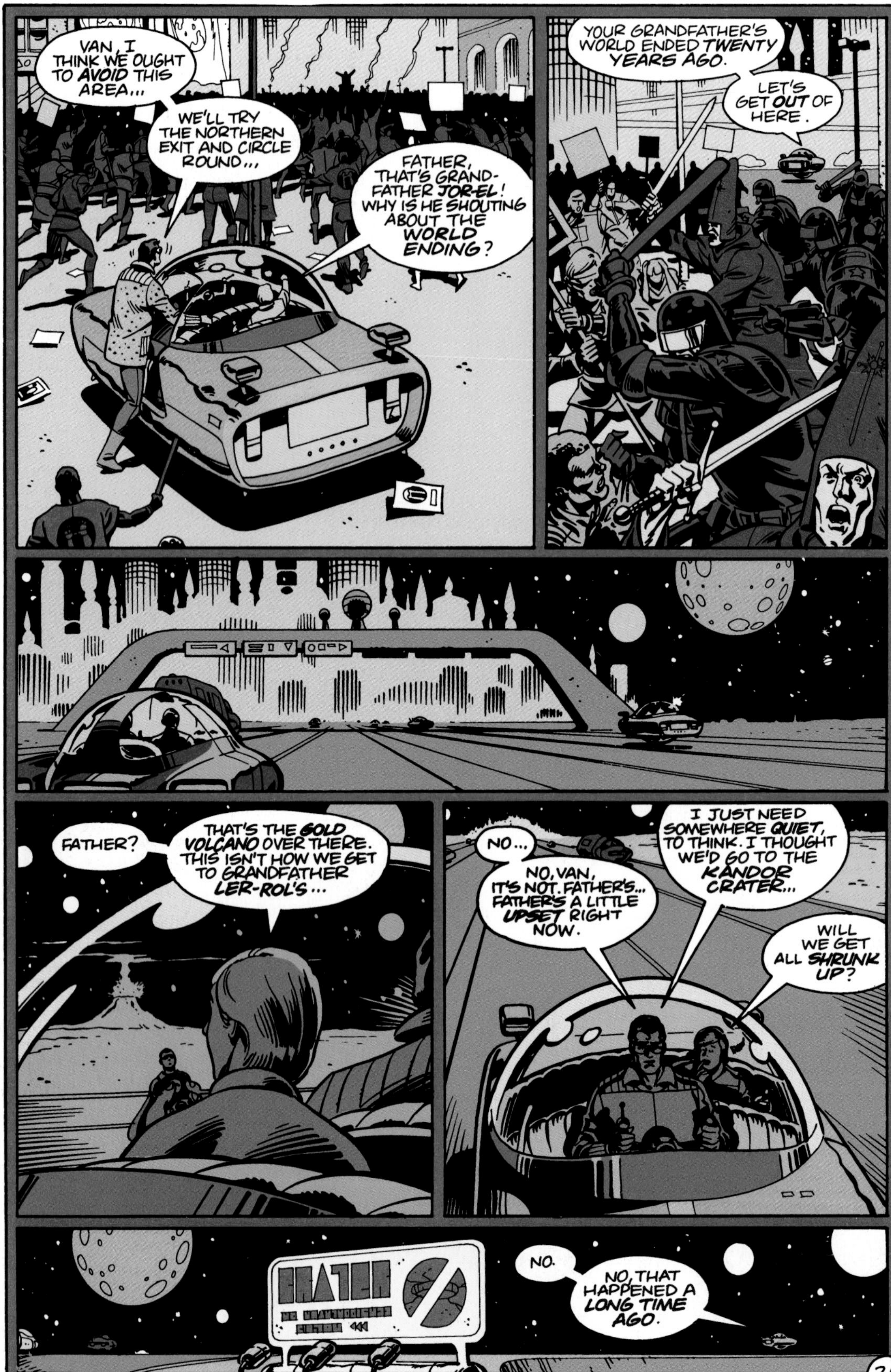
VAN, I THINK WE OUGHT TO AVOID THIS AREA...
WE'LL TRY THE NORTHERN EXIT AND CIRCLE ROUND...
FATHER, THAT'S GRAND-FATHER JOR-EL! WHY IS HE SHOUTING ABOUT THE WORLD ENDING?
YOUR GRANDFATHER'S WORLD ENDED TWENTY YEARS AGO.
LET'S GET OUT OF HERE.
FATHER?
THAT'S THE GOLD VOLCANO OVER THERE. THIS ISN'T HOW WE GET TO GRANDFATHER LER-ROL'S...
NO...
NO, VAN, IT'S NOT. FATHER'S... FATHER'S A LITTLE UPSET RIGHT NOW.
I JUST NEED SOMEWHERE QUIET, TO THINK. I THOUGHT WE'D GO TO THE KANDOR CRATER...
WILL WE GET ALL SHRUNK UP?
NO.
NO, THAT HAPPENED A LONG TIME AGO.
21

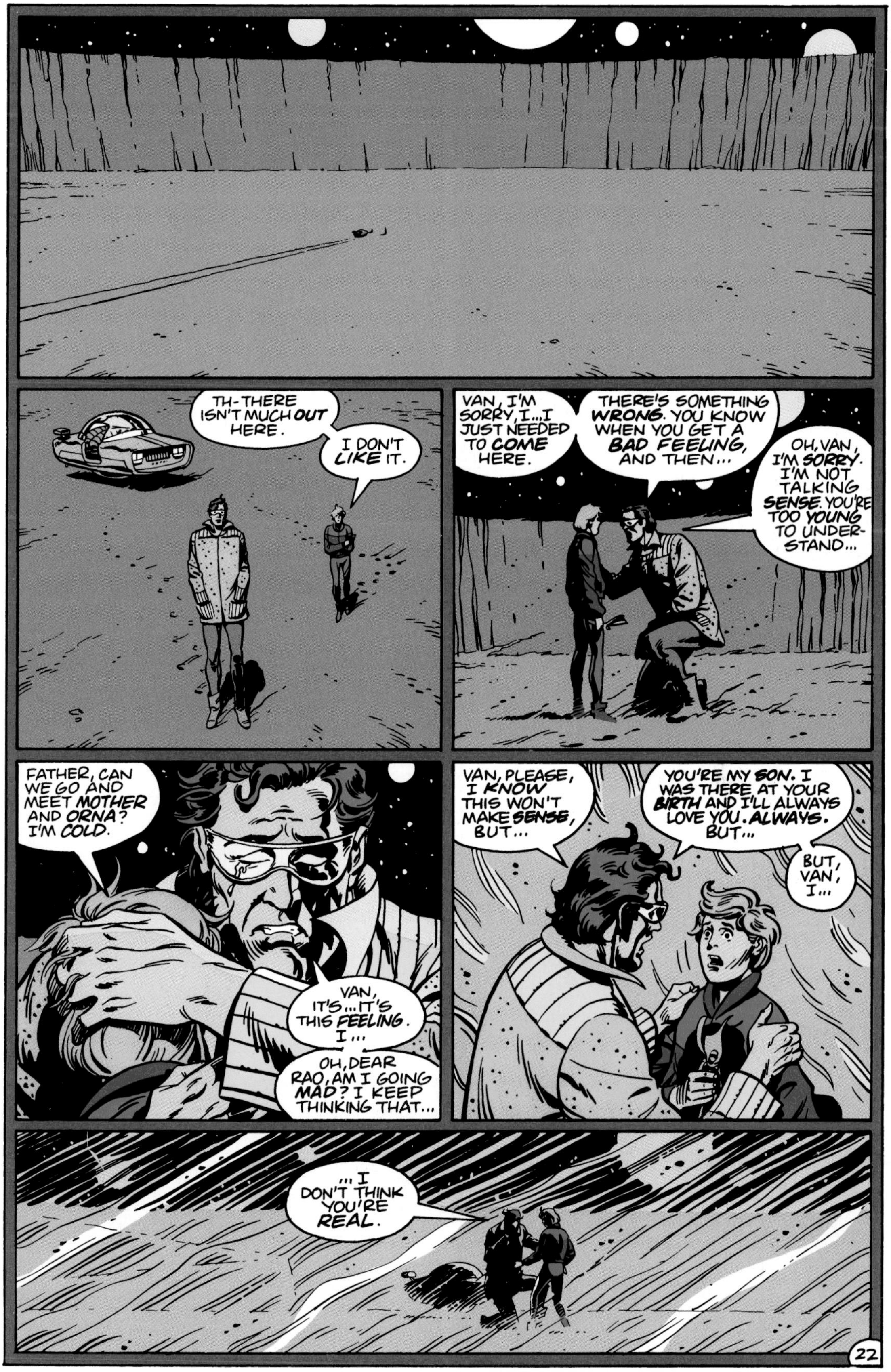

TH-THERE ISN'T MUCH OUT HERE.
I DON'T LIKE IT.
VAN, I'M SORRY, I...I JUST NEEDED TO COME HERE.
THERE'S SOMETHING WRONG. YOU KNOW WHEN YOU GET A BAD FEELING, AND THEN...
OH, VAN, I'M SORRY. I'M NOT TALKING SENSE. YOU'RE TOO YOUNG TO UNDERSTAND...
FATHER, CAN WE GO AND MEET MOTHER AND ORNA? I'M COLD.
VAN, IT'S...IT'S THIS FEELING. I...
OH, DEAR RAO, AM I GOING MAD? I KEEP THINKING THAT...
VAN, PLEASE, I KNOW THIS WON'T MAKE SENSE, BUT...
YOU'RE MY SON. I WAS THERE AT YOUR BIRTH AND I'LL ALWAYS LOVE YOU. ALWAYS. BUT...
BUT, VAN, I...
...I DON'T THINK YOU'RE REAL.
22

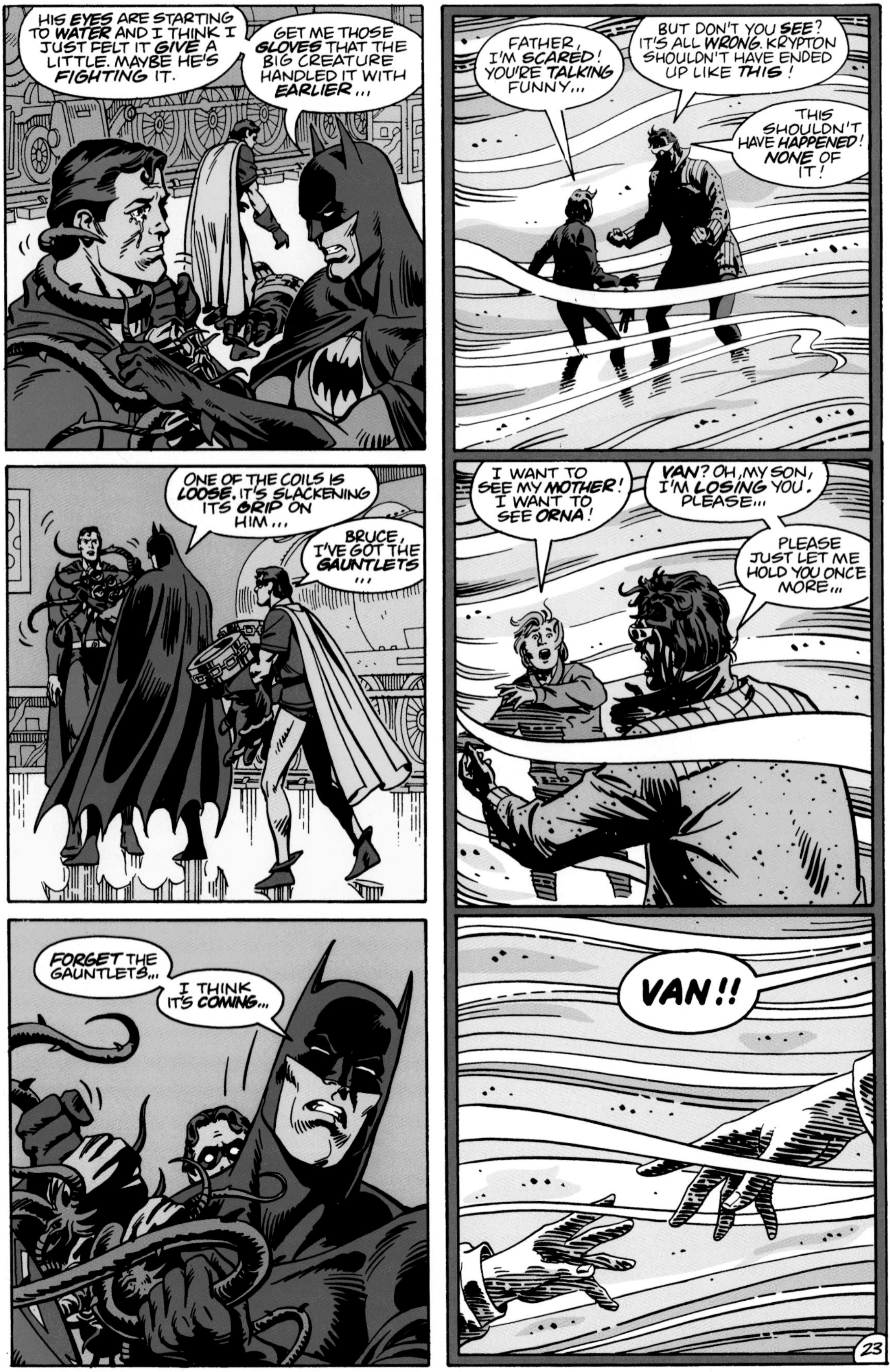
HIS EYES ARE STARTING TO WATER AND I THINK I JUST FELT IT GIVE A LITTLE. MAYBE HE'S FIGHTING IT.
GET ME THOSE GLOVES THAT THE BIG CREATURE HANDLED IT WITH EARLIER...
ONE OF THE COILS IS LOOSE. IT'S SLACKENING ITS GRIP ON HIM...
BRUCE, I'VE GOT THE GAUNTLETS...
FORGET THE GAUNTLETS...
I THINK IT'S COMING...
FATHER, I'M SCARED! YOU'RE TALKING FUNNY...
BUT DON'T YOU SEE? IT'S ALL WRONG. KRYPTON SHOULDN'T HAVE ENDED UP LIKE THIS!
THIS SHOULDN'T HAVE HAPPENED! NONE OF IT!
I WANT TO SEE MY MOTHER! I WANT TO SEE ORNA!
VAN? OH, MY SON, I'M LOSING YOU. PLEASE...
PLEASE JUST LET ME HOLD YOU ONCE MORE...
VAN!!
23

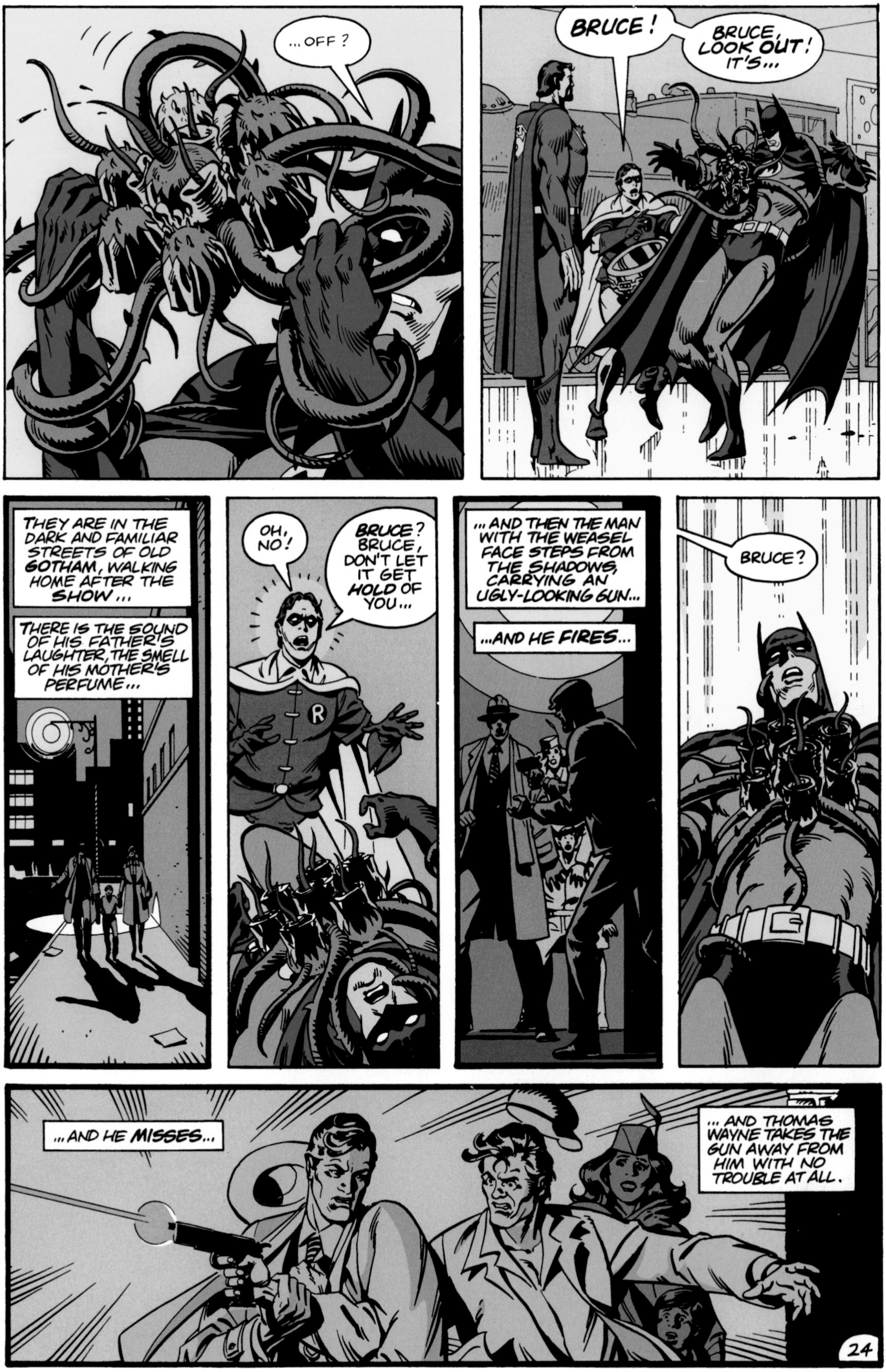

... OFF ?
BRUCE !
BRUCE, LOOK OUT! IT'S...
THEY ARE IN THE DARK AND FAMILIAR STREETS OF OLD GOTHAM, WALKING HOME AFTER THE SHOW...
THERE IS THE SOUND OF HIS FATHER'S LAUGHTER, THE SMELL OF HIS MOTHER'S PERFUME...
OH, NO!
BRUCE? BRUCE, DON'T LET IT GET HOLD OF YOU...
... AND THEN THE MAN WITH THE WEASEL FACE STEPS FROM THE SHADOWS, CARRYING AN UGLY-LOOKING GUN...
...AND HE FIRES...
BRUCE?
...AND HE MISSES...
... AND THOMAS WAYNE TAKES THE GUN AWAY FROM HIM WITH NO TROUBLE AT ALL.
24

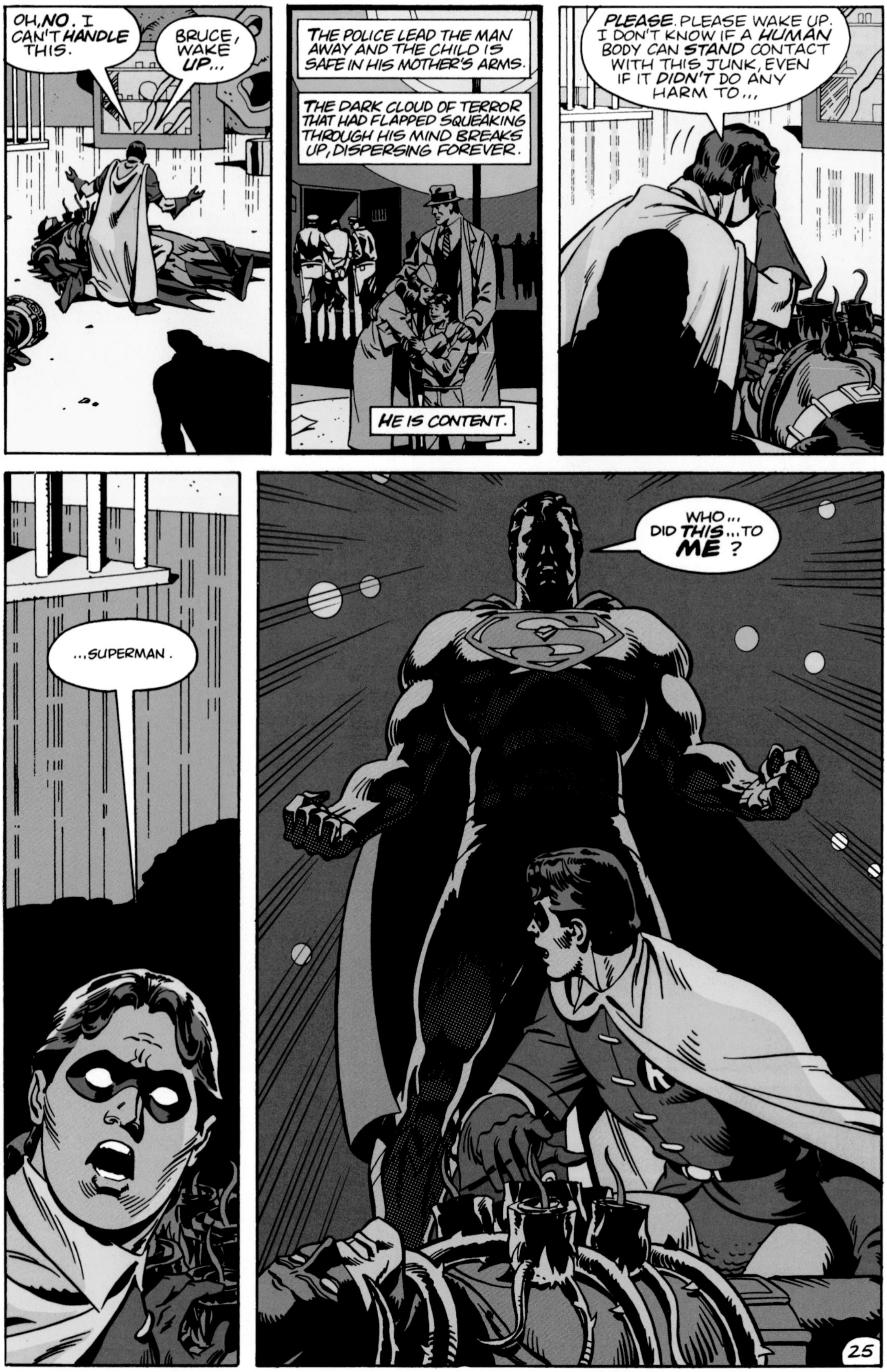
OH, NO. I CAN'T HANDLE THIS.
BRUCE, WAKE UP...
THE POLICE LEAD THE MAN AWAY AND THE CHILD IS SAFE IN HIS MOTHER'S ARMS.
THE DARK CLOUD OF TERROR THAT HAD FLAPPED SQUEAKING THROUGH HIS MIND BREAKS UP, DISPERSING FOREVER.
HE IS CONTENT.
PLEASE. PLEASE WAKE UP. I DON'T KNOW IF A HUMAN BODY CAN STAND CONTACT WITH THIS JUNK, EVEN IF IT DIDN'T DO ANY HARM TO...
...SUPERMAN.
WHO... DID THIS... TO ME?
25

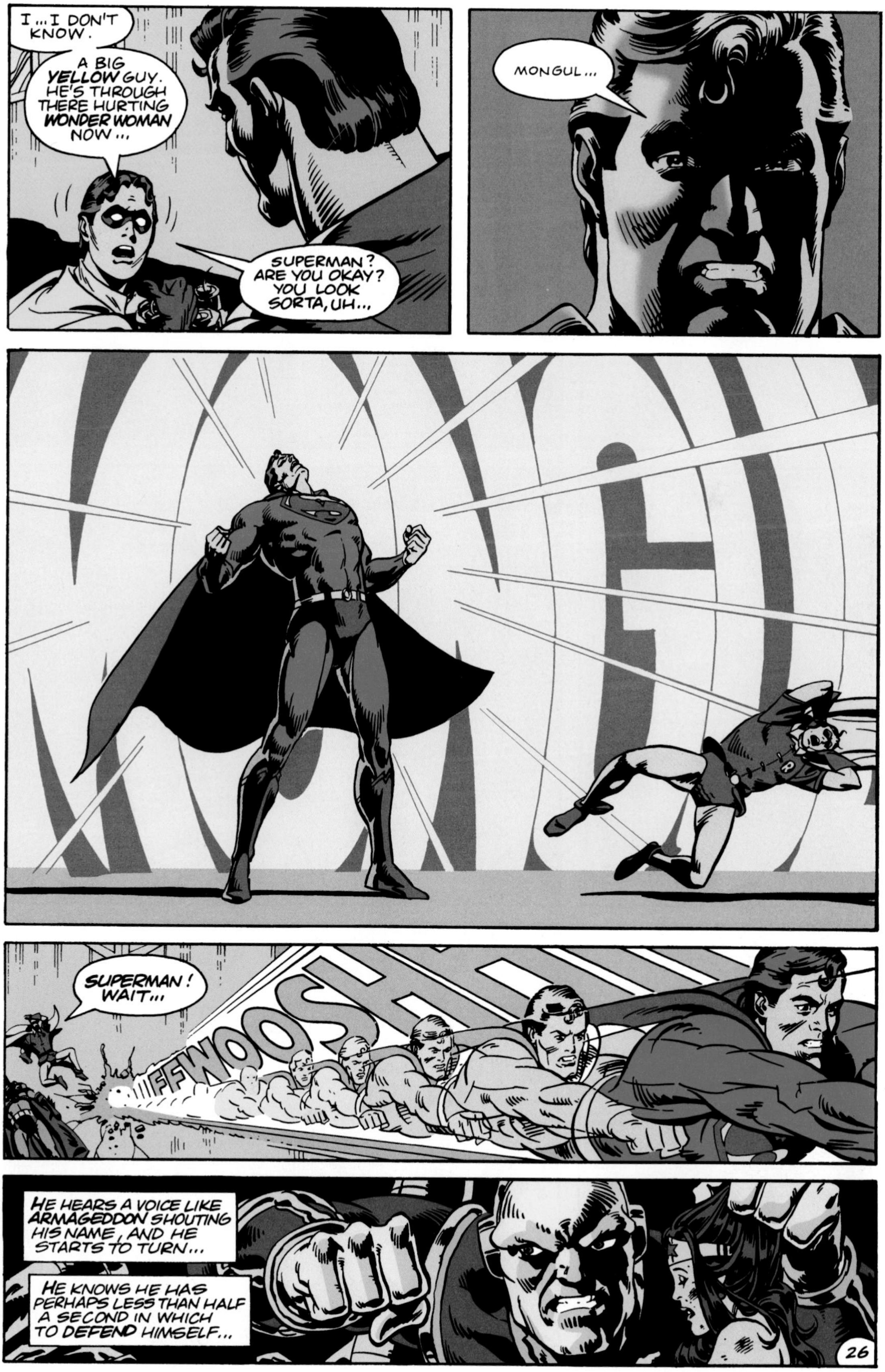
I... I DON'T KNOW.
A BIG YELLOW GUY. HE'S THROUGH THERE HURTING WONDER WOMAN NOW...
SUPERMAN? ARE YOU OKAY? YOU LOOK SORTA, UH...
MONGUL...
SUPERMAN! WAIT...
FFWOOSH
HE HEARS A VOICE LIKE ARMAGEDDON SHOUTING HIS NAME, AND HE STARTS TO TURN...
HE KNOWS HE HAS PERHAPS LESS THAN HALF A SECOND IN WHICH TO DEFEND HIMSELF...
26

WHAT AM I GOING TO DO ABOUT *BRUCE*? I CAN'T...

UH....

HE STARTS TO REACH TOWARDS HIS ARMOR'S *WEAPON SYSTEMS*, LETTING THE UNCONSCIOUS WOMAN *CRUMPLE* TO THE FLOOR...

...BUT THE ROCK OF THE FAR WALL SEEMS TO *RIPPLE* OUTWARDS IN A SUDDEN *CASCADE* OF POWDER...

...AND A *FOUR-HUNDRED-MILE-AN-HOUR* WIND SLAMS INTO HIM LIKE A STEAM HAMMER AS BIG AS THE *WORLD*...

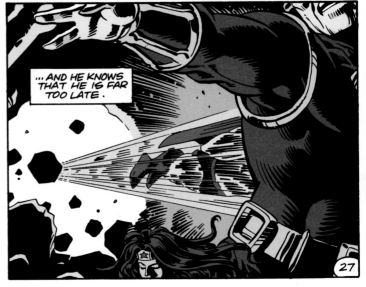

...AND HE KNOWS THAT HE IS *FAR TOO LATE.*

27

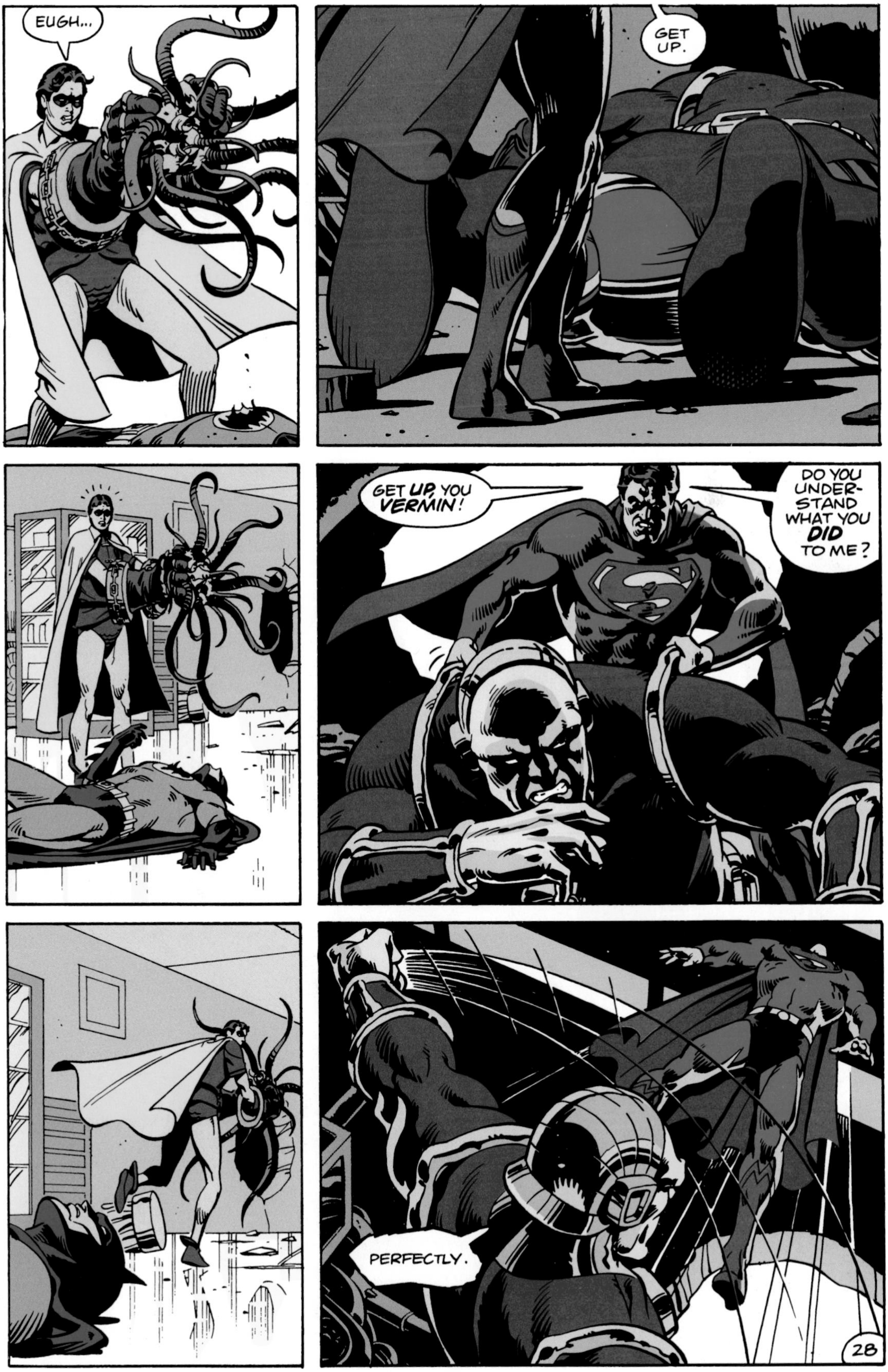
EUGH...
GET UP.
GET UP, YOU VERMIN!
DO YOU UNDERSTAND WHAT YOU DID TO ME?
PERFECTLY.
28

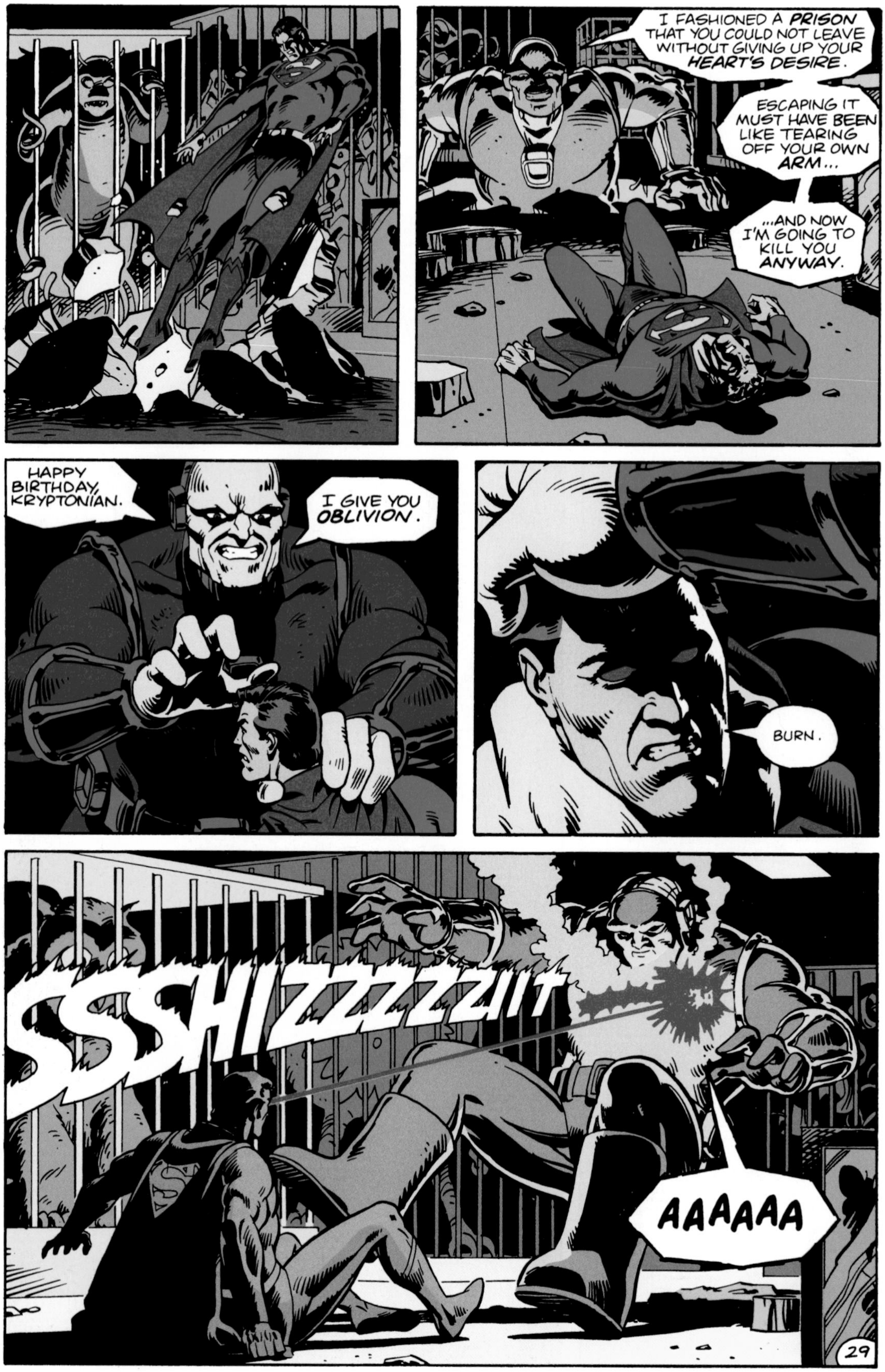

I FASHIONED A PRISON THAT YOU COULD NOT LEAVE WITHOUT GIVING UP YOUR HEART'S DESIRE.
ESCAPING IT MUST HAVE BEEN LIKE TEARING OFF YOUR OWN ARM...
...AND NOW I'M GOING TO KILL YOU ANYWAY.
HAPPY BIRTHDAY, KRYPTONIAN.
I GIVE YOU OBLIVION.
BURN.
SSHIZZZZZZIIT
AAAAAA
29

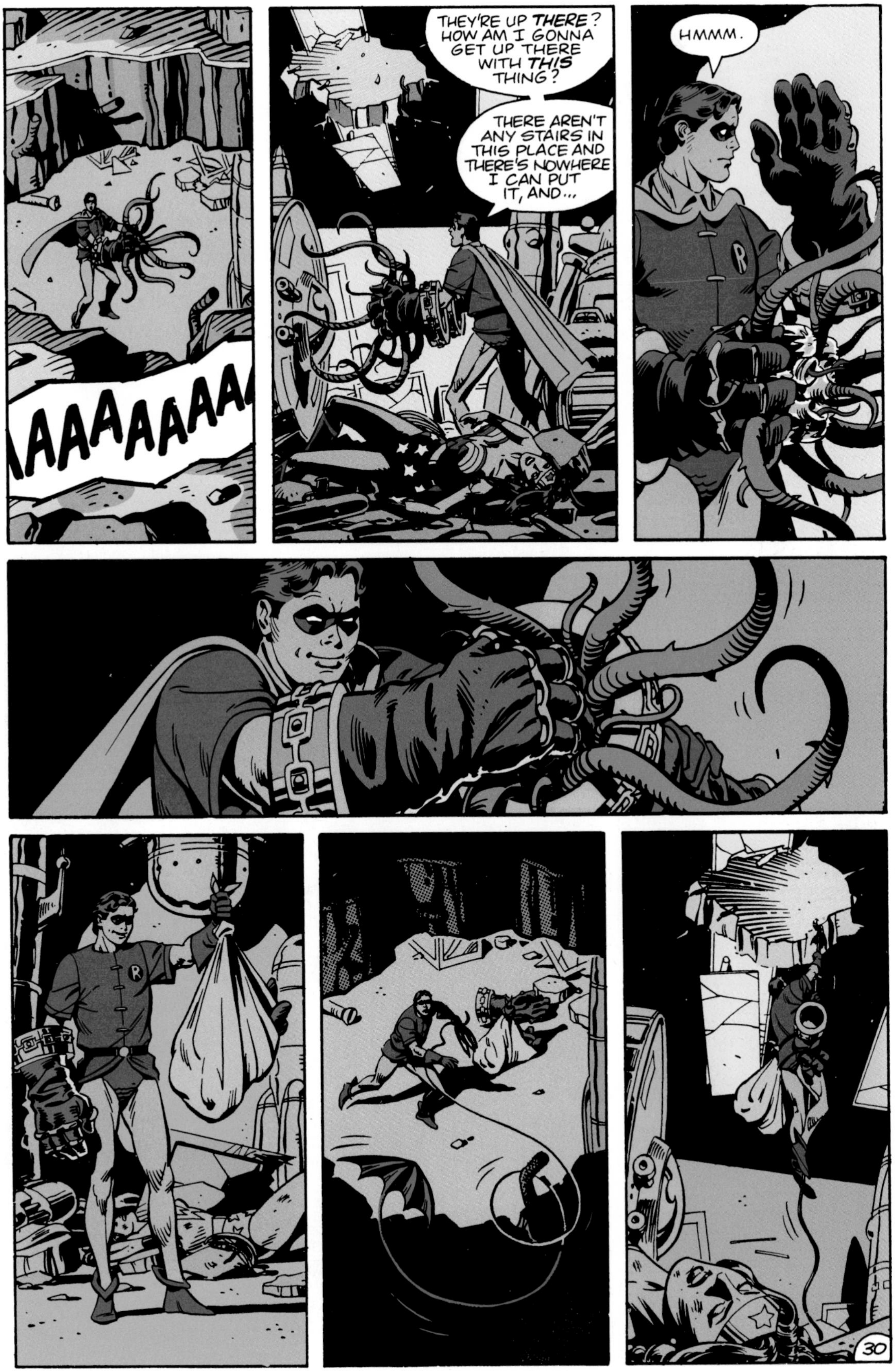
AAAAAAAAA
THEY'RE UP *THERE*? HOW AM I GONNA GET UP THERE WITH *THIS* THING?
THERE AREN'T ANY STAIRS IN THIS PLACE AND THERE'S NOWHERE I CAN PUT IT, AND...
HMMM.
30

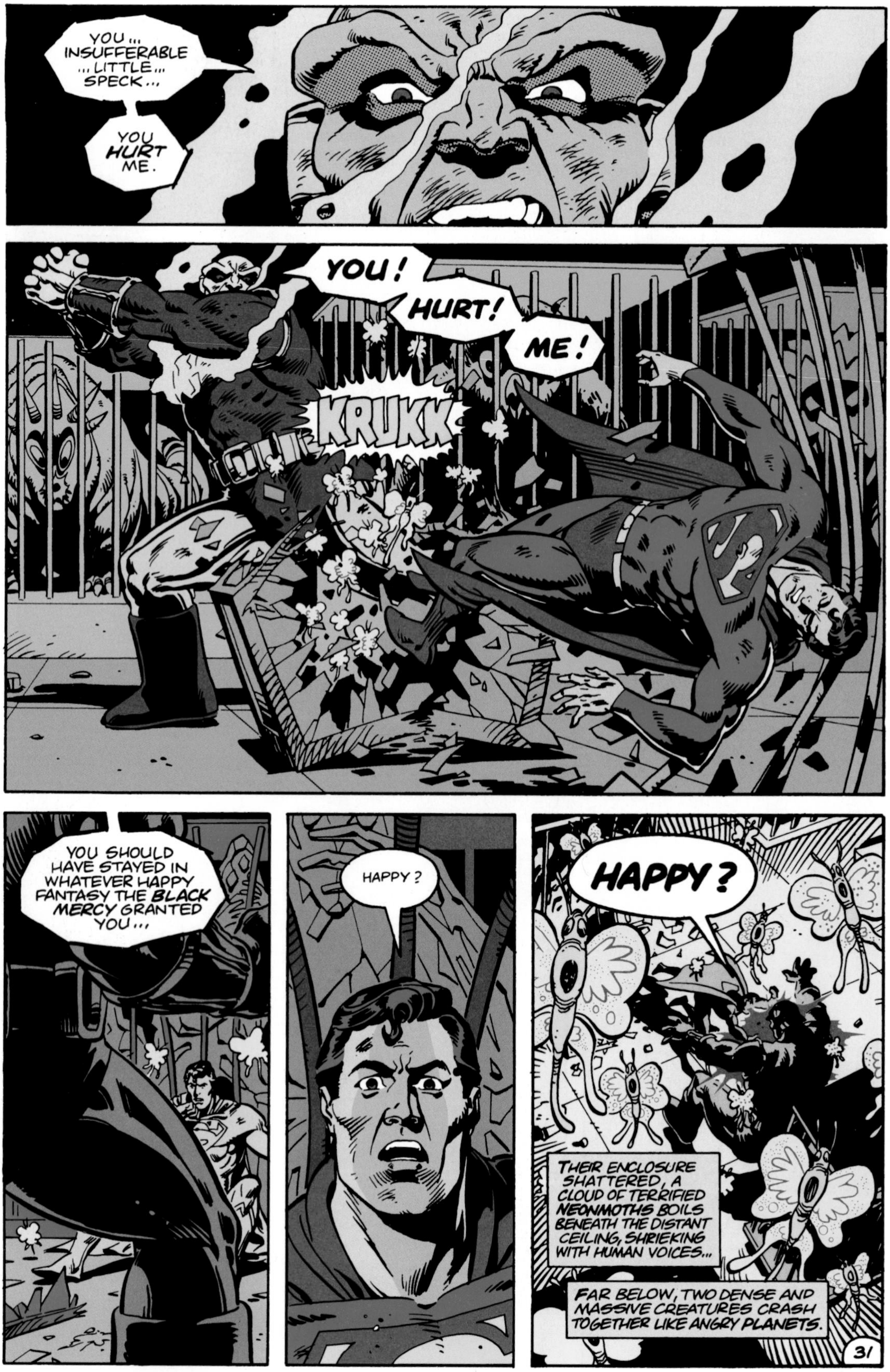
YOU... INSUFFERABLE ...LITTLE... SPECK...,
YOU HURT ME.
YOU!
HURT!
ME!
KRUKK
YOU SHOULD HAVE STAYED IN WHATEVER HAPPY FANTASY THE BLACK MERCY GRANTED YOU...,
HAPPY?
HAPPY?
THEIR ENCLOSURE SHATTERED, A CLOUD OF TERRIFIED NEONMOTHS BOILS BENEATH THE DISTANT CEILING, SHRIEKING WITH HUMAN VOICES...
FAR BELOW, TWO DENSE AND MASSIVE CREATURES CRASH TOGETHER LIKE ANGRY PLANETS.
31

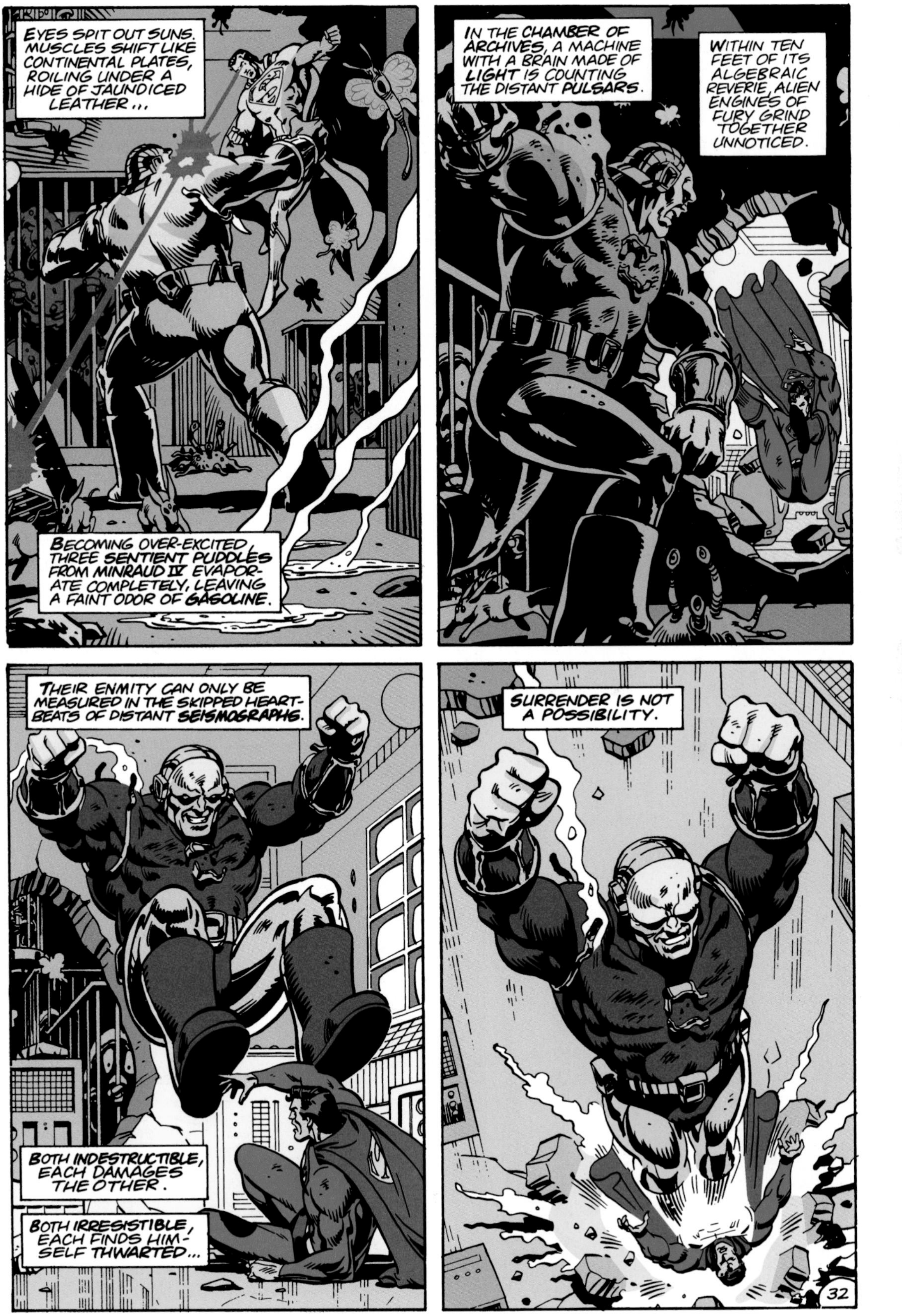
EYES SPIT OUT SUNS. MUSCLES SHIFT LIKE CONTINENTAL PLATES, ROILING UNDER A HIDE OF JAUNDICED LEATHER...
BECOMING OVER-EXCITED THREE SENTIENT PUDDLES FROM MINRAUD IV EVAPORATE COMPLETELY, LEAVING A FAINT ODOR OF GASOLINE.
IN THE CHAMBER OF ARCHIVES, A MACHINE WITH A BRAIN MADE OF LIGHT IS COUNTING THE DISTANT PULSARS.
WITHIN TEN FEET OF ITS ALGEBRAIC REVERIE, ALIEN ENGINES OF FURY GRIND TOGETHER UNNOTICED.
THEIR ENMITY CAN ONLY BE MEASURED IN THE SKIPPED HEART-BEATS OF DISTANT SEISMOGRAPHS.
BOTH INDESTRUCTIBLE, EACH DAMAGES THE OTHER.
BOTH IRRESISTIBLE, EACH FINDS HIMSELF THWARTED...
SURRENDER IS NOT A POSSIBILITY.
32

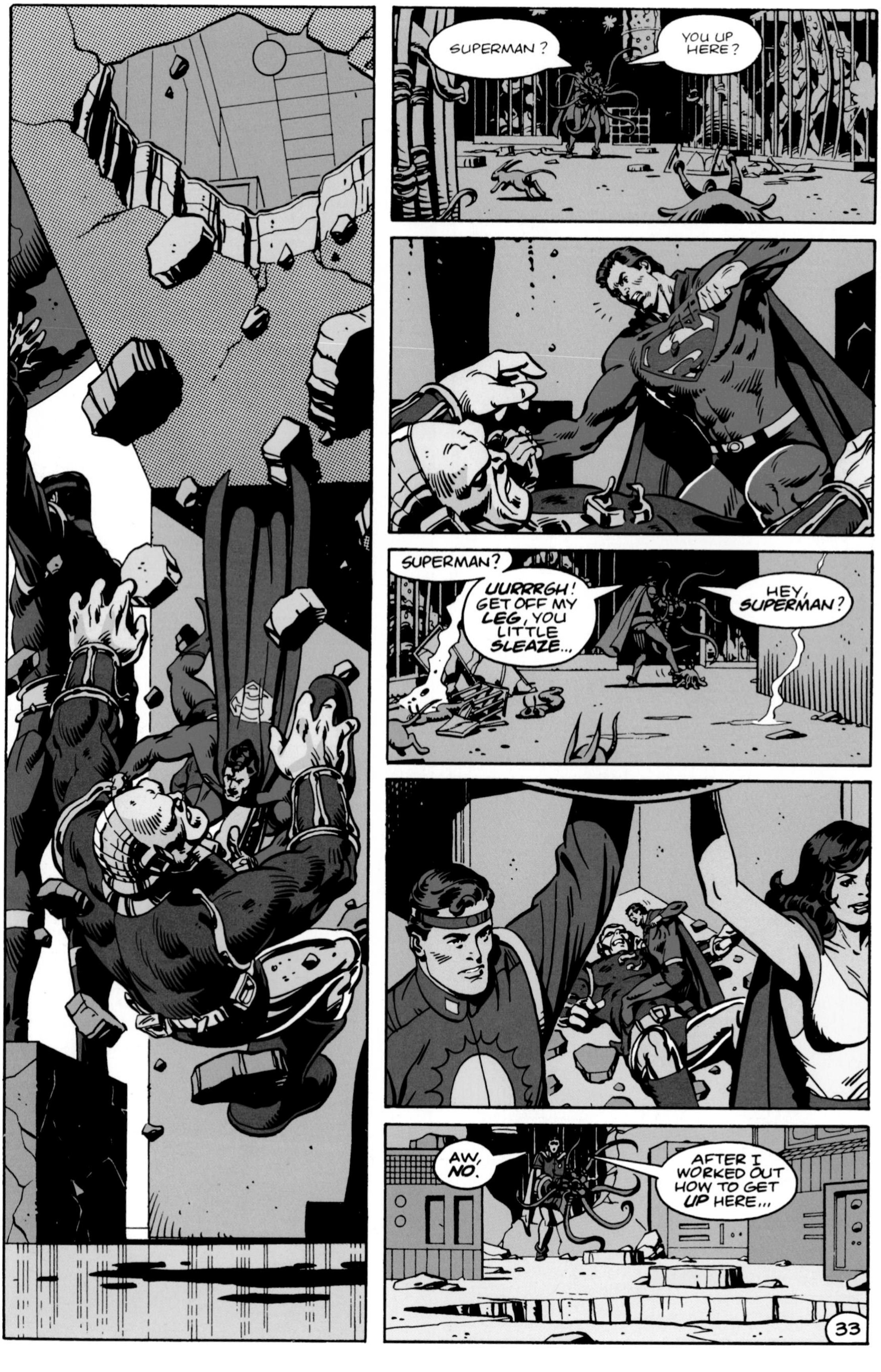
SUPERMAN ?
YOU UP HERE ?
SUPERMAN?
UURRRGH! GET OFF MY LEG, YOU LITTLE SLEAZE...
HEY, SUPERMAN?
AW, NO.
AFTER I WORKED OUT HOW TO GET UP HERE...
33

KRYPTON...?

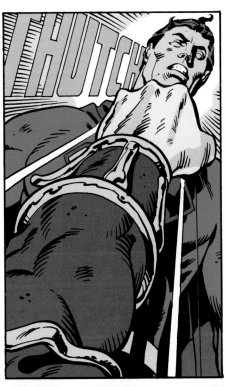

THUTCH

THERE...

DO YOU KNOW, I ALMOST BELIEVED THAT YOU WERE GOING TO *KILL* ME.

HOW STUPID OF YOU TO *HESITATE* LIKE THAT...

NOT A MISTAKE THAT *I'LL MAKE*, I ASSURE YOU...

UH, EXCUSE ME...

34

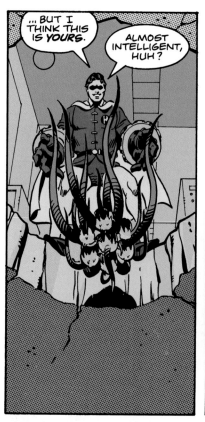

...BUT I THINK THIS IS YOURS.

ALMOST INTELLIGENT, HUH?

AAAAAAA

35

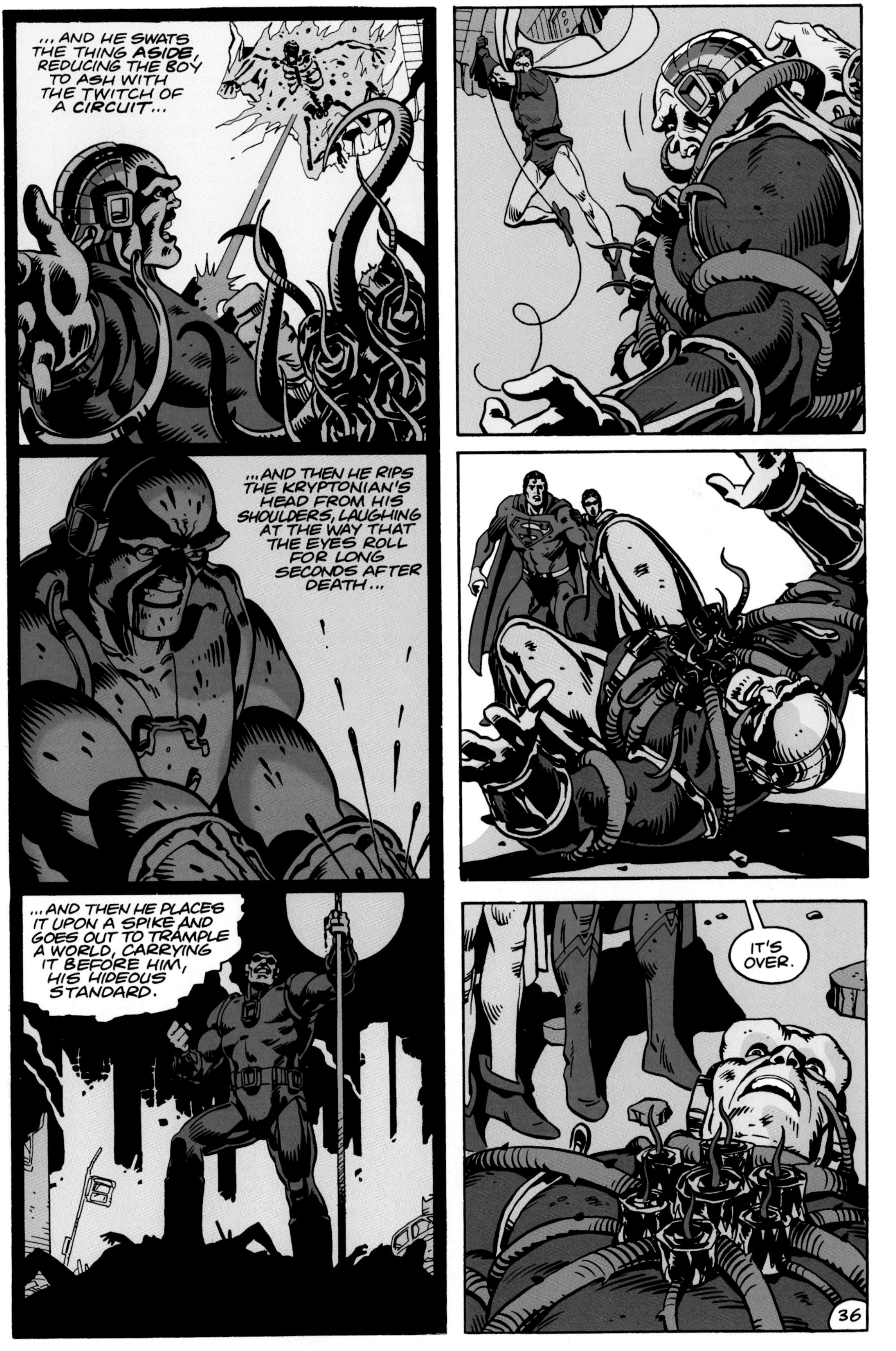
...AND HE SWATS THE THING ASIDE, REDUCING THE BOY TO ASH WITH THE TWITCH OF A CIRCUIT...
...AND THEN HE RIPS THE KRYPTONIAN'S HEAD FROM HIS SHOULDERS, LAUGHING AT THE WAY THAT THE EYES ROLL FOR LONG SECONDS AFTER DEATH...
...AND THEN HE PLACES IT UPON A SPIKE AND GOES OUT TO TRAMPLE A WORLD, CARRYING IT BEFORE HIM, HIS HIDEOUS STANDARD.
IT'S OVER.
36

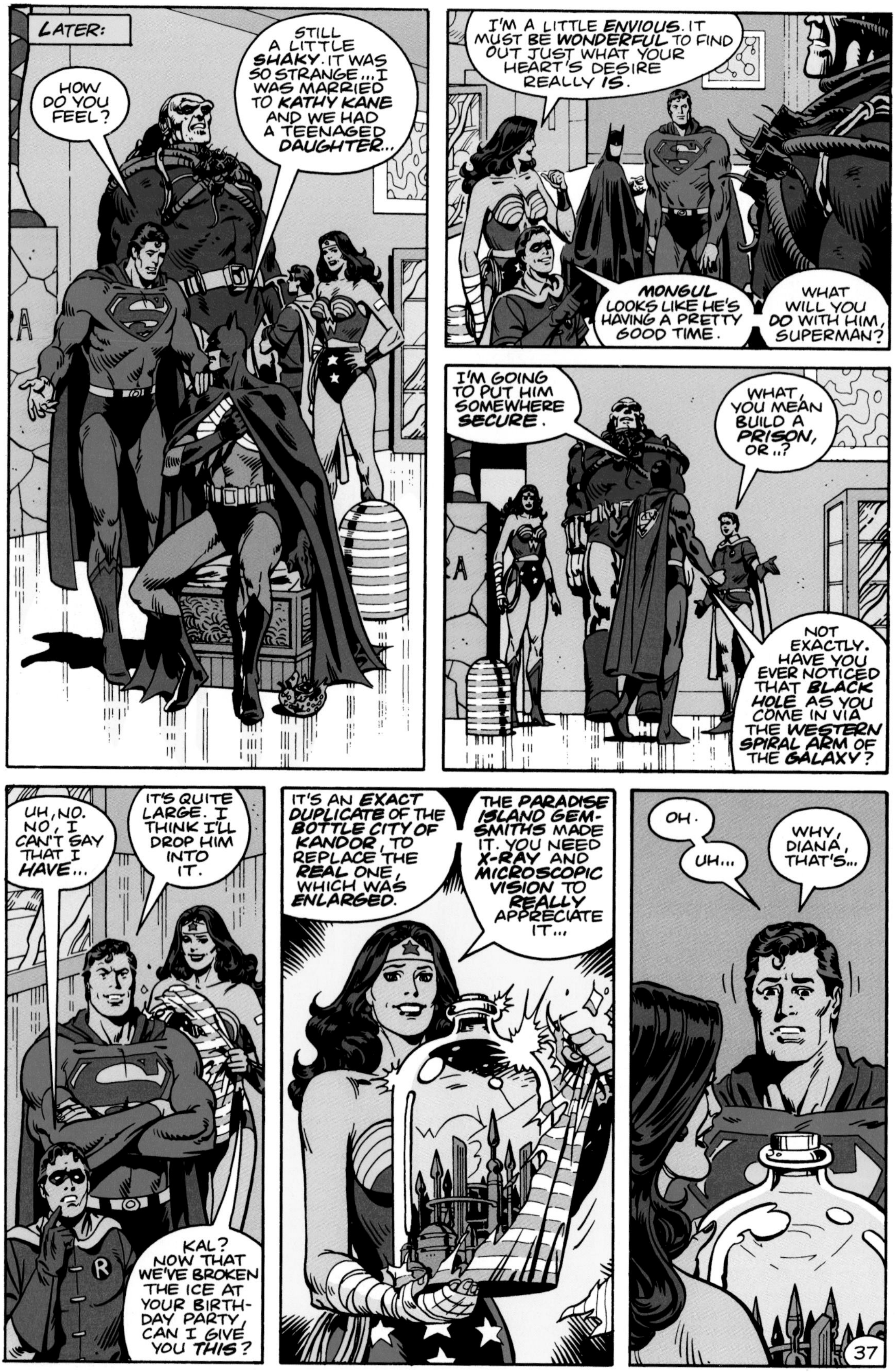
LATER:
HOW DO YOU FEEL?
STILL A LITTLE SHAKY. IT WAS SO STRANGE... I WAS MARRIED TO KATHY KANE AND WE HAD A TEENAGED DAUGHTER...
I'M A LITTLE ENVIOUS. IT MUST BE WONDERFUL TO FIND OUT JUST WHAT YOUR HEART'S DESIRE REALLY IS.
MONGUL LOOKS LIKE HE'S HAVING A PRETTY GOOD TIME.
WHAT WILL YOU DO WITH HIM, SUPERMAN?
I'M GOING TO PUT HIM SOMEWHERE SECURE.
WHAT, YOU MEAN BUILD A PRISON, OR..?
NOT EXACTLY. HAVE YOU EVER NOTICED THAT BLACK HOLE AS YOU COME IN VIA THE WESTERN SPIRAL ARM OF THE GALAXY?
UH, NO. NO, I CAN'T SAY THAT I HAVE...
IT'S QUITE LARGE. I THINK I'LL DROP HIM INTO IT.
KAL? NOW THAT WE'VE BROKEN THE ICE AT YOUR BIRTHDAY PARTY, CAN I GIVE YOU THIS?
IT'S AN EXACT DUPLICATE OF THE BOTTLE CITY OF KANDOR, TO REPLACE THE REAL ONE, WHICH WAS ENLARGED.
THE PARADISE ISLAND GEM-SMITHS MADE IT. YOU NEED X-RAY AND MICROSCOPIC VISION TO REALLY APPRECIATE IT...
OH.
UH...
WHY, DIANA, THAT'S...
37

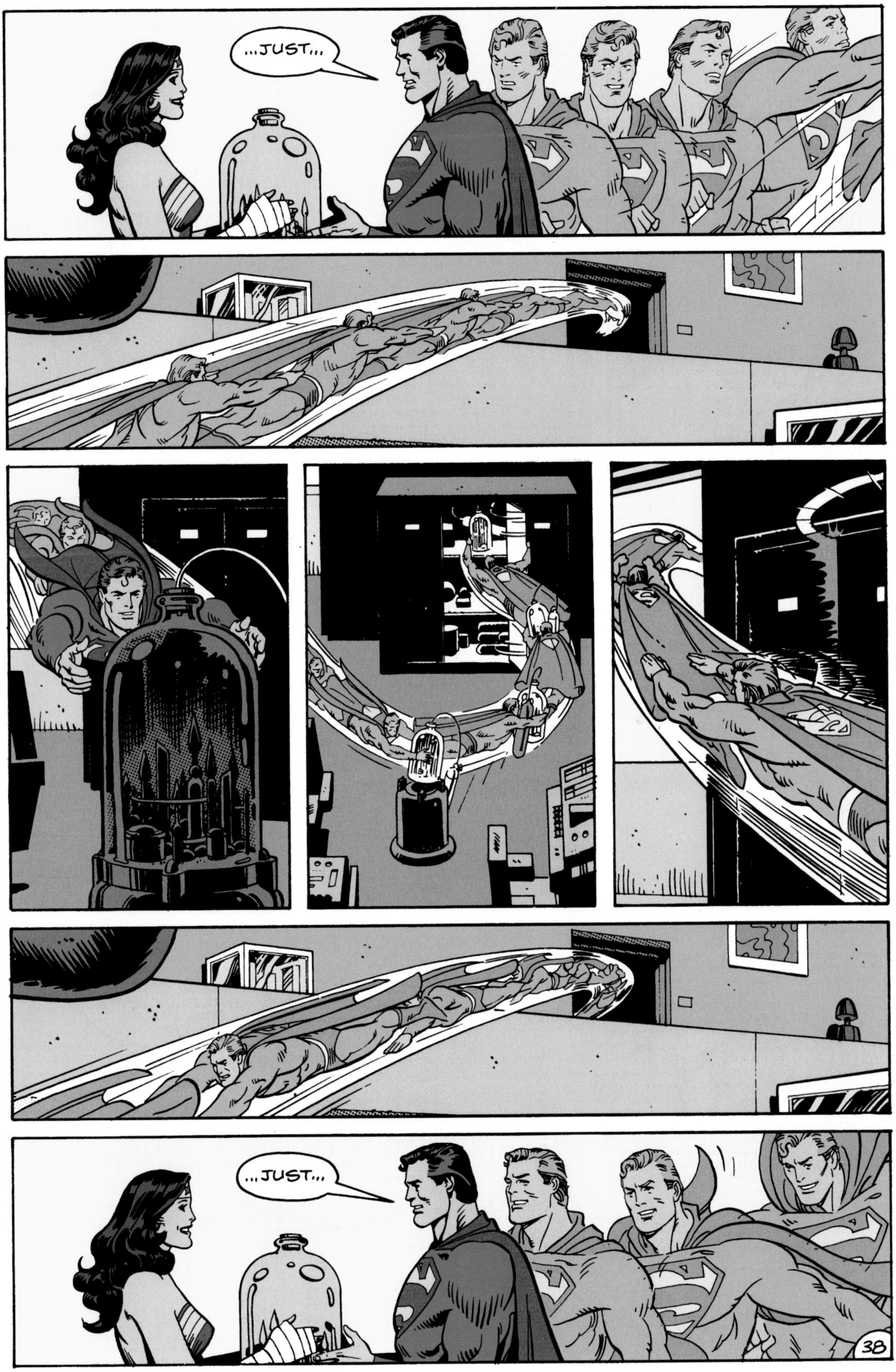
...JUST...
...JUST...
38

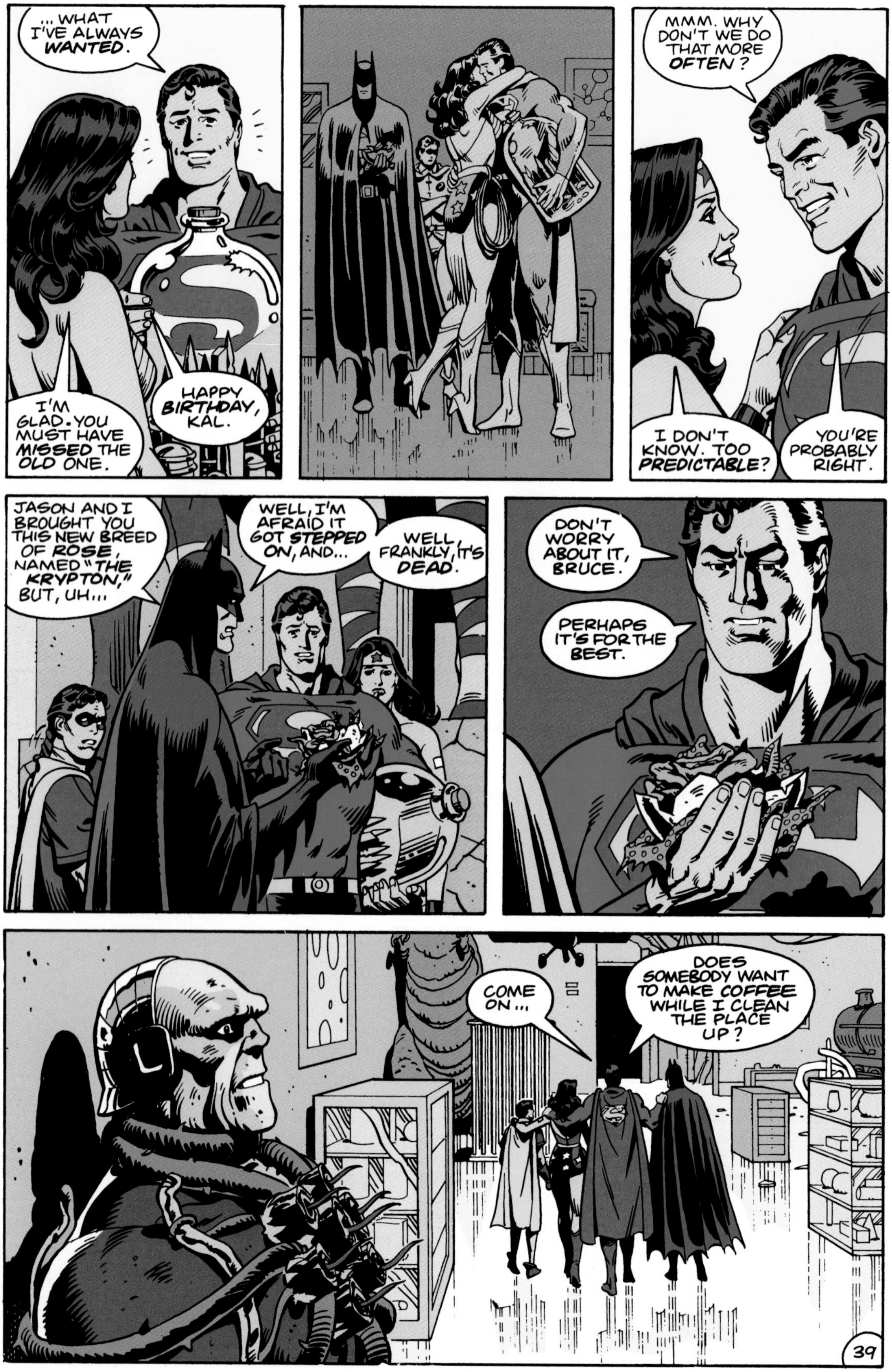
...WHAT I'VE ALWAYS WANTED.
I'M GLAD. YOU MUST HAVE MISSED THE OLD ONE.
HAPPY BIRTHDAY, KAL.
MMM. WHY DON'T WE DO THAT MORE OFTEN?
I DON'T KNOW. TOO PREDICTABLE?
YOU'RE PROBABLY RIGHT.
JASON AND I BROUGHT YOU THIS NEW BREED OF ROSE, NAMED "THE KRYPTON," BUT, UH...
WELL, I'M AFRAID IT GOT STEPPED ON, AND...
WELL, FRANKLY, IT'S DEAD.
DON'T WORRY ABOUT IT, BRUCE.
PERHAPS IT'S FOR THE BEST.
COME ON...
DOES SOMEBODY WANT TO MAKE COFFEE WHILE I CLEAN THE PLACE UP?
39

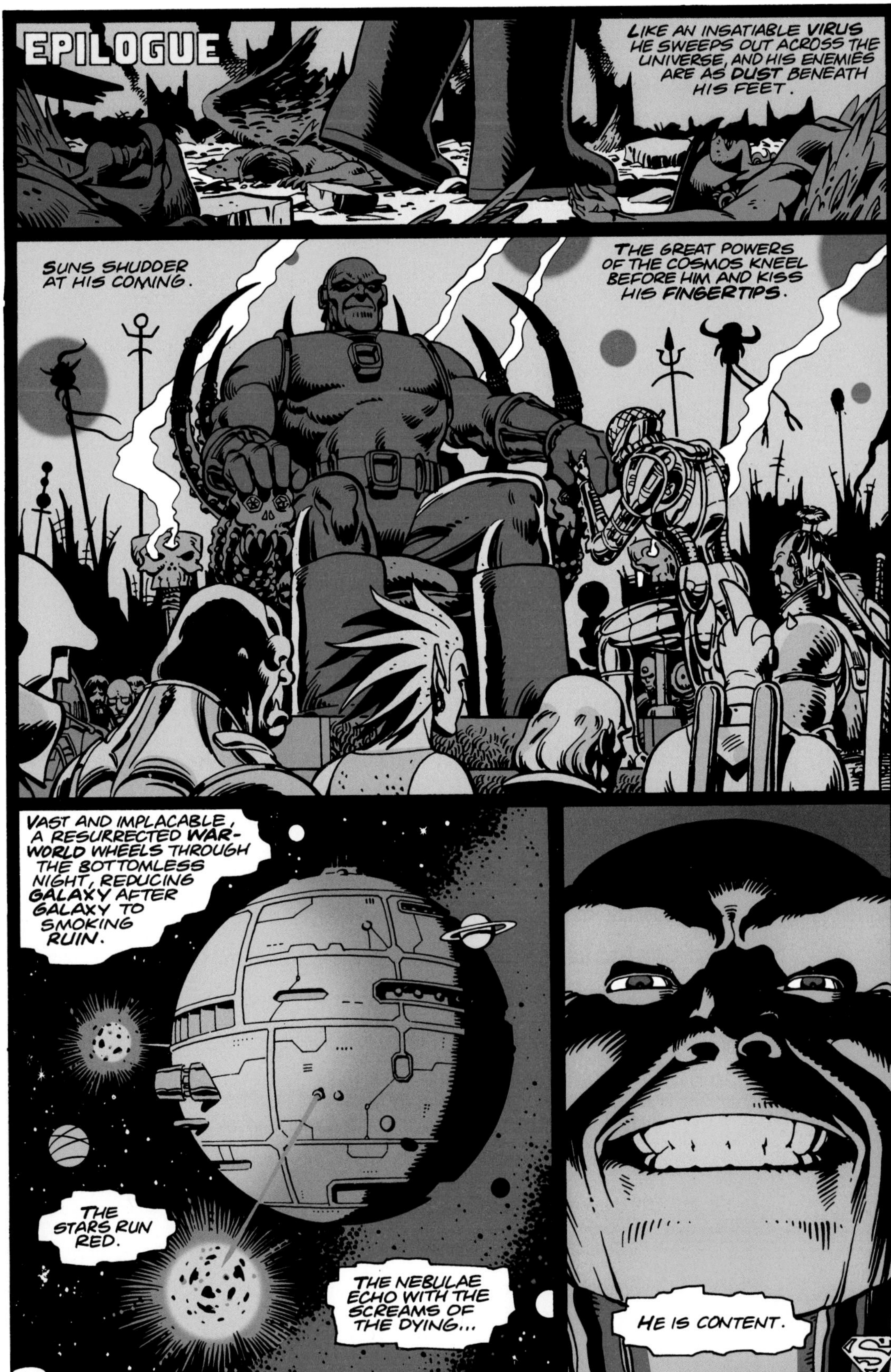
EPILOGUE
LIKE AN INSATIABLE VIRUS HE SWEEPS OUT ACROSS THE UNIVERSE, AND HIS ENEMIES ARE AS DUST BENEATH HIS FEET.
SUNS SHUDDER AT HIS COMING.
THE GREAT POWERS OF THE COSMOS KNEEL BEFORE HIM AND KISS HIS FINGERTIPS.
VAST AND IMPLACABLE, A RESURRECTED WAR-WORLD WHEELS THROUGH THE BOTTOMLESS NIGHT, REDUCING GALAXY AFTER GALAXY TO SMOKING RUIN.
THE STARS RUN RED.
THE NEBULAE ECHO WITH THE SCREAMS OF THE DYING...
HE IS CONTENT.
40

In 1986, DC Comics remodeled its universe completely with CRISIS ON INFINITE EARTHS. From then on, continuity was split for fans between "Pre-Crisis" and "Post-Crisis."

Before this time, the DC Universe contained many alternate worlds with different versions of Earth and its heroes. Thus, there were multiple versions of Superman: the main Superman lived with his "Super-family" on Earth 1, while the 1940s Superman, who worked for the Daily Star and was married to Lois Lane, lived on Earth 2. There were so many character doppelgängers from so many Earths, it had become confusing for new and occasional readers. CRISIS delivered the ultimate solution: tabula rasa!

The maxiseries allowed DC Comics to reboot its entire universe to include only one Earth and created a great jumping-on point for all fans, both existing and new.

Writer/artist John Byrne was assigned to reinvent Superman for a new era. In MAN OF STEEL (1986), Byrne presented a new Krypton: a dryly scientific world on the verge of destruction. In this version, Kryptonians have traded emotion for logic and intellect. Jor-El and Lara weren't passionate lovers, but a couple selected for their unparalleled genes. Despite the mental, social and cultural conditioning he experienced, Jor-El falls in love with Lara and places not a baby but a conception matrix in a ship that will trigger the conception of a baby once it lands on Earth.

The post-Crisis Superman is then born in the USA and feels closer to his Kansas peers than to his Kryptonian heritage. Moreover, unlike the previous version, Clark dons his costume only in adulthood.

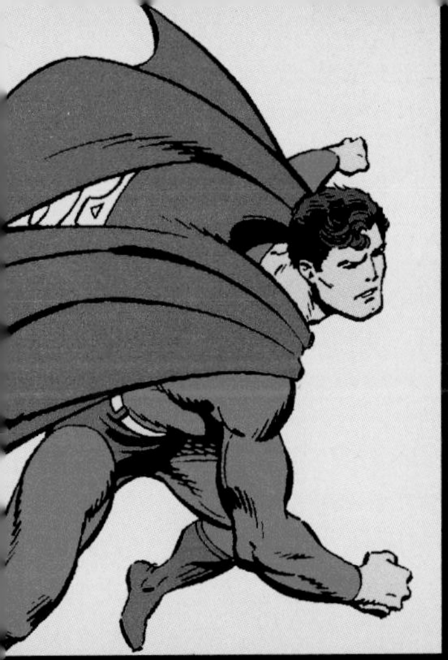

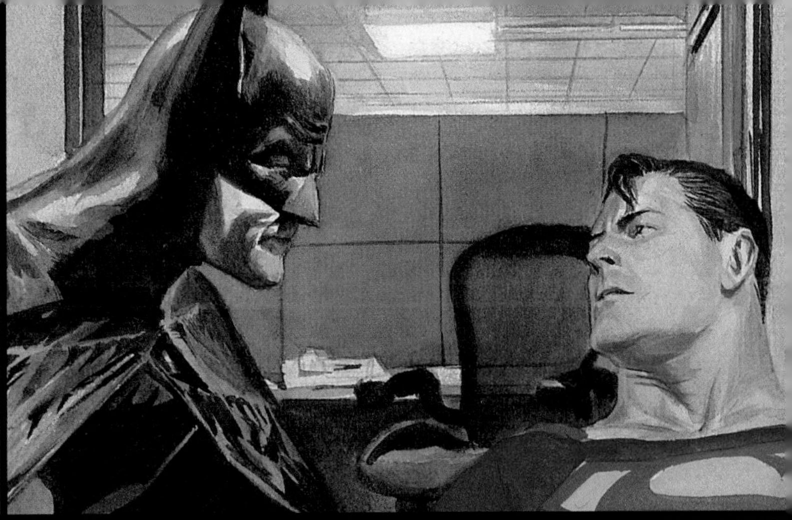

The young man moves to Metropolis where he reveals his powers saving a crashing space shuttle. Lois Lane becomes instantly interested in writing the Superman story, only to be scooped by her new Daily Planet co-worker, Clark Kent.

Just like in the 1940s, Lois and Clark are friends as much as competitors. She resents him for "stealing" the Superman scoop, but with time, learns to appreciate and ultimately love him — an attitude reflected in the popular 1990s TV series *Lois & Clark: The New Adventures of Superman.* In 1996, the two officially tied the knot, and they would remain happily together until DC's next continuity revamp: The New 52.

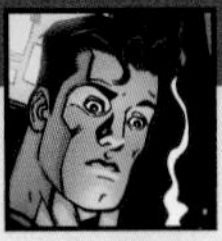

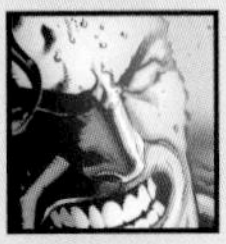

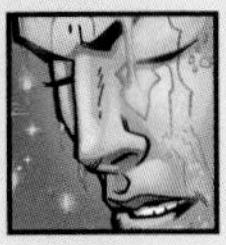

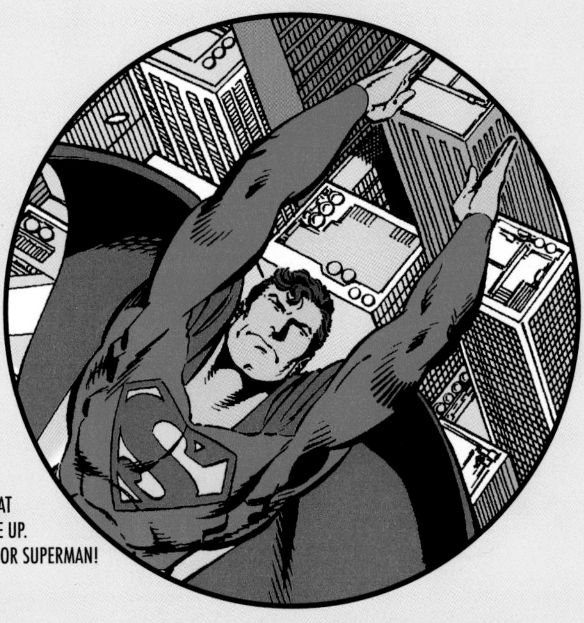

HAVE TO TAKE A RAIN CHECK ON THAT LASAGNA. SOMETHING... JUST CAME UP. SOMETHING THAT MAY BE A JOB... FOR SUPERMAN!

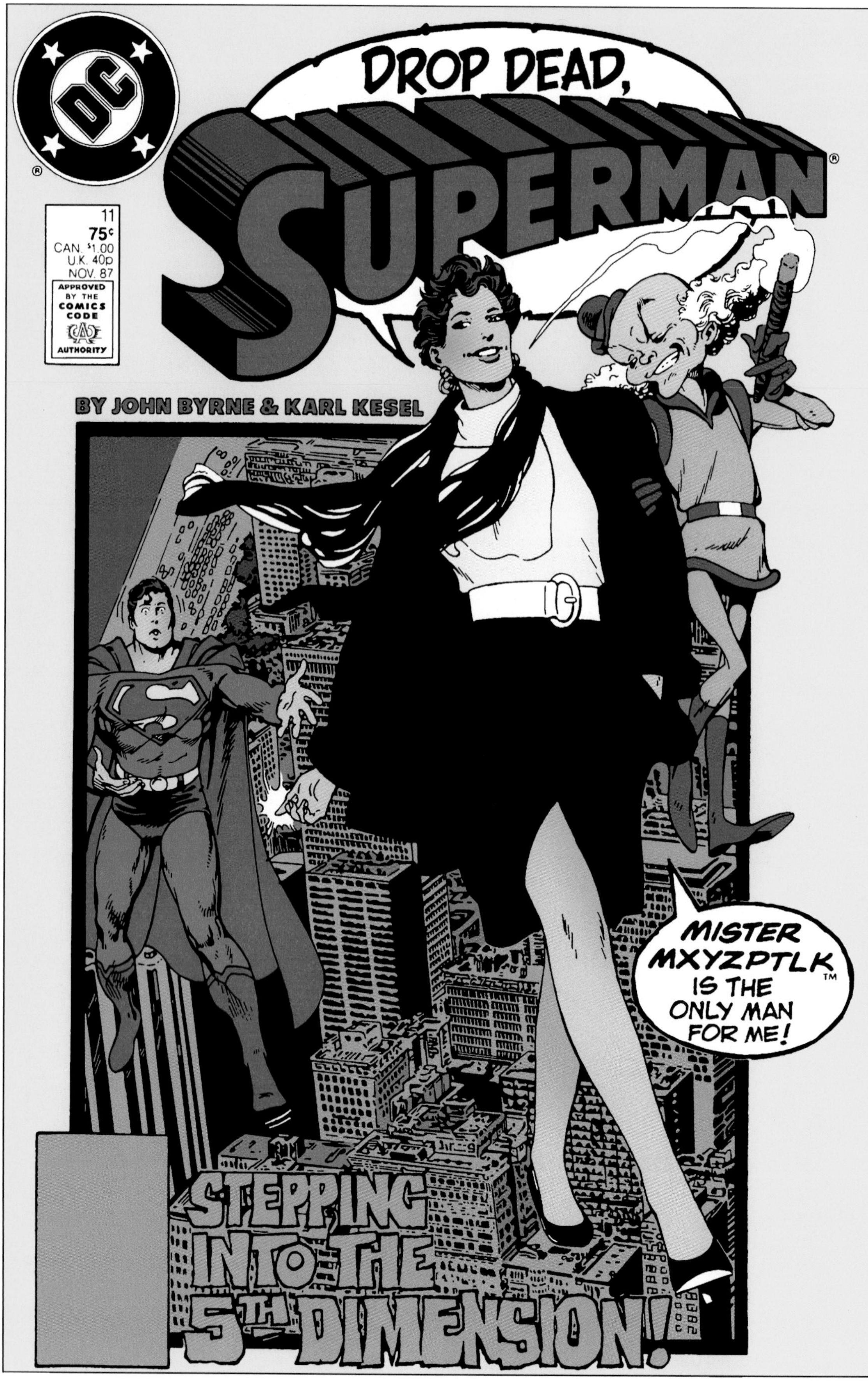
DROP DEAD,
SUPERMAN
11
75¢
CAN. $1.00
U.K. 40p
NOV. 87
APPROVED BY THE COMICS CODE AUTHORITY
BY JOHN BYRNE & KARL KESEL
MISTER MXYZPTLK™ IS THE ONLY MAN FOR ME!
STEPPING INTO THE 5TH DIMENSION!

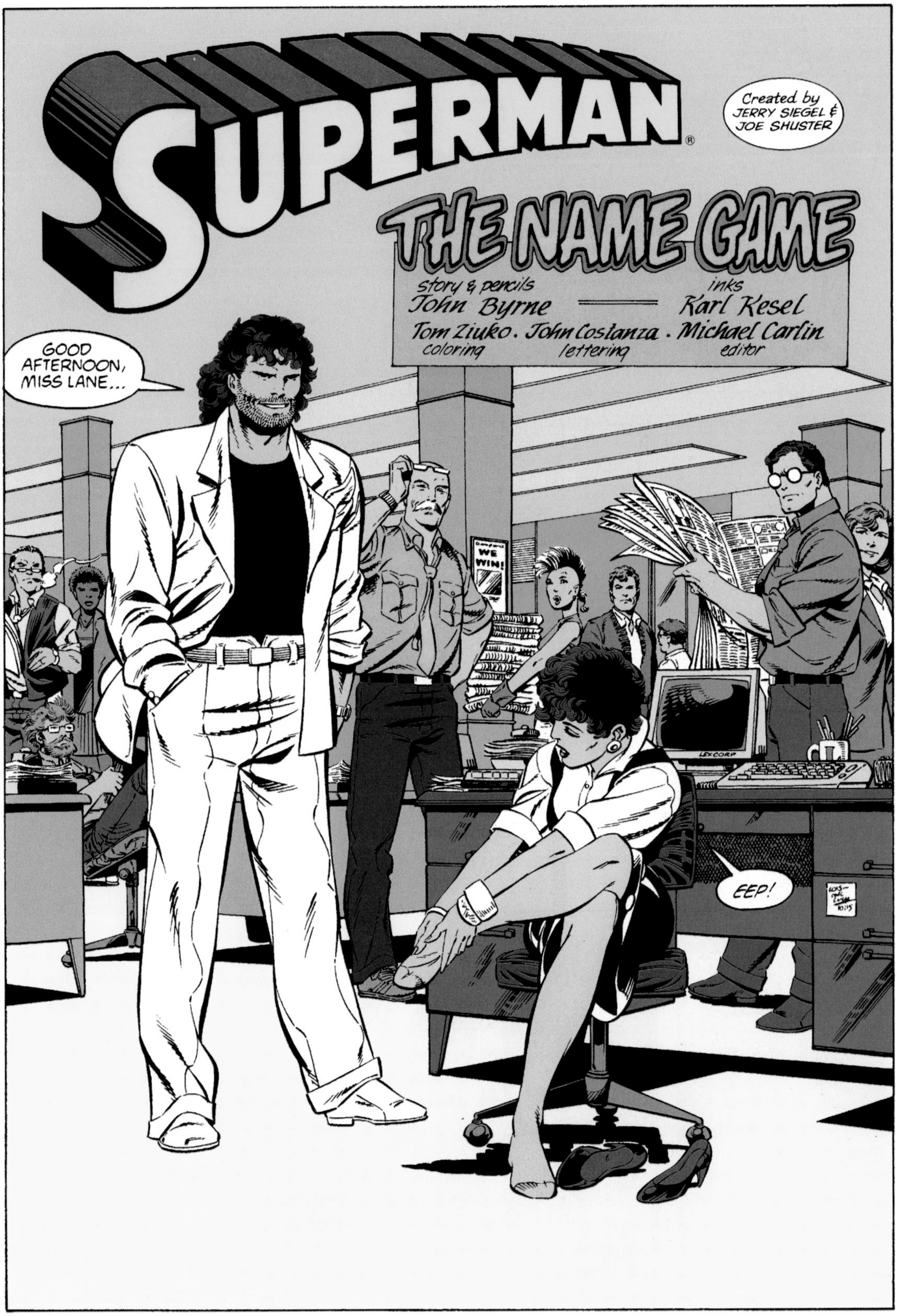
SUPERMAN®
Created by JERRY SIEGEL & JOE SHUSTER
THE NAME GAME
story & pencils John Byrne — inks Karl Kesel
Tom Ziuko . John Costanza . Michael Carlin
coloring lettering editor
GOOD AFTERNOON, MISS LANE...
WE WIN!
LEXCORP
EEP!

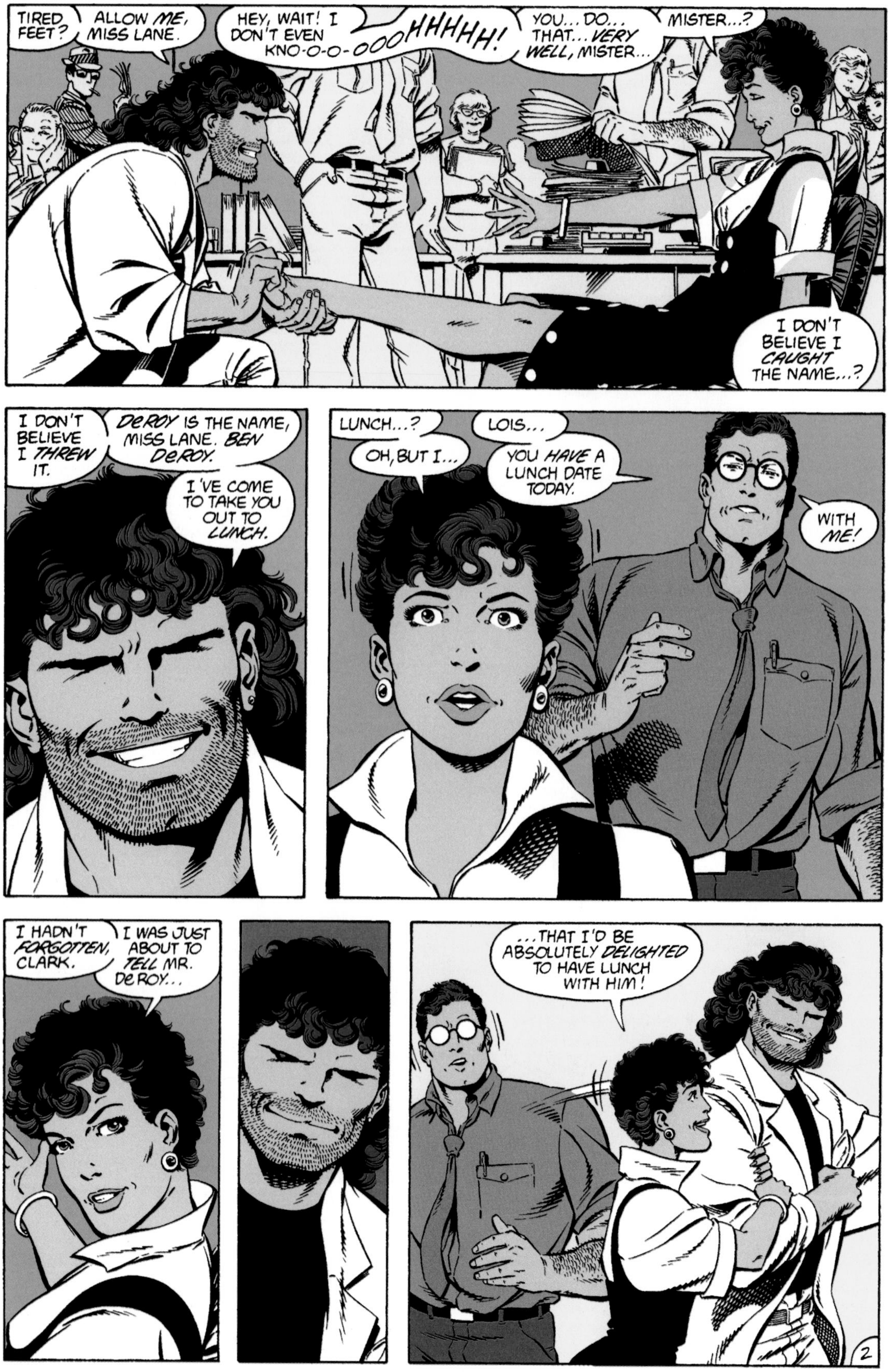

TIRED FEET?
ALLOW ME, MISS LANE.
HEY, WAIT! I DON'T EVEN KNO-O-O-OOOHHHHH!
YOU... DO... THAT... VERY WELL, MISTER...
MISTER...?
I DON'T BELIEVE I CAUGHT THE NAME...?
I DON'T BELIEVE I THREW IT.
DeROY IS THE NAME, MISS LANE. BEN DeROY.
I'VE COME TO TAKE YOU OUT TO LUNCH.
LUNCH...?
OH, BUT I...
LOIS...
YOU HAVE A LUNCH DATE TODAY.
WITH ME!
I HADN'T FORGOTTEN, CLARK.
I WAS JUST ABOUT TO TELL MR. DeROY...
...THAT I'D BE ABSOLUTELY DELIGHTED TO HAVE LUNCH WITH HIM!
2

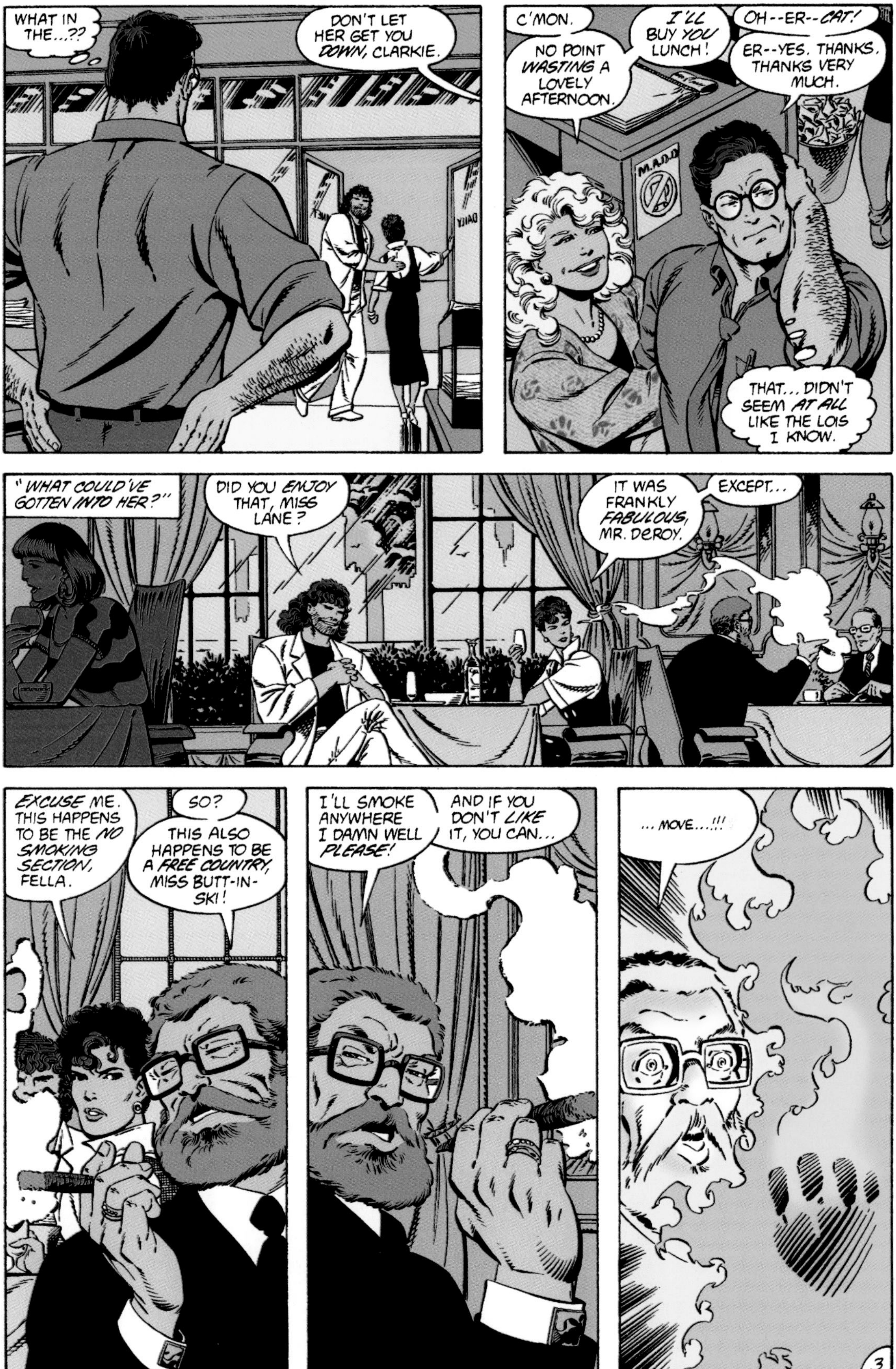
WHAT IN THE...??
DON'T LET HER GET YOU DOWN, CLARKIE.
C'MON.
NO POINT WASTING A LOVELY AFTERNOON.
I'LL BUY YOU LUNCH!
OH--ER--CAT!
ER--YES. THANKS. THANKS VERY MUCH.
M.A.D.D.
THAT... DIDN'T SEEM AT ALL LIKE THE LOIS I KNOW.
"WHAT COULD'VE GOTTEN INTO HER?"
DID YOU ENJOY THAT, MISS LANE?
IT WAS FRANKLY FABULOUS, MR. DeROY.
EXCEPT...
EXCUSE ME. THIS HAPPENS TO BE THE NO SMOKING SECTION, FELLA.
SO? THIS ALSO HAPPENS TO BE A FREE COUNTRY, MISS BUTT-IN-SKI!
I'LL SMOKE ANYWHERE I DAMN WELL PLEASE!
AND IF YOU DON'T LIKE IT, YOU CAN...
... MOVE...!!!
3

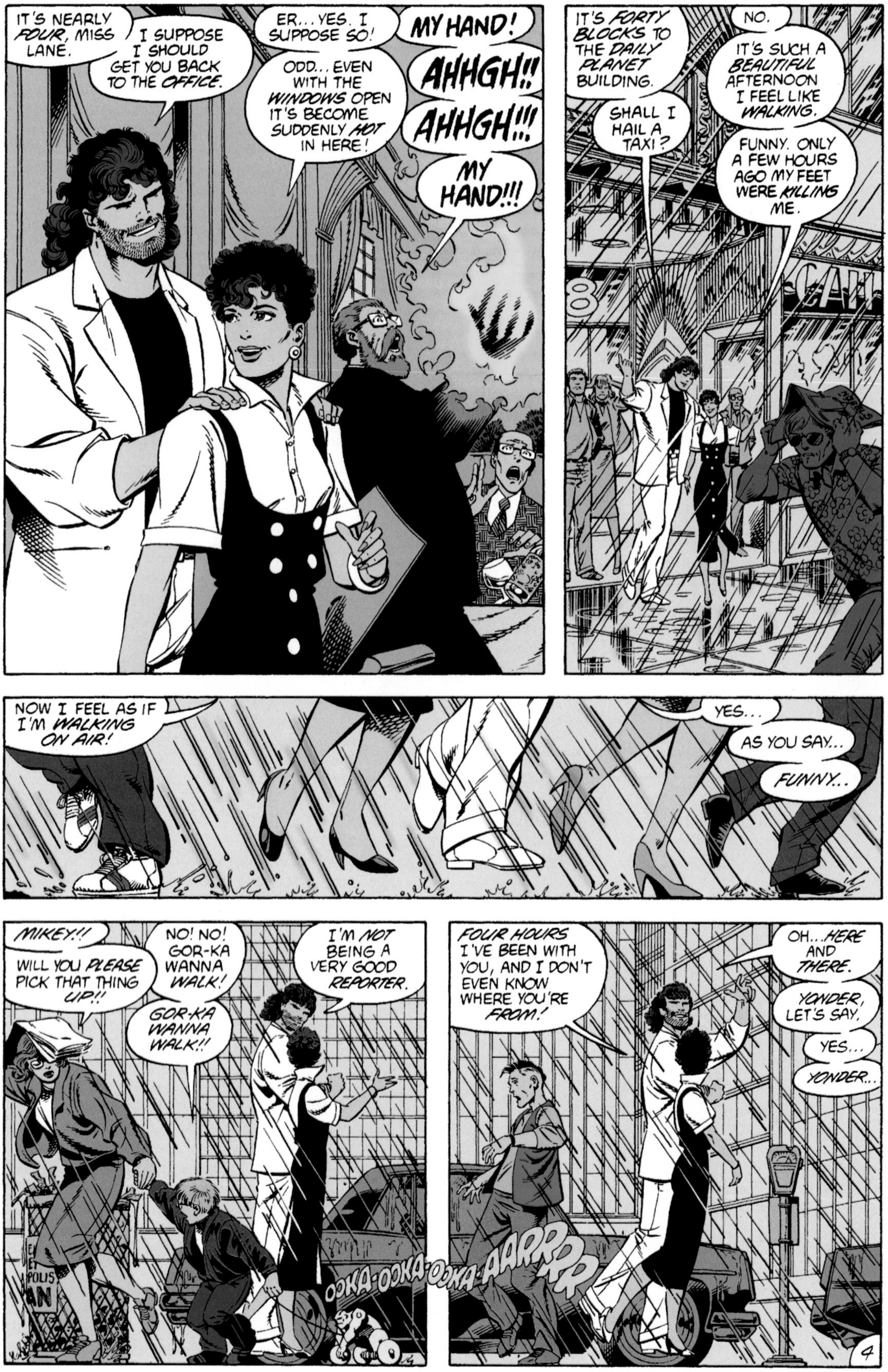
IT'S NEARLY FOUR, MISS LANE.
I SUPPOSE I SHOULD GET YOU BACK TO THE OFFICE.
ER... YES. I SUPPOSE SO!
ODD... EVEN WITH THE WINDOWS OPEN IT'S BECOME SUDDENLY HOT IN HERE!
MY HAND!
AHHGH!!
AHHGH!!!
MY HAND!!!
IT'S FORTY BLOCKS TO THE DAILY PLANET BUILDING.
SHALL I HAIL A TAXI?
NO.
IT'S SUCH A BEAUTIFUL AFTERNOON I FEEL LIKE WALKING.
FUNNY. ONLY A FEW HOURS AGO MY FEET WERE KILLING ME.
NOW I FEEL AS IF I'M WALKING ON AIR!
YES...
AS YOU SAY...
FUNNY...
MIKEY!!
WILL YOU PLEASE PICK THAT THING UP!!
NO! NO! GOR-KA WANNA WALK!
GOR-KA WANNA WALK!!
I'M NOT BEING A VERY GOOD REPORTER.
OOKA-OOKA-OOKA-AARRRR
FOUR HOURS I'VE BEEN WITH YOU, AND I DON'T EVEN KNOW WHERE YOU'RE FROM!
OH... HERE AND THERE.
YONDER, LET'S SAY.
YES...
YONDER...
4

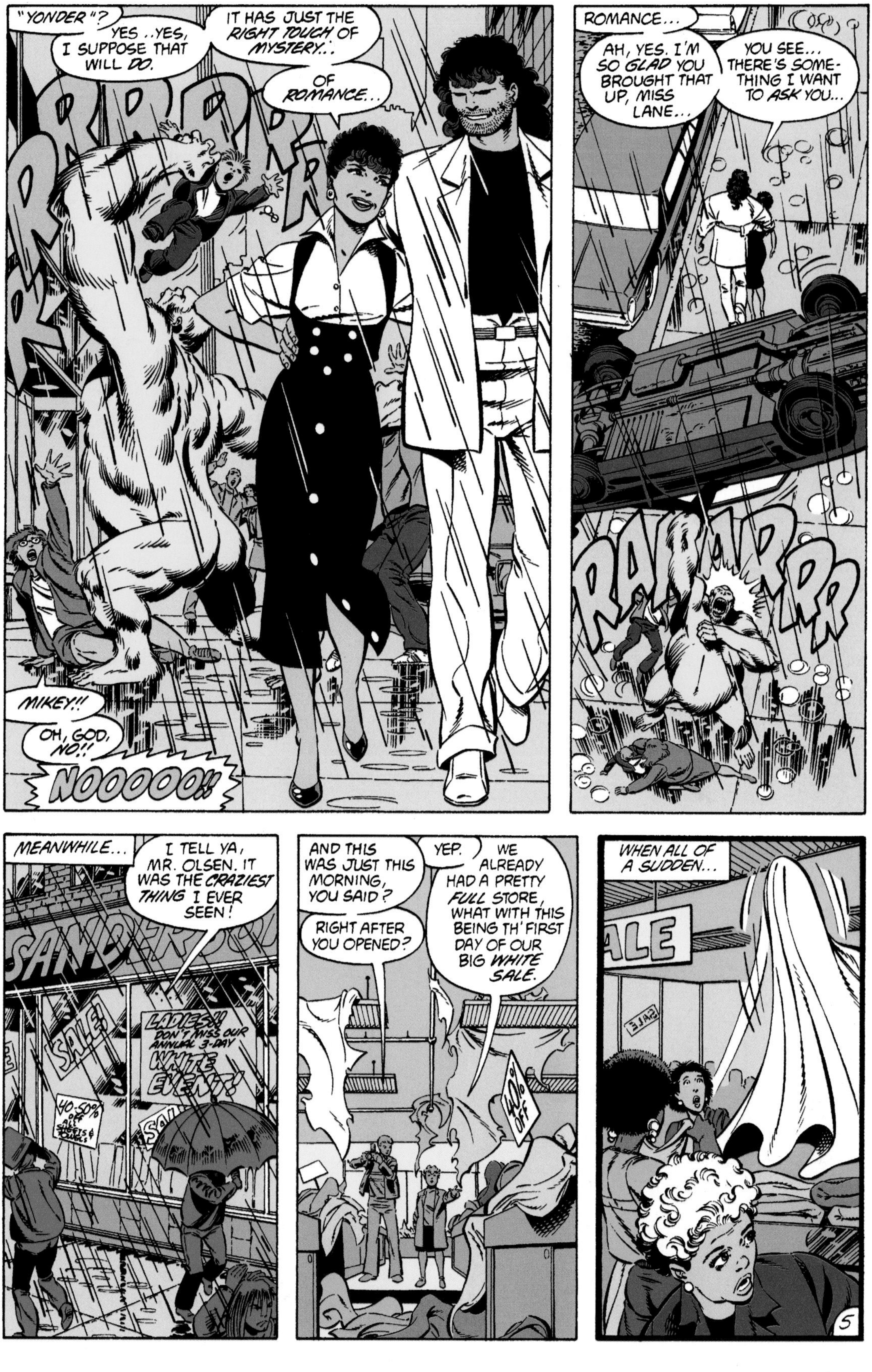
"YONDER"?
YES ..YES, I SUPPOSE THAT WILL DO.
IT HAS JUST THE RIGHT TOUCH OF MYSTERY...
OF ROMANCE...
RRRRR
MIKEY!!
OH, GOD, NO!!
NOOOOO!!
ROMANCE...
AH, YES. I'M SO GLAD YOU BROUGHT THAT UP, MISS LANE...
YOU SEE... THERE'S SOME-THING I WANT TO ASK YOU...
RARRRRRR
MEANWHILE...
I TELL YA, MR. OLSEN. IT WAS THE CRAZIEST THING I EVER SEEN!
SALE
LADIES!! DON'T MISS OUR ANNUAL 3-DAY WHITE EVENT!
40-50% OFF ALL SHEETS & TOWELS
AND THIS WAS JUST THIS MORNING, YOU SAID?
RIGHT AFTER YOU OPENED?
YEP.
WE ALREADY HAD A PRETTY FULL STORE, WHAT WITH THIS BEING TH' FIRST DAY OF OUR BIG WHITE SALE.
40% OFF
WHEN ALL OF A SUDDEN...
ALE
5

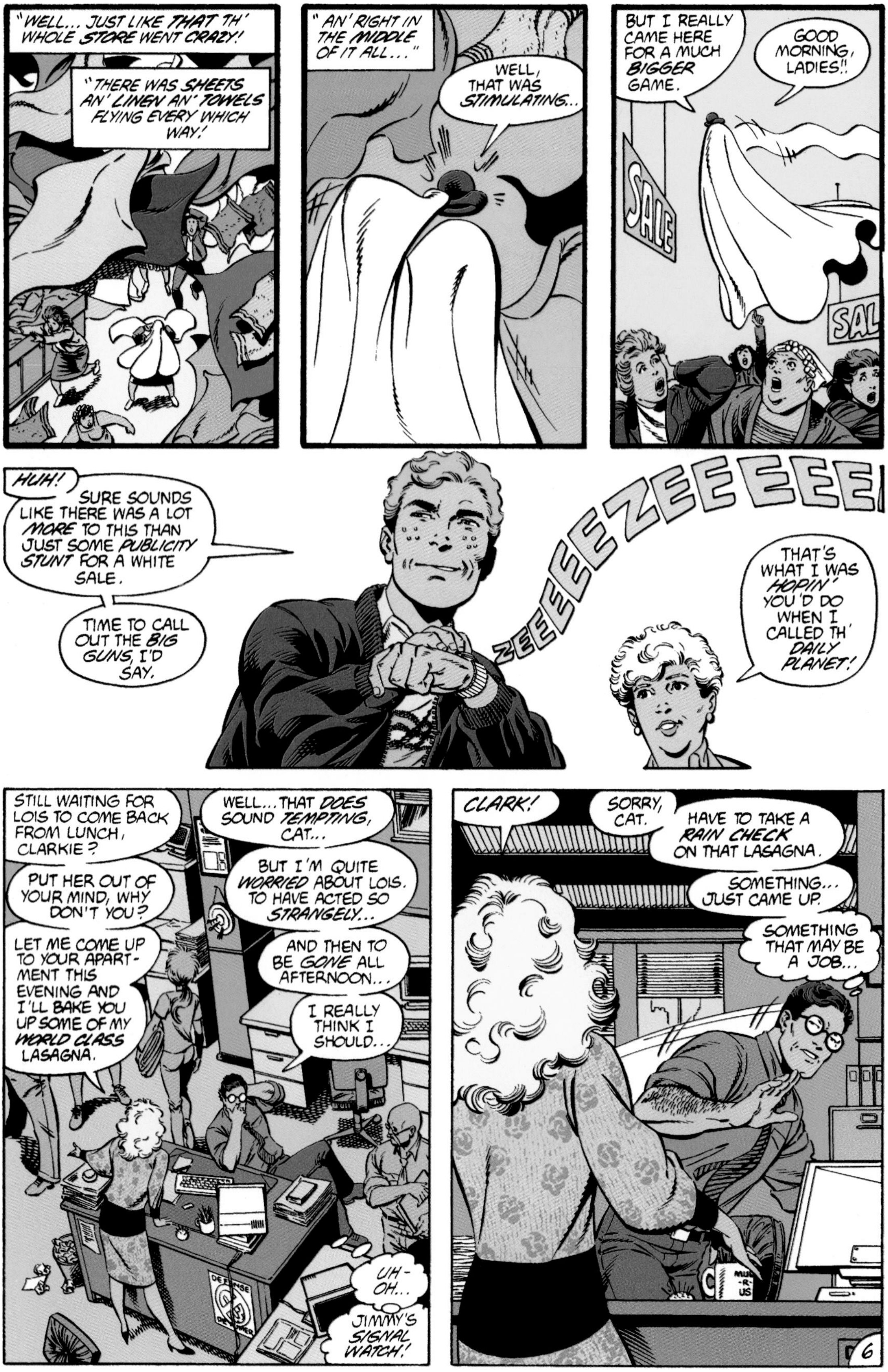
"WELL... JUST LIKE THAT TH' WHOLE STORE WENT CRAZY!
"THERE WAS SHEETS AN' LINEN AN' TOWELS FLYING EVERY WHICH WAY!
"AN' RIGHT IN THE MIDDLE OF IT ALL..."
WELL, THAT WAS STIMULATING...
BUT I REALLY CAME HERE FOR A MUCH BIGGER GAME.
GOOD MORNING, LADIES!!
SALE
SAL
HUH!
SURE SOUNDS LIKE THERE WAS A LOT MORE TO THIS THAN JUST SOME PUBLICITY STUNT FOR A WHITE SALE.
TIME TO CALL OUT THE BIG GUNS, I'D SAY.
ZEEEEEZEEEEEE
THAT'S WHAT I WAS HOPIN' YOU'D DO WHEN I CALLED TH' DAILY PLANET!
STILL WAITING FOR LOIS TO COME BACK FROM LUNCH, CLARKIE?
PUT HER OUT OF YOUR MIND, WHY DON'T YOU?
LET ME COME UP TO YOUR APARTMENT THIS EVENING AND I'LL BAKE YOU UP SOME OF MY WORLD CLASS LASAGNA.
WELL... THAT DOES SOUND TEMPTING, CAT...
BUT I'M QUITE WORRIED ABOUT LOIS. TO HAVE ACTED SO STRANGELY...
AND THEN TO BE GONE ALL AFTERNOON...
I REALLY THINK I SHOULD...
UH-OH...
JIMMY'S SIGNAL WATCH!
CLARK!
SORRY, CAT.
HAVE TO TAKE A RAIN CHECK ON THAT LASAGNA.
SOMETHING... JUST CAME UP.
SOMETHING THAT MAY BE A JOB...
MUG-R-US
6

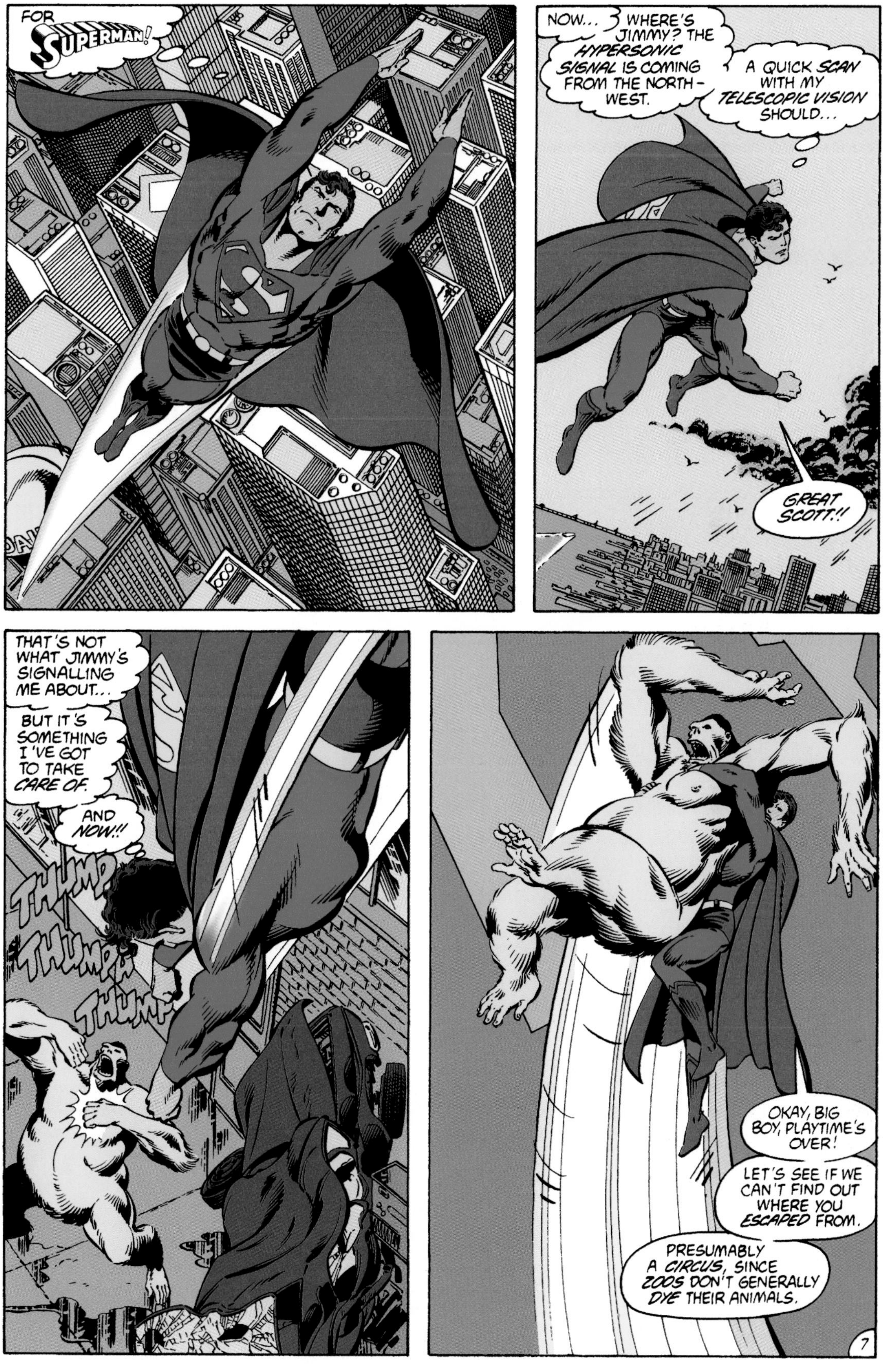
FOR SUPERMAN!
NOW... WHERE'S JIMMY? THE HYPERSONIC SIGNAL IS COMING FROM THE NORTH-WEST.
A QUICK SCAN WITH MY TELESCOPIC VISION SHOULD...
GREAT SCOTT!!
THAT'S NOT WHAT JIMMY'S SIGNALLING ME ABOUT...
BUT IT'S SOMETHING I'VE GOT TO TAKE CARE OF.
AND NOW!!
THUMP
THUMP
THUMP
OKAY, BIG BOY, PLAYTIME'S OVER!
LET'S SEE IF WE CAN'T FIND OUT WHERE YOU ESCAPED FROM.
PRESUMABLY A CIRCUS, SINCE ZOOS DON'T GENERALLY DYE THEIR ANIMALS.
7

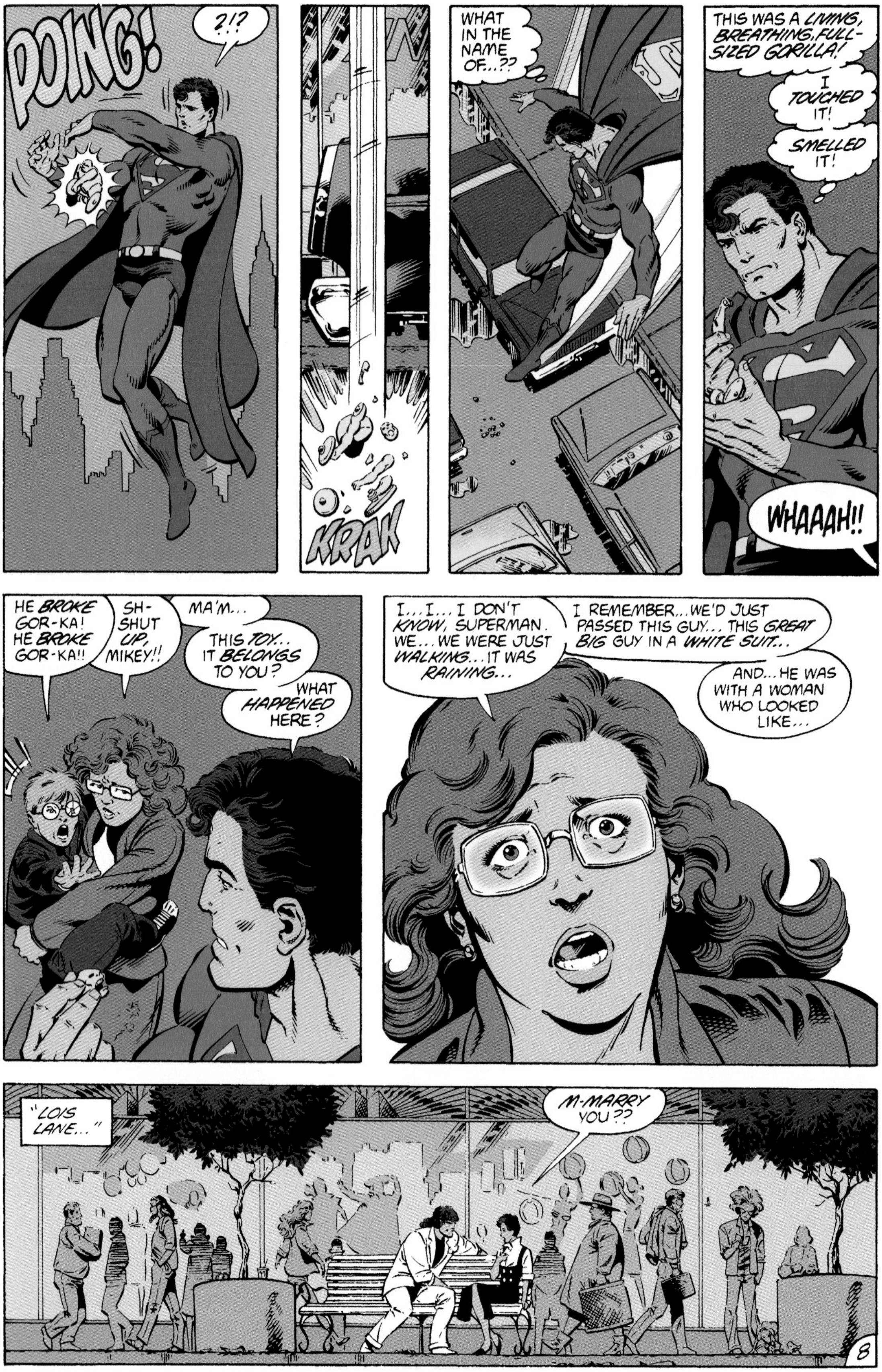
POING!
?!?
KRAK
WHAT IN THE NAME OF...??
THIS WAS A LIVING, BREATHING, FULL-SIZED GORILLA!
I TOUCHED IT!
SMELLED IT!
WHAAAH!!
HE BROKE GOR-KA! HE BROKE GOR-KA!!
SH-SHUT UP, MIKEY!!
MA'M...
THIS TOY... IT BELONGS TO YOU?
WHAT HAPPENED HERE?
I... I... I DON'T KNOW, SUPERMAN. WE... WE WERE JUST WALKING... IT WAS RAINING...
I REMEMBER... WE'D JUST PASSED THIS GUY... THIS GREAT BIG GUY IN A WHITE SUIT...
AND... HE WAS WITH A WOMAN WHO LOOKED LIKE...
"LOIS LANE..."
M-MARRY YOU??
8

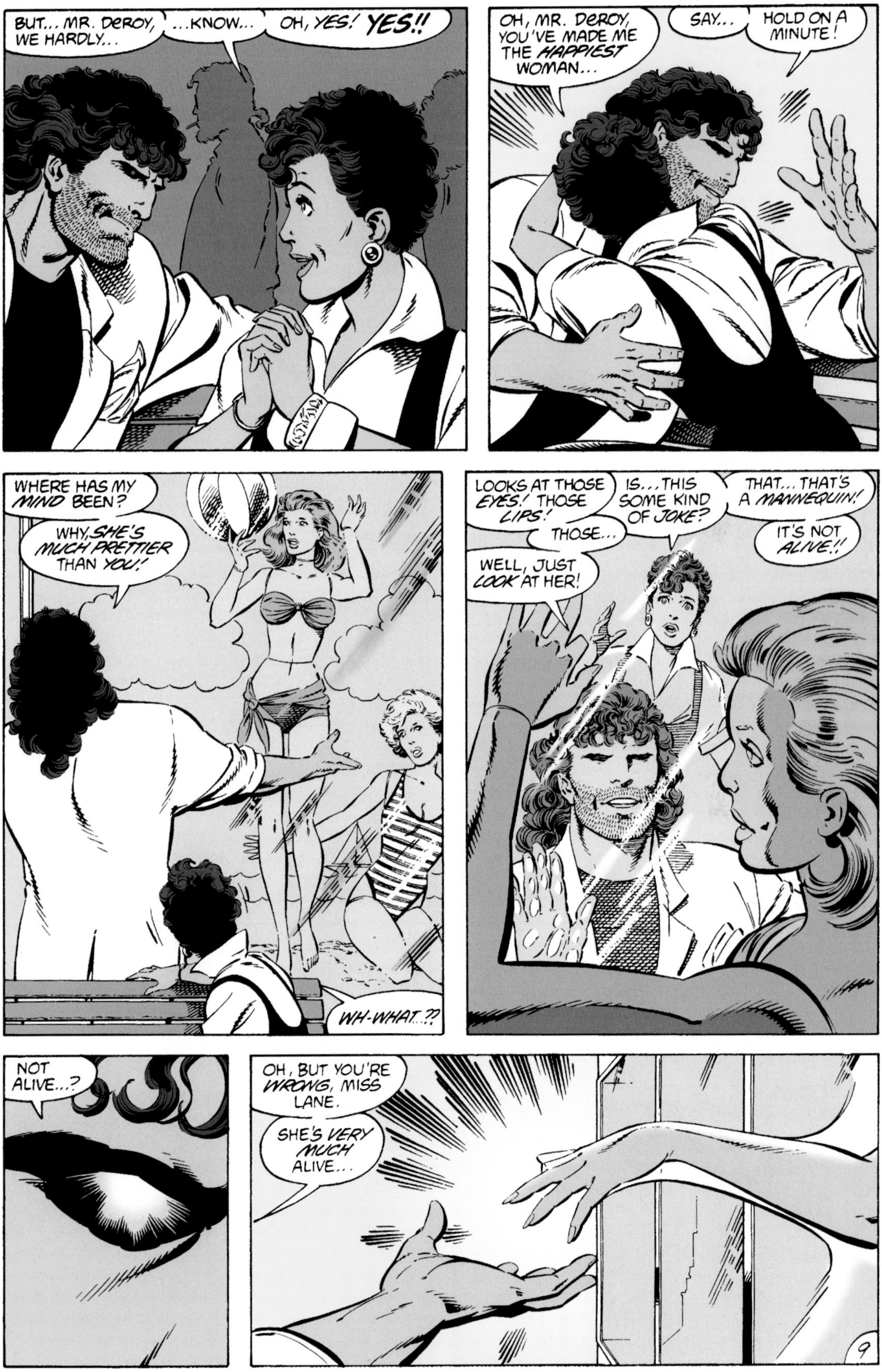
BUT... MR. DEROY, WE HARDLY...
...KNOW...
OH, YES! YES!!
OH, MR. DEROY, YOU'VE MADE ME THE HAPPIEST WOMAN...
SAY...
HOLD ON A MINUTE!
WHERE HAS MY MIND BEEN?
WHY, SHE'S MUCH PRETTIER THAN YOU!
WH-WHAT..??
LOOKS AT THOSE EYES! THOSE LIPS!
THOSE...
IS...THIS SOME KIND OF JOKE?
THAT... THAT'S A MANNEQUIN!
IT'S NOT ALIVE!!
WELL, JUST LOOK AT HER!
NOT ALIVE...?
OH, BUT YOU'RE WRONG, MISS LANE.
SHE'S VERY MUCH ALIVE...
9

ALIVE... AND *EVERYTHING* ANY MAN COULD *WANT!*

OH, BEN HONEY! Y'ALL *DO* SAY TH' *SWEETEST* THAINGS!

AND NOW, IF YOU'LL *EXCUSE* US, MISS LANE, WE...

BEN, HONEY! *WAIT!* Y'ALL *CAIN'T JEST* STROLL OFF WITH ME!

THAT'D BE *STEALIN'!* BUT... BUT...

YOU'RE *RIGHT,* OF COURSE. PERHAPS...

PERHAPS AN *EXCHANGE* WOULD BE MORE *ACCEPTABLE!*

NO SIGN OF LOIS *ANYWHERE!*

AND THAT *BEN DEROY* CHARACTER SEEMS TO HAVE FADED INTO THE *OZONE,* TOO!

EEEEEEEK

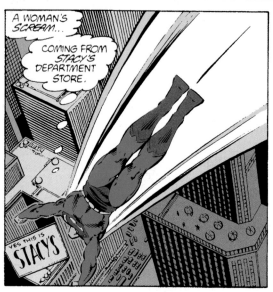

A WOMAN'S *SCREAM...*

COMING FROM *STACY'S* DEPARTMENT STORE.

YES, THIS IS STACY'S

MISS...?

WHAT IS IT? WHAT'S *WRONG?*

TH'... TH'... TH' *WINDOW DISPLAY!!*

I WAS S'POSED TO *CHANGE* THE SETUP T'DAY... BUT... BUT...

10

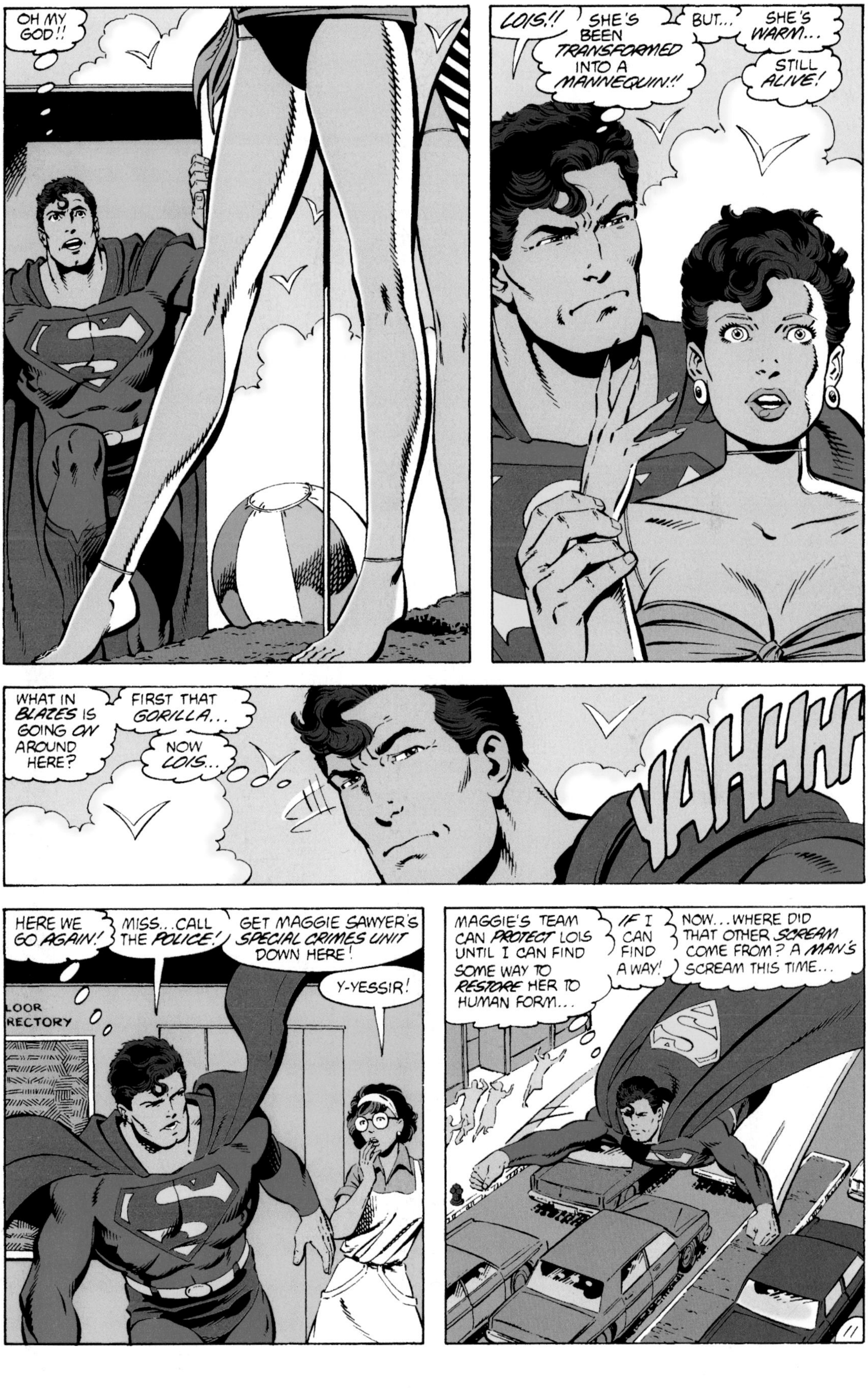
OH MY GOD!!
LOIS!! SHE'S BEEN TRANSFORMED INTO A MANNEQUIN!!
BUT... SHE'S WARM...
STILL ALIVE!
WHAT IN BLAZES IS GOING ON AROUND HERE?
FIRST THAT GORILLA...
NOW LOIS...
YAHHHH
HERE WE GO AGAIN!
MISS...CALL THE POLICE!
GET MAGGIE SAWYER'S SPECIAL CRIMES UNIT DOWN HERE!
Y-YESSIR!
LOOR
RECTORY
MAGGIE'S TEAM CAN PROTECT LOIS UNTIL I CAN FIND SOME WAY TO RESTORE HER TO HUMAN FORM...
IF I CAN FIND A WAY!
NOW...WHERE DID THAT OTHER SCREAM COME FROM? A MAN'S SCREAM THIS TIME...
11

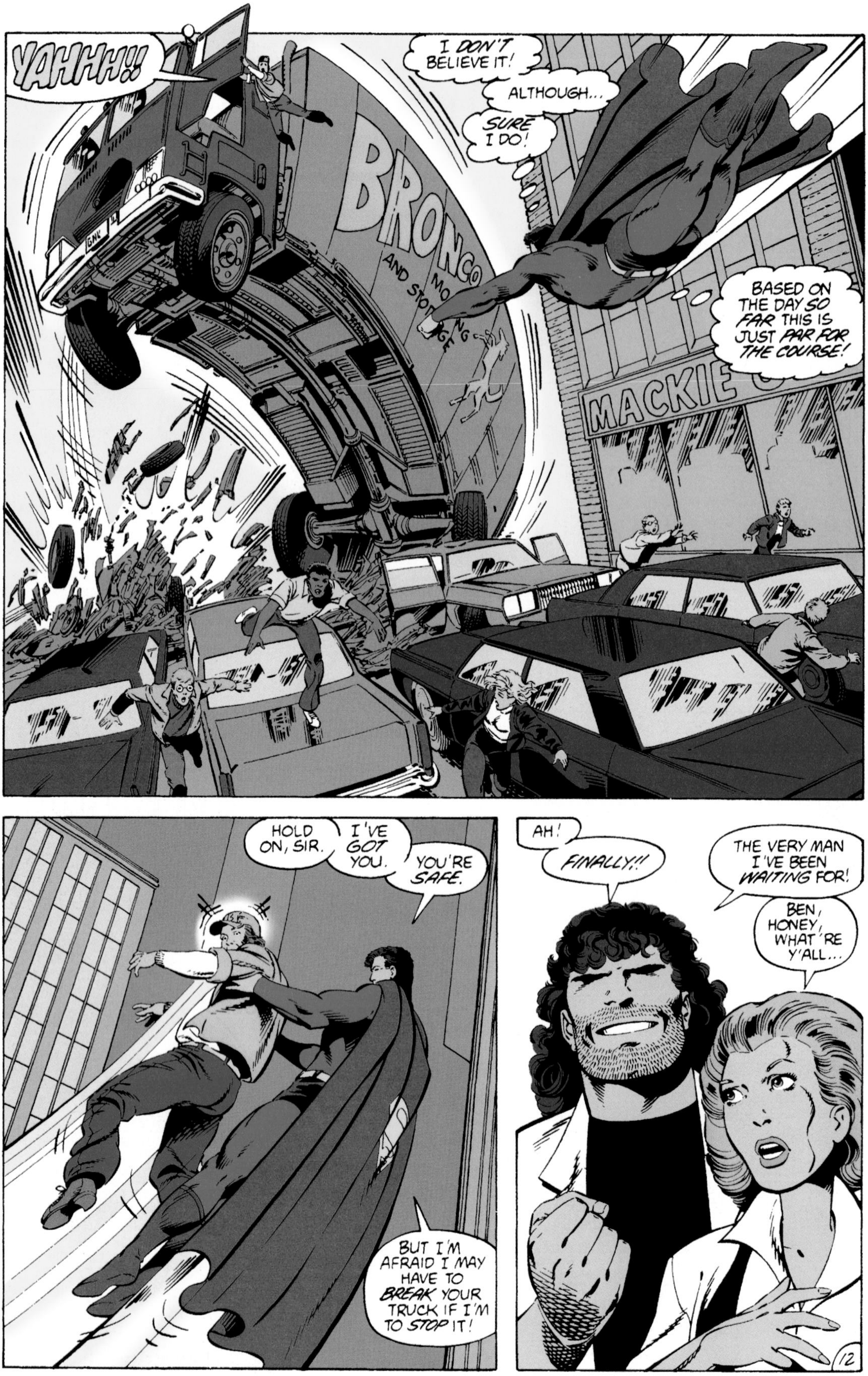
YAHHH!!
I DON'T BELIEVE IT!
ALTHOUGH...
SURE I DO!
BASED ON THE DAY SO FAR THIS IS JUST PAR FOR THE COURSE!
BRONCO MOVING AND STORAGE
MACKIE
HOLD ON, SIR.
I'VE GOT YOU.
YOU'RE SAFE.
BUT I'M AFRAID I MAY HAVE TO BREAK YOUR TRUCK IF I'M TO STOP IT!
AH!
FINALLY!!
THE VERY MAN I'VE BEEN WAITING FOR!
BEN, HONEY, WHAT'RE Y'ALL...
12

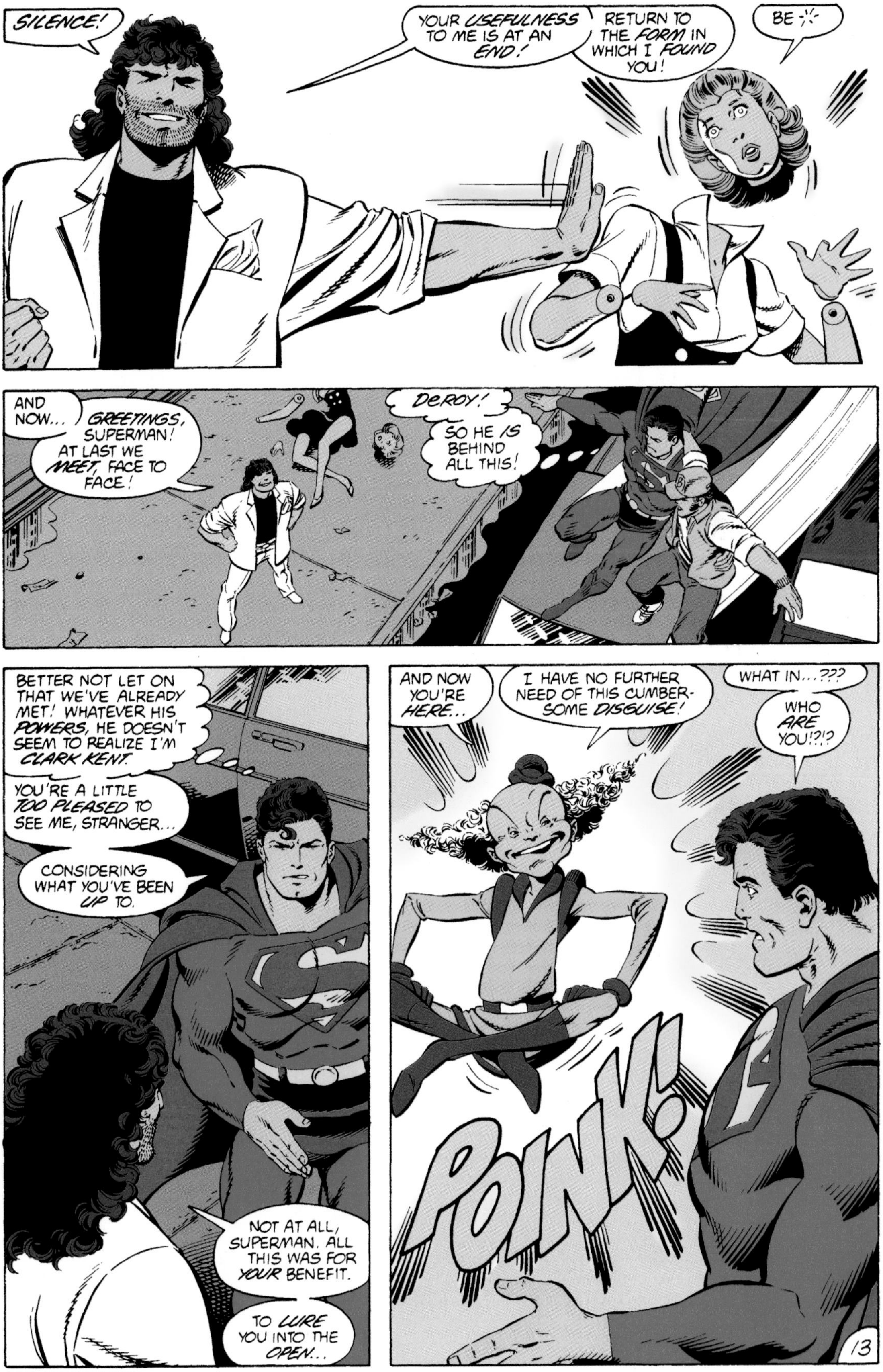
SILENCE!
YOUR USEFULNESS TO ME IS AT AN END!
RETURN TO THE FORM IN WHICH I FOUND YOU!
BE--!
AND NOW... GREETINGS, SUPERMAN! AT LAST WE MEET, FACE TO FACE!
DeROY!
SO HE IS BEHIND ALL THIS!
BETTER NOT LET ON THAT WE'VE ALREADY MET! WHATEVER HIS POWERS, HE DOESN'T SEEM TO REALIZE I'M CLARK KENT.
YOU'RE A LITTLE TOO PLEASED TO SEE ME, STRANGER...
CONSIDERING WHAT YOU'VE BEEN UP TO.
NOT AT ALL, SUPERMAN. ALL THIS WAS FOR YOUR BENEFIT.
TO LURE YOU INTO THE OPEN...
AND NOW YOU'RE HERE...
I HAVE NO FURTHER NEED OF THIS CUMBERSOME DISGUISE!
WHAT IN...???
WHO ARE YOU!?!?
POINK!
13

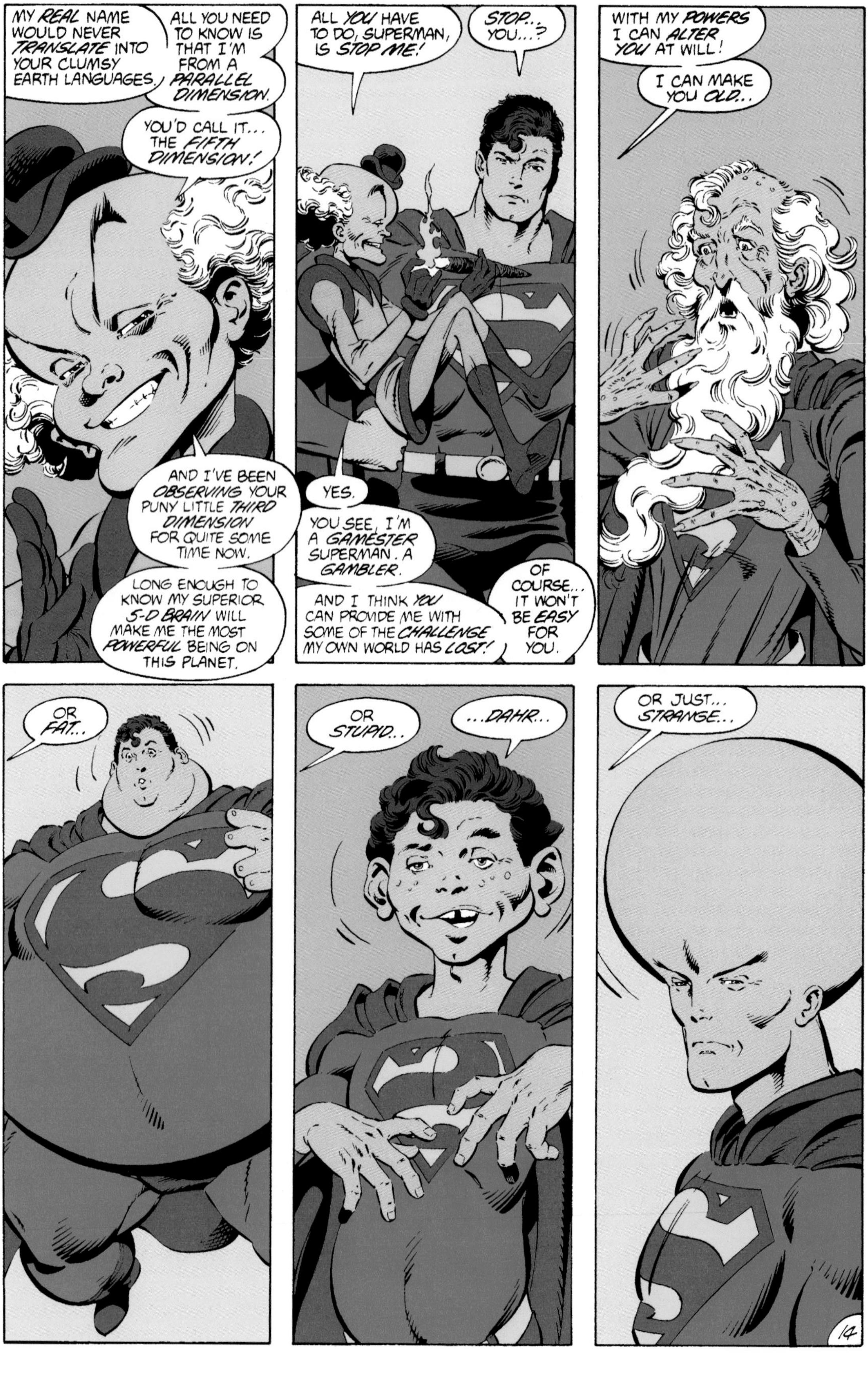
MY REAL NAME WOULD NEVER TRANSLATE INTO YOUR CLUMSY EARTH LANGUAGES.
ALL YOU NEED TO KNOW IS THAT I'M FROM A PARALLEL DIMENSION.
YOU'D CALL IT... THE FIFTH DIMENSION!
AND I'VE BEEN OBSERVING YOUR PUNY LITTLE THIRD DIMENSION FOR QUITE SOME TIME NOW.
LONG ENOUGH TO KNOW MY SUPERIOR 5-D BRAIN WILL MAKE ME THE MOST POWERFUL BEING ON THIS PLANET.
ALL YOU HAVE TO DO, SUPERMAN, IS STOP ME!
STOP... YOU...?
YES.
YOU SEE, I'M A GAMESTER SUPERMAN. A GAMBLER.
AND I THINK YOU CAN PROVIDE ME WITH SOME OF THE CHALLENGE MY OWN WORLD HAS LOST!
OF COURSE... IT WON'T BE EASY FOR YOU.
WITH MY POWERS I CAN ALTER YOU AT WILL!
I CAN MAKE YOU OLD...
OR FAT...
OR STUPID...
...DAHR...
OR JUST... STRANGE...
14

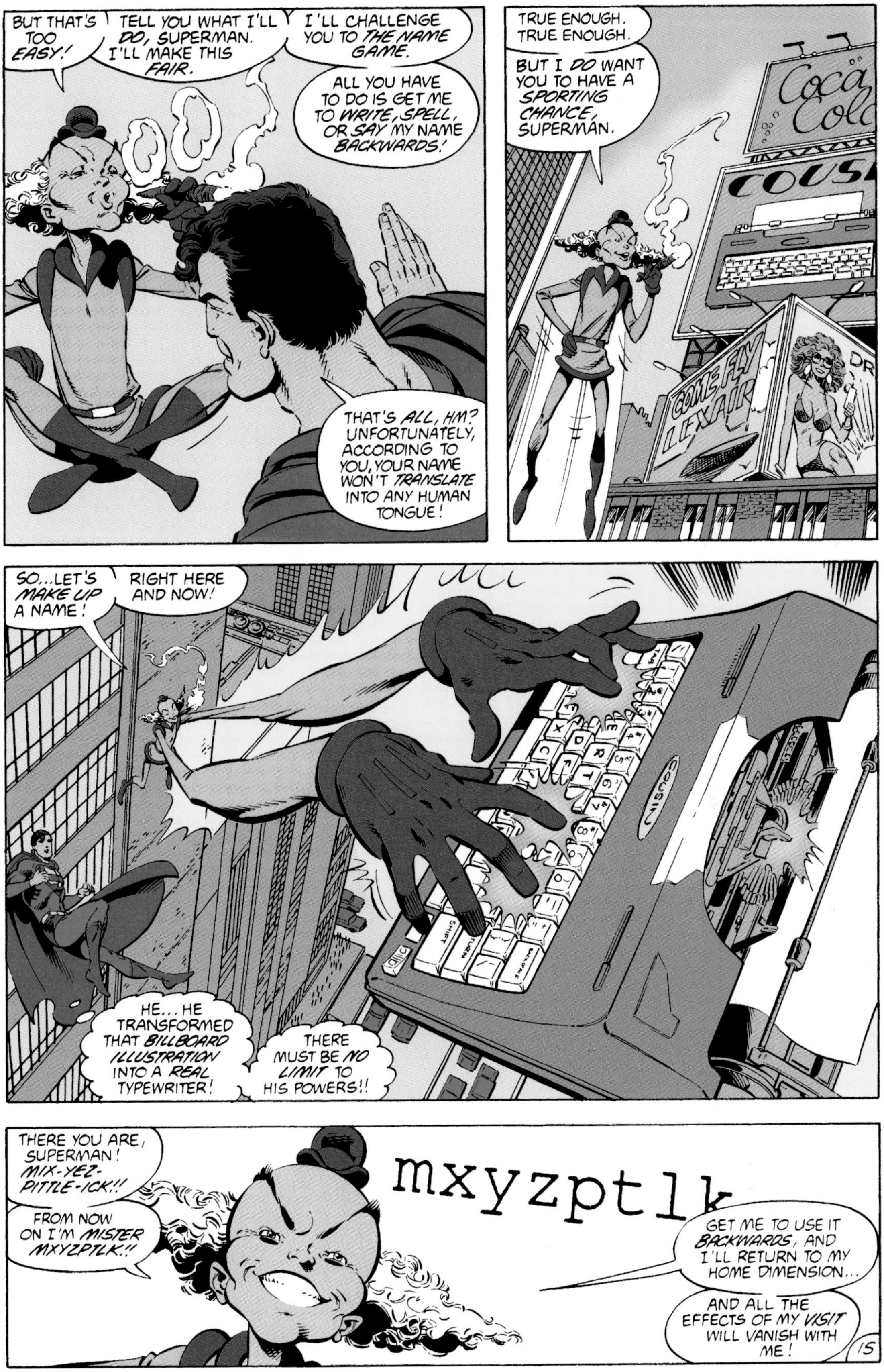

BUT THAT'S TOO EASY!
TELL YOU WHAT I'LL DO, SUPERMAN. I'LL MAKE THIS FAIR.
I'LL CHALLENGE YOU TO THE NAME GAME.
ALL YOU HAVE TO DO IS GET ME TO WRITE, SPELL, OR SAY MY NAME BACKWARDS!
THAT'S ALL, HM? UNFORTUNATELY, ACCORDING TO YOU, YOUR NAME WON'T TRANSLATE INTO ANY HUMAN TONGUE!
TRUE ENOUGH. TRUE ENOUGH.
BUT I DO WANT YOU TO HAVE A SPORTING CHANCE, SUPERMAN.
Coca Cola
COME FLY LEXAIR
SO...LET'S MAKE UP A NAME!
RIGHT HERE AND NOW!
HE... HE TRANSFORMED THAT BILLBOARD ILLUSTRATION INTO A REAL TYPEWRITER!
THERE MUST BE NO LIMIT TO HIS POWERS!!
THERE YOU ARE, SUPERMAN! MIX-YEZ-PITTLE-ICK!!
FROM NOW ON I'M MISTER MXYZPTLK!!
mxyzptlk
GET ME TO USE IT BACKWARDS, AND I'LL RETURN TO MY HOME DIMENSION...
AND ALL THE EFFECTS OF MY VISIT WILL VANISH WITH ME!
15

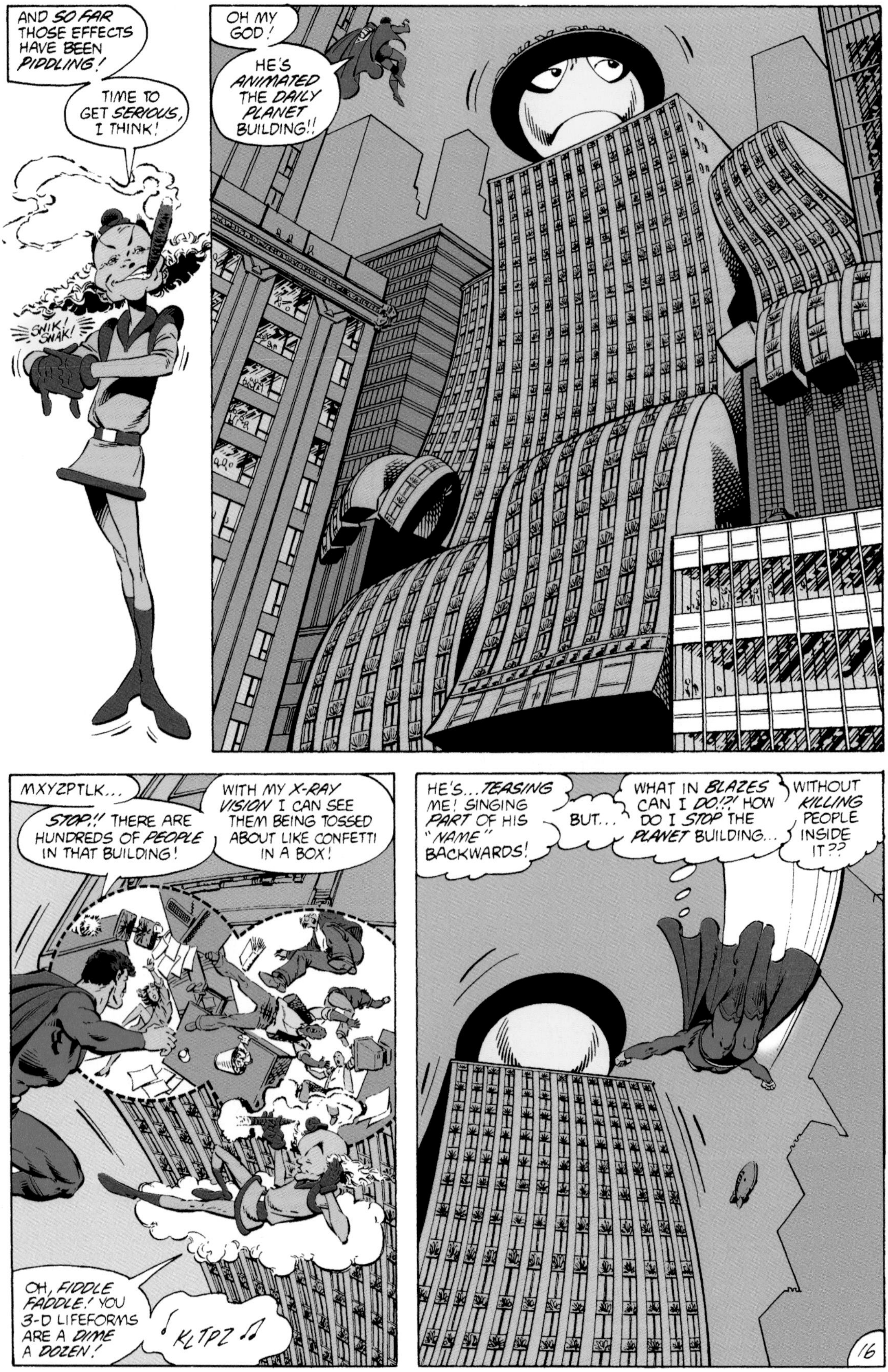
AND SO FAR THOSE EFFECTS HAVE BEEN PIDDLING!
TIME TO GET SERIOUS, I THINK!
SNIK! SNAK!
OH MY GOD!
HE'S ANIMATED THE DAILY PLANET BUILDING!!
MXYZPTLK...
STOP!! THERE ARE HUNDREDS OF PEOPLE IN THAT BUILDING!
WITH MY X-RAY VISION I CAN SEE THEM BEING TOSSED ABOUT LIKE CONFETTI IN A BOX!
OH, FIDDLE FADDLE! YOU 3-D LIFEFORMS ARE A DIME A DOZEN!
KLTPZ
HE'S...TEASING ME! SINGING PART OF HIS "NAME" BACKWARDS!
BUT...
WHAT IN BLAZES CAN I DO!?! HOW DO I STOP THE PLANET BUILDING...
WITHOUT KILLING PEOPLE INSIDE IT??
16

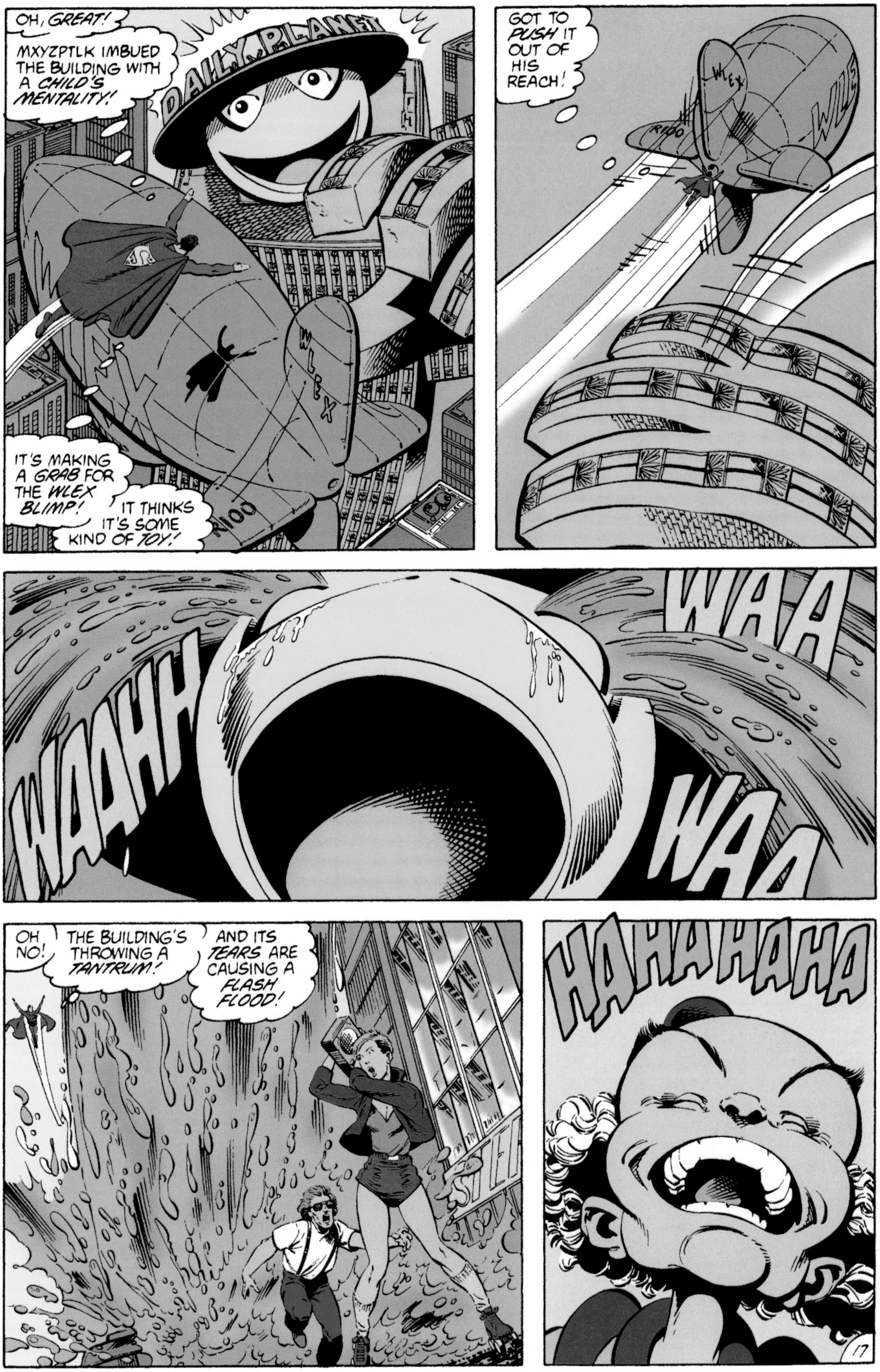

OH, GREAT!
MXYZPTLK IMBUED THE BUILDING WITH A CHILD'S MENTALITY!
DAILY PLANET
IT'S MAKING A GRAB FOR THE WLEX BLIMP!
IT THINKS IT'S SOME KIND OF TOY!
WLEX
R100
GOT TO PUSH IT OUT OF HIS REACH!
WAAHH
WAA
WAA
OH NO!
THE BUILDING'S THROWING A TANTRUM!
AND ITS TEARS ARE CAUSING A FLASH FLOOD!
HAHAHAHAHA
17

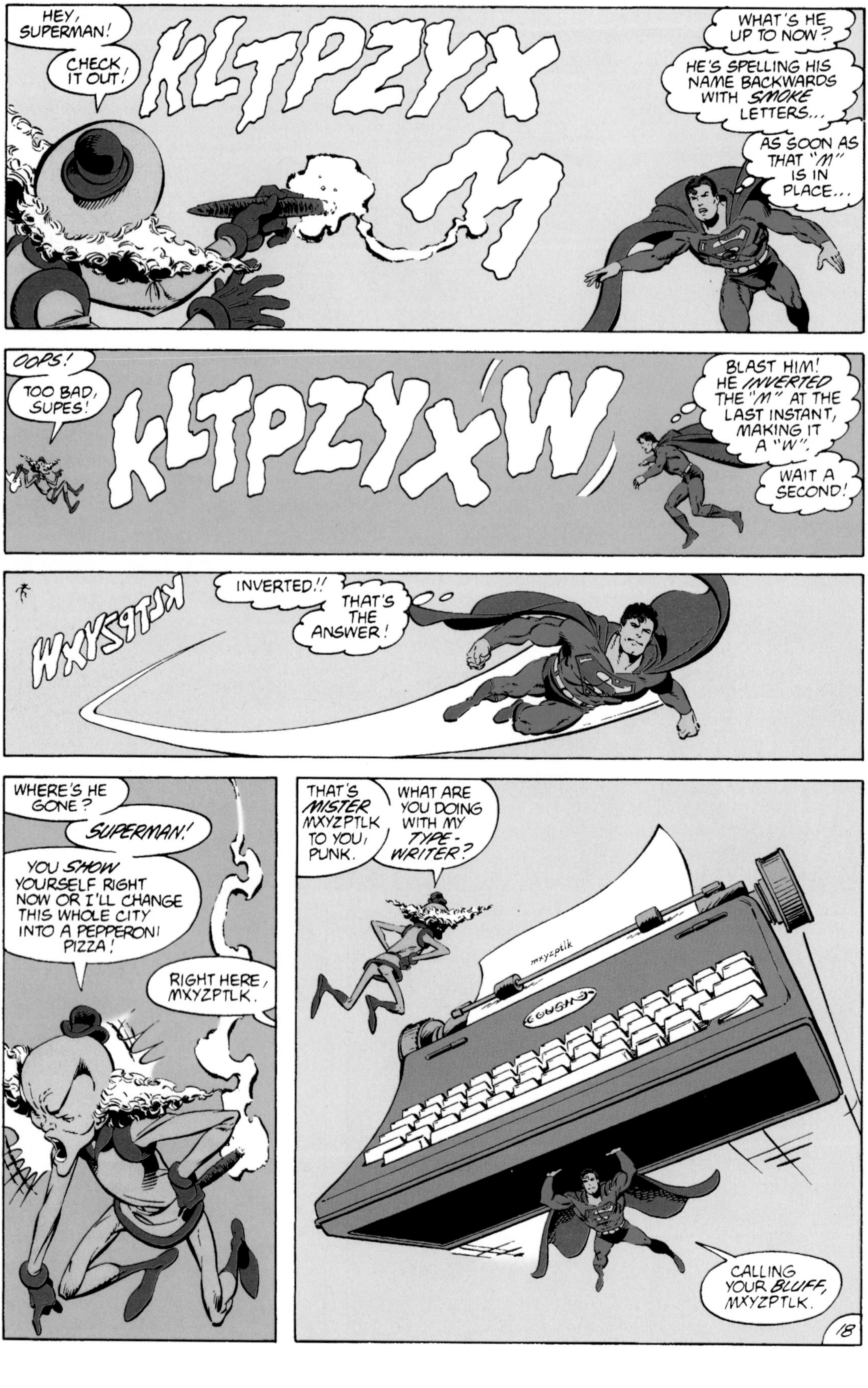
HEY, SUPERMAN!
CHECK IT OUT!
KLTPZYX
M
WHAT'S HE UP TO NOW?
HE'S SPELLING HIS NAME BACKWARDS WITH SMOKE LETTERS...
AS SOON AS THAT "M" IS IN PLACE...
OOPS!
TOO BAD, SUPES!
KLTPZYXW
BLAST HIM! HE INVERTED THE "M" AT THE LAST INSTANT, MAKING IT A "W".
WAIT A SECOND!
INVERTED!!
THAT'S THE ANSWER!
WHERE'S HE GONE?
SUPERMAN!
YOU SHOW YOURSELF RIGHT NOW OR I'LL CHANGE THIS WHOLE CITY INTO A PEPPERONI PIZZA!
RIGHT HERE, MXYZPTLK.
THAT'S MISTER MXYZPTLK TO YOU, PUNK.
WHAT ARE YOU DOING WITH MY TYPE-WRITER?
mxyzptlk
CALLING YOUR BLUFF, MXYZPTLK.
18

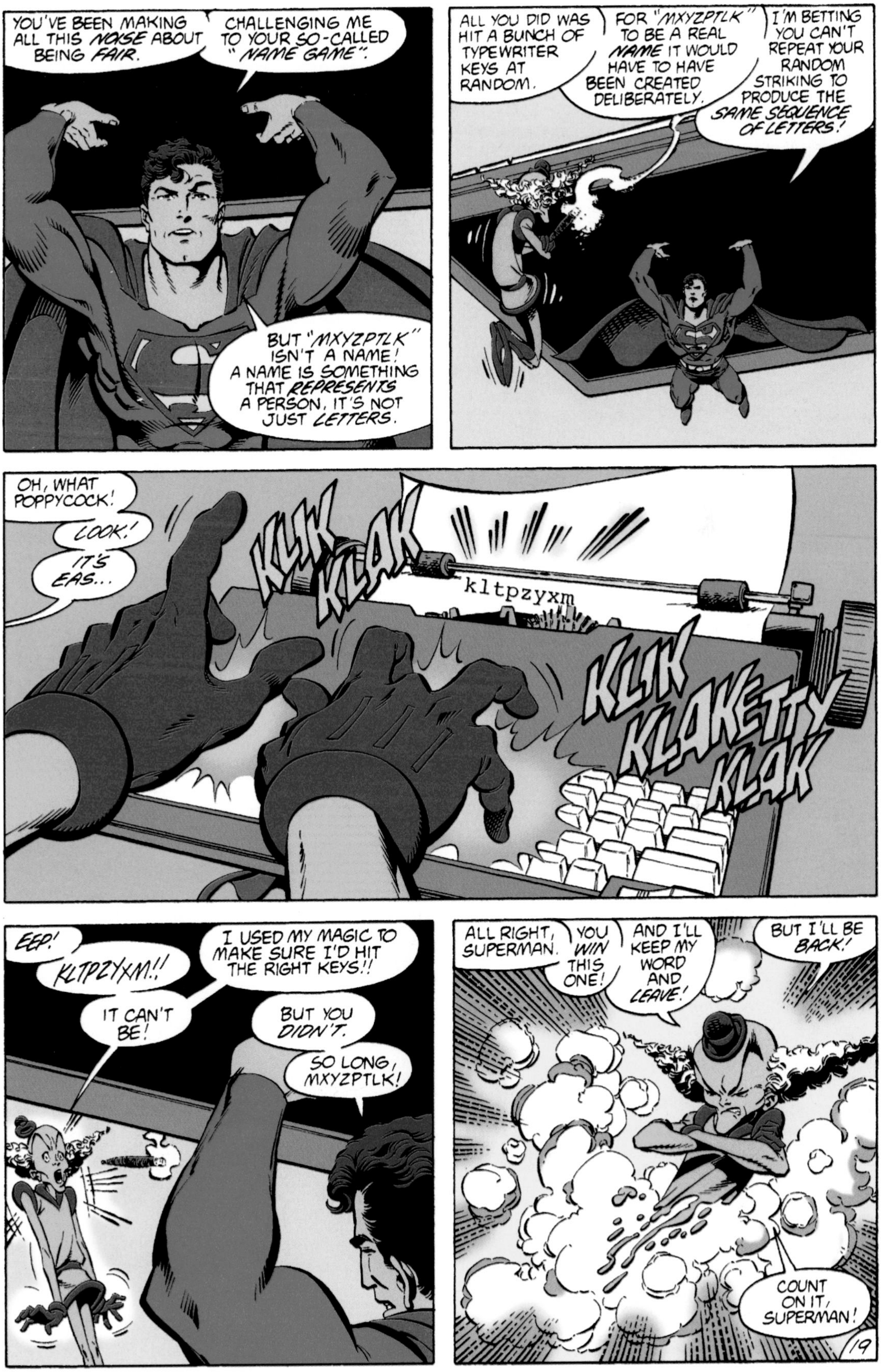
YOU'VE BEEN MAKING ALL THIS NOISE ABOUT BEING FAIR.
CHALLENGING ME TO YOUR SO-CALLED "NAME GAME".
BUT "MXYZPTLK" ISN'T A NAME! A NAME IS SOMETHING THAT REPRESENTS A PERSON, IT'S NOT JUST LETTERS.
ALL YOU DID WAS HIT A BUNCH OF TYPEWRITER KEYS AT RANDOM.
FOR "MXYZPTLK" TO BE A REAL NAME IT WOULD HAVE TO HAVE BEEN CREATED DELIBERATELY.
I'M BETTING YOU CAN'T REPEAT YOUR RANDOM STRIKING TO PRODUCE THE SAME SEQUENCE OF LETTERS!
OH, WHAT POPPYCOCK!
LOOK!
IT'S EAS...
KLIK KLAK
kltpzyxm
KLIK KLAKETTY KLAK
EEP!
KLTPZYXM!!
I USED MY MAGIC TO MAKE SURE I'D HIT THE RIGHT KEYS!!
IT CAN'T BE!
BUT YOU DIDN'T.
SO LONG, MXYZPTLK!
ALL RIGHT, SUPERMAN.
YOU WIN THIS ONE!
AND I'LL KEEP MY WORD AND LEAVE!
BUT I'LL BE BACK!
COUNT ON IT, SUPERMAN!
19

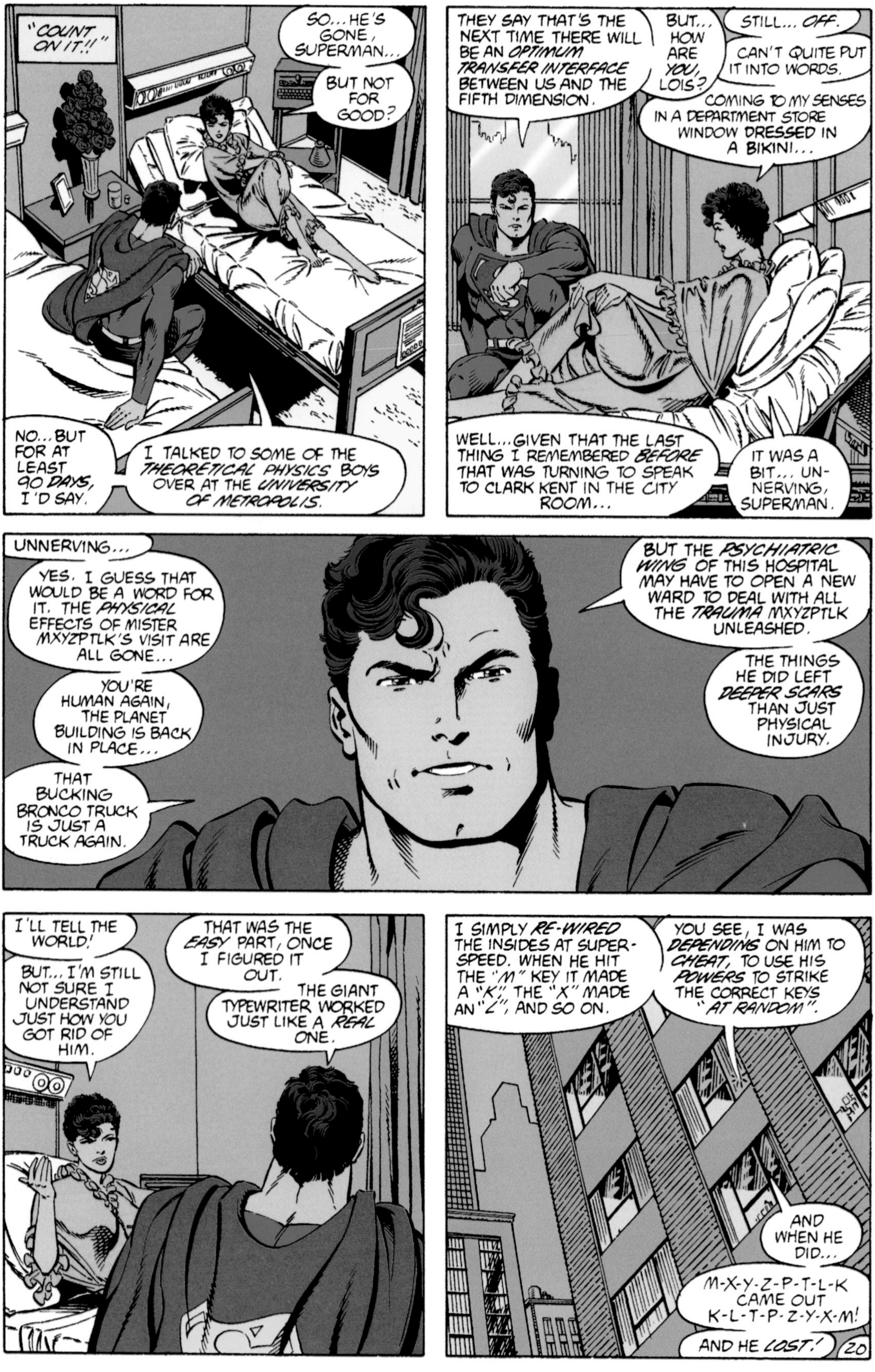
"COUNT ON IT!!"
SO... HE'S GONE, SUPERMAN...
BUT NOT FOR GOOD?
NO... BUT FOR AT LEAST 90 DAYS, I'D SAY.
I TALKED TO SOME OF THE THEORETICAL PHYSICS BOYS OVER AT THE UNIVERSITY OF METROPOLIS.
THEY SAY THAT'S THE NEXT TIME THERE WILL BE AN OPTIMUM TRANSFER INTERFACE BETWEEN US AND THE FIFTH DIMENSION.
BUT... HOW ARE YOU, LOIS?
STILL... OFF.
CAN'T QUITE PUT IT INTO WORDS.
COMING TO MY SENSES IN A DEPARTMENT STORE WINDOW DRESSED IN A BIKINI...
WELL... GIVEN THAT THE LAST THING I REMEMBERED BEFORE THAT WAS TURNING TO SPEAK TO CLARK KENT IN THE CITY ROOM...
IT WAS A BIT... UN-NERVING, SUPERMAN.
UNNERVING...
YES. I GUESS THAT WOULD BE A WORD FOR IT. THE PHYSICAL EFFECTS OF MISTER MXYZPTLK'S VISIT ARE ALL GONE...
YOU'RE HUMAN AGAIN, THE PLANET BUILDING IS BACK IN PLACE...
THAT BUCKING BRONCO TRUCK IS JUST A TRUCK AGAIN.
BUT THE PSYCHIATRIC WING OF THIS HOSPITAL MAY HAVE TO OPEN A NEW WARD TO DEAL WITH ALL THE TRAUMA MXYZPTLK UNLEASHED.
THE THINGS HE DID LEFT DEEPER SCARS THAN JUST PHYSICAL INJURY.
I'LL TELL THE WORLD!
BUT... I'M STILL NOT SURE I UNDERSTAND JUST HOW YOU GOT RID OF HIM.
THAT WAS THE EASY PART, ONCE I FIGURED IT OUT.
THE GIANT TYPEWRITER WORKED JUST LIKE A REAL ONE.
I SIMPLY RE-WIRED THE INSIDES AT SUPER-SPEED. WHEN HE HIT THE "M" KEY IT MADE A "K", THE "X" MADE AN "Z", AND SO ON.
YOU SEE, I WAS DEPENDING ON HIM TO CHEAT, TO USE HIS POWERS TO STRIKE THE CORRECT KEYS "AT RANDOM".
AND WHEN HE DID...
M-X-Y-Z-P-T-L-K CAME OUT K-L-T-P-Z-Y-X-M!
AND HE LOST!
20

$4.25, LADY.

HERE'S A *FIVER.* KEEP THE *CHANGE.*

I SURE HOPE THIS ISN'T A *WASTE OF TIME.*

I'M JUST *ASSUMING* HE'S EVEN *HOME.*

MTA

344 CLINTON

MISS LANE! NICE T'BE SEEIN' YOU AGAIN.

SHALL I BE RINGIN' MR. KENT?

ER...NO THANKS, MR. HARRIGAN.

LET ME *SURPRISE* HIM.

GOOD, HE'S HOME!

NOW ALL I NEED TO WORRY ABOUT IS *WHY* I'M DOING THIS.

I *COULD* TELL MYSELF IT'S BECAUSE THAT *MIXELY-PLIT* CHARACTER CHEATED KENT OUT OF A *LUNCH*...

BUT THAT'S NOT *QUITE* AN EXPLANATION OF WHY I'D GET IT INTO MY HEAD TO COME OVER HERE AND COOK HIM *DINNER.*

APARTMENTS A TO G

3B

COULD IT BE AFTER ALL THESE YEARS HE'S FINALLY *GETTING TO ME* WITH HIS *WORLD'S SEXIEST BOY SCOUT* ROUTINE?

BZZZT

PECAN RICE

YES...

...LOIS...?!?

CAT....!?!

WHAT...??

WHY...??

PECAN RICE

21

267

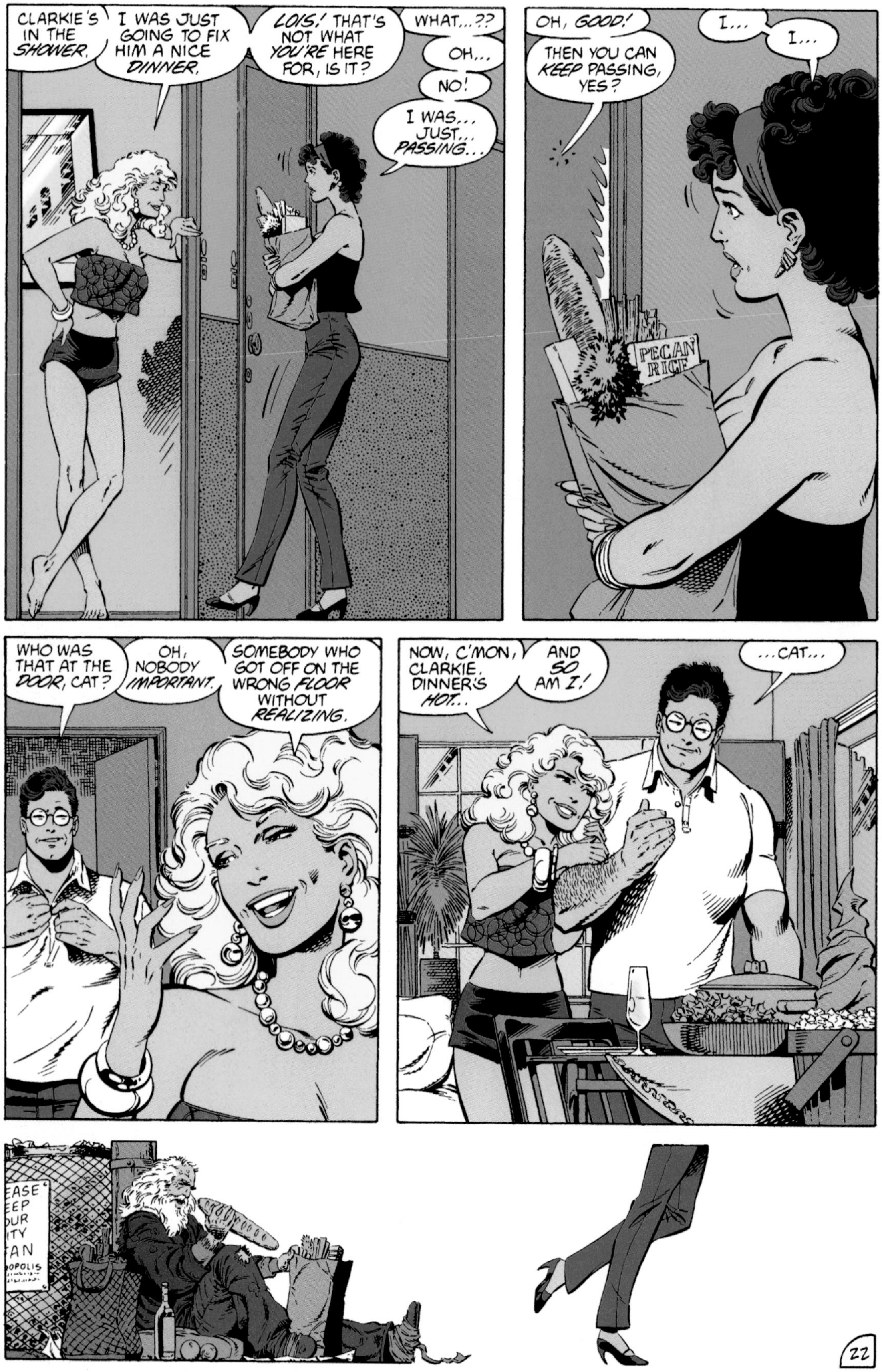
CLARKIE'S IN THE SHOWER.
I WAS JUST GOING TO FIX HIM A NICE DINNER.
LOIS! THAT'S NOT WHAT YOU'RE HERE FOR, IS IT?
WHAT...??
OH...
NO!
I WAS... JUST... PASSING...
OH, GOOD!
THEN YOU CAN KEEP PASSING, YES?
I...
I...
WHO WAS THAT AT THE DOOR, CAT?
OH, NOBODY IMPORTANT.
SOMEBODY WHO GOT OFF ON THE WRONG FLOOR WITHOUT REALIZING.
NOW, C'MON, CLARKIE. DINNER'S HOT...
AND SO AM I!
...CAT...
PECAN RICE
EASE
EEP
UR
ITY
AN
OPOLIS
22

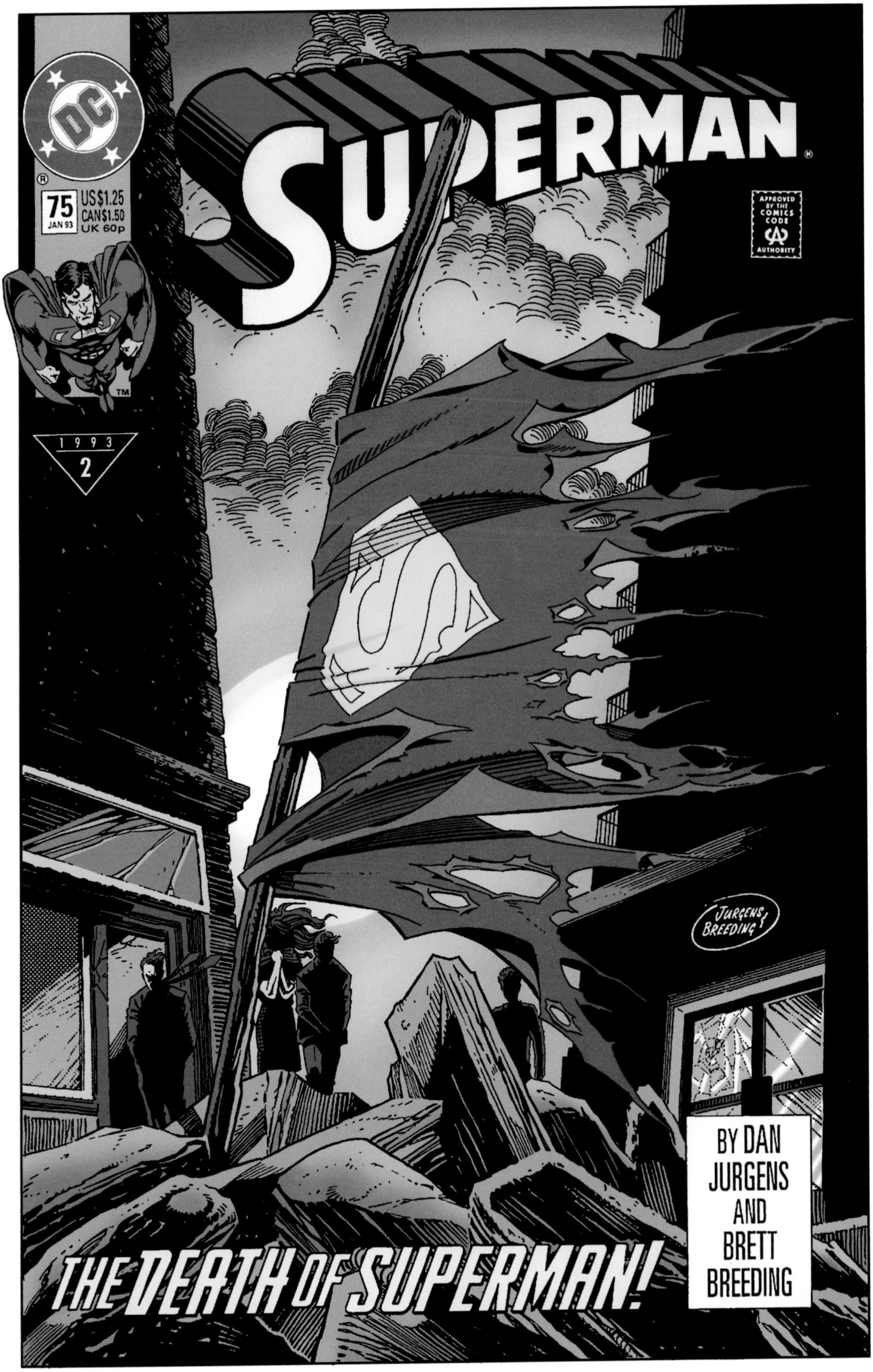
SUPERMAN
75
JAN 93
US$1.25
CAN$1.50
UK 60p
APPROVED BY THE COMICS CODE AUTHORITY
1 9 9 3
2
JURGENS, BREEDING
BY DAN JURGENS AND BRETT BREEDING
THE DEATH OF SUPERMAN!

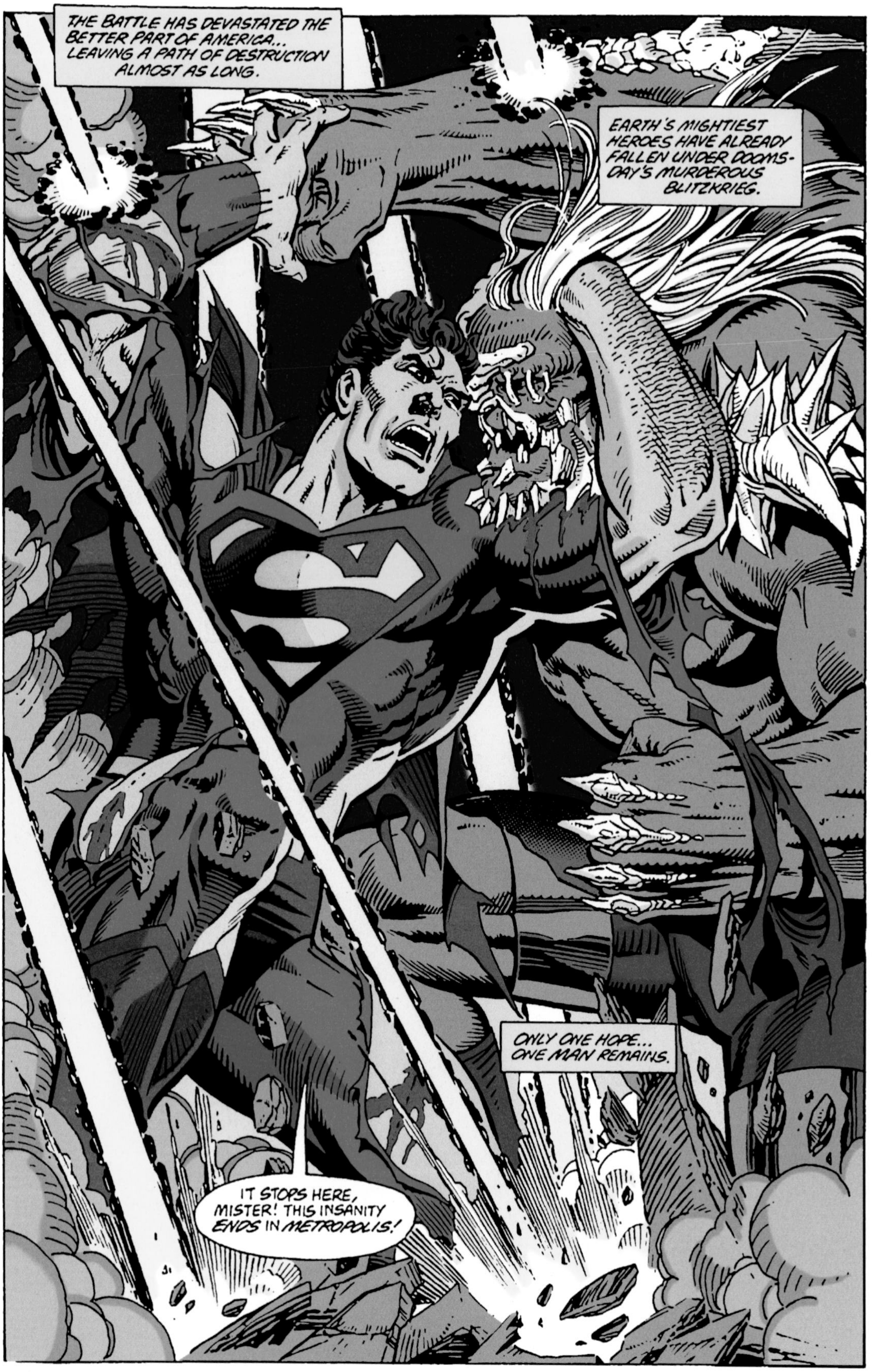
THE BATTLE HAS DEVASTATED THE BETTER PART OF AMERICA... LEAVING A PATH OF DESTRUCTION ALMOST AS LONG.
EARTH'S MIGHTIEST HEROES HAVE ALREADY FALLEN UNDER DOOMSDAY'S MURDEROUS BLITZKRIEG.
ONLY ONE HOPE... ONE MAN REMAINS.
IT STOPS HERE, MISTER! THIS INSANITY ENDS IN METROPOLIS!

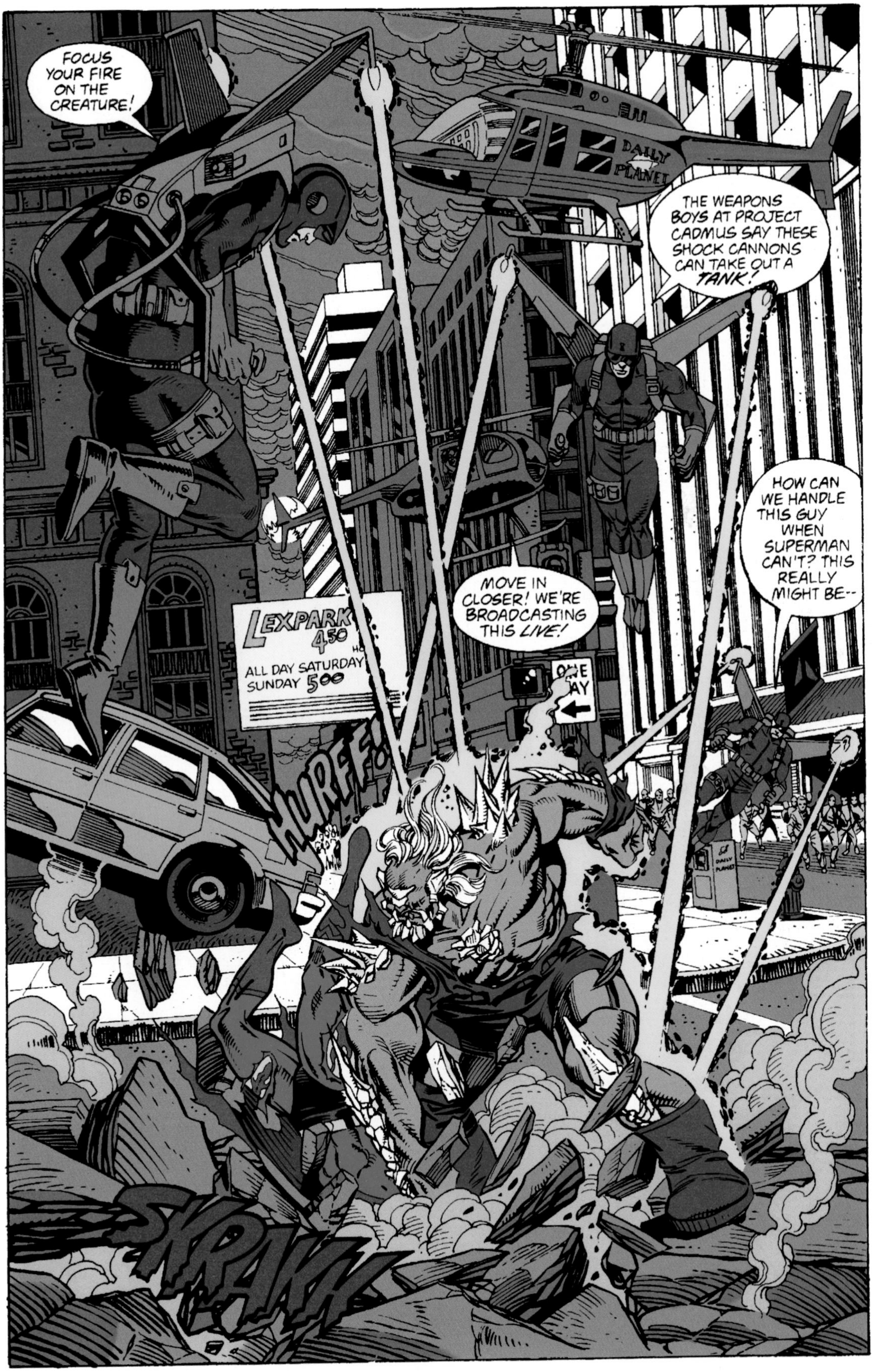
FOCUS YOUR FIRE ON THE CREATURE!
DAILY PLANET
THE WEAPONS BOYS AT PROJECT CADMUS SAY THESE SHOCK CANNONS CAN TAKE OUT A TANK!
HOW CAN WE HANDLE THIS GUY WHEN SUPERMAN CAN'T? THIS REALLY MIGHT BE--
MOVE IN CLOSER! WE'RE BROADCASTING THIS LIVE!
LEXPARK
ALL DAY SATURDAY
SUNDAY
HURFF
SKRAKK

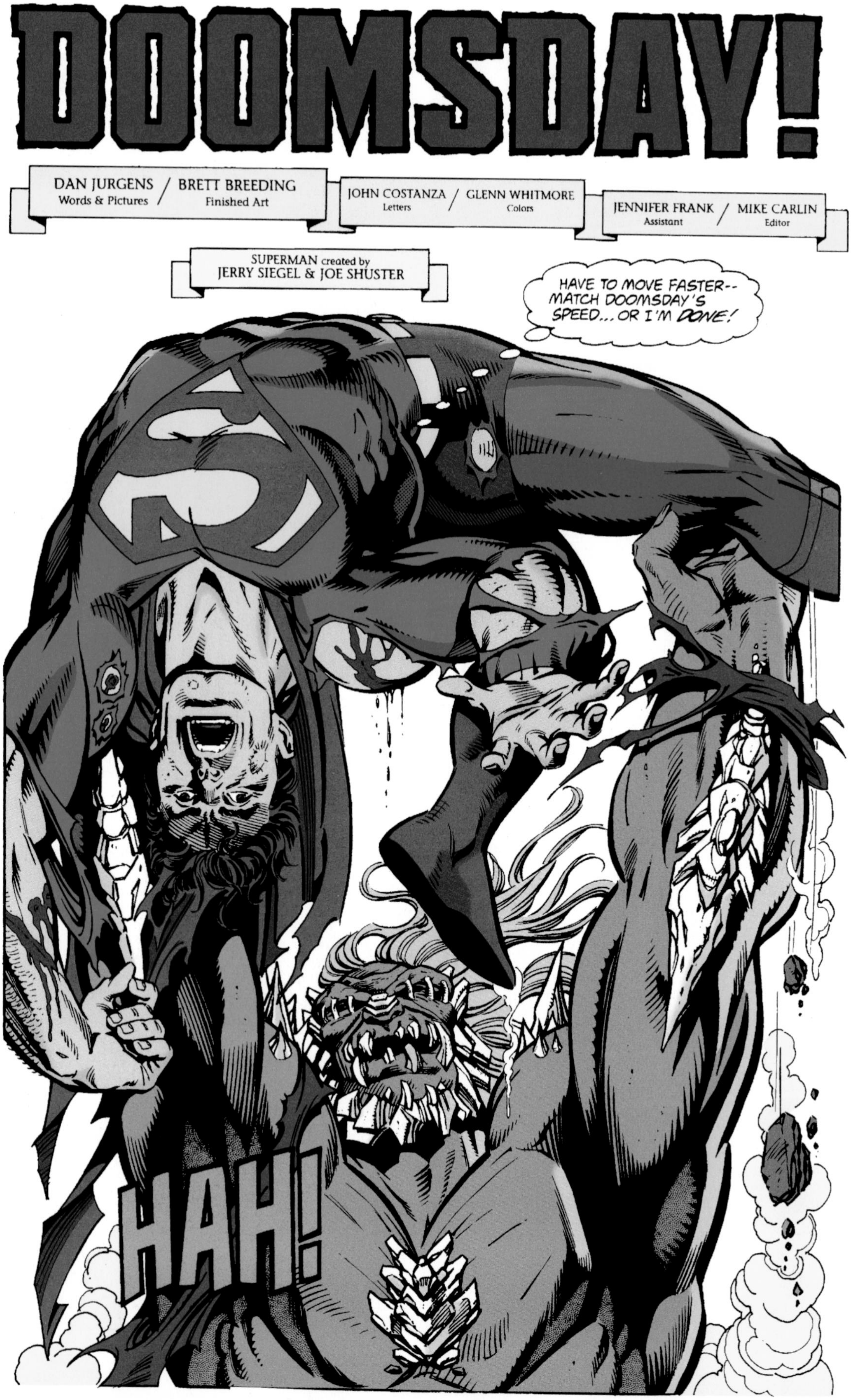
DOOMSDAY!
DAN JURGENS Words & Pictures / BRETT BREEDING Finished Art
JOHN COSTANZA Letters / GLENN WHITMORE Colors
JENNIFER FRANK Assistant / MIKE CARLIN Editor
SUPERMAN created by JERRY SIEGEL & JOE SHUSTER
HAVE TO MOVE FASTER--MATCH DOOMSDAY'S SPEED... OR I'M DONE!
HAH!

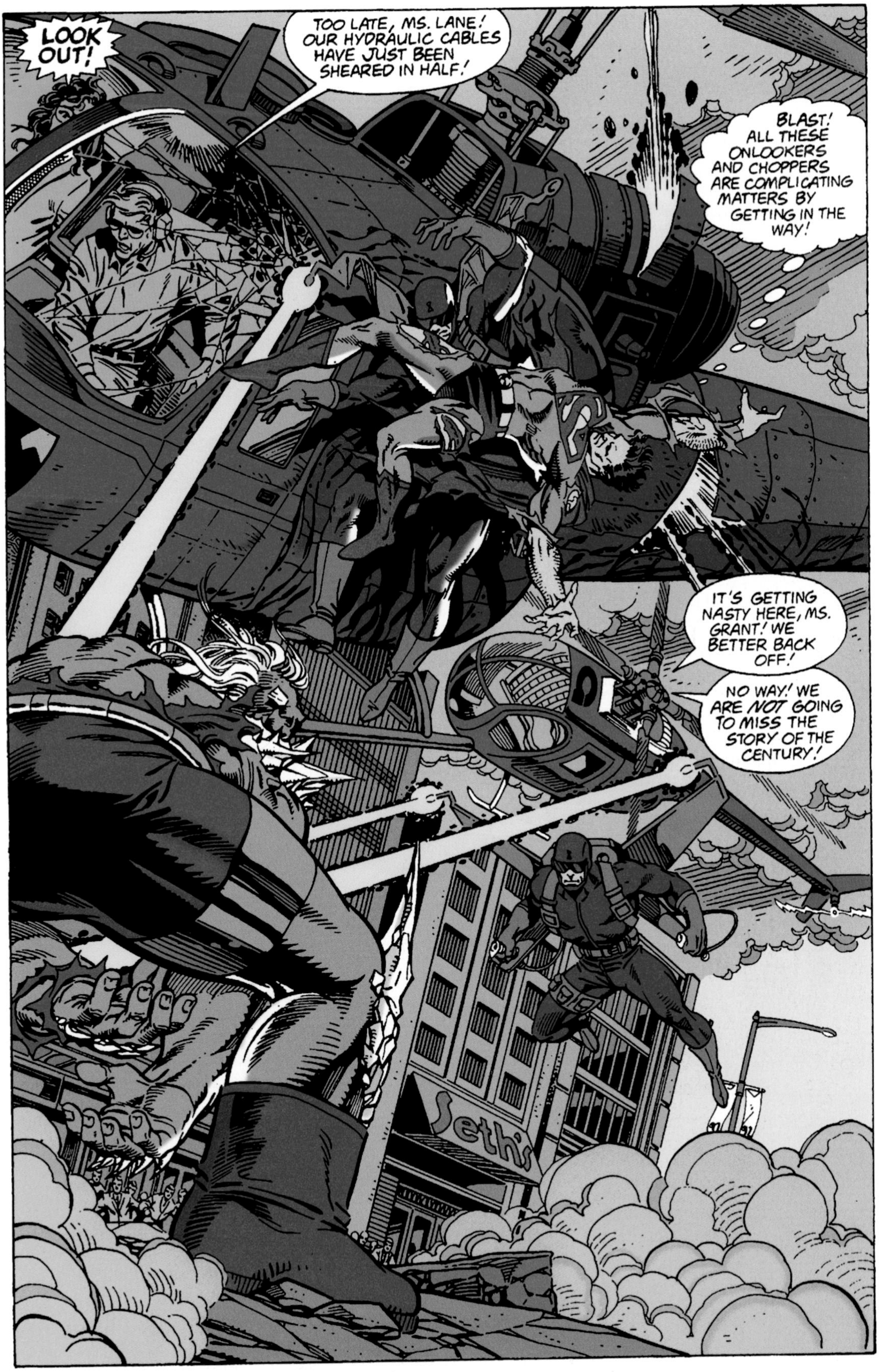
LOOK OUT!
TOO LATE, MS. LANE! OUR HYDRAULIC CABLES HAVE JUST BEEN SHEARED IN HALF!
BLAST! ALL THESE ONLOOKERS AND CHOPPERS ARE COMPLICATING MATTERS BY GETTING IN THE WAY!
IT'S GETTING NASTY HERE, MS. GRANT! WE BETTER BACK OFF!
NO WAY! WE ARE *NOT* GOING TO MISS THE STORY OF THE CENTURY!
Seth's

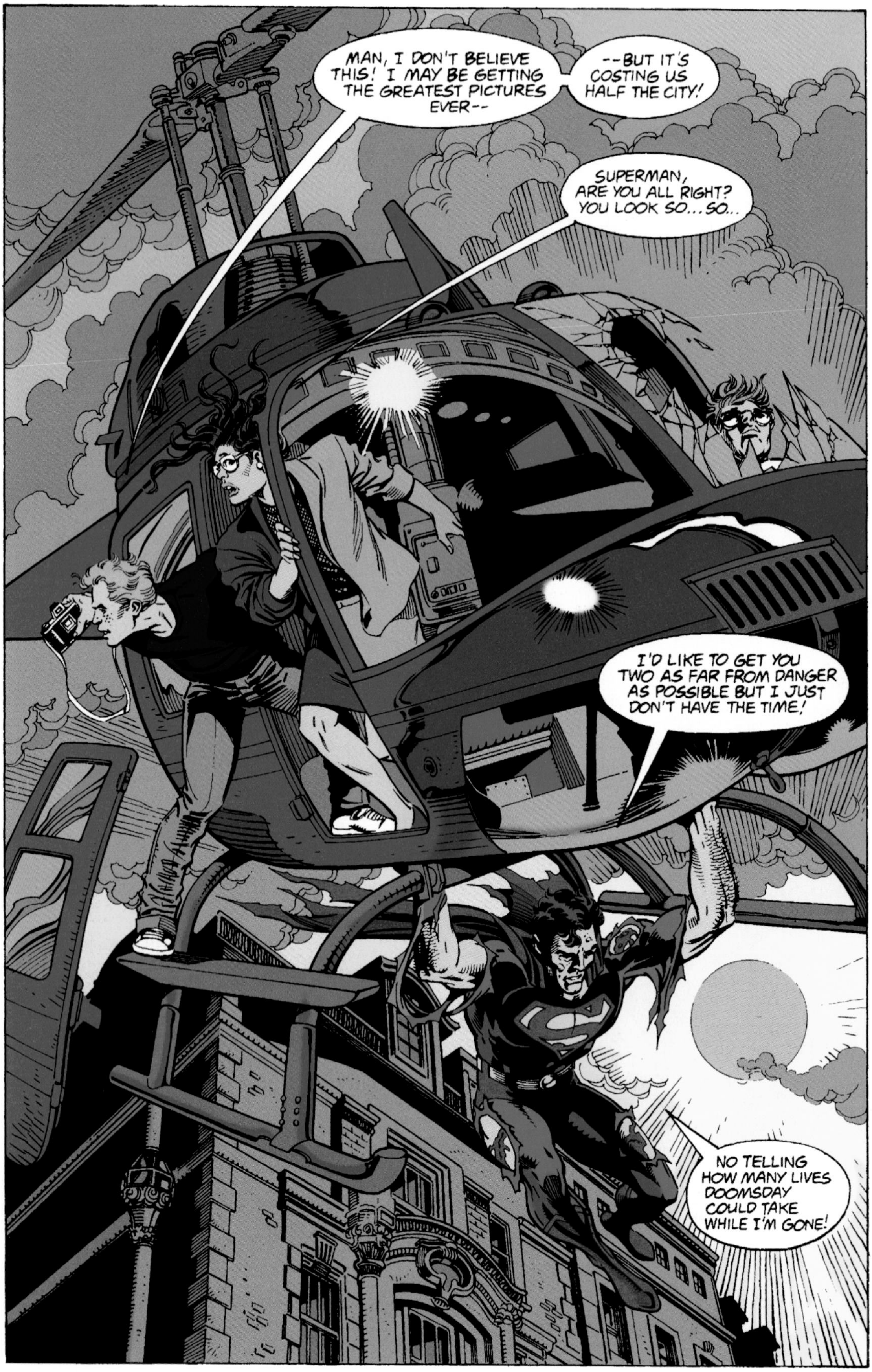
MAN, I DON'T BELIEVE THIS! I MAY BE GETTING THE GREATEST PICTURES EVER--
--BUT IT'S COSTING US HALF THE CITY!
SUPERMAN, ARE YOU ALL RIGHT? YOU LOOK SO... SO...
I'D LIKE TO GET YOU TWO AS FAR FROM DANGER AS POSSIBLE BUT I JUST DON'T HAVE THE TIME!
NO TELLING HOW MANY LIVES DOOMSDAY COULD TAKE WHILE I'M GONE!

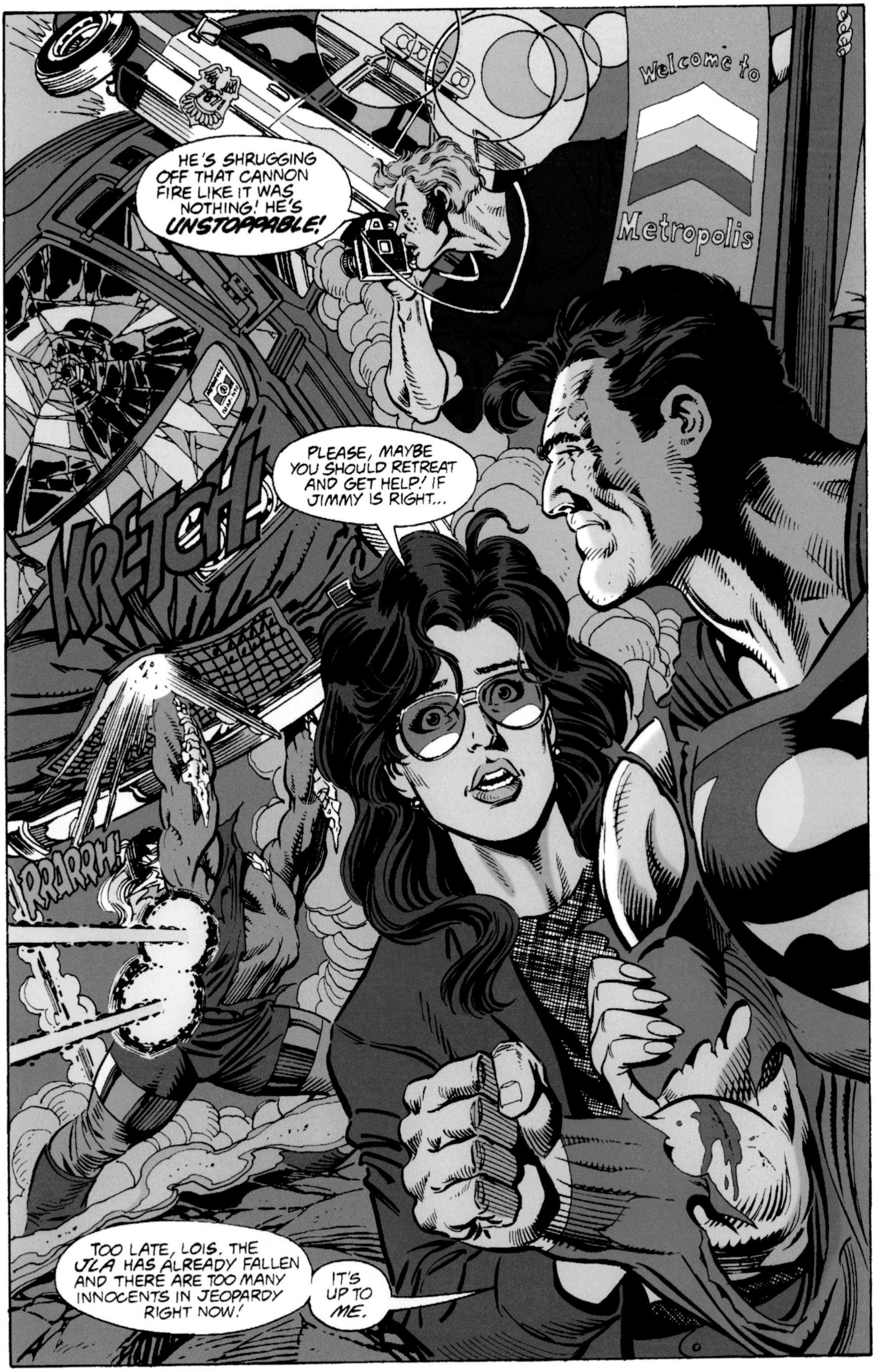
HE'S SHRUGGING OFF THAT CANNON FIRE LIKE IT WAS NOTHING! HE'S UNSTOPPABLE!
Welcome to
Metropolis
PLEASE, MAYBE YOU SHOULD RETREAT AND GET HELP! IF JIMMY IS RIGHT...
KRETCH!
RRARRH!
TOO LATE, LOIS. THE JLA HAS ALREADY FALLEN AND THERE ARE TOO MANY INNOCENTS IN JEOPARDY RIGHT NOW!
IT'S UP TO ME.

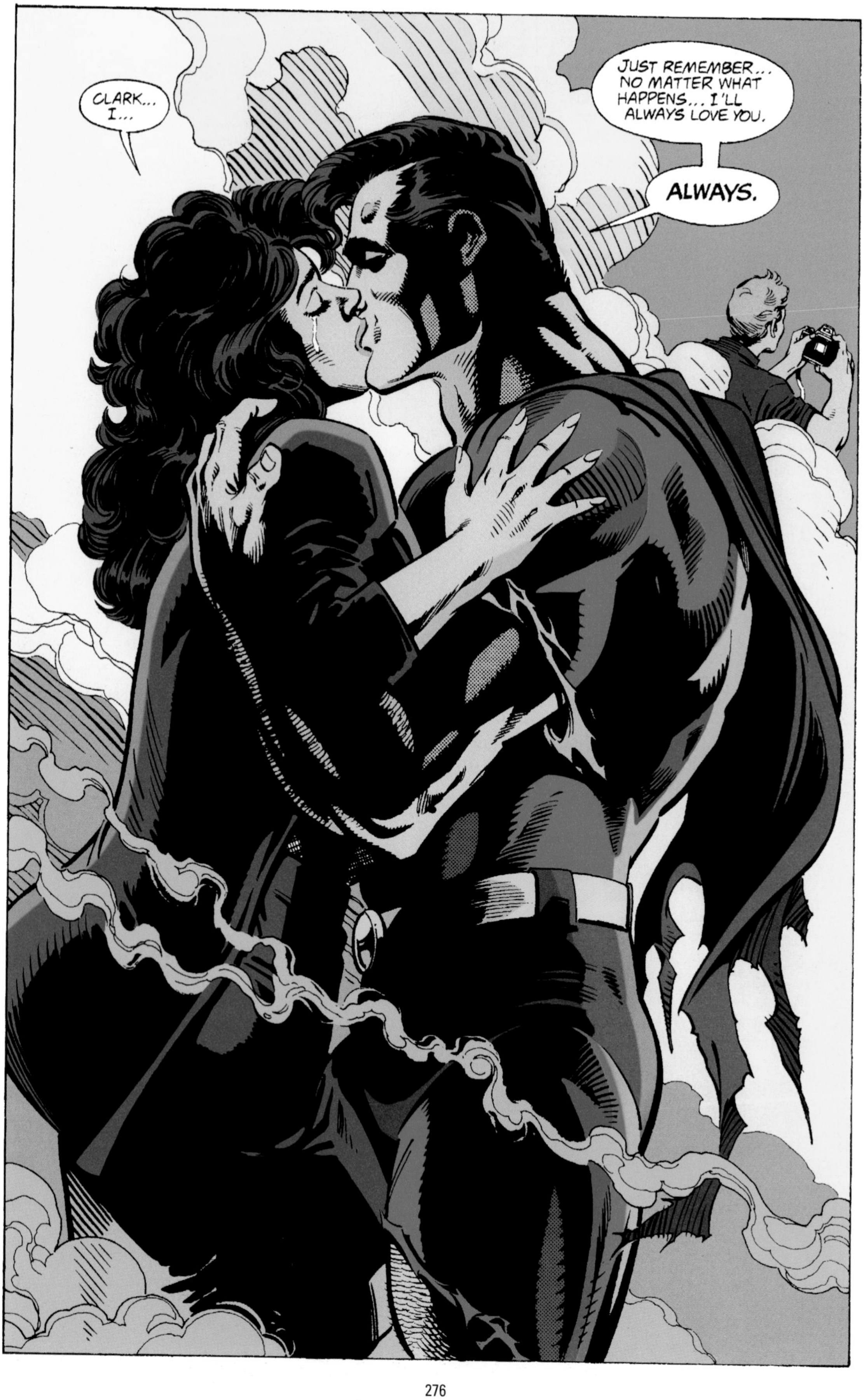
CLARK... I...
JUST REMEMBER... NO MATTER WHAT HAPPENS... I'LL ALWAYS LOVE YOU.
ALWAYS.

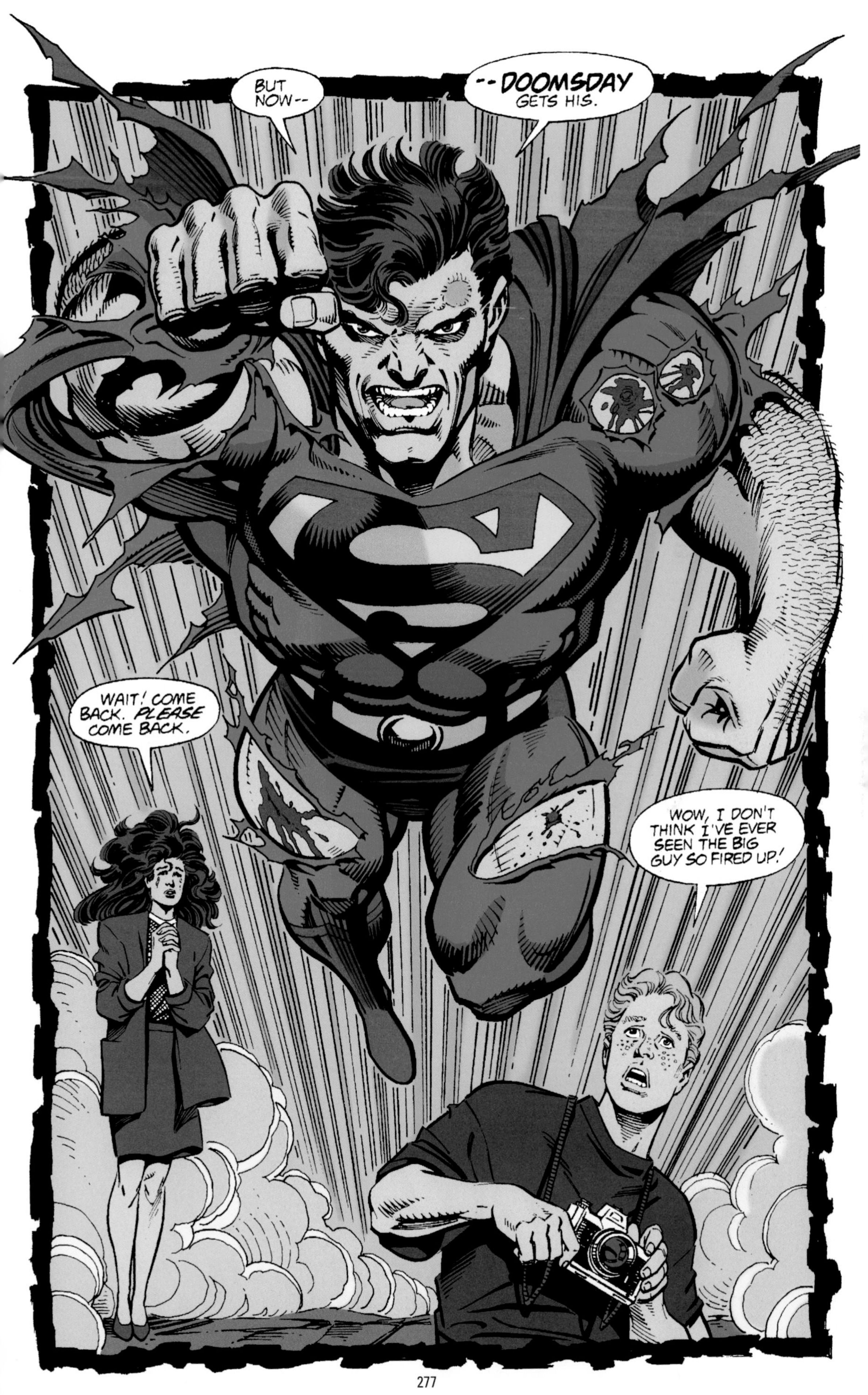
BUT NOW--
--DOOMSDAY GETS HIS.
WAIT! COME BACK. PLEASE COME BACK.
WOW, I DON'T THINK I'VE EVER SEEN THE BIG GUY SO FIRED UP!

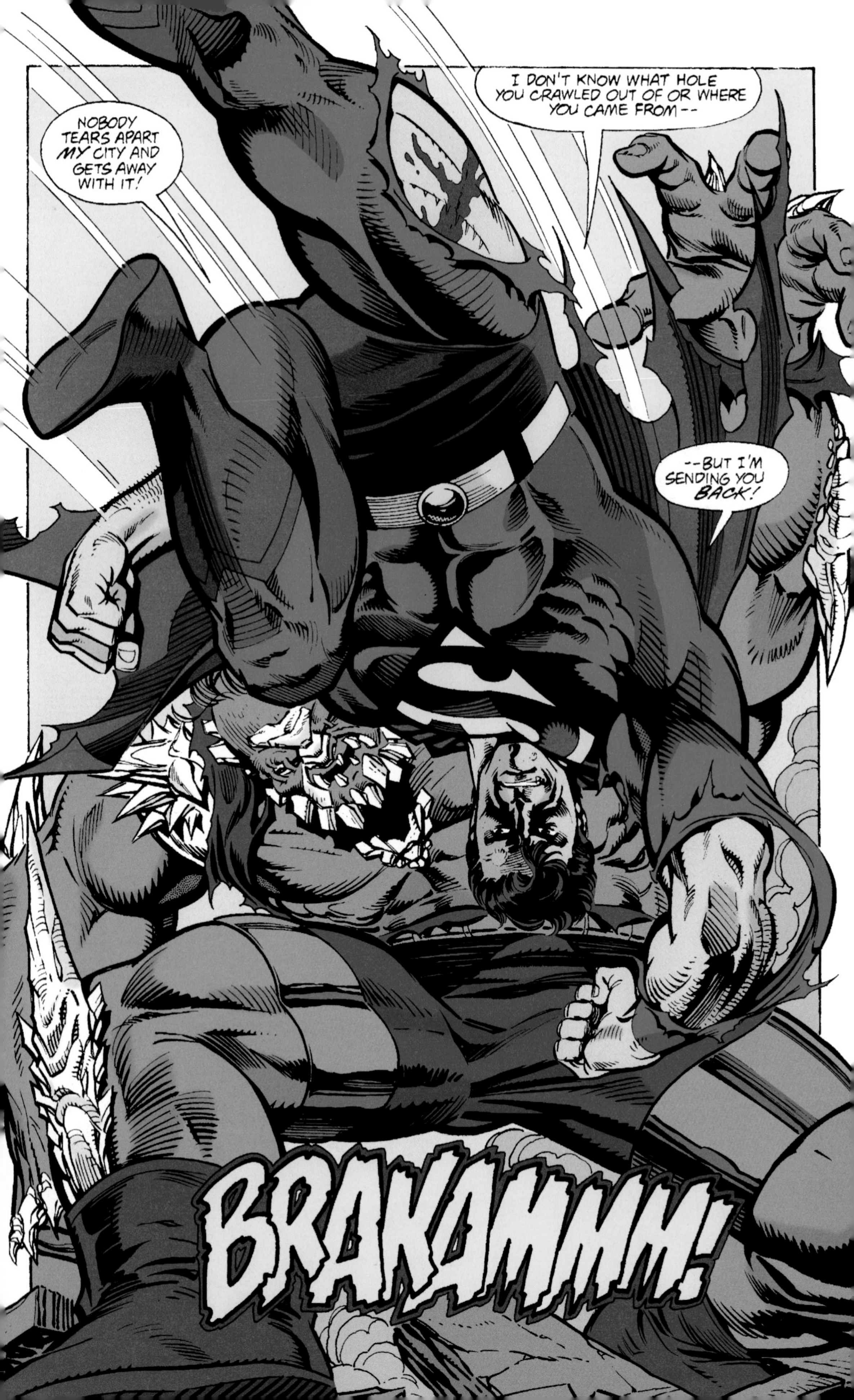
NOBODY TEARS APART MY CITY AND GETS AWAY WITH IT!
I DON'T KNOW WHAT HOLE YOU CRAWLED OUT OF OR WHERE YOU CAME FROM --
--BUT I'M SENDING YOU BACK!
BRAKAMMM!

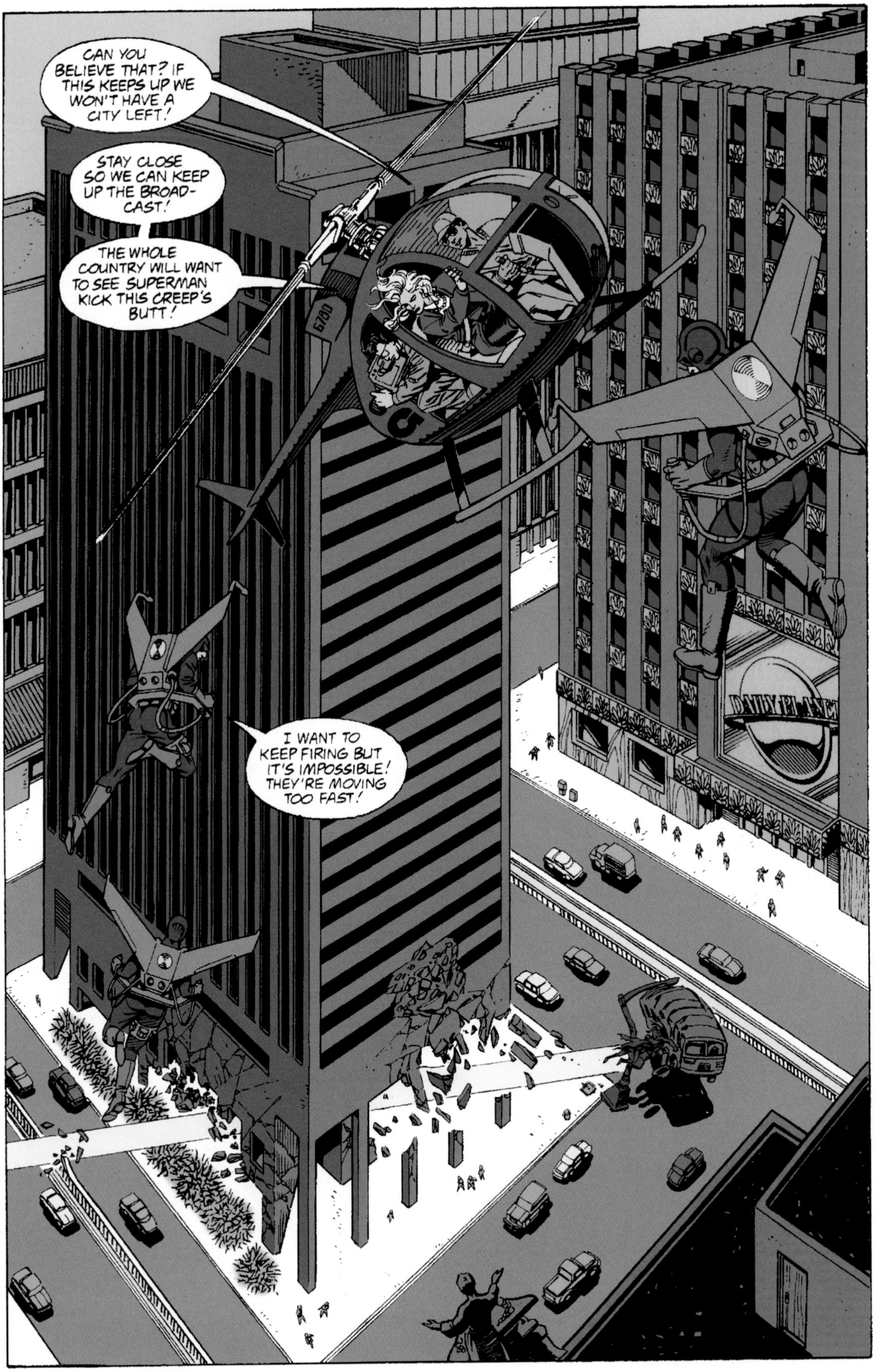
CAN YOU BELIEVE THAT? IF THIS KEEPS UP WE WON'T HAVE A CITY LEFT!
STAY CLOSE SO WE CAN KEEP UP THE BROAD-CAST!
THE WHOLE COUNTRY WILL WANT TO SEE SUPERMAN KICK THIS CREEP'S BUTT!
I WANT TO KEEP FIRING BUT IT'S IMPOSSIBLE! THEY'RE MOVING TOO FAST!
DAILY PLANET

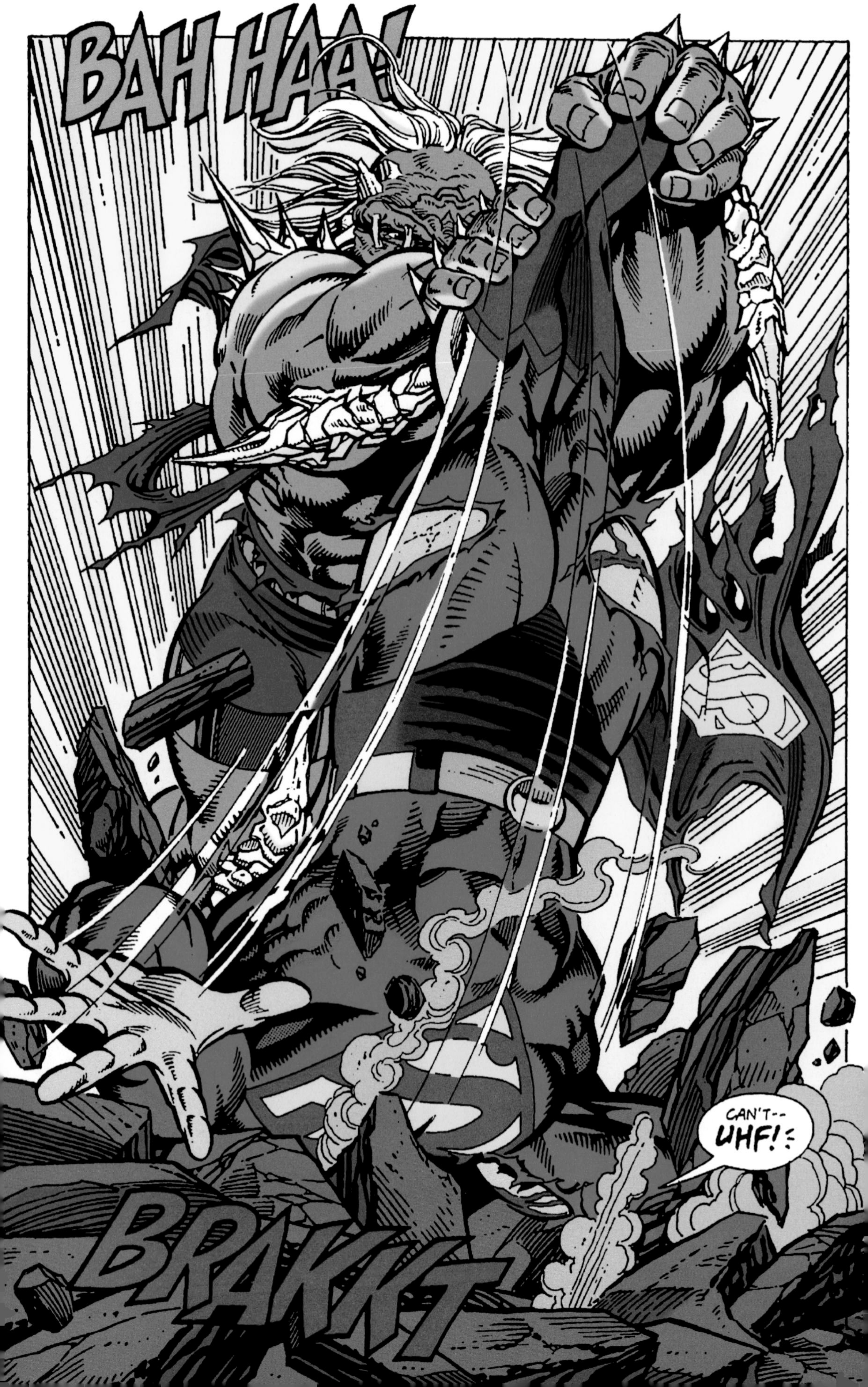
BAH HAA!
CAN'T-- UHF!
BRAKKT

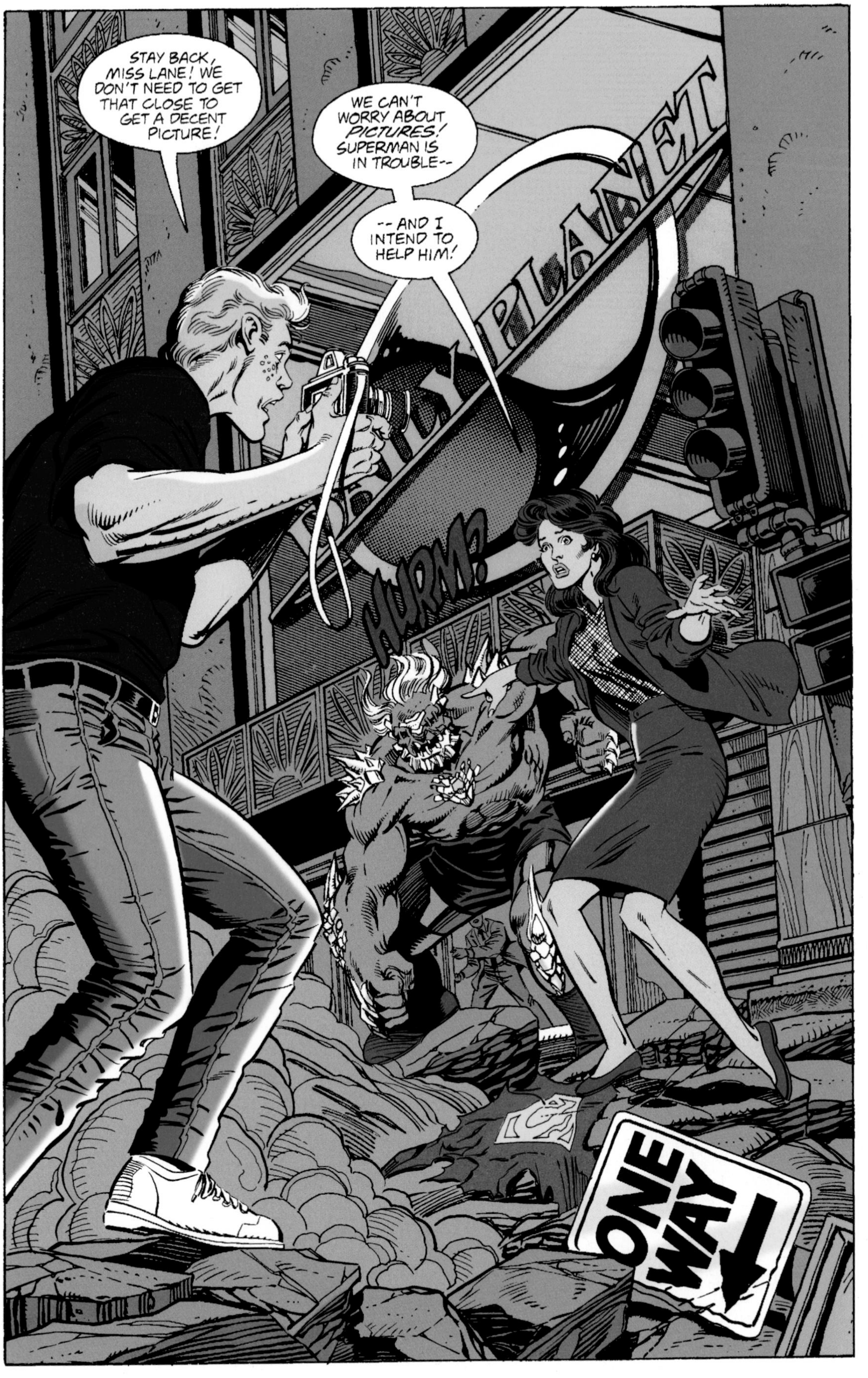
STAY BACK, MISS LANE! WE DON'T NEED TO GET THAT CLOSE TO GET A DECENT PICTURE!
WE CAN'T WORRY ABOUT PICTURES! SUPERMAN IS IN TROUBLE--
--AND I INTEND TO HELP HIM!
DAILY PLANET
HURM?
ONE WAY

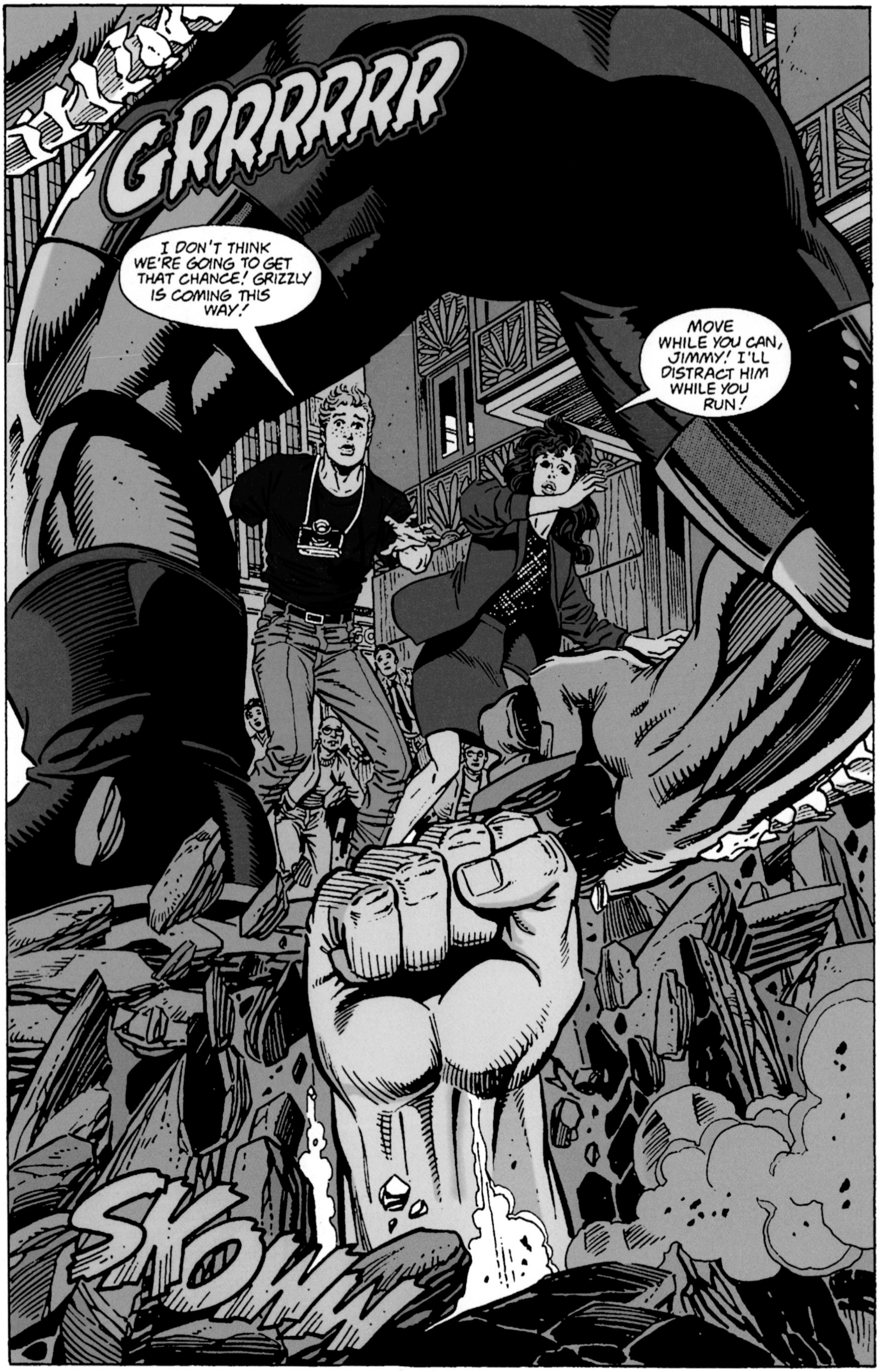
GRRRRRR
I DON'T THINK WE'RE GOING TO GET THAT CHANCE! GRIZZLY IS COMING THIS WAY!
MOVE WHILE YOU CAN, JIMMY! I'LL DISTRACT HIM WHILE YOU RUN!
SKOW

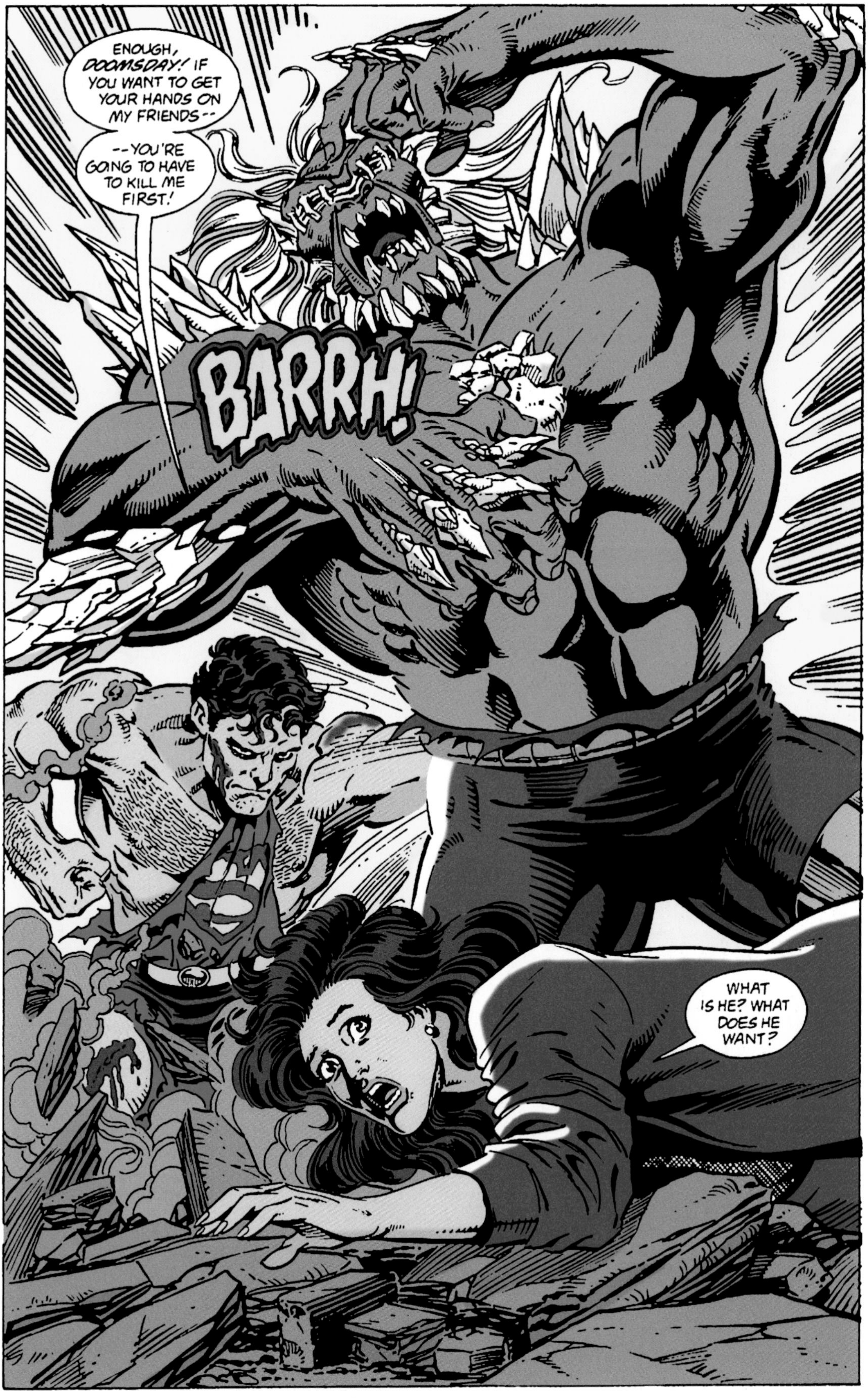
ENOUGH, DOOMSDAY! IF YOU WANT TO GET YOUR HANDS ON MY FRIENDS--
--YOU'RE GOING TO HAVE TO KILL ME FIRST!
BARRH!
WHAT IS HE? WHAT DOES HE WANT?

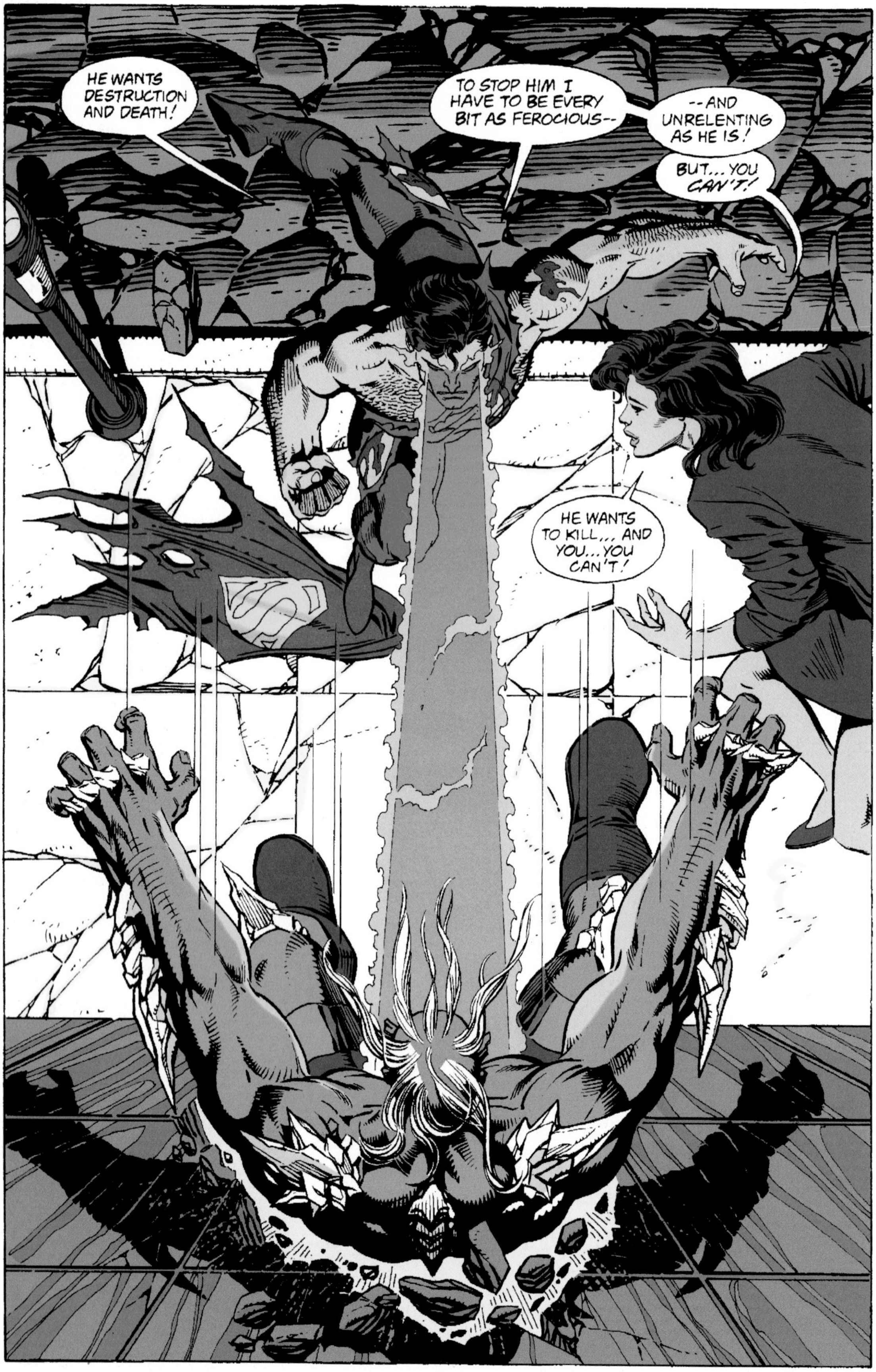
HE WANTS DESTRUCTION AND DEATH!
TO STOP HIM I HAVE TO BE EVERY BIT AS FEROCIOUS--
--AND UNRELENTING AS HE IS!
BUT... YOU CAN'T!
HE WANTS TO KILL... AND YOU... YOU CAN'T!

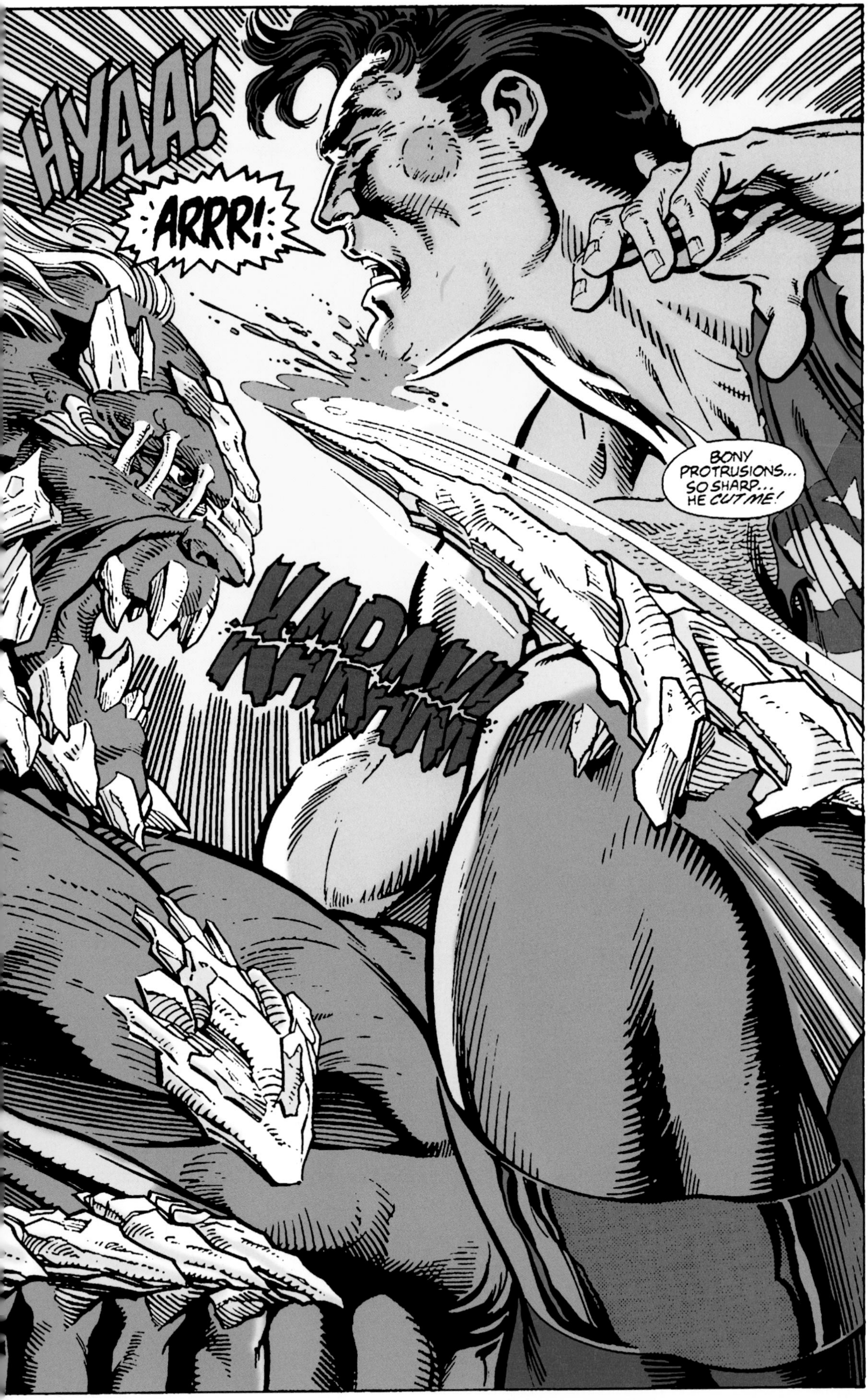
HYAA!
ARRR!
BONY PROTRUSIONS... SO SHARP... HE CUT ME!
KADANNK

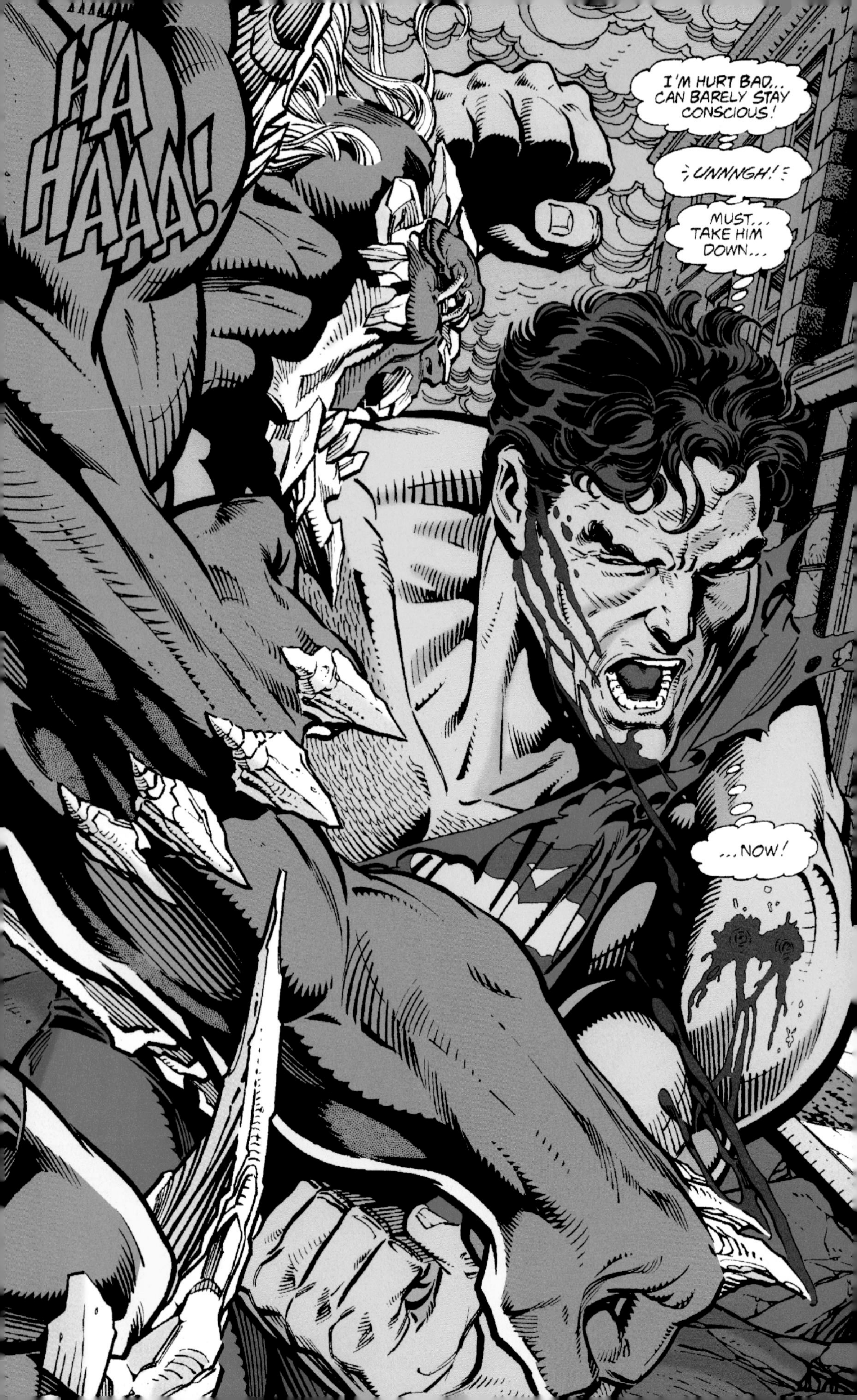
HA HA HAAA!
I'M HURT BAD... CAN BARELY STAY CONSCIOUS!
UNNNGH!
MUST... TAKE HIM DOWN...
...NOW!

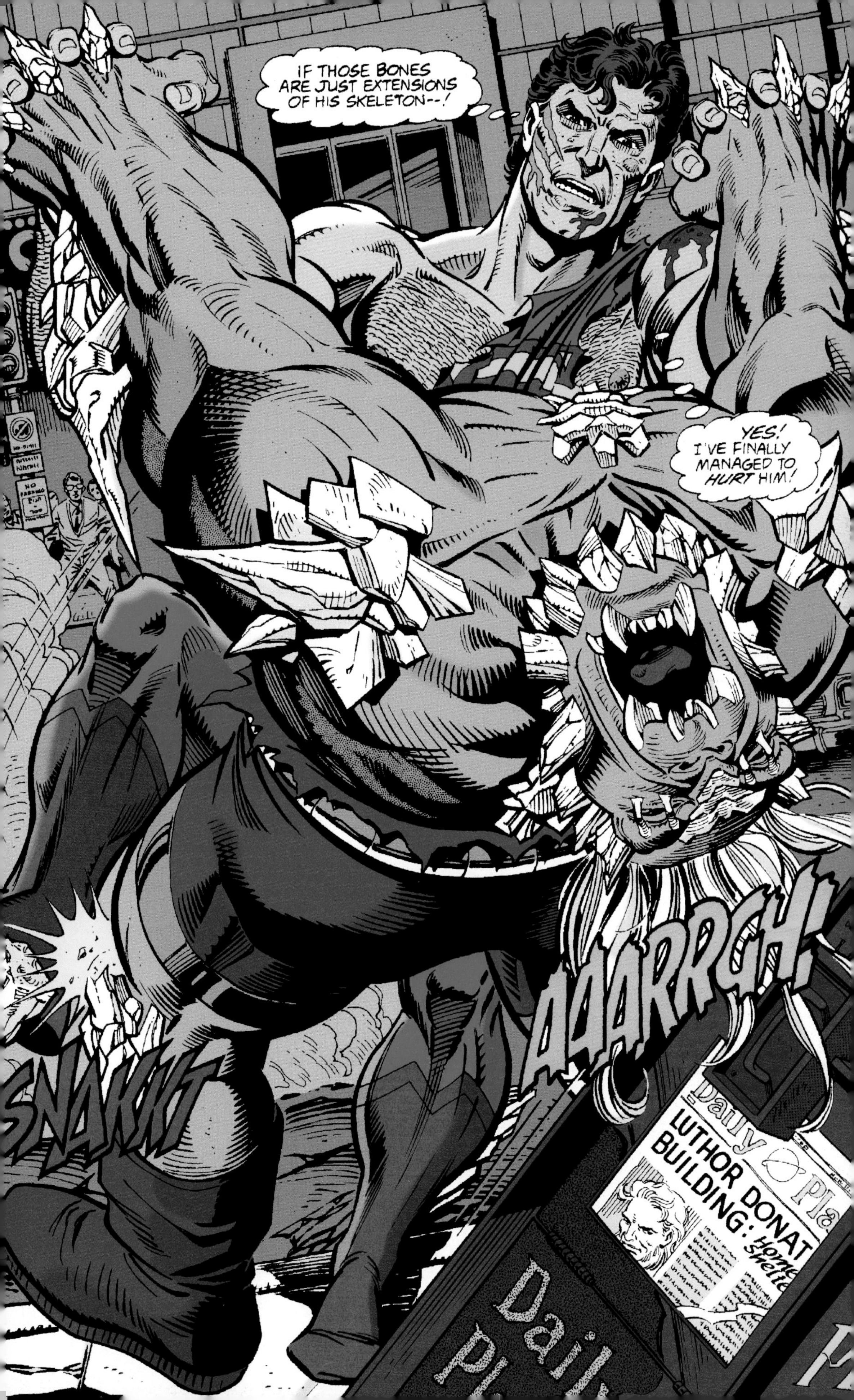
IF THOSE BONES ARE JUST EXTENSIONS OF HIS SKELETON--!
YES! I'VE FINALLY MANAGED TO HURT HIM!
SNAKKT
AAARRGH!
LUTHOR DONAT
BUILDING:

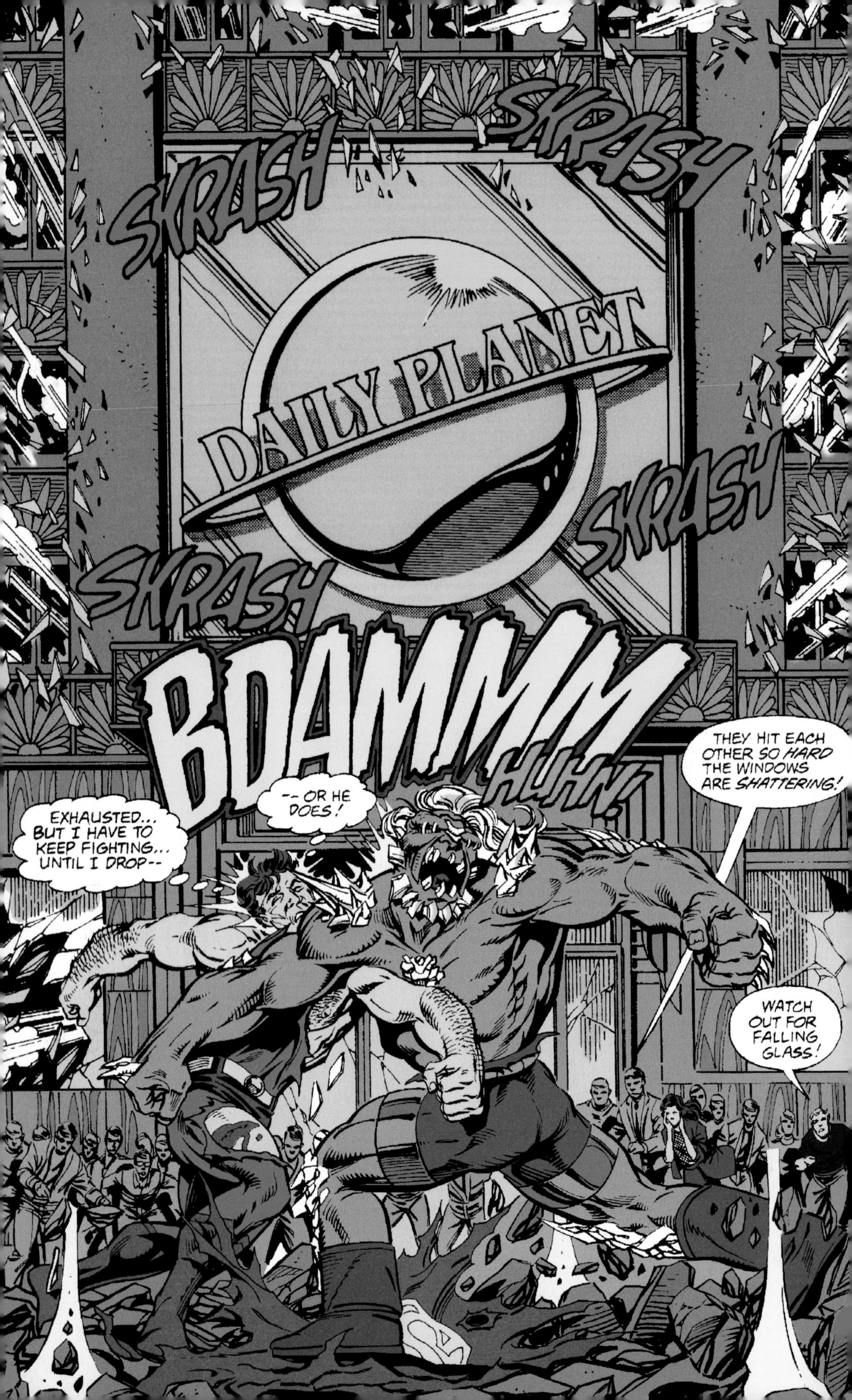
SKRASH
SKRASH
DAILY PLANET
SKRASH
SKRASH
BDAMMM
HUHH!
EXHAUSTED... BUT I HAVE TO KEEP FIGHTING... UNTIL I DROP--
--OR HE DOES!
THEY HIT EACH OTHER SO HARD THE WINDOWS ARE SHATTERING!
WATCH OUT FOR FALLING GLASS!

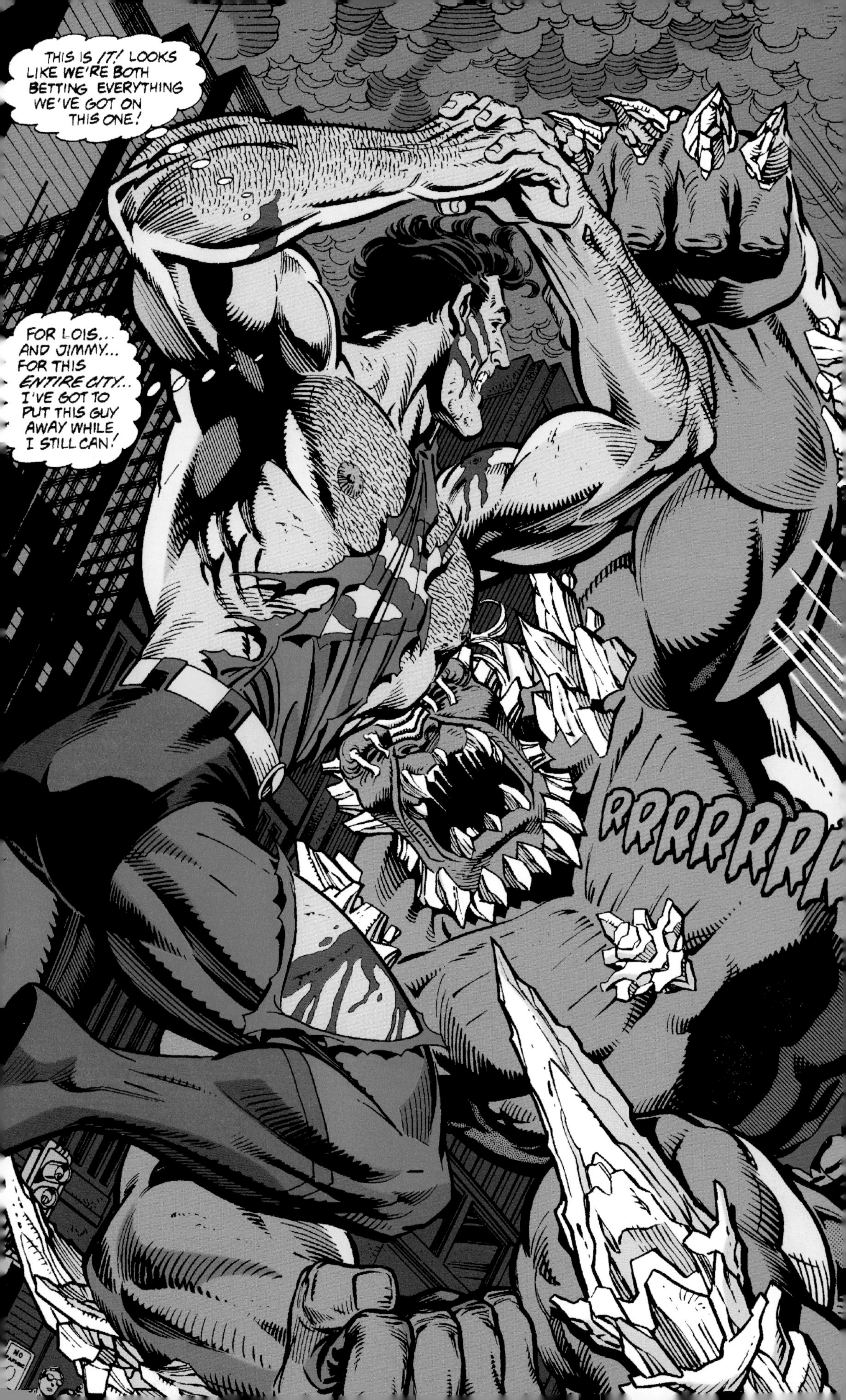
THIS IS *IT!* LOOKS LIKE WE'RE BOTH BETTING EVERYTHING WE'VE GOT ON THIS ONE!
FOR LOIS... AND JIMMY... FOR THIS *ENTIRE CITY*... I'VE GOT TO PUT THIS GUY AWAY WHILE I STILL CAN!
RRRRRRR

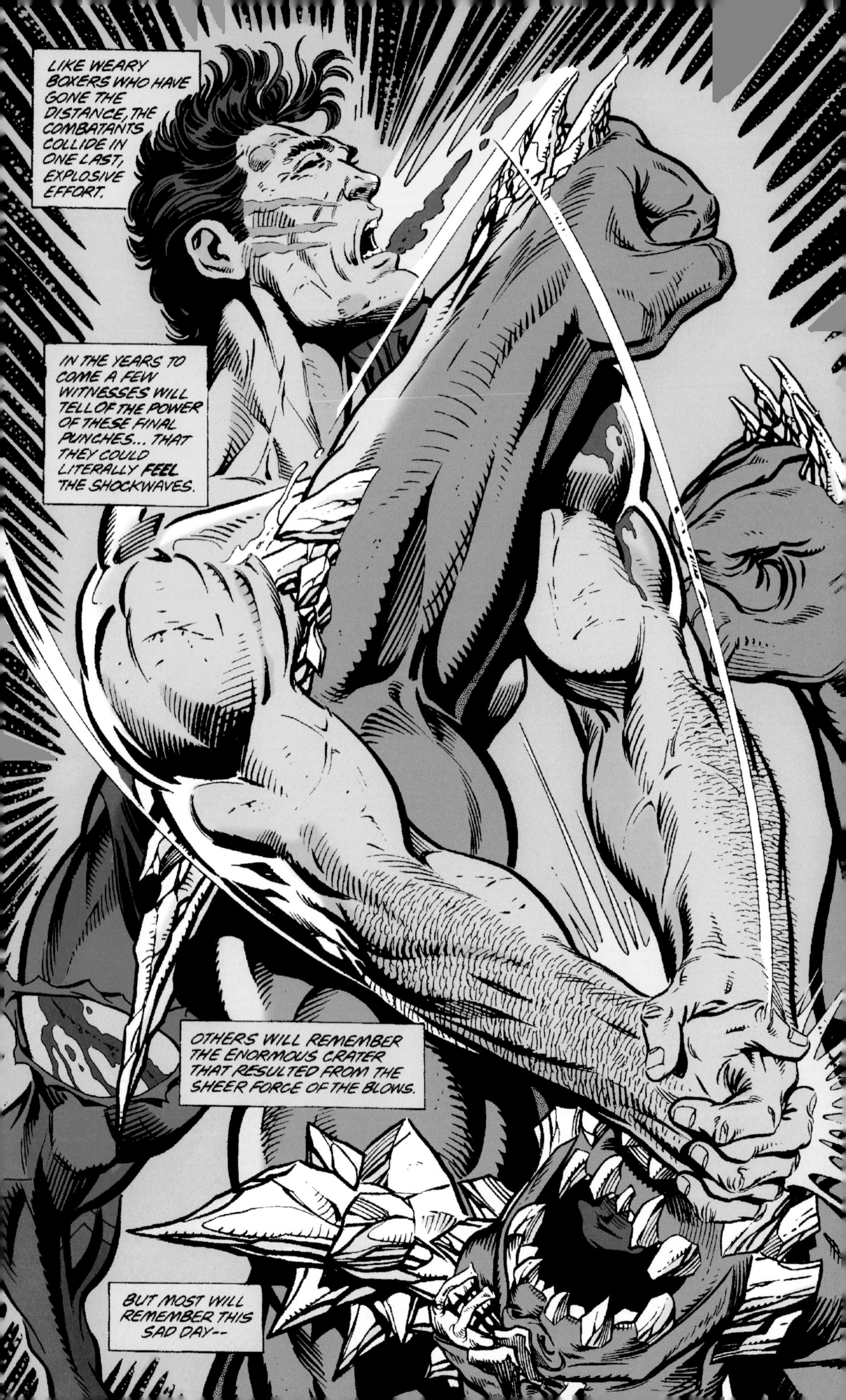
LIKE WEARY BOXERS WHO HAVE GONE THE DISTANCE, THE COMBATANTS COLLIDE IN ONE LAST, EXPLOSIVE EFFORT.
IN THE YEARS TO COME A FEW WITNESSES WILL TELL OF THE POWER OF THESE FINAL PUNCHES... THAT THEY COULD LITERALLY **FEEL** THE SHOCKWAVES.
OTHERS WILL REMEMBER THE ENORMOUS CRATER THAT RESULTED FROM THE SHEER FORCE OF THE BLOWS.
BUT MOST WILL REMEMBER THIS SAD DAY--

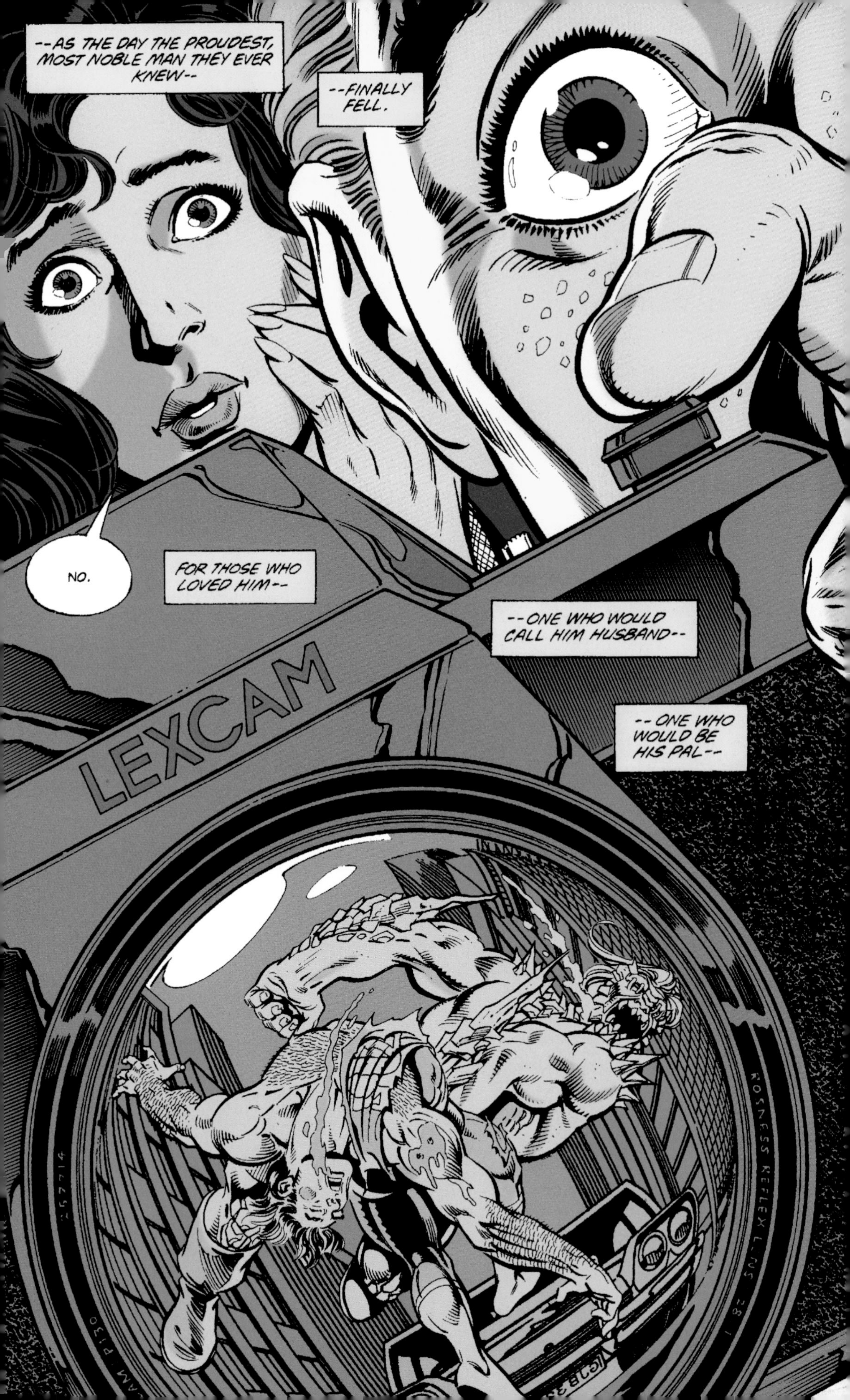

--AS THE DAY THE PROUDEST, MOST NOBLE MAN THEY EVER KNEW--
--FINALLY FELL.
NO.
FOR THOSE WHO LOVED HIM--
--ONE WHO WOULD CALL HIM HUSBAND--
--ONE WHO WOULD BE HIS PAL--
LEXCAM

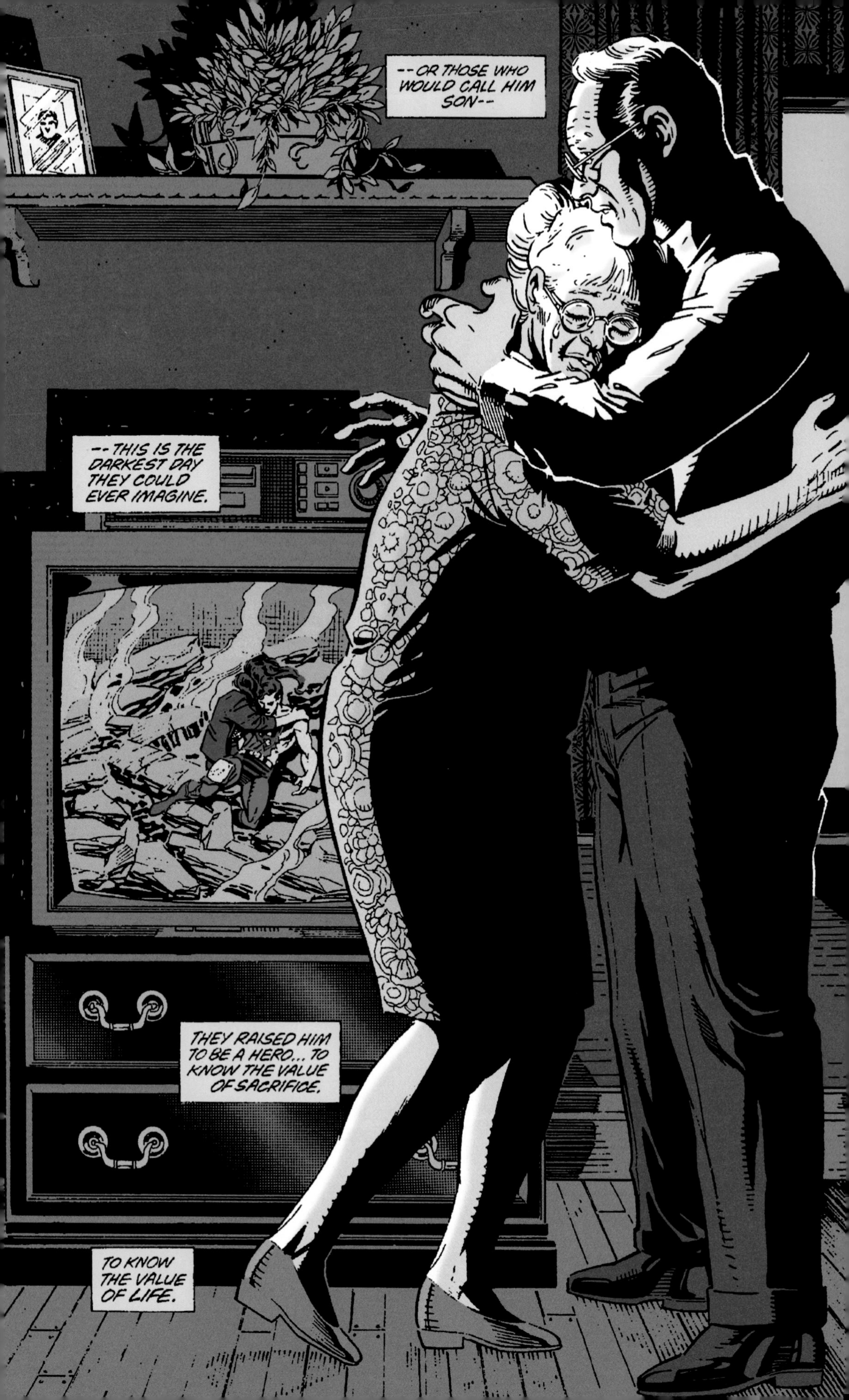
--OR THOSE WHO WOULD CALL HIM SON--
--THIS IS THE DARKEST DAY THEY COULD EVER IMAGINE.
THEY RAISED HIM TO BE A HERO... TO KNOW THE VALUE OF SACRIFICE.
TO KNOW THE VALUE OF LIFE.

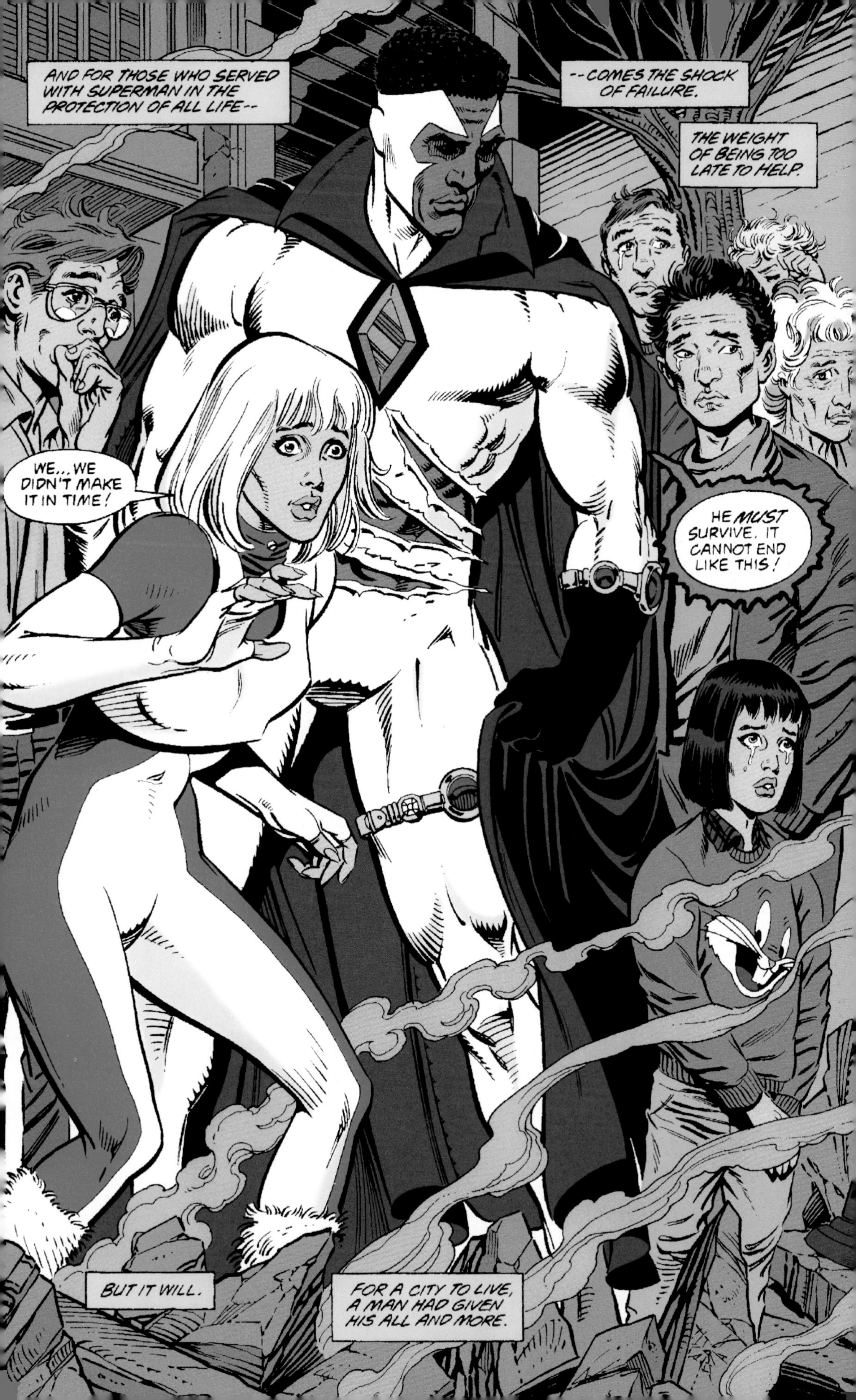
AND FOR THOSE WHO SERVED WITH SUPERMAN IN THE PROTECTION OF ALL LIFE--
--COMES THE SHOCK OF FAILURE.
THE WEIGHT OF BEING TOO LATE TO HELP.
WE...WE DIDN'T MAKE IT IN TIME!
HE MUST SURVIVE. IT CANNOT END LIKE THIS!
BUT IT WILL.
FOR A CITY TO LIVE, A MAN HAD GIVEN HIS ALL AND MORE.

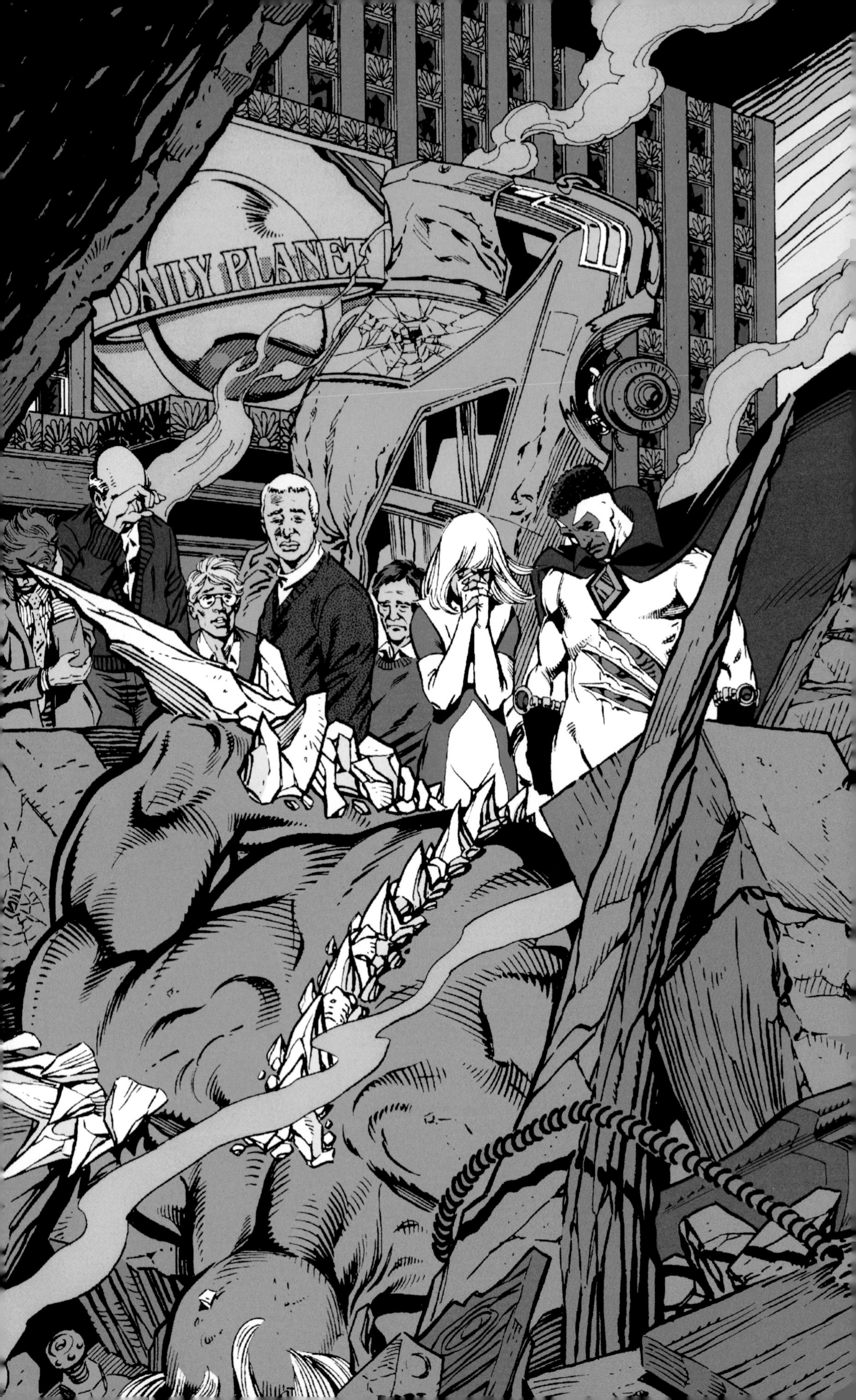
DAILY PLANET

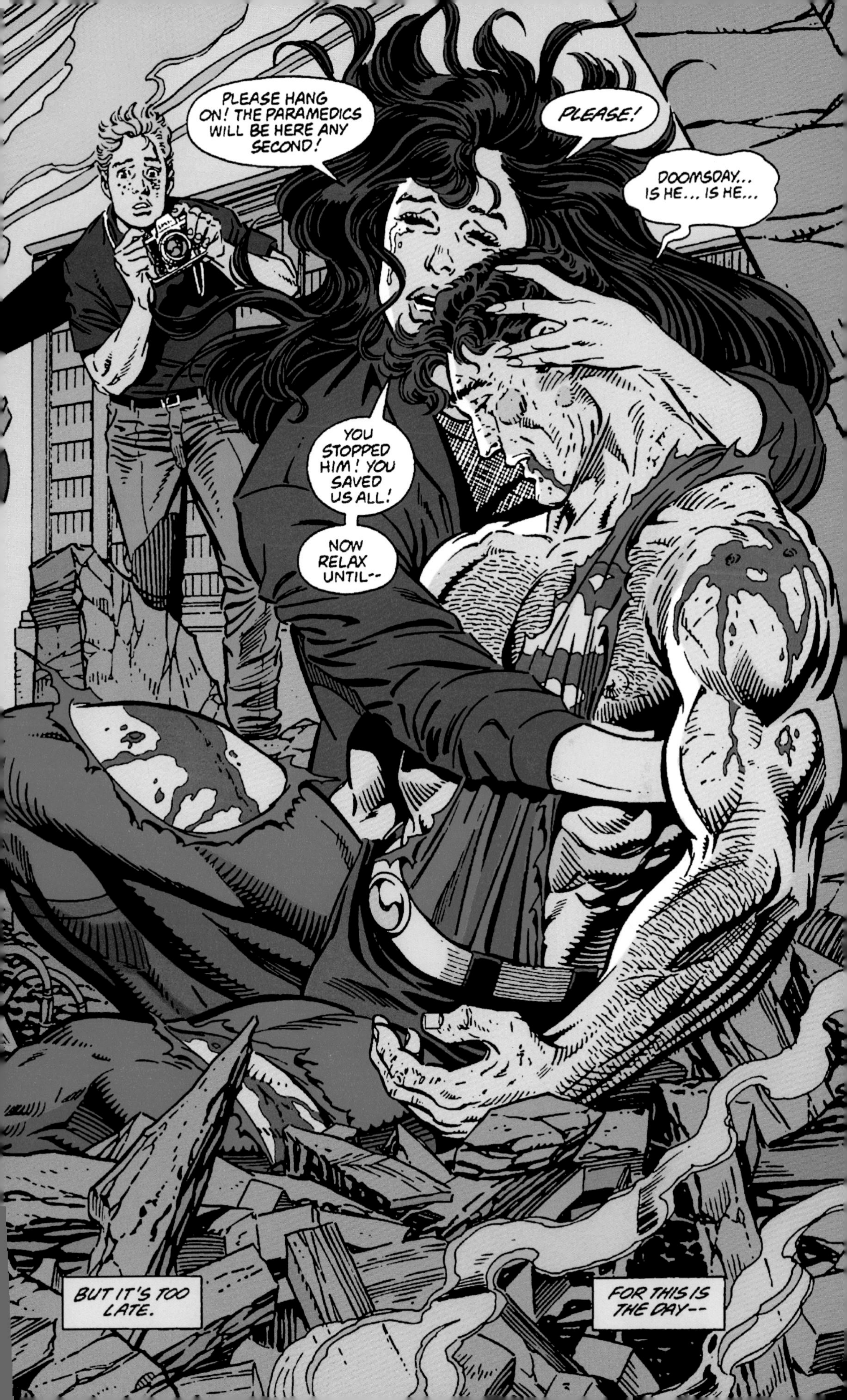
PLEASE HANG ON! THE PARAMEDICS WILL BE HERE ANY SECOND!
PLEASE!
DOOMSDAY... IS HE... IS HE...
YOU STOPPED HIM! YOU SAVED US ALL!
NOW RELAX UNTIL--
BUT IT'S TOO LATE.
FOR THIS IS THE DAY--

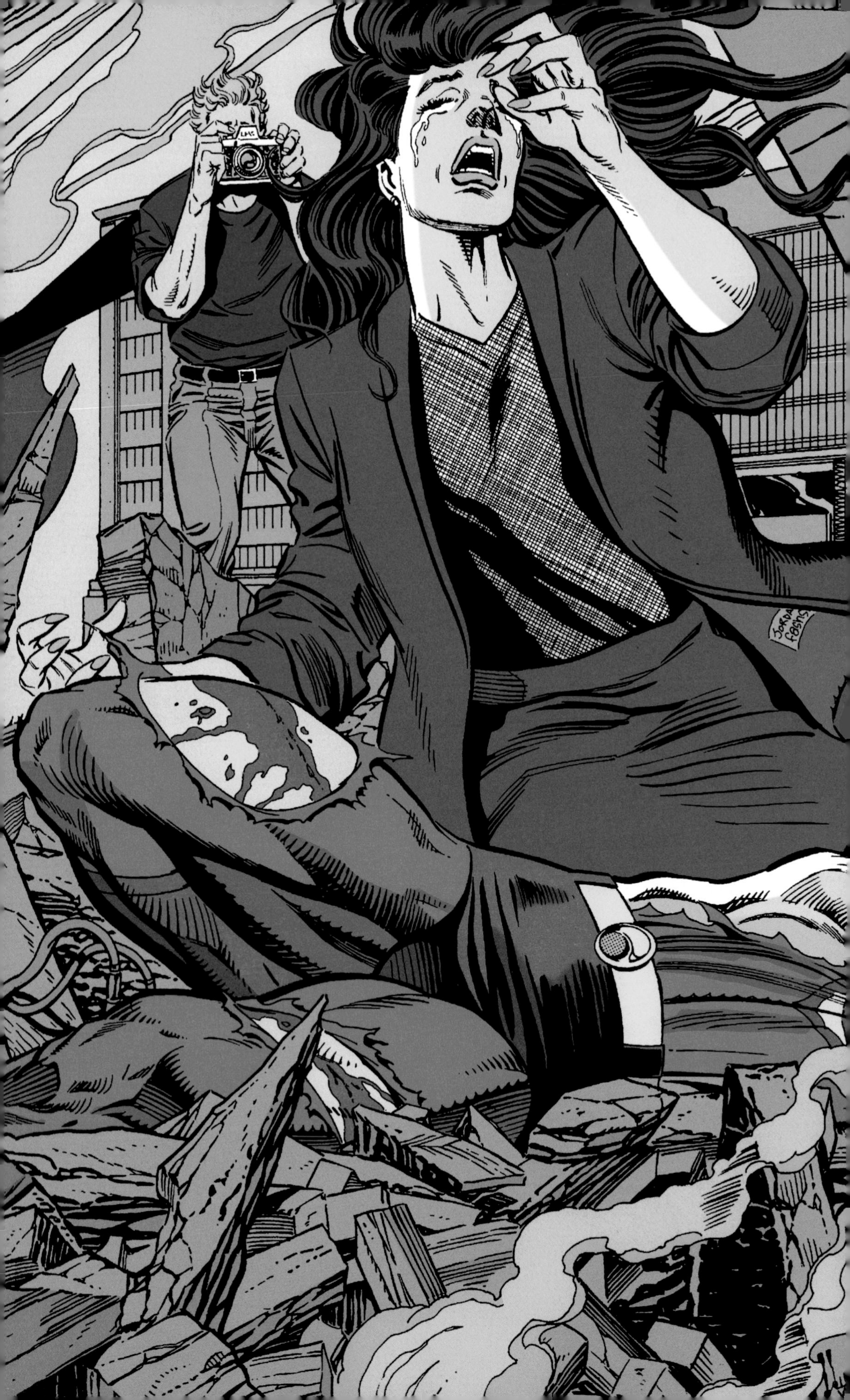

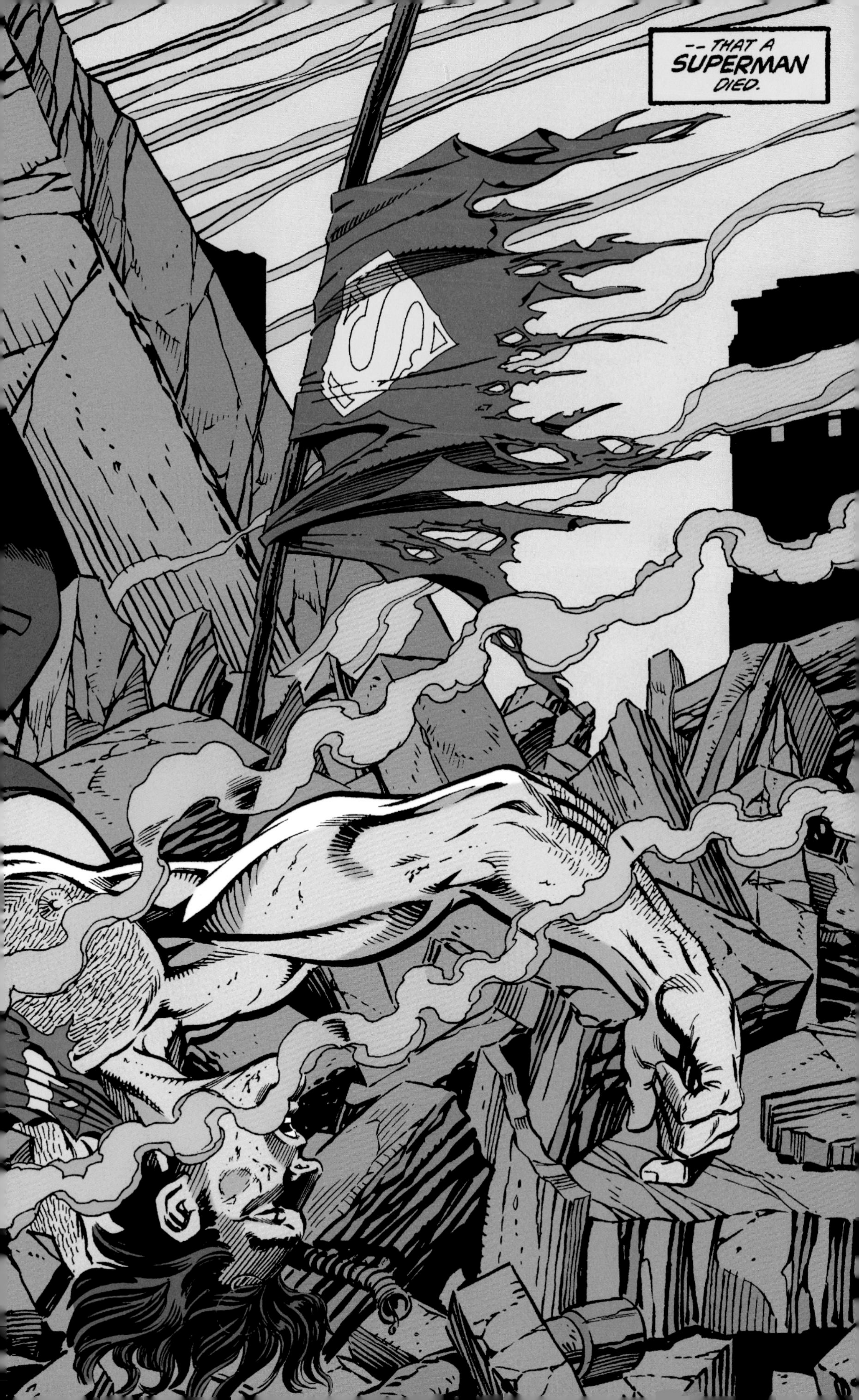
--THAT A SUPERMAN DIED.

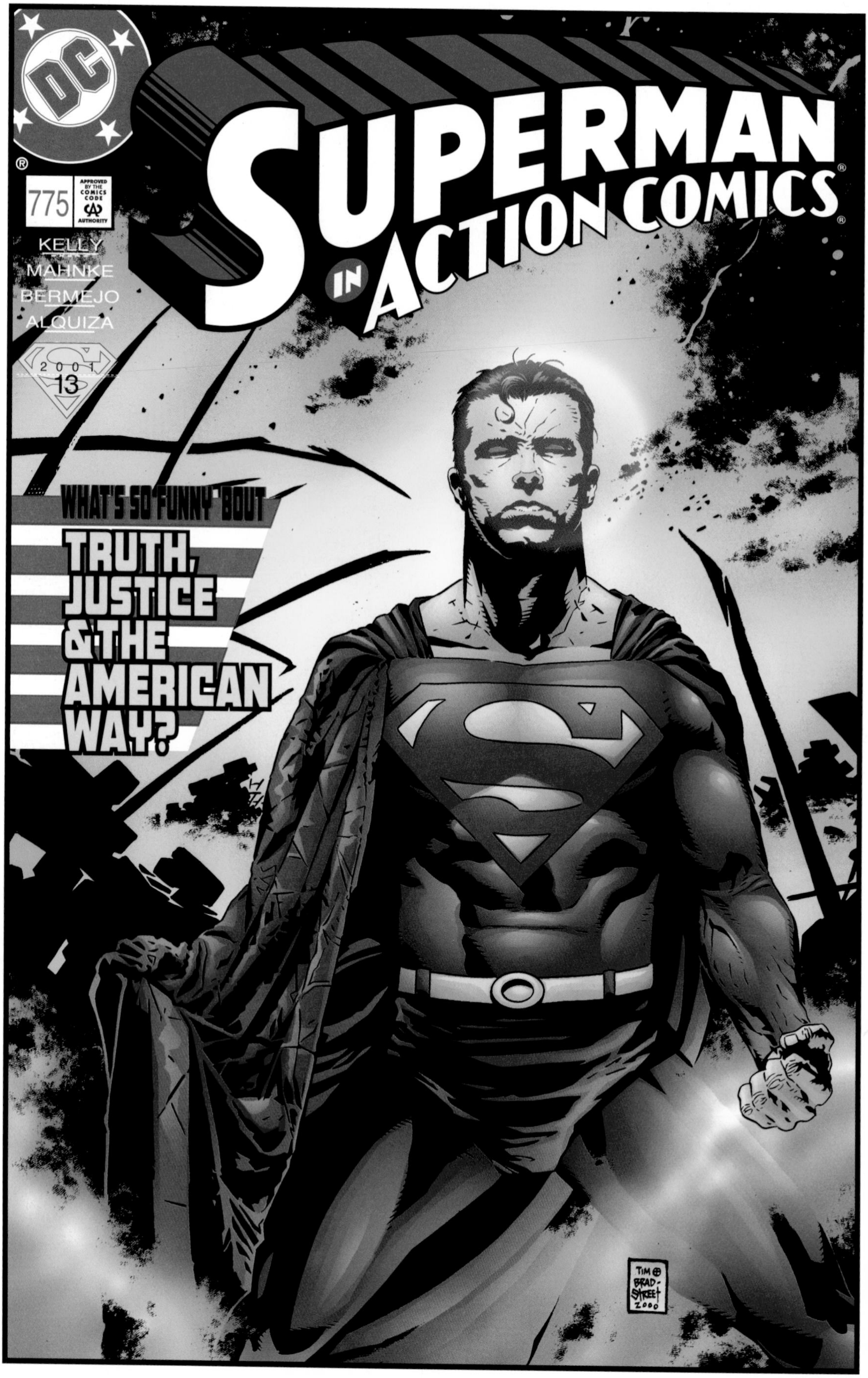
DC
SUPERMAN
IN ACTION COMICS
775
APPROVED BY THE COMICS CODE AUTHORITY
KELLY
MAHNKE
BERMEJO
ALQUIZA
2001
13
WHAT'S SO FUNNY 'BOUT
TRUTH, JUSTICE & THE AMERICAN WAY?
TIM BRADSTREET 2000

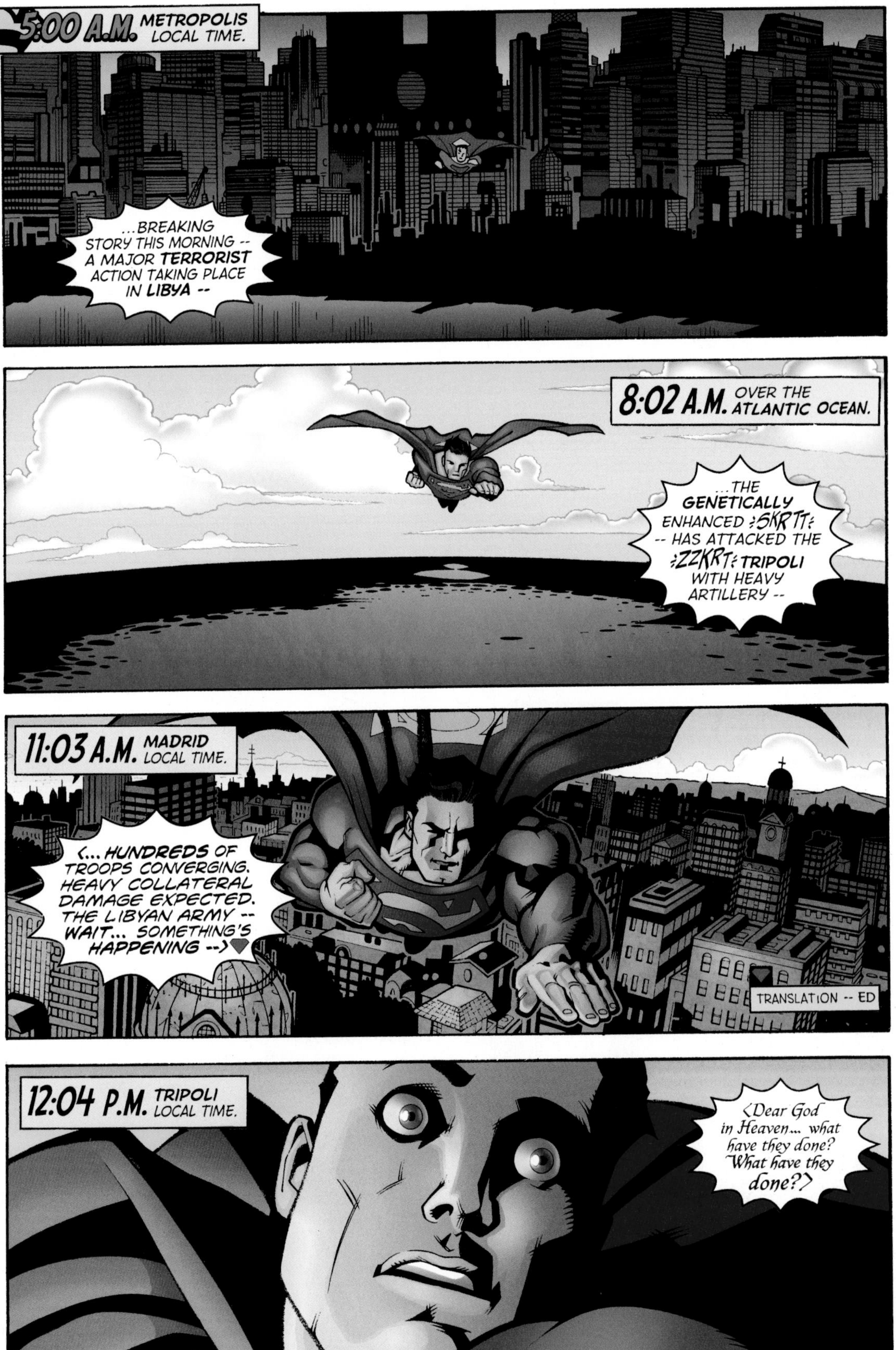
5:00 A.M. METROPOLIS LOCAL TIME.
...BREAKING STORY THIS MORNING -- A MAJOR TERRORIST ACTION TAKING PLACE IN LIBYA --
8:02 A.M. OVER THE ATLANTIC OCEAN.
...THE GENETICALLY ENHANCED SKRTT -- HAS ATTACKED THE ZZKRT TRIPOLI WITH HEAVY ARTILLERY --
11:03 A.M. MADRID LOCAL TIME.
<...HUNDREDS OF TROOPS CONVERGING. HEAVY COLLATERAL DAMAGE EXPECTED. THE LIBYAN ARMY -- WAIT... SOMETHING'S HAPPENING -->
TRANSLATION -- ED
12:04 P.M. TRIPOLI LOCAL TIME.
<Dear God in Heaven... what have they done? What have they done?>

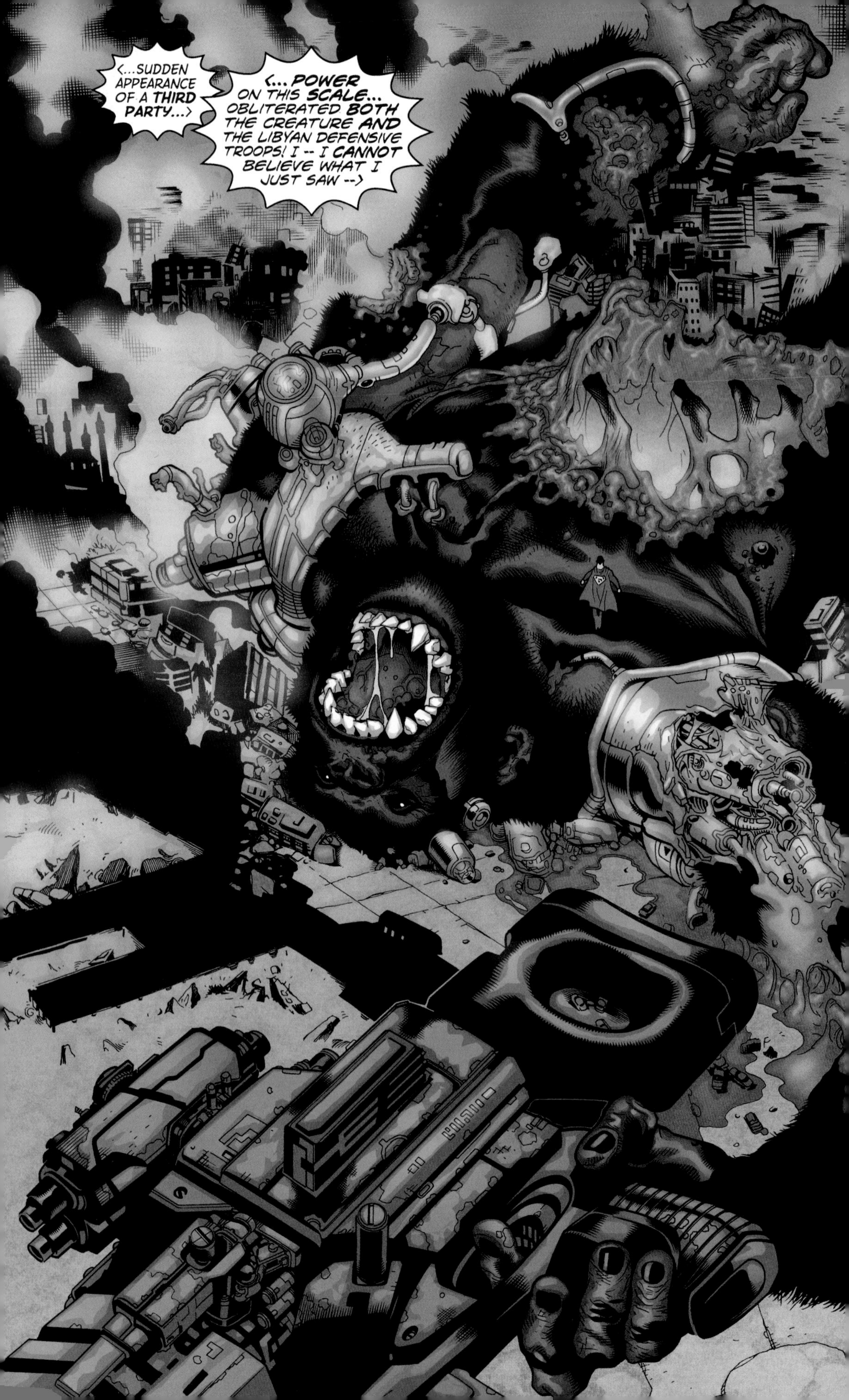

<...SUDDEN APPEARANCE OF A THIRD PARTY...>
<...POWER ON THIS SCALE... OBLITERATED BOTH THE CREATURE AND THE LIBYAN DEFENSIVE TROOPS! I -- I CANNOT BELIEVE WHAT I JUST SAW -->

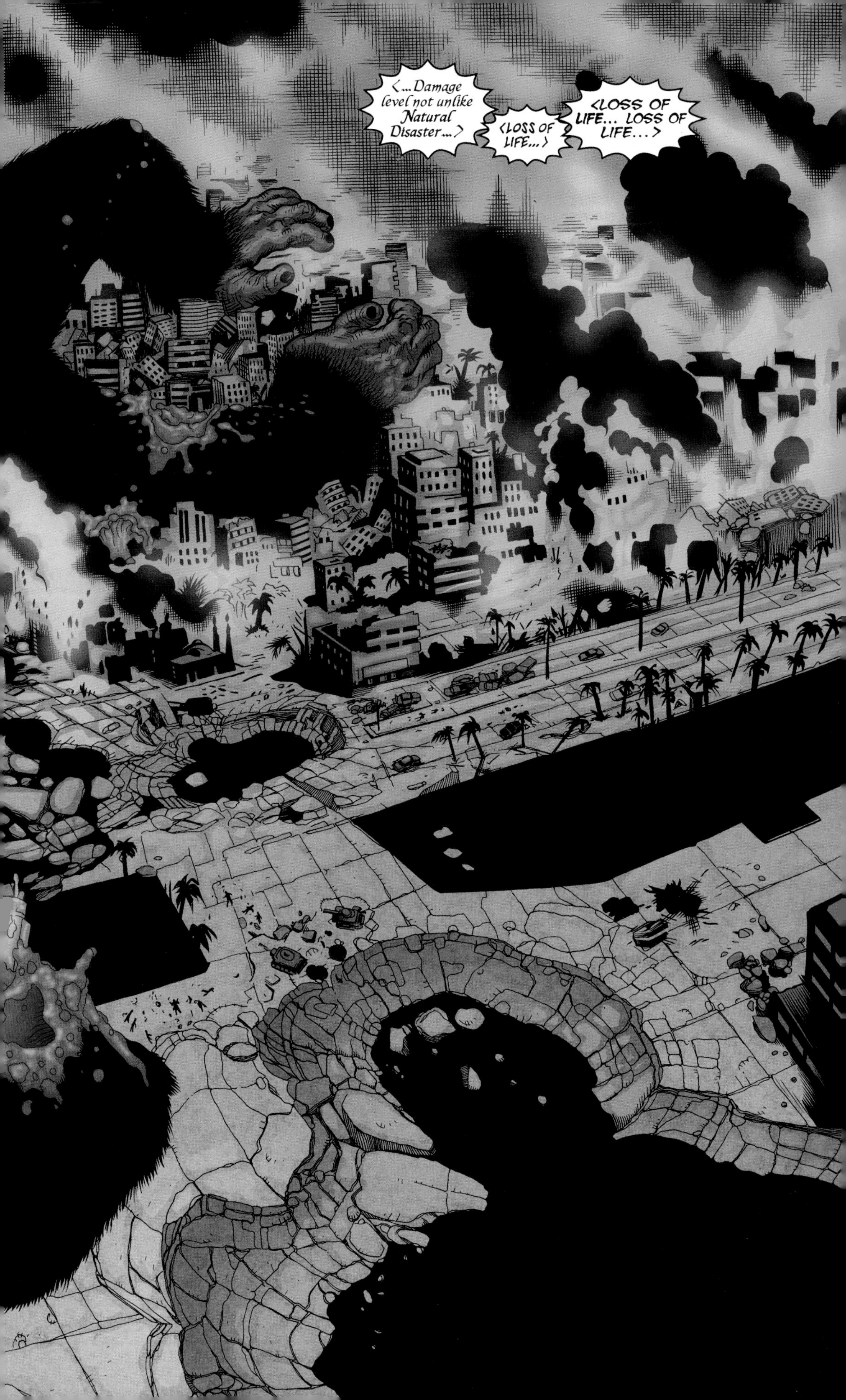
<...Damage level not unlike Natural Disaster...>
<LOSS OF LIFE...>
<LOSS OF LIFE... LOSS OF LIFE...>

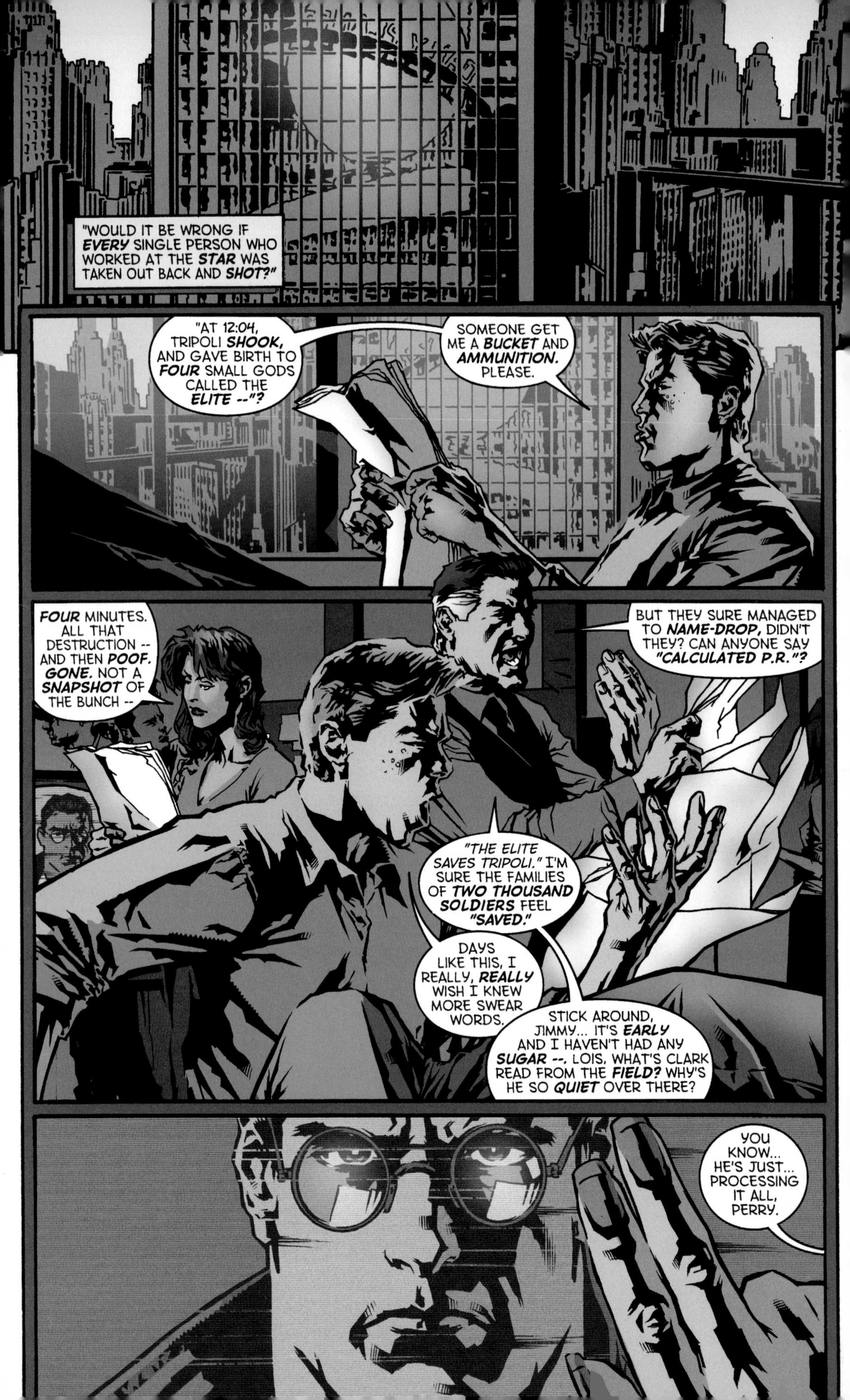
"WOULD IT BE WRONG IF EVERY SINGLE PERSON WHO WORKED AT THE STAR WAS TAKEN OUT BACK AND SHOT?"
"AT 12:04, TRIPOLI SHOOK, AND GAVE BIRTH TO FOUR SMALL GODS CALLED THE ELITE --"?
SOMEONE GET ME A BUCKET AND AMMUNITION. PLEASE.
FOUR MINUTES. ALL THAT DESTRUCTION -- AND THEN POOF. GONE. NOT A SNAPSHOT OF THE BUNCH --
BUT THEY SURE MANAGED TO NAME-DROP, DIDN'T THEY? CAN ANYONE SAY "CALCULATED P.R."?
"THE ELITE SAVES TRIPOLI." I'M SURE THE FAMILIES OF TWO THOUSAND SOLDIERS FEEL "SAVED."
DAYS LIKE THIS, I REALLY, REALLY WISH I KNEW MORE SWEAR WORDS.
STICK AROUND, JIMMY... IT'S EARLY AND I HAVEN'T HAD ANY SUGAR --. LOIS, WHAT'S CLARK READ FROM THE FIELD? WHY'S HE SO QUIET OVER THERE?
YOU KNOW... HE'S JUST... PROCESSING IT ALL, PERRY.

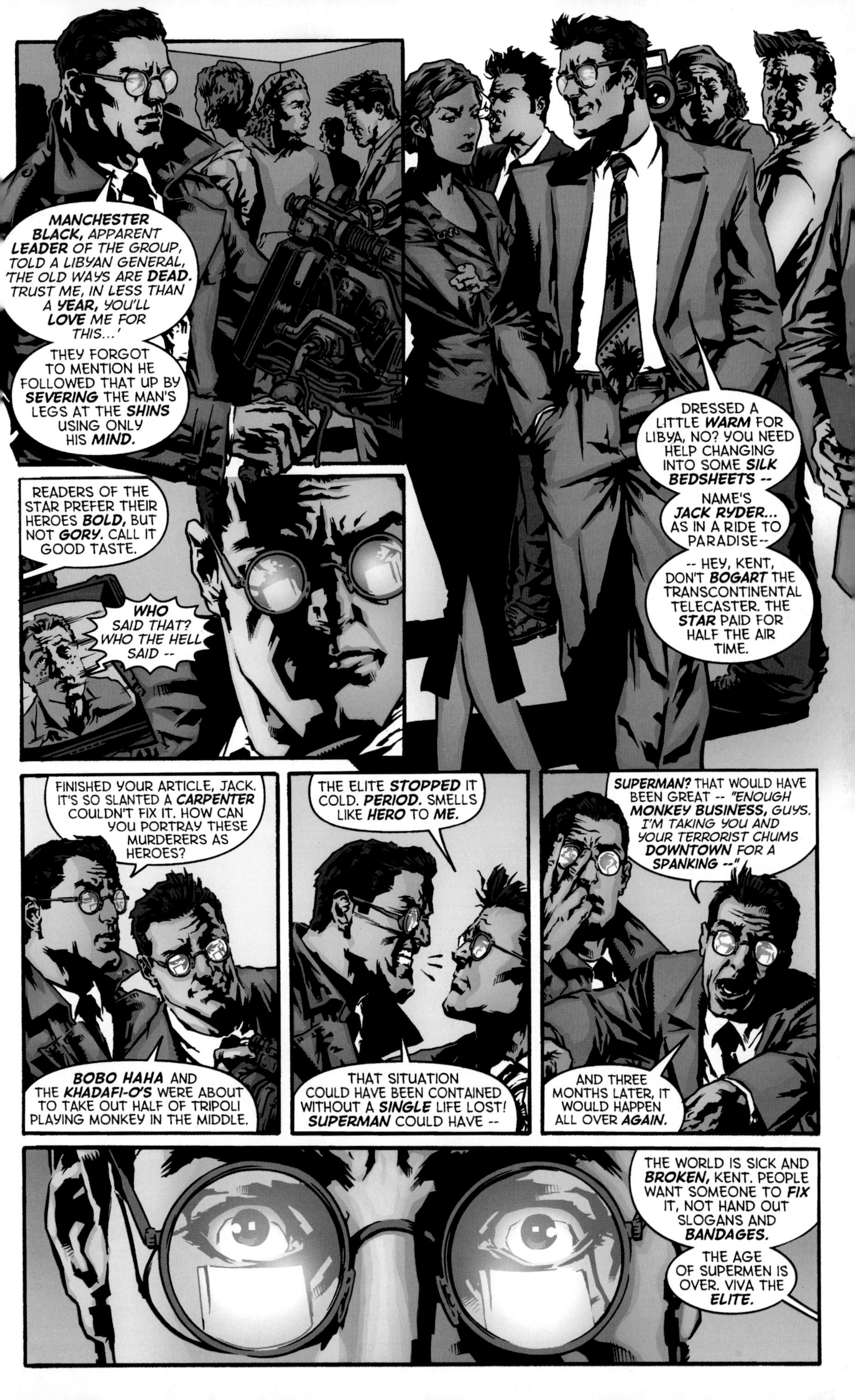

MANCHESTER BLACK, APPARENT LEADER OF THE GROUP, TOLD A LIBYAN GENERAL, 'THE OLD WAYS ARE DEAD. TRUST ME, IN LESS THAN A YEAR, YOU'LL LOVE ME FOR THIS...'
THEY FORGOT TO MENTION HE FOLLOWED THAT UP BY SEVERING THE MAN'S LEGS AT THE SHINS USING ONLY HIS MIND.
DRESSED A LITTLE WARM FOR LIBYA, NO? YOU NEED HELP CHANGING INTO SOME SILK BEDSHEETS --
NAME'S JACK RYDER... AS IN A RIDE TO PARADISE--
READERS OF THE STAR PREFER THEIR HEROES BOLD, BUT NOT GORY. CALL IT GOOD TASTE.
WHO SAID THAT? WHO THE HELL SAID --
-- HEY, KENT, DON'T BOGART THE TRANSCONTINENTAL TELECASTER. THE STAR PAID FOR HALF THE AIR TIME.
FINISHED YOUR ARTICLE, JACK. IT'S SO SLANTED A CARPENTER COULDN'T FIX IT. HOW CAN YOU PORTRAY THESE MURDERERS AS HEROES?
BOBO HAHA AND THE KHADAFI-O'S WERE ABOUT TO TAKE OUT HALF OF TRIPOLI PLAYING MONKEY IN THE MIDDLE.
THE ELITE STOPPED IT COLD. PERIOD. SMELLS LIKE HERO TO ME.
THAT SITUATION COULD HAVE BEEN CONTAINED WITHOUT A SINGLE LIFE LOST! SUPERMAN COULD HAVE --
SUPERMAN? THAT WOULD HAVE BEEN GREAT -- "ENOUGH MONKEY BUSINESS, GUYS. I'M TAKING YOU AND YOUR TERRORIST CHUMS DOWNTOWN FOR A SPANKING --"
AND THREE MONTHS LATER, IT WOULD HAPPEN ALL OVER AGAIN.
THE WORLD IS SICK AND BROKEN, KENT. PEOPLE WANT SOMEONE TO FIX IT, NOT HAND OUT SLOGANS AND BANDAGES.
THE AGE OF SUPERMEN IS OVER. VIVA THE ELITE.

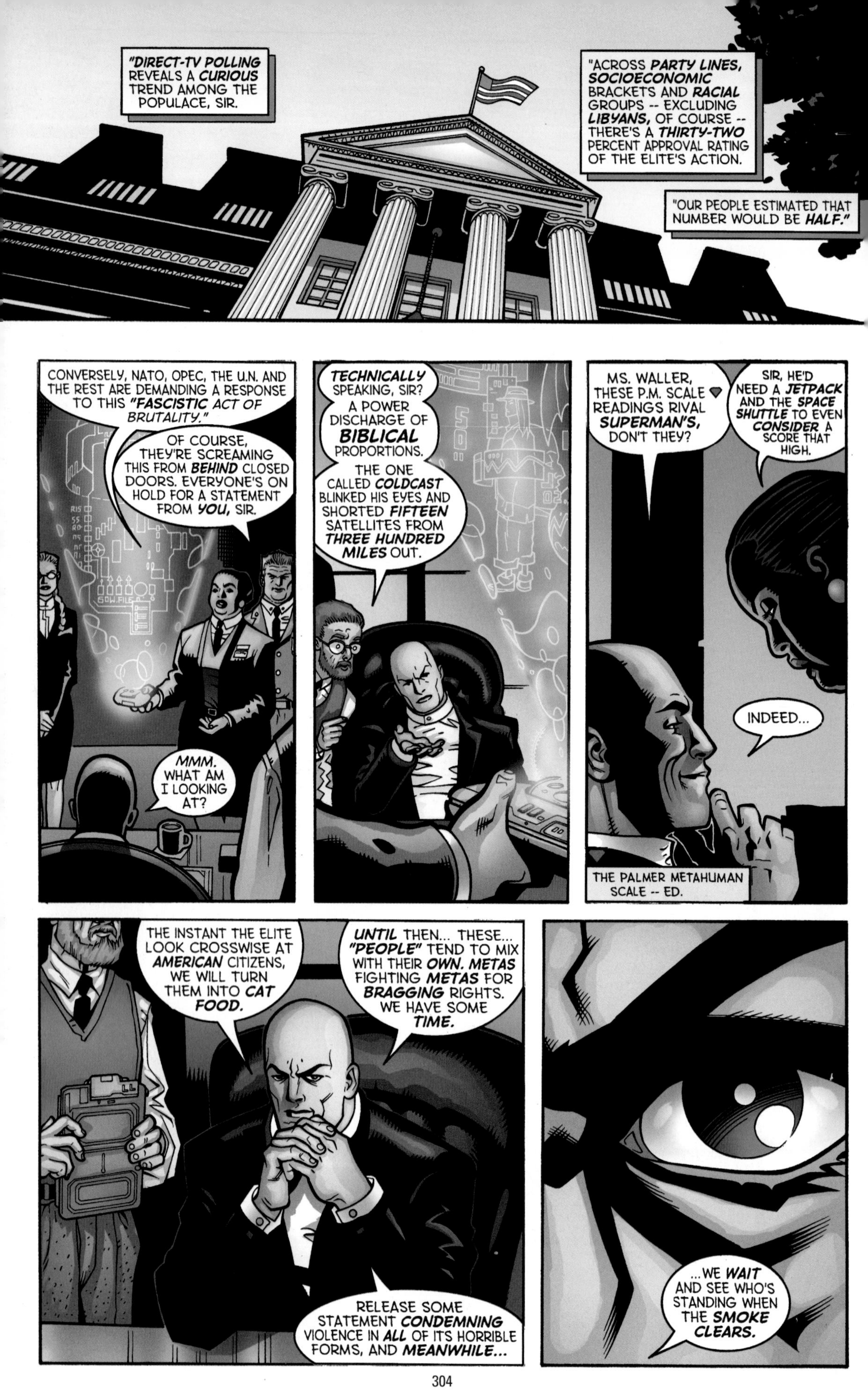
"DIRECT-TV POLLING REVEALS A CURIOUS TREND AMONG THE POPULACE, SIR.
"ACROSS PARTY LINES, SOCIOECONOMIC BRACKETS AND RACIAL GROUPS -- EXCLUDING LIBYANS, OF COURSE -- THERE'S A THIRTY-TWO PERCENT APPROVAL RATING OF THE ELITE'S ACTION.
"OUR PEOPLE ESTIMATED THAT NUMBER WOULD BE HALF."
CONVERSELY, NATO, OPEC, THE U.N. AND THE REST ARE DEMANDING A RESPONSE TO THIS "FASCISTIC ACT OF BRUTALITY."
OF COURSE, THEY'RE SCREAMING THIS FROM BEHIND CLOSED DOORS. EVERYONE'S ON HOLD FOR A STATEMENT FROM YOU, SIR.
MMM. WHAT AM I LOOKING AT?
TECHNICALLY SPEAKING, SIR? A POWER DISCHARGE OF BIBLICAL PROPORTIONS.
THE ONE CALLED COLDCAST BLINKED HIS EYES AND SHORTED FIFTEEN SATELLITES FROM THREE HUNDRED MILES OUT.
MS. WALLER, THESE P.M. SCALE ♥ READINGS RIVAL SUPERMAN'S, DON'T THEY?
SIR, HE'D NEED A JETPACK AND THE SPACE SHUTTLE TO EVEN CONSIDER A SCORE THAT HIGH.
INDEED...
♥ THE PALMER METAHUMAN SCALE -- ED.
THE INSTANT THE ELITE LOOK CROSSWISE AT AMERICAN CITIZENS, WE WILL TURN THEM INTO CAT FOOD.
UNTIL THEN... THESE... "PEOPLE" TEND TO MIX WITH THEIR OWN. METAS FIGHTING METAS FOR BRAGGING RIGHTS. WE HAVE SOME TIME.
RELEASE SOME STATEMENT CONDEMNING VIOLENCE IN ALL OF ITS HORRIBLE FORMS, AND MEANWHILE...
...WE WAIT AND SEE WHO'S STANDING WHEN THE SMOKE CLEARS.

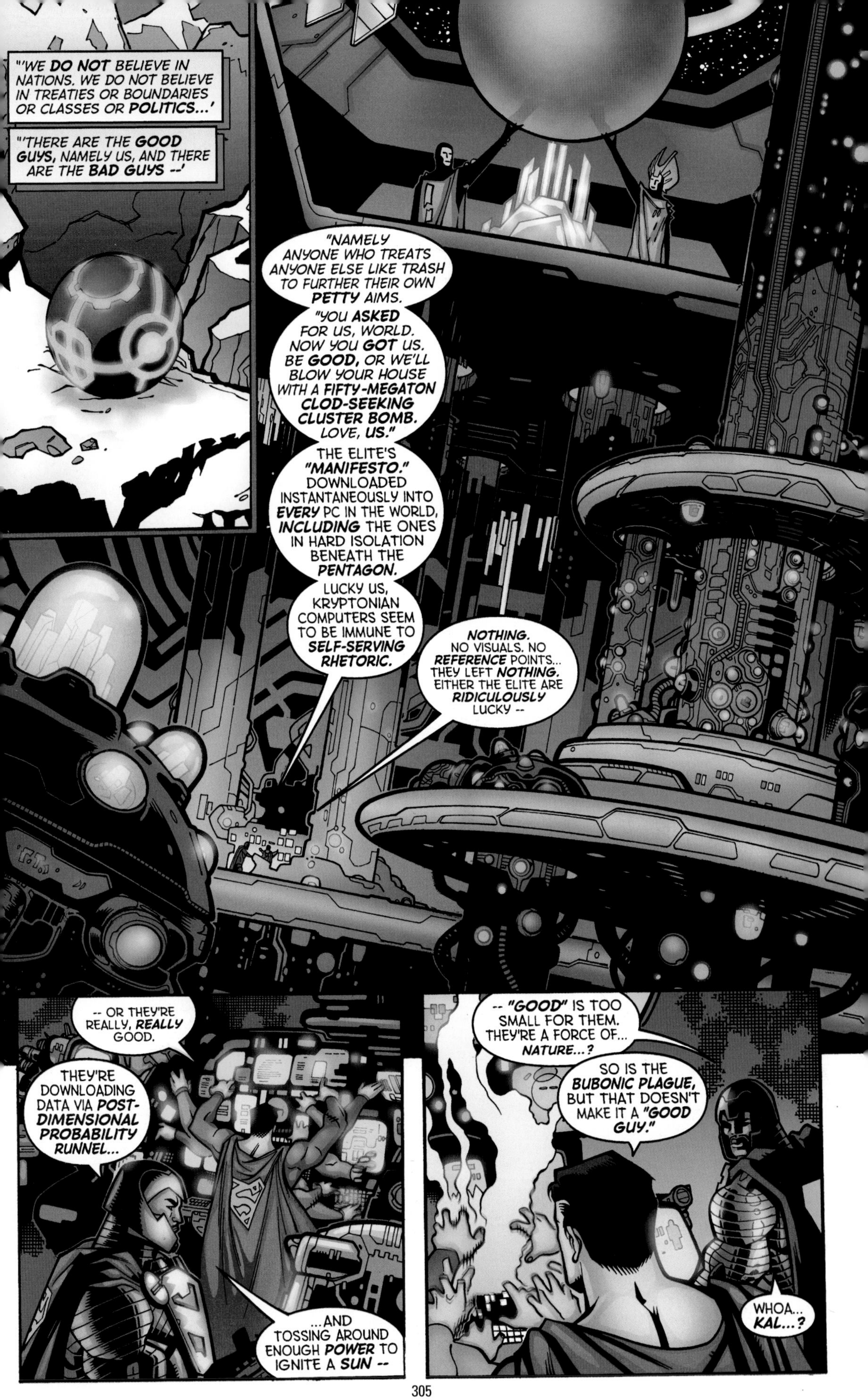
"'WE DO NOT BELIEVE IN NATIONS. WE DO NOT BELIEVE IN TREATIES OR BOUNDARIES OR CLASSES OR POLITICS...'
"'THERE ARE THE GOOD GUYS, NAMELY US, AND THERE ARE THE BAD GUYS --'
"NAMELY ANYONE WHO TREATS ANYONE ELSE LIKE TRASH TO FURTHER THEIR OWN PETTY AIMS.
"YOU ASKED FOR US, WORLD. NOW YOU GOT US. BE GOOD, OR WE'LL BLOW YOUR HOUSE WITH A FIFTY-MEGATON CLOD-SEEKING CLUSTER BOMB. LOVE, US."
THE ELITE'S "MANIFESTO." DOWNLOADED INSTANTANEOUSLY INTO EVERY PC IN THE WORLD, INCLUDING THE ONES IN HARD ISOLATION BENEATH THE PENTAGON.
LUCKY US, KRYPTONIAN COMPUTERS SEEM TO BE IMMUNE TO SELF-SERVING RHETORIC.
NOTHING. NO VISUALS. NO REFERENCE POINTS... THEY LEFT NOTHING. EITHER THE ELITE ARE RIDICULOUSLY LUCKY --
-- OR THEY'RE REALLY, REALLY GOOD.
THEY'RE DOWNLOADING DATA VIA POST-DIMENSIONAL PROBABILITY RUNNEL...
...AND TOSSING AROUND ENOUGH POWER TO IGNITE A SUN --
-- "GOOD" IS TOO SMALL FOR THEM. THEY'RE A FORCE OF... NATURE...?
SO IS THE BUBONIC PLAGUE, BUT THAT DOESN'T MAKE IT A "GOOD GUY."
WHOA... KAL...?

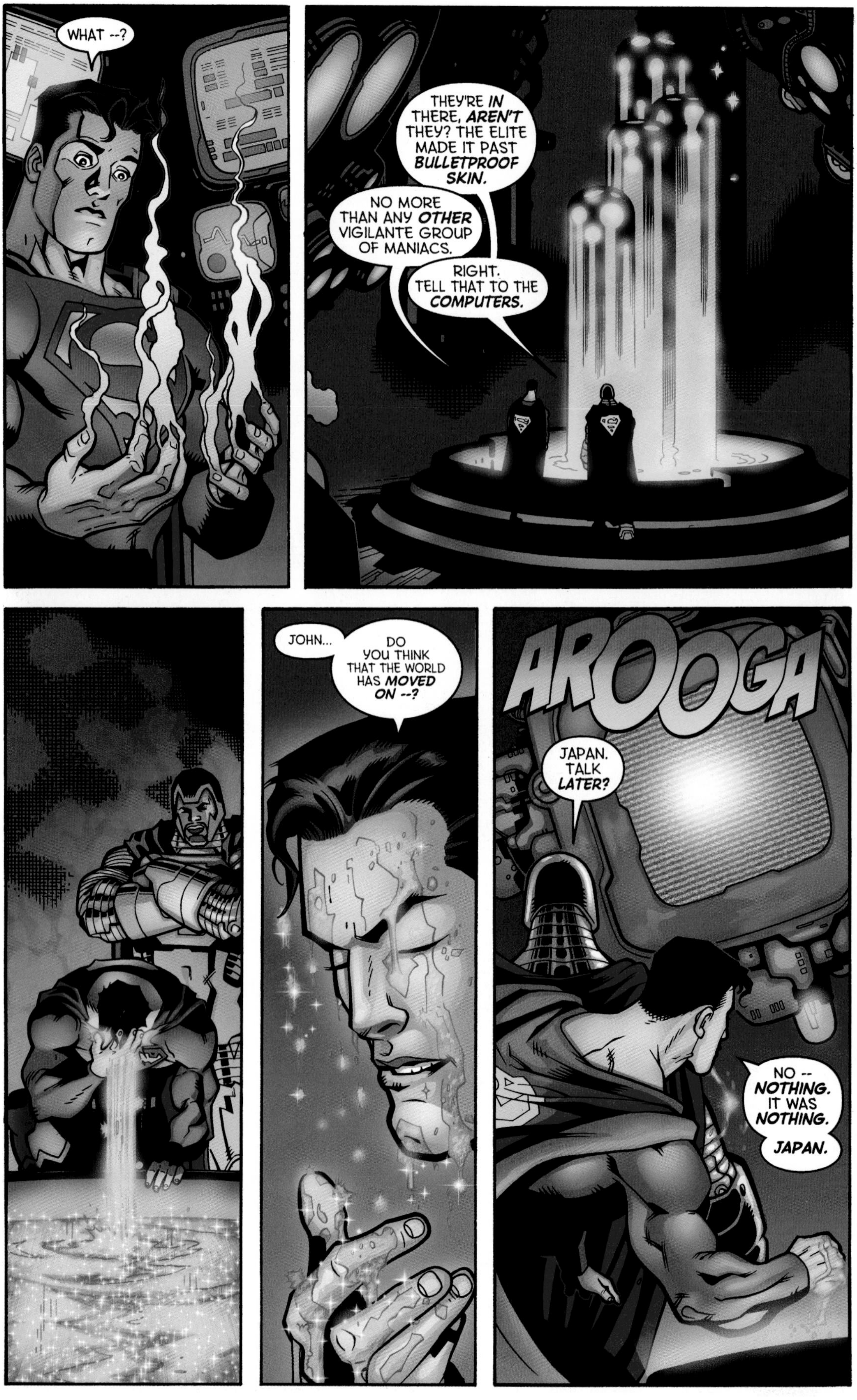
WHAT --?
THEY'RE IN THERE, AREN'T THEY? THE ELITE MADE IT PAST BULLETPROOF SKIN.
NO MORE THAN ANY OTHER VIGILANTE GROUP OF MANIACS.
RIGHT. TELL THAT TO THE COMPUTERS.
JOHN...
DO YOU THINK THAT THE WORLD HAS MOVED ON --?
AROOGA
JAPAN. TALK LATER?
NO -- NOTHING. IT WAS NOTHING.
JAPAN.

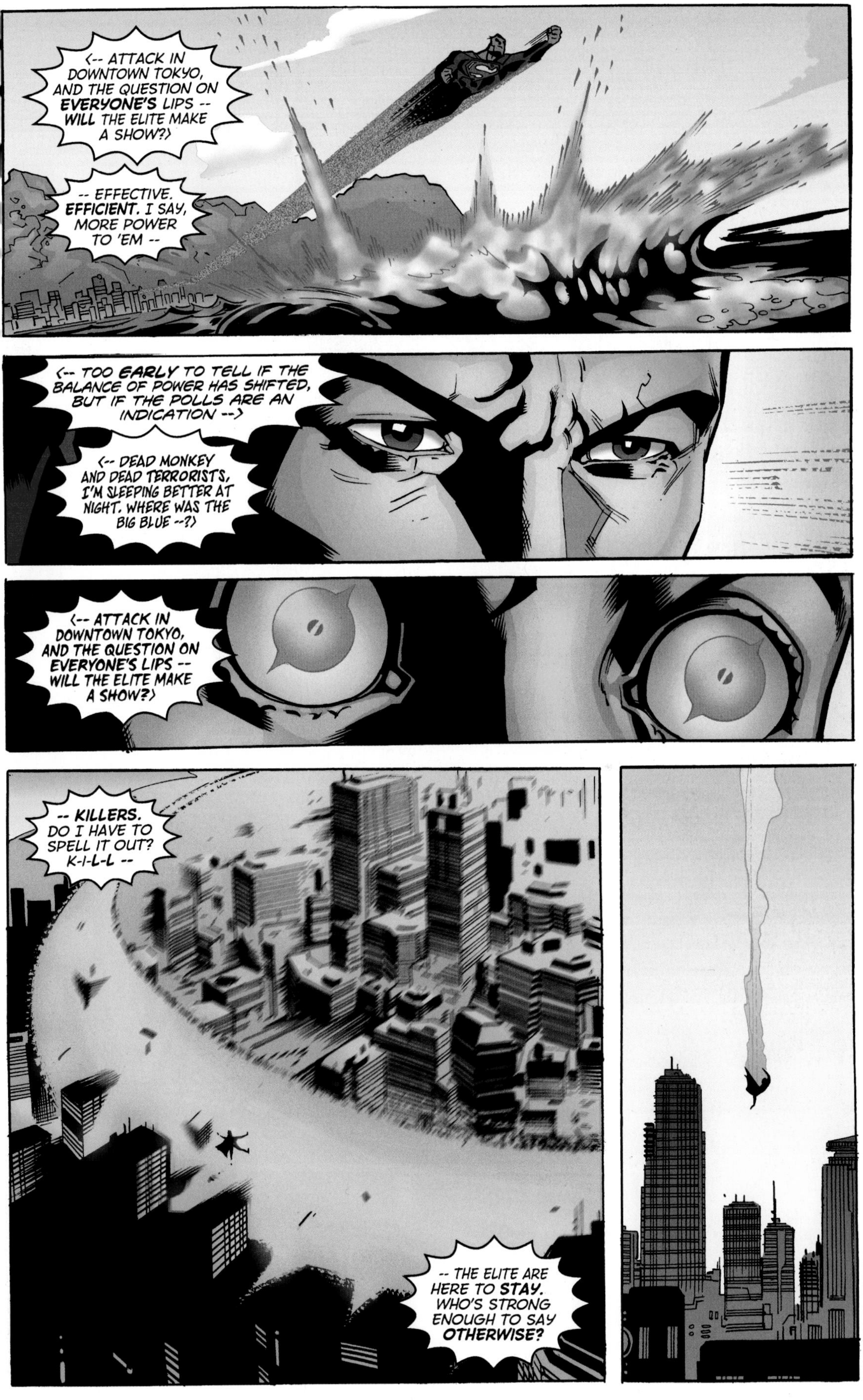

<-- ATTACK IN DOWNTOWN TOKYO, AND THE QUESTION ON **EVERYONE'S** LIPS -- **WILL** THE ELITE MAKE A SHOW?>
-- EFFECTIVE. **EFFICIENT.** I SAY, MORE POWER TO 'EM --
<-- TOO **EARLY** TO TELL IF THE BALANCE OF POWER HAS SHIFTED, BUT IF THE POLLS ARE AN INDICATION -->
<-- DEAD MONKEY AND DEAD TERRORISTS, I'M SLEEPING BETTER AT NIGHT. WHERE WAS THE BIG BLUE --?>
<-- ATTACK IN DOWNTOWN TOKYO, AND THE QUESTION ON EVERYONE'S LIPS -- WILL THE ELITE MAKE A SHOW?>
-- **KILLERS.** DO I HAVE TO SPELL IT OUT? K-I-**L-L** --
-- THE ELITE ARE HERE TO **STAY.** WHO'S STRONG ENOUGH TO SAY **OTHERWISE?**

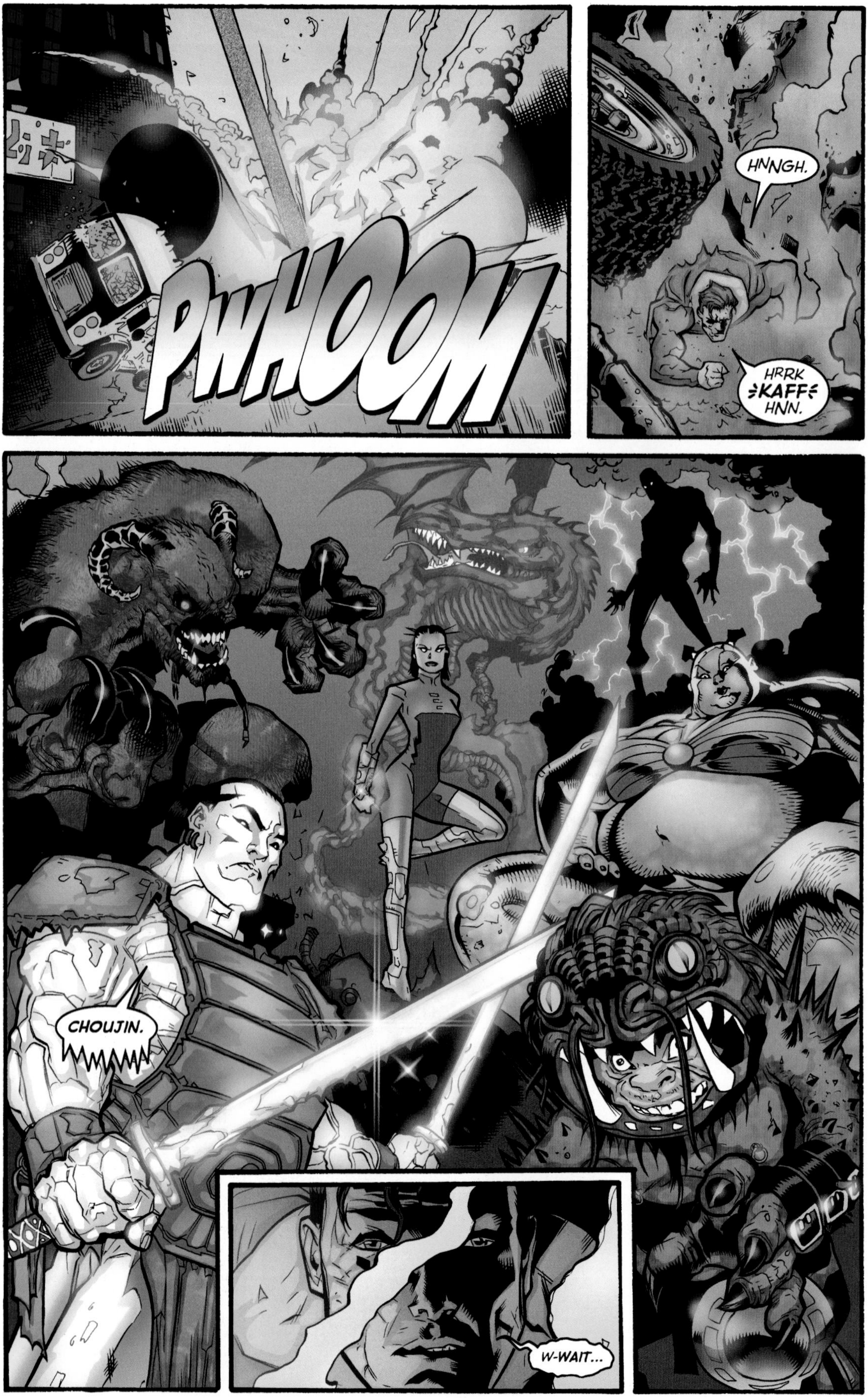

PWHOOOM
HNNGH.
HRRK
KAFF
HNN.
CHOUJIN.
W-WAIT...

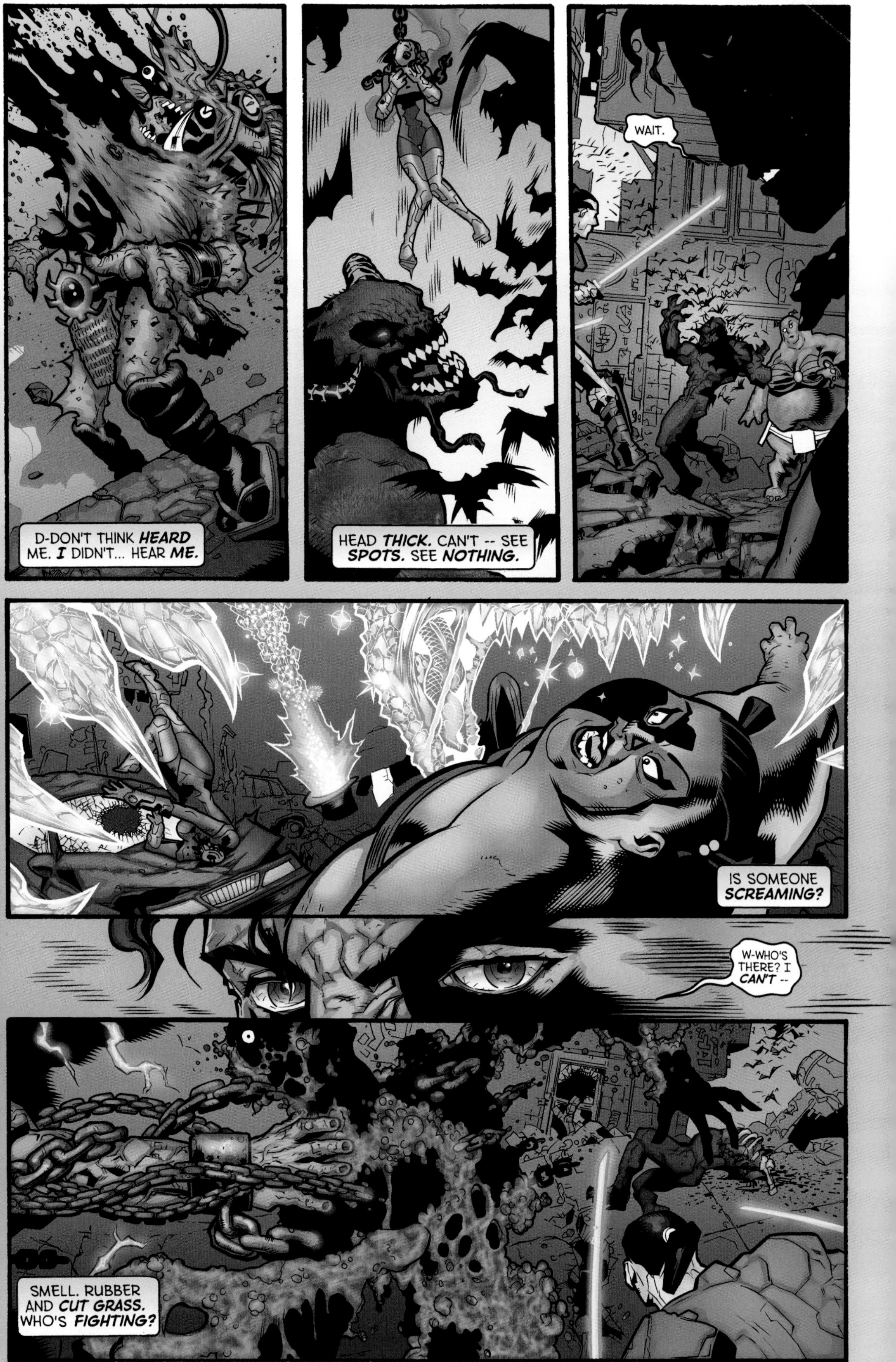
D-DON'T THINK HEARD ME. I DIDN'T... HEAR ME.
HEAD THICK. CAN'T -- SEE SPOTS. SEE NOTHING.
WAIT.
IS SOMEONE SCREAMING?
W-WHO'S THERE? I CAN'T --
SMELL. RUBBER AND CUT GRASS. WHO'S FIGHTING?

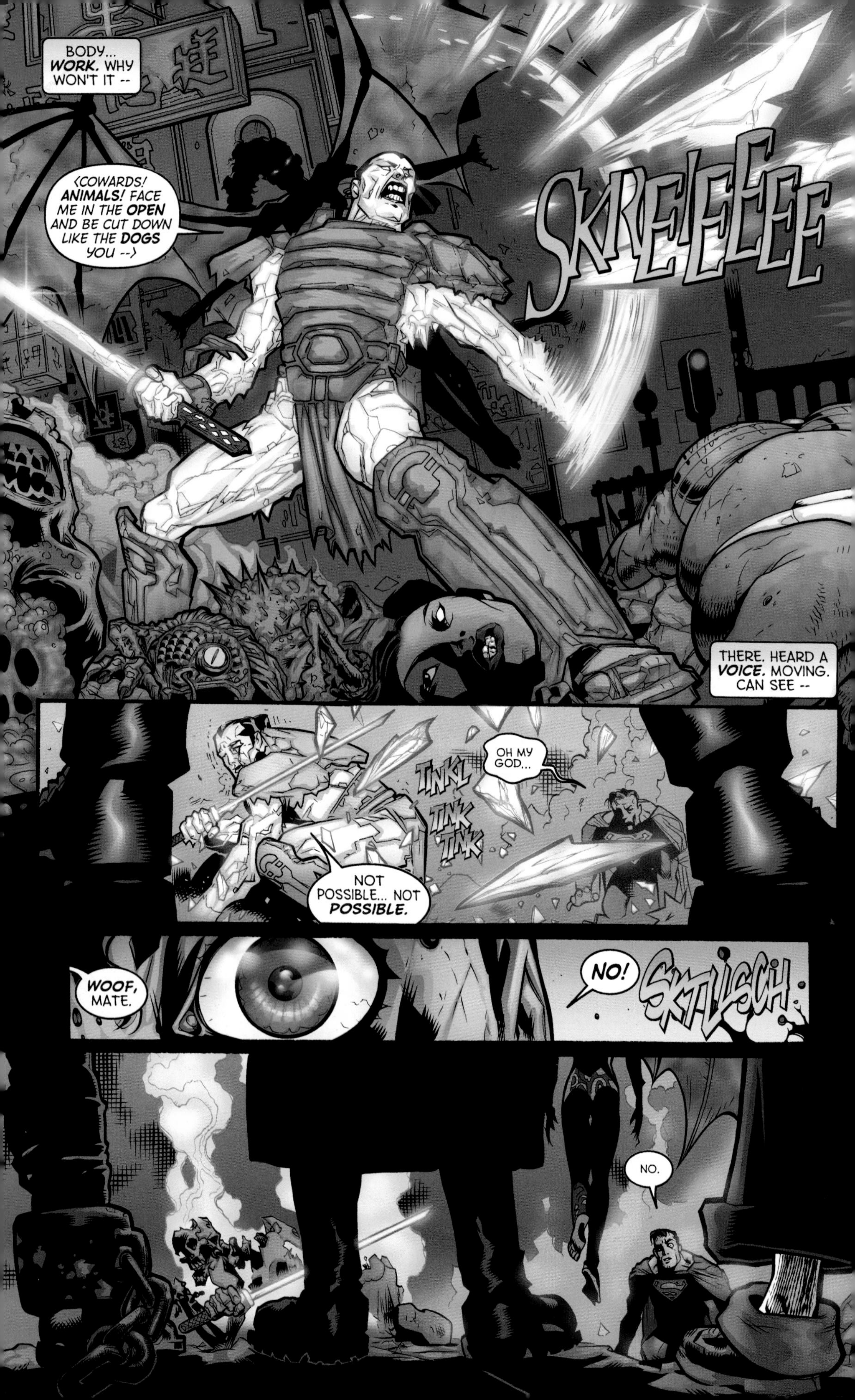
BODY... WORK. WHY WON'T IT --
‹COWARDS! ANIMALS! FACE ME IN THE OPEN AND BE CUT DOWN LIKE THE DOGS YOU --›
SKREIEEEE
THERE. HEARD A VOICE. MOVING. CAN SEE --
OH MY GOD...
TINKL
TINK TINK
NOT POSSIBLE... NOT POSSIBLE.
WOOF, MATE.
NO!
SKTLISCH
NO.

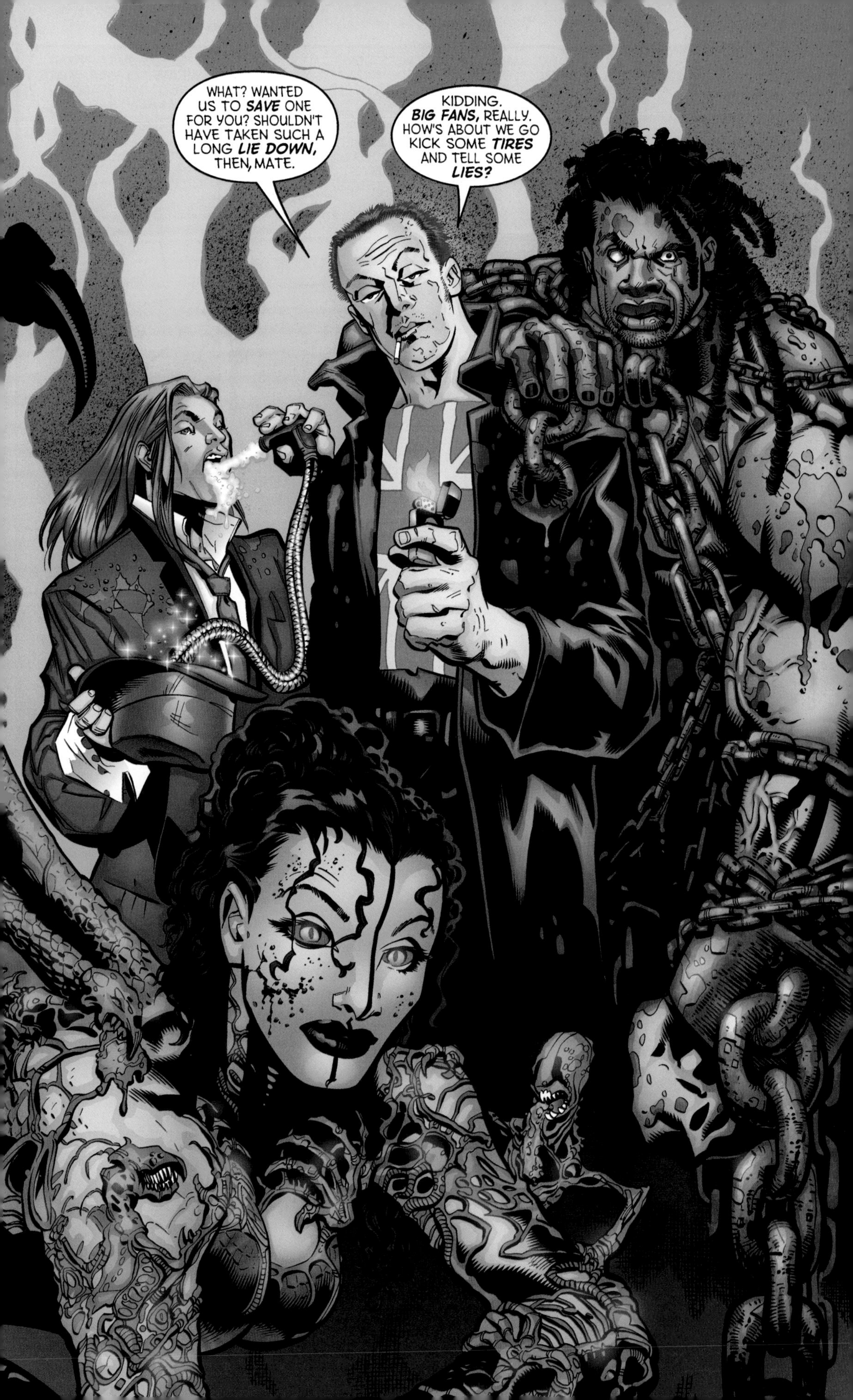
WHAT? WANTED US TO SAVE ONE FOR YOU? SHOULDN'T HAVE TAKEN SUCH A LONG LIE DOWN, THEN, MATE.
KIDDING. BIG FANS, REALLY. HOW'S ABOUT WE GO KICK SOME TIRES AND TELL SOME LIES?

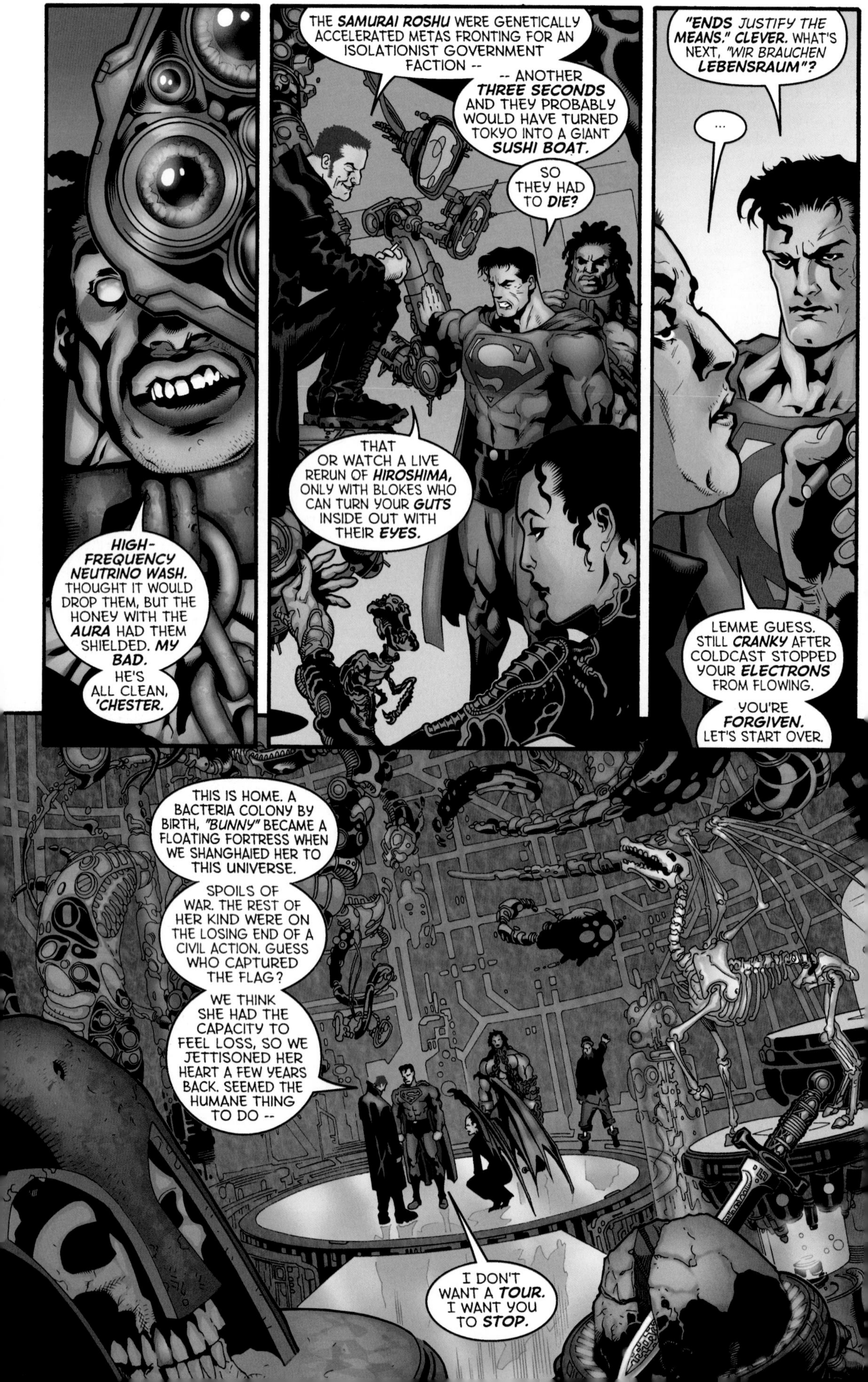

HIGH-FREQUENCY NEUTRINO WASH. THOUGHT IT WOULD DROP THEM, BUT THE HONEY WITH THE AURA HAD THEM SHIELDED. MY BAD.
HE'S ALL CLEAN, 'CHESTER.
THE SAMURAI ROSHU WERE GENETICALLY ACCELERATED METAS FRONTING FOR AN ISOLATIONIST GOVERNMENT FACTION --
-- ANOTHER THREE SECONDS AND THEY PROBABLY WOULD HAVE TURNED TOKYO INTO A GIANT SUSHI BOAT.
SO THEY HAD TO DIE?
THAT OR WATCH A LIVE RERUN OF HIROSHIMA, ONLY WITH BLOKES WHO CAN TURN YOUR GUTS INSIDE OUT WITH THEIR EYES.
"ENDS JUSTIFY THE MEANS." CLEVER. WHAT'S NEXT, "WIR BRAUCHEN LEBENSRAUM"?
...
LEMME GUESS. STILL CRANKY AFTER COLDCAST STOPPED YOUR ELECTRONS FROM FLOWING.
YOU'RE FORGIVEN. LET'S START OVER.
THIS IS HOME. A BACTERIA COLONY BY BIRTH, "BUNNY" BECAME A FLOATING FORTRESS WHEN WE SHANGHAIED HER TO THIS UNIVERSE.
SPOILS OF WAR. THE REST OF HER KIND WERE ON THE LOSING END OF A CIVIL ACTION. GUESS WHO CAPTURED THE FLAG?
WE THINK SHE HAD THE CAPACITY TO FEEL LOSS, SO WE JETTISONED HER HEART A FEW YEARS BACK. SEEMED THE HUMANE THING TO DO --
I DON'T WANT A TOUR. I WANT YOU TO STOP.

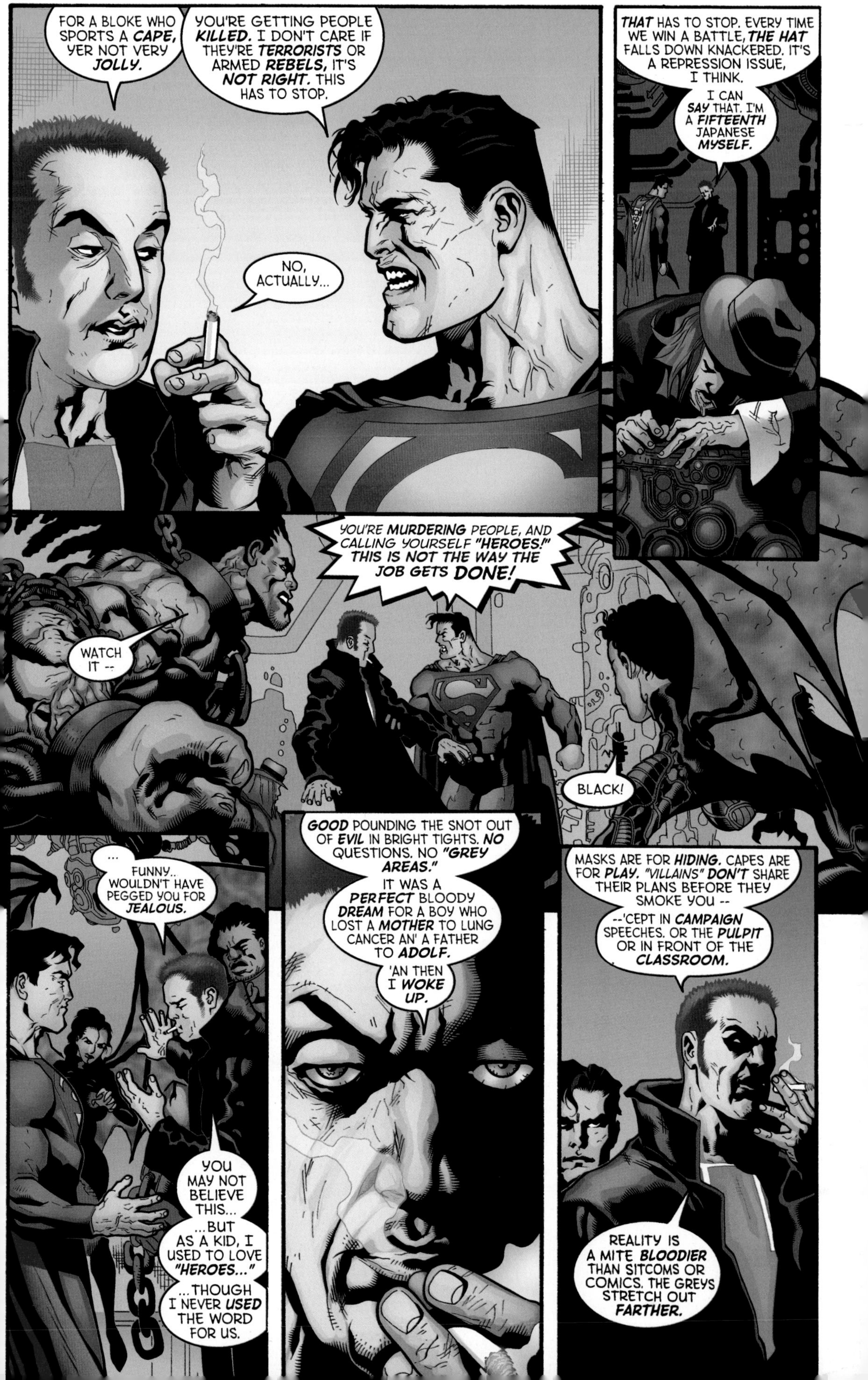

FOR A BLOKE WHO SPORTS A CAPE, YER NOT VERY JOLLY.
YOU'RE GETTING PEOPLE KILLED. I DON'T CARE IF THEY'RE TERRORISTS OR ARMED REBELS, IT'S NOT RIGHT. THIS HAS TO STOP.
NO, ACTUALLY...
THAT HAS TO STOP. EVERY TIME WE WIN A BATTLE, THE HAT FALLS DOWN KNACKERED. IT'S A REPRESSION ISSUE, I THINK.
I CAN SAY THAT. I'M A FIFTEENTH JAPANESE MYSELF.
YOU'RE MURDERING PEOPLE, AND CALLING YOURSELF "HEROES!" THIS IS NOT THE WAY THE JOB GETS DONE!
WATCH IT --
BLACK!
...
FUNNY.. WOULDN'T HAVE PEGGED YOU FOR JEALOUS.
YOU MAY NOT BELIEVE THIS...
...BUT AS A KID, I USED TO LOVE "HEROES..."
...THOUGH I NEVER USED THE WORD FOR US.
GOOD POUNDING THE SNOT OUT OF EVIL IN BRIGHT TIGHTS. NO QUESTIONS. NO "GREY AREAS."
IT WAS A PERFECT BLOODY DREAM FOR A BOY WHO LOST A MOTHER TO LUNG CANCER AN' A FATHER TO ADOLF.
'AN THEN I WOKE UP.
MASKS ARE FOR HIDING. CAPES ARE FOR PLAY. "VILLAINS" DON'T SHARE THEIR PLANS BEFORE THEY SMOKE YOU --
--'CEPT IN CAMPAIGN SPEECHES, OR THE PULPIT OR IN FRONT OF THE CLASSROOM.
REALITY IS A MITE BLOODIER THAN SITCOMS OR COMICS. THE GREYS STRETCH OUT FARTHER.

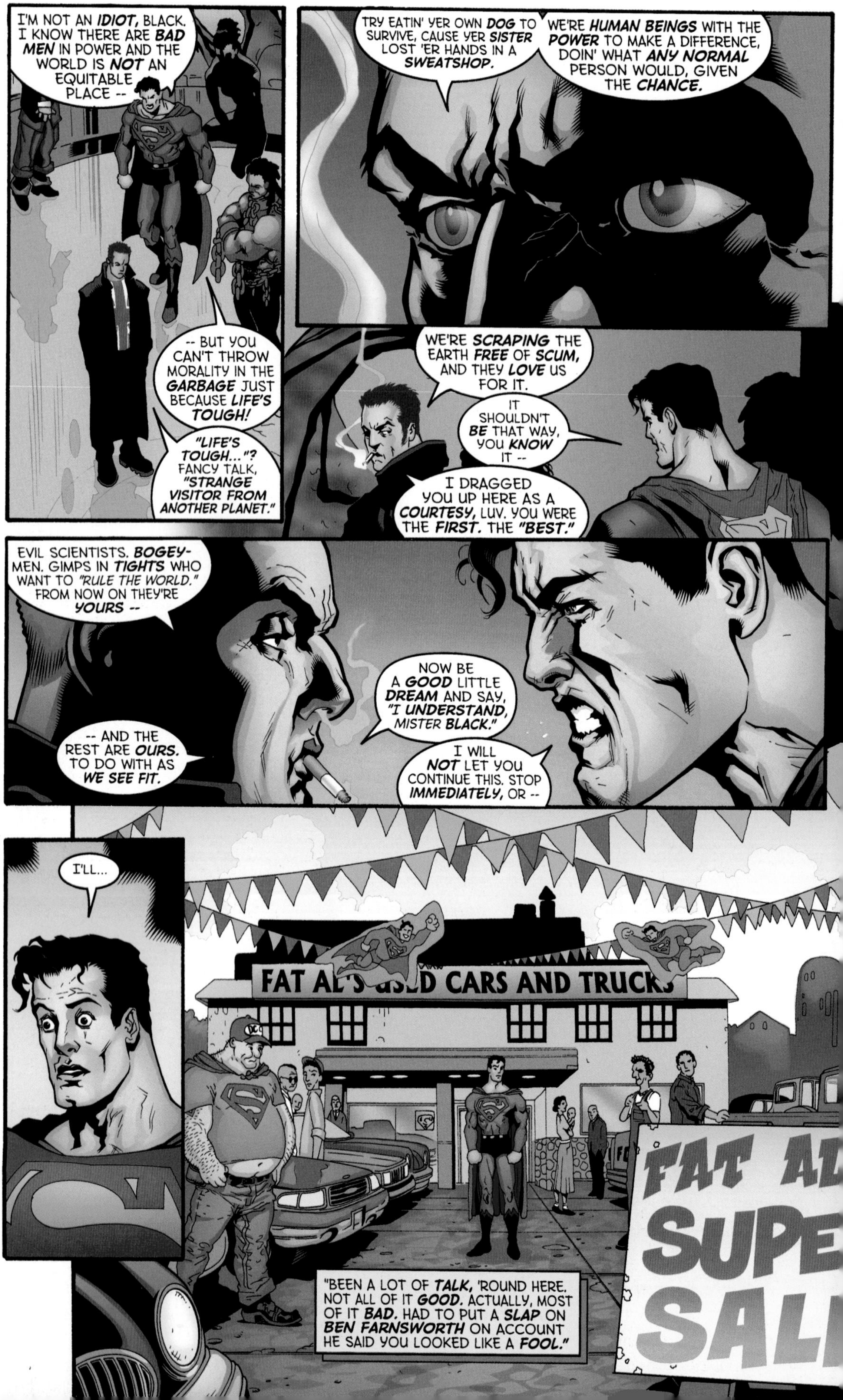
I'M NOT AN IDIOT, BLACK. I KNOW THERE ARE BAD MEN IN POWER AND THE WORLD IS NOT AN EQUITABLE PLACE --
-- BUT YOU CAN'T THROW MORALITY IN THE GARBAGE JUST BECAUSE LIFE'S TOUGH!
"LIFE'S TOUGH..."? FANCY TALK, "STRANGE VISITOR FROM ANOTHER PLANET."
TRY EATIN' YER OWN DOG TO SURVIVE, CAUSE YER SISTER LOST 'ER HANDS IN A SWEATSHOP.
WE'RE HUMAN BEINGS WITH THE POWER TO MAKE A DIFFERENCE, DOIN' WHAT ANY NORMAL PERSON WOULD, GIVEN THE CHANCE.
WE'RE SCRAPING THE EARTH FREE OF SCUM, AND THEY LOVE US FOR IT.
IT SHOULDN'T BE THAT WAY, YOU KNOW IT --
I DRAGGED YOU UP HERE AS A COURTESY, LUV. YOU WERE THE FIRST. THE "BEST."
EVIL SCIENTISTS. BOGEY-MEN. GIMPS IN TIGHTS WHO WANT TO "RULE THE WORLD." FROM NOW ON THEY'RE YOURS --
-- AND THE REST ARE OURS. TO DO WITH AS WE SEE FIT.
NOW BE A GOOD LITTLE DREAM AND SAY, "I UNDERSTAND, MISTER BLACK."
I WILL NOT LET YOU CONTINUE THIS. STOP IMMEDIATELY, OR --
I'LL...
FAT AL'S USED CARS AND TRUCKS
"BEEN A LOT OF TALK, 'ROUND HERE. NOT ALL OF IT GOOD. ACTUALLY, MOST OF IT BAD. HAD TO PUT A SLAP ON BEN FARNSWORTH ON ACCOUNT HE SAID YOU LOOKED LIKE A FOOL."

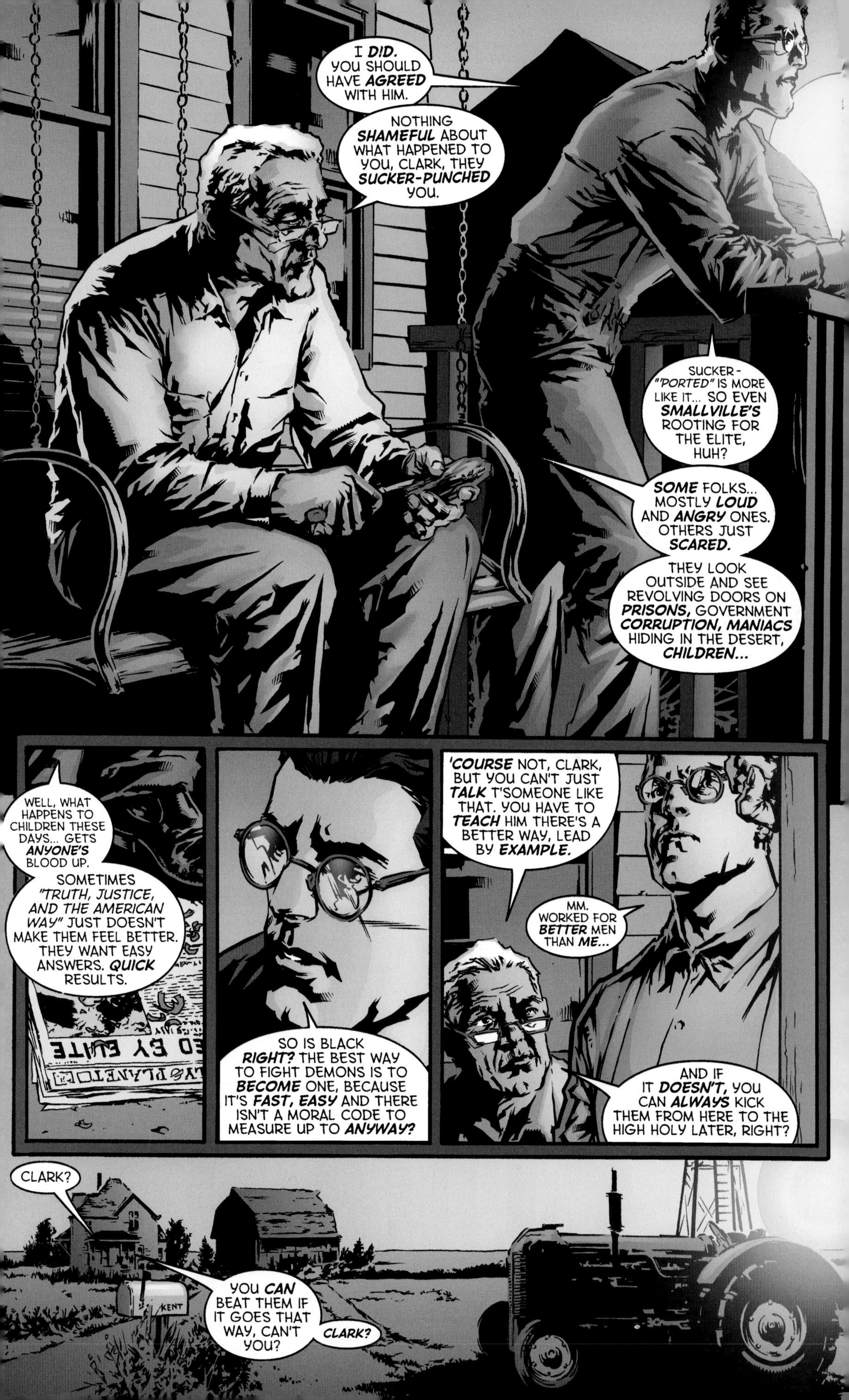
I DID. YOU SHOULD HAVE AGREED WITH HIM.
NOTHING SHAMEFUL ABOUT WHAT HAPPENED TO YOU, CLARK, THEY SUCKER-PUNCHED YOU.
SUCKER-"PORTED" IS MORE LIKE IT... SO EVEN SMALLVILLE'S ROOTING FOR THE ELITE, HUH?
SOME FOLKS... MOSTLY LOUD AND ANGRY ONES. OTHERS JUST SCARED.
THEY LOOK OUTSIDE AND SEE REVOLVING DOORS ON PRISONS, GOVERNMENT CORRUPTION, MANIACS HIDING IN THE DESERT, CHILDREN...
WELL, WHAT HAPPENS TO CHILDREN THESE DAYS... GETS ANYONE'S BLOOD UP.
SOMETIMES "TRUTH, JUSTICE, AND THE AMERICAN WAY" JUST DOESN'T MAKE THEM FEEL BETTER. THEY WANT EASY ANSWERS. QUICK RESULTS.
SO IS BLACK RIGHT? THE BEST WAY TO FIGHT DEMONS IS TO BECOME ONE, BECAUSE IT'S FAST, EASY AND THERE ISN'T A MORAL CODE TO MEASURE UP TO ANYWAY?
'COURSE NOT, CLARK, BUT YOU CAN'T JUST TALK T'SOMEONE LIKE THAT. YOU HAVE TO TEACH HIM THERE'S A BETTER WAY, LEAD BY EXAMPLE.
MM. WORKED FOR BETTER MEN THAN ME...
AND IF IT DOESN'T, YOU CAN ALWAYS KICK THEM FROM HERE TO THE HIGH HOLY LATER, RIGHT?
CLARK?
KENT
YOU CAN BEAT THEM IF IT GOES THAT WAY, CAN'T YOU?
CLARK?

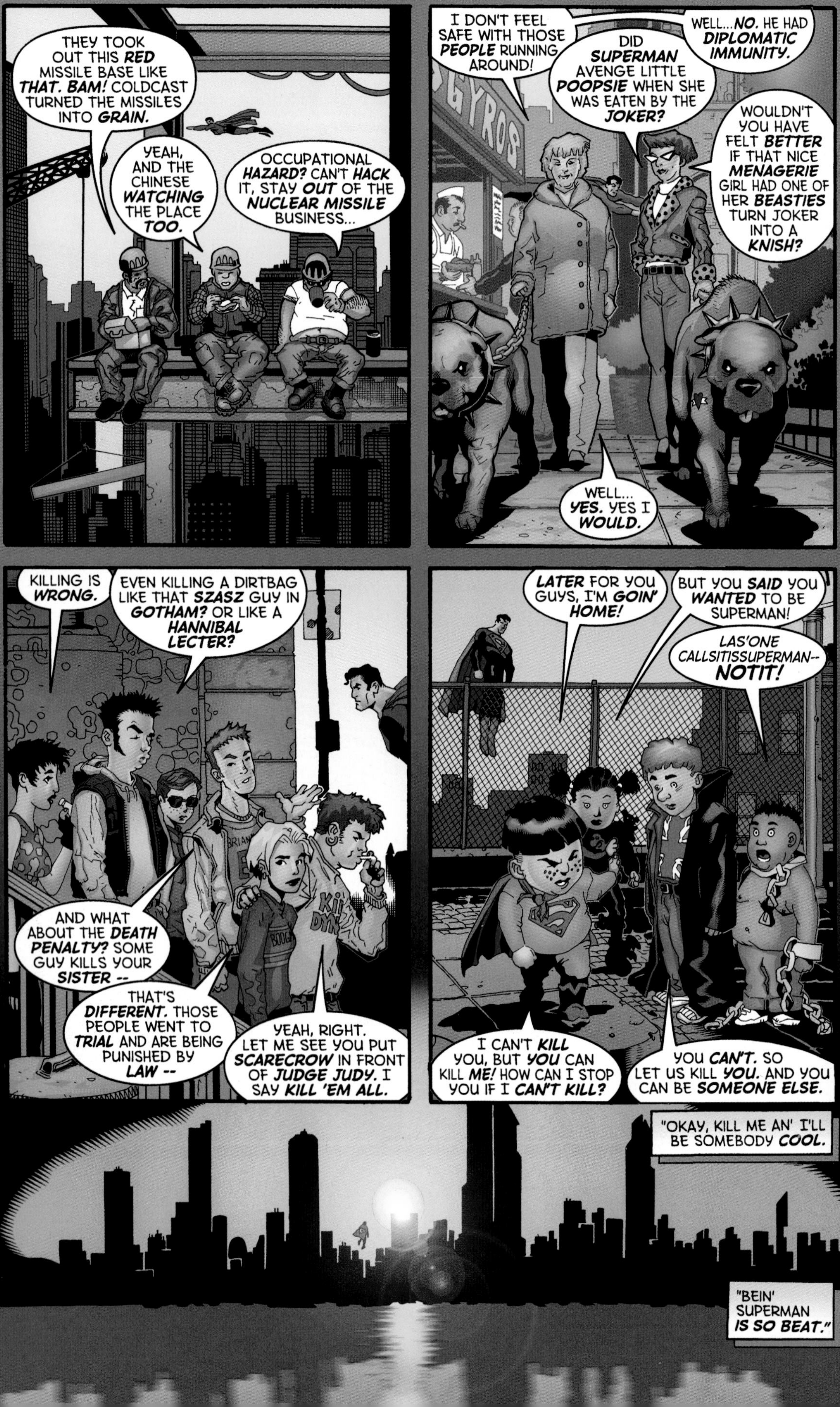
THEY TOOK OUT THIS RED MISSILE BASE LIKE THAT. BAM! COLDCAST TURNED THE MISSILES INTO GRAIN.
YEAH, AND THE CHINESE WATCHING THE PLACE TOO.
OCCUPATIONAL HAZARD? CAN'T HACK IT, STAY OUT OF THE NUCLEAR MISSILE BUSINESS...
I DON'T FEEL SAFE WITH THOSE PEOPLE RUNNING AROUND!
DID SUPERMAN AVENGE LITTLE POOPSIE WHEN SHE WAS EATEN BY THE JOKER?
WELL...NO. HE HAD DIPLOMATIC IMMUNITY.
GYROS
WOULDN'T YOU HAVE FELT BETTER IF THAT NICE MENAGERIE GIRL HAD ONE OF HER BEASTIES TURN JOKER INTO A KNISH?
WELL... YES. YES I WOULD.
KILLING IS WRONG.
EVEN KILLING A DIRTBAG LIKE THAT SZASZ GUY IN GOTHAM? OR LIKE A HANNIBAL LECTER?
AND WHAT ABOUT THE DEATH PENALTY? SOME GUY KILLS YOUR SISTER --
THAT'S DIFFERENT. THOSE PEOPLE WENT TO TRIAL AND ARE BEING PUNISHED BY LAW --
YEAH, RIGHT. LET ME SEE YOU PUT SCARECROW IN FRONT OF JUDGE JUDY. I SAY KILL 'EM ALL.
LATER FOR YOU GUYS, I'M GOIN' HOME!
BUT YOU SAID YOU WANTED TO BE SUPERMAN!
LAS'ONE CALLSITISSUPERMAN-- NOTIT!
I CAN'T KILL YOU, BUT YOU CAN KILL ME! HOW CAN I STOP YOU IF I CAN'T KILL?
YOU CAN'T. SO LET US KILL YOU. AND YOU CAN BE SOMEONE ELSE.
"OKAY, KILL ME AN' I'LL BE SOMEBODY COOL.
"BEIN' SUPERMAN IS SO BEAT."

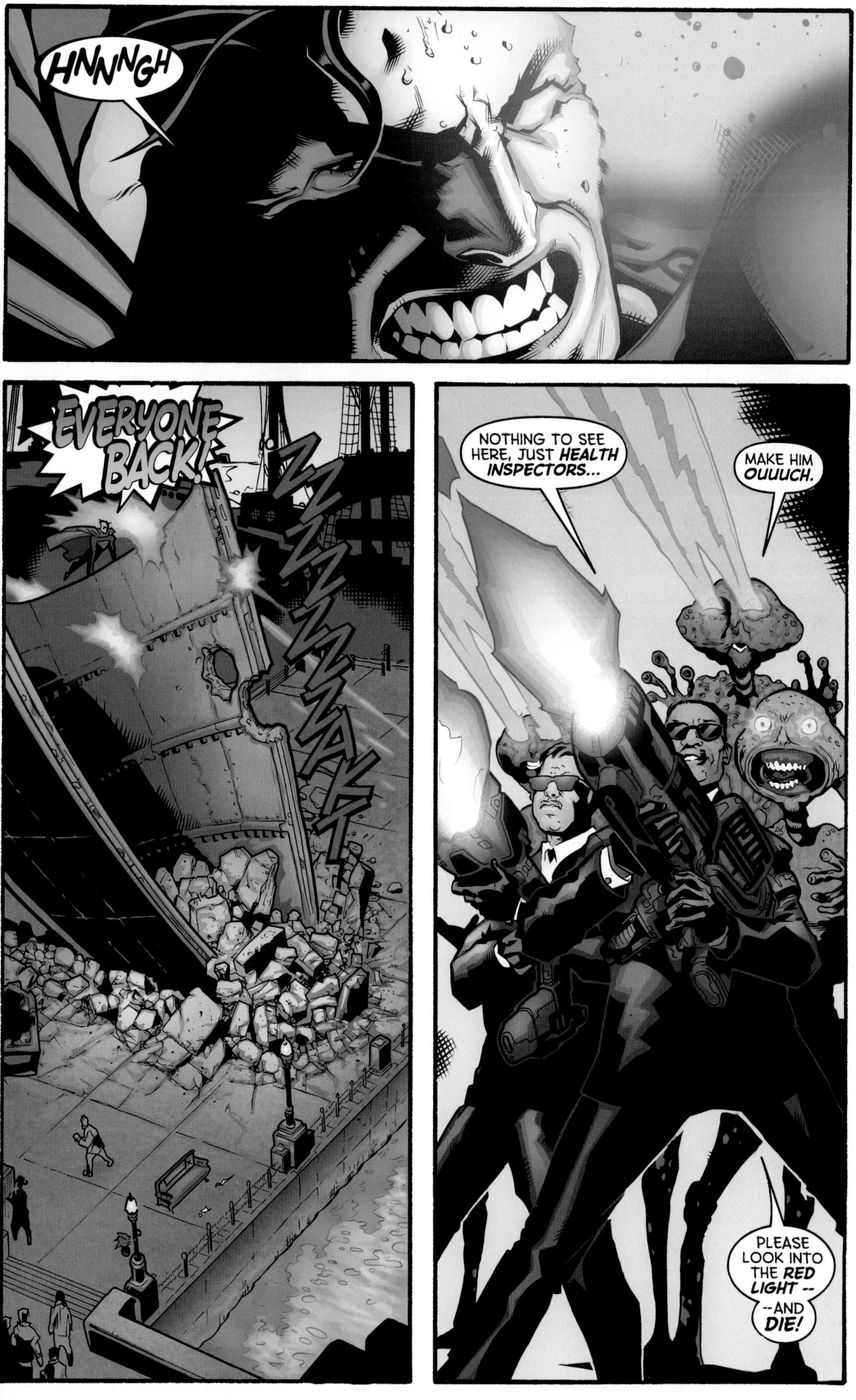
HNNNGH
EVERYONE BACK!
NNNNNNWAK
NOTHING TO SEE HERE, JUST HEALTH INSPECTORS...
MAKE HIM OUUUCH.
PLEASE LOOK INTO THE RED LIGHT --
--AND DIE!

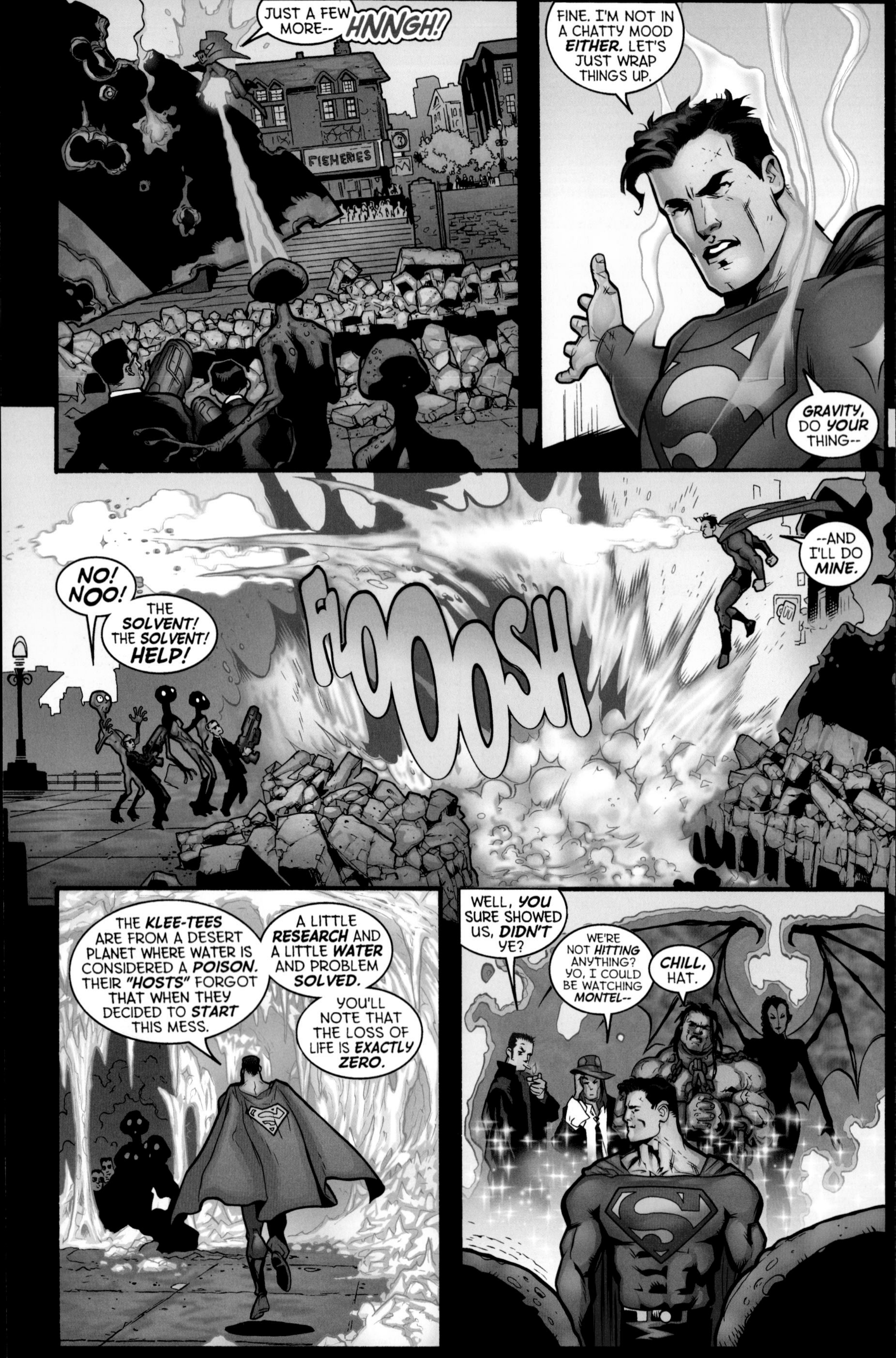
JUST A FEW MORE-- HNNGH!
FINE. I'M NOT IN A CHATTY MOOD EITHER. LET'S JUST WRAP THINGS UP.
GRAVITY, DO YOUR THING--
--AND I'LL DO MINE.
FISHERIES
FLOOOSH
NO! NOO!
THE SOLVENT! THE SOLVENT! HELP!
THE KLEE-TEES ARE FROM A DESERT PLANET WHERE WATER IS CONSIDERED A POISON. THEIR "HOSTS" FORGOT THAT WHEN THEY DECIDED TO START THIS MESS.
A LITTLE RESEARCH AND A LITTLE WATER AND PROBLEM SOLVED.
YOU'LL NOTE THAT THE LOSS OF LIFE IS EXACTLY ZERO.
WELL, YOU SURE SHOWED US, DIDN'T YE?
WE'RE NOT HITTING ANYTHING? YO, I COULD BE WATCHING MONTEL--
CHILL, HAT.

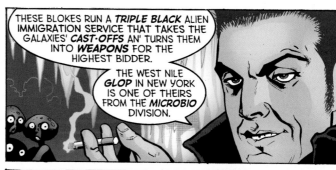

AND WHAT HAPPENS NOW, SWEETHEART?

FIRST, I GET THE JLA DOWN HERE TO DETAIN THE ALIENS. THEN, WE QUESTION THESE ROGUE D.E.O.♡ AGENTS TO DETERMINE WHO THEY ARE AND WHAT THEY--

THESE BLOKES RUN A TRIPLE BLACK ALIEN IMMIGRATION SERVICE THAT TAKES THE GALAXIES' CAST-OFFS AN' TURNS THEM INTO WEAPONS FOR THE HIGHEST BIDDER.

THE WEST NILE GLOP IN NEW YORK IS ONE OF THEIRS FROM THE MICROBIO DIVISION.

IDIOT.

EXCUSE ME?

DEPARTMENT OF EXTRANORMAL OPERATIONS -- EDDIE.

AND YOU KNOW THIS HOW?

YOU THINK PAM BONDED HERSELF TO AN ALIEN WARRIOR CRECHE WITH A HOT GLUE GUN?

TEE.

THESE ARE BAD MEN, SUPES. VERY BAD. AN' LET ME TELL YOU WHAT'LL HAPPEN NEXT. THEY'LL STAND "TRIAL," GET SENT TO A "MAXIMUM SECURITY POKEY," --GASP AND HORROR--!

IT WON'T BE A PRISON, BUT A SHADOW CABINET WORKSHOP WHERE THEY'LL ALL GET JOBS TRAINING SLACK-JAWED YANKS TO DO THE SAME THING.

THEN I'LL STOP THEM AGAIN. AND AGAIN. AND AGAIN IF I HAVE TO--

--UNTIL THEY GET THE MESSAGE.

AND I'LL DO IT WITHOUT MELTING ANY-ONE INTO SLAG FOR KICKS.

DAMN YOU AMERICANS LIKE TO HEAR YOURSELVES YAP.

HAT, TELL THE STREETS TO SWALLOW THEM ALL, THEN RAIN ACID ON THEIR FAMILIES. THAT OUGHT TO SEND A MESSAGE.

AYE AYE, CAP'N BLIGH--

NO!

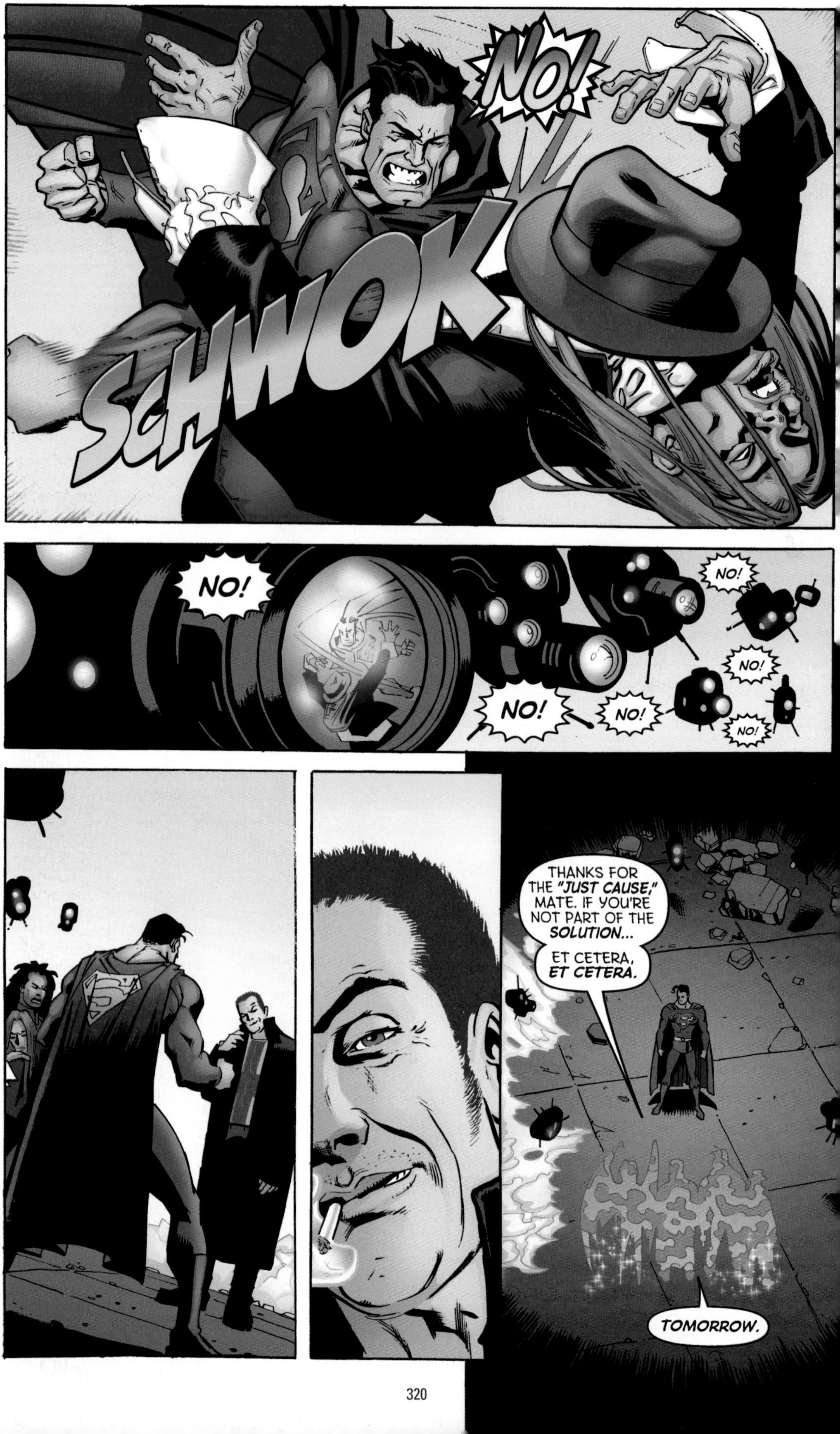
NO!
SCHWOK
NO!
NO!
NO!
NO!
NO!
NO!
THANKS FOR THE "JUST CAUSE," MATE. IF YOU'RE NOT PART OF THE SOLUTION...
ET CETERA, ET CETERA.
TOMORROW.

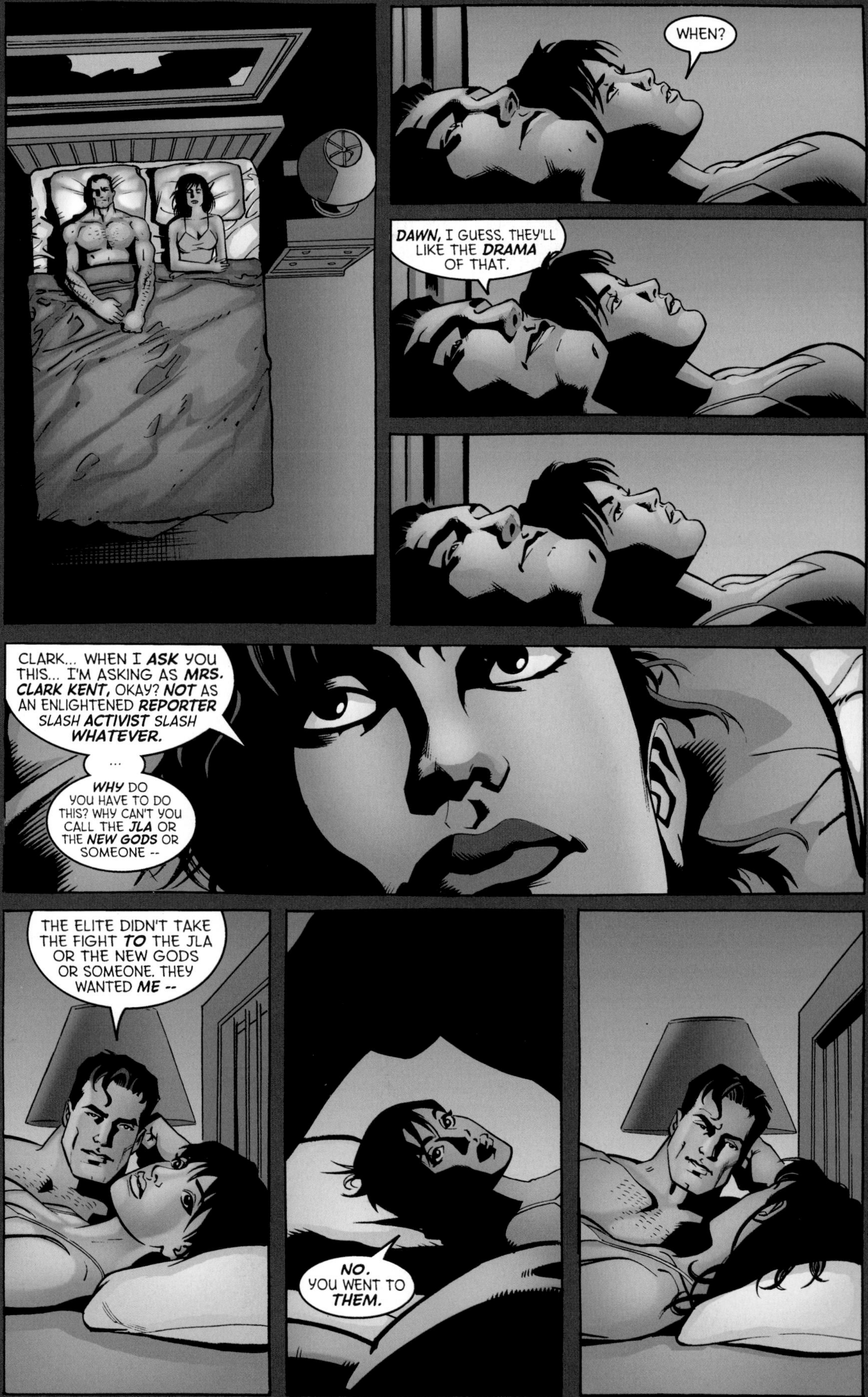
WHEN?
DAWN, I GUESS. THEY'LL LIKE THE DRAMA OF THAT.
CLARK... WHEN I ASK YOU THIS... I'M ASKING AS MRS. CLARK KENT, OKAY? NOT AS AN ENLIGHTENED REPORTER SLASH ACTIVIST SLASH WHATEVER.
...
WHY DO YOU HAVE TO DO THIS? WHY CAN'T YOU CALL THE JLA OR THE NEW GODS OR SOMEONE --
THE ELITE DIDN'T TAKE THE FIGHT TO THE JLA OR THE NEW GODS OR SOMEONE. THEY WANTED ME --
NO. YOU WENT TO THEM.

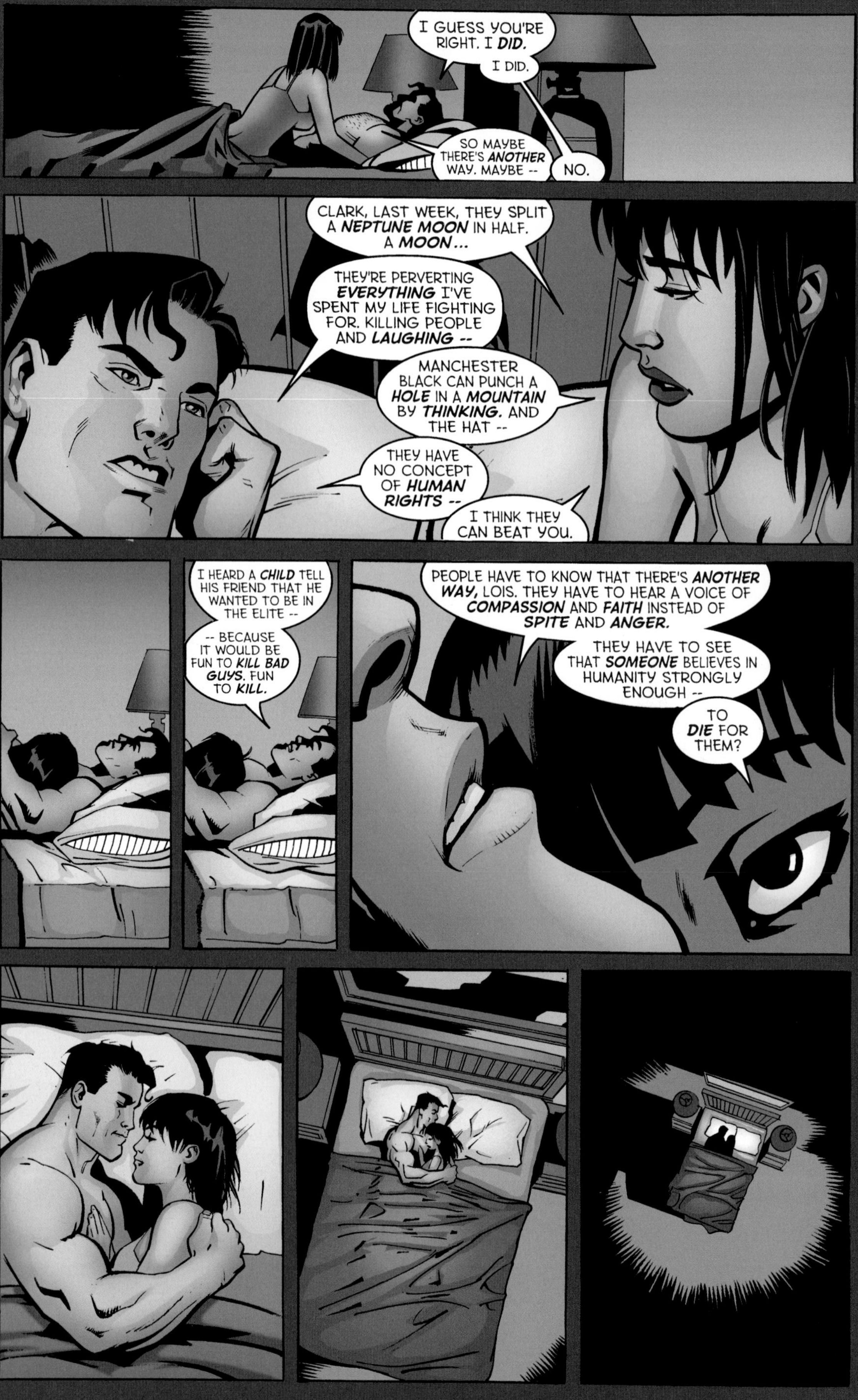
I GUESS YOU'RE RIGHT. I DID.
I DID.
SO MAYBE THERE'S ANOTHER WAY. MAYBE --
NO.
CLARK, LAST WEEK, THEY SPLIT A NEPTUNE MOON IN HALF. A MOON...
THEY'RE PERVERTING EVERYTHING I'VE SPENT MY LIFE FIGHTING FOR. KILLING PEOPLE AND LAUGHING --
MANCHESTER BLACK CAN PUNCH A HOLE IN A MOUNTAIN BY THINKING. AND THE HAT --
THEY HAVE NO CONCEPT OF HUMAN RIGHTS --
I THINK THEY CAN BEAT YOU.
I HEARD A CHILD TELL HIS FRIEND THAT HE WANTED TO BE IN THE ELITE --
-- BECAUSE IT WOULD BE FUN TO KILL BAD GUYS. FUN TO KILL.
PEOPLE HAVE TO KNOW THAT THERE'S ANOTHER WAY, LOIS. THEY HAVE TO HEAR A VOICE OF COMPASSION AND FAITH INSTEAD OF SPITE AND ANGER.
THEY HAVE TO SEE THAT SOMEONE BELIEVES IN HUMANITY STRONGLY ENOUGH --
TO DIE FOR THEM?

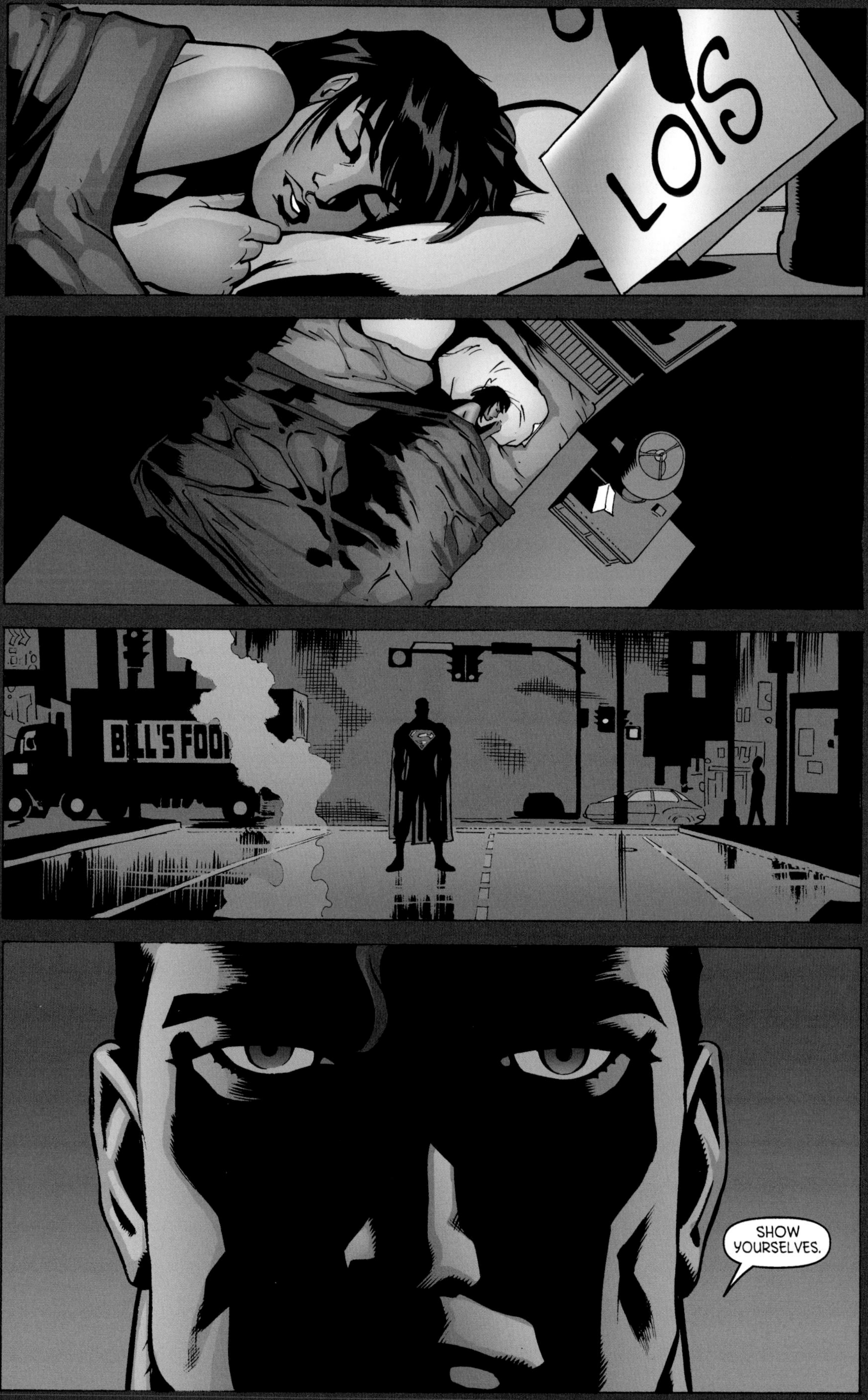
LOIS
BILL'S FOO
SHOW YOURSELVES.

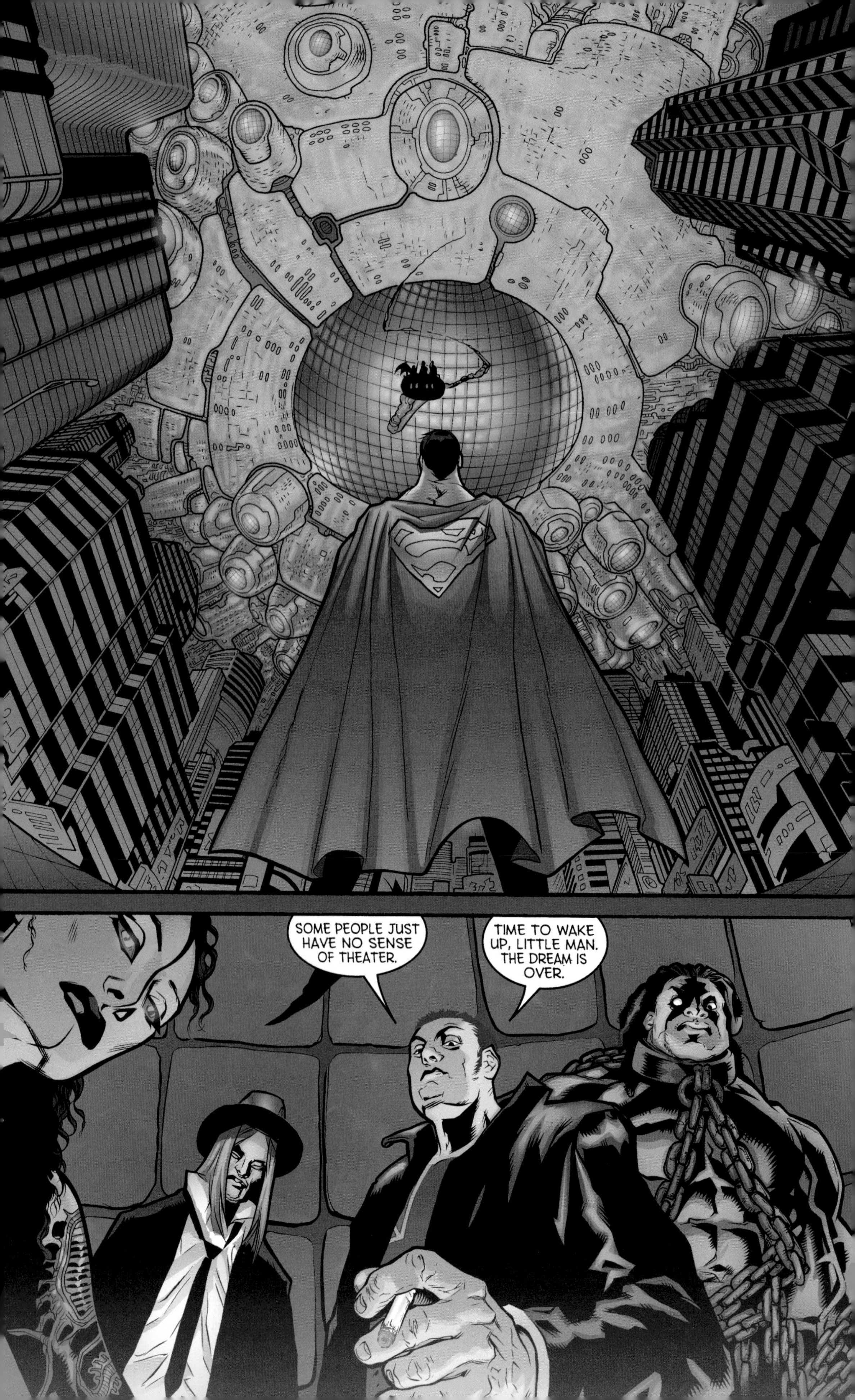
SOME PEOPLE JUST HAVE NO SENSE OF THEATER.
TIME TO WAKE UP, LITTLE MAN. THE DREAM IS OVER.

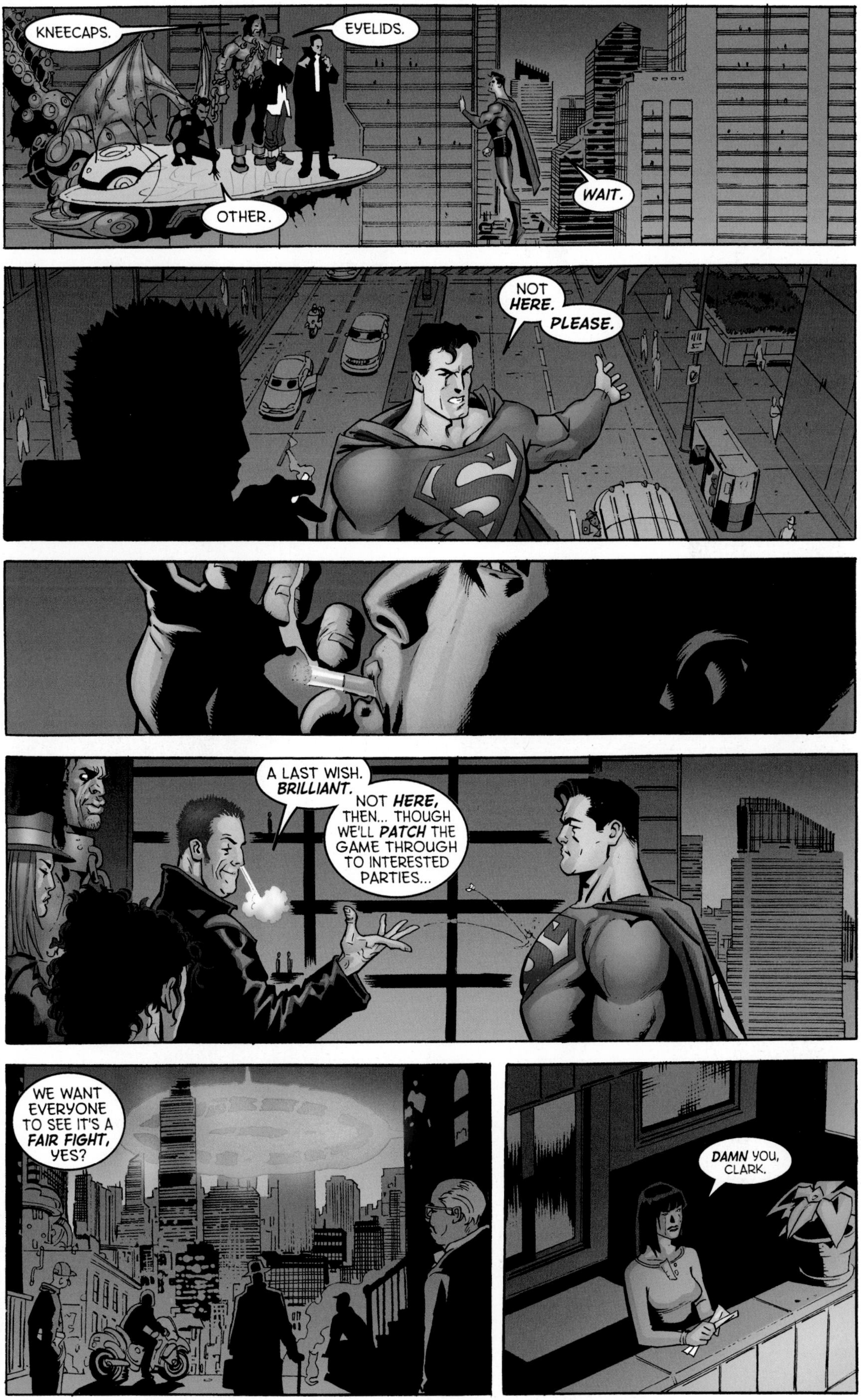
KNEECAPS.
EYELIDS.
OTHER.
WAIT.
NOT HERE. PLEASE.
A LAST WISH. BRILLIANT.
NOT HERE, THEN... THOUGH WE'LL PATCH THE GAME THROUGH TO INTERESTED PARTIES...
WE WANT EVERYONE TO SEE IT'S A FAIR FIGHT, YES?
DAMN YOU, CLARK.

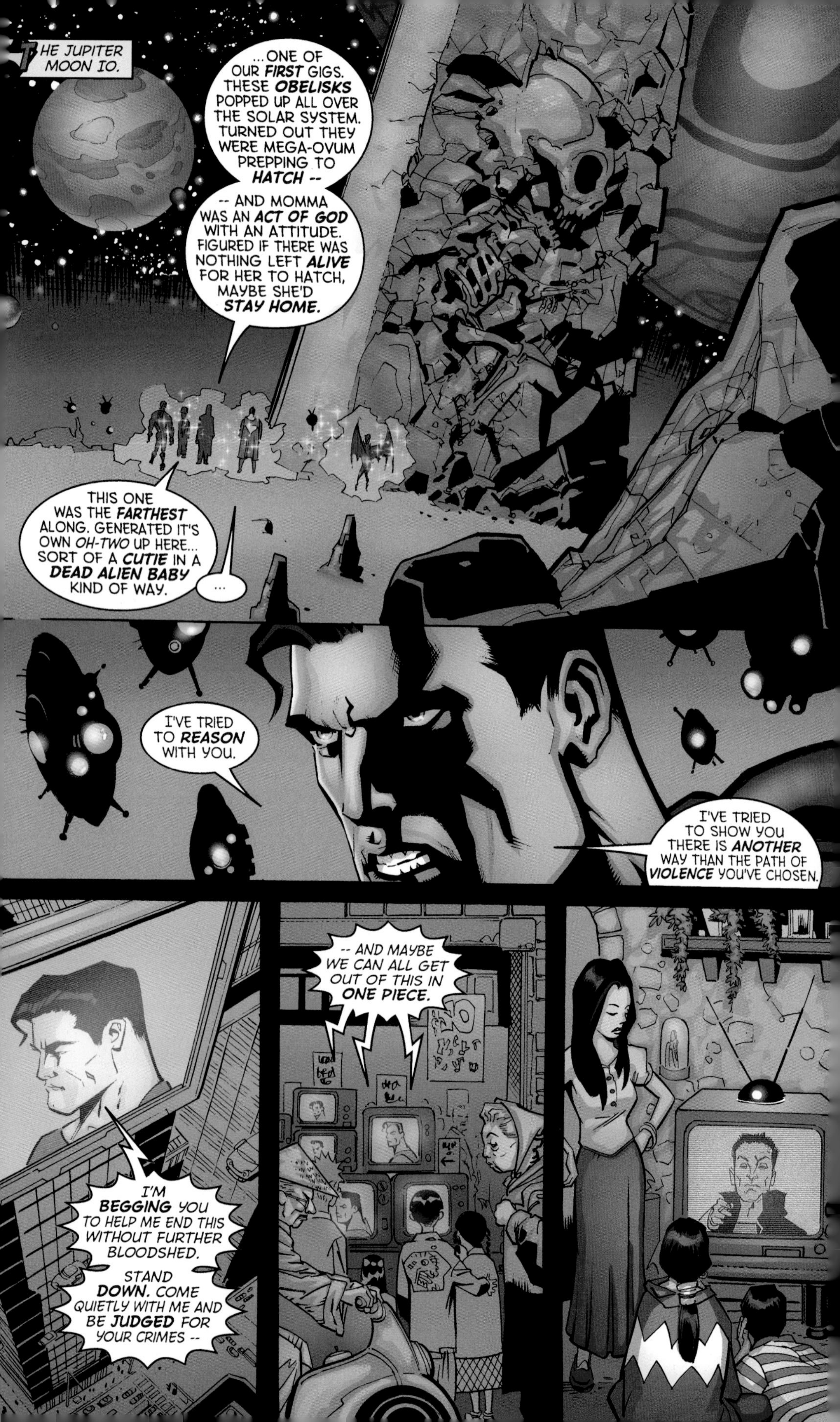
THE JUPITER MOON IO.
...ONE OF OUR FIRST GIGS. THESE OBELISKS POPPED UP ALL OVER THE SOLAR SYSTEM. TURNED OUT THEY WERE MEGA-OVUM PREPPING TO HATCH --
-- AND MOMMA WAS AN ACT OF GOD WITH AN ATTITUDE. FIGURED IF THERE WAS NOTHING LEFT ALIVE FOR HER TO HATCH, MAYBE SHE'D STAY HOME.
THIS ONE WAS THE FARTHEST ALONG. GENERATED IT'S OWN OH-TWO UP HERE... SORT OF A CUTIE IN A DEAD ALIEN BABY KIND OF WAY.
...
I'VE TRIED TO REASON WITH YOU.
I'VE TRIED TO SHOW YOU THERE IS ANOTHER WAY THAN THE PATH OF VIOLENCE YOU'VE CHOSEN.
I'M BEGGING YOU TO HELP ME END THIS WITHOUT FURTHER BLOODSHED.
STAND DOWN. COME QUIETLY WITH ME AND BE JUDGED FOR YOUR CRIMES --
-- AND MAYBE WE CAN ALL GET OUT OF THIS IN ONE PIECE.

UH-UH.

HNNNGH!

"RULE NUMBER *ONE*... HE WHO HAS THE *POWER* MAKES THE RULES.

"*NO ONE* HITS ONE OF MY PEOPLE AND *WALKS*.

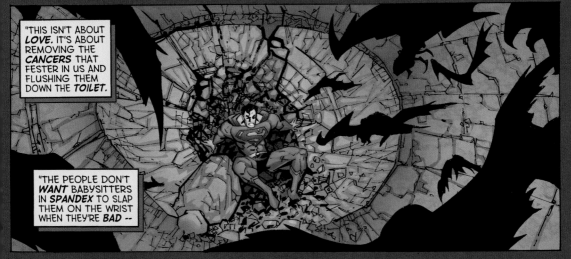

"THIS ISN'T ABOUT *LOVE.* IT'S ABOUT REMOVING THE *CANCERS* THAT FESTER IN US AND FLUSHING THEM DOWN THE *TOILET.*

"THE PEOPLE DON'T *WANT* BABYSITTERS IN *SPANDEX* TO SLAP THEM ON THE WRIST WHEN THEY'RE *BAD* --

"-- THEY WANT *SURGEONS* TO CUT THE UGLY BITS FROM THEM AND *CHARGE* THEM THROUGH THE MORAL *NOSE.*

"*DOCTOR MANCHESTER BLACK* AT YOUR SERVICE.

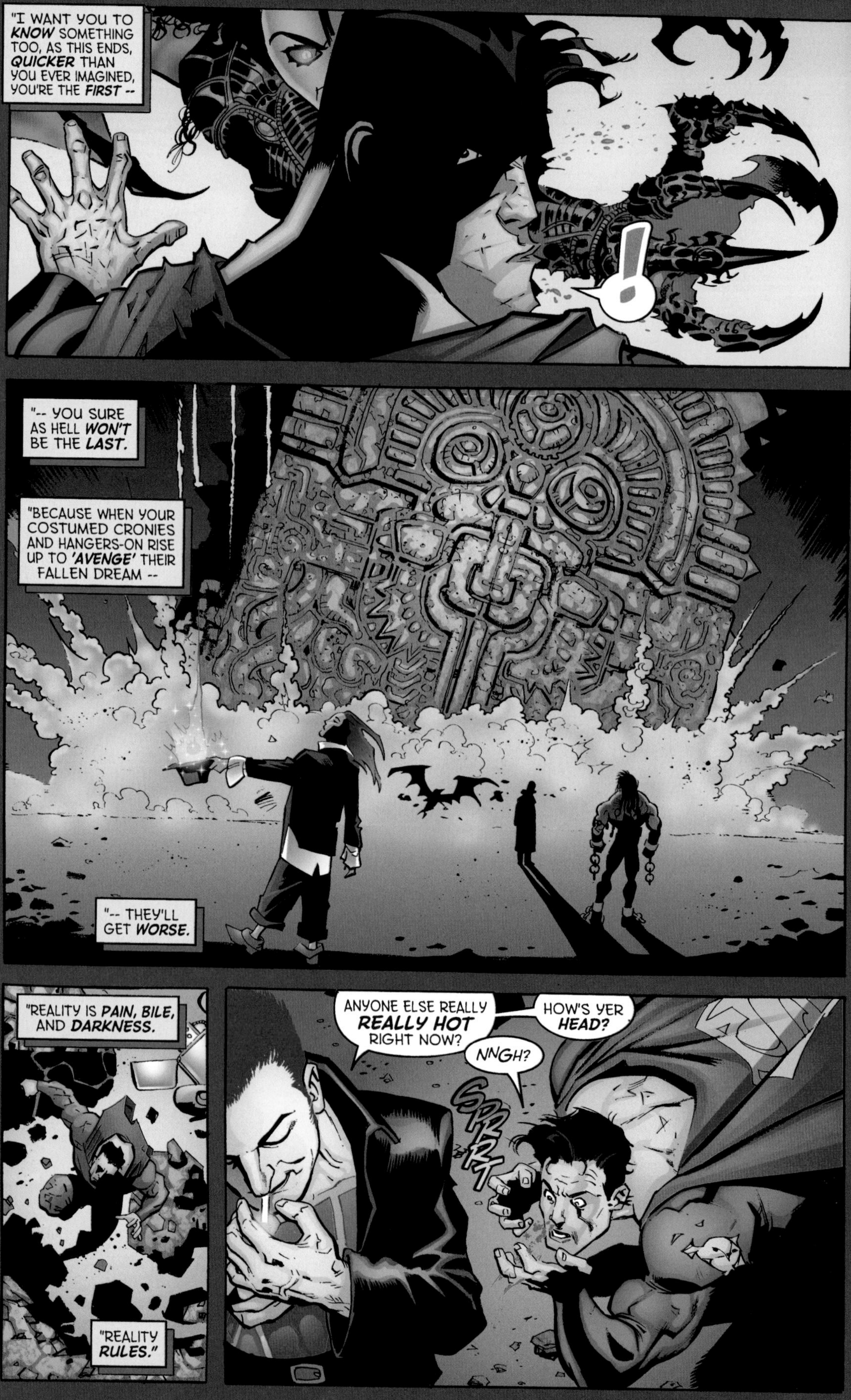
"I WANT YOU TO KNOW SOMETHING TOO, AS THIS ENDS, QUICKER THAN YOU EVER IMAGINED, YOU'RE THE FIRST --
!
"-- YOU SURE AS HELL WON'T BE THE LAST.
"BECAUSE WHEN YOUR COSTUMED CRONIES AND HANGERS-ON RISE UP TO 'AVENGE' THEIR FALLEN DREAM --
"-- THEY'LL GET WORSE.
"REALITY IS PAIN, BILE, AND DARKNESS.
"REALITY RULES."
ANYONE ELSE REALLY REALLY HOT RIGHT NOW?
HOW'S YER HEAD?
NNGH?
SPRRT

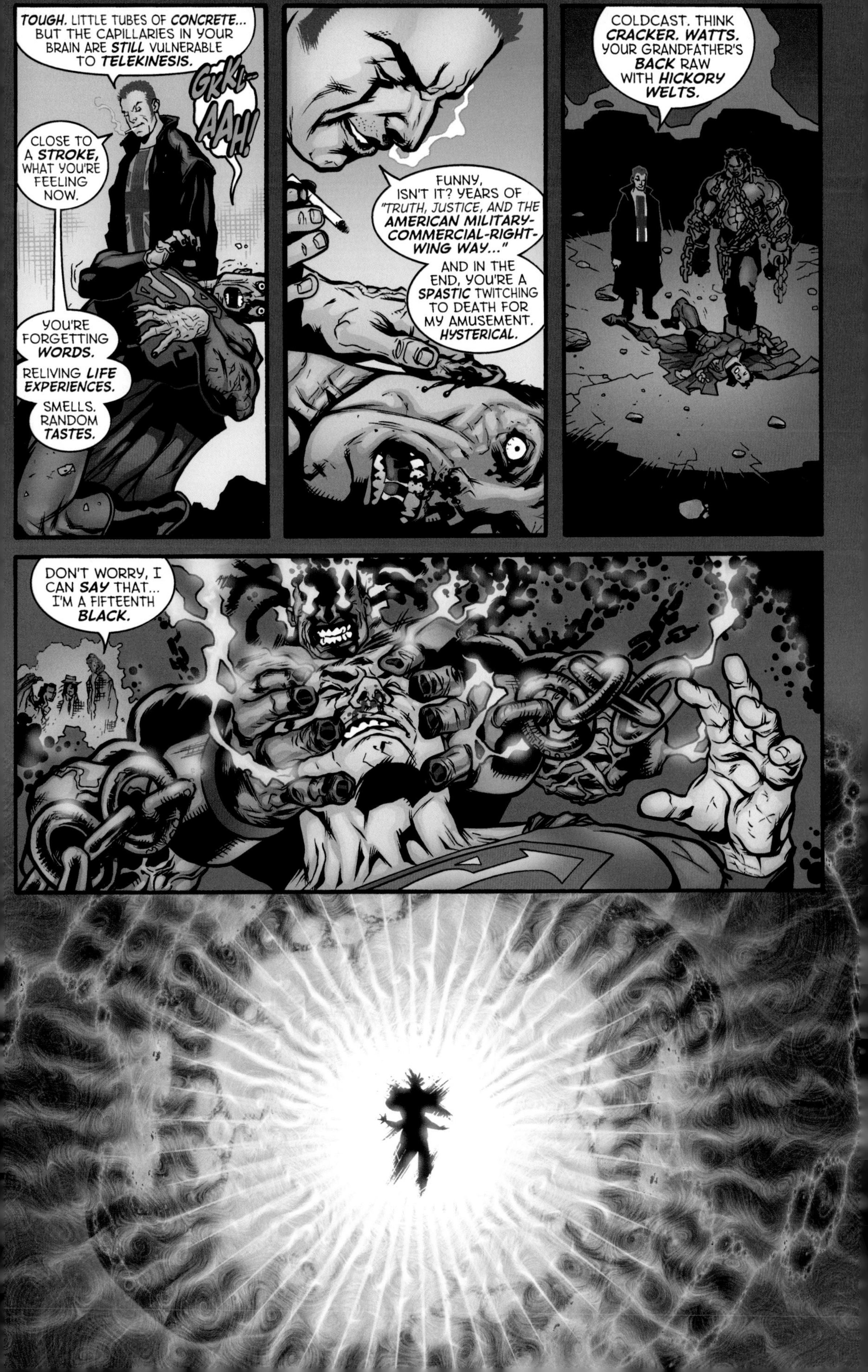
TOUGH. LITTLE TUBES OF CONCRETE... BUT THE CAPILLARIES IN YOUR BRAIN ARE STILL VULNERABLE TO TELEKINESIS.
GKKL-AAH!
CLOSE TO A STROKE, WHAT YOU'RE FEELING NOW.
YOU'RE FORGETTING WORDS.
RELIVING LIFE EXPERIENCES.
SMELLS. RANDOM TASTES.
FUNNY, ISN'T IT? YEARS OF "TRUTH, JUSTICE, AND THE AMERICAN MILITARY-COMMERCIAL-RIGHT-WING WAY..."
AND IN THE END, YOU'RE A SPASTIC TWITCHING TO DEATH FOR MY AMUSEMENT. HYSTERICAL.
COLDCAST. THINK CRACKER. WATTS. YOUR GRANDFATHER'S BACK RAW WITH HICKORY WELTS.
DON'T WORRY, I CAN SAY THAT... I'M A FIFTEENTH BLACK.

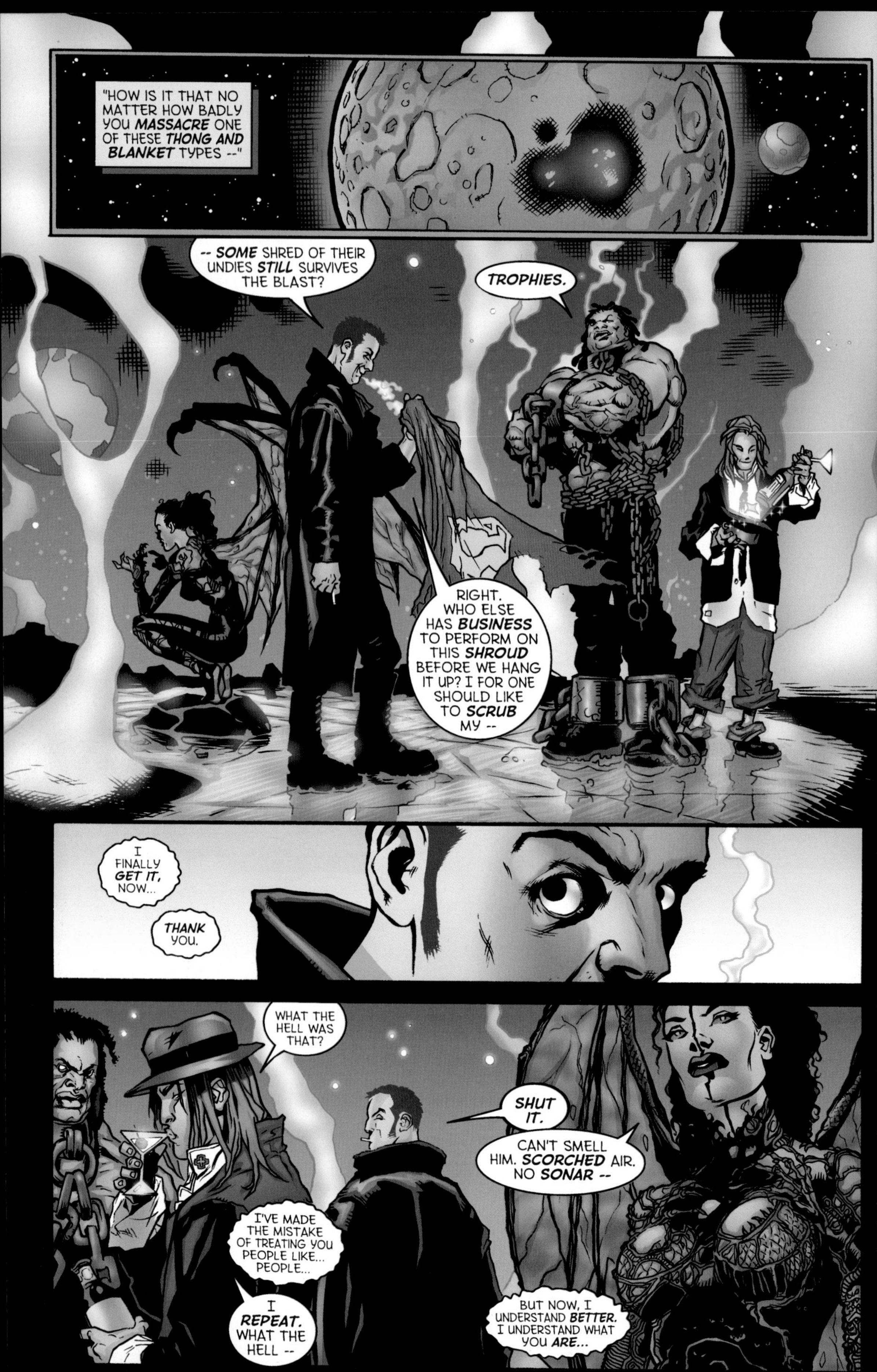
"HOW IS IT THAT NO MATTER HOW BADLY YOU MASSACRE ONE OF THESE THONG AND BLANKET TYPES --"
-- SOME SHRED OF THEIR UNDIES STILL SURVIVES THE BLAST?
TROPHIES.
RIGHT. WHO ELSE HAS BUSINESS TO PERFORM ON THIS SHROUD BEFORE WE HANG IT UP? I FOR ONE SHOULD LIKE TO SCRUB MY --
I FINALLY GET IT, NOW...
THANK YOU.
WHAT THE HELL WAS THAT?
SHUT IT.
CAN'T SMELL HIM. SCORCHED AIR. NO SONAR --
I'VE MADE THE MISTAKE OF TREATING YOU PEOPLE LIKE... PEOPLE...
I REPEAT. WHAT THE HELL --
BUT NOW, I UNDERSTAND BETTER. I UNDERSTAND WHAT YOU ARE...

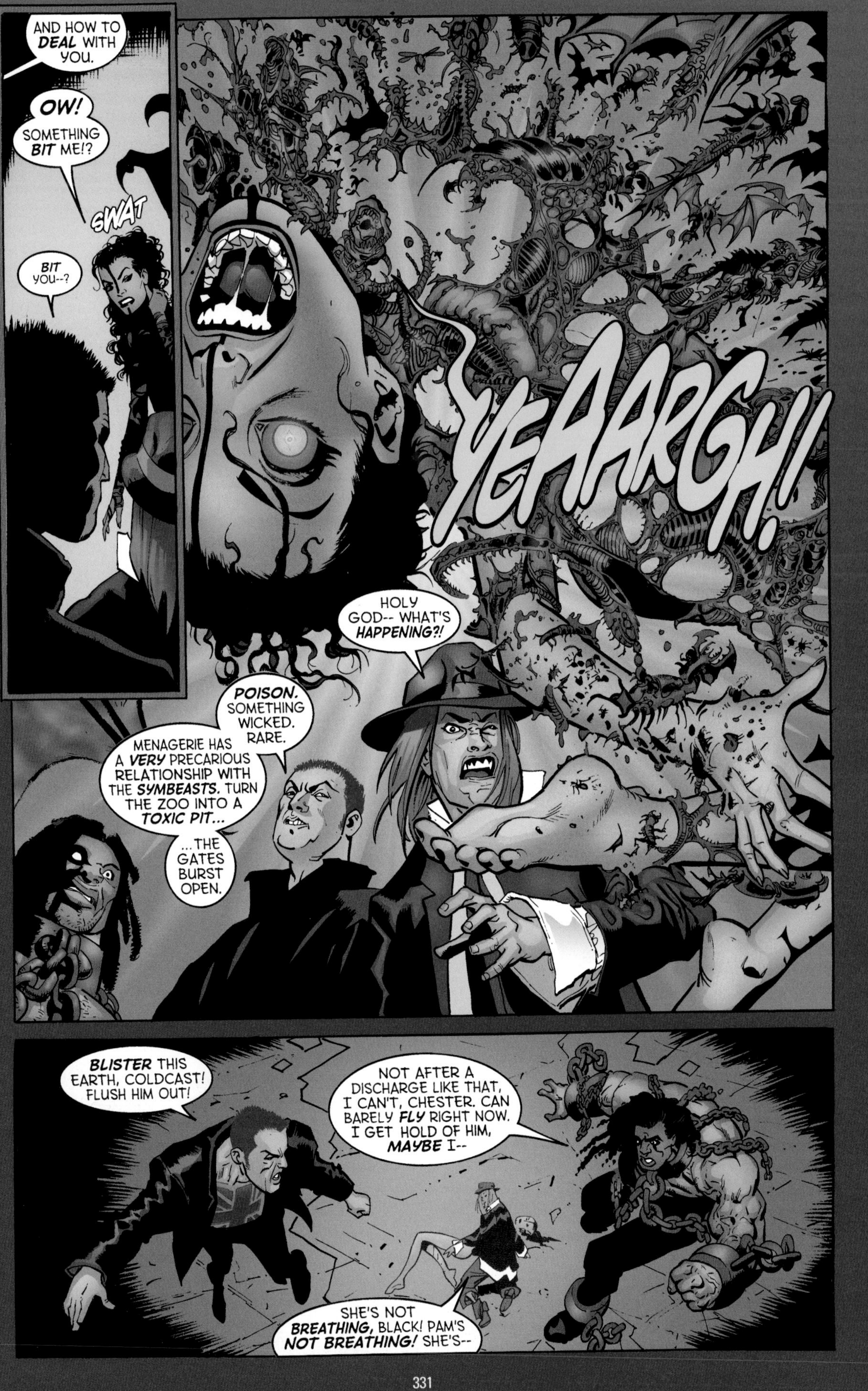
AND HOW TO DEAL WITH YOU.
OW! SOMETHING BIT ME!?
SWAT
BIT YOU--?
YEAARGH!!
HOLY GOD-- WHAT'S HAPPENING?!
POISON. SOMETHING WICKED. RARE.
MENAGERIE HAS A VERY PRECARIOUS RELATIONSHIP WITH THE SYMBEASTS. TURN THE ZOO INTO A TOXIC PIT...
...THE GATES BURST OPEN.
BLISTER THIS EARTH, COLDCAST! FLUSH HIM OUT!
NOT AFTER A DISCHARGE LIKE THAT, I CAN'T, CHESTER. CAN BARELY FLY RIGHT NOW. I GET HOLD OF HIM, MAYBE I--
SHE'S NOT BREATHING, BLACK! PAM'S NOT BREATHING! SHE'S--

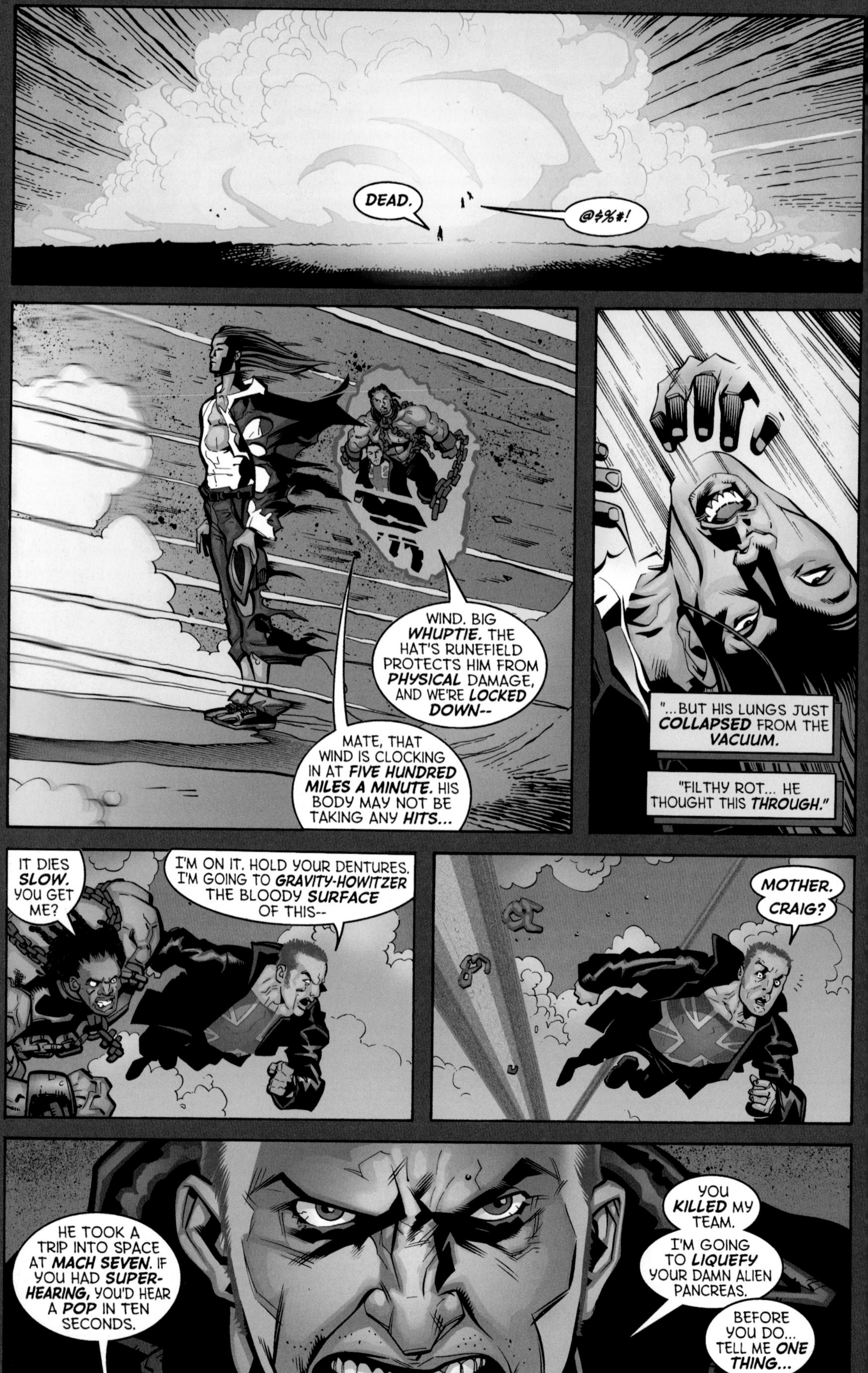
DEAD.
@$%#!
WIND. BIG WHUPTIE. THE HAT'S RUNEFIELD PROTECTS HIM FROM PHYSICAL DAMAGE, AND WE'RE LOCKED DOWN--
MATE, THAT WIND IS CLOCKING IN AT FIVE HUNDRED MILES A MINUTE. HIS BODY MAY NOT BE TAKING ANY HITS...
"...BUT HIS LUNGS JUST COLLAPSED FROM THE VACUUM.
"FILTHY ROT... HE THOUGHT THIS THROUGH."
IT DIES SLOW. YOU GET ME?
I'M ON IT. HOLD YOUR DENTURES. I'M GOING TO GRAVITY-HOWITZER THE BLOODY SURFACE OF THIS--
MOTHER. CRAIG?
HE TOOK A TRIP INTO SPACE AT MACH SEVEN. IF YOU HAD SUPER-HEARING, YOU'D HEAR A POP IN TEN SECONDS.
YOU KILLED MY TEAM.
I'M GOING TO LIQUEFY YOUR DAMN ALIEN PANCREAS.
BEFORE YOU DO... TELL ME ONE THING...

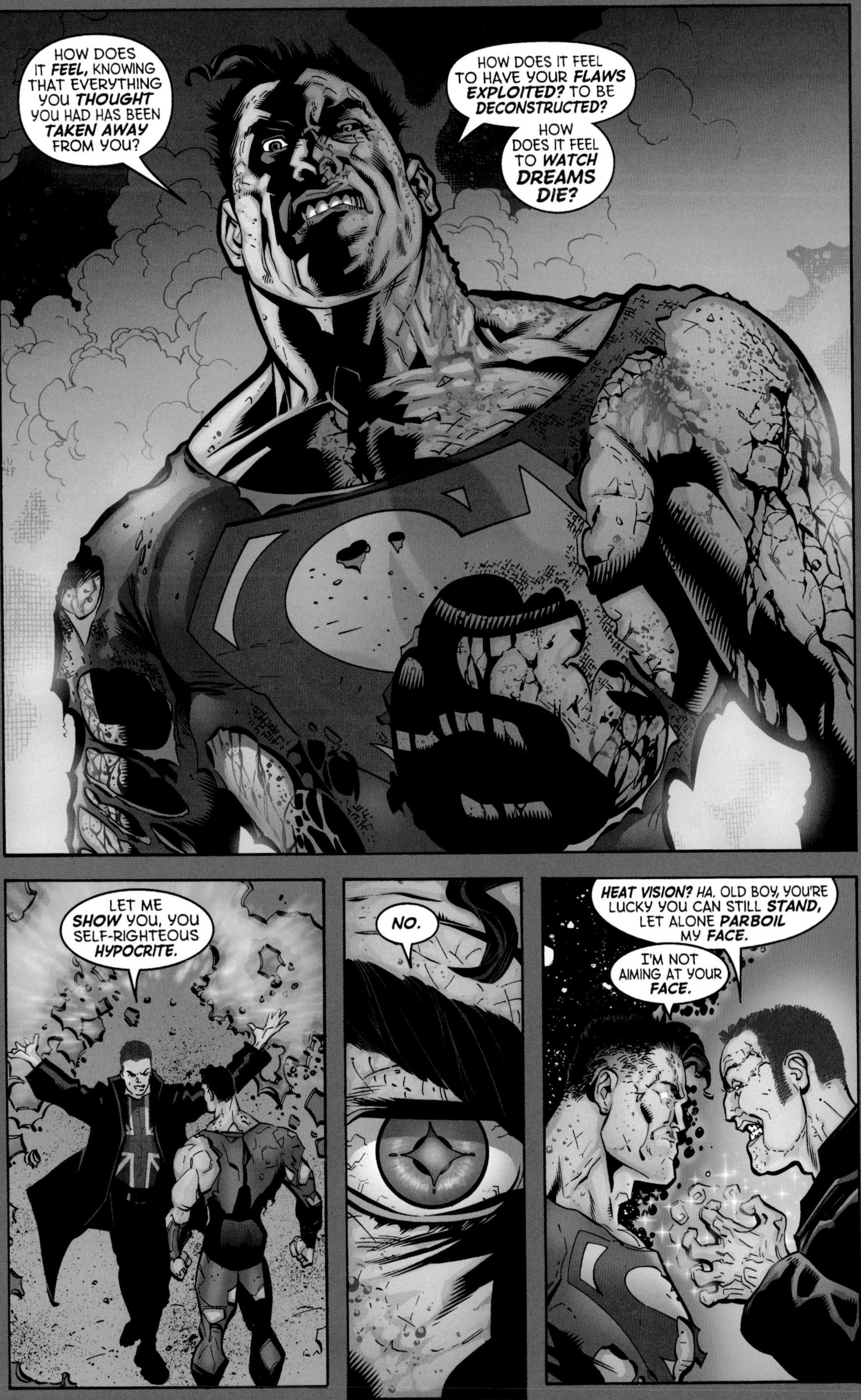
HOW DOES IT FEEL, KNOWING THAT EVERYTHING YOU THOUGHT YOU HAD HAS BEEN TAKEN AWAY FROM YOU?
HOW DOES IT FEEL TO HAVE YOUR FLAWS EXPLOITED? TO BE DECONSTRUCTED?
HOW DOES IT FEEL TO WATCH DREAMS DIE?
LET ME SHOW YOU, YOU SELF-RIGHTEOUS HYPOCRITE.
NO.
HEAT VISION? HA. OLD BOY, YOU'RE LUCKY YOU CAN STILL STAND, LET ALONE PARBOIL MY FACE.
I'M NOT AIMING AT YOUR FACE.

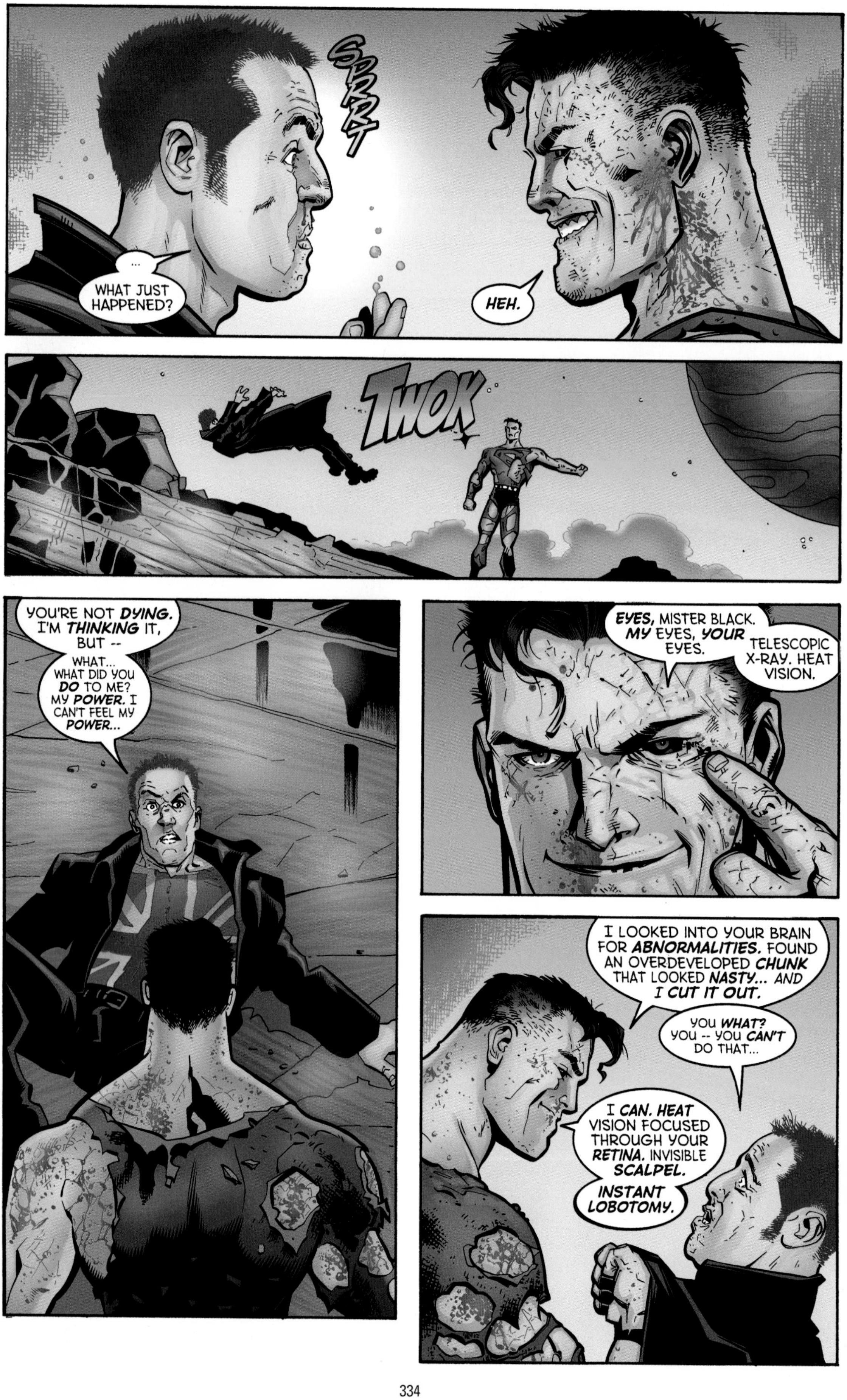
SPRRT
...
WHAT JUST HAPPENED?
HEH.
TWOK
YOU'RE NOT DYING. I'M THINKING IT, BUT --
WHAT... WHAT DID YOU DO TO ME? MY POWER. I CAN'T FEEL MY POWER...
EYES, MISTER BLACK. MY EYES, YOUR EYES.
TELESCOPIC X-RAY. HEAT VISION.
I LOOKED INTO YOUR BRAIN FOR ABNORMALITIES. FOUND AN OVERDEVELOPED CHUNK THAT LOOKED NASTY... AND I CUT IT OUT.
YOU WHAT? YOU -- YOU CAN'T DO THAT...
I CAN. HEAT VISION FOCUSED THROUGH YOUR RETINA. INVISIBLE SCALPEL.
INSTANT LOBOTOMY.

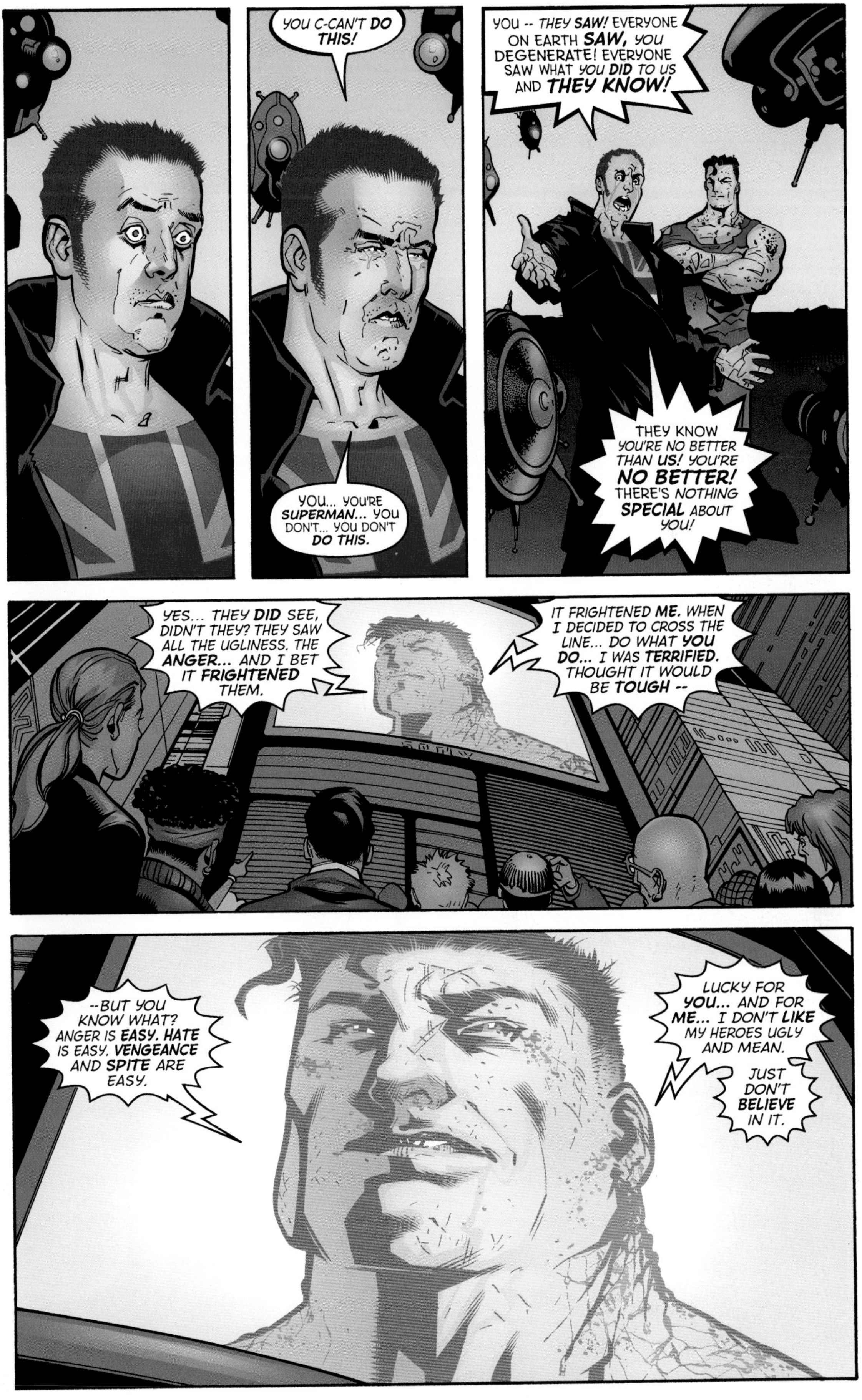
YOU C-CAN'T DO THIS!
YOU... YOU'RE SUPERMAN... YOU DON'T... YOU DON'T DO THIS.
YOU -- THEY SAW! EVERYONE ON EARTH SAW, YOU DEGENERATE! EVERYONE SAW WHAT YOU DID TO US AND THEY KNOW!
THEY KNOW YOU'RE NO BETTER THAN US! YOU'RE NO BETTER! THERE'S NOTHING SPECIAL ABOUT YOU!
YES... THEY DID SEE, DIDN'T THEY? THEY SAW ALL THE UGLINESS. THE ANGER... AND I BET IT FRIGHTENED THEM.
IT FRIGHTENED ME. WHEN I DECIDED TO CROSS THE LINE... DO WHAT YOU DO... I WAS TERRIFIED. THOUGHT IT WOULD BE TOUGH --
--BUT YOU KNOW WHAT? ANGER IS EASY. HATE IS EASY. VENGEANCE AND SPITE ARE EASY.
LUCKY FOR YOU... AND FOR ME... I DON'T LIKE MY HEROES UGLY AND MEAN.
JUST DON'T BELIEVE IN IT.

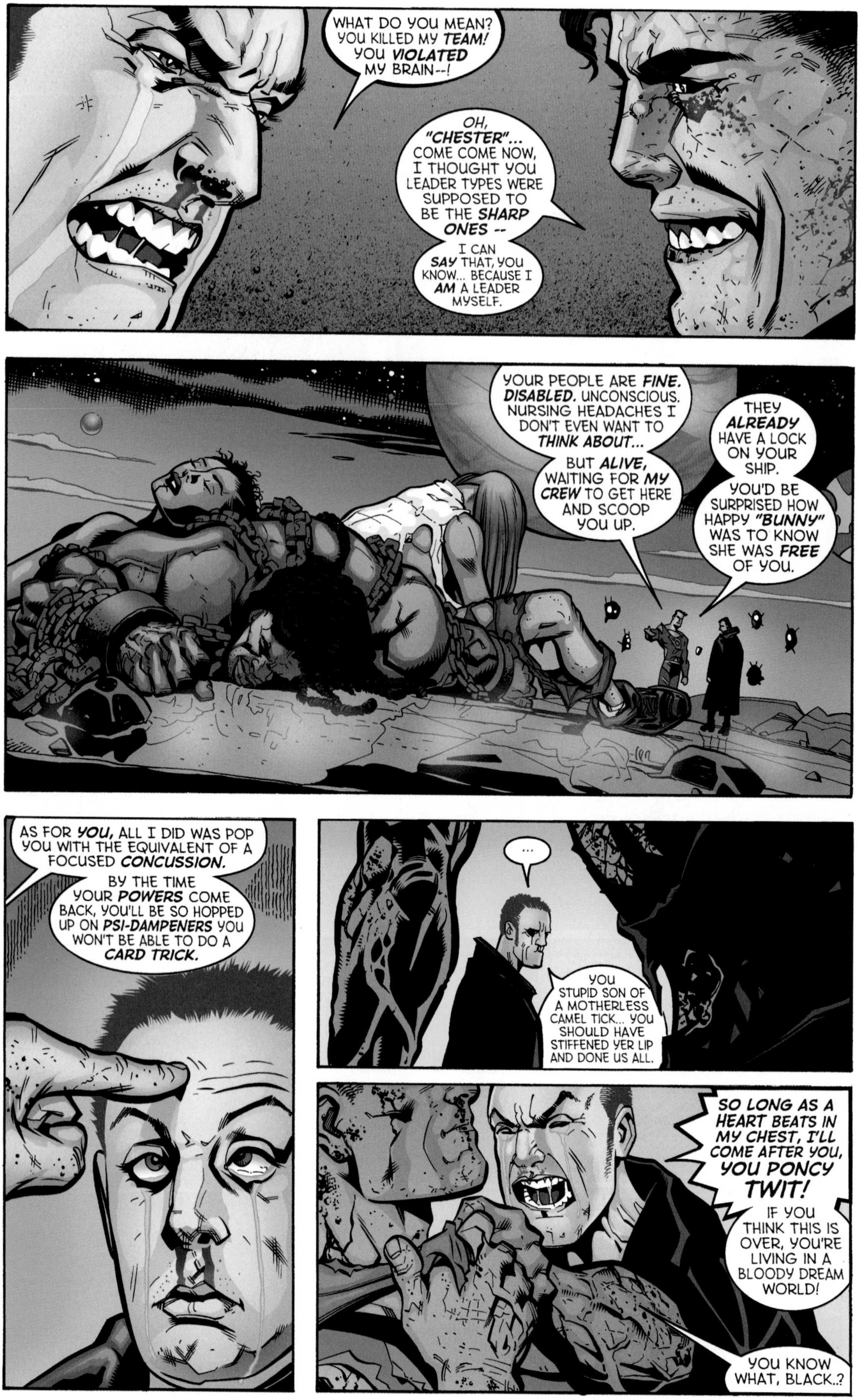
WHAT DO YOU MEAN? YOU KILLED MY TEAM! YOU VIOLATED MY BRAIN--!
OH, "CHESTER"... COME COME NOW, I THOUGHT YOU LEADER TYPES WERE SUPPOSED TO BE THE SHARP ONES --
I CAN SAY THAT, YOU KNOW... BECAUSE I AM A LEADER MYSELF.
YOUR PEOPLE ARE FINE. DISABLED. UNCONSCIOUS. NURSING HEADACHES I DON'T EVEN WANT TO THINK ABOUT...
BUT ALIVE, WAITING FOR MY CREW TO GET HERE AND SCOOP YOU UP.
THEY ALREADY HAVE A LOCK ON YOUR SHIP.
YOU'D BE SURPRISED HOW HAPPY "BUNNY" WAS TO KNOW SHE WAS FREE OF YOU.
AS FOR YOU, ALL I DID WAS POP YOU WITH THE EQUIVALENT OF A FOCUSED CONCUSSION.
BY THE TIME YOUR POWERS COME BACK, YOU'LL BE SO HOPPED UP ON PSI-DAMPENERS YOU WON'T BE ABLE TO DO A CARD TRICK.
...
YOU STUPID SON OF A MOTHERLESS CAMEL TICK... YOU SHOULD HAVE STIFFENED YER LIP AND DONE US ALL.
SO LONG AS A HEART BEATS IN MY CHEST, I'LL COME AFTER YOU, YOU PONCY TWIT!
IF YOU THINK THIS IS OVER, YOU'RE LIVING IN A BLOODY DREAM WORLD!
YOU KNOW WHAT, BLACK..?

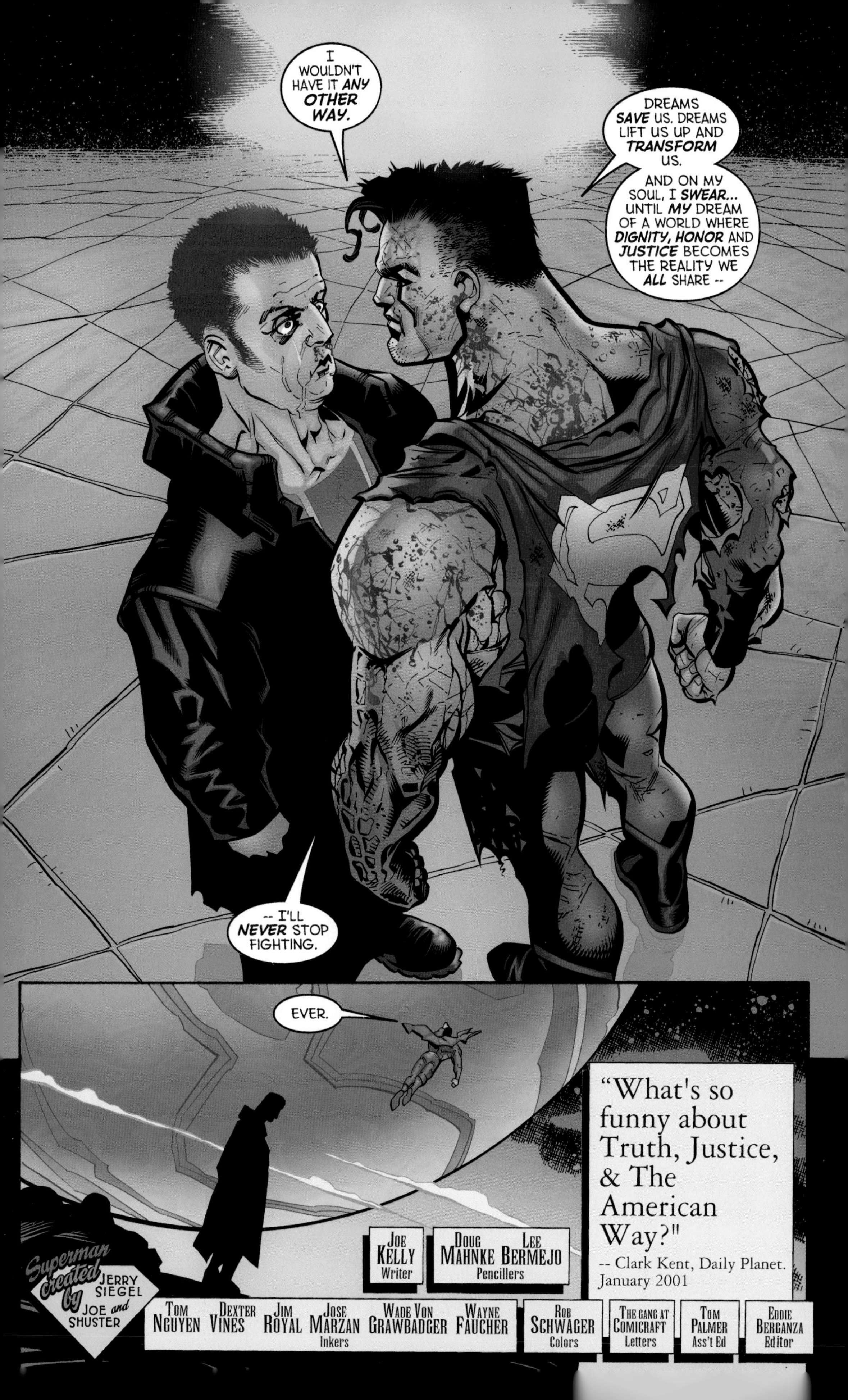

I WOULDN'T HAVE IT ANY OTHER WAY.
DREAMS SAVE US. DREAMS LIFT US UP AND TRANSFORM US.
AND ON MY SOUL, I SWEAR... UNTIL MY DREAM OF A WORLD WHERE DIGNITY, HONOR AND JUSTICE BECOMES THE REALITY WE ALL SHARE --
-- I'LL NEVER STOP FIGHTING.
EVER.
"What's so funny about Truth, Justice, & The American Way?"
-- Clark Kent, Daily Planet. January 2001
JOE KELLY Writer
DOUG MAHNKE LEE BERMEJO Pencillers
Superman created by JERRY SIEGEL JOE and SHUSTER
TOM NGUYEN DEXTER VINES JIM ROYAL JOSE MARZAN WADE VON GRAWBADGER WAYNE FAUCHER Inkers
ROB SCHWAGER Colors
THE GANG AT COMICRAFT Letters
TOM PALMER Ass't Ed
EDDIE BERGANZA Editor

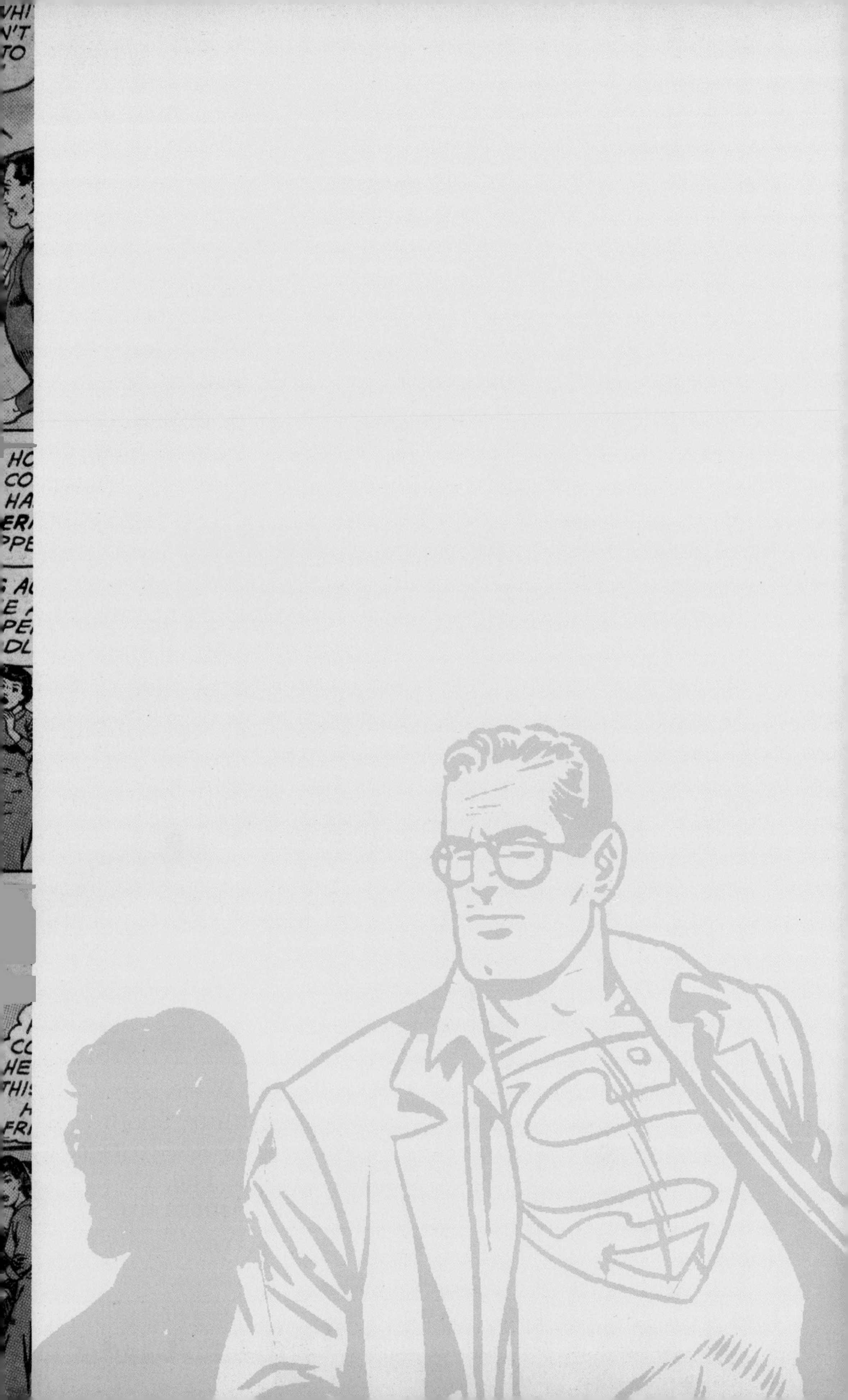

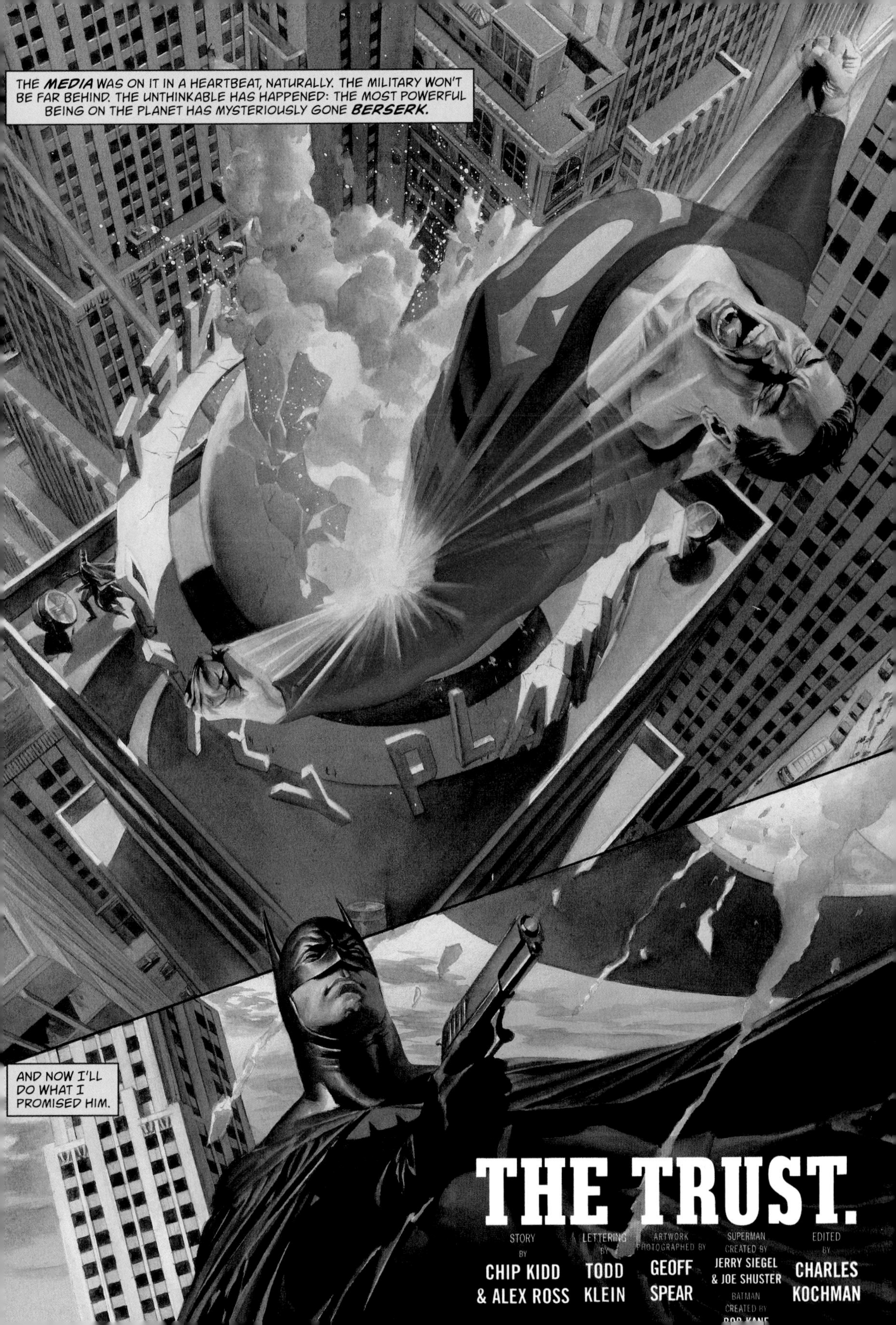

THE MEDIA WAS ON IT IN A HEARTBEAT, NATURALLY. THE MILITARY WON'T BE FAR BEHIND. THE UNTHINKABLE HAS HAPPENED: THE MOST POWERFUL BEING ON THE PLANET HAS MYSTERIOUSLY GONE BERSERK.
AND NOW I'LL DO WHAT I PROMISED HIM.
THE TRUST.
STORY BY CHIP KIDD & ALEX ROSS
LETTERING BY TODD KLEIN
ARTWORK PHOTOGRAPHED BY GEOFF SPEAR
SUPERMAN CREATED BY JERRY SIEGEL & JOE SHUSTER
BATMAN CREATED BY
EDITED BY CHARLES KOCHMAN

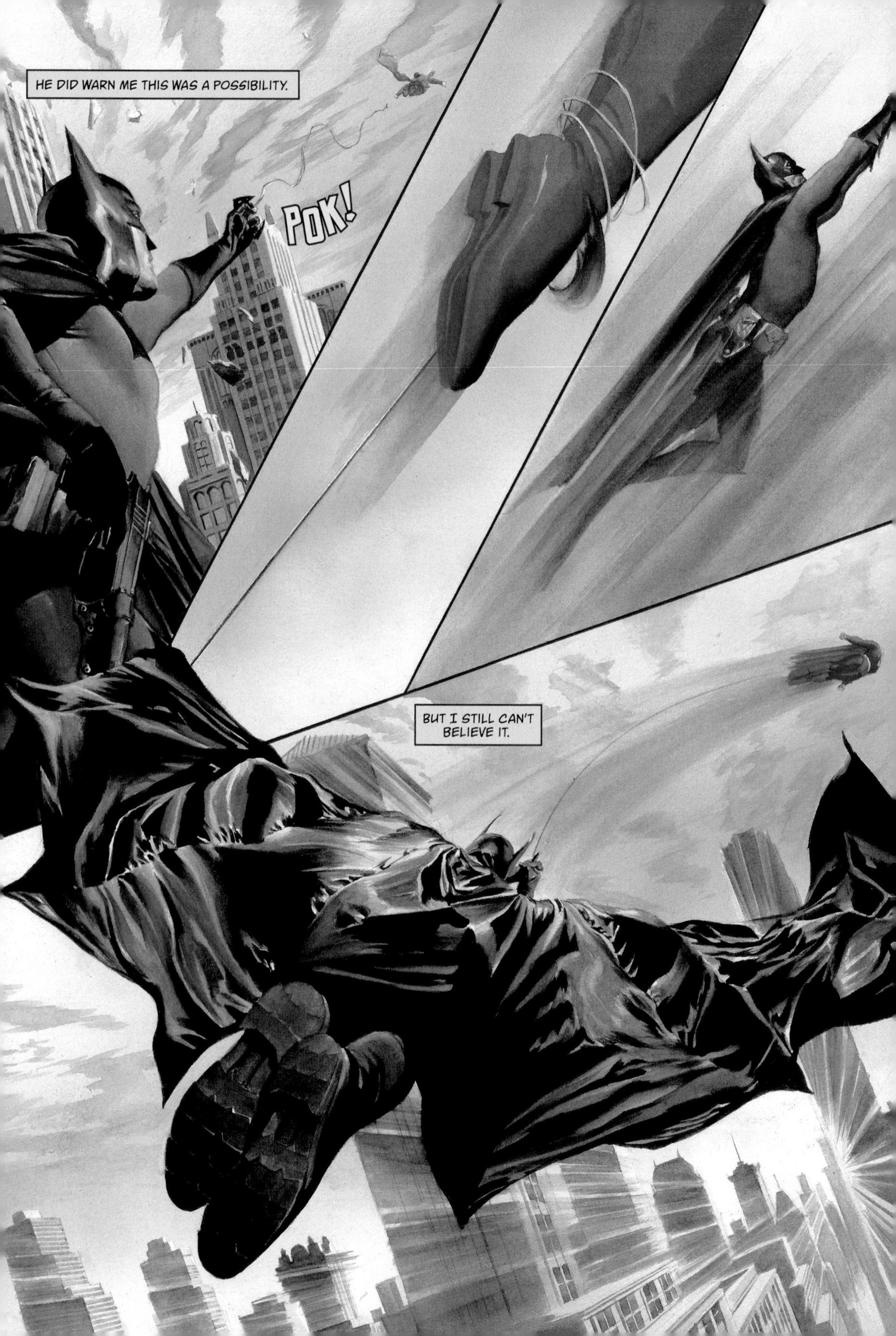
HE DID WARN ME THIS WAS A POSSIBILITY.
POK!
BUT I STILL CAN'T BELIEVE IT.

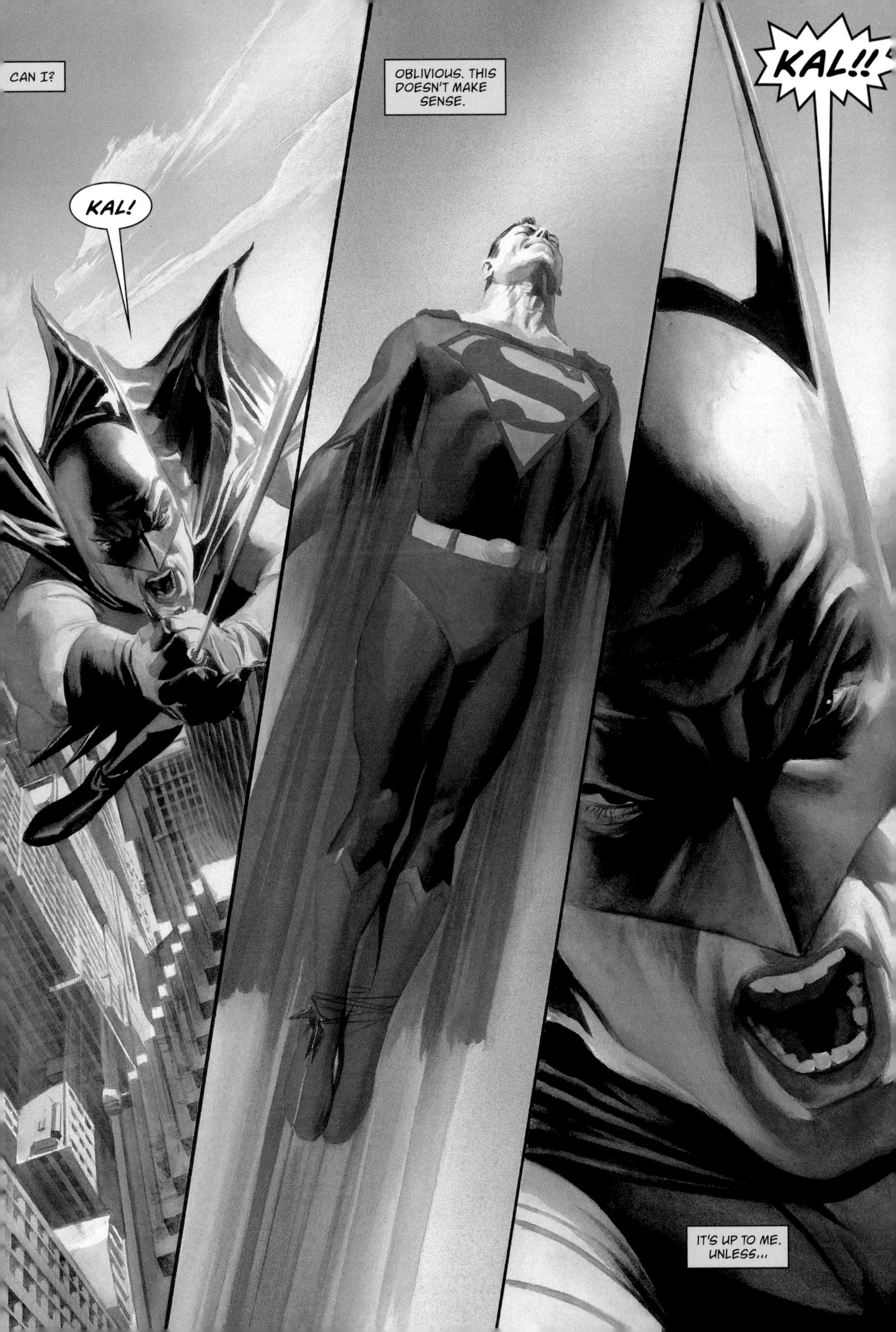
CAN I?
KAL!
OBLIVIOUS. THIS DOESN'T MAKE SENSE.
KAL!!
IT'S UP TO ME. UNLESS...

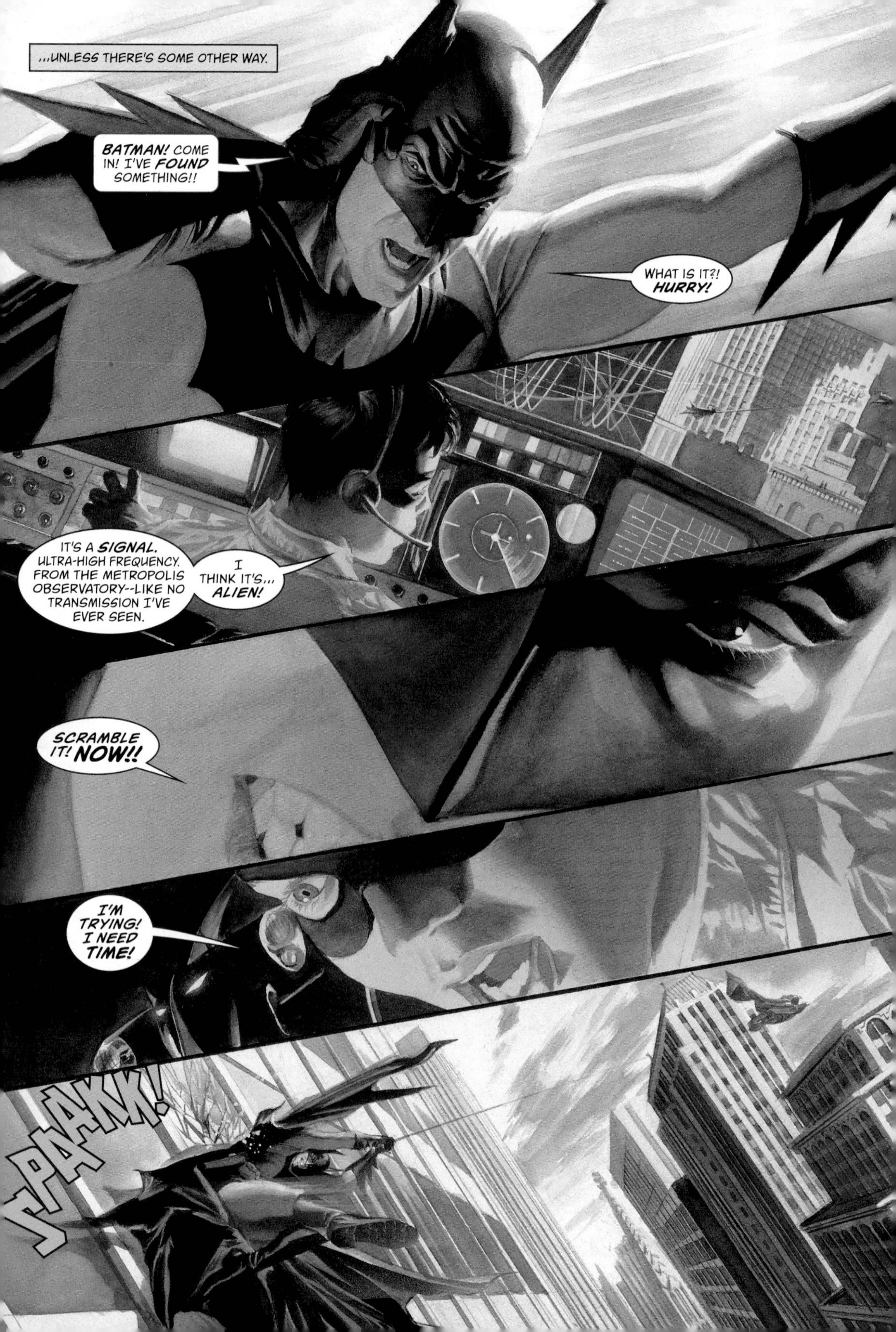
...UNLESS THERE'S SOME OTHER WAY.
BATMAN! COME IN! I'VE FOUND SOMETHING!!
WHAT IS IT?! HURRY!
IT'S A SIGNAL. ULTRA-HIGH FREQUENCY. FROM THE METROPOLIS OBSERVATORY--LIKE NO TRANSMISSION I'VE EVER SEEN.
I THINK IT'S... ALIEN!
SCRAMBLE IT! NOW!!
I'M TRYING! I NEED TIME!
THPAKK!

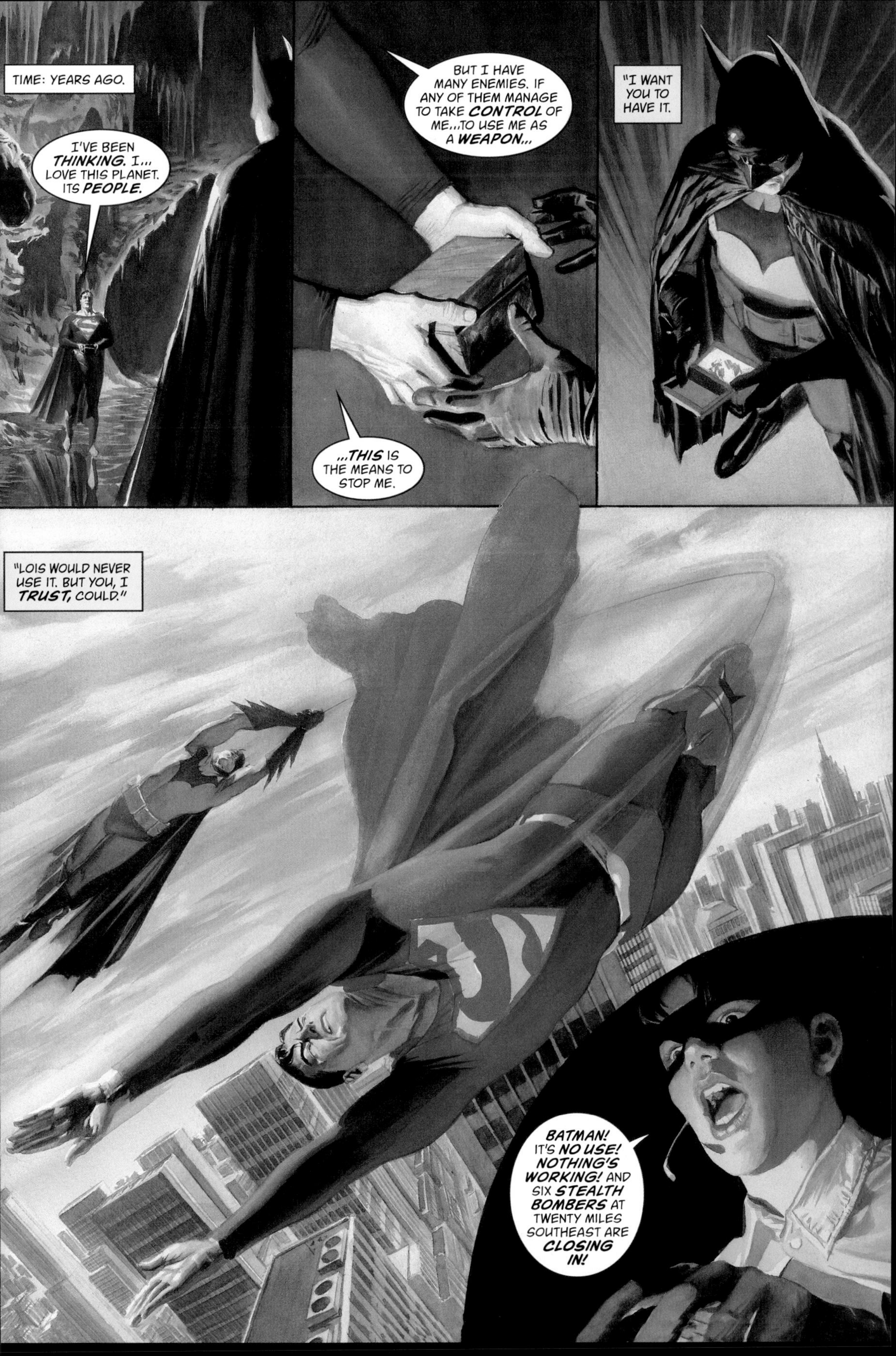
TIME: YEARS AGO.
I'VE BEEN THINKING. I... LOVE THIS PLANET. ITS PEOPLE.
BUT I HAVE MANY ENEMIES. IF ANY OF THEM MANAGE TO TAKE CONTROL OF ME...TO USE ME AS A WEAPON...
...THIS IS THE MEANS TO STOP ME.
"I WANT YOU TO HAVE IT.
"LOIS WOULD NEVER USE IT. BUT YOU, I TRUST, COULD."
BATMAN! IT'S NO USE! NOTHING'S WORKING! AND SIX STEALTH BOMBERS AT TWENTY MILES SOUTHEAST ARE CLOSING IN!

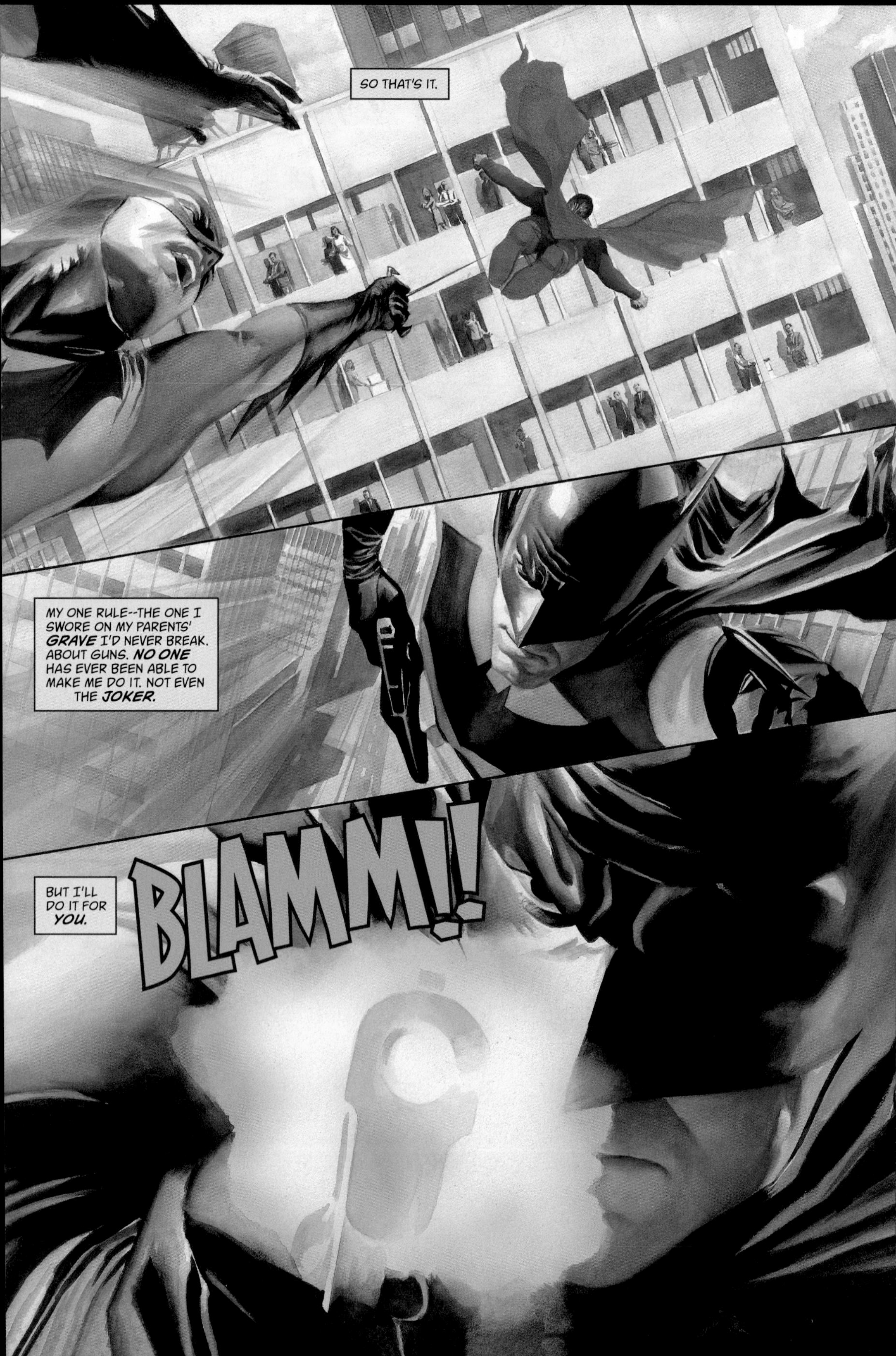
SO THAT'S IT.
MY ONE RULE--THE ONE I SWORE ON MY PARENTS' GRAVE I'D NEVER BREAK. ABOUT GUNS. NO ONE HAS EVER BEEN ABLE TO MAKE ME DO IT. NOT EVEN THE JOKER.
BUT I'LL DO IT FOR YOU.
BLAMM!!

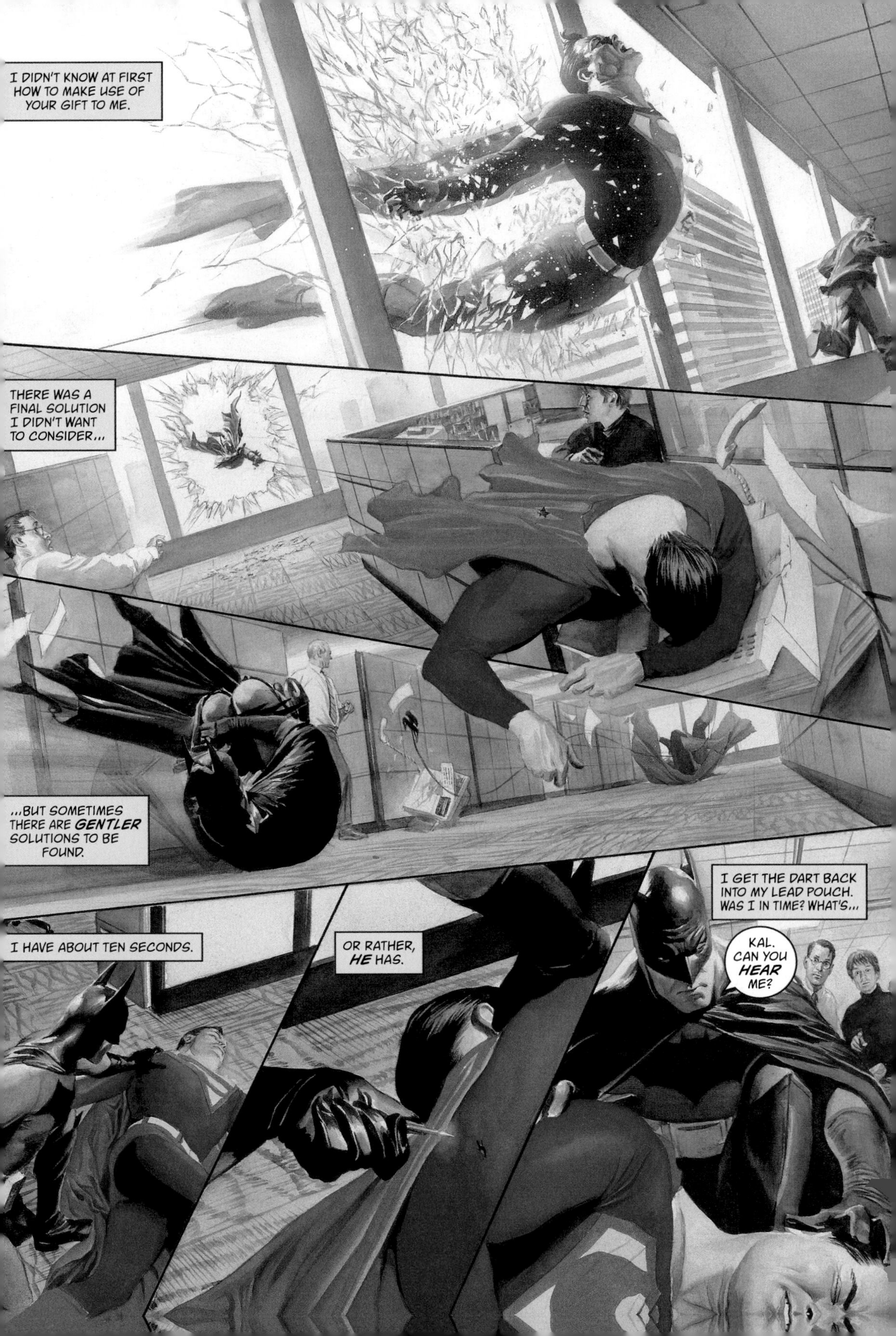
I DIDN'T KNOW AT FIRST HOW TO MAKE USE OF YOUR GIFT TO ME.
THERE WAS A FINAL SOLUTION I DIDN'T WANT TO CONSIDER...
...BUT SOMETIMES THERE ARE GENTLER SOLUTIONS TO BE FOUND.
I HAVE ABOUT TEN SECONDS.
OR RATHER, HE HAS.
I GET THE DART BACK INTO MY LEAD POUCH. WAS I IN TIME? WHAT'S...
KAL. CAN YOU HEAR ME?

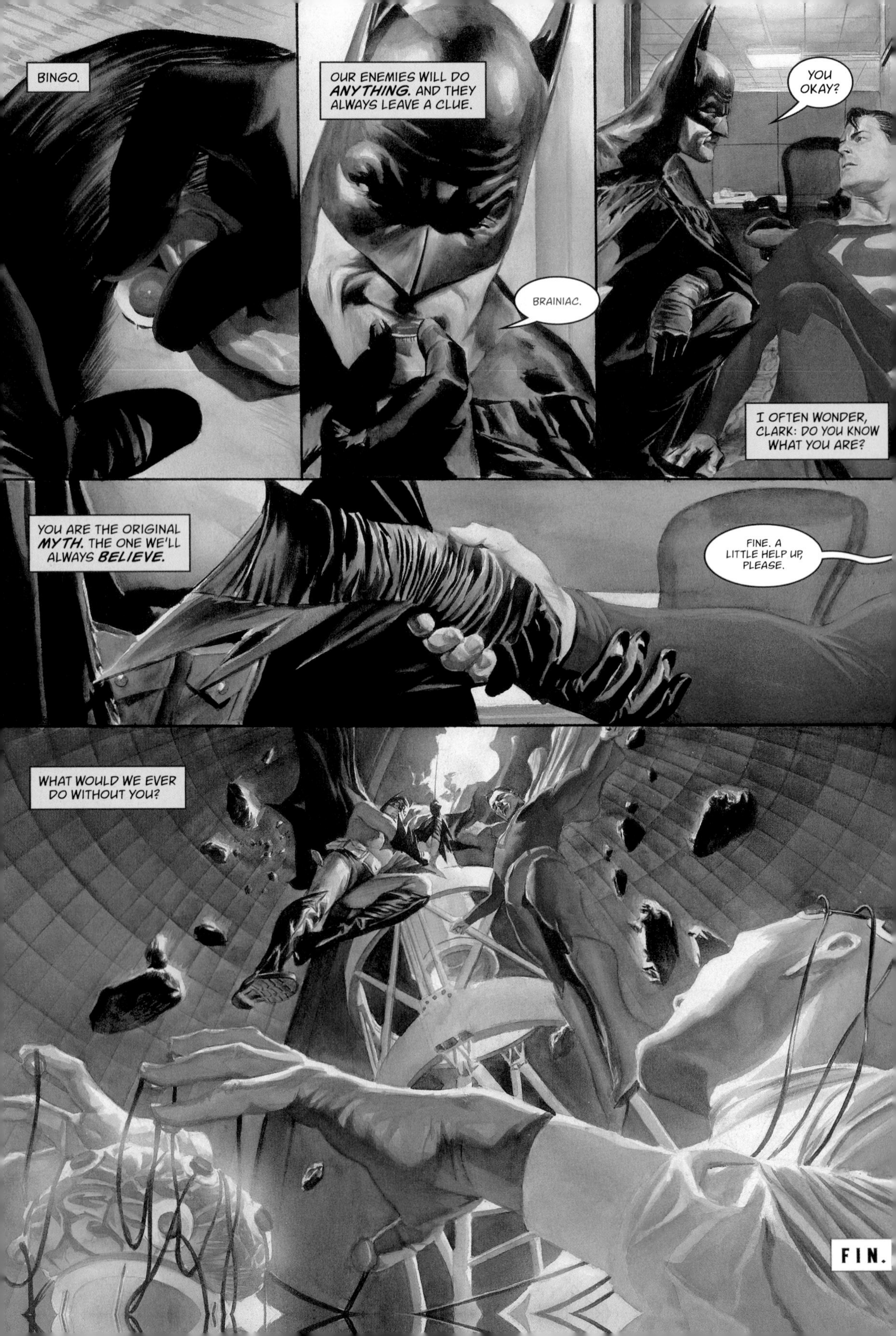
BINGO.
OUR ENEMIES WILL DO ANYTHING. AND THEY ALWAYS LEAVE A CLUE.
BRAINIAC.
YOU OKAY?
I OFTEN WONDER, CLARK: DO YOU KNOW WHAT YOU ARE?
YOU ARE THE ORIGINAL MYTH. THE ONE WE'LL ALWAYS BELIEVE.
FINE. A LITTLE HELP UP, PLEASE.
WHAT WOULD WE EVER DO WITHOUT YOU?
FIN.

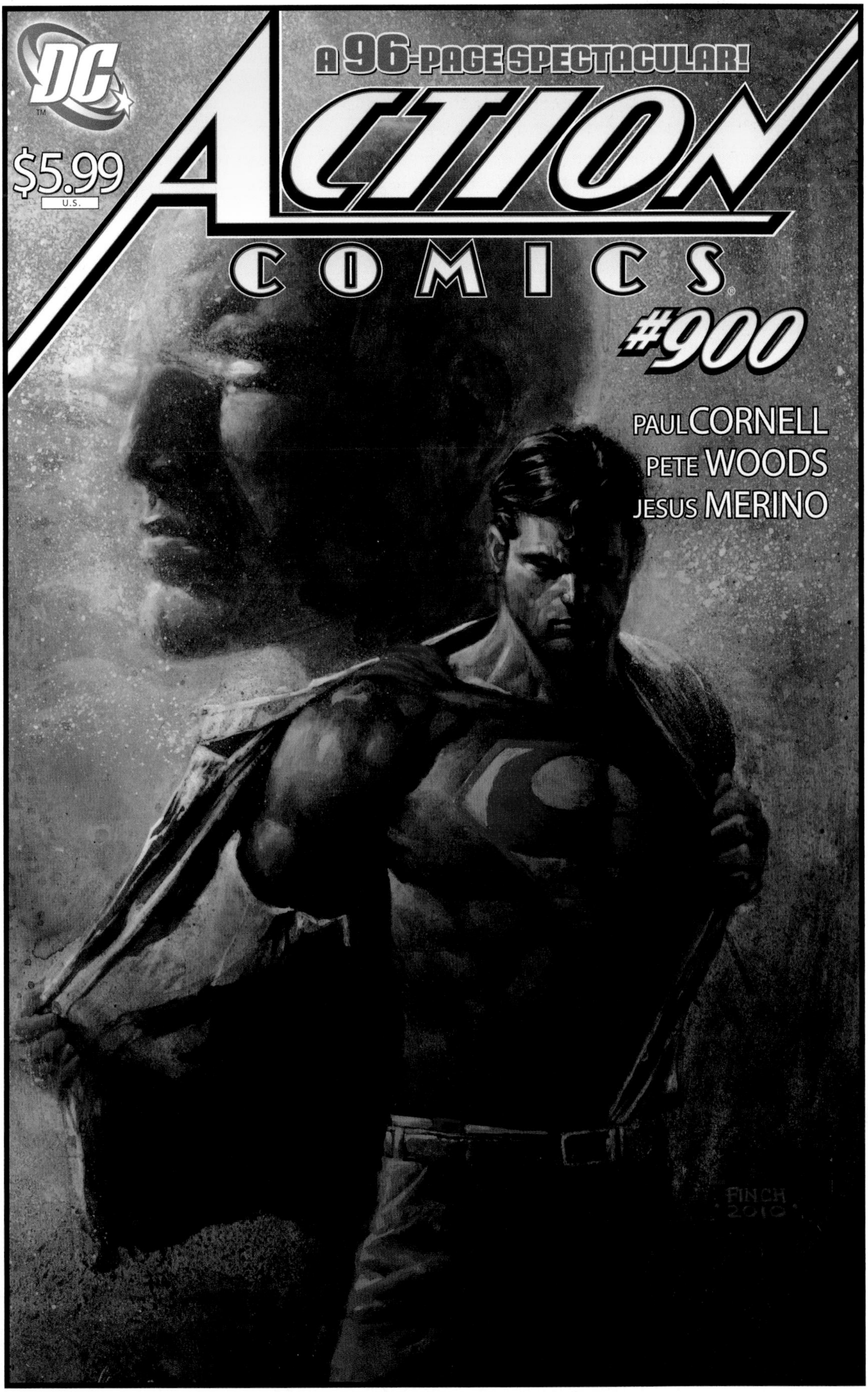
DC
$5.99
U.S.
A 96-PAGE SPECTACULAR!
ACTION COMICS
#900
PAUL CORNELL
PETE WOODS
JESUS MERINO
FINCH 2010

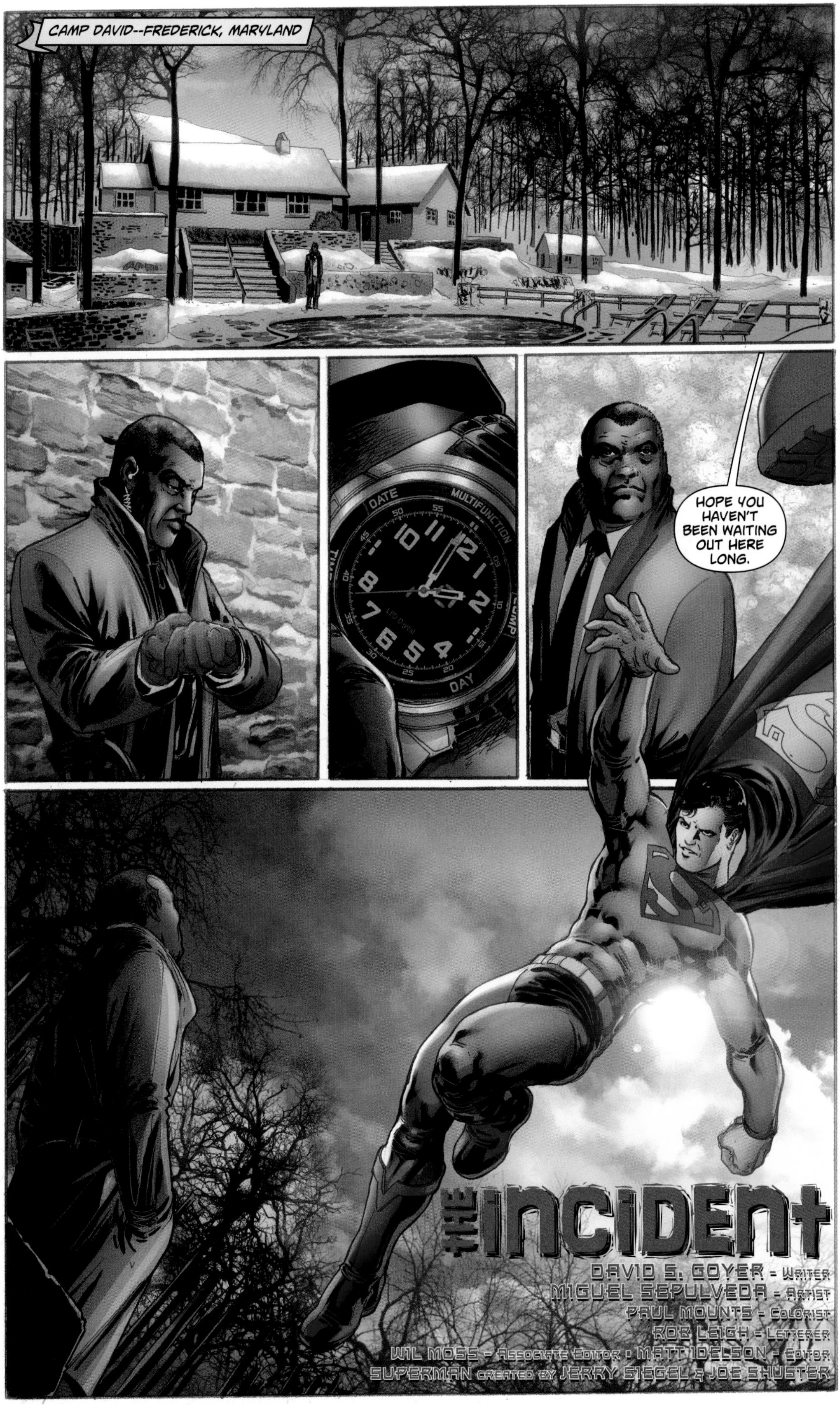
CAMP DAVID--FREDERICK, MARYLAND
HOPE YOU HAVEN'T BEEN WAITING OUT HERE LONG.
THE INCIDENT
DAVID S. GOYER - WRITER
MIGUEL SEPULVEDA - ARTIST
PAUL MOUNTS - COLORIST
ROB LEIGH - LETTERER
WIL MOSS - ASSOCIATE EDITOR : MATT IDELSON - EDITOR
SUPERMAN CREATED BY JERRY SIEGEL & JOE SHUSTER

THANK YOU FOR COMING. MY NAME IS--

GABRIEL WRIGHT, THE PRESIDENT'S NATIONAL SECURITY ADVISOR.

THEN YOU'RE AWARE OF THE GRAVITY OF THE SITUATION.

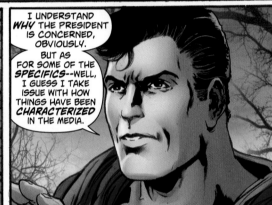

I UNDERSTAND WHY THE PRESIDENT IS CONCERNED, OBVIOUSLY. BUT AS FOR SOME OF THE SPECIFICS--WELL, I GUESS I TAKE ISSUE WITH HOW THINGS HAVE BEEN CHARACTERIZED IN THE MEDIA.

MAYBE YOU COULD SET THE RECORD STRAIGHT FOR US, THEN.

WHY DID YOU DO IT? WHAT IN GOD'S NAME WERE YOU THINKING?

THOSE MARINE SNIPERS YOU'VE GOT STATIONED UP ON THAT RIDGE ABOUT TWO HUNDRED YARDS TO THE NORTH--

"--THEIR *WINTER CAMO* DOESN'T DO MUCH TO HIDE THEM, SINCE I CAN SEE INTO THE *U.V.* AND *INFRARED SPECTRUMS.*

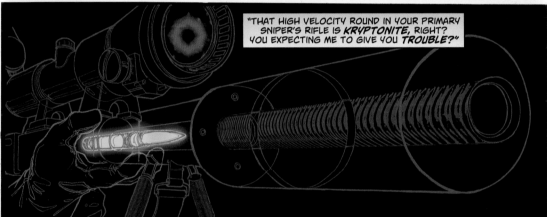

"THAT HIGH VELOCITY ROUND IN YOUR PRIMARY SNIPER'S RIFLE IS *KRYPTONITE*, RIGHT? YOU EXPECTING ME TO GIVE YOU *TROUBLE?*"

BOTTOM LINE? WE DON'T KNOW *WHAT* TO THINK.

WE'RE HOPING YOU HAVEN'T GONE *ROGUE.* WE'RE HOPING YOU CAN PUT OUR MINDS AT *EASE.*

SO I'M GOING TO ASK YOU *ONE MORE TIME:*

WHAT, IN GOD'S NAME, DID YOU THINK YOU WERE DOING FLYING INTO *TEHRAN?*

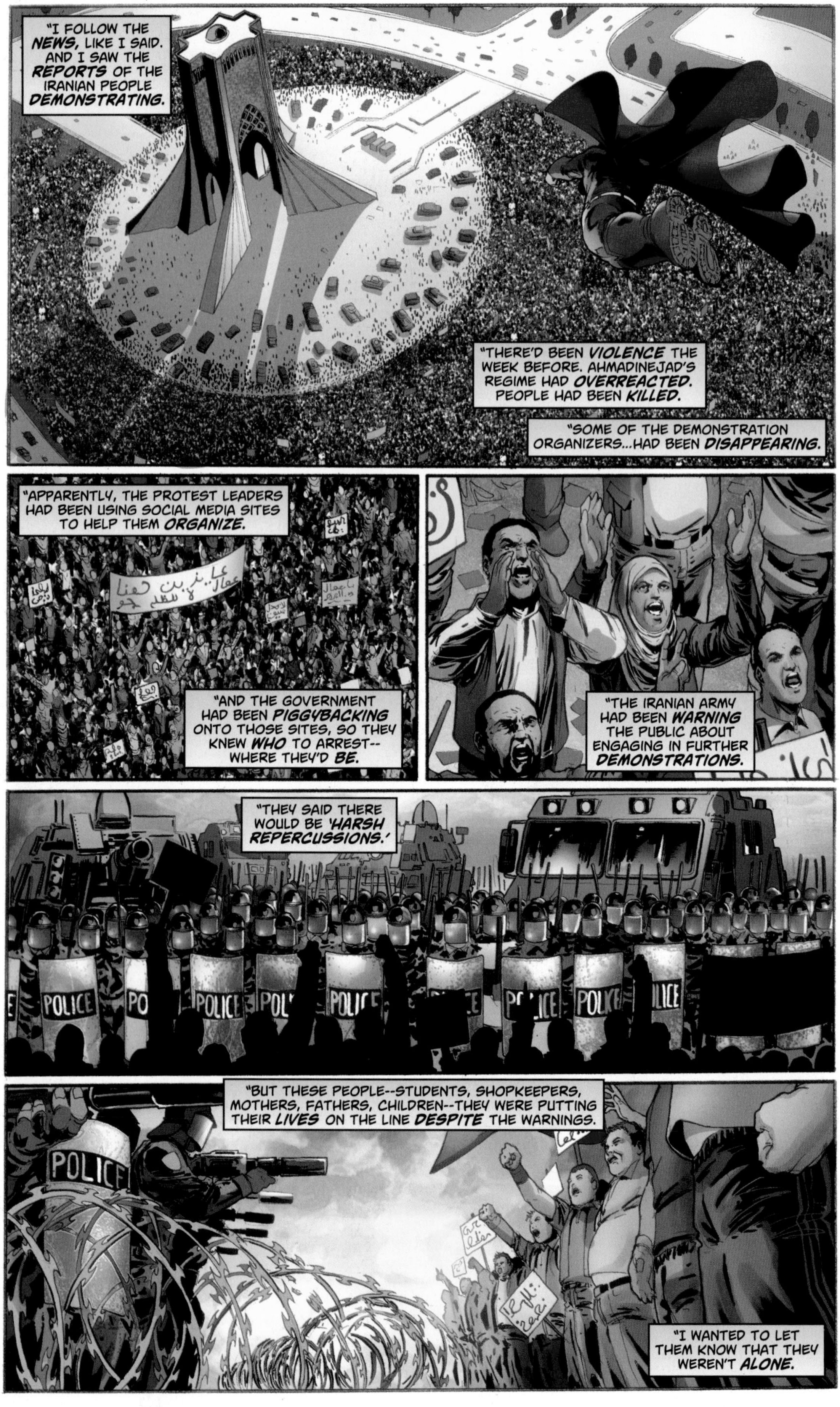
"I FOLLOW THE NEWS, LIKE I SAID. AND I SAW THE REPORTS OF THE IRANIAN PEOPLE DEMONSTRATING.
"THERE'D BEEN VIOLENCE THE WEEK BEFORE. AHMADINEJAD'S REGIME HAD OVERREACTED. PEOPLE HAD BEEN KILLED.
"SOME OF THE DEMONSTRATION ORGANIZERS...HAD BEEN DISAPPEARING.
"APPARENTLY, THE PROTEST LEADERS HAD BEEN USING SOCIAL MEDIA SITES TO HELP THEM ORGANIZE.
"AND THE GOVERNMENT HAD BEEN PIGGYBACKING ONTO THOSE SITES, SO THEY KNEW WHO TO ARREST-- WHERE THEY'D BE.
"THE IRANIAN ARMY HAD BEEN WARNING THE PUBLIC ABOUT ENGAGING IN FURTHER DEMONSTRATIONS.
"THEY SAID THERE WOULD BE 'HARSH REPERCUSSIONS.'
POLICE
"BUT THESE PEOPLE--STUDENTS, SHOPKEEPERS, MOTHERS, FATHERS, CHILDREN--THEY WERE PUTTING THEIR LIVES ON THE LINE DESPITE THE WARNINGS.
POLICE
"I WANTED TO LET THEM KNOW THAT THEY WEREN'T ALONE.

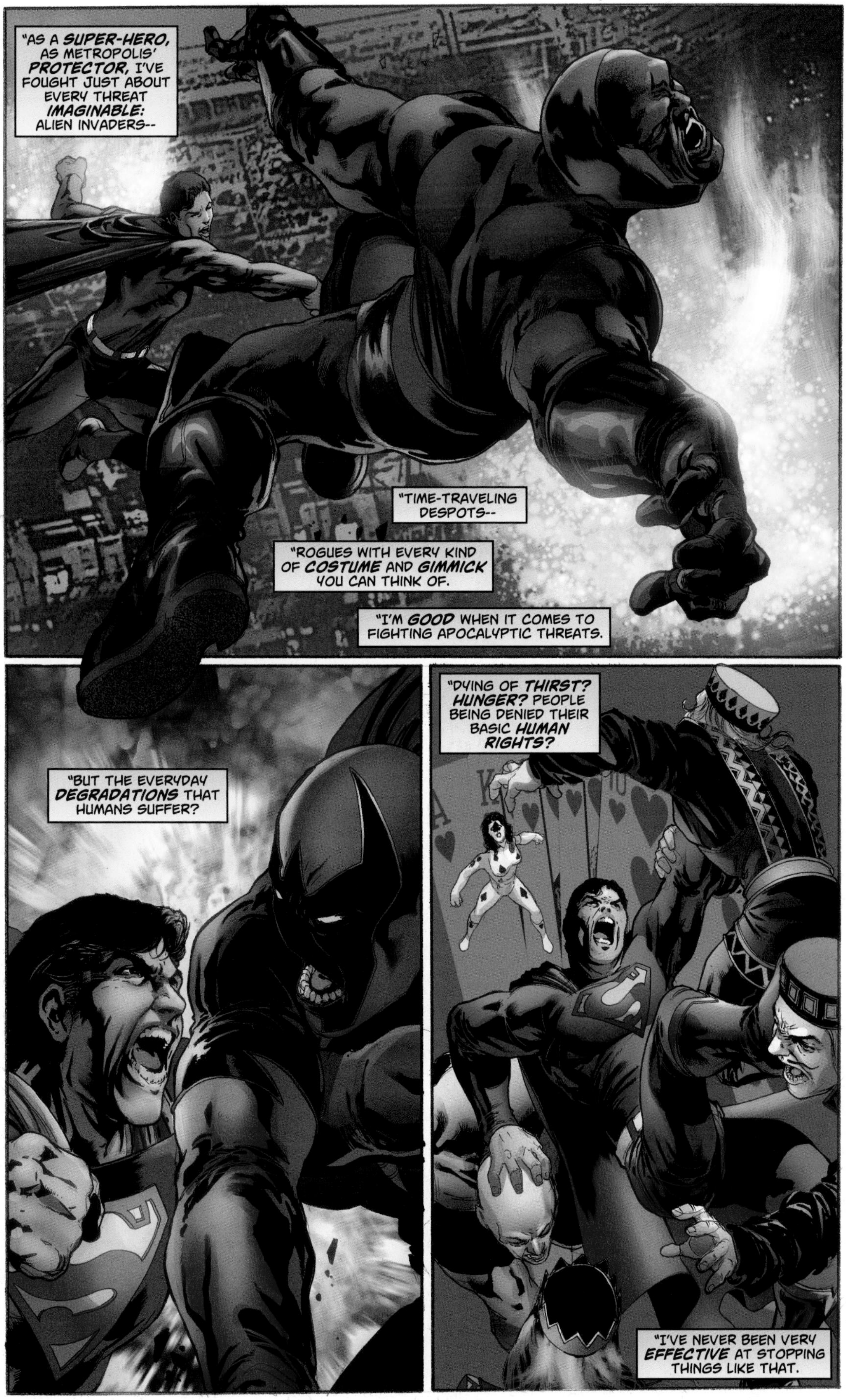
"AS A SUPER-HERO, AS METROPOLIS' PROTECTOR, I'VE FOUGHT JUST ABOUT EVERY THREAT IMAGINABLE: ALIEN INVADERS--
"TIME-TRAVELING DESPOTS--
"ROGUES WITH EVERY KIND OF COSTUME AND GIMMICK YOU CAN THINK OF.
"I'M GOOD WHEN IT COMES TO FIGHTING APOCALYPTIC THREATS.
"BUT THE EVERYDAY DEGRADATIONS THAT HUMANS SUFFER?
"DYING OF THIRST? HUNGER? PEOPLE BEING DENIED THEIR BASIC HUMAN RIGHTS?
"I'VE NEVER BEEN VERY EFFECTIVE AT STOPPING THINGS LIKE THAT.

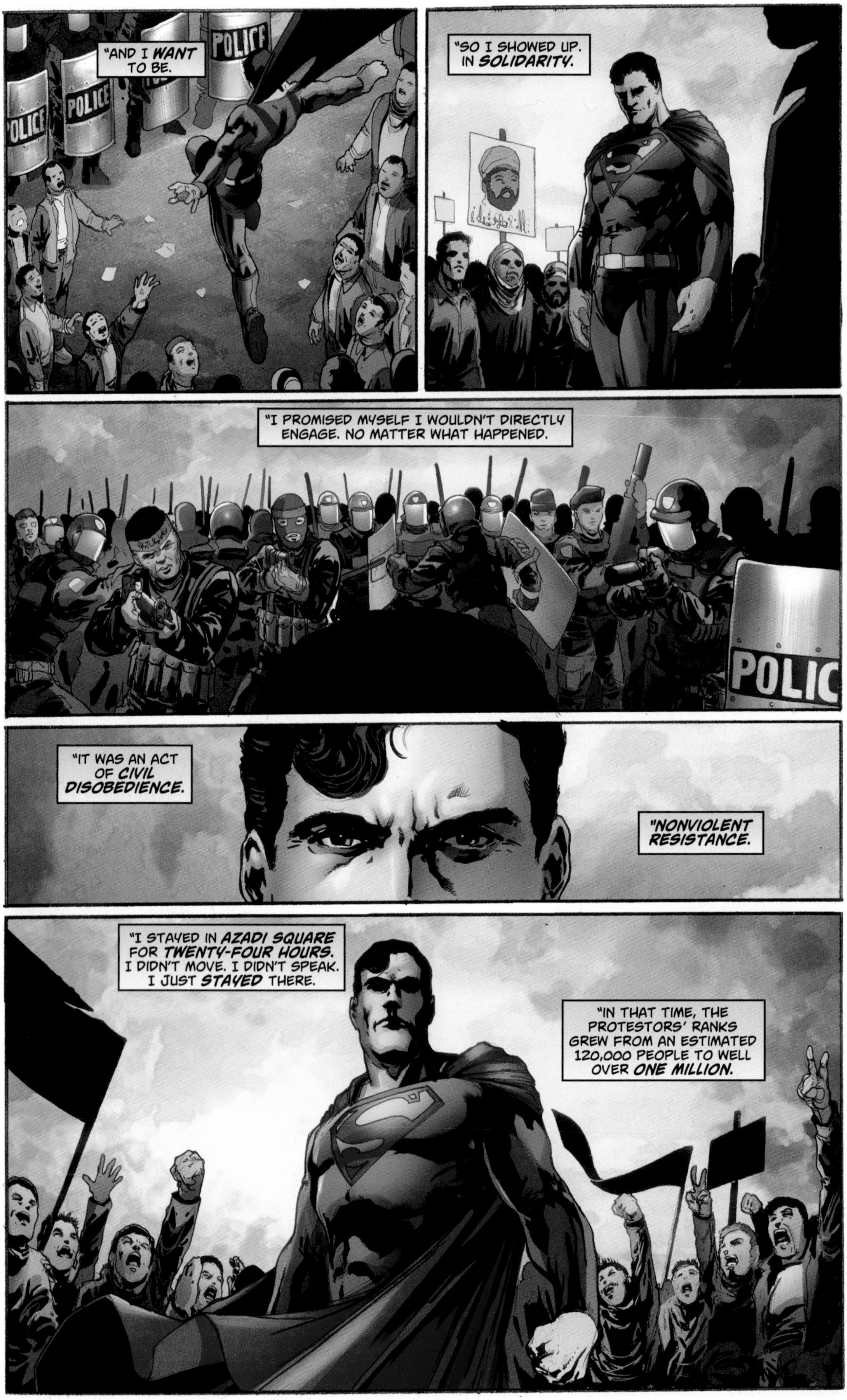
"AND I *WANT* TO BE.
POLICE
"SO I SHOWED UP. IN *SOLIDARITY*.
"I PROMISED MYSELF I WOULDN'T DIRECTLY ENGAGE. NO MATTER WHAT HAPPENED.
POLIC
"IT WAS AN ACT OF *CIVIL DISOBEDIENCE*.
"*NONVIOLENT RESISTANCE*.
"I STAYED IN *AZADI SQUARE* FOR *TWENTY-FOUR HOURS*. I DIDN'T MOVE. I DIDN'T SPEAK. I JUST *STAYED* THERE.
"IN THAT TIME, THE PROTESTORS' RANKS GREW FROM AN ESTIMATED 120,000 PEOPLE TO WELL OVER *ONE MILLION*.

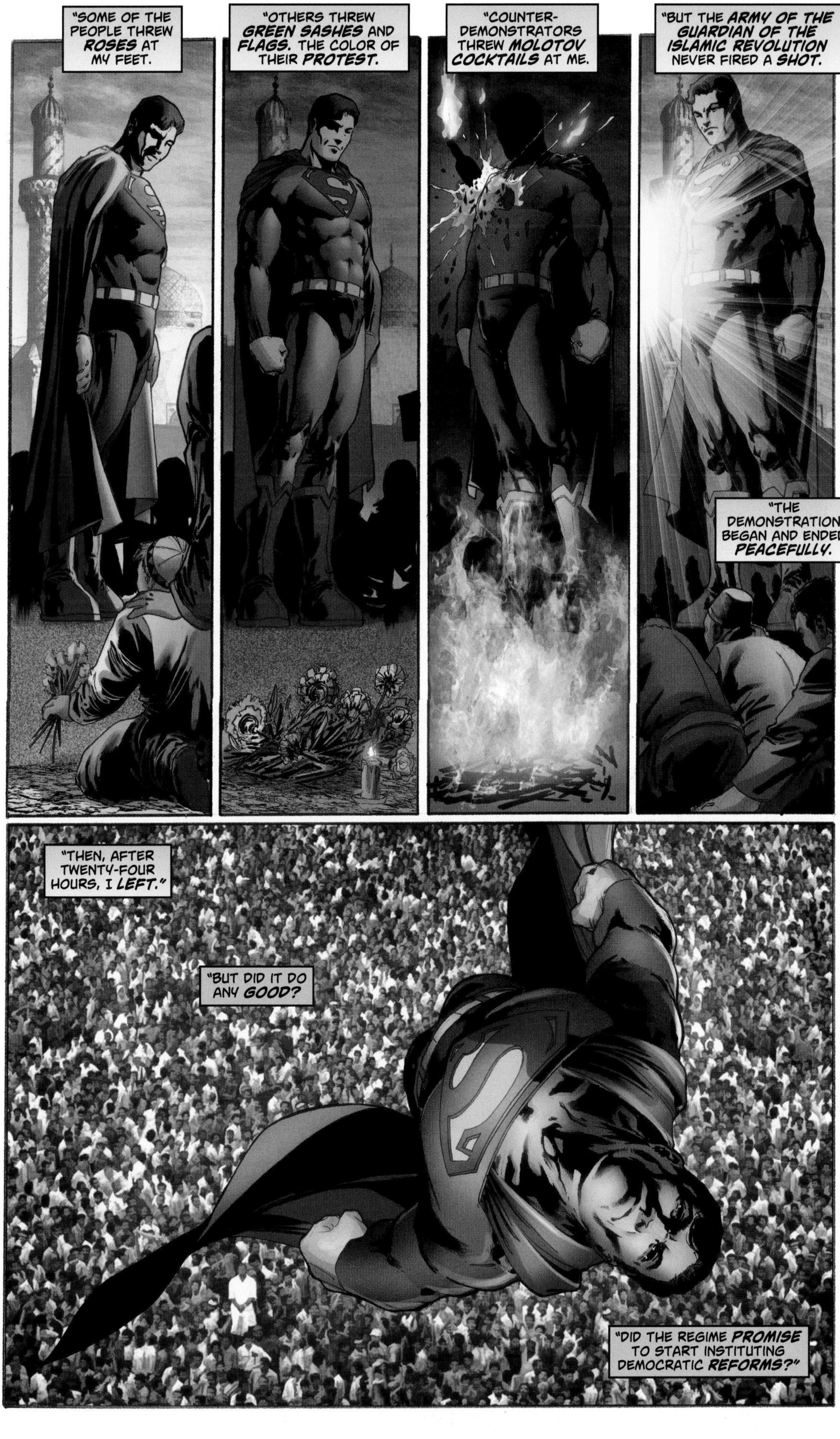
"SOME OF THE PEOPLE THREW ROSES AT MY FEET.
"OTHERS THREW GREEN SASHES AND FLAGS. THE COLOR OF THEIR PROTEST.
"COUNTER-DEMONSTRATORS THREW MOLOTOV COCKTAILS AT ME.
"BUT THE ARMY OF THE GUARDIAN OF THE ISLAMIC REVOLUTION NEVER FIRED A SHOT.
"THE DEMONSTRATION BEGAN AND ENDED PEACEFULLY.
"THEN, AFTER TWENTY-FOUR HOURS, I LEFT."
"BUT DID IT DO ANY GOOD?
"DID THE REGIME PROMISE TO START INSTITUTING DEMOCRATIC REFORMS?"

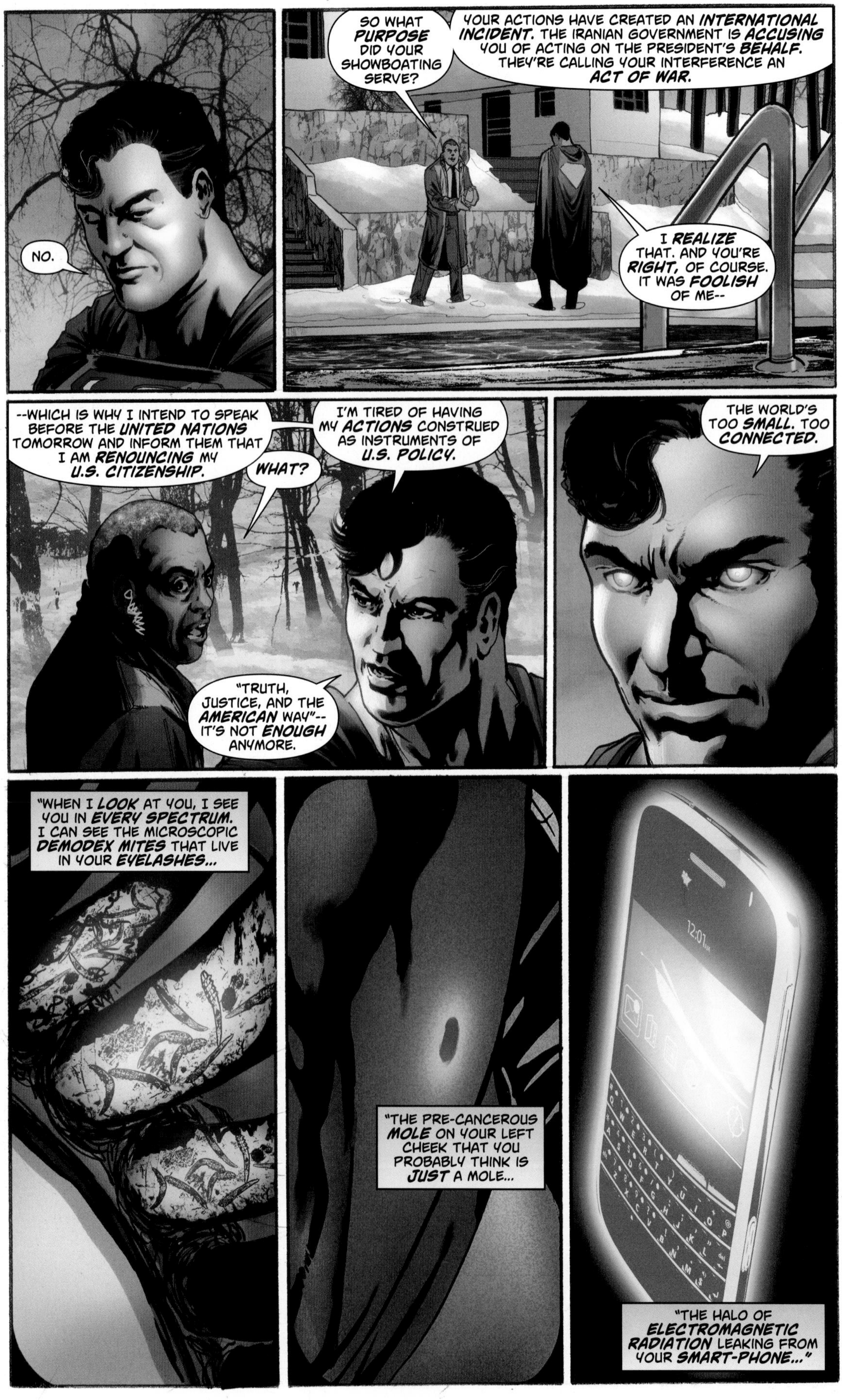
NO.
SO WHAT PURPOSE DID YOUR SHOWBOATING SERVE?
YOUR ACTIONS HAVE CREATED AN INTERNATIONAL INCIDENT. THE IRANIAN GOVERNMENT IS ACCUSING YOU OF ACTING ON THE PRESIDENT'S BEHALF. THEY'RE CALLING YOUR INTERFERENCE AN ACT OF WAR.
I REALIZE THAT. AND YOU'RE RIGHT, OF COURSE. IT WAS FOOLISH OF ME--
--WHICH IS WHY I INTEND TO SPEAK BEFORE THE UNITED NATIONS TOMORROW AND INFORM THEM THAT I AM RENOUNCING MY U.S. CITIZENSHIP.
WHAT?
I'M TIRED OF HAVING MY ACTIONS CONSTRUED AS INSTRUMENTS OF U.S. POLICY.
"TRUTH, JUSTICE, AND THE AMERICAN WAY"-- IT'S NOT ENOUGH ANYMORE.
THE WORLD'S TOO SMALL. TOO CONNECTED.
"WHEN I LOOK AT YOU, I SEE YOU IN EVERY SPECTRUM. I CAN SEE THE MICROSCOPIC DEMODEX MITES THAT LIVE IN YOUR EYELASHES...
"THE PRE-CANCEROUS MOLE ON YOUR LEFT CHEEK THAT YOU PROBABLY THINK IS JUST A MOLE...
"THE HALO OF ELECTROMAGNETIC RADIATION LEAKING FROM YOUR SMART-PHONE..."

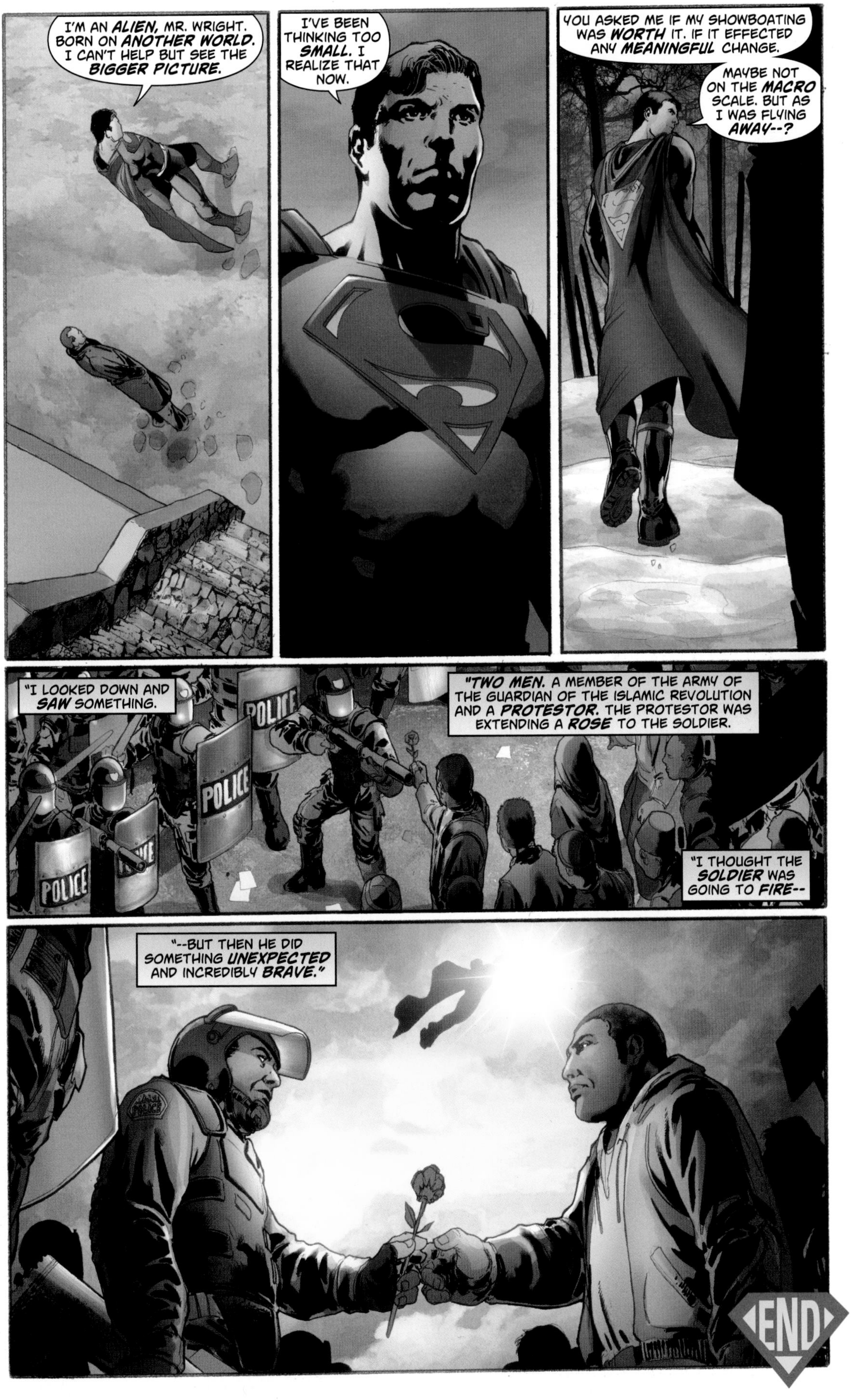
I'M AN ALIEN, MR. WRIGHT. BORN ON ANOTHER WORLD. I CAN'T HELP BUT SEE THE BIGGER PICTURE.
I'VE BEEN THINKING TOO SMALL. I REALIZE THAT NOW.
YOU ASKED ME IF MY SHOWBOATING WAS WORTH IT. IF IT EFFECTED ANY MEANINGFUL CHANGE.
MAYBE NOT ON THE MACRO SCALE. BUT AS I WAS FLYING AWAY--?
"I LOOKED DOWN AND SAW SOMETHING.
"TWO MEN. A MEMBER OF THE ARMY OF THE GUARDIAN OF THE ISLAMIC REVOLUTION AND A PROTESTOR. THE PROTESTOR WAS EXTENDING A ROSE TO THE SOLDIER.
POLICE
POLICE
POLICE
POLICE
"I THOUGHT THE SOLDIER WAS GOING TO FIRE--
"--BUT THEN HE DID SOMETHING UNEXPECTED AND INCREDIBLY BRAVE."
POLICE
END

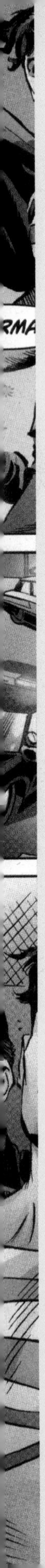

PART V • 2011 and BEYOND
THE MAN OF TOMORROW

In 2011, following the events of the "Flashpoint" crossover storyline, the DC Comics editorial team relaunched their entire line of titles, making sweeping changes to characters and continuity. For the following "New 52" initiative, the Last Son of Krypton was completely reinvented.

Scottish writer Grant Morrison took over the new Man of Steel with ACTION COMICS, the title where it all began, this time exploring the hero's early days and taking the character back to his roots: a champion, fighting for those unable to defend themselves against the corrupted elites. The first story arc showed the hero's adventures during his first five years as a super hero. We see a very young Superman, a rookie, not yet flying.

Of course, ACTION COMICS isn't the only title starring the Man of Steel in "The New 52." The more traditional title, SUPERMAN, is set in the present day and shows a fully empowered Superman. Finally, JUSTICE LEAGUE shows Superman as part of a super hero team, putting more emphasis on the hero's brash attitude than ever before. He also develops a romance with his teammate Wonder Woman.

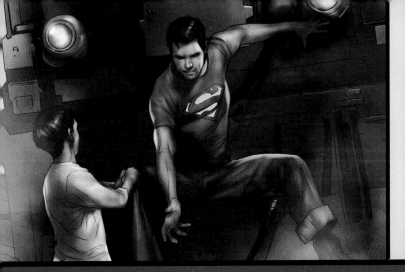

Next to him, a new Superboy and Supergirl debut, creating a modern, more dysfunctional version of the "Superman Family" of old. The former is still a clone but also a living weapon. His artificial nature weighs on him, as he tries, with the Teen Titans, to give his life meaning. Supergirl remains Superman's cousin, but is newly arrived on the planet. Sent to Earth as a teenager by her father, she lived all her childhood on Krypton and has a hard time accepting the loss of her home world.

With new adventures being published every month, the Man of Tomorrow continues his ceaseless fight for truth, justice and the American Way!

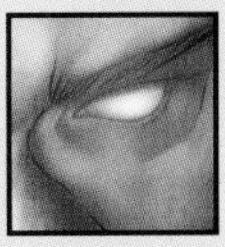

CARE TO WASTE SOME MORE BULLETS, BOYS?
LET THE LADY GO-- AND START RUNNING.

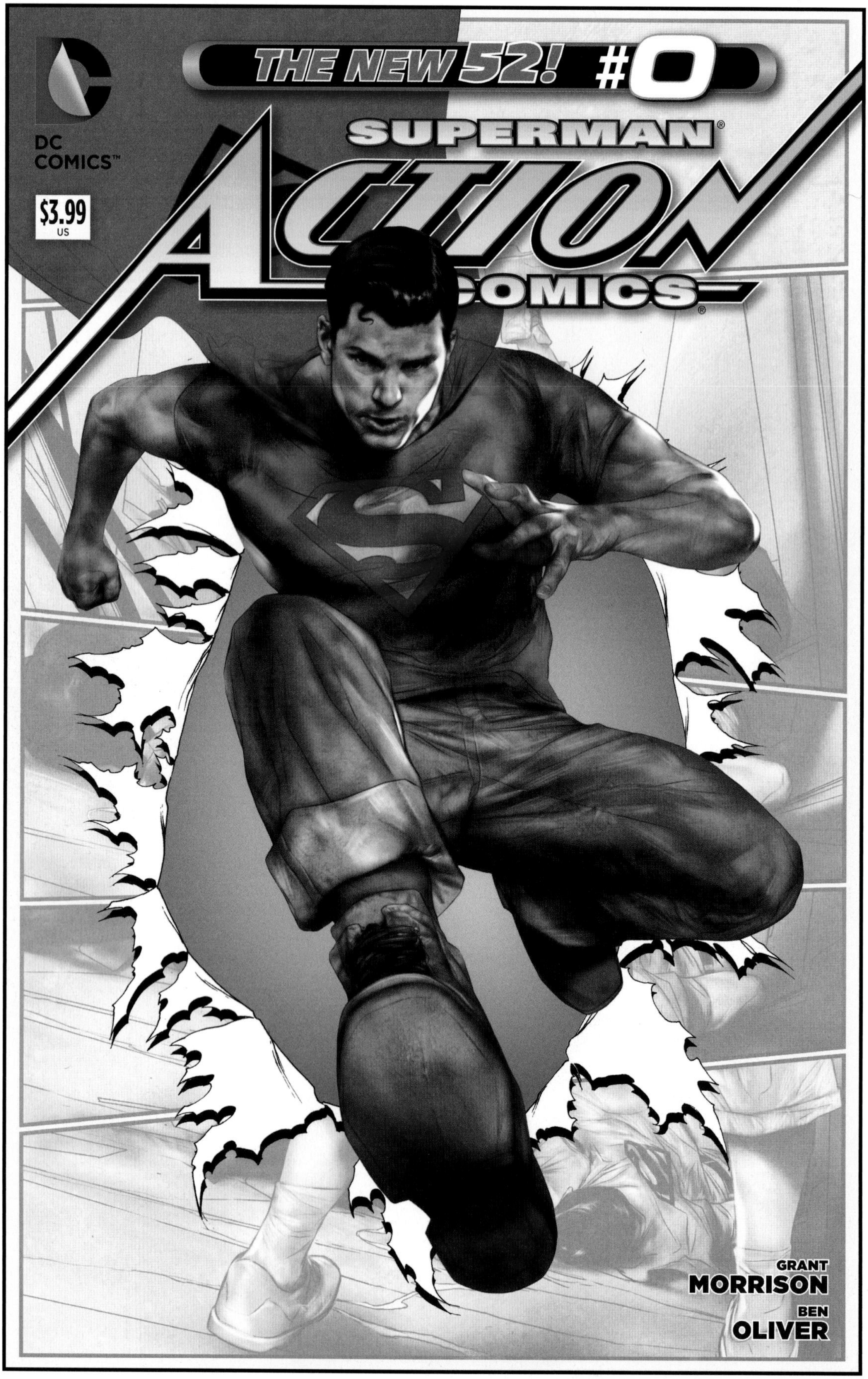
DC COMICS™
THE NEW 52! #0
SUPERMAN®
ACTION COMICS®
$3.99 US
GRANT MORRISON
BEN OLIVER

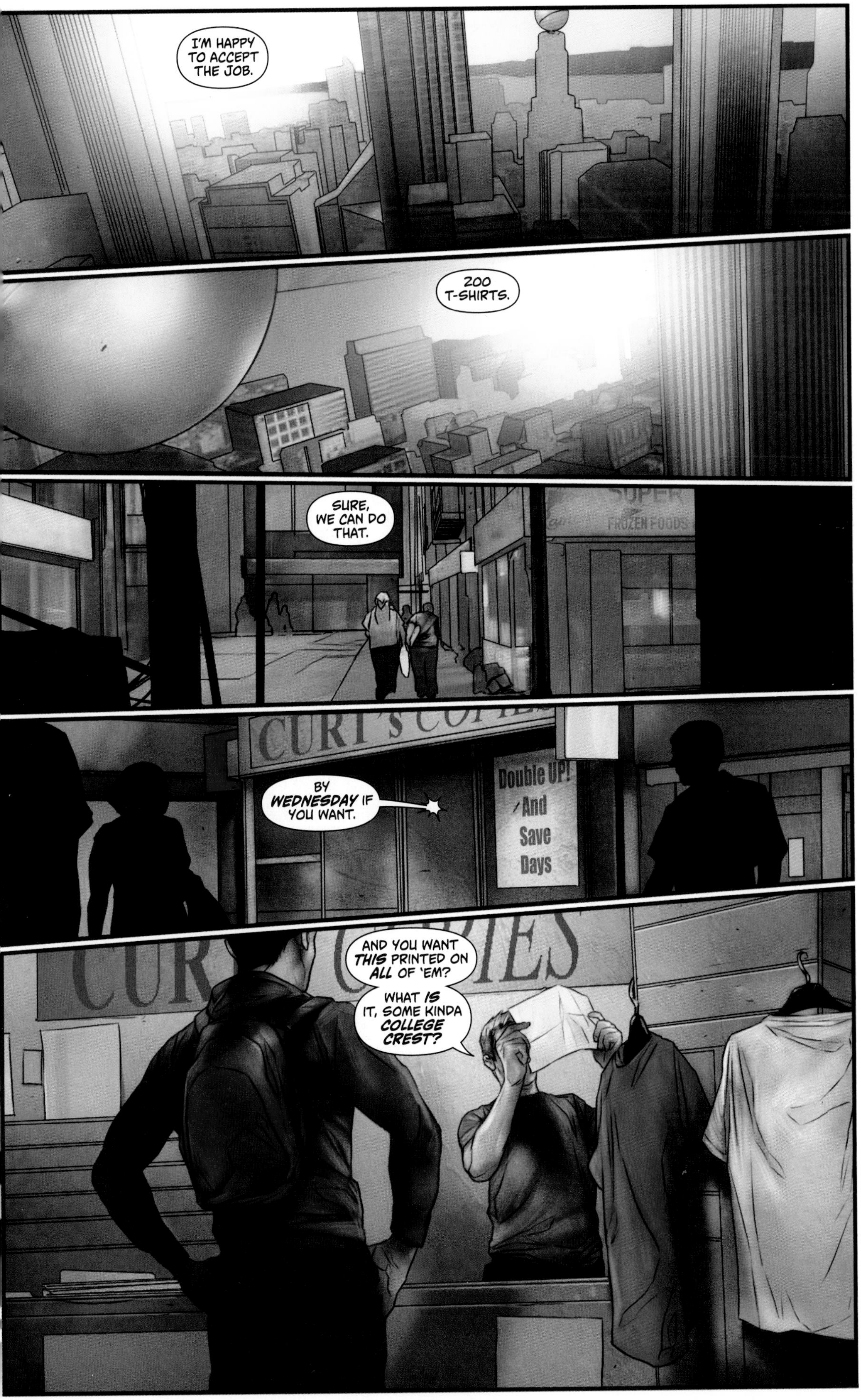

I'M HAPPY TO ACCEPT THE JOB.
200 T-SHIRTS.
SUPER FROZEN FOODS
SURE, WE CAN DO THAT.
CURT'S COPIES
BY WEDNESDAY IF YOU WANT.
Double UP! And Save Days
AND YOU WANT THIS PRINTED ON ALL OF 'EM?
WHAT IS IT, SOME KINDA COLLEGE CREST?

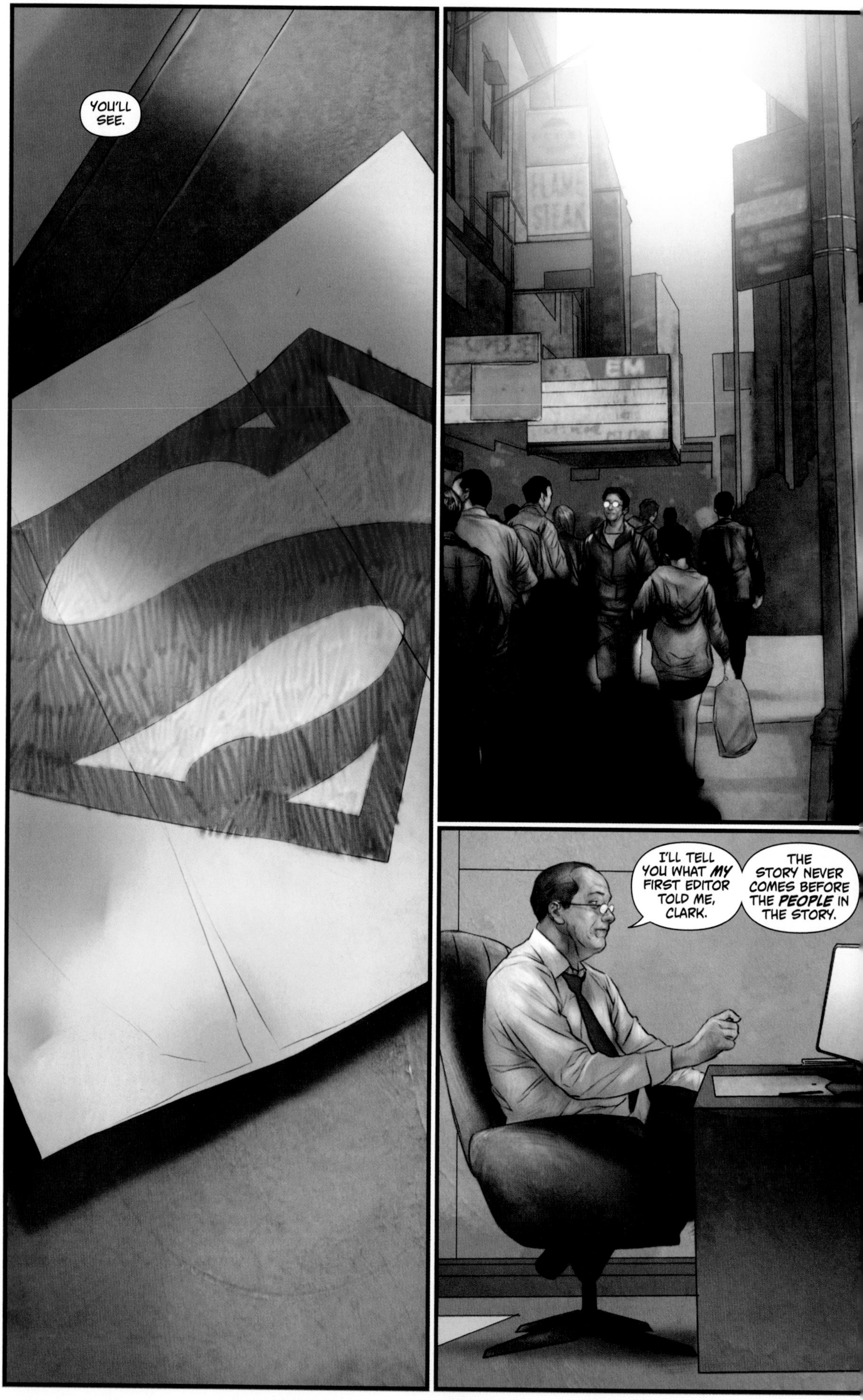
YOU'LL SEE.
I'LL TELL YOU WHAT *MY* FIRST EDITOR TOLD ME, CLARK.
THE STORY NEVER COMES BEFORE THE *PEOPLE* IN THE STORY.

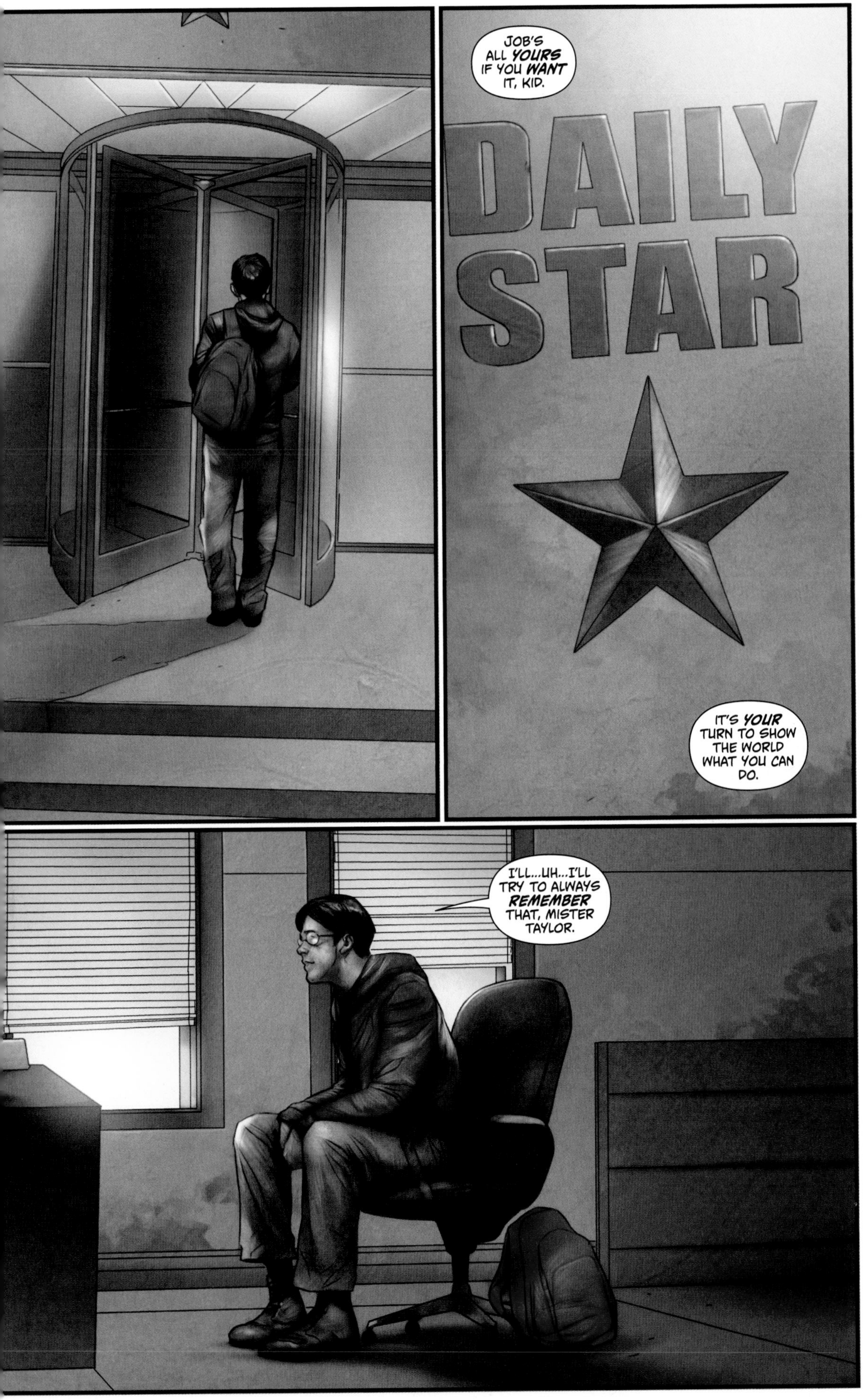
JOB'S ALL YOURS IF YOU WANT IT, KID.
DAILY STAR
IT'S YOUR TURN TO SHOW THE WORLD WHAT YOU CAN DO.
I'LL...UH...I'LL TRY TO ALWAYS REMEMBER THAT, MISTER TAYLOR.

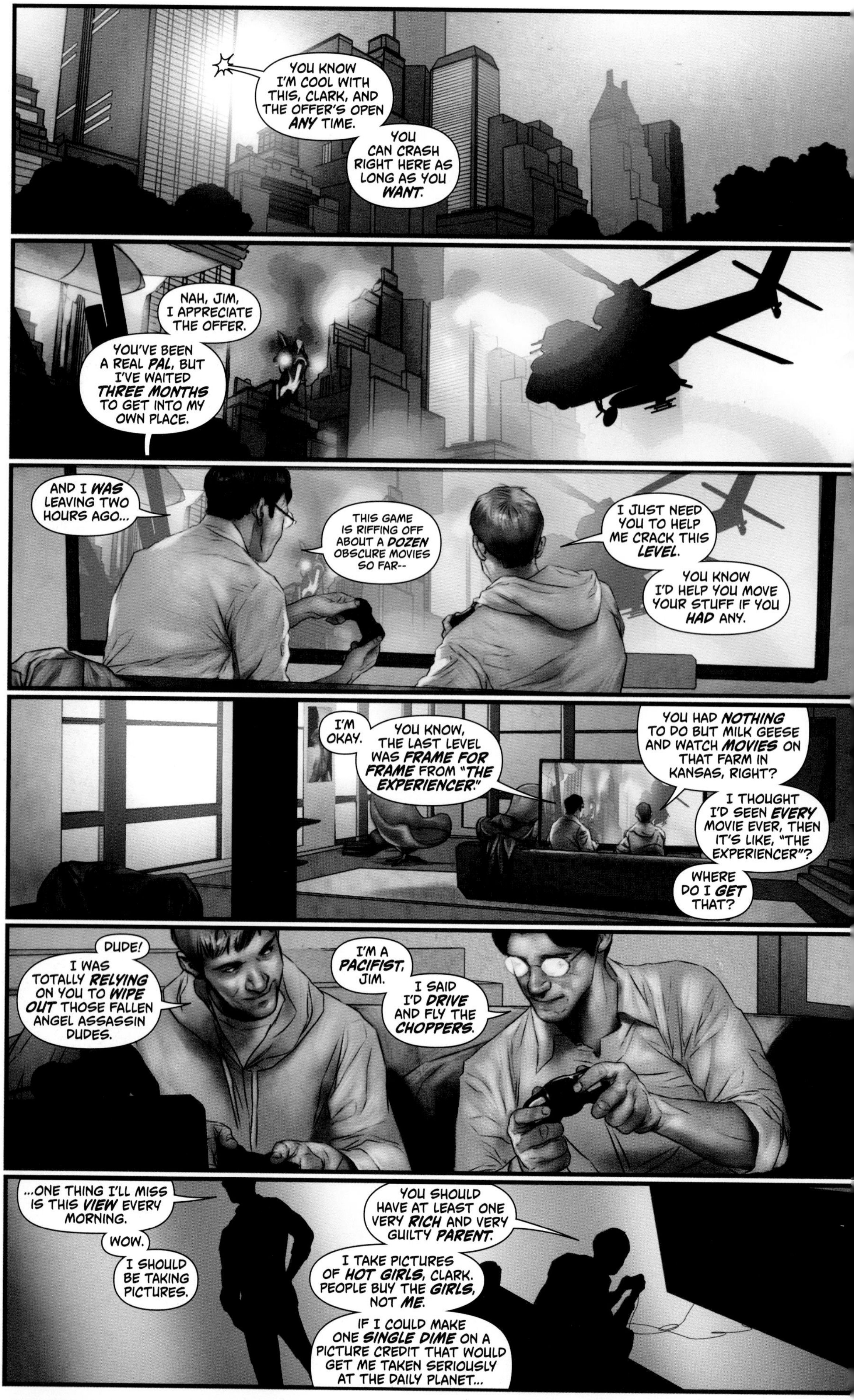
YOU KNOW I'M COOL WITH THIS, CLARK, AND THE OFFER'S OPEN ANY TIME.
YOU CAN CRASH RIGHT HERE AS LONG AS YOU WANT.
NAH, JIM, I APPRECIATE THE OFFER.
YOU'VE BEEN A REAL PAL, BUT I'VE WAITED THREE MONTHS TO GET INTO MY OWN PLACE.
AND I WAS LEAVING TWO HOURS AGO...
THIS GAME IS RIFFING OFF ABOUT A DOZEN OBSCURE MOVIES SO FAR--
I JUST NEED YOU TO HELP ME CRACK THIS LEVEL.
YOU KNOW I'D HELP YOU MOVE YOUR STUFF IF YOU HAD ANY.
I'M OKAY.
YOU KNOW, THE LAST LEVEL WAS FRAME FOR FRAME FROM "THE EXPERIENCER."
YOU HAD NOTHING TO DO BUT MILK GEESE AND WATCH MOVIES ON THAT FARM IN KANSAS, RIGHT?
I THOUGHT I'D SEEN EVERY MOVIE EVER, THEN IT'S LIKE, "THE EXPERIENCER"?
WHERE DO I GET THAT?
DUDE!
I WAS TOTALLY RELYING ON YOU TO WIPE OUT THOSE FALLEN ANGEL ASSASSIN DUDES.
I'M A PACIFIST, JIM.
I SAID I'D DRIVE AND FLY THE CHOPPERS.
...ONE THING I'LL MISS IS THIS VIEW EVERY MORNING.
WOW.
I SHOULD BE TAKING PICTURES.
YOU SHOULD HAVE AT LEAST ONE VERY RICH AND VERY GUILTY PARENT.
I TAKE PICTURES OF HOT GIRLS, CLARK. PEOPLE BUY THE GIRLS, NOT ME.
IF I COULD MAKE ONE SINGLE DIME ON A PICTURE CREDIT THAT WOULD GET ME TAKEN SERIOUSLY AT THE DAILY PLANET...

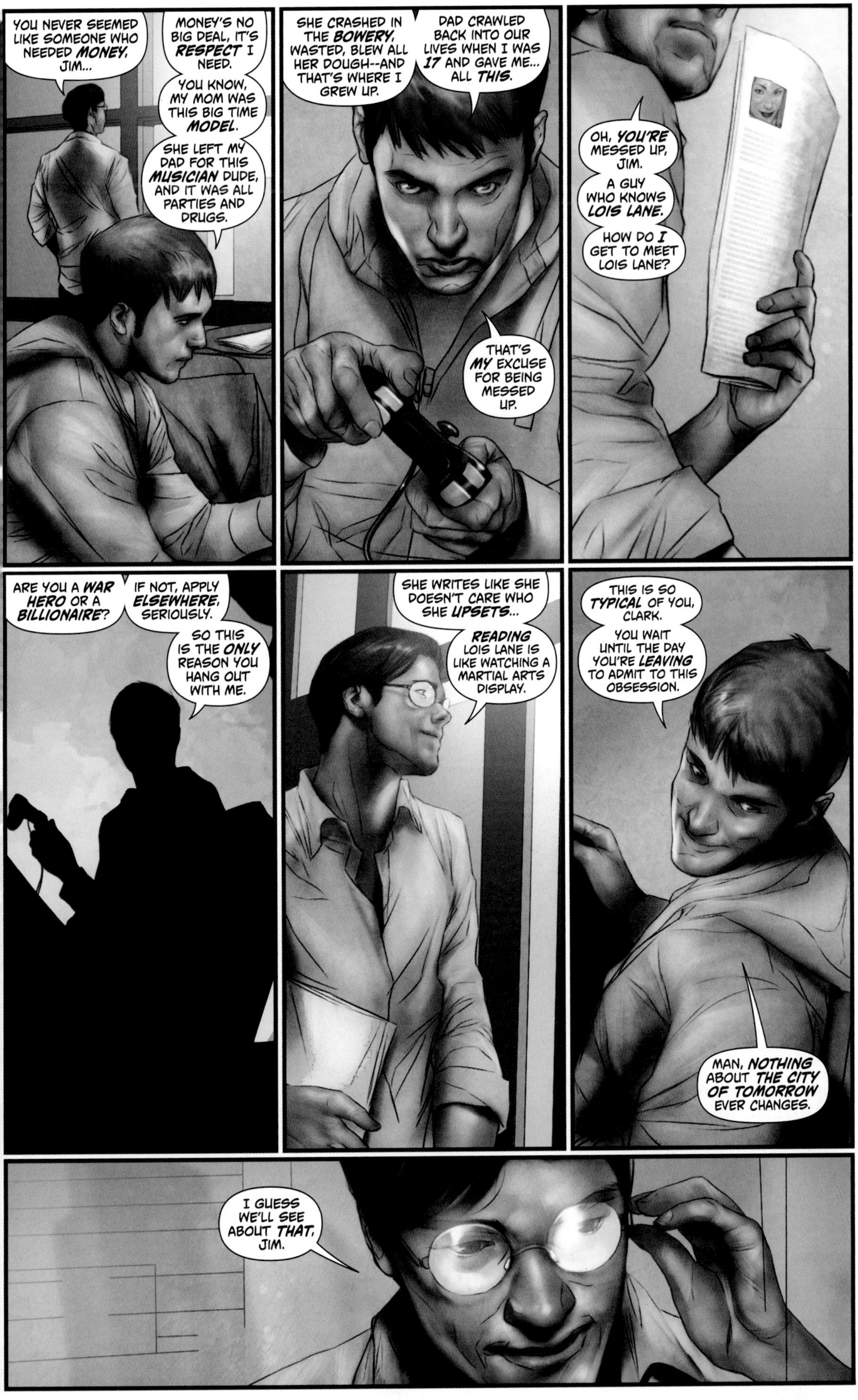
YOU NEVER SEEMED LIKE SOMEONE WHO NEEDED MONEY, JIM...
MONEY'S NO BIG DEAL, IT'S RESPECT I NEED.
YOU KNOW, MY MOM WAS THIS BIG TIME MODEL.
SHE LEFT MY DAD FOR THIS MUSICIAN DUDE, AND IT WAS ALL PARTIES AND DRUGS.
SHE CRASHED IN THE BOWERY, WASTED, BLEW ALL HER DOUGH--AND THAT'S WHERE I GREW UP.
DAD CRAWLED BACK INTO OUR LIVES WHEN I WAS 17 AND GAVE ME... ALL THIS.
THAT'S MY EXCUSE FOR BEING MESSED UP.
OH, YOU'RE MESSED UP, JIM.
A GUY WHO KNOWS LOIS LANE.
HOW DO I GET TO MEET LOIS LANE?
ARE YOU A WAR HERO OR A BILLIONAIRE?
IF NOT, APPLY ELSEWHERE, SERIOUSLY.
SO THIS IS THE ONLY REASON YOU HANG OUT WITH ME.
SHE WRITES LIKE SHE DOESN'T CARE WHO SHE UPSETS...
READING LOIS LANE IS LIKE WATCHING A MARTIAL ARTS DISPLAY.
THIS IS SO TYPICAL OF YOU, CLARK.
YOU WAIT UNTIL THE DAY YOU'RE LEAVING TO ADMIT TO THIS OBSESSION.
MAN, NOTHING ABOUT THE CITY OF TOMORROW EVER CHANGES.
I GUESS WE'LL SEE ABOUT THAT, JIM.

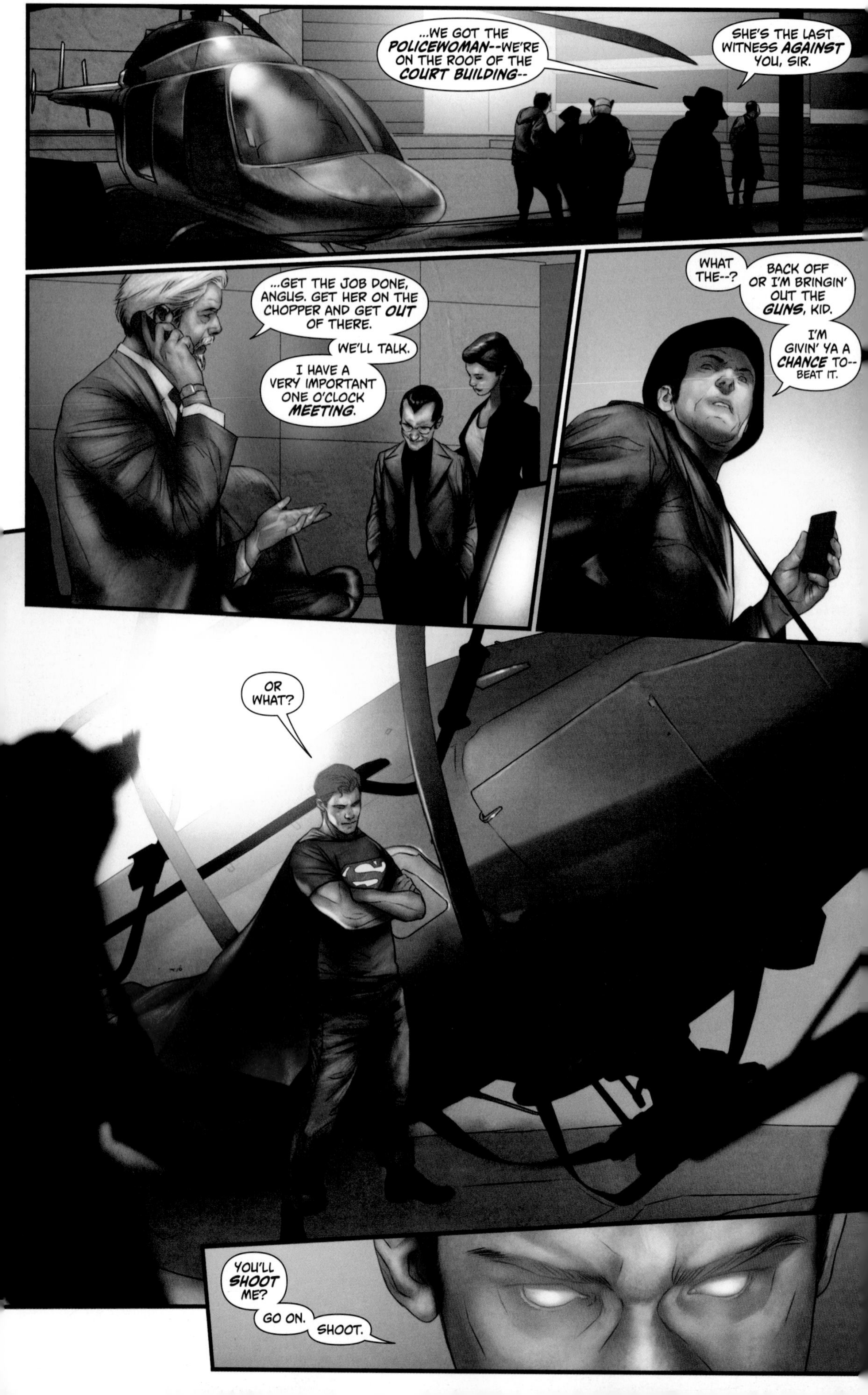
...WE GOT THE POLICEWOMAN--WE'RE ON THE ROOF OF THE COURT BUILDING--
SHE'S THE LAST WITNESS AGAINST YOU, SIR.
...GET THE JOB DONE, ANGUS. GET HER ON THE CHOPPER AND GET OUT OF THERE.
WE'LL TALK.
I HAVE A VERY IMPORTANT ONE O'CLOCK MEETING.
WHAT THE--?
BACK OFF OR I'M BRINGIN' OUT THE GUNS, KID.
I'M GIVIN' YA A CHANCE TO-- BEAT IT.
OR WHAT?
YOU'LL SHOOT ME?
GO ON.
SHOOT.

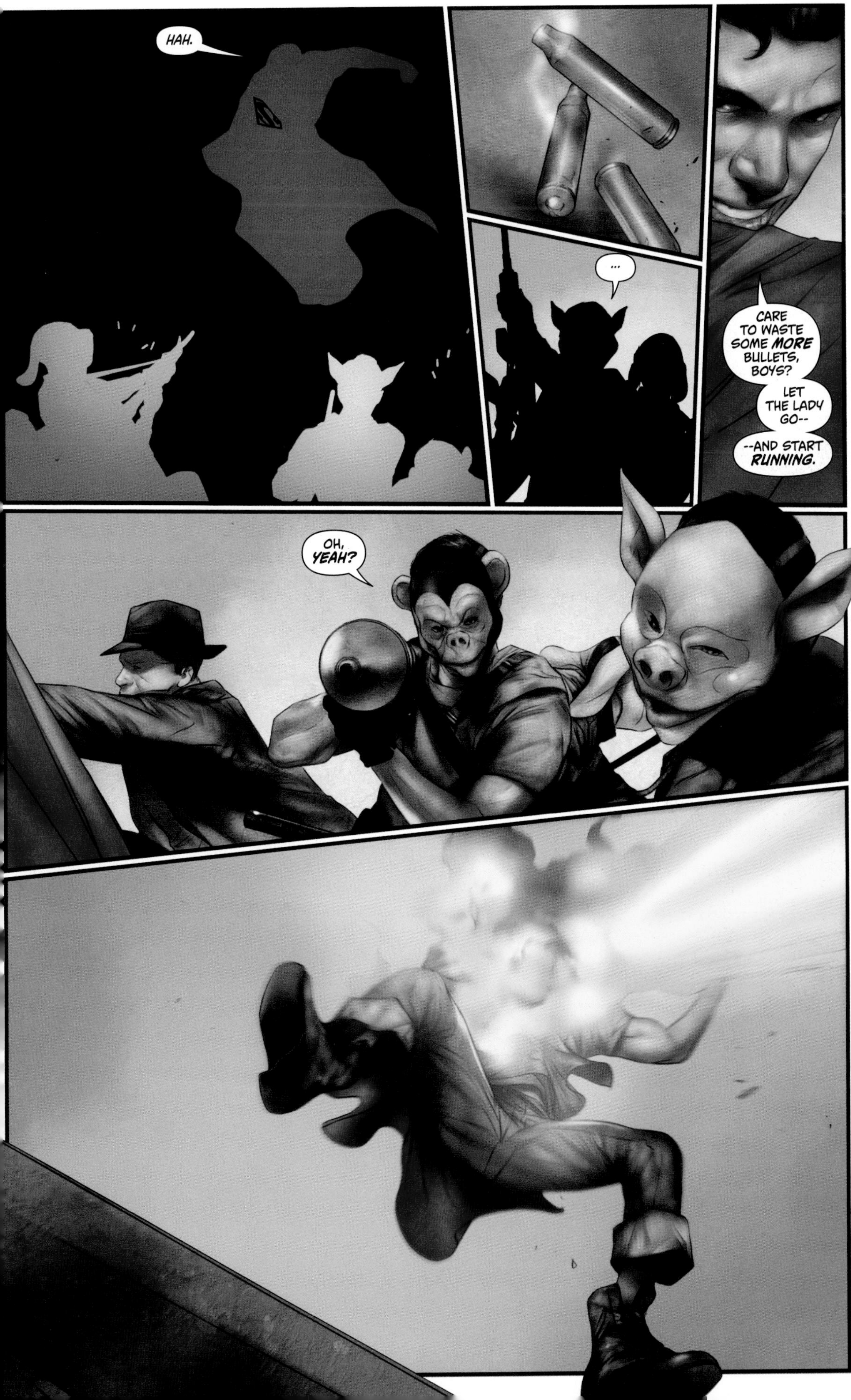
HAH.
...
CARE TO WASTE SOME MORE BULLETS, BOYS?
LET THE LADY GO--
--AND START RUNNING.
OH, YEAH?

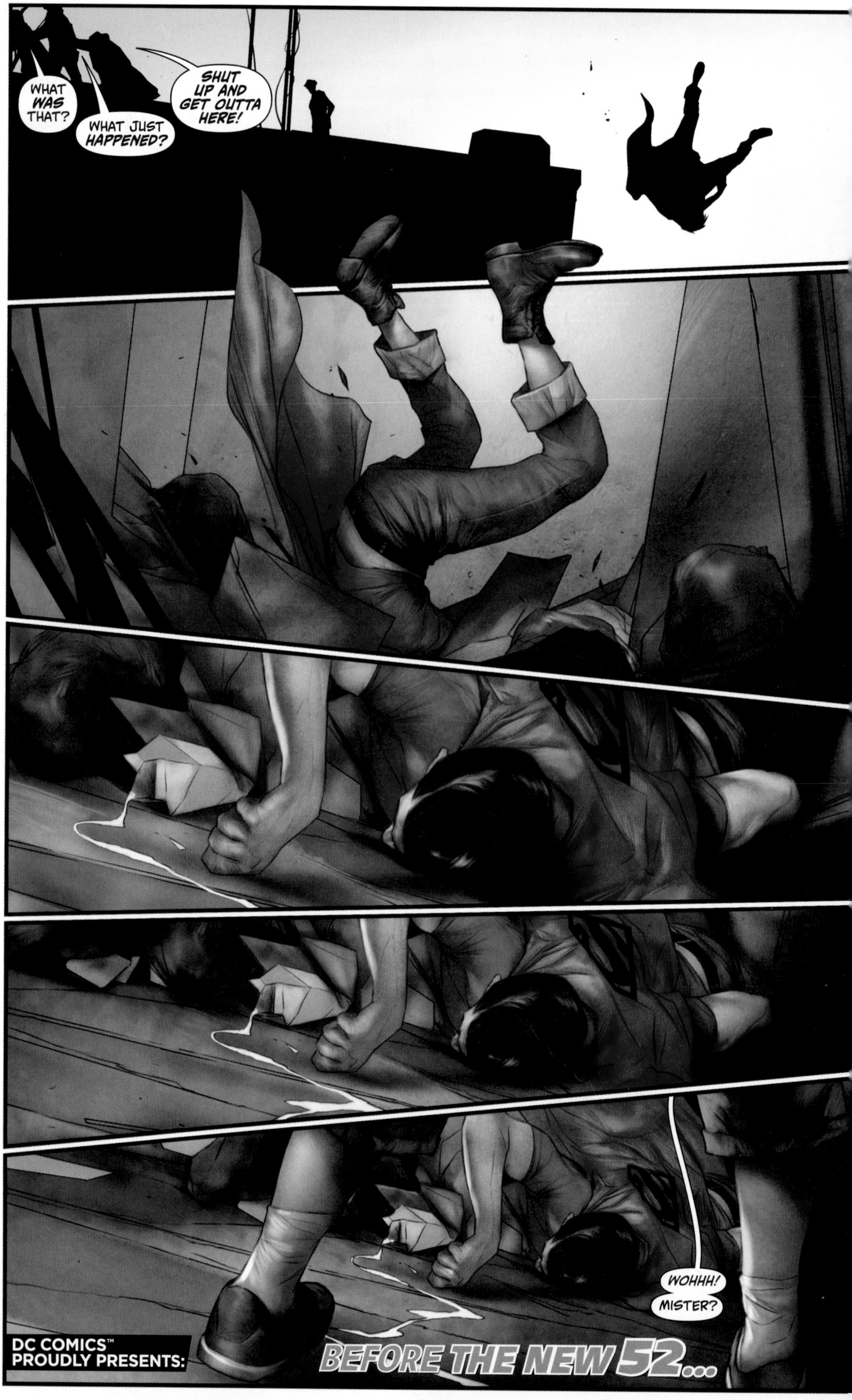
WHAT WAS THAT?
WHAT JUST HAPPENED?
SHUT UP AND GET OUTTA HERE!
WOHHH!
MISTER?
DC COMICS™ PROUDLY PRESENTS:
BEFORE THE NEW 52...

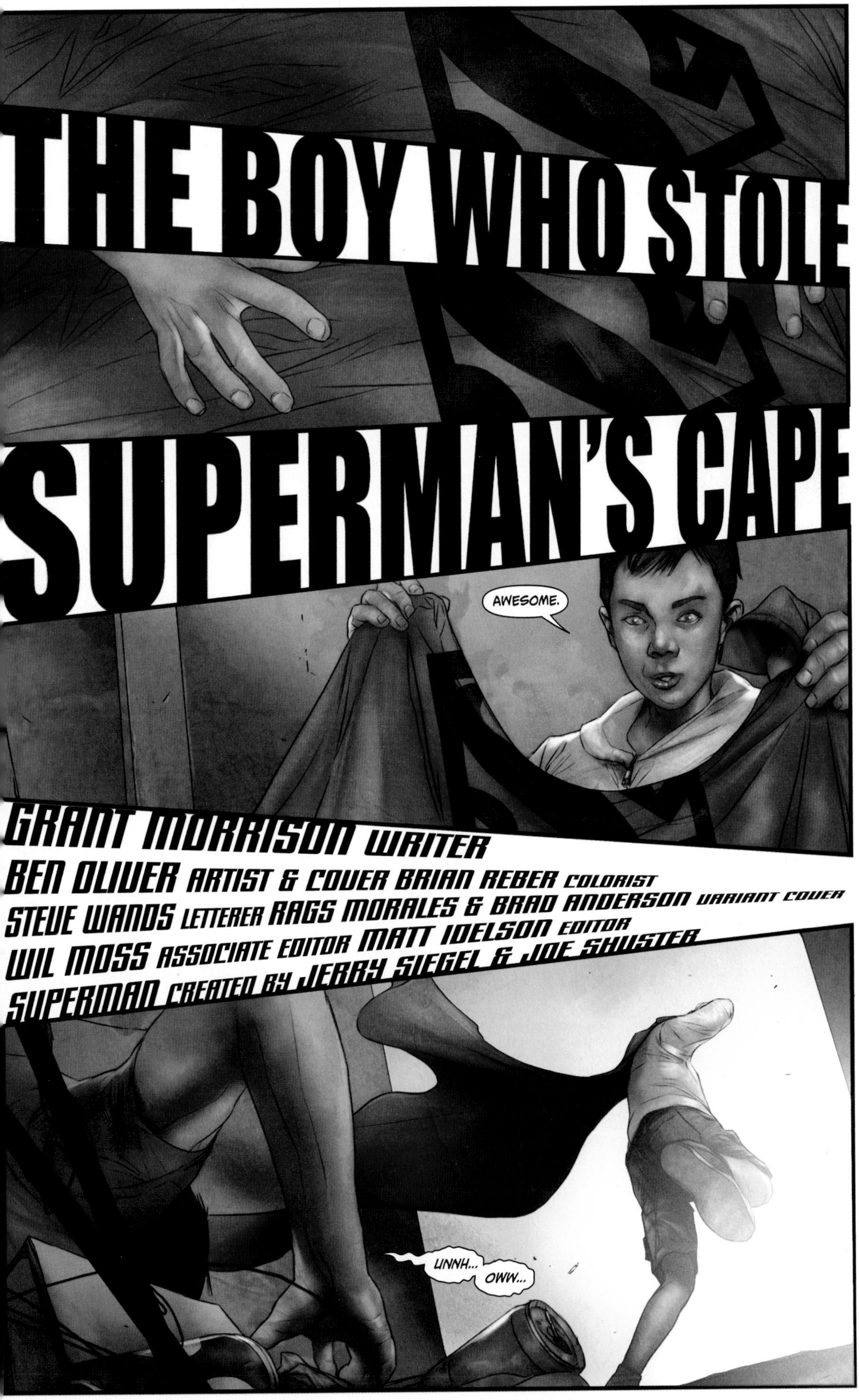
THE BOY WHO STOLE
SUPERMAN'S CAPE
AWESOME.
GRANT MORRISON WRITER
BEN OLIVER ARTIST & COVER BRIAN REBER COLORIST
STEVE WANDS LETTERER RAGS MORALES & BRAD ANDERSON VARIANT COVER
WIL MOSS ASSOCIATE EDITOR MATT IDELSON EDITOR
SUPERMAN CREATED BY JERRY SIEGEL & JOE SHUSTER
UNNH...
OWW...

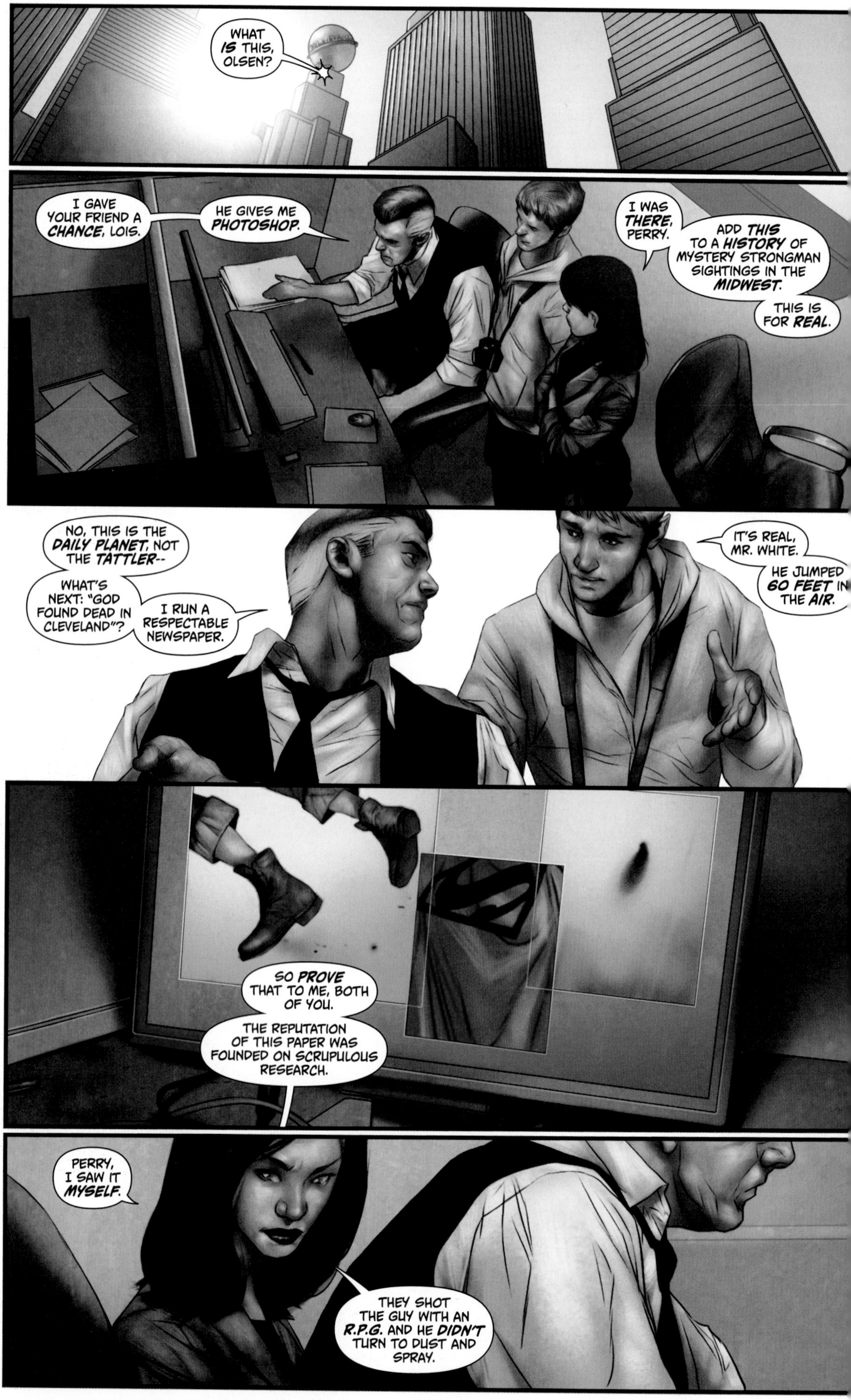
WHAT IS THIS, OLSEN?
I GAVE YOUR FRIEND A CHANCE, LOIS.
HE GIVES ME PHOTOSHOP.
I WAS THERE, PERRY.
ADD THIS TO A HISTORY OF MYSTERY STRONGMAN SIGHTINGS IN THE MIDWEST.
THIS IS FOR REAL.
NO, THIS IS THE DAILY PLANET, NOT THE TATTLER--
WHAT'S NEXT: "GOD FOUND DEAD IN CLEVELAND"?
I RUN A RESPECTABLE NEWSPAPER.
IT'S REAL, MR. WHITE.
HE JUMPED 60 FEET IN THE AIR.
SO PROVE THAT TO ME, BOTH OF YOU.
THE REPUTATION OF THIS PAPER WAS FOUNDED ON SCRUPULOUS RESEARCH.
PERRY, I SAW IT MYSELF.
THEY SHOT THE GUY WITH AN R.P.G. AND HE DIDN'T TURN TO DUST AND SPRAY.

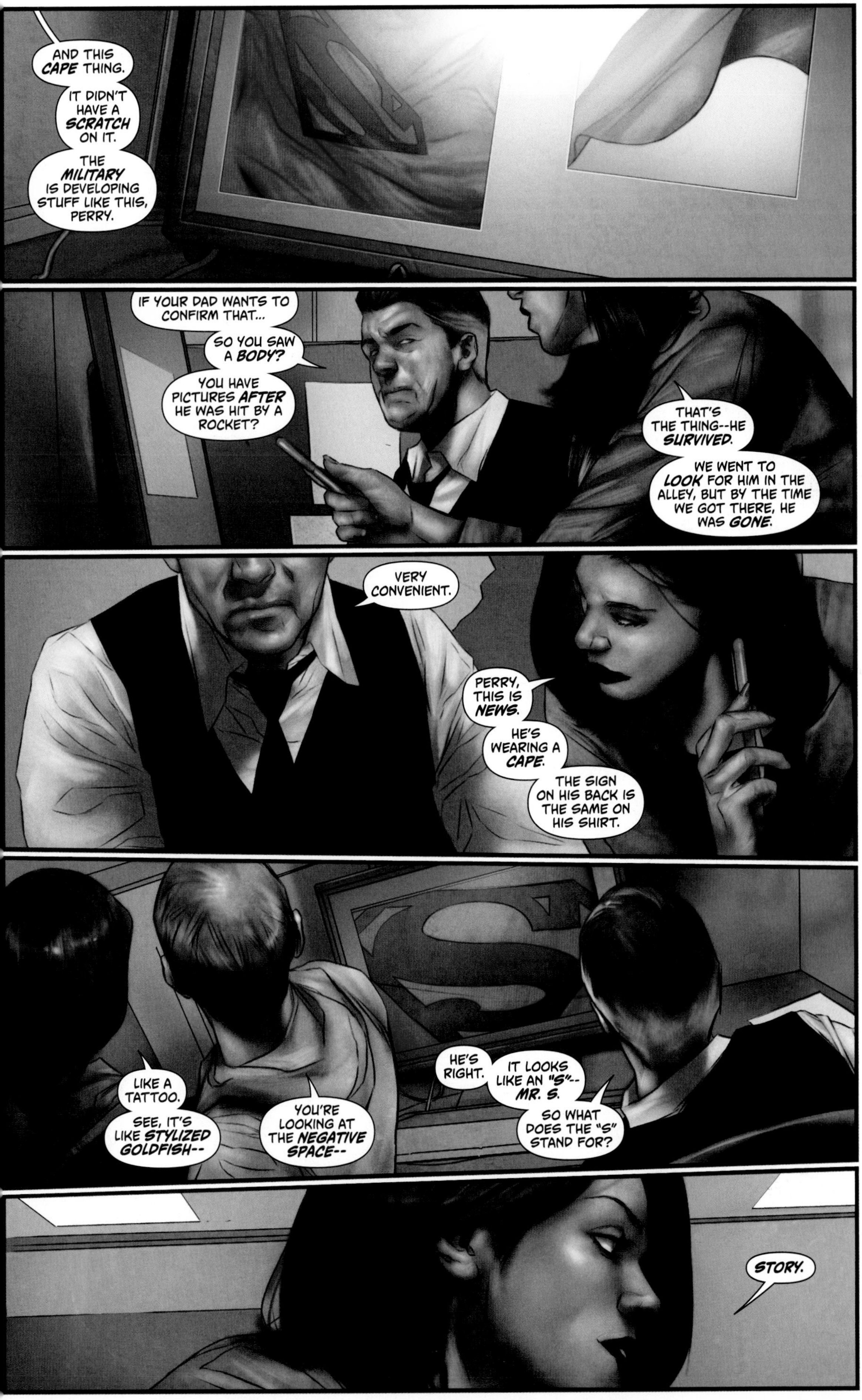
AND THIS CAPE THING.
IT DIDN'T HAVE A SCRATCH ON IT.
THE MILITARY IS DEVELOPING STUFF LIKE THIS, PERRY.
IF YOUR DAD WANTS TO CONFIRM THAT...
SO YOU SAW A BODY?
YOU HAVE PICTURES AFTER HE WAS HIT BY A ROCKET?
THAT'S THE THING--HE SURVIVED.
WE WENT TO LOOK FOR HIM IN THE ALLEY, BUT BY THE TIME WE GOT THERE, HE WAS GONE.
VERY CONVENIENT.
PERRY, THIS IS NEWS.
HE'S WEARING A CAPE.
THE SIGN ON HIS BACK IS THE SAME ON HIS SHIRT.
LIKE A TATTOO.
SEE, IT'S LIKE STYLIZED GOLDFISH--
YOU'RE LOOKING AT THE NEGATIVE SPACE--
HE'S RIGHT.
IT LOOKS LIKE AN "S"-- MR. S.
SO WHAT DOES THE "S" STAND FOR?
STORY.

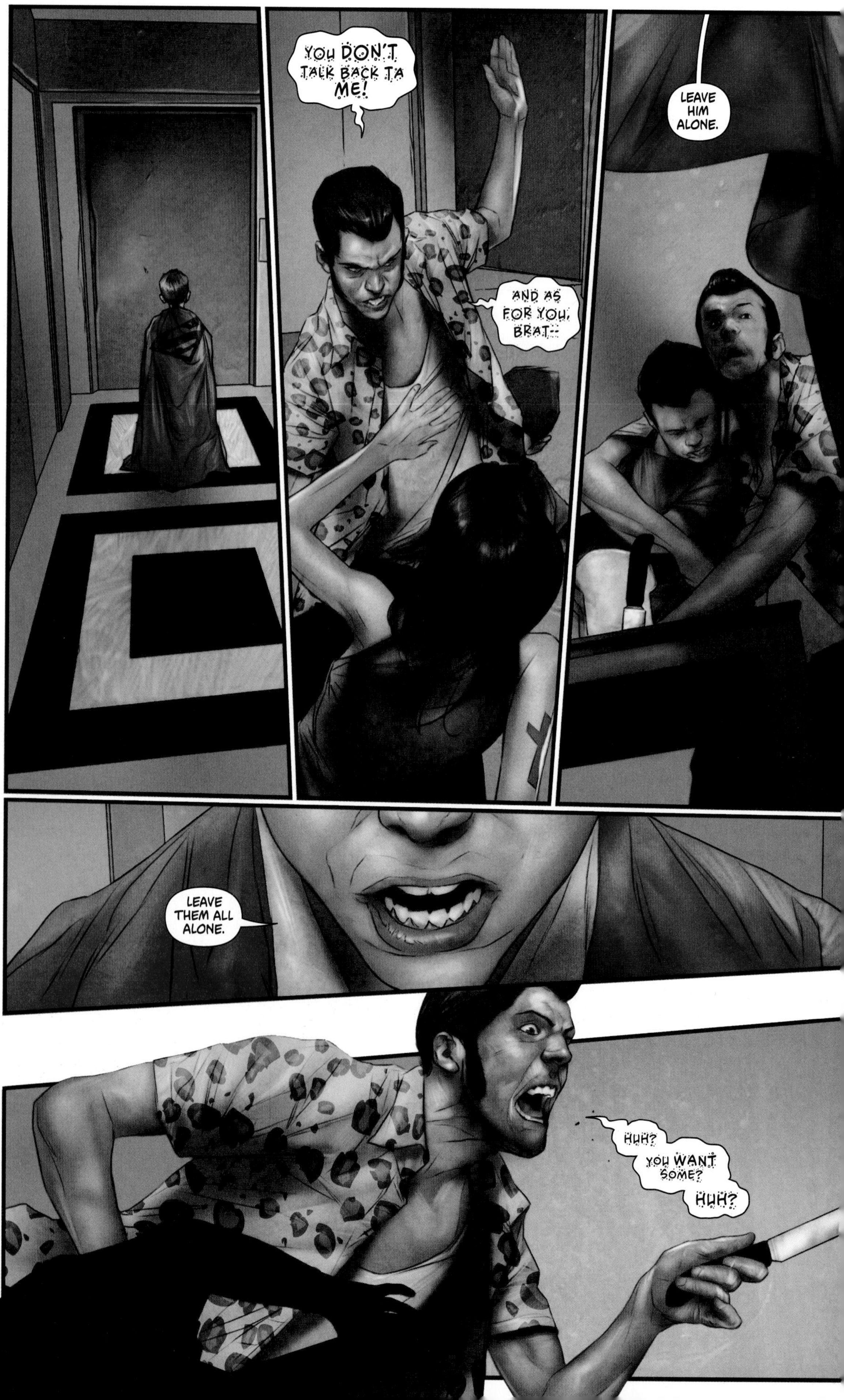
YOU DON'T TALK BACK TA ME!
AND AS FOR YOU, BRAT--
LEAVE HIM ALONE.
LEAVE THEM ALL ALONE.
HUH?
YOU WANT SOME?
HUH?

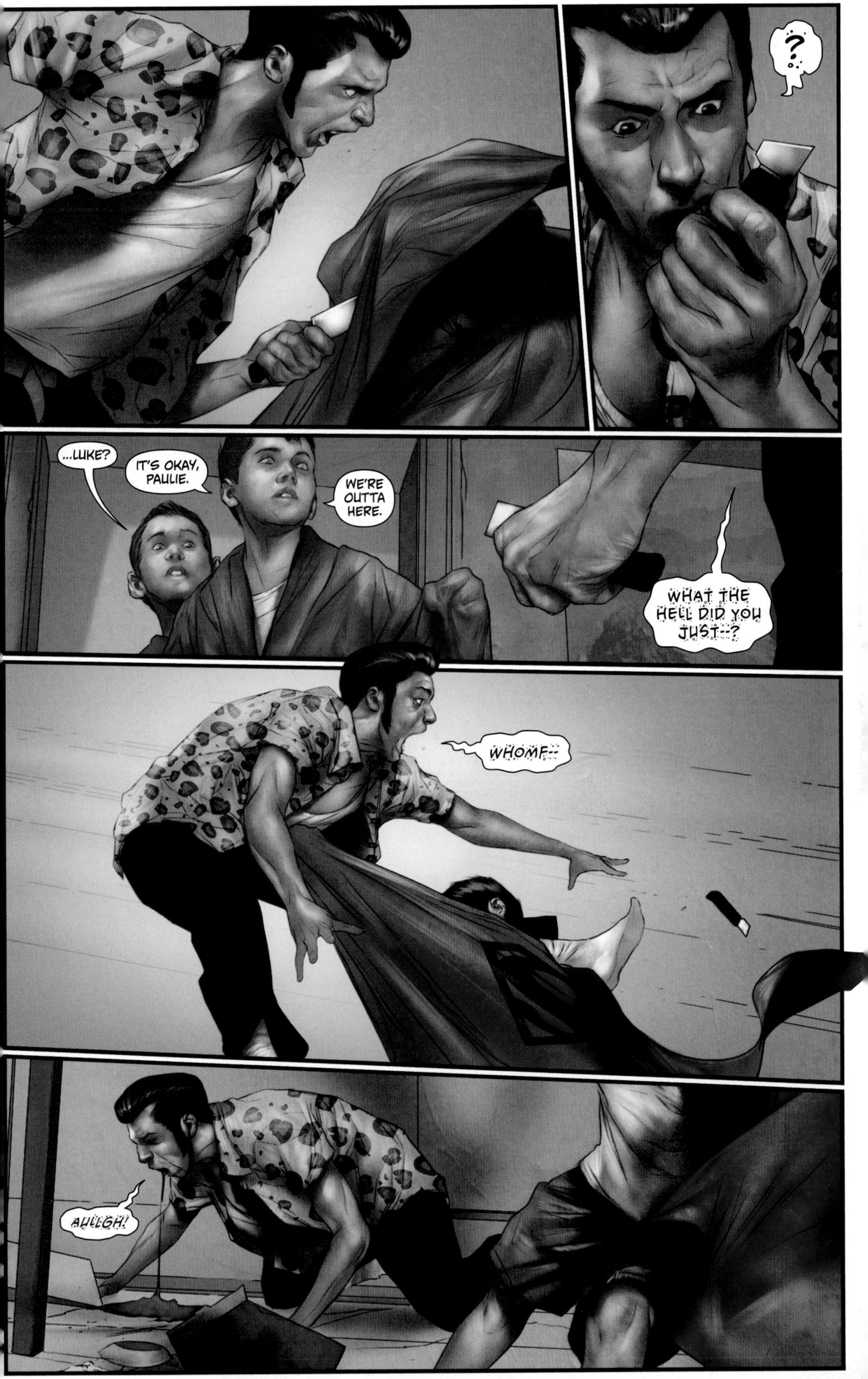
?
...LUKE?
IT'S OKAY, PAULIE.
WE'RE OUTTA HERE.
WHAT THE HELL DID YOU JUST--?
WHOMF--
AUUGH!

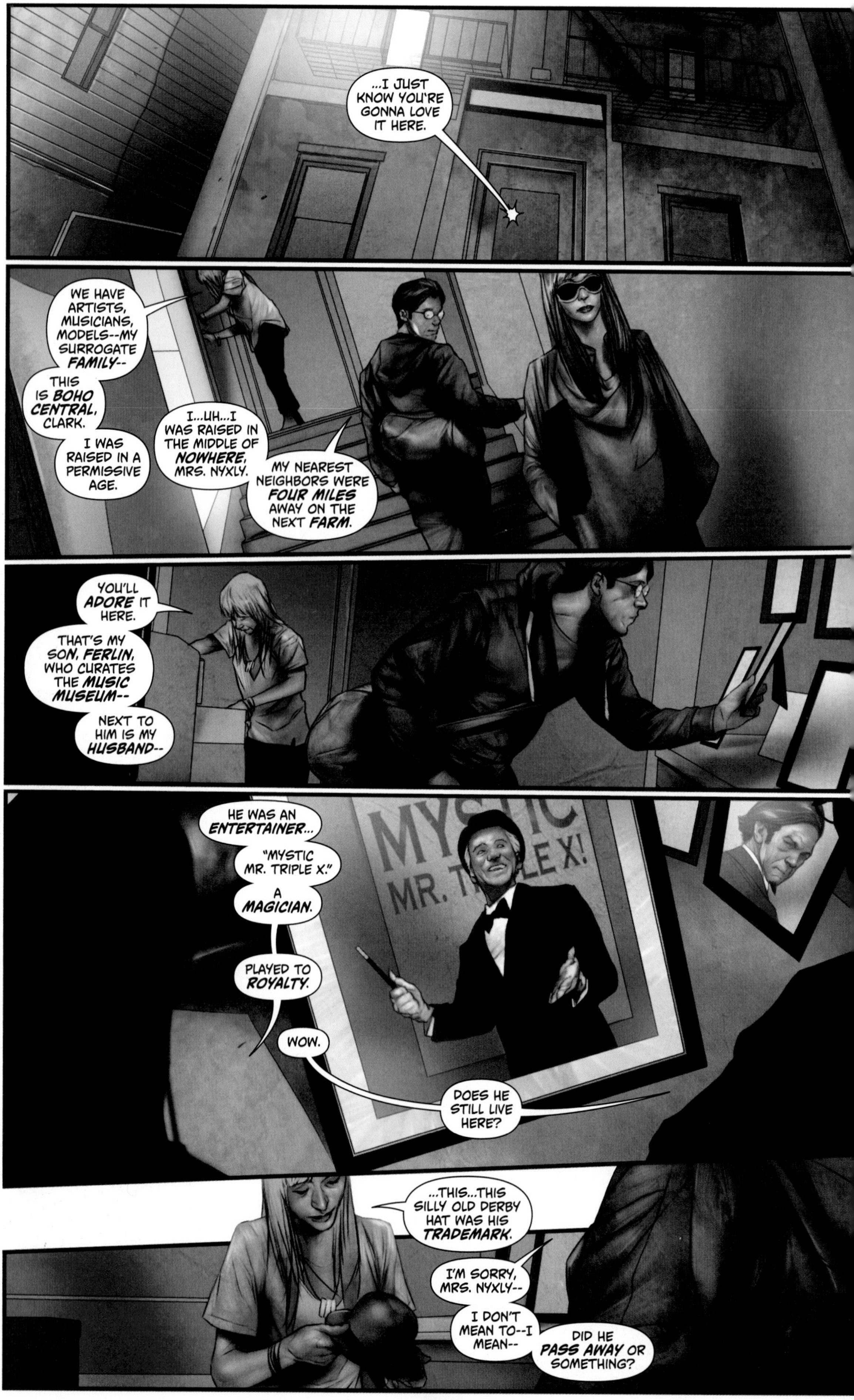

...I JUST KNOW YOU'RE GONNA LOVE IT HERE.
WE HAVE ARTISTS, MUSICIANS, MODELS--MY SURROGATE FAMILY--
THIS IS BOHO CENTRAL, CLARK.
I WAS RAISED IN A PERMISSIVE AGE.
I...UH...I WAS RAISED IN THE MIDDLE OF NOWHERE, MRS. NYXLY.
MY NEAREST NEIGHBORS WERE FOUR MILES AWAY ON THE NEXT FARM.
YOU'LL ADORE IT HERE.
THAT'S MY SON, FERLIN, WHO CURATES THE MUSIC MUSEUM--
NEXT TO HIM IS MY HUSBAND--
MYSTIC MR. T LE X!
HE WAS AN ENTERTAINER...
"MYSTIC MR. TRIPLE X."
A MAGICIAN.
PLAYED TO ROYALTY.
WOW.
DOES HE STILL LIVE HERE?
...THIS...THIS SILLY OLD DERBY HAT WAS HIS TRADEMARK.
I'M SORRY, MRS. NYXLY--
I DON'T MEAN TO--I MEAN--
DID HE PASS AWAY OR SOMETHING?

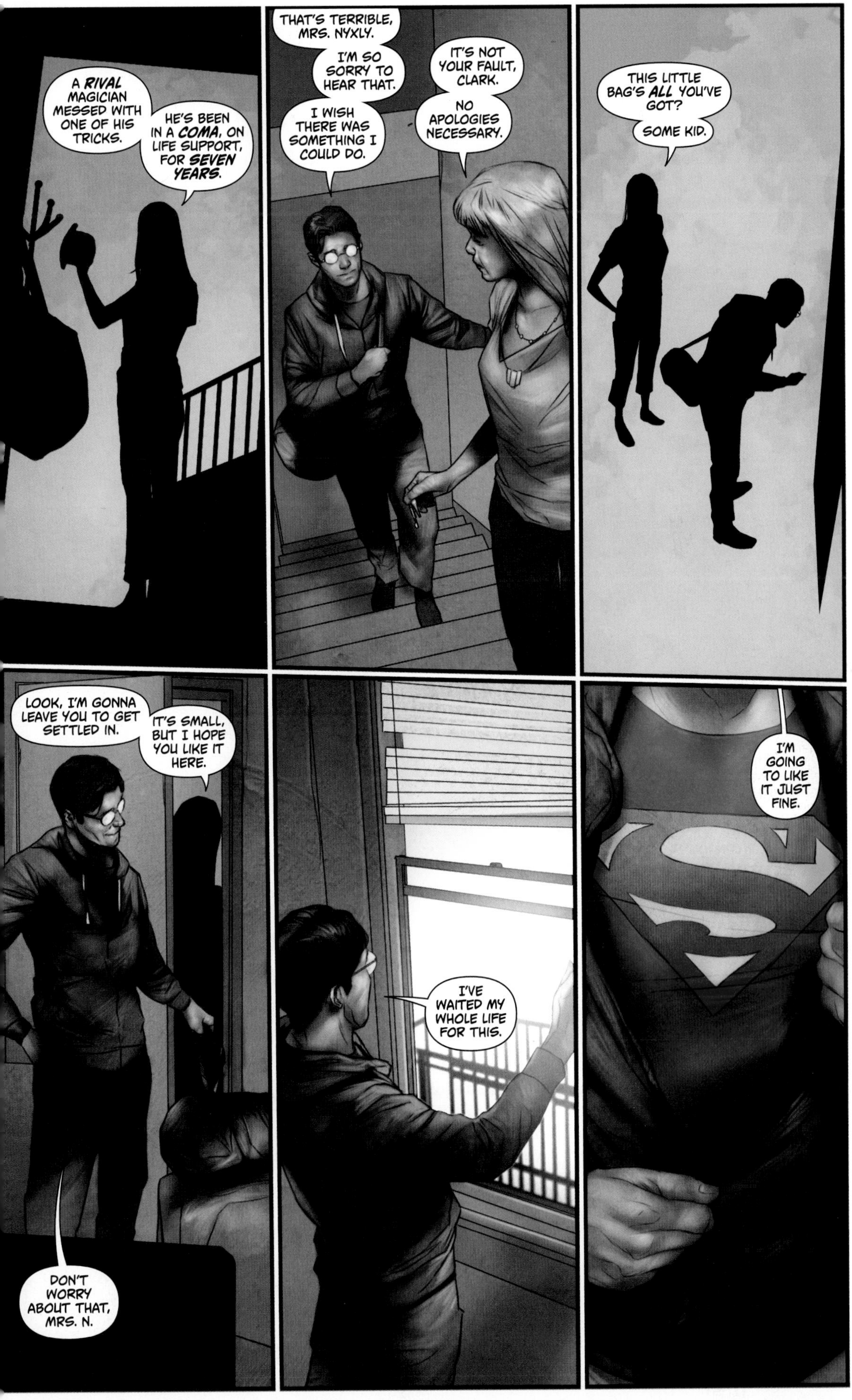
A RIVAL MAGICIAN MESSED WITH ONE OF HIS TRICKS.
HE'S BEEN IN A COMA, ON LIFE SUPPORT, FOR SEVEN YEARS.
THAT'S TERRIBLE, MRS. NYXLY.
I'M SO SORRY TO HEAR THAT.
I WISH THERE WAS SOMETHING I COULD DO.
IT'S NOT YOUR FAULT, CLARK.
NO APOLOGIES NECESSARY.
THIS LITTLE BAG'S ALL YOU'VE GOT?
SOME KID.
LOOK, I'M GONNA LEAVE YOU TO GET SETTLED IN.
IT'S SMALL, BUT I HOPE YOU LIKE IT HERE.
DON'T WORRY ABOUT THAT, MRS. N.
I'VE WAITED MY WHOLE LIFE FOR THIS.
I'M GOING TO LIKE IT JUST FINE.

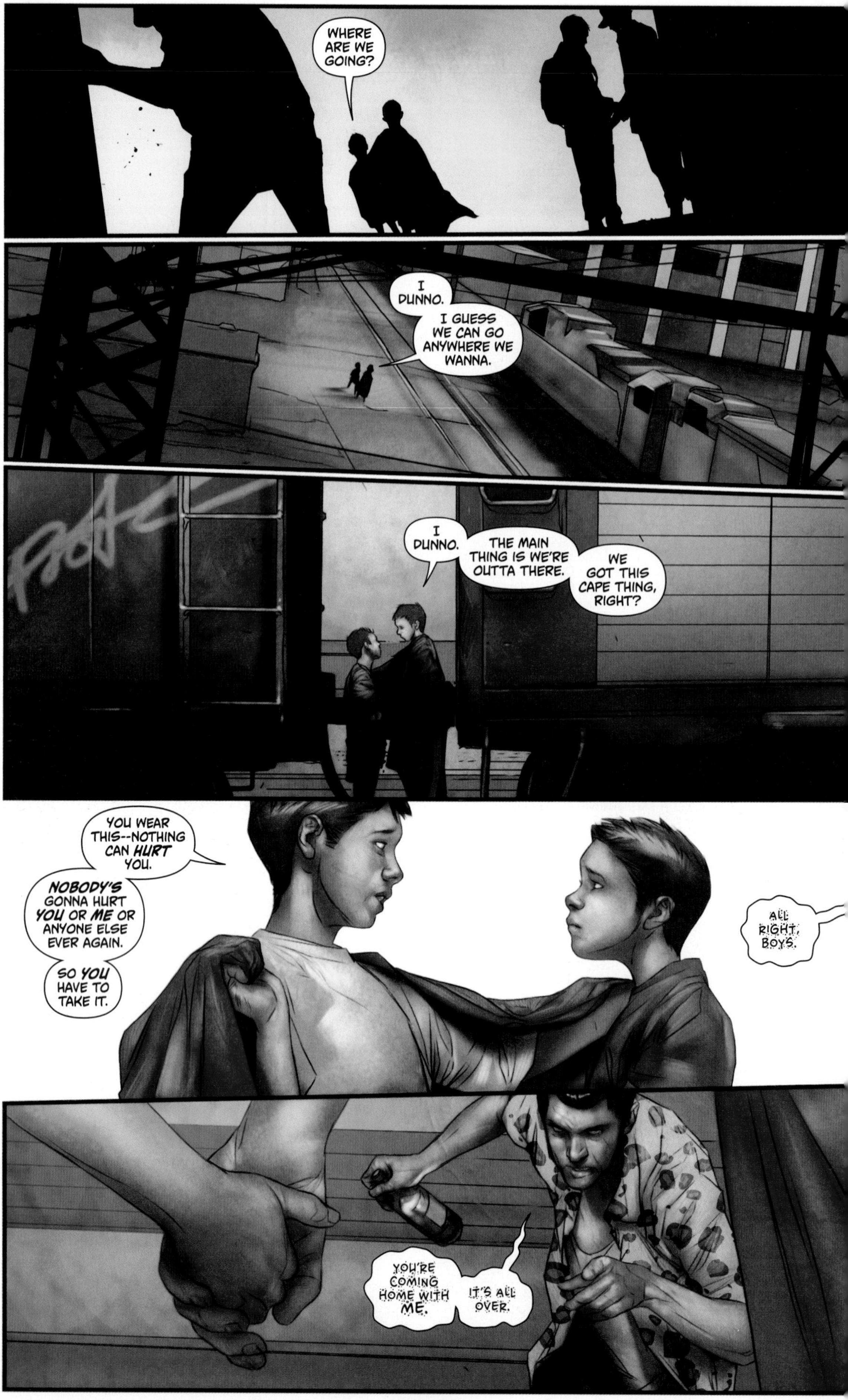
WHERE ARE WE GOING?
I DUNNO.
I GUESS WE CAN GO ANYWHERE WE WANNA.
I DUNNO.
THE MAIN THING IS WE'RE OUTTA THERE.
WE GOT THIS CAPE THING, RIGHT?
YOU WEAR THIS--NOTHING CAN HURT YOU.
NOBODY'S GONNA HURT YOU OR ME OR ANYONE ELSE EVER AGAIN.
SO YOU HAVE TO TAKE IT.
ALL RIGHT, BOYS.
YOU'RE COMING HOME WITH ME.
IT'S ALL OVER.

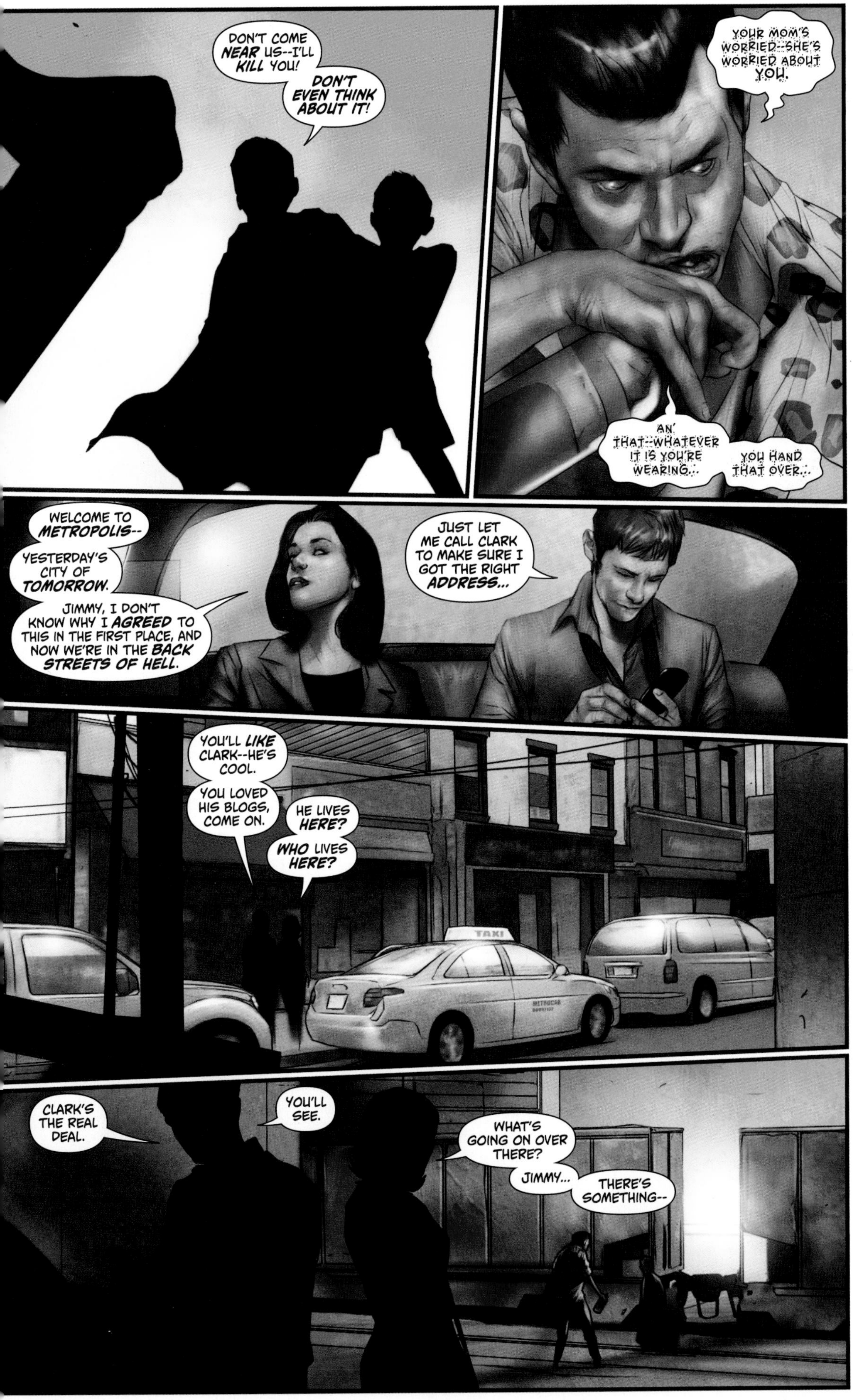
DON'T COME NEAR US--I'LL KILL YOU!
DON'T EVEN THINK ABOUT IT!
YOUR MOM'S WORRIED--SHE'S WORRIED ABOUT YOU.
AN' THAT--WHATEVER IT IS YOU'RE WEARING...
YOU HAND THAT OVER...
WELCOME TO METROPOLIS--
YESTERDAY'S CITY OF TOMORROW.
JIMMY, I DON'T KNOW WHY I AGREED TO THIS IN THE FIRST PLACE, AND NOW WE'RE IN THE BACK STREETS OF HELL.
JUST LET ME CALL CLARK TO MAKE SURE I GOT THE RIGHT ADDRESS...
YOU'LL LIKE CLARK--HE'S COOL.
YOU LOVED HIS BLOGS, COME ON.
HE LIVES HERE?
WHO LIVES HERE?
TAXI
METROCAB
CLARK'S THE REAL DEAL.
YOU'LL SEE.
WHAT'S GOING ON OVER THERE?
JIMMY...
THERE'S SOMETHING--

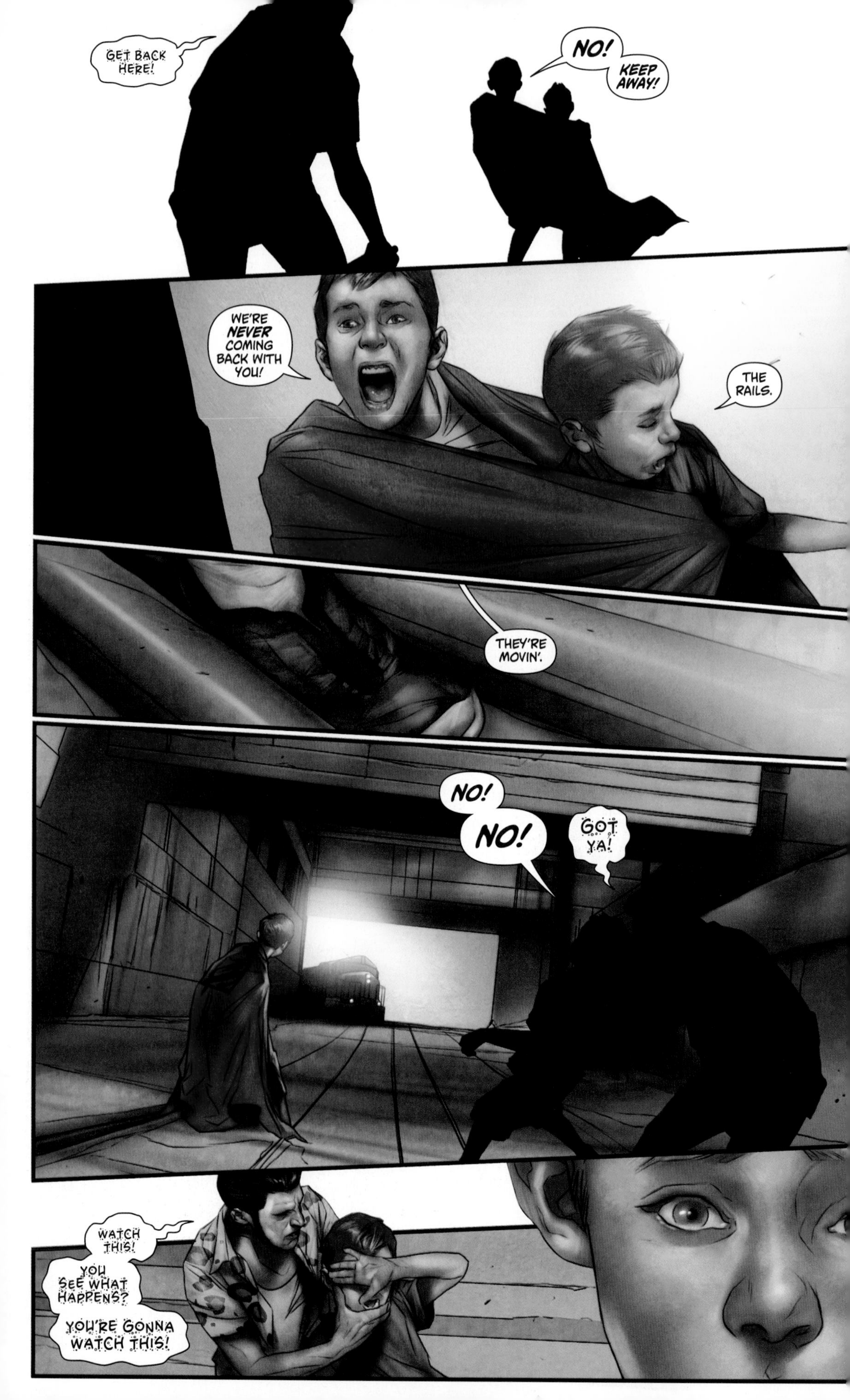
GET BACK HERE!
NO!
KEEP AWAY!
WE'RE NEVER COMING BACK WITH YOU!
THE RAILS.
THEY'RE MOVIN'.
NO!
NO!
GOT YA!
WATCH THIS!
YOU SEE WHAT HAPPENS?
YOU'RE GONNA WATCH THIS!

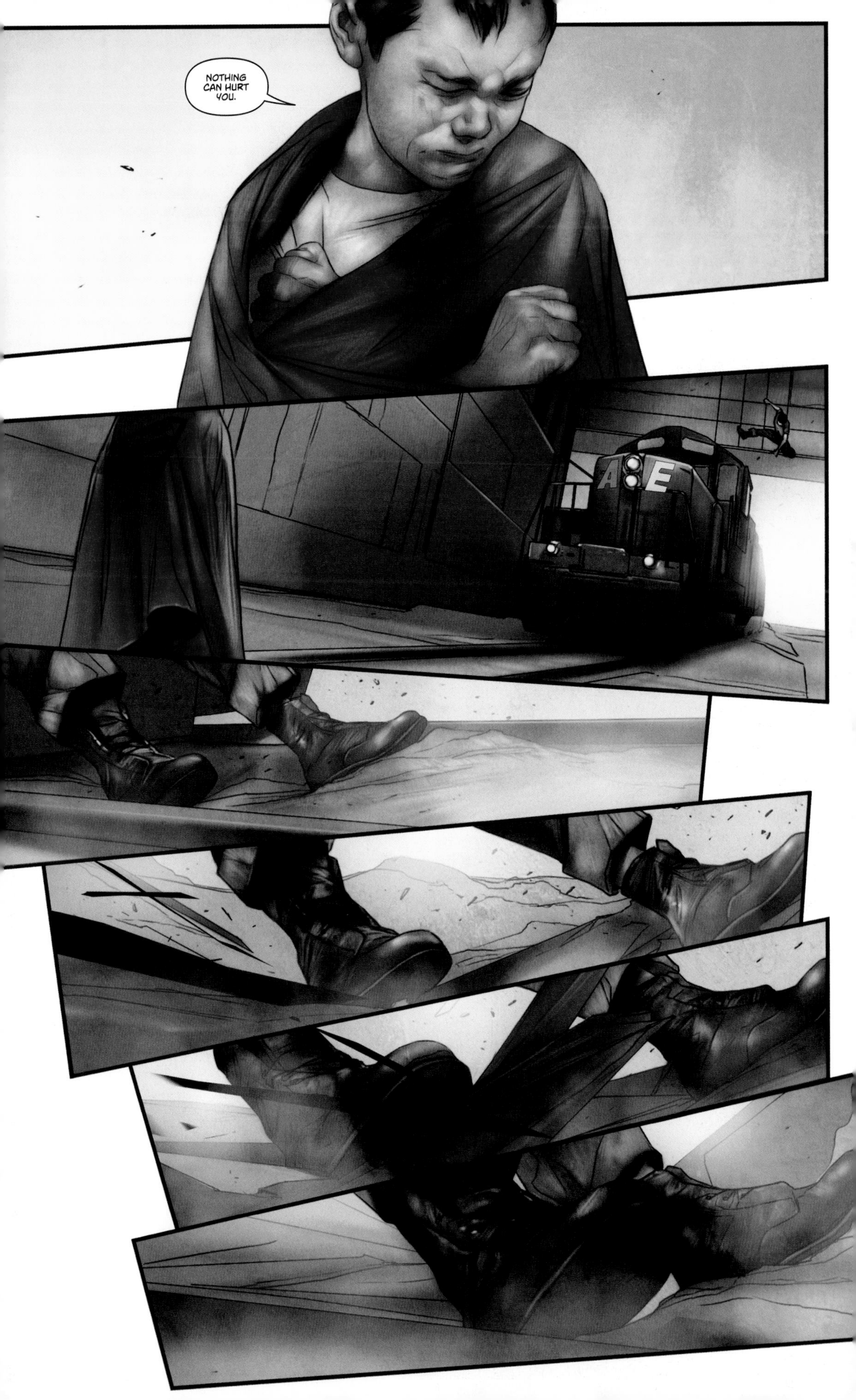
NOTHING CAN HURT YOU.

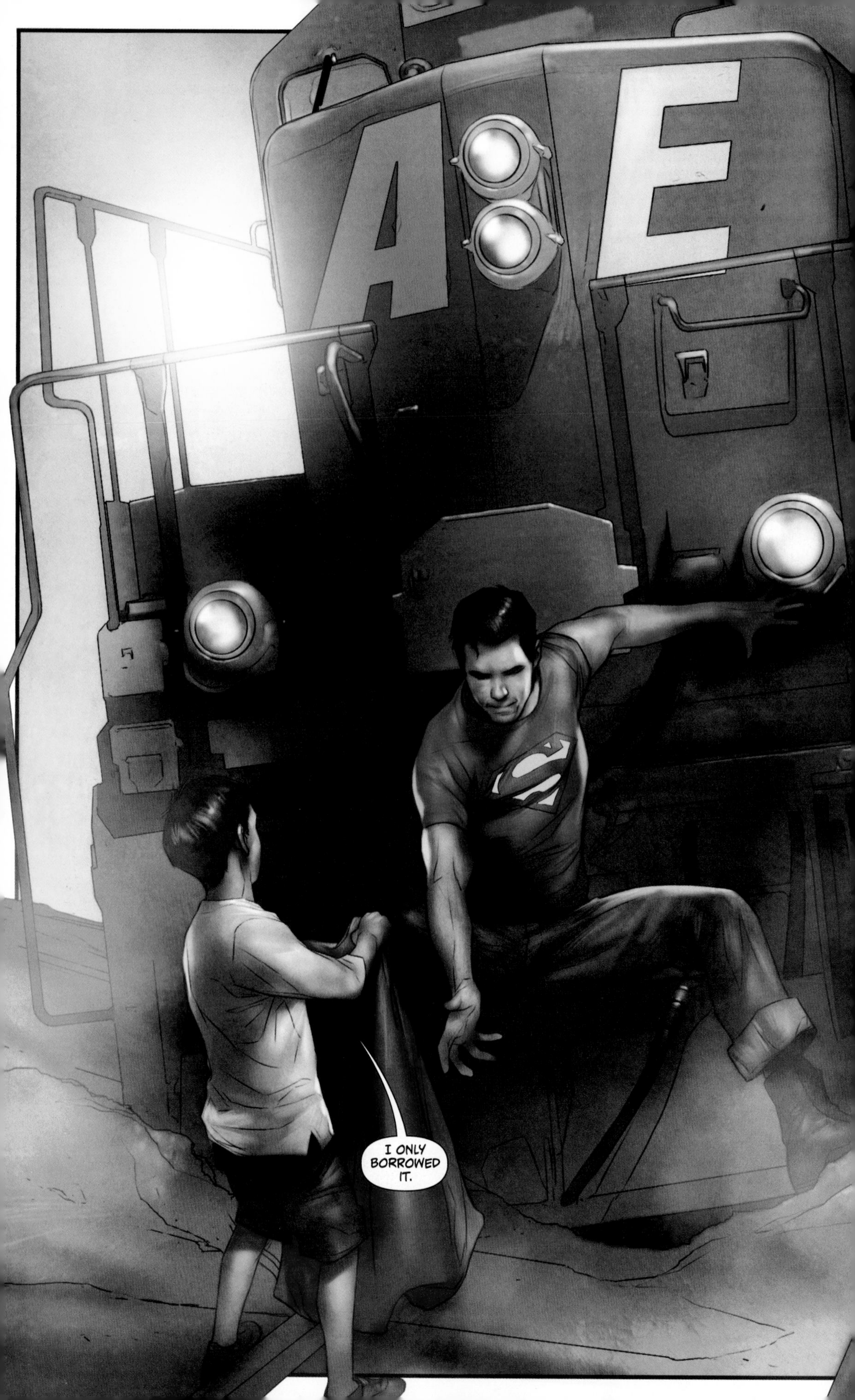
A
E
I ONLY BORROWED IT.

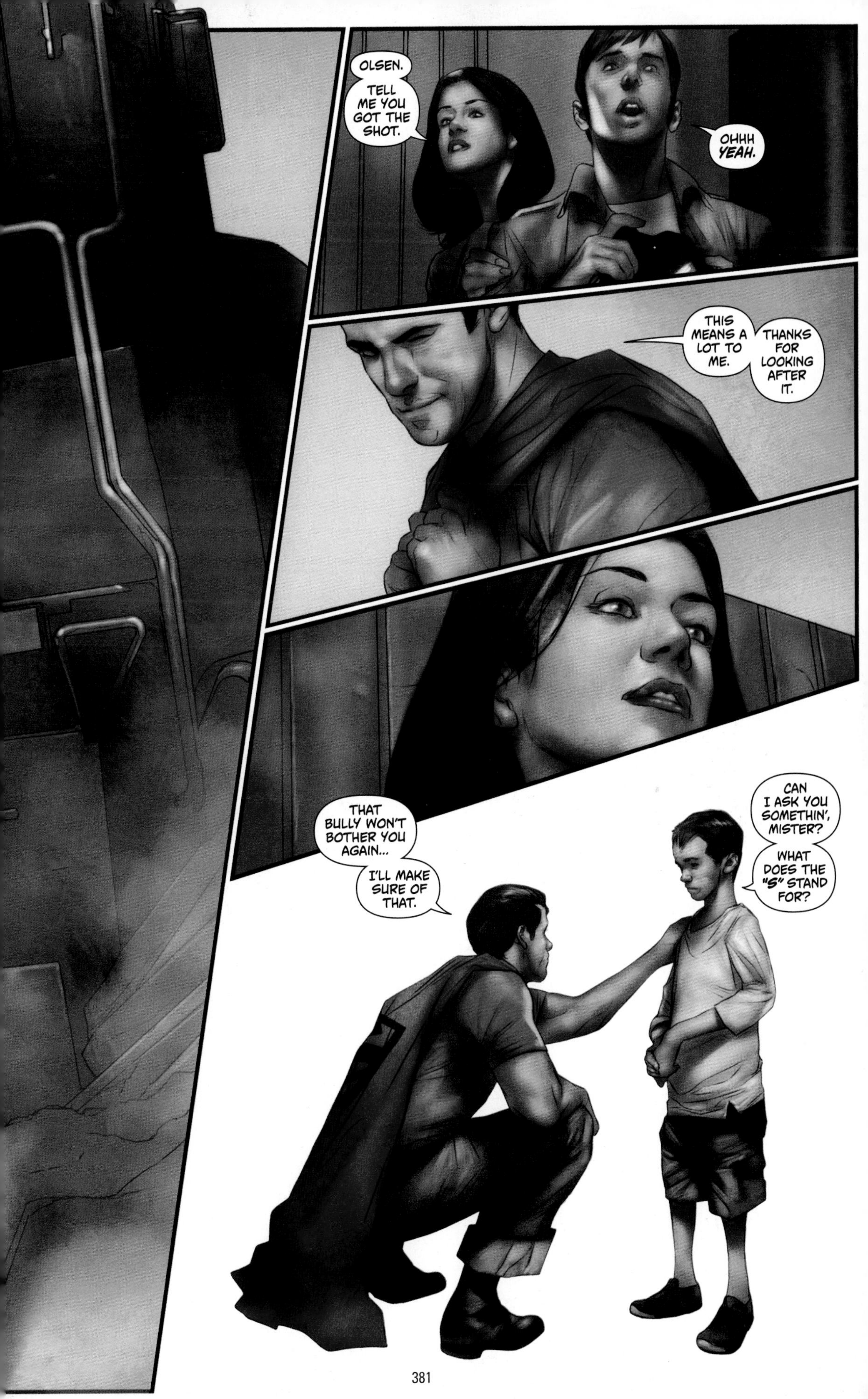
OLSEN.
TELL ME YOU GOT THE SHOT.
OHHH YEAH.
THIS MEANS A LOT TO ME.
THANKS FOR LOOKING AFTER IT.
THAT BULLY WON'T BOTHER YOU AGAIN...
I'LL MAKE SURE OF THAT.
CAN I ASK YOU SOMETHIN', MISTER?
WHAT DOES THE "S" STAND FOR?

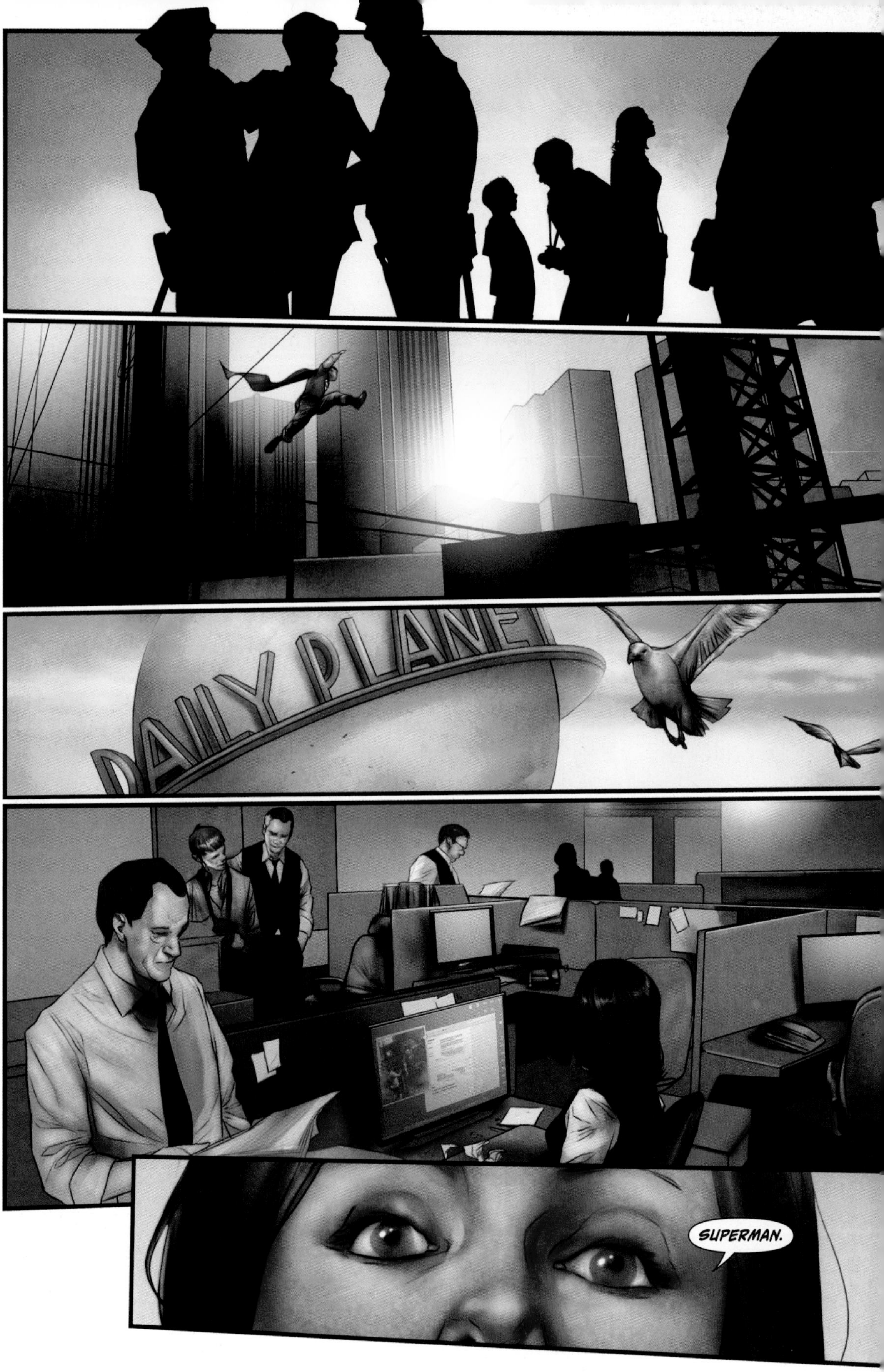
DAILY PLANET
SUPERMAN.

DC COMICS™

"An invigorating, entertaining and modern take on the Man of Steel."
—VARIETY

"Grade: A-."
—ENTERTAINMENT WEEKLY

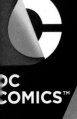

FROM THE WRITER OF *JUSTICE LEAGUE* & *GREEN LANTERN*

GEOFF JOHNS

SUPERMAN: SECRET ORIGIN with GARY FRANK

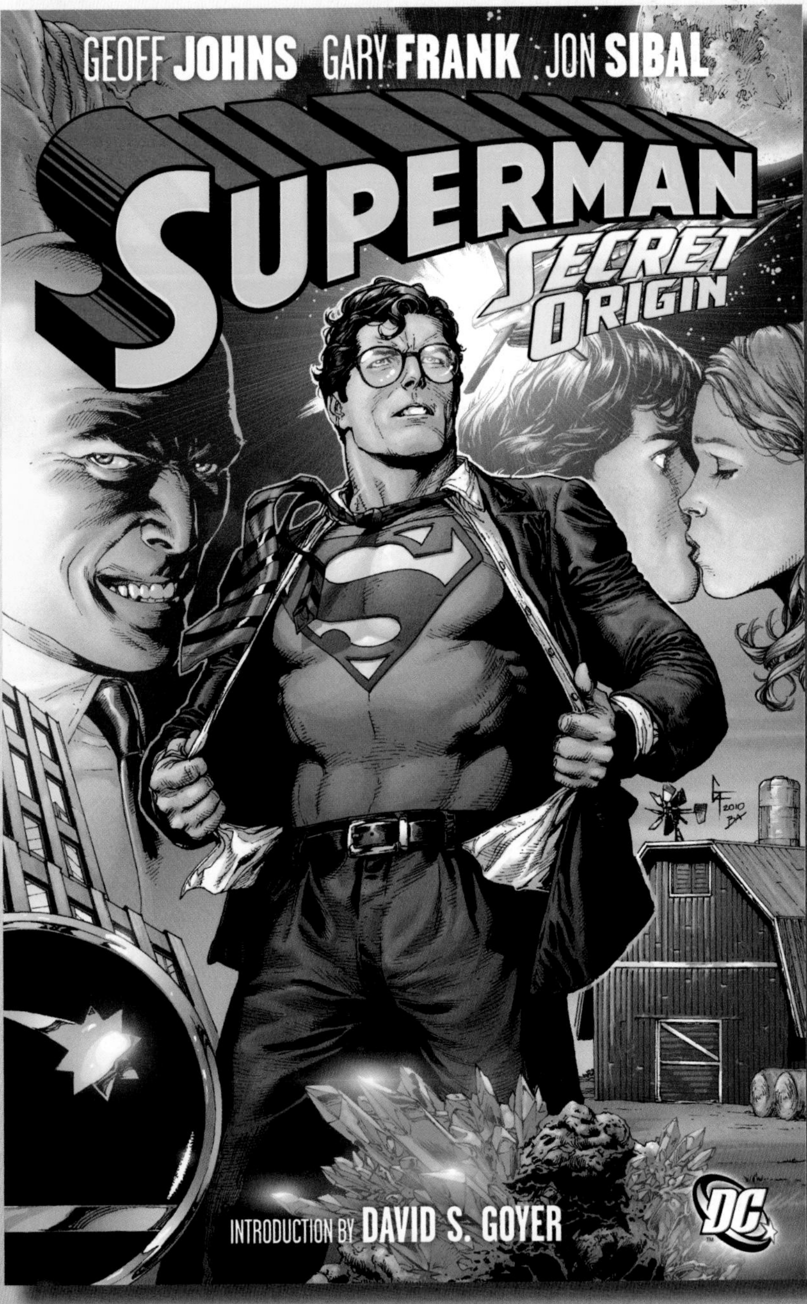
GEOFF JOHNS GARY FRANK JON SIBAL
SUPERMAN
SECRET ORIGIN
INTRODUCTION BY DAVID S. GOYER

SUPERMAN: LAST SON

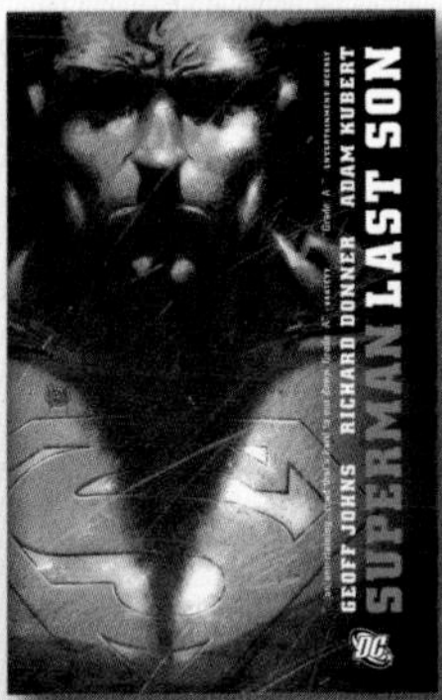
GEOFF JOHNS RICHARD DONNER ADAM KUBERT
SUPERMAN LAST SON

with RICHARD DONNER & ADAM KUBERT

SUPERMAN & THE LEGION OF SUPER-HEROES

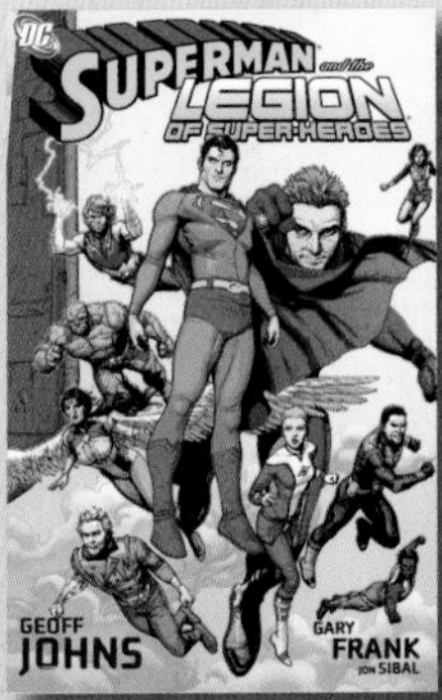
SUPERMAN and the LEGION OF SUPER-HEROES
GEOFF JOHNS
GARY FRANK JON SIBAL

with GARY FRANK

SUPERMAN: BRAINIAC

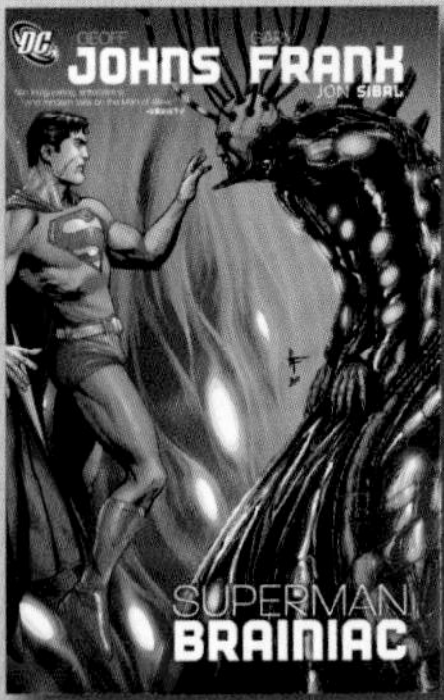
GEOFF JOHNS GARY FRANK JON SIBAL
SUPERMAN BRAINIAC

with GARY FRANK

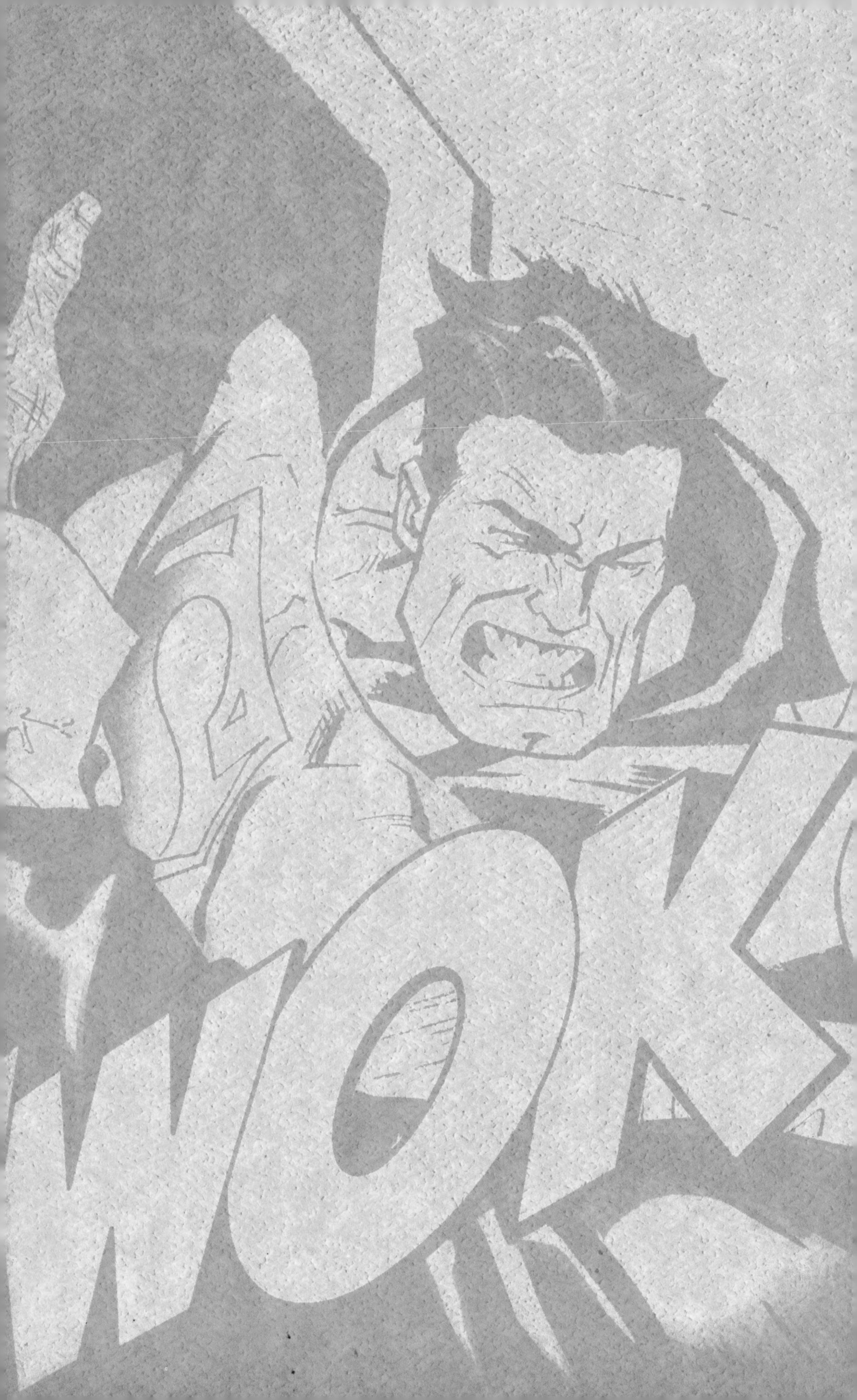